Celebrate Freedom

Celebrate Freedom

Our nation's system of government is based on the Declaration of Independence, the Constitution of the United States, and the Bill of Rights. Each of these declares the rights and freedoms of every American citizen. Parts of each are given on these pages.

Declaration of Independence, 1776

We hold these truths to be self-evident, that all men are created equal, that they are endowed by their Creator with certain unalienable Rights, that among these are Life, Liberty and the pursuit of Happiness. That to secure these rights, Governments are instituted among Men, deriving their just powers from the consent of the governed. . . . It is the Right of the People to [change their government] . . . laying its foundation on such principles and organizing its powers in such form, as to them shall seem most likely to effect their Safety and Happiness.

- **What rights does the Declaration of Independence outline?**
- **Who is entitled to these rights, according to the Declaration?**

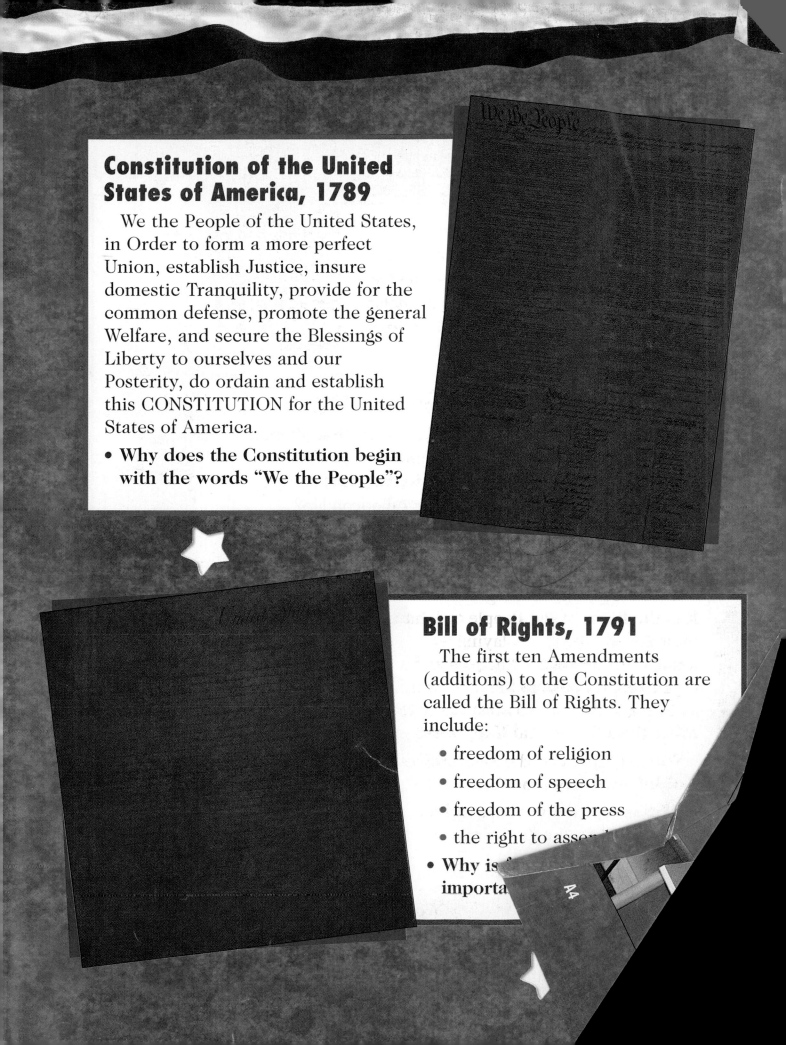

Constitution of the United States of America, 1789

We the People of the United States, in Order to form a more perfect Union, establish Justice, insure domestic Tranquility, provide for the common defense, promote the general Welfare, and secure the Blessings of Liberty to ourselves and our Posterity, do ordain and establish this CONSTITUTION for the United States of America.

- **Why does the Constitution begin with the words "We the People"?**

Bill of Rights, 1791

The first ten Amendments (additions) to the Constitution are called the Bill of Rights. They include:

- freedom of religion
- freedom of speech
- freedom of the press
- the right to assem

- **Why is** importa

A4

Celebrate Freedom

Produce a News Program

In groups, write a short news program to discuss the Declaration of Independence. As you prepare your news story, think about helping your viewers to understand:

- Who wrote the Declaration of Independence?
- Where and when was it written?
- Why was it written?
- How might this event change American life? Will it change everyone's lives?

Make sure everyone has a turn to speak.

Roles:
- Anchor person
- Reporters
- Men and women to interview

Make a Constitutional News Bulletin Board

In the United States, we have many freedoms. We have the right to vote for our leaders. We have the right to freely discuss our ideas. We also have the right to practice any religion we choose.

Go through old newspapers, magazines, and pamphlets to find articles and pictures that deal with American freedoms and rights. Post clippings on a class bulletin board.

Celebrate Freedom

Explore Different Points of View

Americans believe in freedom of speech and freedom of the press. These and other freedoms are part of our Bill of Rights. Some people think that these rights must be protected at all times. Others say there are some times—such as during war—when it is permissible for the government to limit citizens' rights.

What do you think? Is it ever right to limit our freedoms, such as freedom of speech? Or should free speech always be protected?

Choose a side of the debate. List the reasons for your viewpoint. Then take the opposing view and list reasons for that viewpoint.

Materials:
- Paper
- Pen or pencil

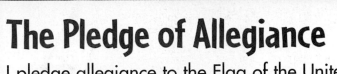

The Pledge of Allegiance

I pledge allegiance to the Flag of the United States of America, and to the Republic for which it stands, one Nation under God, indivisible, with liberty and justice for all.

The National Anthem

Oh, say, can you see, by the dawn's early light,
What so proudly we hailed at the twilight's last gleaming?
Whose broad stripes and bright stars, thro' the perilous fight,
O'er the ramparts we watched, were so gallantly streaming.
And the rockets' red glare, the bombs bursting in air,
Gave proof through the night that our flag was still there.
Oh, say, does that star-spangled banner yet wave
O'er the land of the free and the home of the brave?

A7

History

Throughout our nation's history, Americans have worked to bring liberty and equality to all.

Patrick Henry

American Revolution leader

"Is life so dear, or peace so sweet, as to be purchased at the price of chains and slavery? ...I know not what course others may take; but as for me, give me liberty or give me death!"

Patrick Henry spoke at the Second Virginia Convention at St. John's Church in Richmond, Virginia, March 23, 1775. His words inspired other colonists to join the American Revolution.

Alice Paul

Women's rights leader

"Mr. President, how long must women wait for liberty?"

Alice Paul led the fight for a Constitutional amendment giving women the right to vote. In 1917 she and her followers urged President Woodrow Wilson to support voting rights for women.

Franklin Delano Roosevelt

32nd President of the United States

"In the future days, which we seek to make secure, we look forward to a world founded upon four essential human freedoms."

"The first is freedom of speech and expression—everywhere in the world."

"The second is freedom of every person to worship God in his own way—everywhere in the world."

"The third is freedom from want—which, translated into world terms, means economic understandings that will secure to every nation a healthy peacetime life for its inhabitants—everywhere in the world."

"The fourth is freedom from fear—which, translated into world terms, means a world-wide reduction of armaments to such a point and in such a thorough fashion that no nation will be in a position to commit an act of physical aggression against any neighbor—anywhere in the world."

President Roosevelt proposed the "Four Freedoms" in the President's annual message to the Congress on January 6, 1941.

Barbara Jordan

Congresswoman from Texas

"We are a people trying not only to solve the problems of the present... but we are attempting on a larger scale to fulfill the promise of America. We are attempting to fulfill our national purpose—to create and sustain a society in which all of us are equal."

Barbara Jordan spoke these words at a political meeting in 1976.

Geography

Our national parks tell a story of America's history. Several parks help us to remember and learn about major eras of our history.

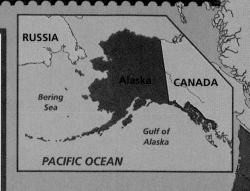

RUSSIA

Bering Sea

Alaska

CANADA

Gulf of Alaska

PACIFIC OCEAN

Washington

Oregon

Idaho

Montana

North

Columbia River

Wyoming

South

Scotts Bluff National Monument

Nevada

Great Salt Lake

Utah

Colorado

California

Mesa Verde National Park

Arizona

New Mexico

MEXICO

Mesa Verde National Park in Colorado gives a picture of what life was like for Native Americans living there more than 1,000 years ago.

Kauai

Nihau

Oahu

Hawaii

Molokai

Maui

USS *Arizona* Memorial

Hawaii

PACIFIC OCEAN

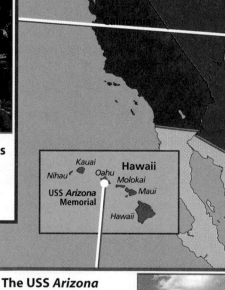

The USS *Arizona* National Memorial in the waters off Pearl Harbor, Hawaii, honors Americans killed during the Japanese attack there on December 7, 1941.

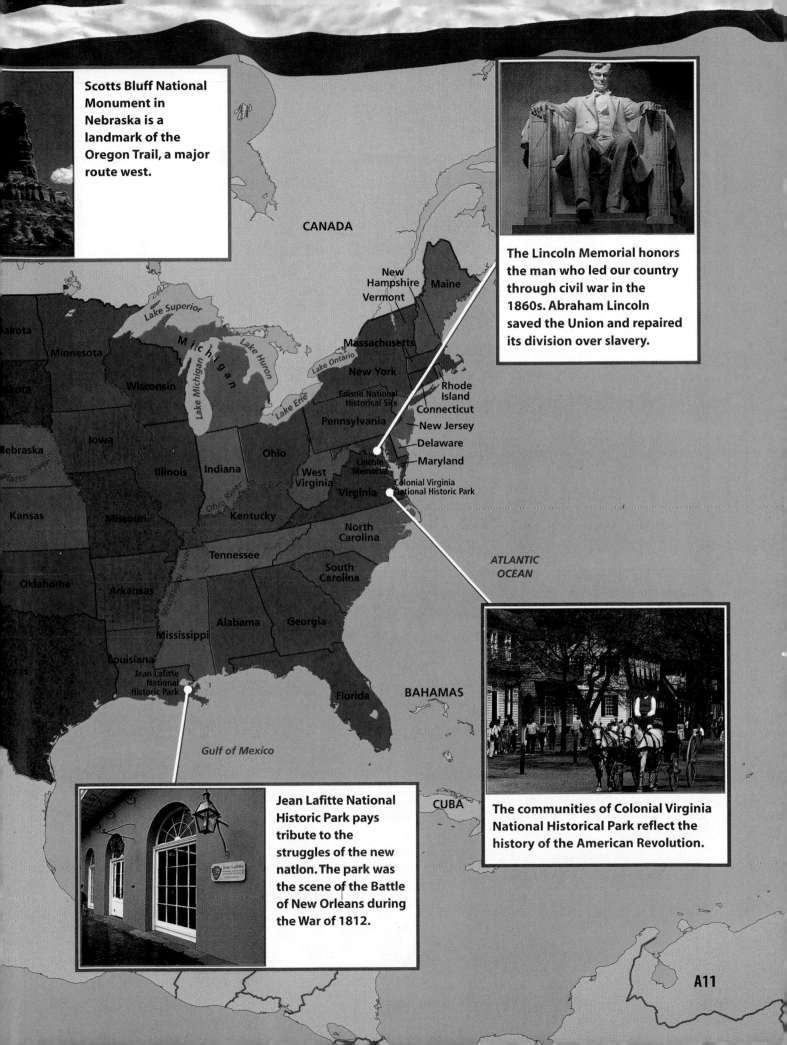

Scotts Bluff National Monument in Nebraska is a landmark of the Oregon Trail, a major route west.

CANADA

The Lincoln Memorial honors the man who led our country through civil war in the 1860s. Abraham Lincoln saved the Union and repaired its division over slavery.

New Hampshire
Maine
Vermont
Massachusetts
Lake Ontario
New York
Rhode Island
Edison National Historical Site
Connecticut
Pennsylvania
New Jersey
Delaware
Lincoln Memorial
Maryland
West Virginia
Colonial Virginia National Historic Park
Virginia
North Carolina
Tennessee
South Carolina
Alabama
Georgia
Mississippi
Louisiana
Jean Lafitte National Historic Park
Florida

Lake Superior
Michigan
Lake Michigan
Lake Huron
Lake Erie

Dakota
Minnesota
Wisconsin
Iowa
Nebraska
Platte River
Illinois
Indiana
Ohio
Ohio River
Kansas
Missouri
Kentucky
Oklahoma
Arkansas
Mississippi River
Texas

ATLANTIC OCEAN

BAHAMAS

CUBA

Gulf of Mexico

Jean Lafitte National Historic Park pays tribute to the struggles of the new nation. The park was the scene of the Battle of New Orleans during the War of 1812.

The communities of Colonial Virginia National Historical Park reflect the history of the American Revolution.

Economics

The United States has the largest economy in the world. Our country has become the world leader in business because of our natural resources, good climate, educated workers, and free enterprise system. Americans work in many industries, including manufacturing, agriculture, services, science and technology, mining, and construction.

READING CHECK What are two industries, or job types, in which Americans work?

Agriculture

Construction

Education

Steel making

Mining

Government

President

Congress

Supreme Court

Our Constitution

The Constitution is the foundation for our nation's government. Our Constitution is based on five principles, or ideas.

Popular Sovereignty

Sovereignty means authority to rule. In our government, citizens have sovereignty. The most important way we rule is by electing leaders to represent us.

Limited Government

The government does not have total authority. The Constitution limits the powers of government. The Bill of Rights protects the freedoms of individuals.

Federalism

The national government and the state governments share power. States have the power to maintain schools, set up local governments, and conduct elections. The national government has the powers to declare war and make peace, regulate trade, print money, and oversee immigration. Both national and state governments make laws, collect taxes, and set up court systems.

Separation of Powers

The national government is divided among three branches: the legislative, which makes laws; the executive, which carries out laws; and the judicial, which interprets laws.

Checks and Balances

Each branch of government has important powers that check, or limit, the power of the other two branches.

READING CHECK What are the three branches of our nation's government?

Citizenship

Voting

The right to vote is one of our most important rights. It is one way that American citizens can take part in government. At the beginning of our country's history, only white men were allowed to elect our leaders by voting. Over time, the right to vote was given to all citizens over age eighteen.

 Who is allowed to vote today?

African American men won the right to vote with the passage of the Fourteenth Amendment in 1868. It granted citizenship to people who had been enslaved.

Women struggled for almost 100 years to gain the right to vote. The Nineteenth Amendment, passed in 1920, gave women that right.

After the Fourteenth Amendment passed, some states began

writing laws that stopped African Americans from voting. One type of law forced African Americans to explain difficult parts of the Constitution. Another forced people to pay a tax to vote. The Civil Rights Act of 1964 and the Voting Rights Act of 1965 removed those barriers.

In the late 1960s, young people under age twenty-one began demanding the right to vote. Many said that if they could serve as soldiers in war, then they should have the right to vote. In 1971, the Twenty-Sixth Amendment gave eighteen-year-old adults the right to vote.

It's All American Food

Americans eat many dishes that were first made someplace else. Often new flavors are brought to our country by immigrants from other parts of the world. When immigrants move to the United States, they bring new flavors and ways of cooking. Many dishes that we think of as "American," such as hot dogs, originally came from other countries.

 How do foods from different parts of the world become popular in the United States?

Where did this "American" dish come from?
Hot dogs - Germany
Ravioli - Italy
Black beans - Brazil and the Caribbean
Tacos and tortillas - Mexico
Egg rolls - China
Sushi - Japan
Gumbo - Africa

Science, Technology, and Society

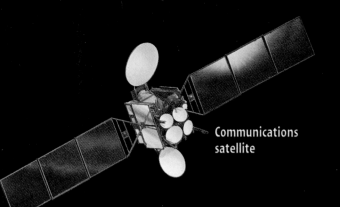
Communications satellite

The greatest changes in technology over the past 100 years may have come in ways we communicate. One hundred years ago, the telephone had been invented, but families did not use it very often. Mail was often the fastest way to communicate across our nation. Today, we have many ways of keeping in close contact, whether we are across a room or across the country.

 How has communication changed in the past century?

Internet communications

Cellular telephone

Text pager

Macmillan/McGraw-Hill

Our Nation

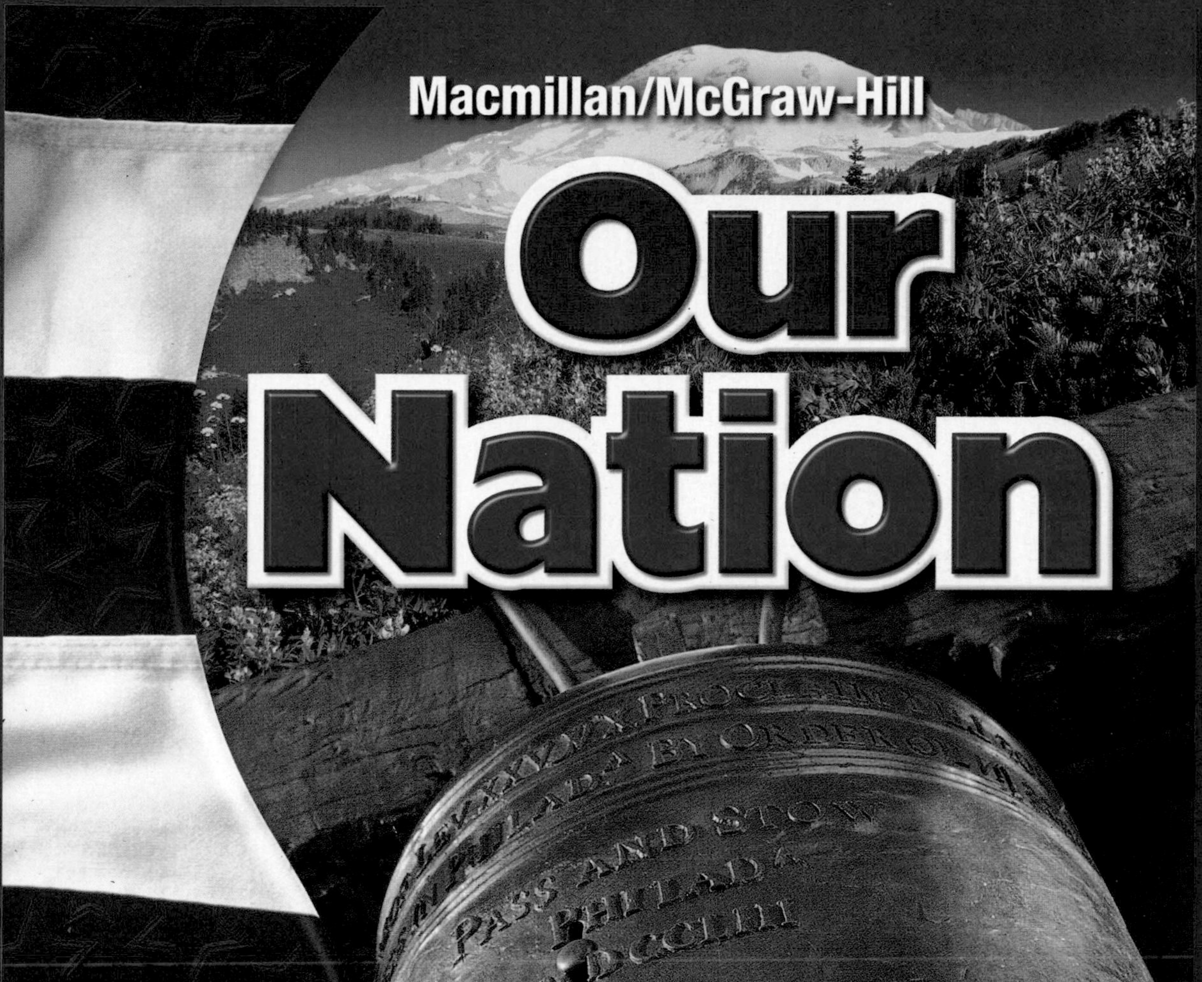

Mc Graw Hill

NATIONAL GEOGRAPHIC

BEING A GOOD CITIZEN

In this textbook you will meet special people and learn many important things. On the BIOGRAPHY pages and in the POINTS OF VIEW lessons, you will see eight important words that help define what it means to be a good citizen. These words are listed below. They help us understand how to be better citizens in our home, neighborhood, school, community, country, and world.

★**COURAGE**★
being brave in the face of difficulty

★**FREEDOM**★
making choices and holding beliefs of one's own

★**HONESTY**★
telling the truth

★**JUSTICE**★
working toward fair treatment for everyone

★**LEADERSHIP**★
showing good behavior worth following
through example

★**LOYALTY**★
showing support for people and one's country

★**RESPECT**★
treating others as you would like to be treated

★**RESPONSIBILITY**★
being worthy of trust

Macmillan/McGraw-Hill

Our Nation

James A. Banks

Richard G. Boehm

Kevin P. Colleary

Gloria Contreras

A. Lin Goodwin

Mary A. McFarland

Walter C. Parker

 NATIONAL GEOGRAPHIC

Macmillan
McGraw-Hill

New York   Farmington

PROGRAM AUTHORS

Dr. James A. Banks
Russell F. Stark University Professor and Director of the Center for Multicultural Education
University of Washington
Seattle, Washington

Dr. Richard G. Boehm
Jesse H. Jones Distinguished Chair in Geographic Education and Director, The Gilbert M. Grosvenor Center for Geographic Education
Southwest Texas State University
San Marcos, Texas

Dr. Kevin P. Colleary
Curriculum and Teaching Department
Hunter College
City University of New York
New York, New York

Dr. Gloria Contreras
Professor of Education
University of North Texas
Denton, Texas

Dr. A. Lin Goodwin
Associate Professor of Education
Department of Curriculum and Teaching
Teachers College
Columbia University
New York, New York

Dr. Mary A. McFarland
Social Studies Education Consultant, K–12
St. Louis, Missouri

Dr. Walter C. Parker
Professor of Education and Chair of Social Studies Education
University of Washington
Seattle, Washington
Washington, D.C.

NATIONAL GEOGRAPHIC

HISTORIANS/SCHOLARS

Dr. Joyce Appleby
Professor of History
University of California, Los Angeles
Los Angeles, California

Dr. Alan Brinkley
Professor of American History
Columbia University
New York, New York

Dr. Nancy Cott
Stanley Woodward Professor of History and American Studies
Yale University
New Haven, Connecticut

Dr. James McPherson
George Henry Davis Professor of American History
Princeton University
Princeton, New Jersey

Dr. Donald A. Ritchie
Associate Historian of the United States Senate Historical Office
Washington, D.C.

PROGRAM CONSULTANTS

Betty Ruth Baker, M.Ed
Assistant Professor of Curriculum and Instruction
Early Childhood Specialist
School of Education
Baylor University
Waco, Texas

Dr. Randolph B. Campbell
Regents' Professor of History
University of North Texas
Denton, Texas

Dr. Steven Cobb
Director, Center for Economic Education
Chair, Department of Economics
University of North Texas
Denton, Texas

Frank de Varona, Ed.S.
Visiting Associate Professor
Florida International University
Miami, Florida

Dr. John L. Esposito
Professor of Religion and International Affairs, and Director of the Center for Christian-Muslim Understanding
Georgetown University
Washington, D.C.

READING INSTRUCTION CONSULTANTS

M. Frankie Dungan , M.Ed
Reading/Language Arts Consultant, K-6
Mansfield, Texas

Antonio A. Fierro
Program Director for the Texas Reading Initiative, Region 19
El Paso, Texas

Dr. William H. Rupley
Professor of Reading Education
Distinguished Research Fellow
Department of Teaching, Learning and Culture
College of Education
Texas A&M University
College Station, Texas

GRADE LEVEL CONSULTANTS

Linda Blanchard
Fifth Grade Teacher
Williams Elementary School
Pasadena, Texas

Steve Harvel
Social Studies Consultant
Northwest Regional Education Service Alliance, North Carolina Public Schools
Wilkesboro, North Carolina

Barbara Hett
Intermediate Project C.H.I.L.D. Teacher
Glendale Elementary School
Vero Beach, Florida

Larry Howell
Fifth Grade Teacher
Giberson Elementary School
Colorado Springs, Colorado

Bruce Jelley
Assistant Principal
Bakersville Elementary School
Manchester, New Hampshire

Jim McConnell
Social Studies Consultant
Dearborn Public Schools
Dearborn, Michigan

Juan Salazar
Fifth Grade Teacher
Resaca Elementary School
Brownsville, Texas

Yvonne Thornton
Fifth Grade Teacher
Thomas Tolbert Elementary School
Dallas, Texas

Nancy Volpe
Instructional Coordinator
Buder School
St. Louis Public Schools
St. Louis, Missouri

Kirk Waller
Fifth Grade Teacher
Smith Academy
Duncanville, Texas

Dr. Christine Yeh
Child Psychologist
Columbia University
New York, New York

CONTRIBUTING WRITERS

Dinah Zike
Comfort, Texas

Reyna Eisenstark
Ghent, New York

Matt Goodman
Brooklyn, New York

Howard Gutner
Brooklyn, New York

Linda Scher
Raleigh, North Carolina

RFB&D
learning through listening

Students with print disabilities may be eligible to obtain an accessible, audio version of the pupil edition of this textbook. Please call Recording for the Blind & Dyslexic at 1-800-221-4792 for complete information.

Acknowledgments The publisher gratefully acknowledges permission to reprint the following copyrighted material:

From **North Star to Freedom: The Story of the Underground Railroad** by Gena Kinton Gorrell. Copyright © 1996 by Gena K. Gorrell. Random House, Inc., Delacorte Press. Used by permission.

From **The Glorious Cause: The American Revolution, 1763–1789** by Robert Middlekauff. Copyright © 1982 by Oxford University Press, Inc. Used by permission.

From **The Mighty Leaf: Tobacco Thru the Centuries** by J. E. Brooks. Copyright © 1952. Little, Brown & Co. Used by permission.

From **Through My Eyes** by Ruby Bridges. Copyright © 1999 by Ruby Bridges. Scholastic Press. Used by permission.

From **Pioneer Women: Voices from the Kansas Frontier** by Joanna L. Stratton. Copyright © 1981 by Joanna L. Stratton. Simon and Schuster. Used by permission.

(continued on page R101)

Macmillan/McGraw-Hill

A Division of The **McGraw·Hill** Companies

Published by Macmillan/McGraw-Hill, of McGraw-Hill Education, a division of The McGraw-Hill Companies, Inc., Two Penn Plaza, New York, New York 10121.

Printed in the United States of America

ISBN 0-02-149267-0

4 5 6 7 8 9 027/043 06 05 04 03

Contents

CHARTS, GRAPHS & DIAGRAMS

TIME LINES

MAPS

Social Studies Handbook

The Social Studies Strands are a way of thinking about Social Studies. Social Studies is the study of people and the world we live in. This is a very big subject! One way to think about Social Studies is to break it into parts. We call these parts strands.

The pie chart on the next page shows the eight strands of Social Studies. Each strand teaches us something about the world. Studying all of the strands together leads to an understanding of our world, past and present. The only thing left is the future. That will be up to you!

The Eight Strands
of Social Studies

Economics
Wants and needs, goods and services. Basic human needs are met in a variety of ways.

Citizenship
Rights, responsibilities, pride and hope. Our beliefs and principles help make up our national identity.

Culture
Holidays, traditions and stories. We learn about ourselves and our families through the customs we share and celebrate.

Geography
Location, place, maps and more. People and environments surround us and are ever changing.

Science, Technology, and Society
Inventions, computers and ideas. Technology has changed how people live together in the world

Social Studies Skills
Many special skills are needed to better understand the world around you.

History
Time and chronology, years and dates. Historical figures and ordinary people help shape our lives.

Government
People work to make the laws that influence our lives. People work with citizens to govern.

Thinking About Reading

Your social studies book traces the history of the United States through the present time. In order to understand the information and ideas that are presented, it is important to read your book carefully. The strategies below describe some of the ways that can help you become a more effective social studies reader.

Preview ⟩ Ask ⟩ Read ⟩ Review

How to Preview, Ask, Read, and Review:

1 **Preview the lesson.** Read the title, headings, and highlighted words. Look at the photographs, illustrations, and maps, and read their captions. Think about what you already know about the topic. Form a general idea of what the lesson is about.

2 **Ask yourself questions before you read and as you read.** For example, you might ask, "What will I learn about the War of 1812?"

3 **Read and reread.** Read carefully. Figure out the main ideas and pay attention to the details. When necessary, look up the meanings of unfamiliar words.

4 **Review what you have read by summarizing, either aloud or in writing.** Focus on the most important points. Make sure you have answers to the questions you raised.

1

Preview.
The title, the photograph, and its caption tell me this lesson will be about fishing for salmon.

2

Ask yourself questions.
I can turn the title into a question: "What is a salmon run?"

3

Read and reread.
The main idea will help focus my reading.

4

Review.
A good way to review is to write down the answers to my questions.

The Salmon Run

Every year salmon would swim from the sea against the flow of freshwater rivers, such as the Columbia, to lay their eggs. This event, known as the *salmon run*, was an important event for the Northwest Coast peoples.

During the salmon run a family could catch over 1,000 pounds of fish. Men and women put aside their tasks and went to the river to catch salmon. Some of it was eaten then. Most was dried or smoked and then stored for meals throughout the year.

Native Americans fishing for salmon

Use Visuals

When you use the **visuals** in this book, you can learn more from your reading. Visuals are the pictures, maps, charts, and graphs throughout your book. They provide useful information in an easy-to-study form.

Tip!

★ When looking at graphs, maps, or charts, read the legend or key to find out the meanings of special symbols.

★ Look for objects in the picture that might give additional information.

How to Use Visuals

Look closely at the visual. Then ask yourself the following questions:

- What does the picture, map, chart, or graph show?

- How does it help me understand what I have read?

- How does it add to the information I have read?

- What information does the caption or label provide?

Study the picture below:

The town has many buildings. The town has a large population.

The town has a harbor. Boats are used for transportation.

New York City, 1679

The caption tells us that the town is New York City in 1679.

Try It!

Study the photograph below. Then copy the diagram on a sheet of paper. Think about the information given in the photograph and caption. Then complete the diagram.

WILL SENATOR O'GORMAN VOTE 'YES' ON THE NATIONAL SUFFRAGE AMENDMENT ?

Suffragists in 1915 hold a banner urging a New York senator to support the Nineteenth Amendment.

Keep in Mind

For more help in reading social studies, keep these strategies in mind:

Use the pictures.
Photographs and drawings of people and places will make your reading more meaningful.

Study the charts and graphs.
Charts and graphs provide information in a form that is easy to understand.

Summarize.
In your own words, briefly describe what your reading is about.

Visual Information

The photo shows women in a group holding a protest sign.

The sign says "WILL SENATOR O'GORMAN VOTE 'YES' ON THE NATIONAL SUFFRAGE AMENDMENT?"

Visual Information

Visual Information

The group is dressed in clothes that women wore in the past.

Caption Information

Practice Activities!

1. **Use Visuals** Find a photograph in your book. Tell what information the photograph and the caption provide.

2. **Create Visuals** Find another visual in your book. Use information from the visual to complete a diagram like the one above.

Context Clues

As you read a sentence or paragraph in your book, you may find a word or term that you don't know. One way to figure out the meaning of an unfamiliar word is by looking for **context clues**. Context clues are the words and sentences that are near the unfamiliar word. Using context clues will give you a better understanding of what you read.

★ Have you heard this word before? How was it used?

★ Write down the context clues you used to find the meaning of the new word.

★ Use the new word in a sentence of your own to help you remember it.

How To Use Context Clues

Ask yourself the following questions:

● Are any parts of this word familiar?

● Are there other words, phrases, or sentences in the paragraph that can help me figure out the meaning of the word?

● What information do the other words, phrases, or sentences provide?

● Do the pictures give me any information about the word?

Read the paragraph below. What context clues would you use to identify the meaning of the word *conservation*?

The growth of cities has made it necessary for people in the United States to practice conservation. Without conservation, most of Earth's resources would be wasted or destroyed.

One way we can all practice conservation is by recycling. Recycling saves natural resources and energy. It reduces air pollution that can harm the environment. Recycling just one glass jar saves enough energy to keep a light bulb lit for four hours.

Context Clue:
Earth's resources would be wasted or destroyed.

Context Clue:
Practice conservation by recycling.

Context Clue:
Recycling saves natural resources and energy.

 **Try It!**

Read the paragraph below about cattle herds. Then copy and complete the diagram to find context clues for the word *stampede.*

Cowboys faced many dangers on the trail. These included thieves and Native Americans who did not want the herds trampling their land. The most dangerous part of the drive was usually controlling the herd. Anything, even lightning streaking across the sky, could scare a heard into stampeding. Once a stampede started, the cattle could trample anything in their path. To keep the herd calm, cowboys often sang to them. Cattle drives could last around 100 days.

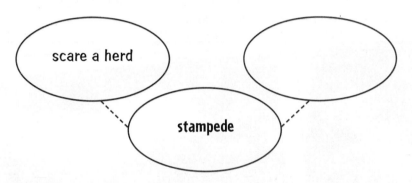

• What steps did you take to find the meaning of **stampede**?

 **Keep in Mind**

For more help in reading social studies, keep these strategies in mind:

Reread.
Review each sentence carefully. Make sure you understand what you have read before going further.

Find the main idea.
As you read, think about the topic and the most important information in each paragraph or section.

Make predictions.
As you read, think about what might come next in your reading.

Practice Activities!

1. **Read** Find an unfamiliar word or term in your book. Look for context clues to help you figure out its meaning.
2. **Write** Write one or two sentences about the word *computer.* Use context clues in your sentences.

WELCOME TO Washington, D.C.

Human Systems:
Many people use the Metro system to travel from where they live to where they work in Washington, D.C.

Physical Systems:
Great Falls is a famous waterfall on the Potomac River that provides a habitat to plants, fish, birds, and other animals.

Places and Regions:
Washington, D.C. has many memorials that honor special events and people from American history.

The World in Spatial Terms:

This satellite photo gives a close-up view of where buildings, monuments, and roads are in Washington, D.C.

Environment & Society:

People have changed the natural landscape along the waterfront, so that it meets their needs for places to live, work and play.

Uses of Geography

Cartographers use computer technology and other tools to create maps.

H10

Understanding Earth

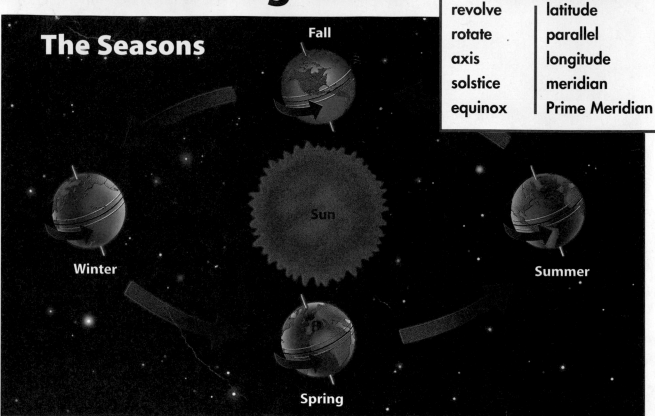

The Seasons

Fall

Sun

Winter

Summer

Spring

What is the relationship between Earth and the Sun?

- Earth **revolves** around the sun once a year. To revolve means to move in a circle around an object. As Earth revolves around the sun, it also **rotates.** To rotate means to turn around on an **axis.** An axis is an imaginary line through the center of an object. Earth's axis is tilted 23.5 º from due north. That tilt, plus the revolution of Earth around the sun, causes our seasons.

- Once a year the sun appears at its northernmost point. On that day, around June 22 in the Northern Hemisphere, the North Pole is tilted toward the sun and the sun appears directly overhead at the Tropic of Cancer. This day is the beginning of summer and has the most hours of daylight. In the Southern Hemisphere, June 22

has the year's fewest hours of daylight and is the beginning of winter. Winter begins around December 22 in the Northern Hemisphere. On that day, the North Pole is tilted away from the sun and the sun appears overhead at its southernmost point, the Tropic of Capricorn. The days on which the sun appears at its northernmost and southernmost points are called **solstices.** What is the shortest day of the year in the Northern Hemisphere?

- The time when the sun is directly over the equator is called an **equinox**. During an equinox, day and night are equal. This occurs in the Northern Hemisphere around March 21, the beginning of spring, and about September 21, which is the beginning of autumn. The dates are opposite in the Southern Hemisphere.

Understanding the Global Grid

What are latitude and longitude?

- Maps and globes use a system of imaginary lines to help us locate places.

- **Latitude** lines run east and west. They measure distance north or south of the equator. Latitude lines are also called **parallels**. Look at the latitude map below. What parallel is at 0º?

- **Longitude** lines run north and south. They are also called **meridians**. They measure distance east and west from the **Prime Meridian**. They also connect the North and South poles. Look at the longitude map below. Where do the longitudes all meet?

- Together the latitude and longitude lines form a global grid.

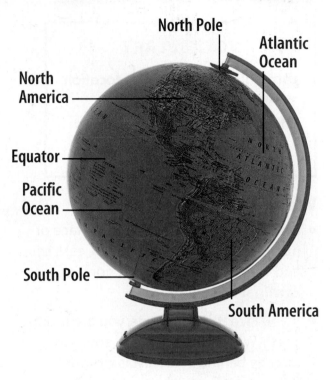

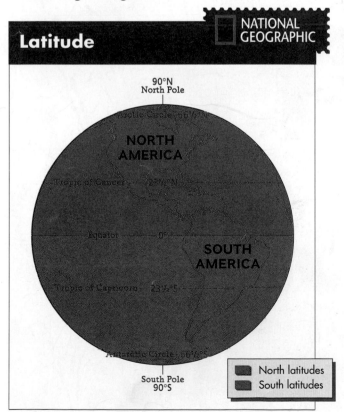

Latitude

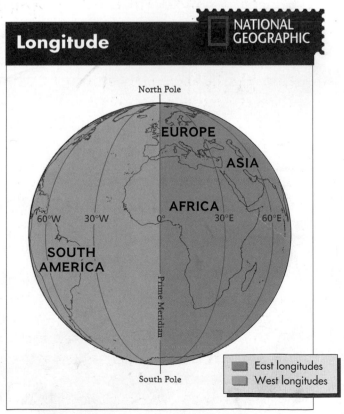

Longitude

Using Maps

VOCABULARY

cardinal directions	relative location
intermediate directions	scale
	map symbol
	locator

What are directions?

- Directions describe the way you face or move to get somewhere. North, east, south, and west are the main directions, or **cardinal directions**.

- If you face the North Pole, you are facing north. When you face north, south is directly behind you. West is to your left. What direction will be to your right?

- Look at the compass rose on the map below. The cardinal directions are written as **N**, **E**, **S**, and **W**. In which direction is Lynchburg from Richmond?

- The spikes between the cardinal directions on the compass rose show **intermediate**, or in-between **directions**.

- The intermediate directions are northeast, southeast, southwest, and northwest. The direction northwest is often written as **NW**. What letters are used for the other intermediate directions?

- Intermediate directions help us describe **relative location**. When we use relative location, we describe one place in relation to another. For example, you can say that Lynchburg is southwest of Charlottesville.

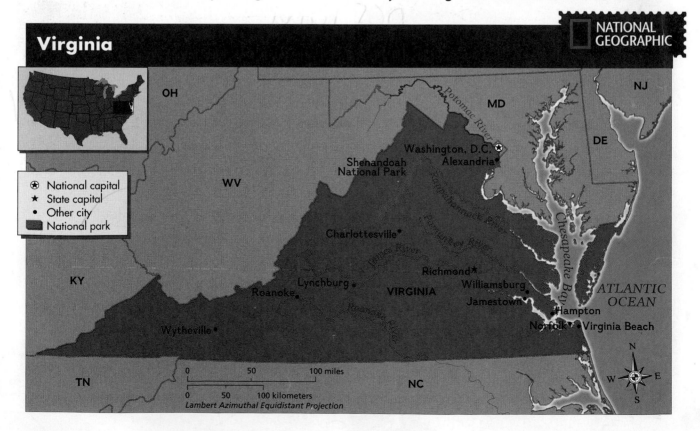

Virginia

NATIONAL GEOGRAPHIC

- ⊛ National capital
- ★ State capital
- • Other city
- ▬ National park

OH
MD
NJ
DE
WV
Potomac River
Washington, D.C.
Shenandoah National Park
Alexandria
KY
Charlottesville
Rappahannock River
Chesapeake Bay
Richmond
Lynchburg
VIRGINIA
Williamsburg
Jamestown
Roanoke
ATLANTIC OCEAN
Hampton
Norfolk
Virginia Beach
Wytheville

0 50 100 miles
0 50 100 kilometers
Lambert Azimuthal Equidistant Projection

TN
NC

N
W E
S

What is a map scale?

- All maps are smaller than the real area that they show. To figure out real distance between places, most maps include a scale. The scale shows the relationship between distances on a map and real distances.

- The scales on the maps in this book are drawn with two horizontal lines. The top line shows distance in miles. What unit of measurement does the bottom line use?

How do you use a map scale?

- You can use a ruler to measure distances on a map. You can also make a scale strip.

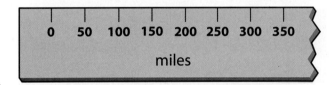

```
0   50  100  150  200  250  300  350
                 miles
```

Place the edge of a strip of paper under the scale lines on map A. Mark the distances in miles.

- Use the scale strip to measure the distance between two places on Map A. Place the zero on Kauai. What is the distance in miles between the island of Kauai and the city of Honolulu?

- Maps are drawn at different scales. Maps A and B both show the Hawaiian Islands, but the islands look larger on Map B. They look larger because Map B has a larger scale. This means that it shows more detail.

- The scales are different, but the distance between places on both maps is the same. On both maps, what is the distance in miles between Niihau and Molokai?

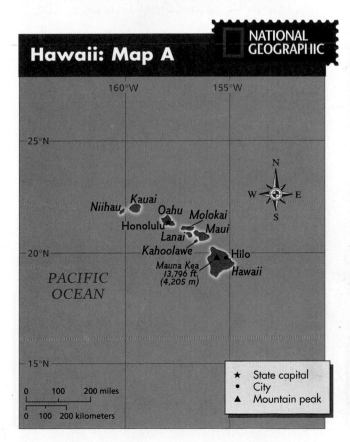

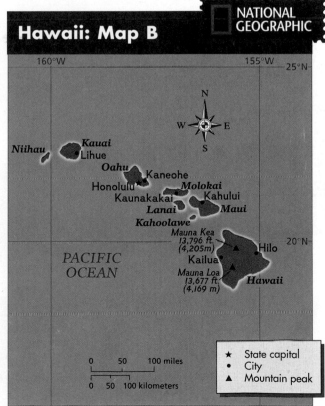

Reviewing Geography Skills

Why do maps include symbols?

- A **map symbol** is a drawing that stands for real things.

- On a map common symbols include dots, lines, triangles, and colors. Many maps use the color blue to stand for water. What do dots sometimes stand for?

- Maps often use symbols that are small drawings of the things they stand for. A drawing of a tree might stand for a forest. What might an airplane stand for?

- Often the same symbol stands for different things on different maps. For this reason many maps have a map key to explain the symbol on the map.

- You should always study the map key on a map. Look at the map keys on the maps below. What does the color green show in each map?

What do locators show?

- A **locator** is a small map set into the main map. It shows where the area of the main map is located. Where on the maps below are the locators placed?

- Most of the locators in this book show either the United States or the Western Hemisphere. Look at the maps below. What area do these locators show?

- The area of the main map is shown in red on the locator. Look at the locators below. Where do they locate the main maps?

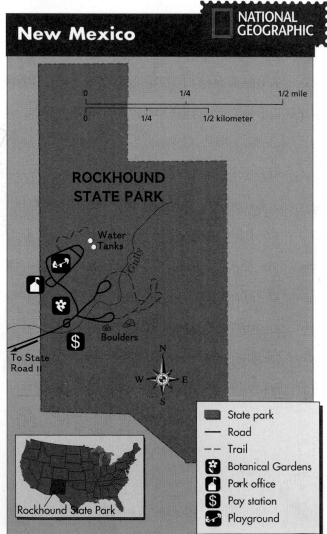

Using Maps to Find Geographic Information

Why do maps have titles?

- The map title names the area the map shows. It may also tell you the kind of information shown on the map.

What is a political map?

- A **political map** shows cities, states, and countries. What symbol is used to show state capitals on the map below? What is the capital of Montana?

- Political maps use lines to show borders. States or countries may be shown in different colors. What color is used on the map to show Idaho? How many colors are used to show the Mountain States?

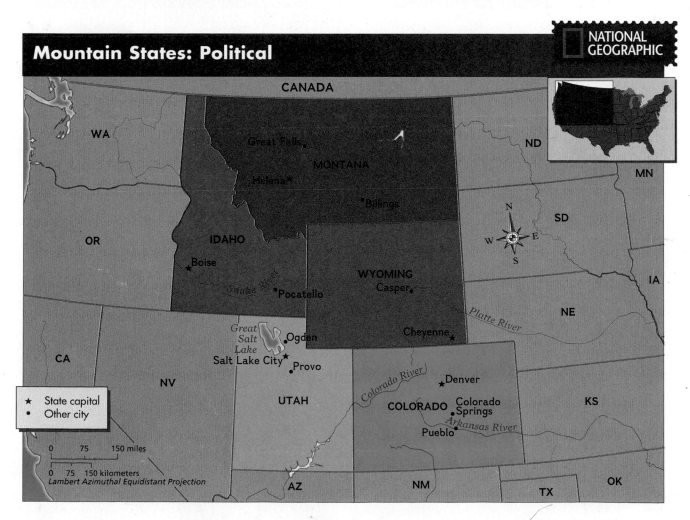

Mountain States: Political

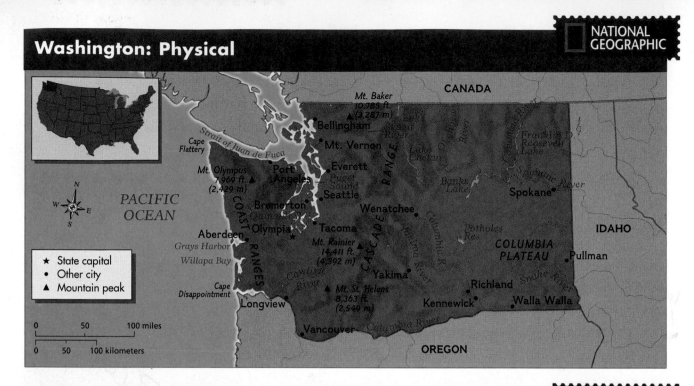

Washington: Physical

NATIONAL GEOGRAPHIC

★ State capital
• Other city
▲ Mountain peak

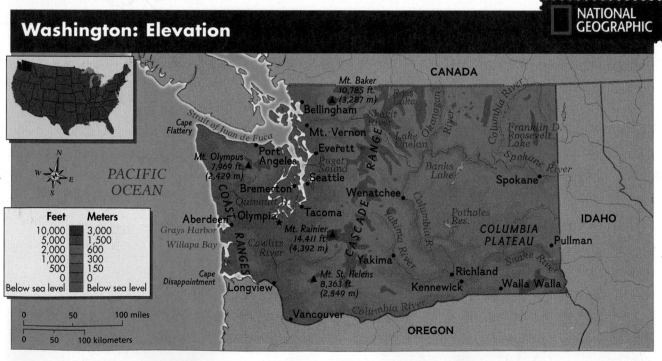

Washington: Elevation

NATIONAL GEOGRAPHIC

Feet	Meters
10,000	3,000
5,000	1,500
2,000	600
1,000	300
500	150
0	0
Below sea level	Below sea level

What are physical maps?

- A **physical map** shows the characteristics of the physical environment, such as landforms.

- **Relief** is shading on a map to show mountains or hilly areas. Highlands are shaded to appear higher than lowlands. Look at the relief on the physical map above . Which parts of Washington state have the greatest relief?

- An **elevation map** is a physical map that uses colors to show the elevation, or height of land above sea level. The height is usually measured in feet or meters. What color does the elevation map use to show elevations between 5,000 feet and 10,000 feet? What is the elevation of Mount Rainier?

What is a historical map?

- A **historical map** is a map that shows information about past events and where they occurred. Look at the historical map to the right. In which group of colonies is Virginia shown? What color is used to show the New England colonies?

What is a road map?

- A **road map** shows you how to get from one place to another. Road maps usually show different types of roads, cities, points of interest, and natural features such as rivers. Look at the road map. What road would you take to get from Raleigh to Wilmington?

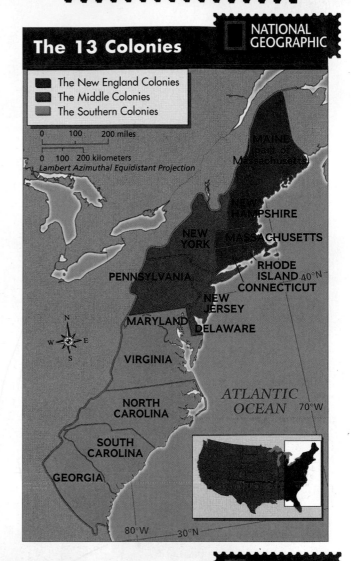

The 13 Colonies

- The New England Colonies
- The Middle Colonies
- The Southern Colonies

Lambert Azimuthal Equidistant Projection

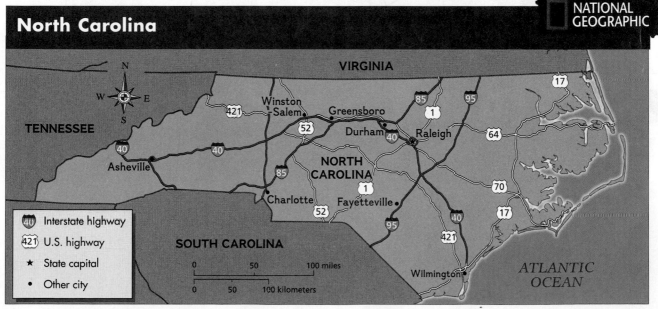

North Carolina

- 🛡 Interstate highway
- 🛡 U.S. highway
- ★ State capital
- • Other city

Land and People of the United States

The United States is a country of great natural beauty. One of our national treasures is Yosemite National Park. John Muir wrote, "Yosemite Park is … a refuge [shelter] from the roar and dust… This one noble [impressive] park is big enough and rich enough for a whole life of study and… enjoyment." John Muir was a conservationist. A conservationist works to preserve, or protect, the wilderness.

In this introduction, you will learn about our magnificent land. You will also learn how different groups of people have made the United States a great nation.

America's Land

The United States has several kinds of landforms. A landform is a shape on Earth's surface. Some landforms in the United States are: mountains, plains, plateaus, and basins.

MOUNTAINS

The writer Mark Twain once said, "A [mountain] climber's appetite… is hard to satisfy; when it comes upon him he is like a starving man with a feast before him." Mountain climbing is one way people use landforms. Mountains protect settlements by making them difficult to reach. They can also get in the way of people who want to go places and do things. America's longest mountain range is the **Rocky Mountains**. It stretches from Alaska to Mexico. One of the highest mountain ranges is the Coast Ranges in the West. Our country's highest mountain, Mount McKinley, is located in the Alaska Range. The lowest mountain range is the Appalachian Mountains. This range stretches from Maine to Alabama. Many of the mountains in the United States are rich in natural resources such as minerals and forests.

READING CHECK **Which is the longest mountain range in the United States?**

PLAINS

The Interior Plains are a vast area of flat land stretching between the Appalachian and Rocky Mountains. The Great Plains, in the west, are drier than the rest of the area. However, much of this region has rich soil. This makes it ideal for growing corn and wheat. The interior lowland has our country's largest river system. It includes the Great Lakes and the Mississippi River.

A flat lowland lies along the Atlantic Coast and the Gulf Coast. This **Coastal Plain** has sandy beaches, wetlands, and rich farmland. Many deep harbors and large cities are on the Coastal Plain.

NATIONAL GEOGRAPHIC

United States: Landforms

BROOKS RANGE

ALASKA CANADA
ALASKA RANGE
Mt. McKinley
20,320 ft.
(6,194 m)
0   300   600 miles
0   300 600 kilometers
170°W   160°W   150°W

CANADA

Superior

L. Ontario

CASCADE RANGE

COLUMBIA PLATEAU

ROCKY MOUNTAINS

GREAT PLAINS

CENTRAL PLAINS

Michigan

Huron

Erie

APPALACHIAN MOUNTAINS

N
W   E
S

40°N

COAST RANGES

SIERRA NEVADA

GREAT BASIN
Mt. Whitney
(4,404 ft.
(4,418 m)

PACIFIC OCEAN

COLORADO PLATEAU

INTERIOR PLAINS

PIEDMONT

ATLANTIC COASTAL PLAIN

ATLANTIC OCEAN

▲ Highest point
▼ Lowest point

Death Valley
-282 ft.
(-86 m)

SONORAN DESERT

0   250   500 miles
0   250   500 kilometers
Lambert Azimuthal
Equal-Area Projection

130°W

30°N

120°W

70°W

HAWAII
Maupa Kea
13,796 ft.
(4,205 m)
0   100   200 miles
0 100 200 kilometers
160°W

20°W

MEXICO

Gulf of California

GULF COASTAL PLAIN

Gulf of Mexico

BAHAMA ISLANDS

80°W

110°W

90°W

CUBA

Map Skill

What are the names of some landforms along the coasts of the United States?

PLATEAUS AND BASINS

The Western Plateaus and Basins region stretches from Washington State to Mexico. It is the driest region of the United States. The Colorado Plateau in the south has some of the most unusual landforms in our nation, including natural bridges, the **Grand Canyon** (above), and huge, flat-topped rocks. The Grand Canyon is a huge canyon that has been carved out by the fast-moving waters of the Colorado River.

 Which is the driest region of the United States?

7

America's Climate

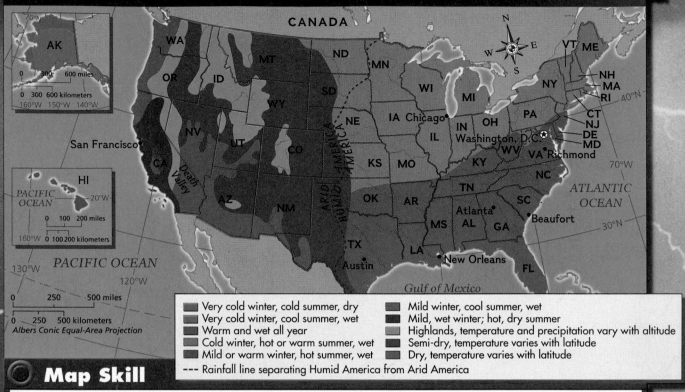

Map Legend:
- Very cold winter, cold summer, dry
- Very cold winter, cool summer, wet
- Warm and wet all year
- Cold winter, hot or warm summer, wet
- Mild or warm winter, hot summer, wet
- Mild winter, cool summer, wet
- Mild, wet winter; hot, dry summer
- Highlands, temperature and precipitation vary with altitude
- Semi-dry, temperature varies with latitude
- Dry, temperature varies with latitude
- --- Rainfall line separating Humid America from Arid America

Map Skill

1. Which states have a wet climate with warm winters and cool summers?

2. Which state is warm and wet all year?

The weather in the United States differs from place to place. That is because different parts of our nation have different **climates**. Climate is the weather an area has over a number of years. The climate of a place includes its general temperature, and amount of **precipitation**. Precipitation (prih sihp ih TAY shun) is the moisture that falls to Earth as rain or snow.

Climate varies for many reasons. A region's distance from the equator affects its climate. Places near the equator are warmer than places that are farther away from it.

One way to study the nation's climate is to divide it into two areas of precipitation, arid and humid. Arid regions are dry. Humid regions are wet. The East is humid and receives more than 20 inches of precipitation a year. The West is arid. It gets less than 20 inches of precipitation a year.

READING CHECK

Which area of the United States is humid?

United States Vegetation

The five vegetation regions of the United States are shown on the map. The kinds of plant life found in each region are shown in the table. Study these graphics, then answer the questions below.

NATIONAL GEOGRAPHIC

U.S. VEGETATION REGIONS

Legend:
- Forests
- Grasslands
- Desert
- Tropical
- Tundra

VEGETATION REGION	TYPES OF PLANTS
Forests	needleleaf trees, broadleaf trees, ferns, fungi, mosses
Grassland	bluestem grass, buffalo grass, gamma grass
Deserts	cactuses, desert palm, sagebrush, wildflowers
Tropical	rubber, mahogany, tropical palm, ferns, orchids
Tundra	mosses, shrubs, wild-flowers, low-growing grasses

QUESTIONS:

1. Which plants are found in deserts?
2. What types of vegetation grow in Texas?
3. Which state has a tundra?

To learn more, visit our Website: www.mhschool.com

9

Using Latitude and Longitude Maps

To help people locate places on Earth, geographers have drawn lines on maps and globes. They are called lines of **latitude** and **longitude**. The lines of latitude run east and west and measure distance north and south of the equator. The equator is labeled 0°. The symbol ° stands for degree, which is a unit of measurement. Lines of longitude run north and south. They are called **meridians** and measure distance east and west of the prime meridian. The **prime meridian** is labeled 0°. These lines identify the absolute location of place. Absolute location is the exact location of a place expressed by latitude and longitude.

VOCABULARY

latitude
longitude
meridian
prime meridian
parallel
grid

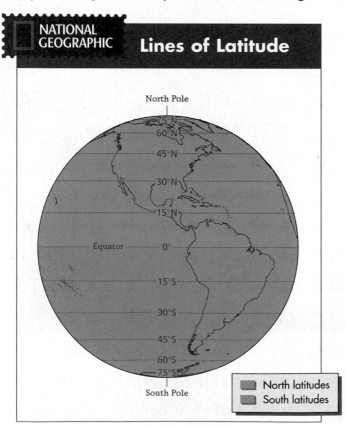

NATIONAL GEOGRAPHIC — Lines of Latitude

North Pole
75°N
60°N
45°N
30°N
15°N
Equator 0°
15°S
30°S
45°S
60°S
75°S
South Pole

■ North latitudes
■ South latitudes

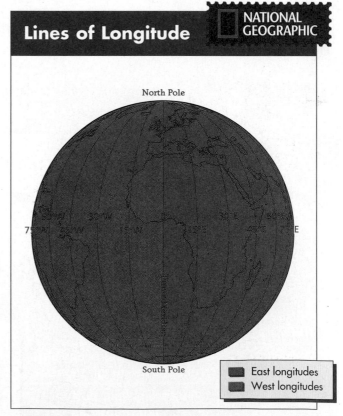

Lines of Longitude — **NATIONAL GEOGRAPHIC**

North Pole
South Pole

■ East longitudes
■ West longitudes

LEARN THE SKILL

Follow these steps to better understand latitude and longitude lines.

1. **Identify the lines of latitude.**
   Lines of latitude run east and west and are called **parallels**. Parallel lines are always the

same distance apart and never meet. Those north of the equator are labeled **N**. Those south of the equator are labeled **S**.

2. **Identify lines of longitude.**
Lines of longitude run north and south. Those east of the prime meridian are labeled **E**. Those west of the prime meridian are labeled **W**.

3. **Look at the grid to find where the lines intersect.**
A grid is a set of criss-crossing lines that helps you find the latitude and longitude of a place on a map. For example, the map below shows Memphis, Tennessee at 35°N latitude and 90°W longitude.

TRY THE SKILL

Use the grid on the map below to locate New Orleans, Louisiana, and Miami, Florida. Then answer the following questions.

1. What is the latitude of New Orleans?

2. What is the longitude of New Orleans?

3. What city is near 32°N and 90°W?

4. What is the grid location of Miami, Florida?

5. When would it be helpful to find latitude and longitude on a map?

EXTEND THE SKILL

You can learn more about places by comparing latitude and longitude maps with other kinds of maps. Look at the map below.

- What is the major mountain range?

- What is the approximate grid location of Mt. Mitchell?

- Between which two parallels does the Savannah River flow?

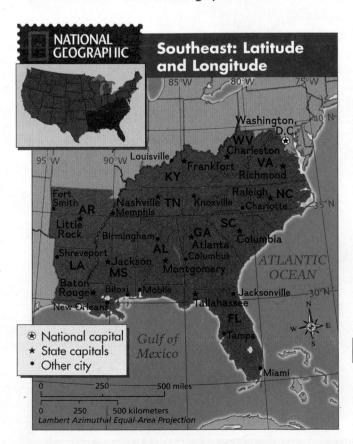

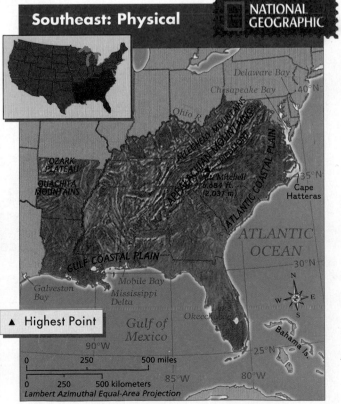

Environment

Climate and vegetation are parts of our **environment**. The environment is all the surroundings in which people, plants, and animals live.

NATURAL RESOURCES

Natural resources can be **renewable** or **nonrenewable**. Renewable resources, such as trees, can be replaced. Nonrenewable resources, such as minerals, cannot be replaced. **Fossil fuels** such as coal, oil, and natural gas are also nonrenewable. They are formed from plants and animals.

Natural Resources of the U.S.

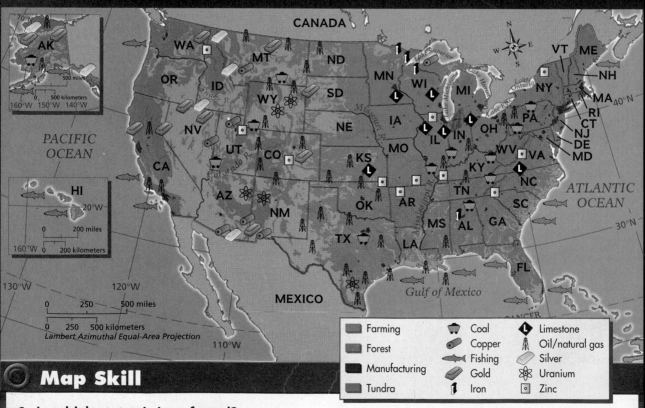

Farming	Coal	Limestone
Forest	Copper	Oil/natural gas
Manufacturing	Fishing	Silver
Tundra	Gold	Uranium
	Iron	Zinc

Map Skill

1. In which states is iron found?
2. What is a natural resource of Florida?

ECOSYSTEMS

Our environment is divided into many smaller special environments called **ecosystems**. An ecosystem is all the living and nonliving things in a certain area. Soil, water, tiny plants called algae (AL jee), insects, fish, and frogs, are some of the things that make up the ecosystem of a pond. The six major kinds of ecosystems are croplands, forests, coasts and oceans, urban and suburban areas, arid and rangeland areas, and fresh-water areas.

Ecosystems are in a biological balance. The living and non-living things in an ecosystem affect one another. For example, in a pond, many animals get their food from pond plants. The plants get nutrients from the pond and energy from the sun. Without the plants, the animals could not live there. Sometimes **pollution** can threaten this balance. Pollution is unclean matter.

READING CHECK How do people change their environment?

ECOSYSTEM OF A POND

1. heron
2. dragonfly
3. cattail
4. waterlily
5. fish
6. turtle
7. Mallard duck
8. algae
9. frog
10. water bug

Diagram Skill

1. What kinds of insects live in or near ponds?

2. Which plants are found in ponds?

13

Changing Our Land

People have been changing the American land for thousands of years. Native Americans cleared spaces in forests to build villages and farms. Later, settlers built canals, dams, mines, and factories.

When we build a home, a highway, or a city, we add physical features to the land. We change the land.

We also change the air and water on the earth. We change the air when we drive a car or use a machine. We change the flow of water over the land when we build dams. Dams are often built to help stop flooding where people live. They help keep people safe. Dams can also direct water to areas where water is needed.

Although our changes to the land have sometimes caused changes to ecosystems, government and private business are trying to prevent harming our ecosystems.

CITIES

One of the biggest changes in the American land came with **urbanization**. Urbanization is the development and growth of cities. Less than a century ago, most people in the United States lived in **rural** areas. Rural means "of the countryside." Cities are central places. They often help businesses grow. People began to start businesses and build factories in cities. As businesses began to grow in cities, more people began moving to **urban** areas, or cities, for better-paying jobs. The cities also became diverse, with immigrants who arrived from many different countries.

During the 1800s thousands of people came to Chicago to work in its factories and steel mills. Today Chicago is the largest city in the Middle West. It has many tall buildings, the largest grain market, and the second-busiest airport in the nation.

CONSERVATION

The growth of cities has made it necessary for people in the United States to practice **conservation**. Conservation is the protection and careful use of natural resources.

One way that we conserve is by **recycling**. Recycling is the reuse of materials. Recycling saves natural resources and energy. Today, government, businesses, and everyday people work together to practice conservation.

READING CHECK What is urbanization?

Problem Solving

Every day you face problems. Problem solving is a process you can use to find solutions. It can help you figure out how to learn more about an issue or how to get your message across to other people.

LEARN THE SKILL

Follow these steps to solve a problem.

1. **Identify the problem.**
   Here is an example. Sue is a fifth-grader who has noticed that the bald eagle appears on coins and bills. She would like to find out about how the bald eagle became a national symbol, and then share this information with her class. She is not sure what method to use to inform other students.

2. **Gather information.**
   Sue goes to the library and does research. She finds out that the bald eagle was declared the National Emblem of the United States by the Second Continental Congress in 1782, and that it is a symbol of freedom.
   She finds out that bald eagles live in most of North America. She finds photographs and maps. Then Sue asks students if they know about national symbols, maybe from bulletin boards or from students' reports. She asks them which methods they think gave the best information.

3. **Identify the options.**
   To solve the problem, Sue thinks she could write a poem. She also could make a speech about the topic in class. A third solution would be to make a bulletin board illustrating the topic.

4. **List the possible consequences.**
   Each option, or choice, has a **consequence**, or result, and should be considered against values, lawfulness, and whether it can be done. Reciting a poem might get people interested in the topic. However, Sue wants to give more information than a poem would allow. Making a speech might be better because she can give more information. However, people may not remember all of the information. Sue thinks that making a bulletin board might be the best solution because it can include explanations, photographs, and maps. She thinks more people will remember the information this way.

5. **Choose a solution. Check it with your parents, teacher, or other adult.**
   Sue decides to make a bulletin board at school. She checks with her parents and they agree. Sue includes words, photos, and maps in the display.

6. **Evaluate the solution.**
   A year later, many students at school knew about the bald eagle and how it became the national emblem. Based on this result, Sue **evaluates**, or judges her solution best.

TRY THE SKILL

The Science Club at Washington Elementary School has a problem. It does not have enough money for all club members to enter projects in the annual Science Fair.

Enrique suggests waiting until next year, when the club will have more money. Lucia suggests choosing two projects to enter on behalf of the entire club. Frances suggests washing cars to make money so all members of the club can participate in the fair.

Follow the steps on the previous page, to help the students solve their problem.

1. How would you identify the problem?

2. What information would help solve it?

3. What are the possible options?

4. What are the possible consequences?

5. What is the best solution and why? Talk with your parents, teacher, or other adult about your solution.

6. What was the best solution?

EXTEND THE SKILL

Knowing how to solve problems can help you figure out how to get a message across to others. Suppose you will go to the library to do research on whether there is a plant or tree that is a national symbol. You want to make a bulletin board using the research. You have one hour at the library and need to choose how to spend your time. Use the problem-solving process. Answer the questions.

- Which display methods would best get your point across?

- What sources are available at the library? How long does it take to use these sources?

- How will you spend your time at the library? What do your parents, teacher, or other adult think?

- How can using the problem-solving process help you figure out how to get your message across to other people?

The American People

"Give me your tired, your poor, your huddled masses yearning to breathe free," wrote poet Emma Lazarus in 1883. Her words appear on the Statue of Liberty, a symbol of freedom to millions of **immigrants**. An immigrant is a person who comes to a country from another country to live.

The United States has been described as a nation of immigrants. In fact, most Americans have someone in their family background who was an immigrant. Over the years, immigrants from all over the world have made contributions to the United States. Their differences have brought a great deal of cultural **diversity** (dih VUR sih tee) to our country. Diversity is variety.

This diversity can be seen in the many religions, languages, **values**, and traditions that are found in our nation. Values are the beliefs that guide the way people live. One important value is patriotism, or love for and loyal support of one's country.

MANY DIFFERENT PEOPLE

Part of our nation's diversity is due to its many different **ethnic groups**. An ethnic group is a group of people who share the same customs and language. Many also have a common history.

Unlike other ethnic groups in the United States, the Native Americans have lived here for thousands of years. It was not until the 1500s that Europeans and Africans began coming to what is now the United States. The Africans did not choose to come. They were brought here as captives.

Since then, ethnic groups from many areas have come to this country. They include Jews, Italians, Scots, Irish and Germans. Today the largest number of immigrants come from Asia and Latin America (Mexico, Central America, the Caribbean Islands, and South America). People whose ancestors are from Spanish or Portuguese-speaking countries in the Western Hemisphere are called Hispanics or Latinos. An ancestor is a relative who lived before you.

What contributions have immigrants made to the United States?

People of the United States

The population of the United States has grown from less than 4 million people in 1790 to over 281 million in 2001. We know this because every ten years our country takes a  census. A census is an official study of the people of a country. It provides us with information about the number of people in an area, where they live, and how they live. This information helps the government plan for our future needs. Study the graphics on these pages. Then answer the questions.

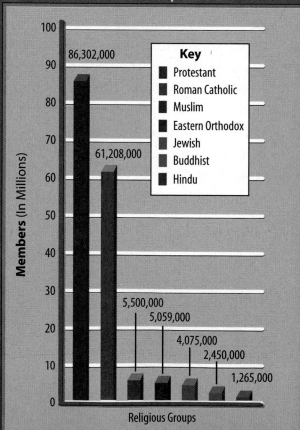

Major Religious Groups in the United States, 2000

Members (In Millions)

Religious Group	Members
Protestant	86,302,000
Roman Catholic	61,208,000
Muslim	5,500,000
Eastern Orthodox	5,059,000
Jewish	4,075,000
Buddhist	2,450,000
Hindu	1,265,000

Key
- Protestant
- Roman Catholic
- Muslim
- Eastern Orthodox
- Jewish
- Buddhist
- Hindu

Religious Groups

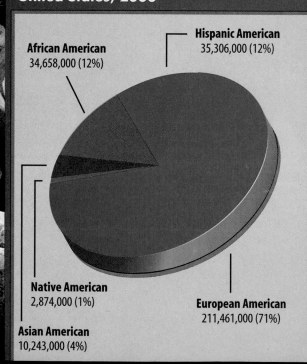

Ethnic Groups in the United States, 2000

- **African American** 34,658,000 (12%)
- **Hispanic American** 35,306,000 (12%)
- **Native American** 2,874,000 (1%)
- **Asian American** 10,243,000 (4%)
- **European American** 211,461,000 (71%)

QUESTIONS:

1 In 2001 over half of the foreign-born population lived in just three states—California, New York, and Florida. Name the other state that has a foreign-born population of more than 15%.

2 Which is the third largest religious group in the United States?

3 What do these graphics tell you about the United States?

PERCENT OF FOREIGN BORN BY STATE

CANADA

MEXICO

■	15% or more
■	10.0%–14.9%
■	5.0%–9.9%
■	4.9% or less

Lambert Azimuthal Equal-Area Projection

To learn more,
visit our Web site:
www.mhschool.com

21

Government

Our nation's government is responsible for protecting the diverse people who make up the United States. Our nation's people take part in our government.

"We the people of the United States… ." These famous words begin the **Constitution** of the United States. A constitution is a plan of government for a country. Our plan serves the people by providing ways to make, carry out, and interpret the laws of our land.

Our constitution calls for a **democratic republic**. In a democratic republic, people choose representatives to run the **federal**, or national, government. A representative is a person chosen to speak or act for others. Like the federal government, representatives elected by the people run all of our state and local governments.

Every four years voters in the United States elect a President. The President is the highest elected official in the United States. Every President except George Washington has worked and lived in the White House. It was designed by James Hoban, an Irish-born immigrant.

A PATRIOTIC OATH

The Pledge of Allegiance is a patriotic oath that was written more than 100 years ago. By reciting it, we promise our allegiance, or loyalty, to our flag and to our nation.

Primary Source:

The Pledge of Allegiance
by Francis Bellamy, 1892

I pledge allegiance (uh LEE juhns) to the flag of the United States of America and to the Republic for which it stands, one Nation under God, indivisible, with liberty and justice for all.

What do we promise when we recite the Pledge of Allegiance?

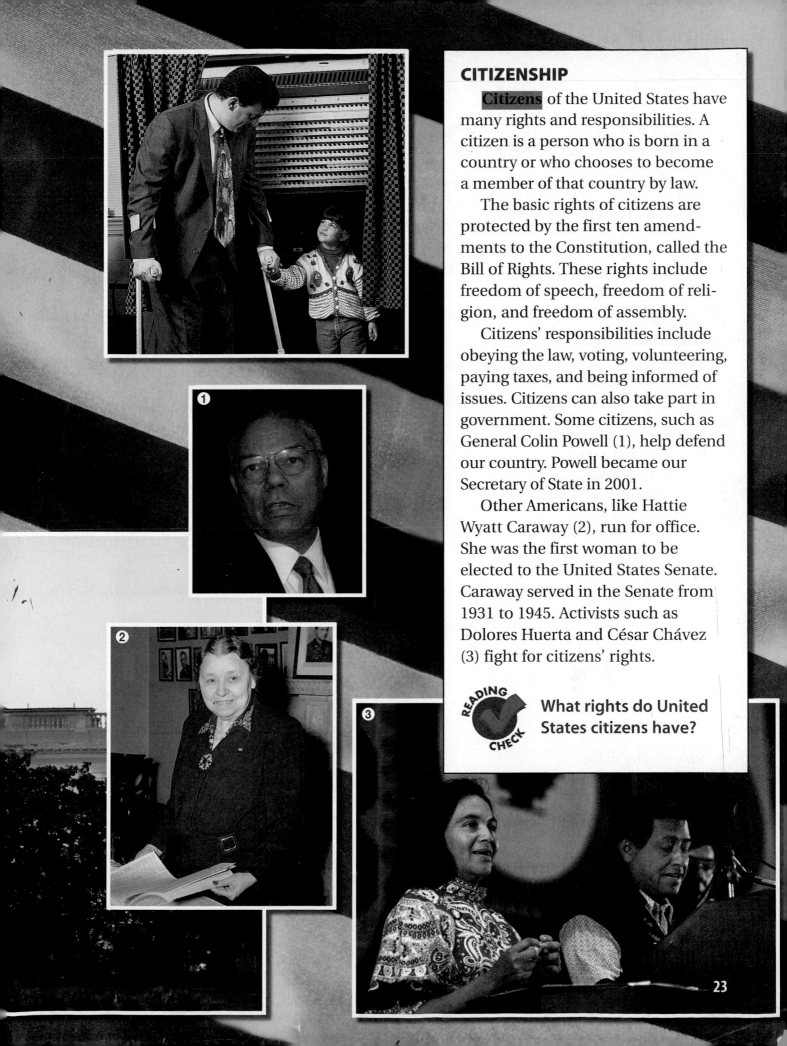

CITIZENSHIP

Citizens of the United States have many rights and responsibilities. A citizen is a person who is born in a country or who chooses to become a member of that country by law.

The basic rights of citizens are protected by the first ten amendments to the Constitution, called the Bill of Rights. These rights include freedom of speech, freedom of religion, and freedom of assembly.

Citizens' responsibilities include obeying the law, voting, volunteering, paying taxes, and being informed of issues. Citizens can also take part in government. Some citizens, such as General Colin Powell (1), help defend our country. Powell became our Secretary of State in 2001.

Other Americans, like Hattie Wyatt Caraway (2), run for office. She was the first woman to be elected to the United States Senate. Caraway served in the Senate from 1931 to 1945. Activists such as Dolores Huerta and César Chávez (3) fight for citizens' rights.

READING CHECK What rights do United States citizens have?

23

Writing an Outline

Suppose you were asked to write a report based on what you just read about government and citizenship. You would need to organize your information. Making an **outline** helps you to group facts and see how they are related. An outline is a plan that presents ideas about a subject in an organized way.

GOVERNMENT AND CITIZENSHIP
I. Constitution
        A. Plan for our government
        B. Makes our country a democratic republic
        C. Protects the rights of citizens
II. Rights of Citizens
        A. Freedom of speech
        B. Freedom of religion
        C. Freedom of assembly
III. Responsibilities of Citizens
        A. Obeying the law
        B. Voting
        C. Paying taxes
        D. Staying informed of issues
        E. Volunteering

LEARN THE SKILL

Use the following steps to create an outline, such as the one above.

1. **Identify the topic.**
   The topic is "Government and Citizenship."

2. **Identify the main ideas.**
   The main ideas for the topic are "The Constitution," "The Rights of Citizens," and "The Responsibilities of Citizens."

3. **Identify the facts that support the main idea.**
   Look back at pages 22–23. There are several details and important facts that support each main idea. "Plan for our government," for example, is a detail that supports the main idea "Constitution."

4. **Organize the information.**
   When you create an outline, first use Roman numerals to show the sequence of the main ideas. Then, under each of your main ideas, group the facts that support it. Place a capital letter beside each fact. How does the outline help you to understand the information you just read?

TRY THE SKILL

Read the following article about Supreme Court Justice Thurgood Marshall.

> *Thurgood Marshall was born in Baltimore in 1908 where he attended African American-only public schools. Marshall graduated from Howard University with a degree in law. From 1936 to 1961 Marshall served as chief legal advisor for the National Association for the Advancement of Colored People. In 1954 Marshall went before the Supreme Court to argue for an end to separate schools for blacks and whites. The resulting Supreme Court decision ended the practice. In 1967 President Lyndon B. Johnson chose Marshall to become the first African American to serve on the Supreme Court. Marshall was a strong voice for civil rights on the Court until he retired in 1991.*

Look back over the passage above and identify the topic and main ideas. Now, create an outline organizing the information found in the article. Include detailed facts for each of the main ideas. Then use your outline to answer the following questions.

1. What is the topic of the article?

2. What are the main ideas?

3. What are the facts related to Marshall's career?

4. How can writing an outline help you understand information that you read?

EXTEND THE SKILL

Use the following outline to write a short report about César Chávez, who worked to help migrant farm workers in California.

I. Early years of César Chávez
   A. Born in Yuma, Arizona, 1927
   B. Served in the Navy
   C. Worked in community action programs
II. Organizing the farm workers
   A. Fasted, marched, rallied, and organized boycotts
   B. Formed the United Farm Workers
   C. Obtained union contracts and improved conditions for farm workers
III. Honors
   A. Honorary Doctorate, Arizona State University
   B. Presidential Medal of Freedom
   C. Hall of Heroes

• How can creating outlines help you to **draw conclusions** about what you read?

Our Nation's Economy

Citizens of the United States share other things in addition to customs and civil rights. They also benefit from the American **free enterprise** system. This system allows equal opportunity for people to own and operate their own businesses. Each business person makes their own economic decisions. For example, the owner of a factory decides what to make, how much to produce, and what price to charge. A street vendor decides which items to sell, where to sell them, and what price to charge.

People who form and run a business are called **entrepreneurs**. Entrepreneurs use their ideas and savings to start a business. Entrepreneurs need skilled and hard-working people to produce their goods and services. They are an important part of free enterprise and make our economy strong and growing.

Examples of free enterprise can be found in many places—suburban shopping malls, big cities, even farms. The laws of the United States help and protect both businesses and **consumers**. A consumer is a person who buys and uses goods and services. The United States Department of Agriculture, for example, helps farmers protect their business. Our laws help consumers by making businesses list what is in the products we eat. Many products must also list the amount of fat, salt (sodium) and other contents that affect our health.

READING CHECK How has equal opportunity helped our economy?

U.S.
INSPECTED
AND PASSED BY
DEPARTMENT OF
AGRICULTURE
EST.38

nas
)¢

Preserving Our History

"History is who we are and why we are the way we are," said author David McCullough. History is the study or record of what happened in the past.

Historians, people who study the past, examine clues and records that people have left behind. Historians use this information to understand why people do what they do, and then write books to keep history alive.

Museums help keep the stories of hard times and successes of entire groups of people alive. Ellis Island was the gateway through which over 12 million immigrants passed. Today it is a museum from which over 100 million Americans can trace their ancestors.

Historians also study **primary sources** and **secondary sources**. A primary source is information that comes from the time being studied: It could be a letter, an official document, or a photograph. A secondary source is an account written by someone who did not witness the event being studied.

The Library of Congress is working to preserve important primary sources. For example, two copies of the Gettysburg Address have been preserved in special environmental containers. These containers allow future generations to enjoy and study the documents.

Another way of preserving history is by preserving historic districts, or areas in towns and cities. Red brick buildings in the historic district of Beacon Hill, Massachusetts date back to the 1700s.

READING CHECK How do people preserve history?

Regions of the United States

Most nations are divided into regions. Each region is a mixture of physical and cultural features. The six regions of the United States are examples of this. Each region has its own environment. Tall redwood forests are found only in the West, for example.

Each region also shares a history and other features. In the 1800s, for example, whaling was important to the Northeast's economy.

NATIONAL GEOGRAPHIC

Six Regions of the United States

MOUNTAIN   MIDDLE WEST   NORTHEAST

ALASKA

WASHINGTON

VERMONT   MAINE

MONTANA

NORTH DAKOTA   MN   MICHIGAN   NEW HAMPSHIRE

OREGON

IDAHO   SOUTH DAKOTA   WI   NEW YORK   MA   RHODE ISLAND   CONNECTICUT

WYOMING   NEBRASKA   IOWA   PA   NEW JERSEY   DELAWARE

NEVADA   ILLINOIS   IN   OHIO   MARYLAND

UTAH   COLORADO   KANSAS   MISSOURI   WV   VIRGINIA

WEST   CALIFORNIA   KENTUCKY   NORTH CAROLINA

TENNESSEE

ARIZONA   NEW MEXICO   OKLAHOMA   AR   SC

MS   AL   GEORGIA

HAWAII   TEXAS   LA   FLORIDA

SOUTHWEST   SOUTHEAST

Lambert Azimuthal Equal-Area Projection

Map Skill

1. Which regions border the Great Lakes?   **2.** Which region has the fewest states?

CULTURAL REGIONS

Our nation has other kinds of regions also. Among them are **cultural regions**. Cultural regions are areas where people share the same language, beliefs, and customs.

The Gullah people of coastal South Carolina and Georgia make up a cultural region. They speak a language like that of Sierra Leone in Africa. They also tell African folktales and make African-style handicrafts.

The Cajun people of Louisiana and Mississippi also form a cultural region. They are known for their spicy style of cooking. Cajun dishes include a thick soup called *gumbo* and a rice dish called *jambalaya*. Originally from a French-speaking region in Canada called Acadia, the Cajuns settled in an area on the Gulf Coast that has swamps and slow moving streams called *bayous*.

ECONOMIC REGIONS

Economic regions are another kind of region. Economic regions are formed when many people are affected by a natural resource or product of an area. The corn belt of the Middle West and the Silicon Valley in California are examples of economic regions.

READING CHECK **What is a cultural region?**

VOCABULARY REVIEW

Number a sheet of paper from 1 to 5. Beside each number write the word or term from the list below that best completes the sentence.

citizen	**environment**
cultural region	**immigrant**
	urban

1. Someone who comes to a country from another country to live is a(n) ____.

2. The Cajun people of southern Louisiana are part of a ____ because they share the same language, beliefs, and customs.

3. You are a(n) ____ of this country if you are born here or choose to be a member of the country by law.

4. All the surroundings in which people, plants, and animals live is their ____.

5. A city is a(n) ____ area.

TECHNOLOGY

For more resources to help you learn more about the people and places you studied in this unit, visit
www.mhschool.com
and follow the links for Grade 5, Introduction.

SKILL REVIEW

6. **Reading/Thinking Skill** What is one way to solve a problem about informing other people about something?

7. **Reading/Thinking Skill** Why is identifying options a good step to use in solving problems?

8. **Study Skill** What is a good first step in preparing an outline?

Latitude and Longitude of Puerto Rico

NATIONAL GEOGRAPHIC

ATLANTIC OCEAN

67°W 66°W

19°N

18°N

Arecibo   San Juan

PUERTO RICO (U.S.)

Mayagüez   Ponce

Vieques

Guayama

Caribbean Sea

0   25   50 miles
0   25   50 kilometers
Albers Conic Equal-Area Projection

9. **Geography Skill** What is the approximate latitude and longitude of Guayama, Puerto Rico?

10. **Geography Skill** How can a grid map help you locate a city or a specific area?

Language Arts

- Working with a partner, pretend that one of you is an entrepreneur who owns an American business that produces a kind of good or service.

- Have your partner interview you about your business. Then switch and interview your partner about another business he or she has chosen.

Make a Map of Regions

- Trace a map of the United States and cut and paste it across a large piece of oaktag.

- Using different colors, divide your map into the six regions of the United States.

- Research the types of natural resources that are found in each of the six regions from the map on page 12.

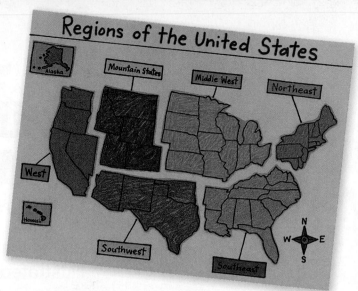

Regions of the United States

- Draw or cut out pictures of these natural resources and paste them onto the appropriate region on your map.

- Present your map to the class.

WRITING ACTIVITIES

Writing to Express *Write* a journal entry of an immigrant who has just moved to the United States.

Writing to Inform *Write* a paragraph that explains how primary sources are important to the study of history.

Writing to Persuade Suppose you wanted a recycling program in your community. *Write* a letter to a local or national government official that will persuade him or her to help get the program started.

LITERATURE

THE GROUNDHOG DANCE

A Cherokee Legend

Edited by Katharine B. Judson
Illustrated by David Diaz

Around 1910 Katharine Judson collected this Cherokee legend in her book NATIVE AMERICAN LEGENDS OF THE GREAT LAKES AND THE MISSISSIPPI VALLEY. *Native peoples told stories to teach, to explain, or to entertain. This story tells why groundhogs have short tails.*

Seven wolves once caught a **groundhog**. They said, "Now we'll kill you and have something to eat." Groundhog said, "When we find good food, we should **rejoice** over it, as people do in the green-corn dances. You will kill me, and I cannot help myself. But if you want to dance, I'll sing for you. Now this is a new dance. I will lean up against seven trees in turn. You will dance forward and then go back. At the last turn you may kill me."

Now the wolves were very hungry, but they wanted to learn the new dance. Groundhog leaned up against a tree and began to sing. He sang, and all the Wolves danced forward. When he shouted *"Yu!"* they turned and danced back in line.

---

groundhog (ground′ hog) a small animal with short legs and brown fur that lives in a hole

rejoice (rē jois′) to show or feel great joy

At each song, Groundhog took another tree, getting closer and closer to his hole under a stump. At the seventh song, Groundhog said, "Now this is the last dance. When I shout '*Yu!*' all come after me. The one who gets me may have me."

Then he sang a long time, until the Wolves were at quite a distance in a straight line. Then he shouted *"Yu!"* and darted for his hole.

At once the Wolves turned and were after him. The **foremost** Wolf caught his tail and gave it such a jerk he broke it off. That is why Groundhog has such a short tail.

---

foremost (fôr′ mōst) first in position

Write About It!

Write a tale to explain why an animal looks a certain way. Then, tell your story to your class.

The First Americans

TAKE A LOOK

Long ago, how did people use resources to meet their needs?

The Anasazi used stone to build houses two or three stories high. Today, people use steel to put up buildings as high as 110 stories.

For more information about early American cultures, visit our Web site at www.mhschool.com

37

THE Big IDEAS ABOUT...

Peopling the Western Hemisphere

The first people to come to the Americas arrived between 27,000 and 32,000 years ago. They came from Asia and Europe when ice covered much of the North. Slowly they moved throughout the Americas, hunting animals for food. When the climate changed, they developed new ways to meet their needs. Read on to find out how the first Americans lived.

EARLY NATIVE AMERICAN CULTURES

Americans learned to live in different environments. People like the Mound Builders, Anasazi, Olmec, and Maya settled in environments rich in natural resources. They built large communities.

AZTEC AND INCA FLOURISH

The Aztec and Inca built great empires in the Valley of Mexico and the mountains of Peru. Both groups founded cities, built great stone monuments, and traded across large areas.

Foldables

Make this Foldable to help organize what you learn about "Peopling the Western Hemisphere."

1. Fold a sheet of paper like a hot dog, but make one side I" longer than the other.

2. On the short side of the paper, make two cuts equal distances apart to form three tabs.

3. Draw two ovals that overlap in the middle section, and label the tabs.

Early Cultures

How did farming and trade lead to the development of early civilizations?

Lesson Outline
- The First Americans
- The Olmec and the Maya
- The Mound Builders and the Anasazi

VOCABULARY

Ice Age
glacier
specialize
civilization
irrigation

READING STRATEGY

Make a chart like this one to organize information. In the first column, write the names of each of the peoples you read about in this chapter. In the second, write one special feature of each.

BUILD BACKGROUND

"America, it seems, was a mosaic of peoples and cultures even 11,000 years ago," according to scientists Douglas Ocosly and Richard Jantz. Scientists now believe that the Americas were once home to people from Asia, Polynesia, and Europe. However, these groups died out. The ancestors of the Native Americans appeared later and spread throughout the Americas.

40,000 B.C.	35,000 B.C.	30,000 B.C.	25,000 B.C.	20,000 B.C.	15,000 B.C.	10,000 B.C.	5000 B.C.	A.D. 1	5000 A.D.

You Are Here
30,000 B.C. – A.D.1300

THE FIRST AMERICANS

Thousands of years ago, Earth went through periods of extreme cold called the Ice Ages. During the Ice Ages, much of Earth's water was frozen into huge sheets of ice called glaciers. Glaciers moving slowly over the land caused water in the oceans to lower, and some land covered by water to appear. Some of this land connected areas once separated by water.

Hunters and animals walked across these natural "land bridges" where large bodies of water are found today. One of these land bridges is called Beringia. Scientists believe that some people crossed Beringia from Asia and arrived in the Americas. It is also thought that some people from Europe may have come to North America along a North Atlantic route.

Hunter-Gatherers

The first settlers in the Americas survived by hunting animals and gathering wild plants. Some early settlers hunted animals called mammoths, which looked like elephants with long, curved tusks and thick, shaggy hair. Early settlers also dug up roots and gathered wild fruits, nuts, and mushrooms from forests.

The Earliest Farmers

By 10,000 B.C., the glaciers began to melt. This caused the oceans to rise and cover the land bridges. Hunter-gatherers in the Americas could not return to Asia and Europe. Some continued to move. Others began to settle in one area.

Discoveries in South America and central Mexico show that people started to plant seeds there as early as 7000 B.C. This area had a warm climate and was rich in natural resources. It had few large animals left to hunt. For food, the first farmers grew corn, beans, squash, tomatoes, and sunflowers.

READING CHECK Why did land bridges form in the north during the Ice Ages?

The woolly mammoth was hunted by groups of hunters working together.

THE OLMEC AND THE MAYA

Once people learned to farm, they were able to grow more food than they needed. Because people no longer hunted for all their food, they could **specialize**, or spend most of their time doing one kind of job. This led to the development of more complex communities, or societies. One of the earliest places this development occurred was in what today is Mexico.

The Olmec

The Olmec were one of the earliest **civilizations** in the Americas. A civilization is a kind of culture that has complex systems of government, education, and religion. From 1300 to 400 B.C., the Olmec

ECONOMICS

Olmec Trade

The Olmec had many specialized jobs. They were farmers, fishers, artists, sculptors, and priests. Each of their cities also specialized in certain goods. The cities **bartered** these goods with one another. That is, people traded goods and services instead of using money. It is thought they exchanged the following goods:

- La Venta, near the coast, traded cacao, rubber, and salt.
- San Lorenzo traded pottery made from its rich clay deposits as well as red hematite, an abundant red coloring used in religious ceremonies.
- Laguna de los Cerros specialized in trading basalt, a stone used to build monuments.

Activity

Draw a map of the Olmec land and show on it the goods that came from its major cities.

people lived along the Gulf coast of what is now southern Mexico. They grew corn, beans, and squash along the riverbanks that flooded in the summer. One city the Olmec built was called **La Venta**. It is thought to have been a trading city.

Most archaeologists believe that the Olmec culture had an influence on other cultures that followed in the region. The Olmec were among the first Americans to use stone in sculpture and architecture. The Olmec are known for creating a calendar and for playing ceremonial ball games.

The Maya

Archaeologists believe that the Maya began to develop a complex culture around 300 B.C. in what is now southern Mexico and Guatemala. Mayan farmers grew an abundant supply of food for a large population. Farmers grew corn, beans, squash, yucca, and sweet potato. Corn (maize) was the main source of food

The Olmec carved large stone heads of their gods and leaders.

for the Maya. They made corn dough into flat cakes, like the tortillas people eat today.

The Maya were not only good farmers. They were artists, scientists, and historians. They formed large cities, such as Tikal, Copán, and Chichén Itzá. The cities had stone temples, palaces, and other buildings. Thousands of people lived in them. Archaeologists have found calendars divided into 260 days. They have also figured out how to read written records of the Maya noting dates, times, and events such as conquests. The Maya also invented the idea of the number zero. Mayan temples and religious centers were the largest at that time in the Americas.

The Maya traded a variety of goods within their region. These goods included jade, flint, obsidian—a glassy black rock formed from lava—oyster shells, cacao beans, cotton cloth, spices, salt, pelts, rubber, wood, and ceramics.

The End of Maya Civilization

By around A.D. 909, the Maya civilization disappeared for reasons we do not know. They left their cities and built no more stone temples, palaces, or other monuments. Today, some experts believe that food shortages and wars were the causes. Descendants of the Maya live in present-day Guatemala and Mexico. They speak a Maya language and follow many customs and traditions of their ancestors.

READING CHECK **In what ways were the Olmec and Maya similar?**

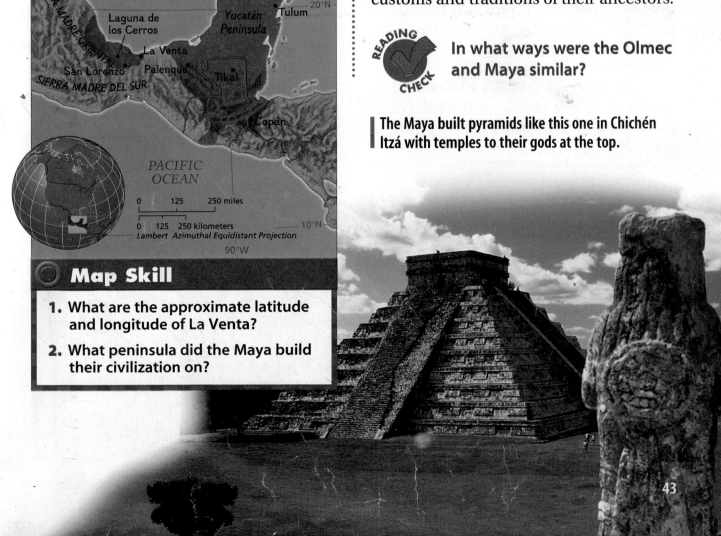

NATIONAL GEOGRAPHIC

The Olmec and the Maya

- Olmec lands
- Maya lands
- • City

Tropic of Cancer

Gulf of Mexico

SIERRA MADRE ORIENTAL

Chichén Itzá

Tulum

20°N

Laguna de los Cerros

Yucatán Peninsula

La Venta

San Lorenzo

Palenque

Tikal

SIERRA MADRE DEL SUR

Copán

PACIFIC OCEAN

0   125   250 miles

0   125   250 kilometers
Lambert Azimuthal Equidistant Projection

10°N

90°W

Map Skill

1. **What are the approximate latitude and longitude of La Venta?**

2. **What peninsula did the Maya build their civilization on?**

The Maya built pyramids like this one in Chichén Itzá with temples to their gods at the top.

43

THE MOUND BUILDERS AND THE ANASAZI

Two of the earliest civilizations that lived in what is now the United States were the Mound Builders and the Anasazi. The Mound Builders settled in the southeast around 3,000 B.C.

The Mound Builders

One of the first groups of Mound Builders, the Adena people, settled along the Ohio River between 800 B.C. and 100 B.C. The Hopewell Mound Builders settled in the same area around 100 B.C. to A.D. 500. A third group, the Cahokia, lived along the Mississippi River around A.D. 1000.

Archaeologists believe the Mound Builders first built small rounded piles of earth to bury their dead. Later, mounds were used for religious purposes. The largest, Great Serpent Mound near present-day Cincinnati, Ohio, was built by the Adena around 100 B.C.

Anasazi

Around A.D. 200, the Anasazi culture began to flourish in the Southwest. The Anasazi lived in an area known as the Four Corners from about A.D. 200 to 1300. The area is called the Four Corners because Utah, Colorado, New Mexico, and Arizona all meet there. They developed villages beneath rock cliffs, on the sides of canyons, and on the tops of tall, flat hills, or mesas.

The Anasazi were able to farm in the desert by using irrigation to water their crops. Irrigation is a method by which water is brought into dry areas.

Anasazi dwellings were built on cliffs for defense. Ladders were pulled up at night.

READING CHECK How were the Mound Builders and the Anasazi different?

HISTORY MYSTERY

Why did the Anasazi leave their homes?

In A.D. 900, the town of Pueblo Bonito had 800 rooms in what is now New Mexico. But by about 1300, the Anasazi had abandoned their towns and villages.

Many archaeologists believe that a drought lasting from 1276 to 1299 may have driven the Anasazi from their homes. Other archaeologists think that invaders from the north may have caused some Anasazi to leave their homes.

What are some other reasons the Anasazi might have left their homes?

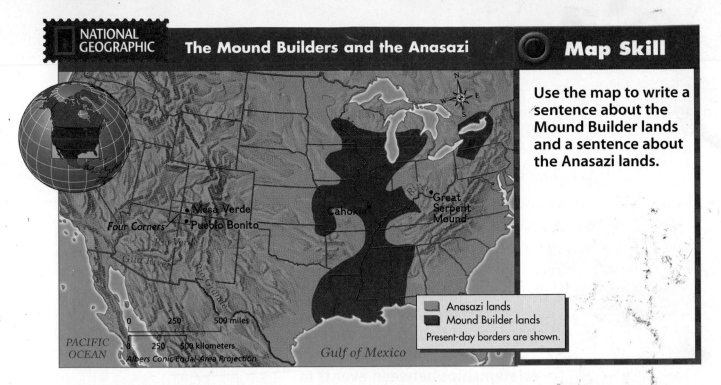

Use the map to write a sentence about the Mound Builder lands and a sentence about the Anasazi lands.

Mesa Verde
Four Corners
Pueblo Bonito
Rio Verde
Gila River
Rio Grande
Cahokia
Great Serpent Mound

Anasazi lands
Mound Builder lands
Present-day borders are shown.

PACIFIC OCEAN
0 250 500 miles
0 250 500 kilometers
Albers Conic Equal-Area Projection
Gulf of Mexico

PUTTING IT TOGETHER

Many of North America's earliest societies lived in what is now the Southwest United States. For many reasons, these civilizations no longer exist. However, the descendants of many Native Americans still follow some traditional customs.

Over time, the Anasazi moved or joined with other Native Americans in the Southwest. At the same time, other highly advanced civilizations were growing in what is now Mexico, Central America, and South America.

Many historians believe that the Hopi and other Pueblo people are descendants of the Anasazi. As you read about our country's history, keep your knowledge of these early North Americans in mind.

Review and Assess

1. Write three sentences using the vocabulary terms from this list.

   civilization   Ice Age   specialize

2. What was Beringia?

3. In what ways did farming and trade lead to the start of civilizations?

4. What did the Maya and the Anasazi have in common?

5. **Compare** the Mound Builders to the Anasazi. How did their environments affect their way of life?

Using the map above, determine a possible route the Mound Builders might have used to reach each other in different states. Draw your route.

Write a story about what you think really happened to the Anasazi. Use standard grammar, spelling, sentence structure, and punctuation.

Reading Time Lines

The Anasazi began to build their "apartment house" villages in the early 600s. The Maya Empire reached its height at about the same time. How could you show the time relationship of these events? A time line is a diagram of several events arranged in the order in which they took place. A time line helps you organize information in an easy, visual way. It can help you organize, summarize, and see the relationships between events in your reading.

VOCABULARY

time line
century
decade
B.C.
A.D.

LEARN THE SKILL

Use the following steps to read the time line below.

1. **Identify the time span.**
   This time line begins in the year A.D. 1 and ends at A.D. 1500.

2. **Identify the periods into which the time line is divided.**
   The time periods for this time line are 300 years each. Usually the periods of time on a time line are equal.

3. **Identify the important events on the time line.**
   The events on this time line are for A.D. 200, 250, 600, 900, 1300.

EARLY CIVILIZATIONS OF THE AMERICAS

250—Maya culture flourishes

900—Maya culture ends

A.D. 1   A.D. 300   A.D. 600   A.D. 900   A.D. 1200   A.D. 1500

200—Anasazi culture begins

600—Anasazi begin to build large village buildings

900—Anasazi culture flourishes

1300—Anasazi culture ends

All time lines are divided into time periods. A **century**, or 100 years, is one time period. A ten-year time period is called a **decade**. A jagged break in a time line means that a number of years have been left out. Some time lines have the abbreviation "**B.C.**". It stands for before Christ. The event took place before Jesus Christ was born. The abbreviation "**A.D.**" means *anno Domini*, or in the year of the Lord. A.D. is used for dates after the birth of Christ.

TRY THE SKILL

Read the following paragraph.

The Anasazi arrived in the Four Corners area around 100 B.C., but they did not settle until close to A.D. 500. About 100 years later they started to build the pueblo homes they are known for. One of the most famous pueblos, Cliff Palace at Mesa Verde, was built around A.D. 1150 and abandoned about 150 years later. Chaco Canyon was their economic and political center at the height of their civilization, around A.D. 1000. Their culture flourished until A.D. 1130.

1. What is the time span in the paragraph?

2. What are the important events in it?

3. What date would be in the middle of the time span?

4. How can making a time line help you understand information that you read?

EXTEND THE SKILL

Look at the dates below about Native Americans. Use the dates to make a time line.

● How does making this time line help you to understand the relationship of events in the Maya and the Mound Builders' history?

The Maya

800 B.C.	Maya settle in Mexico
A.D. 250	Maya culture flourishes
A.D. 900	Maya culture ends

The Mound Builders

700 B.C.	Adena people build burial mounds
A.D. 500	Hopewell people build many mounds
A.D. 1000	Cahokia people build flat-topped temple mounds
A.D. 1700	Mound Builder culture ends

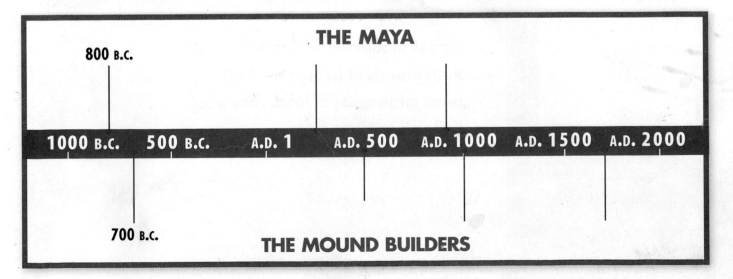

THE MAYA

800 B.C.

1000 B.C.   500 B.C.   A.D. 1   A.D. 500   A.D. 1000   A.D. 1500   A.D. 2000

700 B.C.

THE MOUND BUILDERS

Aztec and Inca

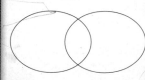

How did the Aztec and Inca build their powerful empires?

Lesson Outline
• The Aztec
• The Inca

READING STRATEGY

On a separate sheet of paper, draw two connecting circles as seen below. In the area where they meet, write the things the Inca and Aztec cultures have in common. Where the circles do not touch, write their differences.

BUILD BACKGROUND

"Our drums are ready, already the eagles and jaguars dance. Already you are on your feet, flower song." This Aztec poem was written sometime around the mid 1400s. By then the Aztec had gained control of a large part of the **Valley of Mexico**.

Around the same time another Indian group, the Inca, ruled an area that stretched over 1,000 miles in the **Andes** Mountains of South America. Both groups of people not only ruled large areas of land, they also had rich cultures.

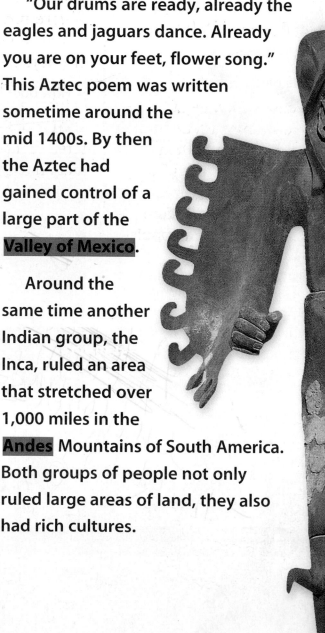

eagle knight

48

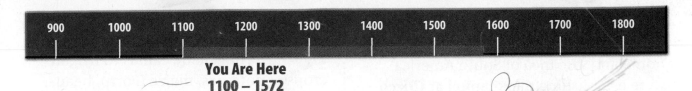
THE AZTEC

The Aztec moved into the **Valley of Mexico** around A.D. 1100. About 225 years later they settled in the area around Lake Texcoco. The Aztec called their new home **Tenochtitlán** (te noch tee TLAHN), which means "land of the prickly pear cactus" in Nahuatl (NAH wah tuhl). Nahuatl was their language.

Tenochtitlán

The people of Tenochtitlán began building a city on a swampy island in the middle of the lake. For most of their food, they built "floating gardens," or "chinampas" (chee NAHM pass) in the marshes near the lake. Before long, Tenochtitlán served a population of more than 200,000.

Around 1430 the Aztec joined other people of Lake Texcoco to defeat the Tepanec (tay pah NAYK). The Tepanec had ruled the Valley of Mexico.

Within ten years Tenochtitlán became the capital of the Aztec **Empire** as shown on the map. An empire is a large area of different peoples controlled by one ruler or government.

War was an important part of Aztec life. Boys trained to become soldiers from an early age. Their goal was to become a knight. Jaguar and eagle knights were leaders of the Aztec army. Soldiers captured their enemies, and forced some of them into **slavery**, the practice of owning people and forcing them to work.

READING CHECK

Where did the Aztec make their home?

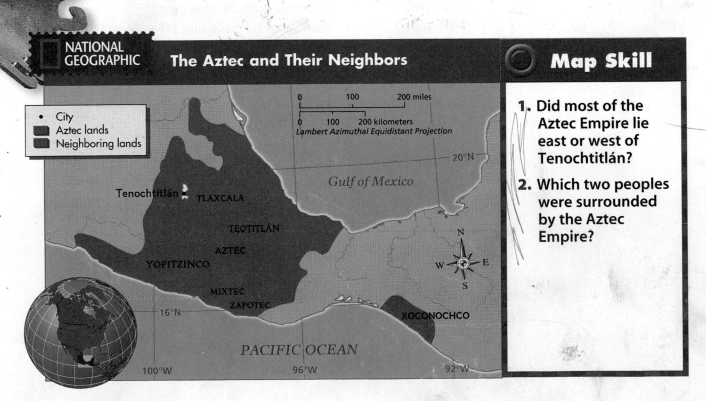

NATIONAL GEOGRAPHIC

The Aztec and Their Neighbors

Map Skill

- • City
- ■ Aztec lands
- ■ Neighboring lands

0   100   200 miles
0   100   200 kilometers
Lambert Azimuthal Equidistant Projection

20°N

Gulf of Mexico

Tenochtitlán   TLAXCALA

TEOTITLÁN

AZTEC

YOPITZINCO

MIXTEC

ZAPOTEC

16°N

XOCONOCHCO

N
W   E
S

PACIFIC OCEAN

100°W   96°W   92°W

1. **Did most of the Aztec Empire lie east or west of Tenochtitlán?**

2. **Which two peoples were surrounded by the Aztec Empire?**

THE INCA

While the Aztec were searching for a homeland, the Inca of South America were establishing their capital at Cuzco (KOOS koh) in a rich mountain valley in southern Peru. Like the Aztec, the Inca built an empire by conquering neighboring peoples. Look at the map. By 1525 the Inca Empire stretched from present-day Ecuador to central Chile.

Strong Leaders

In 1435 the Inca Empire was greatly expanded under the rule of Pachakuti (pah chah KOO tee) Inca. Later, his son enlarged it yet again. An especially gifted leader, Pachakuti set about organizing the empire. He cleared land for settlement, appointed governors for each region, and required every citizen to work toward enlarging the empire and the spread of the Inca religion. The Inca worshiped the sun god Inti.

Skilled Builders

The Inca built more than 19,000 miles of roads within their empire. They also built straw bridges between high mountain peaks. The Inca were skilled farmers who built terraces up the steep mountainsides. They made canals to irrigate crops of potatoes, maize (corn), beans, and peppers. They were skilled in many crafts, including the making of textiles, pottery, and gold and silver jewelry. They recorded information using colored and knotted strings called "quipu."

Inca farmers used stone and earth terraces for their crops.

READING CHECK What skills helped the Inca build their empire?

Inca Empire, about 1500

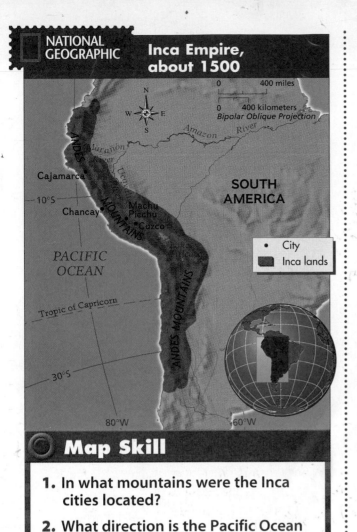

SOUTH
AMERICA

Cajamarca

10°S

Chancay

Machu
Picchu
Cuzco

PACIFIC
OCEAN

Tropic of Capricorn

30°S

ANDES MOUNTAINS

Amazon River

Marañon

0   400 miles
0   400 kilometers
Bipolar Oblique Projection

• City
■ Inca lands

80°W   60°W

Map Skill

1. **In what mountains were the Inca cities located?**

2. **What direction is the Pacific Ocean from the Inca Empire?**

PUTTING IT TOGETHER

The Aztec civilization had great beauty as well as great cruelty. Aztec wars created many enemies. These enemies later helped bring about the end of the Aztec Empire. However, Aztec culture has continued into the present. Many Mexicans still speak the Nahuatl language and follow Aztec traditions.

In about 1532 the Inca Empire was weakened by a civil war. When the Spanish invaded in 1533 the Inca were already at war among themselves. The Spanish fought to win the wealth of the Inca Empire. By 1572 the Inca Empire had come to an end.

Inca quipu

Review and Assess

1. Write one sentence for each of the vocabulary words below.

   empire   slavery

2. Where did the Aztec build Tenochtitlán?

3. How did Pachakuti expand the Inca Empire?

4. Analyze how the Aztec and the Inca built their powerful empires.

5. What **generalization** could you make about the Aztec and Inca empires?

Look at the map on page 49. Using the scale, determine how far the Aztec capital was from the Gulf of Mexico.

Write a paragraph about an Aztec battle from the point of view of an Aztec warrior.

51

VOCABULARY REVIEW

Number a sheet of paper from 1 to 5. Beside each number write the word or term from the list below that matches the description.

civilization   Ice Age

empire   slavery

glacier

1. A huge sheet of ice
2. The practice of owning people and forcing them to work
3. A culture with complex systems of government, education, and religion
4. A large area of different peoples controlled by one ruler or government
5. A period when much of Earth's water was frozen into huge sheets of ice

CHAPTER COMPREHENSION

6. How did farming allow people to specialize in different jobs?
7. Where are the descendants of the Maya?
8. Where did the Mound Builders live?
9. Where did the Anasazi live?
10. How did the people of Tenochtitlán build their city?
11. How did the agriculture techniques of the Inca contribute to the growth of the empire?
12. What led to the end of the Inca Empire?
13. Suppose you were interviewing a descendant of the Maya. **Write** a series of questions about what customs or traditions can be traced back to his or her ancestors.

SKILL REVIEW

Early Ways of Life

Types of Buildings

Olmec	Stone buildings
Maya	Monuments, Temples
Aztec	Palaces, Temples
Mound Builders	Mounds
Anasazi	Underground houses, multi-story stone "apartments"

Ways of Farming

Olmec	Planting along riverbanks
Maya	Terraces, raised islands
Aztec	Floating gardens
Mound Builders	Planting along riverbanks
Anasazi	Irrigation

14. **Chart Skill** Which groups of early Americans did not use special farming methods?
15. **Chart Skill** Why might the Anasazi have built the type of buildings they did?
16. **Chart Skill** Which group made buildings out of rounded piles of earth?
17. **Study Skill** What is the first thing you should do when reading a time line?
18. **Study Skill** How can a time line help you understand historical events?

USING A TIME LINE

10,000 B.C.	1500 B.C.	1000 B.C.	500 B.C.	A.D. 1	A.D. 500	A.D. 1000	A.D. 1500	A.D. 2000

10,000 B.C. Glaciers begin to melt

1200 B.C. The Olmec live along the Gulf of Mexico

1000 B.C. The Maya live in small villages

A.D. 1 The Mound Builders begin settling in permanent villages

A.D. 250 The Maya begin building cities

A.D. 1100 The Aztec settle in the Valley of Mexico

A.D. 1500 Aztec civilization spreads

19. How many years passed between the Aztec settlement of the Valley of Mexico and the spread of their civilization?

20. Which people of Mexico lived around the same time as the Mound Builders?

 **Activity**

***Writing* About Culture** Suppose you were a member of a group hundreds of years ago that had just begun to farm. Another group that lives nearby has not yet begun farming. How would you explain to the second group the ways that farming could change and improve their lives?

Foldables

Use your Foldable to review what you have learned about the early people who came to the Americas and to compare and contrast their lifestyles and cultures. As you look at the Venn diagram on the front of your Foldable, mentally recall what you learned in each of the two lessons. Then review your notes under the tabs to check your memory and responses. Find similarities between these two groups of early people, and record your answers under the "Both" tab.

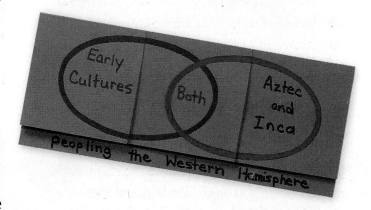

THE Big IDEAS ABOUT....

Native Americans

The ancestors of the Native Americans developed individual cultures in the regions they settled. Many of the major cultures in North America had related languages. Some had similar beliefs and customs. Read on to find out how Native Americans in each environment of North America lived.

NATIVE AMERICANS OF THE SOUTHWEST

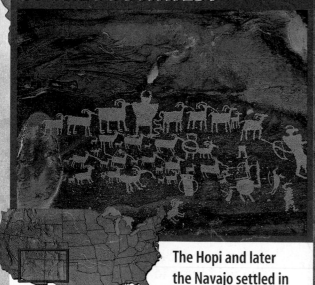

The Hopi and later the Navajo settled in areas where the Anasazi once lived. The mesas and canyons provided materials for homes, clothes, tools, and works of art.

NATIVE AMERICANS OF THE WOODLANDS

The Mohawk settled around what later became New York State. The Eastern Woodlands provided many natural resources to support their way of life.

NATIVE AMERICANS OF THE PLAINS

Native Americans of the Plains hunted buffalo to live. They used different parts of the buffalo for food, homes, clothes, tools, and fine jewelry.

NATIVE AMERICANS OF THE WEST

Many Western peoples settled between the Pacific Ocean and the coastal mountains. Cedar trees and salmon were important natural resources.

Foldables

Make this Foldable study guide and use it to record what you learn about "Native Americans."

1. Fold a large sheet of paper into a shutter fold.
2. Fold the shutter fold in half like a hamburger.
3. Form four tabs by cutting along the fold lines in the middle of the two long tabs.
4. Label the four tabs with lesson titles.

Native Americans of the Southwest

How did the Hopi and Navajo use their environment to enrich their lives?

Lesson Outline
• The Hopi
• Daily Life
• A New Home

VOCABULARY

pueblo
mesa
adobe
kiva
kachina
hogan

READING STRATEGY

Use a Venn diagram to compare and contrast some of the ways the Hopi and Navajo use their environments.

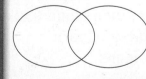

BUILD BACKGROUND

The area around you is hot, dry desert. Yet before you is an unbelievable sight—rows and rows of tall, green corn plants. The scene described above is seen today in many places inhabited by the Hopi, Zuni (ZOO nee), and other Pueblo people. They are descendants of the Anasazi.

Also living in the Southwest are non-Pueblo people such as the Navajo (NAH vuh hoe). The Navajo were mainly hunters and herders.

Taos, New Mexico

56

THE HOPI

Hopi call themselves *Hopiti*, which in their language means "the gentle people." They are one of the Native American Pueblo groups. When the Spanish arrived in the 1500s, they called the Hopi apartment-style homes **pueblos**, which means "villages" in Spanish. The Spanish used the word *pueblo* to describe both the people and the type of home in which they lived. One pueblo, **Old Oraibi** (oh rah EE bee), is one of the oldest settlements in the United States. It is about 800 years old.

Dry Farming

Northeastern Arizona where the Hopi live has many tall mountains, deep canyons, and steep **mesas**. A mesa is a mountain or hill with a flat top and steep sides. Some years the area receives about 20 inches of rain, but it may only receive about 4 inches in other years.

The Hopi are among the most successful farmers in North America. To grow their crops, the Hopi use a method called *dry farming*. This is a way of growing crops in places where there is little water. Even generations ago the Hopi built dams and irrigation canals. They also grew special corn plants with long roots to reach the water underground. The following primary source describes how every person in the community helped.

What farming method did the Hopi use?

excerpt from **"The Life Story of Helen Sekaquaptewa,"** *— published in 1969*

The Hopis knew how to make their corn grow in sandy, arid soil .... One aimed to have on hand a supply of corn, enough to last two years, so that if there was a dry year, one's family would not starve .... [W]hen summer brought the hoped-and-prayed for rains, the community responded .... Hoeing and cultivating ... was also done by all the people.

... [T]here were no lazy ones. All worked hard and prayed as well for a good harvest, the father led his family to the fields daily to make sure no weed was allowed to rob the soil of any drop of moisture.

Why did the Hopi care for their crops so carefully?

DAILY LIFE

Both the Hopi and the Navajo learned to survive in their desert environment. However, their cultures and ways of life were very different.

Hopi Life

In addition to being skilled farmers, the Hopi were and still are excellent builders and potters. The Hopi have long built homes made of **adobe** (uh DOH bee). Adobe is a type of clay. It protects houses from the desert's extreme heat and cold as well as floods and blizzards.

The Hopi built the first floor of most pueblos without doors or windows to keep out invaders. To get in and out of their pueblos, people climbed ladders to doors in the roofs. Most pueblo towns had round structures called **kivas** for their religious ceremonies.

Art has long been an important part of daily life for the Hopi. All of the Pueblo peoples are known for the beautiful pottery they create. Artists today still use the traditional designs created by their ancestors. Parents teach their children these designs and techniques. Some favorite designs include elaborate birds, insects, and rain symbols.

Kachina Ceremonies

The Hopi are also known for their **kachina** ceremonies, which are an important part of the Hopi religion. The Hopi kachinas are spirits who can visit Hopi villages for half of every year. The kachinas are believed to bring rain and help crops grow. They also show people how to live and behave. There are hundreds of different kachinas.

Kachina ceremonies are held during the six months the kachinas are said to dwell in the Hopi villages. Kachina dances are an important part of these ceremonies. Being a dancer is an honor, and each dancer represents one of the hundreds of different kachinas. One dancer represents the Crow Mother, the mother of all kachinas. Other dancers represent clowns who follow the kachinas and cause mischief.

During the kachina festivals, some kachina dancers give out colorful wooden dolls that look like the kachinas they represent. Kachina dolls are used to teach Hopi children about their culture, land, and religious beliefs.

This **kachina** doll represents Crow Mother, one of the most important kachinas. Navajo weavers (above, right) pass traditional skills to the younger generation.

The Navajo

The Navajo, or Diné, are the largest group of non-Pueblo people in the Southwest. The Spanish took the word "Navajo" from the Pueblo word for "great planted fields." Diné means "the people." Today many Navajo live in the Four Corners area. This is where the states of Utah, Colorado, Arizona, and New Mexico meet.

Living Together Peacefully

The Navajo are related to the Apache, hunter-gatherers who originated in present-day Canada and Alaska. The Navajo arrived in northern New Mexico in the late 1300s. Throughout the 1600s their raids on other groups' lands created conflicts with their neighbors. However, they managed to live with the peaceful Hopi people. The Navajo learned farming methods from the Pueblo people. They also learned Pueblo weaving and jewelry making techniques.

Unlike the Pueblo peoples, the Navajo lived in **hogans**. Hogans are dome shaped dwellings made with log or stick frames that are covered with mud or sod. Traditionally hogans have six or eight sides and face east. Archeologists have found hogans near pueblos. This is why they think the Navajo and the Hopi lived together peacefully at one time.

What did the Navajo learn from the Hopi?

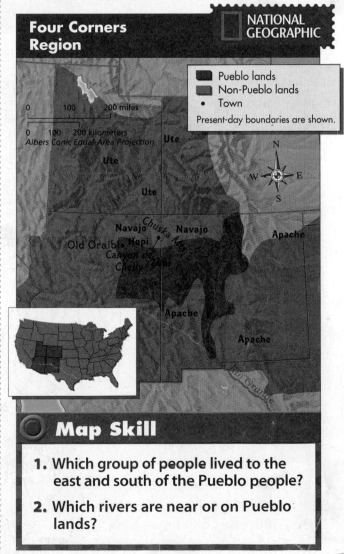

Four Corners Region

NATIONAL GEOGRAPHIC

Pueblo lands
Non-Pueblo lands
• Town
Present-day boundaries are shown.

0   100   200 miles
0   100   200 kilometers
Albers Conic Equal-Area Projection

Ute
Ute
Ute
Navajo
Chuska Mts.
Navajo
Apache
Old Oraibi   Hopi
Canyon de
Chelly   Zuni
Apache
Apache
Rio Grande
Colorado

Map Skill

1. Which group of people lived to the east and south of the Pueblo people?

2. Which rivers are near or on Pueblo lands?

A NEW HOME

In the 1500s the Spanish introduced sheep, goats, cattle, and horses into the Southwest region. Once again, the Navajo adapted their lifestyle to their changing environment. They became expert horse riders and shepherds.

Still, the Navajo continued their raids. These raids angered the Spanish as well as neighboring tribes. During the 1700s the conflicts grew worse and large numbers of Navajo moved their homes to **Canyon de Chelly** in northeastern Arizona. The canyon's fertile floor provided excellent farmland. Its steep walls protected the Navajo in some battles.

READING CHECK

Why did the Navajo leave northern New Mexico?

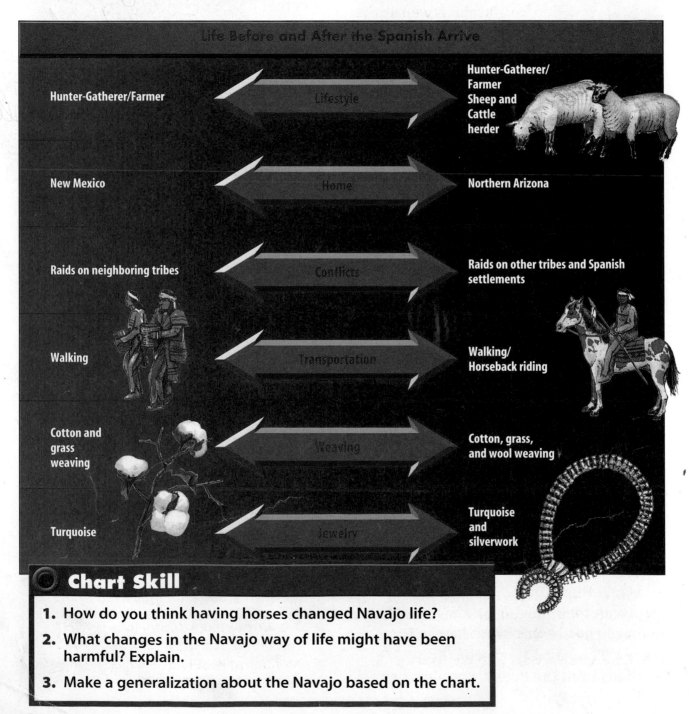

Life Before and After the Spanish Arrive

Before		After
Hunter-Gatherer/Farmer	Lifestyle	Hunter-Gatherer/Farmer Sheep and Cattle herder
New Mexico	Home	Northern Arizona
Raids on neighboring tribes	Conflicts	Raids on other tribes and Spanish settlements
Walking	Transportation	Walking/Horseback riding
Cotton and grass weaving	Weaving	Cotton, grass, and wool weaving
Turquoise	Jewelry	Turquoise and silverwork

Chart Skill

1. How do you think having horses changed Navajo life?

2. What changes in the Navajo way of life might have been harmful? Explain.

3. Make a generalization about the Navajo based on the chart.

PUTTING IT TOGETHER

Today, the Navajo population is growing. Navajo people still live in Canyon de Chelly and farm the way their ancestors did. Once reduced to about 8,000 people, the Navajo Nation now numbers in the hundreds of thousands.

The way of life for Navajo as well as the Hopi and other Native Americans of the Southwest region includes a mix of the traditional and modern. Cities like Phoenix, Arizona, for example, use both modern irrigation canals and those built hundreds of years ago.

The Hopi and Navajo maintain many of their traditional ways. These include ceremonies, government, social organizations, religious practices, and artwork. The Hopi still perform kachina dances in their sacred ceremonies.

The Navajo used dyes made from plants to color their woven rugs (above). A Navajo wedding basket shows a special design.

Review and Assess

1. Write one sentence for each of the vocabulary words below.

   hogan   kachina   kiva   pueblo

2. What is the Four Corners area?

3. Explain how the Native Americans of the Southwest used their environment to enrich their lives.

4. Identify the main reasons Canyon de Chelly was a good home for the Navajo.

5. **Compare** the Hopi with the Anasazi.

Activities

Create an ad designed to interest people in visiting the Four Corners area. It should include information about the geography of the area.

Write a journal entry for a Hopi or Navajo child around A.D. 1400–1700. Mention at least two activities and what you felt about them.

Native Americans of the Woodlands

Find Out!

How did the Iroquois bring peace to their people?

Lesson Outline
• A Rich Environment
• The Hodenosaunee
• The Grand Council

VOCABULARY

wigwam
longhouse
wampum
clan
Iroquois
  Confederacy
compromise

PEOPLE

Deganawida
Hiawatha

READING STRATEGY

Use the sequence of events chart. List the steps that led to the formation of the Iroqouis Confederacy. Keep track of the steps.

BUILD BACKGROUND

As you walk, fallen leaves crunch beneath your feet. An endless maze of trees surrounds you while beams of sunlight stream through the leaves high above.

The land east of the Mississippi River was once almost completely covered by forests. This area was home to many groups of Native Americans. The languages spoken by these Native Americans of the Eastern Woodlands belonged to one of two language groups. The larger group was Algonkian (al GAHNG kee un). The other group was Iroquoian.

1300	1350	1400	1450	1500	1550	1600	1650	1700	1750

You Are Here
1500 – 1700

A RICH ENVIRONMENT

The Eastern Woodlands is a vast area. It extends roughly from the Atlantic Ocean to the Mississippi River and from Canada to Florida. Its forests, lakes, rivers, and the Atlantic Ocean provided abundant natural resources for the many different peoples who lived there.

In the forests were many kinds of animals to hunt for food. Forests also provided wood for building homes and canoes. Many of the wild plants and berries could be eaten or used for medicine. The soil of the coastal plains and river valleys was ideal for farming. Its bodies of water were filled with fish, shellfish, and sea animals.

North and South

Various parts of the woodlands had different seasons and types of land. The Native Americans who lived in these areas adapted to and used their different environments. For example, the Penobscot (puh NAHB skaht) lived in mountainous areas of what is now Maine. Since farming was difficult there, they moved from place to place to hunt. The Penobscot also gathered fruits, nuts, and berries from the forests. In winter they wore warm clothes made from deerskin.

In the south, where the climate is mild much of the year, the Natchez and other peoples mostly farmed. The Natchez were descendants of the Mound Builders. They lived along the east side of the lower Mis-

Wigwams had holes in the roof to allow smoke from cooking fires to escape.

sissippi river. To keep cool in their warm climate, the Natchez wore light clothes woven from plant fibers.

The Native Americans of the Eastern Woodlands were mostly farmers who lived in permanent villages. Many woodlands people built **wigwams**. Wigwams were homes with bent sapling frames. They were covered with cattail mats or elm bark. Many people fished and traveled far in canoes made of birch bark.

How did the people of the Eastern Woodlands use their environments?

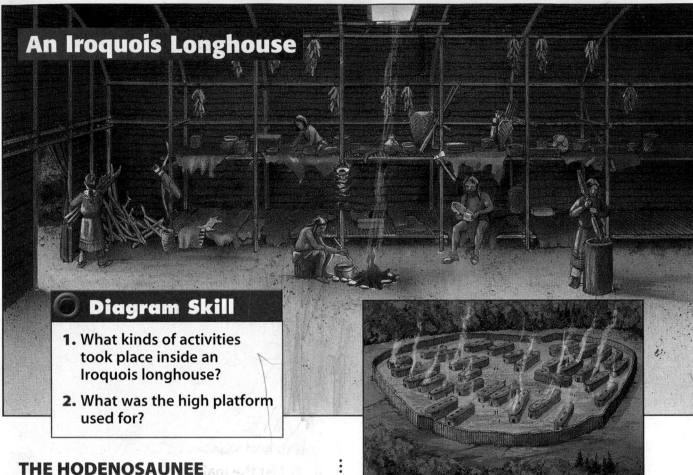

An Iroquois Longhouse

Diagram Skill

1. What kinds of activities took place inside an Iroquois longhouse?

2. What was the high platform used for?

THE HODENOSAUNEE

Today we know the Hodenosaunee (hoh den oh SAH nee) as the Iroquois, mostly because they spoke an Iroquoian language. The Hodenosaunee lived mainly in what is now New York State. They included five groups, the Seneca (SE nih kuh), the Mohawk, the Cayuga (kah YOO guh), the Onondaga (ahn un DAW gah), and the Oneida (oh NĪ duh).

Hodenosaunee means "people of the longhouse" in Iroquoian. Longhouses are long buildings made of poles covered with sheets of bark. Each longhouse held several families.

Hodenosaunee made fine beadwork, called wampum. Wampum was a belt or necklace of small polished beads made from shells and strung or woven together. Wampum was used in ceremonies, to cement agreements, or as a gift.

During the 1500s the Hodenosaunee lands were connected. One route, the Hodenosaunee Trail, connected the main villages of all five peoples.

Clan Mothers

Hodenosaunee women were the leaders of their clans. A clan is a group of families who share the same ancestor. Clans controlled the land. Women also owned the longhouses. After marriage, a husband moved into his wife's longhouse and lived with her family.

The consent of the clan mother had to be given for all important decisions. She also chose the village leaders.

READING CHECK

What were some important features of Hodenosaunee culture?

Iroquois Confederacy

The Hodenosaunee mainly cooperated with each other until around 1300 when their numbers began to grow. Then fighting began, often over hunting grounds. According to tradition the conflict ended when two leaders came up with a bold idea. These leaders were **Deganawida** (day gahn uh WEE duh) and **Hiawatha**.

Around 1452 Hiawatha and Deganawida spoke before the Hodenosaunee. They convinced them to form the **Iroquois Confederacy**, also known as the Iroquois League. A confederacy is a union of people who join together for a common purpose. Its goal was to maintain peace among the five Hodenosaunee groups, or nations. After the Tuscarora joined in 1722, the Confederacy was called the *Six Nations*.

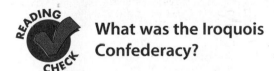

READING CHECK What was the Iroquois Confederacy?

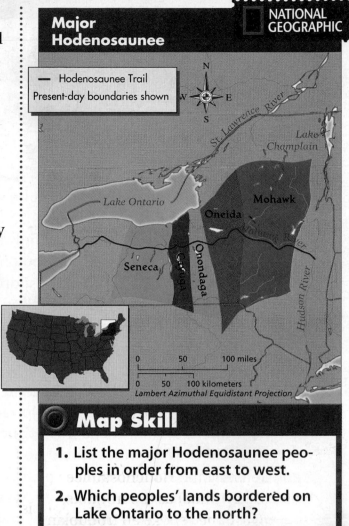

Major Hodenosaunee

NATIONAL GEOGRAPHIC

— Hodenosaunee Trail
Present-day boundaries shown

St. Lawrence River
Lake Champlain
Lake Ontario
Mohawk
Oneida
Onondaga
Cayuga
Seneca
Hudson River

0   50   100 miles
0   50   100 kilometers
Lambert Azimuthal Equidistant Projection

Map Skill

1. List the major Hodenosaunee peoples in order from east to west.

2. Which peoples' lands bordered on Lake Ontario to the north?

Present-day Native Americans often play traditional instruments in community celebrations.

BIOGRAPHY

Focus On: Leadership

Hiawatha Hiawatha was one of history's great peacemakers. Historians believe that he was a Mohawk and lived during the mid-1400s.

At that time, there was continual fighting among the five Iroquois tribes. During one raid on his village, Hiawatha's wife and children were killed. Grieving, Hiawatha left his village and lived alone in the woods. One day a man named Deganawida stopped by. He also was known as a peacemaker.

As the two men talked it became clear they shared similar ideas. They then developed a fair government system called the Iroquois League. All of the five tribes would be represented in a Grand Council, which would settle all arguments among them. Hiawatha and Deganawida also created a set of laws. Their ideas marked a new beginning for the Iroquois people.

Link to Today Think about a leader today who worked to create a new government or organization. Then write a paragraph comparing and contrasting this person's ideas to the ideas of Hiawatha and Deganawida.

THE LIFE OF HIAWATHA	Around 1430 Hiawatha is born.	Around 1450 Hiawatha's family is killed in a raid.	Around 1452 Hiawatha meets Deganawida.	Around 1454 The Iroquois League is formed.		
	1425	**1440**	**1455**	**1470**	**1485**	
LIFE AROUND THE WORLD	1429 Joan of Arc fights to end English rule in France.		1450 Johannes Gutenberg invents a printing press with movable type.		1485 The Plague strikes England, causing many deaths.	

THE GRAND COUNCIL

To keep peace Deganawida and Hiawatha developed the Great Law—the Constitution of the Iroquois Nation. Deganawida also set up a Grand Council. The clan mothers of each nation chose representatives to the council. The council made decisions through discussion and **compromise**. A compromise is the settling of a dispute by each side agreeing to give up something.

The Great Law was more than a set of rules. It was also a set of guidelines for the Iroquois nations to live together in peace. Deganawida described the Iroquois Confederacy as a great longhouse that stretched the length of the Hodenosaunee Trail. The Grand Council continues to make decisions for the Iroquois today.

How did the Iroquois Grand Council make decisions?

PUTTING IT TOGETHER

The history of Native Americans is woven into the history of all Americans. Algonkian words such as *moose, skunk, chipmunk* and *raccoon*, became modern English words. Some scholars believe the authors of the United States Constitution were aware of the Constitution of the Iroquois Nation and used some of its ideas.

The Iroquois often used **wampum** to celebrate events and treaties.

Review and Assess

1. Write one sentence for each of the vocabulary words below.

   clan　　　　　　　**longhouse**
   Iroquois Confederacy　**wigwam**

2. What natural resources were available to the peoples of the Eastern Woodlands?

3. How did the government formed by the Iroquois Confederacy help keep the peace?

4. What role do clan mothers play in Iroquois communities?

5. Based on what you have read, what **generalizations** might you make about the Eastern Woodlands peoples?

Using the map on page 65, list the five major Hodenosaunee areas of settlement in order from east to west. Then make an illustrated chart with the main physical features of each area.

Write a law that you think might help the Iroquois Confederacy keep peace among its members. Research and make notes listing the laws that Deganawida already made. Also note what problems you think still need to be solved.

Identifying Cause and Effect

In this lesson you learned how the Penobscot adapted to their mountainous environment. Because they could not farm, they often moved as they hunted animals. Their inability to farm is the cause that made them hunt. A **cause** is something that makes something else happen.

The event that happens as a result of a cause is the **effect**. The effect of the harsh Maine environment was that the Penobscot had to move constantly to hunt animals. Being able to identify cause and effect makes it easier to understand history.

LEARN THE SKILL

Read the passage below.

Native Americans of the Eastern Woodlands often lived in wigwams. In summer, cattails and bark were fine coverings. Because Maine winters can be fierce, however, the coverings often blew off. As a result, snow fell inside and the winds caused damage to the wigwam. Yearly, the wigwams had to be rebuilt instead of just repaired. One winter, they had extra animal skins and tried these as coverings. Because the skin was heavy, the wind did not lift it. The furs were very thick. So, the snow and rain was kept out as well. As a result of this discovery, the Native Americans now changed their roof coverings with the seasons.

Follow these steps to identify cause and effect. Learn how they work together.

1. **Identify the cause of an event.**
   In the above example, the summer roofs are too thin and light to withstand the windy, snowy winter. The winter weather makes the roofs fall apart.

2. **Identify the effect.**
   As a result of the roofs falling apart, the Native Americans discovered that animal skins kept heat in, and kept them dry through the winter. The result of the roof covering coming undone lead to a new and better covering.

3. **Look to see if an effect becomes a cause.**
   Often, an effect causes something else in turn. Because the Native Americans found skins effective in winter, they began chang-

ing their roof coverings each season. Now, the winter skins are a cause, and the seasonal cover changes are the effect.

4. **Identify clue words.**
   Clue words can help you find causes and effects. Clue words that show causes include *because, as a result of,* and *since.* Clue words that show effects include *so, therefore,* and *as a result.* How does identifying clue words help you understand the wigwam story?

TRY THE SKILL

Now read another passage.

> Before the Hodenosaunee learned to make canoes with birch bark, they experimented with the heavy bark of cherry trees and formed it into rafts. Because of the shape and weight of the boat, they could not travel as fast as they liked or control their direction. As a result, they tried different kinds of woods and shapes. Soon they began to build canoes.

1. What is the cause and what is the effect?

2. Which might be seen as both a cause and an effect?

3. What are some clue words that help you identify cause and effect?

4. How can identifying cause and effect help you in your daily life?

EXTEND THE SKILL

Understanding cause and effect is a very useful skill. In history, it has helped many leaders avoid making the same mistakes as leaders before them. It has also helped them make wise decisions that helped their people. In the last lesson, you learned about a historic decision made by Deganawida and Hiawatha. Because the Hodenosaunee peoples began fighting among themselves, their leaders spoke to them, urging them to unite and cease fighting. Deganawida and Hiawatha understood that to stop all the fighting, something needed to be done. As a result, the Iroquois Confederacy was formed.

- What causes led Deganawida and Hiawatha to speak to the Hodenosaunee?

- What were the effects?

- How can understanding cause and effect throughout history help leaders to make wise decisions? Avoid bad decisions?

Native Americans of the Plains

How did the Native Americans of the Plains use their resources to survive?

Lesson Outline
- Life on the Plains
- The Lakota
- Importance of the Buffalo

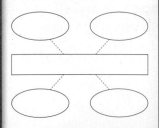
BUILD BACKGROUND

You are a young hunter on the Great Plains 400 years ago. You are looking for animals when suddenly you hear something. The sound becomes louder until it is a great pounding in your ears. It is a stampede of frightened buffalo.

The scene above takes place on the Great Plains when it was the home of many Native Americans. They mostly lived in villages near rivers, where there was plenty of water for farming. In summer, however, the men left their villages to hunt buffalo, or bison.

LIFE ON THE PLAINS

The Great Plains region is east of the Rocky Mountains and stretches north to south from Canada to Texas. It is made up of dry **prairies** and hills. A prairie is flat or rolling land covered mostly with grass. Prairies have few trees because they receive little rain. Summers in the Great Plains can be extremely hot, while winters tend to be very cold. Until the 1800s, large herds of buffalo roamed the Great Plains.

People of the Plains

Although the Plains people did some farming they were mainly hunters. They hunted many kinds of animals, but the buffalo provided them with their basic needs of food, clothing, and shelter.

This painting was done in the 1800s.
It shows a typical Plains camp.

In their villages some Plains people built **lodges**. Lodges are homes made of logs covered with grasses, sticks, and soil. In a traditional Lakota lodge, there is a fireplace in the center. The door faces east, giving honor to the rising sun.

When some Native Americans moved, they placed their belongings on a **travois** (truh VOY). A travois was a sled-like device that was used for carrying people and belongings. Before the arrival of the horse to the plains, dogs often pulled the travois.

The Arrival of Horses

By the 1600s horses that had escaped from their Spanish owners roamed freely across the plains. By the 1700s the Lakota had tamed some of these wild horses. Many Plains peoples became expert riders, breeders, and trainers. Most important, having horses allowed many Plains people to hunt buffalo as their main source of food. Some groups left their villages and stopped farming completely. They traded for other items they needed.

READING CHECK

How did acquiring horses change the life of the Native Americans of the Plains?

71

THE LAKOTA

The Lakota were one of three groups of Sioux living on the Great Plains. In the 1700s the Lakota lived in the **Black Hills** of South Dakota, which they called "the heart of everything that is." The Black Hills were and still are a sacred place to the Sioux. People met there for religious ceremonies and social gatherings.

Training at Early Ages

The Lakota trained boys and girls from early ages in their traditions and ways of life. Young boys were given bows and arrows as toys. As they got older, they were given larger bows and were taught how to hit moving objects. The qualities the Lakota most valued in a person were courage, fortitude, wisdom, and generosity. One way to show courage was to touch an enemy without killing him. To do this, a special stick called a **coup** (KOO) **stick** was needed. *Coup* is the French word for "strike" or "hit." The Sioux used *coup* to mean *war count*.

Mothers taught daughters how to prepare buffalo hide, sew the hides together, and how to erect the **teepee**. Teepees are cone-shaped tents made by leaning long poles together, trying them at the top, and then covering them with animal skins. Girls also learned how to cure buffalo meat and to search for herbs.

The Winter Count

The Lakota kept track of important events by making special calendars called winter counts. The one below was made in the 1800s. Each winter the Lakota met to choose an important event of the past year. The event was recorded on buffalo hide, and events were read counterclockwise. Some winter counts had as many as 200 symbols. The winter count below tells you that during the 1800s the Lakota often interacted with other peoples.

READING CHECK ✓ How did the Lakota pass on their heritage?

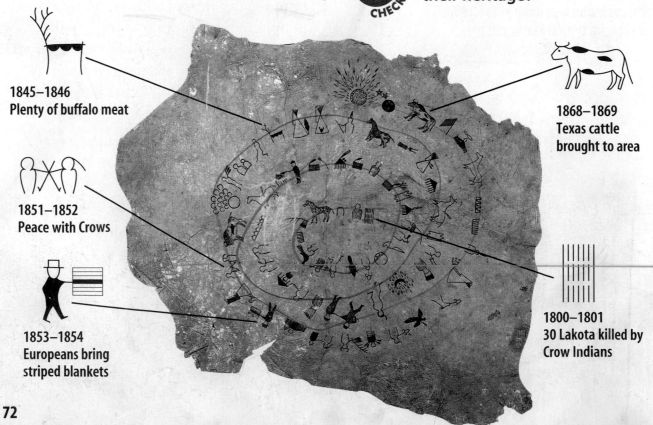

1845–1846
Plenty of buffalo meat

1851–1852
Peace with Crows

1853–1854
Europeans bring striped blankets

1868–1869
Texas cattle brought to area

1800–1801
30 Lakota killed by Crow Indians

DATAGRAPHIC

Horses Come to North America

About 450 years ago horses began to spread across North America. The horses changed the lives of the Plains peoples. After the Plains people began to hunt buffalo on horseback, the buffalo became the center of their way of life. Study the graphics on this page. Then answer the questions below.

NATIONAL GEOGRAPHIC

QUESTIONS:

1. Describe the spread of horses through North America.

2. Which Plains peoples might have been the first to have horses?

3. How does **comparing** and **contrasting** the graphics help you understand the spread of horses among the Native American people?

To learn more, visit our Web site: **www.mhschool.com**

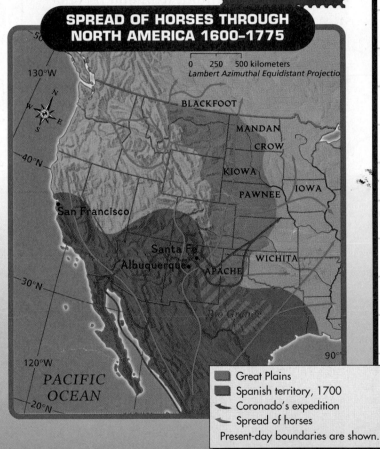

SPREAD OF HORSES THROUGH NORTH AMERICA 1600–1775

0   250   500 kilometers
Lambert Azimuthal Equidistant Projection

130°W

40°N

30°N

120°W

20°N

90°

BLACKFOOT
MANDAN
CROW
KIOWA
PAWNEE
IOWA
San Francisco
Santa Fe
Albuquerque
APACHE
WICHITA
Rio Grande
PACIFIC OCEAN

- Great Plains
- Spanish territory, 1700
- Coronado's expedition
- Spread of horses
- Present-day boundaries are shown.

Spanish and Horses Spread North

1541 Coronado's expedition to the Great Plains.

1609 Spanish found Santa Fe, New Mexico.

1706 Spanish found Albuquerque.

1885 Moving to reservations makes horses less important to Indians.

1500   1600   1700   1800   1900

1598 Juan de Oñate leads settlers from Mexico to upper Rio Grande.

1640 Horses begin to spread throughout North America.

1776 Spanish found San Francisco.

1750 Horses reach the northern part of the Great Plains.

73

IMPORTANCE OF THE BUFFALO

During the 1700s there were between 30 million to 100 million buffalo roaming the Great Plains. As you read, the buffalo provided food and material for clothing, shelter, tools, and weapons for the Plains people. The buffalo was so important to the Native Americans of the Plains that they created stories, songs, and dances about them.

Food, Shelter, and Clothing

After a buffalo hunt, women and children joined the hunters to bring the meat back to camp. The meat had to be cut and cured quickly. Sausages were made and meat was roasted or boiled with vegetables. Meat that was not eaten right away was cut into strips and hung on racks to dry in the sun. This dried meat is called **jerky**.

The buffalo skin would be used for clothing and shelter. Women and young girls would first prepare the buffalo hide by cleaning and scraping the skin, rubbing the skin with a mixture containing fat several times, then washing it in a stream. Finally it was softened by pulling it back and forth through a loop of rope. The hide was then ready to be turned into clothing, shoes, bags, or the covering for a teepee.

No part of the buffalo went to waste. The horns were used to make spoons, cups, and toys. Tools and weapons were made from the bones. The tails were used as a fly brush or whip. Even the stomach and intestines were cleaned, then used to carry water.

READING CHECK How were the many parts of the buffalo used?

PUTTING IT TOGETHER

The buffalo was central to the Plains peoples' way of life. Their existence depended on the large buffalo herds on the Great Plains.

Luther Standing Bear was Chief of the Oglala Lakota from 1905 to 1939. He said, "We did not think of the great open plains, the beautiful rolling hills, the winding streams with tangled growth as 'wild.' To us it was tame. Earth was bountiful and we were surrounded with the blessings of the Great Mystery." He was talking about the times before Europeans started moving to the Plains.

The Lakota of the Great Plains hunted buffalo to meet their food and shelter needs (far left). Traditional Lakota doll and flute are shown above.

Review and Assess

1. Write one sentence for each of the vocabulary words below.

   jerky   lodge   prairie   teepee

2. What kinds of homes did Plains people live in?

3. Explain how the Plains peoples used natural resources to survive.

4. In what ways were the two animals that were most important to the Plains peoples around 1700 useful? What difficulties did they present?

5. **Predict** how life for the Plains peoples would be affected by a big reduction in the buffalo population.

Activities

Look at the map on page 73. What kinds of data can you read on this map? Use this information to make another map about Plains life at this time.

Write a song about the Great Plains from the viewpoint of a Native American living there 300 years ago.

Find Out!

How did the Tlingit use the environment of the Northwest Coast?

VOCABULARY

technology
potlatch
totem pole

READING STRATEGY

Use a word map like the one below. Write the word *Tlingit* in the middle, then write features of their culture in the surrounding circles. Create more circles if you need them.

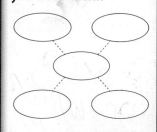

Lesson Outline
• The Northwest Coast
• The Tlingit
• Arrival of the Europeans

BUILD BACKGROUND

The Native Americans of the West lived in a variety of environments. In the Great Basin, east of California, the Paiute (pī OOT) and others lived in deserts. In southern California, where the climate is mild, Native Americans such as the Mojave (moh HAH vee) farmed. The Northwest Coast has a wet climate. Here the Chinook, Tsimshian (TSHIM shee un), Tlingit, and others lived on the sea's resources.

THE NORTHWEST COAST

The Northwest Coast region extends about 2,000 miles from Anchorage, Alaska, south to San Francisco, California. The widest part of the area is no more than 150 miles across. It is a mountainous area with many offshore islands and dense forests with tall trees. It also has a wet climate with mild winters and cool summers.

Abundant Resources

The Northwest Coast has abundant natural resources. People could live there without farming because berries, roots and other plants grew plentifully in the wet climate. In the forests were beaver, bears, deer, and elk. The Native Americans of the area, however, got almost everything they needed from the sea.

The area's ocean, rivers, and streams teemed with salmon, herring, halibut, and cod. Groups would take to the ocean in large canoes to catch seals, sea lions, and whales. From the shore people gathered clams, seaweed, and shellfish. However, salmon became their most important food.

The Salmon Run

Every year salmon would swim from the sea against the flow of freshwater rivers, such as the Columbia, to lay their eggs. This event, known as the *salmon run*, was an important event for the Northwest Coast peoples.

During the salmon run a family could catch over 1,000 pounds of fish. Men and women put aside their tasks to go to the river to catch salmon. Some of it was eaten then. Most was dried or smoked and then stored for meals throughout the year.

READING CHECK How did the peoples of the Northwest Coast live without farming?

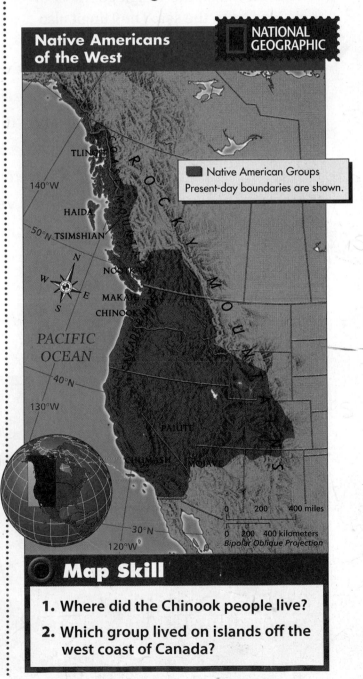

Native Americans of the West

NATIONAL GEOGRAPHIC

■ Native American Groups
Present-day boundaries are shown.

TLINGIT

140°W

HAIDA

50°N TSIMSHIAN

NOOTKA

MAKAH

CHINOOK

PACIFIC OCEAN

40°N

130°W

ROCKY MOUNTAINS

CASCADE RANGE

PAIUTE

CHUMASH

MOJAVE

0   200   400 miles
0   200   400 kilometers
Bipolar Oblique Projection

30°N

120°W

Map Skill

1. **Where did the Chinook people live?**

2. **Which group lived on islands off the west coast of Canada?**

THE TLINGIT

What is today the busy city of Sitka, Alaska, was once the heart of the Tlingit [KHLING iht] homeland. In the 1700s the Tlingit controlled an area that stretched about 400 miles along the coast. Although this area was in the north, the warm Japan Current kept its weather mild and wet.

Like many Native Americans of the Northwest Coast, the Tlingit got most of their food from the sea. The Tlingit also traded their surplus resources with other peoples to the north and south and inland along the rivers. Trade helped to make the Tlingit a wealthy people.

Tlingit villages hugged the water's edge, and their homes faced the sea. The Tlingit built wooden plank houses large enough for several related families. This house, meaning both the building and the related families who lived there, was an important part of each clan. Symbols that identified the clan were owned by the families and were passed on to descendants. Highly skilled woodworkers, the Tlingit decorated most of the items they made.

Technology and Potlatches

Because food was plentiful, the Tlingit had the time to develop the technology they needed. Technology is the design and use of tools, ideas, and methods to solve problems. The Tlingit used their technology to build dams and traps for catching salmon. They also made large canoes that could travel long distances and could be used during war.

Important events were often celebrated with a potlatch (PAHT lach). Potlatches are special feasts at which the guests, not the hosts, receive gifts. The host might distribute hundreds of gifts at the feast. In return, the host received the respect of the community.

How did the Tlingit use technology to improve their lives?

This potlatch was held to celebrate the carving of a totem pole.

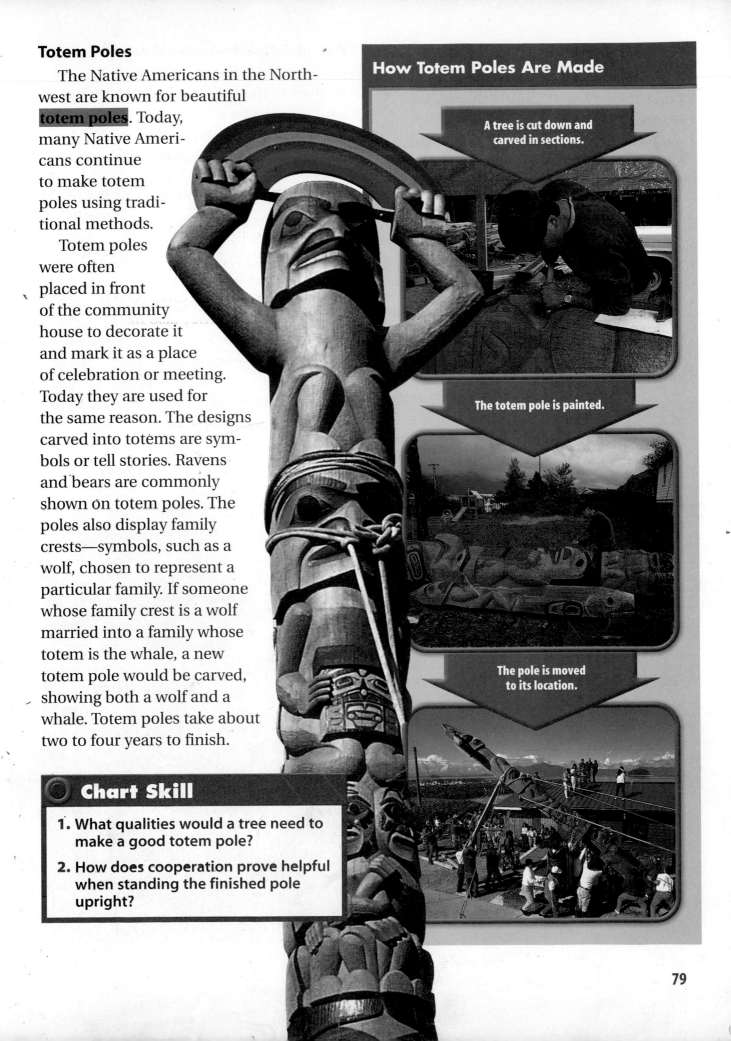

Totem Poles

The Native Americans in the Northwest are known for beautiful **totem poles**. Today, many Native Americans continue to make totem poles using traditional methods.

Totem poles were often placed in front of the community house to decorate it and mark it as a place of celebration or meeting. Today they are used for the same reason. The designs carved into totems are symbols or tell stories. Ravens and bears are commonly shown on totem poles. The poles also display family crests—symbols, such as a wolf, chosen to represent a particular family. If someone whose family crest is a wolf married into a family whose totem is the whale, a new totem pole would be carved, showing both a wolf and a whale. Totem poles take about two to four years to finish.

How Totem Poles Are Made

A tree is cut down and carved in sections.

The totem pole is painted.

The pole is moved to its location.

Chart Skill

1. What qualities would a tree need to make a good totem pole?
2. How does cooperation prove helpful when standing the finished pole upright?

79

ARRIVAL OF THE EUROPEANS

Europeans arrived in the Northwest Coast region later than in other parts of North America. In 1741 a Danish explorer named Vitus Bering sailed from Russia to Alaska, across the waterway now known as the Bering Strait. Alaska became a Russian colony. Russian, Spanish, French, British, and American explorers and fur traders soon arrived.

In 1867 the United States purchased Alaska from Russia. The Tlingit found it hard to keep their way of life. Settlers, missionaries, educators, and gold prospectors streamed into their homeland. Fish canneries were opened in sev-eral areas. In some areas the American government forced the Northwest Coast peoples to move away from the ocean on which they relied.

The Tlingit and other Native Americans in the area struggled to preserve their culture. As a result of efforts by Native Americans and the Inuit, the United States government passed the Alaska Native Claims Settlement Act in 1971. This law returned control of over 44 million acres of Native American home-lands in Alaska to the original owners.

READING CHECK What effect did the arrival of Europeans have on the way of life of the Tlingit?

Tlingit children attended this school in Sitka, Alaska, in the late 1800s.

Exploring ECONOMICS

Changing Economies

For hundreds of years the Northwest Coast people had *traditional economies*. They earned their livings in the same way their ancestors did—by fishing, hunting, and trading. The Tlingit sailed upriver to trade for moose hides, snowshoes, and copper ore. They also went north to trade with the Inuit for copper.

Today the Tlingit still trade but they have modern businesses. Some Tlingit fish for a living and make traditional items, much as their ancestors did. However, these items are often exported or sold to visitors to Sitka and nearby areas. To export means to send to other countries for sale.

Write a poem in which you express your feelings about the way in which fishing or trading has changed in your Pacific Northwest Coast homeland.

PUTTING IT TOGETHER

Native Americans of the West lived in different environments, but they shared certain values. Many native cultures of Alaska share the values of respect for others, sharing, self-knowledge, and the ability to see the connections among all things.

Today, the Central Council of the Tlingit and Haida Indian Tribes of Alaska represents over 24,000 people. Some of them live in the Pacific Northwest and work at logging and fishing. Others have relocated. However, many carry on the traditions of their ancestors such as making beautiful jewelry and holding potlatches.

Carved Tlingit headdresses were used in special ceremonies.

Courtesy of the Division of Anthropology, American Museum of Natural History

Review and Assess

1. Write one sentence for each of the vocabulary words below.

   potlatch   technology   totem pole

2. What opportunities did the Northwest Coast peoples have?

3. Analyze how the Tlingit use the environment of the Northwest Coast to enrich their lives.

4. What effect did the 1971 Alaska Native Claims Settlement Act have on people in the area?

5. **Draw a conclusion** about why the environment is important to the Tlingit way of life. Use what you have read.

Look at the map on page 77. What mountain ranges are shown? Research one of these ranges and make a travel brochure praising its beautiful scenery.

Write a news item about how the potlatch event in a Tlingit community today is celebrated. Include a description of how the Tlingit people remember their culture through this event.

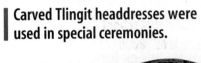

81

Being a Good Citizen
Preserving Traditions

As you read in Lesson 4, Native Americans of the West Coast have preserved many of their traditional ways of life. Preserving traditions can be a source of pride in one's self and an opportunity to show leadership.

In the Pacific Northwest, the Tulalip (Too LAY lip) Indians and other coastal groups are bringing back customs of long ago. Every year Tulalip families take part in a two-week long canoe trip known as the Canoe Journey. Canoes have long been an important form of transportation for Pacific Coast Native Americans. "For centuries," says Marie Zackuse, "our people went by canoe from one village to another, stopping to visit other Native American groups along the way, sharing food, stories, and friendship. We are doing that again."

" ...by canoe ... sharing food, stories, and friendship ...**"**

The idea for the Canoe Journey began a decade ago, when a Tulalip elder, who is a skilled canoe builder, made a large family canoe from a cedar log. The Tulalip named the canoe "Gift from the Ancestors." A few years later they built a second one called "Little Sister."

Each canoe holds 10 paddlers. In the summer of 2001, the Canoe Journey began near Tacoma, Washington, at the home of the Puyallup Indians

"I want to see it carried on for generations ...**"**

and ended north of the city of Vancouver in Canada. Many Tulalip families followed along in cars and trailers. Each night a different group such as the Lummi and Suquamish welcomed the canoes to their longhouse or community center.

Zackuse's granddaughter Sheniece Lane says, "At each place we stop, the people welcome us with a special greeting. The paddlers answer back in our native language. We eat a feast together. Then they perform their cultural dances and songs and we do ours." All year Sheniece and other Tulalip young people learn special songs for the Canoe Journey. "Going on the Canoe Journey made me proud. I want to see it carried on for generations to come."

Be a Good Citizen

Making Connections

- What are some traditions of your school or community?

- How are these traditions preserved? How could you be a leader in preserving this custom for future students?

Talk About it!

- Why did the Tulalip Indians want to preserve the tradition of the Canoe Journey?

- Why do you think Marie Zackuse had her grandchildren take part in the Canoe Journey?

Act On It

In the Community

Identify an event that has become a tradition in your community such as a parade, a fair, or a picnic. Research the history of the event and create a flyer that explains how the event began, and perhaps how it has changed over the years.

In the Classroom

As a class, discuss traditions that are shared at school. Agree on one that you would like to preserve. Draft a paragraph explaining what the tradition is and why it is important. Persuade future students to keep up this tradition.

VOCABULARY REVIEW

Number a sheet of paper from 1 to 5. Beside each number write the word from the list below that matches the description.

longhouse   **pueblo**

mesa   **technology**

prairie

1. Design and use of tools, ideas, and methods to solve problems
2. Flat or rolling land covered mostly with grass
3. Hopi apartment-style homes
4. A long building made of poles covered with sheets of bark
5. A mountain or hill with a flat top and steep sides

CHAPTER COMPREHENSION

6. What material did the Hopi use to build their homes? Describe this material.
7. How do the Navajo differ from the Hopi?
8. What were the two major language groups in the Eastern Woodlands?
9. In what present-day state did the Hodenosaunee live? What five groups made up the Hodenosaunee?
10. How did the Lakota use a coup stick?
11. What was the meaning of the potlatch to the Tlingit?
12. What did the Alaska Native Claims Settlement Act say?
13. **Write** a paragraph in which you describe the importance of the natural environment to one of the Native American peoples you have read about.

SKILL REVIEW

How to Make a Teepee, about 1800
1. A buffalo hide is scraped clean to prepare it for making a teepee.
2. Several buffalo hides are sewn together to make the teepee cover.
3. Wooden poles are used to form the teepee frame.
4. The buffalo hides are stretched over the poles to cover the teepee.

14. **Diagram Skill** What is used to make a cover for the teepee?
15. **Diagram Skill** What are the wooden poles used for?
16. **Diagram Skill** What is the final step in making a teepee?
17. **Reading/Thinking Skill** What caused the Hopi to use the dry farming method?
18. **Reading/Thinking Skill** What effect did the arrival of Europeans to the Northwest Coast have on the Native Americans living there?

USING A TIME LINE

900	1000	1100	1200	1300	1400	1500	1600	1700	1800

1000
The Navajo and Apache begin arriving in the Southwest

1200
The Hopi settle in Old Oraibi

1500
The Spanish begin settling North America

1570
The Hodenosaunee form Iroquois Confederacy

1640
Horses begin to spread throughout Great Plains

1760
The Tlingit begin trading with Europeans

19. Which event on the time line tells the cause of the spread of horses throughout the Great Plains?

20. Did the Hopi settle in Old Oraibi before or after the Apache arrived in the Southwest?

Writing **About Economics** Suppose that you are an archaeologist who has uncovered these artifacts from a Native American culture in Arizona: a canoe, seashells, and a buffalo blanket. What would these artifacts tell you about the trading patterns of the culture? What additional questions would you have about this trade?

Foldables

Use your Foldable to review what you have learned about the Native Americans. As you look at the map on the front of your Foldable, mentally recall how each of these groups used their environment to provide for their basic needs—food, shelter, clothing, and transportation. Record any questions that you have. Then discuss them with classmates or review the chapter to find answers.

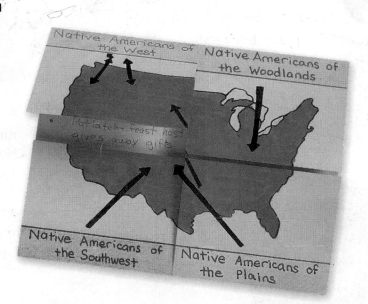

VOCABULARY REVIEW

Number a sheet of paper from 1 to 5. Beside each number write the word from the list below that best completes the sentence.

civilization   pueblos

empire   technology

mesa

1. Hopi lived in ____, or apartment-style homes.

2. A culture with complex systems of government, education and religion is called a ____.

3. A(n) ____ is a large area of different peoples controlled by one ruler or government.

4. ____ is the design or use of tools, ideas, and methods to solve problems.

5. A mountain or hill with a flat top and steep sides is called a(n) ____.

TECHNOLOGY

For resources to help you learn more about the people and places you studied in this unit, visit **www.mhschool.com** and follow the links for Grade 5, Unit 1.

SKILL REVIEW

6. **Reading/Thinking Skill** What caused certain Native American groups to move from place to place to get food?

7. **Reading/Thinking Skill** What was the effect of the Spanish arriving in Mexico in 1521?

8. **Study Skill** What does the last date on a time line stand for?

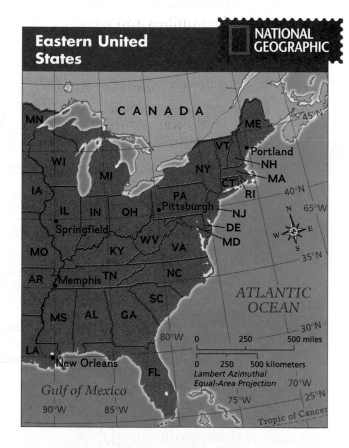

Eastern United States

9. **Geography Skill** Which line of longitude runs through the state in which the Hodenosaunee lived?

10. **Geography Skill** In which state do the following lines of latitude and longitude intersect:

   • 40°N, 90°W (state in which the Mound Builders lived)

1   Tlingit villages hugged the water's edge, and their homes faced the sea. The Tlingit built wooden plank houses large enough for several related families. This house, meaning both the building and the related families who lived there, was an important part of each clan. Symbols that identified the clan were owned by the families and were passed on to descendants. Highly skilled woodworkers, the Tlingit decorated most of the items they made.

2   Because food was plentiful, the Tlingit had the time to develop the technology they needed. Technology is the design and use of tools, ideas, and methods to solve problems. The Tlingit used their technology to build dams and traps for catching salmon. They also made large canoes that could travel long distances and could be used during war.

1   Which sentence about the paragraphs above is an opinion?

  A   Tlingit homes faced the sea.
  B   Families owned clan symbols.
  C   The Tlingit were highly skilled woodworkers.
  D   Tlingit canoes could travel long distances.

2   According to the passage, why did the Tlingit build large canoes?

  A   to travel long distances
  B   to trade tools
  C   to catch salmon
  D   to build dams

WRITING ACTIVITIES

Writing to Persuade Suppose you are an Olmec trader in the town of San Lorenzo. *Write* a newspaper ad in which you persuade traders from other towns to buy your goods.

Writing to Inform Suppose that you are a reporter assigned to write about the founding of the Iroquois Confederacy. Be sure to include as many details as possible.

Writing to Express Choose one event from the picture of the Lakota winter count on page 72. *Write* a story that tells what happened during that event.

Unit 2

LITERATURE

The LOG of CHRISTOPHER COLUMBUS

Selections by Steve Lowe
Illustrated by Bleu Turrell

Here are Christopher Columbus's own words revealing the day-to-day drama, the disappointments, and the wonder of the voyage and discovery that changed the history of the world. At times sad, at times exciting, always interesting, THE LOG OF CHRISTOPHER COLUMBUS *is a personal account of Columbus's first voyage across the Atlantic Ocean. As you read, ask yourself, in what ways was Columbus's journey difficult?*

The Log of
Christopher Columbus
by CHRISTOPHER COLUMBUS
selections by STEVE LOWE illustrations by ROBERT SABUDA

the FIRST VOYAGE

SPRING, SUMMER, AND FALL 1492

Spring and summer 1492

I left Grenada on Saturday, the twelfth day of the month of May in the same year of 1492 and went to the Palos, which is a seaport.

There I fitted out three vessels, very suited to such an enterprise. I left the said port well supplied with a large quantity of provisions and with many seamen on the third day of the month of August of the same year, on a Friday, half an hour before sunset. I set my course for the Canary Islands of Your Highnesses, which are in the Ocean Sea, from there to

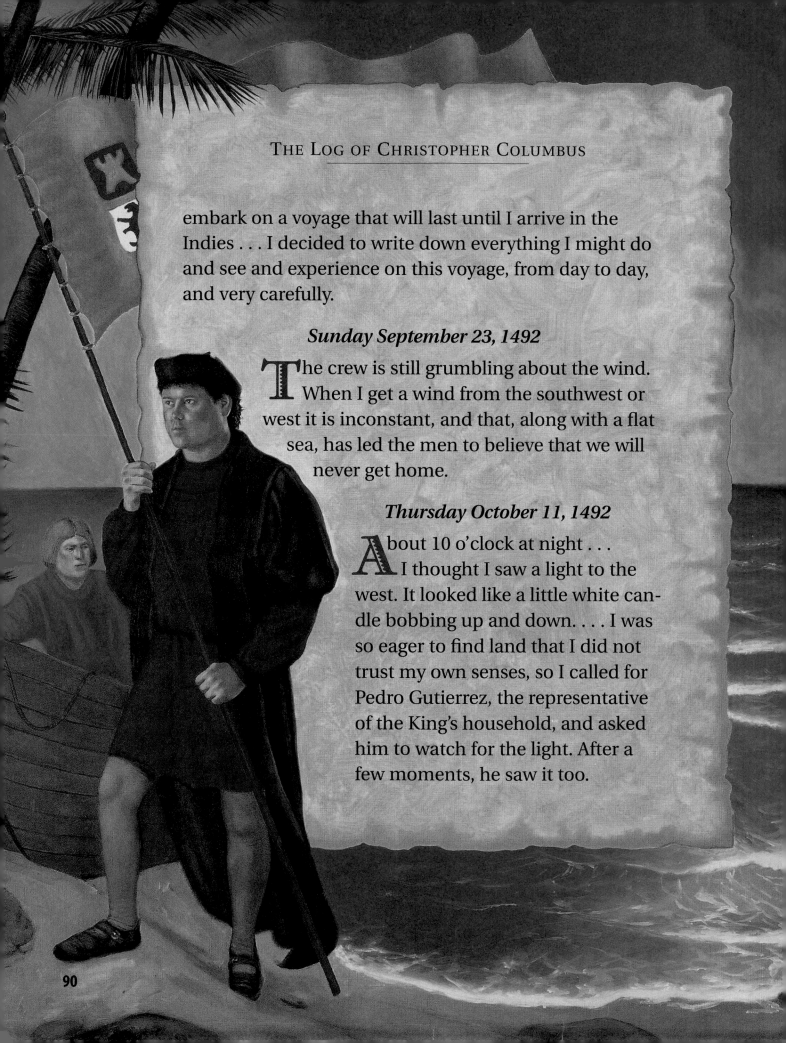

embark on a voyage that will last until I arrive in the Indies . . . I decided to write down everything I might do and see and experience on this voyage, from day to day, and very carefully.

Sunday September 23, 1492

The crew is still grumbling about the wind. When I get a wind from the southwest or west it is inconstant, and that, along with a flat sea, has led the men to believe that we will never get home.

Thursday October 11, 1492

About 10 o'clock at night . . . I thought I saw a light to the west. It looked like a little white candle bobbing up and down. . . . I was so eager to find land that I did not trust my own senses, so I called for Pedro Gutierrez, the representative of the King's household, and asked him to watch for the light. After a few moments, he saw it too.

The Log of Christopher Columbus

Friday October 12, 1492

At dawn . . . I went ashore in the ship's boat. I **unfurled** the royal **banner**. . . . To this island I gave the name, *San Salvador.* . . .

[Soon] people began to come to the beach. . . . They are very friendly.

Tuesday November 27, 1492

As I went along the river it was marvelous to see the forests and greenery, the very clear water, the birds, and the fine situation, and I almost did not want to leave the place. I told the men with me that, in order to make a report to the Sovereigns of the things they saw, a thousand **tongues** would not be sufficient to tell it, nor my hand to write it, for it looks like an enchanted land.

Columbus's signature (above) was written in Greek and Latin.

---

unfurled (un fûrld') opened or spread out; unrolled
banner (ban'ər) a flag
tongues (tungz) people

Write About It!

What if you were a crew member on Columbus's ship? Write a journal entry about a day on your voyage.

Worlds Meet

TAKE A LOOK

How has exploration changed today?

It took Christopher Columbus 70 days to sail from Spain to the Bahamas. Today a space shuttle travels around the world 16 times a day.

For more information about explorers, visit our Web site at www.mhschool.com

THE Big IDEAS ABOUT...

The Age of Exploration

For 1000 years, from 500 to 1500, Europe went through a period of little

growth or expansion. People knew little about the world outside their own.

However, all that soon changed. Explorers like Marco Polo made Europeans

curious about far off places like China, Africa, and Arabia. Read

on to discover how that curiosity led to international trade for Europeans.

EUROPE AND MARCO POLO

During Marco Polo's travels to China, he becomes friendly with the Emperor Kublai Khan.
When he returns to Italy, Marco Polo writes a book describing the riches of China's Empire in great detail.

EXPANSION OF TRADE

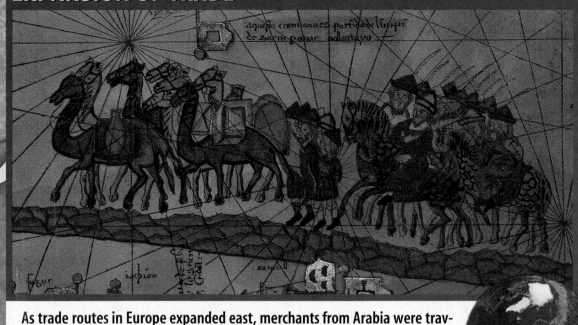

As trade routes in Europe expanded east, merchants from Arabia were traveling to Africa, bringing with them new goods to sell and buy.

THE SEARCH FOR NEW TRADE ROUTES

Prince Henry of Portugal helped create a better sailing ship. Explorers used this ship to sail around the southernmost point of Africa. Soon they reached Asia's trade cities.

Foldables

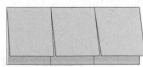

Make this Foldable study guide and use it to record what you learn about "The Age of Exploration."

1. Fold a sheet of paper like a hot dog, but make one side 1" longer than the other.

2. On the short side of the paper, make two cuts equal distances apart to form three tabs.

3. Label the 1" tab with the chapter title. Label the three small tabs with the lesson titles.

Europe and Marco Polo

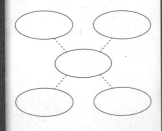

How did Marco Polo's travels to Asia make Europeans interested in the rest of the world?

Lesson Outline
- Thirteenth-Century Europe
- Marco Polo's Journey
- Interest in the World Grows

VOCABULARY

Middle Ages
merchant
expedition

PEOPLE

Marco Polo
Kublai Khan

READING STRATEGY

Place Marco Polo's name in the center of the word map below. List places, people, and items that are associated with him.

BUILD BACKGROUND

In 1298, Marco Polo wrote: "All people who wish to know the . . . diversities of the different regions of the world . . . take this book . . . here you will find all the greatest marvels."

When Marco Polo wrote his book, Europeans were just becoming interested in lands outside of Europe. His account inspired many to broaden their travels.

THIRTEENTH-CENTURY EUROPE

During the thirteenth century, Native American cultures were growing and developing in North America. Across the Atlantic Ocean in Europe, major cultural and economic changes were taking place.

Changes in Agriculture

For hundreds of years people from outside the continent had invaded Europe. Travel between areas lessened and Europeans became less interested in the world beyond their walls. We call this period of European history, from about 500 to about 1500, the **Middle Ages**.

By the twelfth century, Europe began a time of change. Technology improved and a different way of life emerged. Farmers drained marshes and cut down forests, making more land available for growing crops. Many farmers used a new plow that could dig deeper, which increased crop production. They also began to use more metal tools, which were stronger than tools made of wood. Watermills and windmills were built. Women no longer had to grind flour by hand. Work became easier and people had more leisure time.

Growth of Cities

Towns and cities began to appear throughout Europe in the Middle Ages. The greatest number of these were in the Netherlands, Germany, France, and Italy.

Some towns developed out of trading sites. First permanent trading settlements were built. Then innkeepers opened hotels for travelers, and other people built homes nearby.

Genoa, Florence, and Venice were among the most important commercial towns and cities. **Merchants**—people who buy and sell to earn a living—from these cities traded spices, cloth, perfume, medicine, and dyes throughout the Mediterranean region. They also had trading posts in cities along the Black Sea. This sea was an important trading route between Europe and Asia. Here merchants traded for silk, porcelain, and other goods that came over from China.

READING CHECK How did towns and cities develop in Europe in the Middle Ages?

Venice (left) in the thirteenth century. **Merchants** (right) traveled great distances to buy and sell goods.

97

MARCO POLO'S JOURNEY

One of the merchants who traveled to distant lands was a young man named Marco Polo. In 1271, he traveled from Europe through Persia and on to China. When he returned to Europe in 1295, he knew more about China than any other European of his time.

The Court of Kublai Khan

Marco Polo was born in 1254 in Venice. His father and uncle were jewel merchants. They had left Venice in 1260 on a business trip to the Black Sea. In 1262, a war prevented them from returning home, so they traveled farther east to

Central Asia. They reached the court of Kublai Khan, (KOO bli KAHN) who was the ruler of China.

After seven years in China, the brothers returned to Europe. Then in 1271 they set out for Asia again, this time with Marco. They reached the court of Kublai Khan in 1275, in what is now Beijing.

The Polos spent the next 17 years in China. Marco Polo entertained Kublai Khan with stories about the lands he had visited along the way. Kublai Khan liked Marco Polo so much, he sent the young man to represent him at political meetings throughout the empire.

In 1292, the Polos set out for home. They traveled over land to Turkey, then took several ships, and arrived in Venice in 1295. There Marco Polo became known as *il milione*, or "the man with a million stories." People often gathered at his home to hear about his adventures.

Marco Polo (left) returned to Venice with Mongol artifacts including plates (above) and coins (next page).

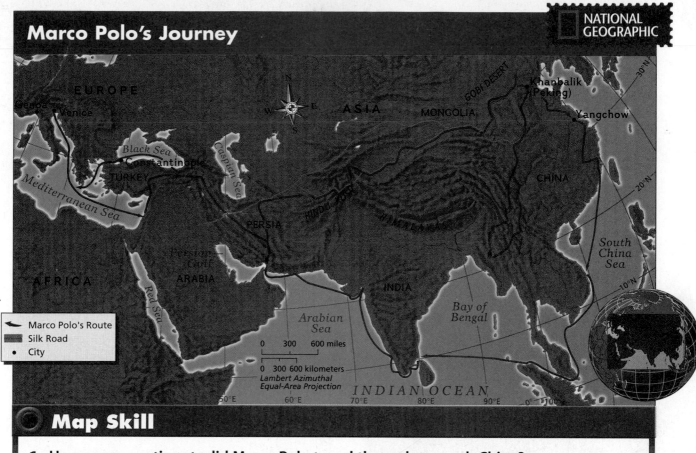

Map Skill

1. How many continents did Marco Polo travel through to reach China?

2. Which bodies of water did he sail through?

The Description of the World

Marco Polo's stories might have been lost to history after his death in 1324. Instead something happened that would change the world forever.

In 1298, three years after his return to Europe, Marco Polo was captured by the Genoese in a war between Venice and Genoa. He was put in prison for a year. Here he passed the time by telling stories. A writer from Pisa named Rustichello became interested in Marco Polo's adventure tales. Eventually Rustichello wrote down these stories and made them into a book.

The book was called *The Description of the World*. It has also been called *The Book of Marvels* and *The Travels of Marco Polo*. Translations of the book became available in many other languages.

Not only did Marco Polo's book describe what life was like in lands outside Europe, it also contained valuable information about the geography of Asia. Mapmakers studied the book when drawing maps of Asia. Merchants used the book to plan trading **expeditions**, or purposeful journeys, farther east.

READING CHECK

What was the significance of Marco Polo's journey to Asia?

99

INTEREST IN THE WORLD GROWS

Marco Polo's account of his travels had a great influence on Europe. News of his journey increased interest in Asia. Europeans began to look outside their borders for new sources of trade.

Marco Polo's Influence

Many Europeans believed that Marco Polo's book was the most important

account of the world outside of Europe available at the time.

It was also the first European account of Chinese society. It included details about the Silk Road, a network of trade routes that connected China to various parts of Europe and India, more than 4,000 miles away. It also described their postal systems and important cities in the empire.

Some of the things Marco Polo had seen in Asia were totally new to him. For example, people in China used paper money instead of the gold and silver that was used in Europe. Marco Polo was also impressed with their use of coal, which he called "stones that burn like logs." He wrote that " . . . these stones, being very plentiful and very cheap, effect a great saving of wood."

Marco Polo described many new and unusual scenes he saw in Asia.

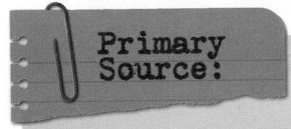
Primary Source:

excerpt from
The Description of the World
— as told by Marco Polo in 1298

*With this currency [Kublai Khan] orders all payments to be made throughout . . . his empire. . . . All the people . . . who are subject to his rule are perfectly willing to accept these papers in payment, . . . whether for goods or for pearls or precious stones or gold or silver. With these pieces of paper they can buy anything and pay for anything. I can tell you that the papers that **reckon** as ten **bezants** do not **weight** as one.*

Why was Marco Polo so amazed by paper money?

reckon: count
bezants: ancient gold coins
weight: weigh

Mapmakers developed maps based on Marco Polo's account of his travels.

When he died in 1324, Marco Polo said: "I have only told the half of what I saw!" He left it up to the next generation to explore the rest of the world. Countries such as Portugal and Spain would soon send many explorers in search of a direct sea route to Asia.

What were some of the things Marco Polo's book described?

PUTTING IT TOGETHER

By the end of the thirteenth century Europe was beginning to look beyond its borders to the rest of the world. Marco Polo's account of his travels in Asia led to a renewed interest in the world outside of Europe. Everyday citizens read his book for its foreign descriptions. Explorers depended on it when planning new routes. Merchants set off eagerly to trade along the Silk Road they had heard about. A new age of European exploration was about to begin.

Review and Assess

1. Write one sentence for each of the vocabulary terms from this list.

   expedition   merchant   Middle Ages

2. Who was Kublai Khan?

3. Analyze how Marco Polo's travels to Asia led to a European interest in the rest of the world.

4. What effect did the inventions of the windmill and watermill have on European farmers in the Middle Ages?

5. **Predict** what might have happened if a book had never been written about Marco Polo's adventures.

Using the map on page 99, draw an illustrated map that shows why the Black Sea was an important trade route.

Think about the first meeting between Marco Polo and Kublai Khan. **Write** a short dialogue between the two men at the moment of their first meeting.

Reading Graphs

Line and Circle Graphs

The population of Europe had been increasing. Then in 1348, disaster struck. The bubonic plague, or the "Black Death," swept across Europe, killing hundreds of thousands of people.

One way to study the changes in Europe's population is to look at a graph. A **graph** is a diagram that presents information in a way that is easy to understand.

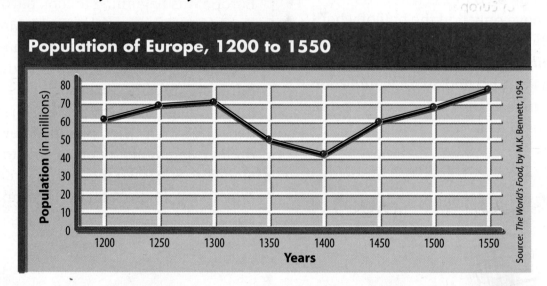

Population of Europe, 1200 to 1550

Population (in millions) — Years

Source: *The World's Food,* by M.K. Bennett, 1954

LEARN THE SKILL

Look at the graphs on these pages as you follow the steps.

1. **Identify the types of graphs.**
   The graph on this page is a **line graph**. It shows patterns and amounts of change over time. The graph on the next page is a **circle graph**. It shows how something can be divided into parts. All of these parts together make up the whole. Circle graphs are called pie graphs because the parts look like slices of a pie.

2. **Identify the titles of the graphs.**
   The title of the line graph is, "Population of

Europe, 1200 to 1550." The title of the circle graph is, "Population of Europe, 1450."

3. **Study labels on the graphs.**
   Labels on the line graph include the years on the bottom and "Population (in millions)" on the left side. The labels on the slices within the circle graph show different countries, their populations, and percentages of the total population.

4. **Compare facts and figures.**
   On the line graph you can tell that the population grew until after 1300. The population then began to decrease. If you compare this graph to the circle graph you can see what percentage of the total population a country had in 1450.

TRY THE SKILL

Look at the graph on this page. Then study the labels. Use the graph to answer the following questions.

1. What kind of graph is it?

2. What is the date on the graph?

3. What does each slice of the pie represent?

4. What was the population of Italy? What percentage of Europe's total population was it?

5. What are some ways that line and circle graphs are useful to you?

EXTEND THE SKILL

Suppose that you have been preparing to run in a race this fall. To practice, you have been running about 4 miles a day. You ran fewer miles when you had a cold and when you had other activities or chores to do. Make a graph showing the number of miles you ran every week for two months. Use your graph to answer the following questions.

- What kind of graph is it?

- What do the labels tell you?

- How do the number of miles change?

- How can circle and line graphs help you to compare and contrast information?

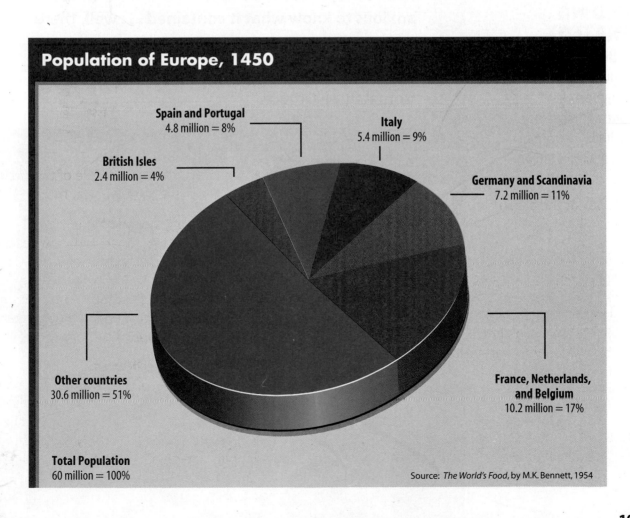

Population of Europe, 1450

Spain and Portugal
4.8 million = 8%

Italy
5.4 million = 9%

British Isles
2.4 million = 4%

Germany and Scandinavia
7.2 million = 11%

Other countries
30.6 million = 51%

France, Netherlands, and Belgium
10.2 million = 17%

Total Population
60 million = 100%

Source: *The World's Food*, by M.K. Bennett, 1954

The Expansion of Trade

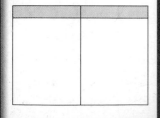
How did trade expand during the Middle Ages?

Lesson Outline
• European Trade Grows
• African and Chinese Trade

BUILD BACKGROUND

An unknown writer who lived around A.D. 1200 describes a Middle Ages trade fair: "I made my way up to a height close by the scene of the fair. What I saw there was a number of merchants' booths set up in parallel rows opposite one another. If you are anxious to know what it contained . . . well, there was every kind of material woven or spun by men or women . . . all that are brought in trading ships from Italy to Greece."

You Are Here
1400 – 1464

EUROPEAN TRADE GROWS

By the 1400s, Italian merchants were traveling great distances to trade with people in Southeastern Europe. The cities of Genoa, Pisa, and Venice built large fleets of ships that carried goods across the Mediterranean Sea to Spain and northern Africa. Once there, they traded their goods for those from seaports and countries as far away as India and China.

European merchants also traded at international fairs held along the main trade routes. Each fair was held at a different time of the year, and merchants traveled most of the year from one fair to another. Italian merchants brought silks, spices, and perfumes from the Middle East, India, and China. Merchants from northern and eastern Europe brought furs, lumber, and stone. Merchants at the fairs often wrote letters that promised payment at a future fair and that could be signed over to another person.

The merchants not only traded their goods, but they also traded ideas. They shared news about technology, new methods of farming, cultures, and events in their own parts of the world.

Banking Develops

With the growth of European trade, there was soon a need for places to hold money. It was neither convenient nor safe for people to carry all their gold with

them. Merchants also needed a way to convert coins from one country's **currency** into another's. Currency is the coins, paper, or gold used as money and it usually varies from country to country. People known as money changers began to hold large sums of money for people. They also loaned money to merchants for trade with other countries. The Medici (MED i chee) family of Florence was one of the first families in Europe to become wealthy from their banking practices in the fifteenth century.

How did the expansion of European trade lead to the development of banks?

At trade fairs (left) early bankers like those above converted foreign money and gave out loans.

105

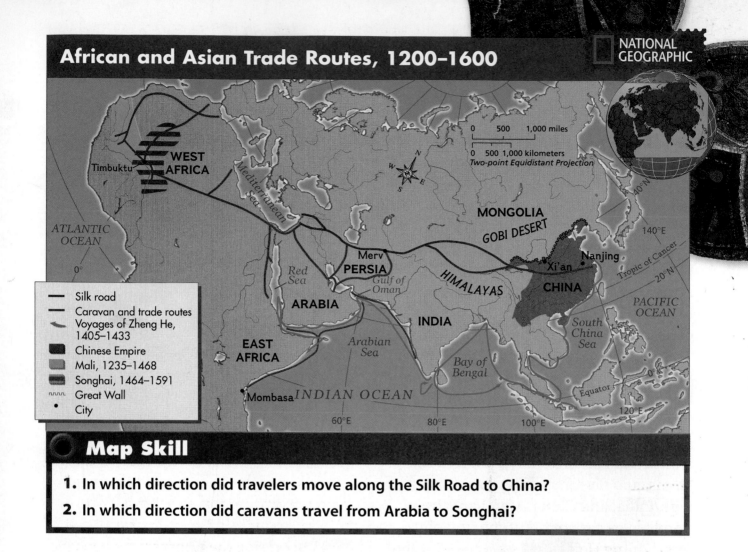

African and Asian Trade Routes, 1200–1600

NATIONAL GEOGRAPHIC

Legend:
- Silk road
- Caravan and trade routes
- Voyages of Zheng He, 1405–1433
- Chinese Empire
- Mali, 1235–1468
- Songhai, 1464–1591
- Great Wall
- • City

Map Skill

1. In which direction did travelers move along the Silk Road to China?
2. In which direction did caravans travel from Arabia to Songhai?

AFRICAN AND CHINESE TRADE

Europe was not the only continent experiencing economic growth during the 1400s. West Africa became a major trading center for gold and salt. Chinese explorers searched for new markets.

Africa

In the 1200s, caravans of traders from Arabia began riding across the Sahara. A caravan is a group of people traveling together, especially through desert areas. It was a difficult journey across the largest desert in the world. By the 1400s, most caravans were headed for Songhai (SAWNG hī), the powerful kingdom that ruled most of West Africa.

In 1464, Sunni Ali became king of Songhai. He turned Songhai into a huge empire. At its peak, Songhai stretched more than 1,000 miles across West Africa. During the 1400s, it controlled most trade as well as the valuable salt and gold regions of the area. The trading of salt and gold with Europe and Egypt to the north and east made Songhai wealthy.

The city of Timbuktu in Songhai became an important trade city because of its location between the salt mines in northern Africa and the gold fields in the south. It was also a great cultural center. Many scholars came to Timbuktu to study astronomy, mathematics, music, and literature.

Mongol silk covers such as this one were used for vases and pottery.

China

By 1368, the Chinese had defeated the Mongols and retaken control of China. In 1402, the new emperor of China, Zhu Di (Zhoo Dee), began to increase trade on the ancient Silk Road named after the most important item carried over it, silk. Through a chain of Chinese, Indian, Arab, and Italian traders, the silk made its long journey over Asia's mountains and deserts to Europe. In exchange, oranges, gold, and horses were brought to China.

Zheng He's Voyages

In 1403, Emperor Zhu Di ordered thousands of sailing ships built. He put Zheng He (ZHAHNG HUH), a Chinese Muslim sea captain, in command of the fleet. Zheng He first set sail in 1405 with 62 large ships and a crew of 27,800 men.

From 1405 to 1433, Zheng He made seven voyages. He explored Southeast Asia, India, Ceylon, present-day Sri Lanka, the Persian Gulf, East Africa, and Egypt.

In 1525, a new emperor ordered that the empire's sailing ships be destroyed. China's days of exploration were over.

READING CHECK **What did Sunni Ali and Zhu Di accomplish as rulers of their empires?**

PUTTING IT TOGETHER

Until about the 1400s, China had done little trading with Europe. During the voyages of Zheng He, China began exploring trade with other countries. At the same time, Songhai increased trade with people from Europe. As Europe increased its international trade, it began to search for better and faster routes to other continents. Countries all over the world were looking outside their borders for new and exciting goods to trade.

Review and Assess

1. Write a paragraph that uses the following vocabulary terms.

   caravan   currency

2. Who was Sunni Ali?

3. Analyze how trade grew during the Middle Ages.

4. Why was Timbuktu an important trade city?

5. **Predict** what might have happened if the new emperor of China had not destroyed the sailing ships of Zheng He.

Using the scale on the Atlas of the World on pages R4–R5, figure out approximately how many miles China is from Europe.

Write a postcard to a frien[d] international fair of the Middl[e] Describe all the things you se[e]

The Search for New Trade Routes

Find Out!

How did advances in technology lead to the expansion of exploration?

Lesson Outline
• Prince Henry Aids Navigation
• Portuguese Explorers

VOCABULARY

navigation
caravel

PEOPLE
Prince Henry
Bartolomeu Dias
Vasco da Gama

READING STRATEGY

Use the sequence-of-events chart to explain how Prince Henry's interest in exploration led to lower prices for Asian spices.

BUILD BACKGROUND

During the Middle Ages, Europeans used Asian spices, such as pepper and cloves, to preserve food over the winter. However, these spices were very expensive. European traders wanted to find another, cheaper route by which they could get goods from Asia. To find this route, they looked to the sea.

SELECTED PORTUGUESE TRADE ROUTES—red
PORTUGUESE EMPIRE BUILDERS:
Diogo Cão (1482, 1485)—green
Bartolomeu Dias (1487-88)—purple
Vasco da Gama (1497-98)—orange
Pedro Álvares Cabral (1500)—yellow
Afonso de Albuquerque (1503-1515)—blue
Francisco Serrão (1512)—pink

0   500
MILES AT EQUATOR

NGS CARTOGRAPHIC DIVISION
ARTWORK BY KINUKO Y. CRAFT

PRINCE HENRY AIDS NAVIGATION

In the early 1400s, Portugal sent explorers farther out into the Atlantic Ocean. **Prince Henry** of Portugal set out to prove that there was a way to reach Asia by ship. Henry soon became known as Henry the Navigator, because of improvements scientists working for him made in **navigation**. Navigation is the science of determining a ship's sailing direction and location. The scientists improved such inventions as the magnetic compass, invented by the Chinese; and the astrolabe. The astrolabe was an instrument used for measuring the positions of stars.

Henry also brought together European shipbuilders, scientists, mapmakers, and ship captains. Together they created a new type of ship called the **caravel**. It was about 70 feet long and could be steered more easily than other ships. The caravel had a hold for carrying large amounts of cargo.

READING CHECK What did Prince Henry do to find a sea route to Asia?

Exploring
TECHNOLOGY

The Three-Masted Ships

The technology of shipbuilding began to improve greatly by the 1400s.

Shape European ships were built wider and rounder at one end. They were not the fastest ships, but were strong and could sail for long distances.

Control This ship, the *caravel*, had a rudder, the movable board for guiding the ship, in the back. Now, the ship turned faster.

Flexibility Caravels had three masts, the tall poles on which sails are hung. Sailors could lower, raise, or slant different sails to sail with the wind or against it.

Why was the caravel an improvement over earlier types of ships?

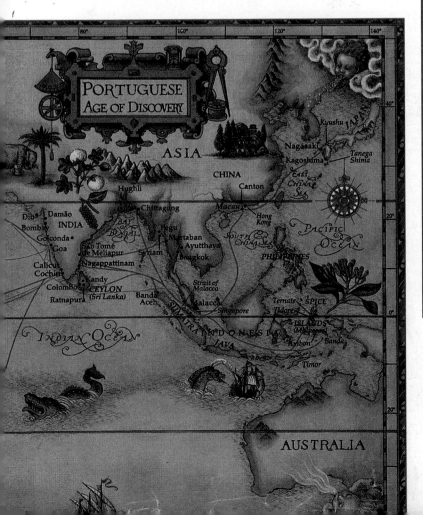

This map shows knowledge European explorers gained in their travels.

PORTUGUESE EXPLORERS

Using new technologies, Henry's caravels first sailed the coast of West Africa. In 1441, a caravel returned from the West African coast with some gold dust, proving that Henry's explorations were worth the expense. In 1445, Henry paid for voyages that reached Cape Verde, the westernmost point of Africa.

By 1460, when Prince Henry died, his ships still had not reached southern Africa. As you can see on the map, though, later European explorers achieved Henry's goal.

From 1470 to 1484, Portuguese explorations led to the discovery of Africa's Gold Coast and the Congo River. Then in 1488, a Portuguese explorer named **Bartolomeu Dias** became the first European to sail around the southern tip of Africa. He named it "Cape of Storms" because of the strong winds that had blown the ships past the tip and into the Indian Ocean. The cape was later renamed the "Cape of Good Hope" by the Portuguese because of its importance as a new route to the east.

Dias had intended to continue his journey to the east, but his exhausted crew insisted that they return home. The map below shows where the ships turned back. Still, Dias brought back valuable information about thousands of miles of ocean waters that Europeans knew nothing about.

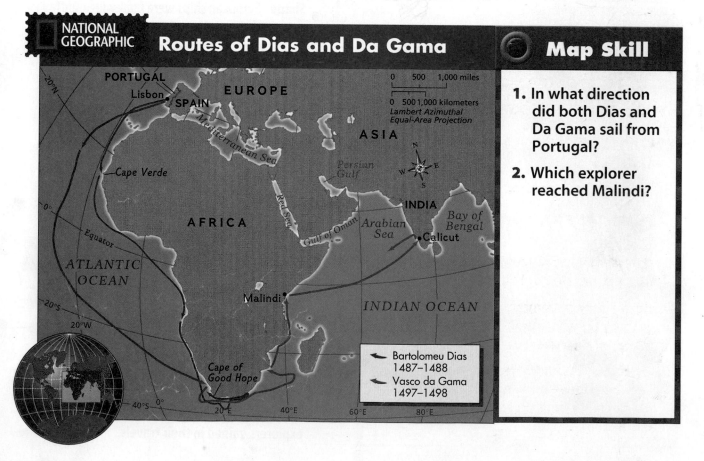

NATIONAL GEOGRAPHIC
Routes of Dias and Da Gama

0 500 1,000 miles
0 500 1,000 kilometers
Lambert Azimuthal
Equal-Area Projection

PORTUGAL
Lisbon
SPAIN
EUROPE
ASIA
Mediterranean Sea
Cape Verde
Persian Gulf
Red Sea
INDIA
AFRICA
Gulf of Oman
Arabian Sea
Bay of Bengal
Calicut
Equator
ATLANTIC OCEAN
Malindi
INDIAN OCEAN
Cape of Good Hope

Bartolomeu Dias
1487–1488
Vasco da Gama
1497–1498

Map Skill

1. In what direction did both Dias and Da Gama sail from Portugal?

2. Which explorer reached Malindi?

In 1497, **Vasco da Gama**, another Portuguese sea captain, set out for India with four ships. He rounded the Cape of Good Hope and stopped on the east coast of Africa. Then he traveled farther east, and in 1498 reached Calicut, India. He was the first European ever to reach Asia by sea.

 READING CHECK Why was the discovery of the Cape of Good Hope important?

Vasco da Gama was the first European explorer to reach India by sea.

PUTTING IT TOGETHER

Vasco da Gama's voyage showed Europe a way to Asia without using the Silk Road. By 1503 the price of pepper in Portugal dropped to less than half of what it had been when Portugal's explorations first began.

Portugal made huge profits from the new sea routes. Spain, seeking an even shorter route to Asia, began to sail the Atlantic Ocean. This would lead to one of the most important voyages of Europe's age of exploration.

Review and Assess

1. Write two sentences using the vocabulary in this list.

   caravel   navigation

2. Why was Prince Henry called "Henry the Navigator?"

3. Analyze how advances in technology led to the expansion of European exploration.

4. How did improvements in such inventions as the magnetic compass and astrolabe make sailing easier?

5. List the **cause** and **effect** connections between the new sea routes to Asia and the decrease in the price of spices.

Using the map on page 110, determine how much longer da Gama's route was than that of Dias.

Suppose you were a crew member on one of Bartolomeu Dias's ships. **Write** a journal entry that describes the discovery of the Cape of Good Hope.

Chapter 3 REVIEW

VOCABULARY REVIEW

Number a sheet of paper from 1 to 5. Beside each number write the word from the list below that matches the description.

caravan   **caravel**   **merchant**
expedition   **navigation**

1. A person who buys and sells to earn a living
2. A group of people traveling together, especially through desert areas
3. The science of determining a ship's sailing direction and location
4. A new kind of ship that could be steered more easily
5. A purposeful journey

CHAPTER COMPREHENSION

6. What changes in agriculture took place in Europe in the twelfth century?
7. What were some things that Marco Polo was introduced to in Asia?
8. What goods were traded in the Songhai Empire?
9. How did the emperor Zhu Di increase contact between China and other countries?
10. Which European countries sent explorers to find a sea route to Asia in the 1400s?
11. What kind of people did Prince Henry bring together in the early 1400s? What was their goal?
12. How did the Cape of Good Hope get its name?
13. Reread the sections in the chapter about Prince Henry and Zheng He. **Write** a paragraph in which you compare and contrast the ocean explorations involving them.

SKILL REVIEW

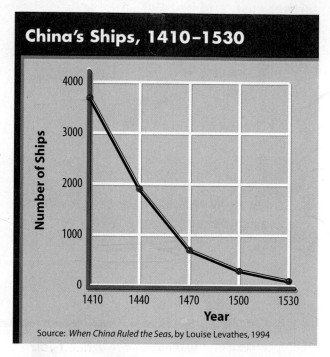

China's Ships, 1410–1530

Source: *When China Ruled the Seas,* by Louise Levathes, 1994

14. **Study Skill** About how many ships did China have in 1470?
15. **Study Skill** When did China have the largest number of ships?
16. **Study Skill** In what 30-year period did the greatest drop in the number of Chinese ships occur? How do you know?
17. **Study Skill** In what year did the number of Chinese ships reach zero?
18. **Study Skill** How are line graphs useful?

USING A TIME LINE

| 1250 | 1275 | 1300 | | 1400 | 1425 | | 1450 | 1475 | 1500 | 1525 | 1550 |

mid-1200s
Arab caravans travel across the Sahara

1274
Marco Polo visits China

1405
Zheng He begins voyages West

1445
Prince Henry's ships reach Cape Verde

1464
Sunni Ali rules Songhai

1488
Bartolomeu Dias reaches the Cape of Good Hope

1498
Vasco da Gama sails to India

19. How many years passed between Zheng He's voyages and Prince Henry's ships reaching Cape Verde?

20. In 1503 the price of pepper in Portugal had dropped to more than half of what it had been in the 1400s. What event on the time line led to this drop in price?

Writing About Exploration What if you were an astronaut about to visit a planet that had never been explored before? How would this visit have an impact on your home planet? What would you be looking for? Write about how this new exploration would change people's lives in the years to come.

Use your Foldable to review what you have learned about The Age of Exploration. As you look at the "East" and "West" labels on the front of your Foldable, mentally recall what you now know about the importance of establishing secure trade routes between the East and West. Review your lesson notes under the tabs of your Foldable to check your memory and responses. Record any questions that you have. Then discuss them with classmates or review the chapter to find answers.

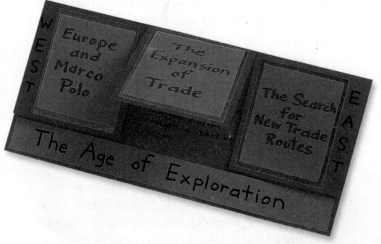

THE Big IDEAS ABOUT...

Contact and Exploration

The meeting of cultures from Europe and the Americas caused a great change in the way people lived on five continents. It led to the deaths of thousands, mostly Indians and Africans. It also led to a new knowledge of Earth. Domestic animals, such as horses, cows, and sheep, were introduced to the Americas, and many important foods and crops were introduced to Europe, Africa, and Asia.

EUROPEANS COME TO THE AMERICAS

In 1492, Columbus landed in the Americas. His voyage was the first of many that brought explorers and settlers from Europe.

EXPLORERS AND CONQUERORS

In the 1500s, other Spanish explorers reach the Americas. They make the Aztec and Inca empires into Spanish colonies.

THE SPANISH BUILD AN EMPIRE

As the Spanish search for gold and land, they expand New Spain to the north and south. The first captive Africans are brought to the Americas.

Foldables

Make this Foldable study guide and use it to record what you learn about "Contact and Exploration."

1. Fold a sheet of paper like a hot dog, but make one side 1" longer than the other.
2. On the short side of the paper, make two cuts equal distances apart to form three tabs.
3. Label the 1" tab with the chapter title. Label the small tabs with the lesson titles.

Europeans Come to the Americas

Find Out!

What happened when the peoples of Europe and the Americas met?

VOCABULARY

log
colony
Columbian
    Exchange

PEOPLE

Christopher
    Columbus
King Ferdinand
Queen Isabella
Amerigo Vespucci

explorer

READING STRATEGY

Make a chart like this one to organize information. Write items from the west in the Columbian Exchange in one column, and items from the east in the other column.

BUILD BACKGROUND

The world of the 1400s was a good place for discoveries. In the Western Hemisphere, the Aztec advanced into what is today Central America. The Inca were building an empire in South America. In the Eastern Hemisphere, Africans were trading with people from Asia and Europe. Chinese sailors were exploring Africa's east coast; and a sailor from Italy was planning a very important voyage.

PEOPLE OF THE CARIBBEAN

By A.D. 1200 the islands of the Caribbean Sea and nearby Atlantic Ocean were home to several groups of Arawak Indians. They had probably come from northeastern South America about 7,000 years earlier. The Arawak were a peaceful people who ate mostly fish and shellfish. Some Arawak groups also farmed the land and hunted and gathered wild plants for additional food. The Taino were the largest Arawak group living on the Caribbean islands at the time.

Around A.D. 1200, groups of Carib Indians from Venezuela sailed north and settled on the islands. The Carib were a more warlike people. For the next 300 years, they raided the Taino villages and took captives.

Helping Each Other

In the late 1400s the Taino lived in villages of 500 to 1,000 people. The climate of their islands made farming easy all year round. One of their main foods was a root crop called cassava. It is the original source of tapioca and probably of sweet potatoes. The Taino were good farmers and had more food than they needed. They often fed neighboring people who were not good farmers. Some of these people were less peaceful than the Taino. They paid for their food by helping the Taino in their conflicts with the Caribs.

 READING CHECK   **What groups of people lived in the Caribbean Islands in the 1400s?**

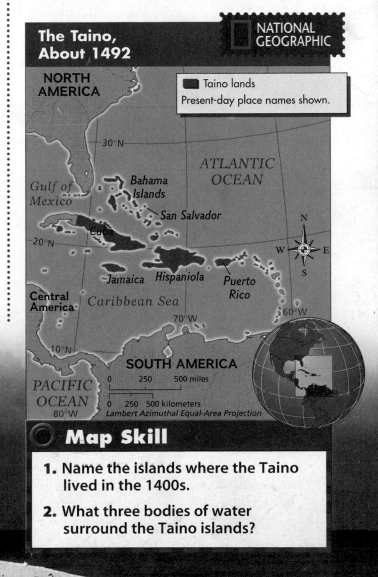

The Taino, About 1492

NATIONAL GEOGRAPHIC

■ Taino lands
Present-day place names shown.

NORTH AMERICA

30°N

ATLANTIC OCEAN

Gulf of Mexico

Bahama Islands

San Salvador

Cuba

20°N

N
W   E
S

Jamaica   Hispaniola   Puerto Rico

Central America   *Caribbean Sea*

70°W

60°W

10°N

SOUTH AMERICA

0   250   500 miles
0   250   500 kilometers
Lambert Azimuthal Equal-Area Projection

PACIFIC OCEAN

80°W

Map Skill

1. Name the islands where the Taino lived in the 1400s.

2. What three bodies of water surround the Taino islands?

THE TAINO

The lives of the Taino and other people of the Caribbean would change suddenly and forever in the fall of 1492. On the morning of October 12 of that year, explorers from Spain arrived on one of the islands that were home to the Taino.

We do not know what the Taino thought about their visitors. In fact, we do not know very much about the Taino at all. They left no written records. Historians have had to study Taino artifacts and other clues to construct a picture of their lives before Columbus arrived.

The Taino Language

The Taino gave several words to the English language. Most of these words described the way the Taino lived. By studying these words and examining other clues and artifacts, historians can learn something about the life of the Taino people.

The word *canoe*, for example, is a Taino word. The Taino made their canoes by hollowing out the centers of tree trunks. The Taino used their canoes to fish and to trade with their neighbors. Since the Taino lived on islands, they needed canoes to get from place to place. These canoes could hold more than 30 people and could travel great distances across open sea. Sometimes, canoes were used when the Taino went to war.

Another Taino word is *hamaca*, or *hammock*. This simple bed was woven from cotton or other plant fibers. It was perfect for the tropical climate where the Taino lived. It was easy to set up and it kept them cool in the warm night air.

The hammocks people use today have changed little since the time of the Taino.

Taino Ceremonies

◀ During ceremonies, a chief sat in a *dujo*, a chair valued as a symbol of power. The circular carving in the center represented Earth.

At religious ceremonies, the Taino greeted *zemis*, statues representing spirits. This *zemi* was made from wood, bone, shell, and glass. ▲

Museo Nazionale Preistorico ed Etnografico, Rome

In medical ceremonies a Taino healer often used *amulets*, or charms, such as this one. They were thought to protect the wearer ◀ from illness or harm.

Chart Skill

1. Why might a Taino wear an amulet?
2. Why do you think the chief sat in a special chair for religious ceremonies?

Taino Ceremonies

Religious ceremonies were an important part of the Taino culture. The Taino believed in many different gods. For example, they believed in a god of the sky. They also believed in a god who caused hurricanes. Our word *hurricane* comes from the Taino name of this god, Hurakan.

A chief or other leader might hold a ceremony to give thanks to the gods or to ask for protection from sickness, war, or hurricanes. The Taino also prayed to the spirits of their ancestors for guidance and protection.

What parts of Taino culture do we still have today?

CHRISTOPHER COLUMBUS

Although the Taino did not know who their visitors were in 1492, we know that the newcomers were led by an Italian captain named Christopher Columbus. His three small Spanish ships—the *Niña*, the *Pinta*, and the *Santa María*—had left Spain two months earlier. Columbus was leading this expedition, a journey for a special purpose, to find a sea route to the Indies.

A New Route to the Indies

The Indies were the islands of Southeast Asia. They were a source of gold, jewels, and valuable spices. European traders traveled to the Indies and returned with cargo that sold for high prices. This made the traders and their countries rich.

These European traders had always traveled east to reach the Indies. For thousands of years, traders had walked or traveled with pack animals across the deserts of central Asia. Columbus believed the world was round. He decided to sail *west* to reach the Indies. Because the cost of shipping by water was lower, Columbus and his backers would make more money when their cargo was sold.

For years Columbus tried to raise money for an expedition across the Atlantic. In 1486, he traveled to Spain to present his plan to King Ferdinand and Queen Isabella. They discussed his plan with their advisers for six years and finally gave him the money for his expedition in 1492.

Queen Isabella

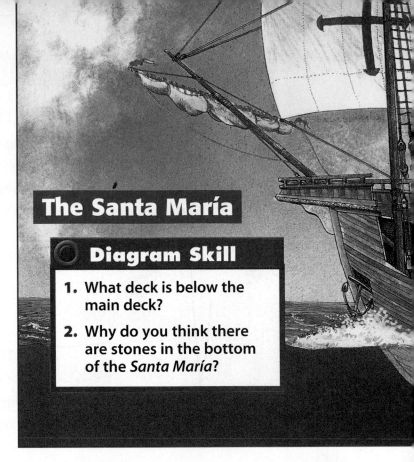

The Santa María

◉ Diagram Skill

1. What deck is below the main deck?

2. Why do you think there are stones in the bottom of the *Santa María*?

Reaching the Americas

On August 3, 1492, Columbus left Spain with his three ships and sailed west. After weeks of sailing, he still had not found land. His crew began to grumble. They were afraid that they would never see their homes again.

Columbus was keeping two logs, or records of their voyage. In the first log, he recorded the actual distance they had traveled each day. The second log showed much shorter distances. Many historians thought he used the false log to fool his sailors. Recently, other historians have argued that Columbus was actually using the second log to fool other explorers. He did not want them to know the route

mainmast

main deck

gun deck

galley

ship's boat

cargo hold

sleeping quarters

captain's quarters

rudder

he was following. In either case, a lookout in the ship finally sighted land. Columbus was sure that they were near Asia.

Today we know that he had reached the **Bahama Islands.** Later, explorer **Amerigo Vespucci** realized these lands were not part of Asia. Europeans then began calling the lands America.

A Historic Meeting

Many historians today believe that they had reached Watling Island. Columbus named it **San Salvador**, or Holy Savior, claimed the island for Spain, and met the Taino for the first time. Thinking he was near Asia, he called the people "Indios," the Spanish word for Indians. Columbus found that the Taino were friendly, but he was disappointed not to find the riches of Asia as he had expected.

READING CHECK

Why did Columbus keep two ship's logs?

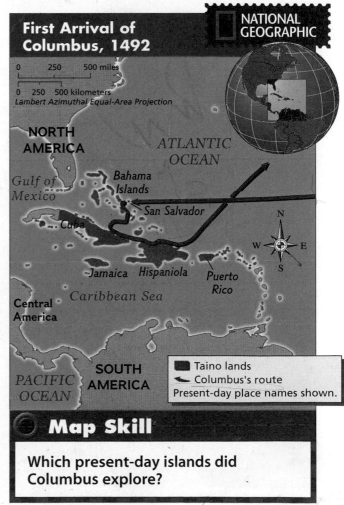

First Arrival of Columbus, 1492

NATIONAL GEOGRAPHIC

0   250   500 miles

0   250   500 kilometers
Lambert Azimuthal Equal-Area Projection

NORTH AMERICA

ATLANTIC OCEAN

Gulf of Mexico

Bahama Islands

San Salvador

Cuba

Jamaica   Hispaniola   Puerto Rico

Caribbean Sea

Central America

N
W   E
S

SOUTH AMERICA

PACIFIC OCEAN

☐ Taino lands
← Columbus's route
Present-day place names shown.

Map Skill

Which present-day islands did Columbus explore?

THE COLUMBIAN EXCHANGE

Columbus sailed south from San Salvador to other islands in the Caribbean Sea. He returned to Spain a few months later with items new to Europe. King Ferdinand and Queen Isabella asked Columbus to return to the Caribbean to found a colony. A colony is a settlement far away from the country that rules it.

The Columbian Exchange began when Columbus landed in the Americas. An exchange is a barter or swap. *Columbian* refers to Columbus. In the Columbian Exchange, products from the Americas and Europe were traded.

The Exchange Continues

When Columbus made a second voyage in 1493, he sailed with 17 ships carrying colonists. The ships also carried horses, cattle, sheep, seeds, and cuttings to grow wheat, onions, sugar, and other European crops. Unknowingly, the colonists also brought germs of diseases such as smallpox and measles.

His ships returned to Spain with turkeys, corn, potatoes, tomatoes, chili peppers, pumpkins, beans, peanuts, avocados, tobacco, and pineapples.

The Europeans also brought the wheel to the Americas. Some Indian toys had wheels, but the wheel was not used for transportation or travel. In addition, Europe sent iron-making technology and plows to prepare fields for planting.

READING CHECK How did the Columbian Exchange change life in Europe and the Americas?

This is a re-creation of an Arawak village in what is now San Salvador, Bahamas.

The Columbian Exchange

The Columbian Exchange carried tomatoes, potatoes, corn, and chili peppers from South America. Tobacco and pineapples came from the Caribbean.

From the East, the Columbian Exchange included animals from Europe such as horses, cows, and sheep. Plants like sugar cane also came from the East.

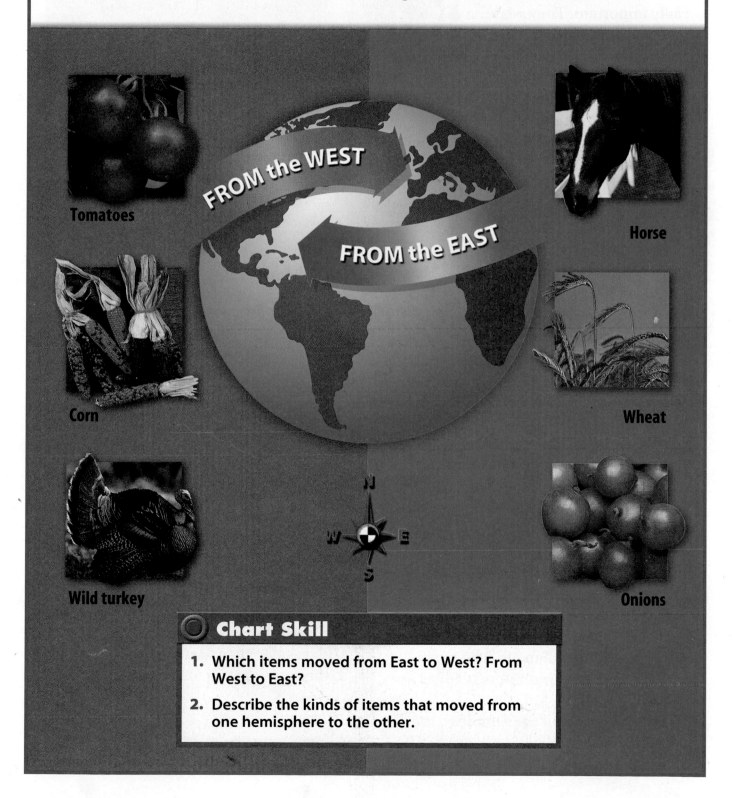

FROM the WEST

FROM the EAST

Tomatoes

Corn

Wild turkey

Horse

Wheat

Onions

Chart Skill

1. Which items moved from East to West? From West to East?

2. Describe the kinds of items that moved from one hemisphere to the other.

THE SEEDS OF CHANGE

The Columbian Exchange changed life around the world. Among the items included in the exchange were five that were especially important. They were potatoes and maize from the Western Hemisphere, and sugar, horses, and diseases from the Eastern Hemisphere. Once they arrived in new lands, these items changed the lives of millions of people. For this reason they are called the "seeds of change."

As you can see, four of these "seeds" were welcome. American foods, such as maize, improved the diets and the health of people in the Eastern Hemisphere. The new foods grew so well in the Eastern Hemisphere that they increased food supplies and led to a rapid increase in the populations of Asia, Africa, and Europe.

Similarly, the horse helped the people of North America. Before the horse arrived with Spanish colonists, Plains Indians had hunted buffalo on foot. The hunters were at a great disadvantage because the buffalo is stronger and faster than a human. The arrival of the horse changed Plains Indian life. The horse made it possible for hunters to travel as fast as the buffalo.

For the people of the Americas, the exchange had good and bad effects. The horse had helped the Plains Indians, but

new germs and diseases killed millions of Native Americans who had no resistance to them.

 **How did the horse change life for Plains Indians?**

124

PUTTING IT TOGETHER

When Christopher Columbus returned to Europe with six Taino and many new and exciting food products and animals, Europeans decided he had discovered a "new world." They began to call the Americas the "New World," but it wasn't a "new world" to the Native Americans who had been living in the Americas for thousands of years.

However, a "New World" developed after Columbus met the Taino. It was the New World made by joining two old worlds—east and west—that had not known about each other before this time.

Columbus took great risks in his expeditions to the west. He knew that ship-wrecks, storms, drowning, and injuries were common when ships sailed across the Atlantic Ocean. He faced the risks and he also showed the people of Europe the way to the Americas. Soon, people from Spain and other European countries began sailing west across the Atlantic Ocean to the Americas. You will read about some of the people who followed Columbus in the next lessons of this book. You will also find out what happened to the native peoples of the Americas.

Special harnesses (left) protected horses from injury during ocean crossings. A mariner's compass is above.

Review and Assess

1. Write one sentence for each vocabulary word.

   colony   Columbian Exchange   log

2. Why did Columbus look for a new route to Asia?

3. Analyze how the meeting of the Taino and Columbus changed the world.

4. How was the understanding of **geography** changed by the voyage of Columbus?

5. What was the **effect** of Columbus's voyage to the Americas?

What advantages would an overseas colony give Spain? What would be the disadvantages? Make a chart to show your ideas.

Write an article for a European newspaper in 1492. Describe the voyage of Columbus and tell what he found.

Points of View
Should Columbus Day Be Celebrated as a National Holiday?

Every October, our country celebrates Columbus's voyage to America as a national holiday. People disagree about whether we should celebrate Columbus Day. While many feel Columbus's legacy should be honored, others do not. Read and think about these different points of view, then answer the questions that follow.

HENRIETTA MANN
Professor, Native American Studies, Montana
Excerpt from an interview, 2001

66 Columbus Day should not be a holiday out of respect for Native American peoples. When Columbus arrived in 1492 we lost an entire continent. Our land, religious beliefs, and many ways of living were taken from us. We need a holiday that celebrates the many different customs and cultures that Americans have and shows respect for them. 99

EMANUELE ALFANO
Italian-American service organization, New Jersey
Excerpt from an interview, 2001

66 Columbus Day is a celebration of diversity and of the time when people of the Americas first met people from Europe. Over time each learned from the other. The unique American culture that was produced by the blending of many different cultures is something we can all be proud of. Columbus showed courage, a spirit of adventure, and a curiosity about the world that I greatly admire. 99

IRENE VERNON
Professor, Colorado
Excerpt from an interview, 2001

66 Many good things came to the Americas as a result of Columbus's voyages, but he isn't a person we should be celebrating with a national holiday. We should pick people to honor that all Americans can agree on and respect. Columbus wiped out many cultures. His ties to Spain influenced the development of Latin America and the Southwestern United States, but had less influence on the rest of our nation. 99

Thinking About the Points of View

1. Like Columbus, Emanuele Alfano's family comes from Italy. He is proud to be an Italian-American. How do you think this influenced his point of view?

2. Henrietta Mann is a Cheyenne Indian and a professor of Native American history. How do you think this influenced her point of view?

3. Irene Vernon studies different groups of people, their customs and cultures. Do you think this may have affected her opinion? How?

4. What other points of view might people have on this issue?

 Building Citizenship

Respect
Discuss ways that you might treat a new neighbor or student at your school in a respectful manner.

How would you carry out Henrietta Mann's idea for a holiday?

 Write About It!

Suppose you were a member of Congress in 1971 voting on whether or not to make Columbus Day a national holiday. Write a letter to the citizens of your district, explaining how you voted and why.

Explorers and Conquerors

How did the arrival of the Spanish explorers change life in the Americas?

Lesson Outline
- The Aztec Empire
- Cortés Reaches Tenochtitlán
- Conquest of the Aztec
- Pizarro Conquers the Inca

VOCABULARY

tribute
conquistador

PEOPLE
Moctezuma II
Hernando Cortés
Doña Marina
Cuauhtemoc
Francisco Pizarro
Atahualpa

READING STRATEGY

Make a chart like this one and write causes and effects for the events you read about in this lesson.

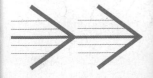

BUILD BACKGROUND

Some of the Spanish soldiers who came after Columbus reached a place called Tenochtitlán. It seemed "like the enchantment they tell of in . . . legend . . . [with] great towers . . . arising from the water . . . some [soldiers] asked whether the things that we saw were not a dream."

The Aztec ruler wore a crown of feathers from the quetzal bird, much like this one.

THE AZTEC EMPIRE

The Aztec city of **Tenochtitlán** (te noch te TLAHN) had been the capital of the empire since the early 1300s. The emperor Moctezuma I, who ruled from 1440 to 1468, led the Aztec as they conquered their neighbors to the south and east. The three emperors who followed him expanded the empire to include most of present-day Mexico.

Challenges to the Empire

The great-grandson of Moctezuma I was chosen as emperor in 1502. He was **Moctezuma II**, or Moctezuma the Younger. The new emperor faced challenges to his power from the very beginning of his rule. Conquered people within the empire were beginning to rebel. They did not want to give prisoners to the Aztec or pay **tribute**, or taxes, to them. Moctezuma also had enemies outside his empire. The Tlaxcalan (tlahs KAH lahn), who lived less than 100 miles east of Tenochtitlán, hated the Aztec. For years, the Tlaxcalan had fought against Aztec conquest. In spite of these challenges, Moctezuma was firmly in control of his empire.

The Strangers Arrive

More than 500 Spanish troops landed on the east coast of Mexico in spring of 1519. They were following rumors of gold. Aztec messengers spied on the Spanish and reported all their movements to Moctezuma.

Moctezuma did not know who the strangers were. He thought they might be friends. He sent them two disks, one of gold and one of silver. This was his first mistake. Now the Spanish were determined to reach Tenochtitlán.

What were the challenges to Moctezuma's power?

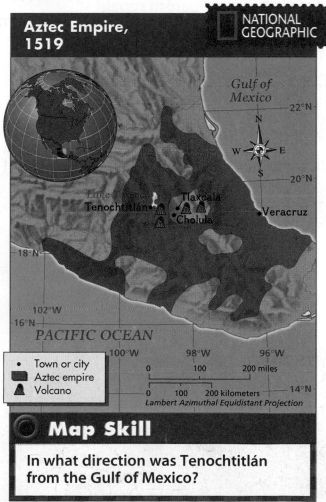

Aztec Empire, 1519

NATIONAL GEOGRAPHIC

Gulf of Mexico

Tlaxcala
Tenochtitlán
Cholula
Veracruz
Lake Texcoco

PACIFIC OCEAN

- Town or city
- Aztec empire
- Volcano

0   100   200 miles
0   100   200 kilometers
Lambert Azimuthal Equidistant Projection

Map Skill

In what direction was Tenochtitlán from the Gulf of Mexico?

129

BIOGRAPHY

Focus On: Respect

Moctezuma II had been educated at a religious school. He was deeply respectful of the Aztec religious traditions. One Aztec legend predicted that a blond, bearded god would return to Mexico one day from the east. Moctezuma thought that Cortés, who was blond, might be this god.

Moctezuma welcomed the Spanish into his own palace. He treated them as honored guests. His beliefs were shattered when the Spanish repaid his hospitality by arresting him and killing many of his people.

Link to Today Think of a political ruler today. Research this leader. Write a paragraph comparing the leader to Moctezuma.

THE LIFE OF MOCTEZUMA II	Around 1480 Moctezuma is born in Tenochtitlán		1502 Moctezuma is elected head of the Aztec Empire	1519 Hernando Cortés arrives in Mexico	1520 Moctezuma dies
	1480	**1490**	**1500**	**1510**	**1520**
LIFE AROUND THE WORLD			1502 Columbus begins his fourth voyage to the Americas	Early 1500s Benin and Songhai Empires flourish in Africa	1519 Magellan begins his voyage around the world

CORTÉS REACHES TENOCHTITLÁN

Hernando Cortés came from Spain to the Caribbean island of Cuba at the age of 19. Cortés was given land to farm, but he had other ideas. "I don't want land," he wrote. "I came for gold." The Spanish governor of Cuba asked Cortés to lead an expedition to Mexico to see if the rumors about gold were true. The young adventurer jumped at the chance. The governor, afraid that Cortés was too eager, took back his order. However, Cortés had already left secretly.

The Road to Tenochtitlán

Cortés did not want his troops to consider retreat, so he burned the boats that had brought them to Mexico. Then he led his troops inland from the coast. The Spanish came to Indian cities where the people were enemies of the Aztec. At one city, Cortés met an Indian woman who was called Malinche (mah LEEN chay) by the Indians and **Doña Marina** (DOHN yah mah REE nah) by the Spanish.

Doña Marina was the daughter of a chief. She was sold as a captive after her father died. She had learned several languages, including those of the Aztec and the Maya. Doña Marina persuaded many Indians to join Cortés. Soon his army was big enough to challenge the Aztec.

Doña Marina (right) acted as interpreter between Hernando Cortés (above) and Moctezuma.

In November 1519, Cortés and his followers reached Tenochtitlán. They were greeted with gifts of food (beans, meat, fish, maize cakes, turkeys), cloaks, and plates of copper and silver. Moctezuma sent someone to meet Cortés. He brought enough food to last the whole group several days and even brought jewels. Huts were built for the visitors. Cortés was given 2,000 servants. Among his crew, and all his gifts, Cortés waited for a meeting with Moctezuma.

READING CHECK How did Doña Marina help Cortés?

CONQUEST OF THE AZTEC

Moctezuma did not understand the Spaniards. Cortés easily took the emperor prisoner and gained control of his capital. The Aztec rose up in fury. They attacked the emperor's palace and drove the Spanish out of their city. During the fighting, Moctezuma was killed.

Cortés retreated to the east and gathered more troops. In 1521, his new army attacked the city. A young man named

HISTORY MYSTERY

Why did Moctezuma welcome Cortés?

Many people are puzzled by Moctezuma's odd behavior. Why did he let an enemy army into his capital? Why did he not defeat the Spanish on the road where his troops outnumbered them?

Moctezuma was a deeply religious man. He thought that Cortés might be a god predicted by Aztec legend to return, coincidentally, at the time Cortés arrived.

Also the Aztec ruler was puzzled by the Spanish horses—he had never seen any before. The rumors were that the men and the horses were one animal. He wanted to see what this strange animal was!

What would you have done in Moctezuma's place?

Cuauhtemoc (kwah TAY mahk) had been elected ruler of the Aztec. He led them in a desperate battle for the city of Tenochtitlán. The many enemies of the Aztec helped Cortés. The Spaniards and their Indian allies closed off all the entrances to the city. No food or water could reach the Aztec defenders. The suffering inside the city was terrible. One Aztec remembered:

> [m]any died of hunger . . . The people ate anything—lizards, barn swallows, corn leaves, saltgrass. They gnawed . . . leather and buckskin, cooked or toasted; or . . . adobe bricks. Never had such suffering been seen.

The End of Tenochtitlán

After 75 days, the city could hold out no longer. Cuauhtemoc was captured and later killed. The Spanish conquerors, or **conquistadors** (kahn KEES tuh dohrz), destroyed the great Aztec temples and smashed the statues of their gods. They also burned all the Aztec sacred books. They declared Mexico a colony of Spain, called New Spain.

The Secret Ally

How was a small army of Spaniards able to conquer the mighty Aztec empire? One important reason was technology. The Spaniards had steel weapons and gunpowder. The Aztec warriors fought with wooden spears and arrows tipped with sharp stones. They were no match for the Spanish weapons.

The Spaniards were also helped by their Indian allies who supported the Spanish against the hated Aztec.

Another Spanish ally was invisible. The Spanish had unknowingly brought new diseases to Mexico with them. The Aztec

Aztec and Spanish Fighting Equipment

AZTEC WARRIOR

1. Carved wooden club edged with sharp pieces of stone

2. Spear

3. Padded cotton armor

4. Shield made of woven reed

5. Atlatl (a stick used to launch a spear)

6. Bow and arrow

SPANISH SOLDIER

1. Andalusian horses

2. Spanish Morion (helmet)

3. Steel armor

4. Steel sword

5. Arquebus(old-fashioned firearm)

6. Cavalry lance (long, wooden pole with a metal tip)

Chart Skill

1. What advantage would fighting on horseback have over fighting on foot?

2. Describe two advantages of Aztec and Spanish fighting equipment.

had no resistance to these diseases. Many Aztec warriors were too sick to fight. Tenochtitlán could not be defended.

Fall of the Maya

About five years after Tenochtitlán fell, Spanish soldiers headed southeast to the **Yucatán peninsula** to find Mayan treasures. You read about the Maya in Chapter 1. By this time the great Maya civilization had ended. However, Maya groups still lived throughout the Yucatán Peninsula. Their determined fighters and thick rain forest environment helped them defend parts of their land for 20 years. But by 1546 the surviving Maya fell under Spanish rule.

To the Maya's horror the Spanish burned their valuable collection of books—books that contained their knowledge of history, math, and science. In one act much of Maya civilization went up in smoke. Only three Mayan books survive today.

READING CHECK How did their weapons give the Spanish an advantage?

PIZARRO CONQUERS THE INCA

In 1531, a conquistador named **Francisco Pizarro** led 180 Spanish soldiers against another powerful Indian empire. This empire was located in South America. It was named for its people, the Inca.

The Inca lived high in the Andes Mountains and ruled an empire that extended from present-day Colombia to Chile. Their leader was named **Atahualpa** (ah tuh HWAL puh); he had just won a war against his brother when the Spanish troops arrived.

Pizarro reached Cajamarca in 1532. Here he met Atahualpa in a great square. The Inca ruler was surrounded by nobility and soldiers. However, the Spanish were ready for them. In a surprise ambush, they massacred 1,500 of Atahualpa's followers and took the Inca ruler prisoner.

Atahualpa realized that the Spanish desired gold. He reached as high as he could on the wall of a room. He offered to fill the room to that height with gold if Pizarro would then release him. It was a fatal mistake. Astonishing amounts of gold poured into Atahualpa's prison. The Spanish watched greedily as golden objects filled the room.

In the end, Pizarro broke his word and murdered the Inca ruler. Then he and his followers conquered **Cuzco**, the Inca capital and the rest of the Inca Empire. Pizarro's troops had the same advantages that Cortés had in Mexico—steel weapons, horses, and germs.

READING CHECK

Why did Pizarro travel to the Inca Empire?

The Inca city of Machu Picchu, high in the Andes, was discovered in 1911.

Inca Empire, 1530

Central America

Panama City

Quito

Cajamarca

Cuzco

SOUTH AMERICA

Equator

0°

20°S
Tropic of Capricorn

PACIFIC OCEAN

ATLANTIC OCEAN

40°S

Strait of Magellan

100°W   80°W   60°W   40°W   20°W

0   500   1,000 miles
0   500   1,000 kilometers
Bipolar Oblique Projection

N W E S

Legend:
⊛ Inca capital
■ Inca Empire
• Other city

Map Skill

1. **Along which body of water was the Inca Empire located?**

2. **Approximately how long was the Inca Empire from north to south?**

PUTTING IT TOGETHER

By 1535, Spain had built one of the world's largest empires. It stretched from Mexico to the southern tip of South America. Inca and Aztec gold and silver poured into Spain. The Spanish authorities organized their new colonies to make Spain rich. This caused many changes in the way the people of the Americas lived.

The Spanish used the gold and silver of the land of present-day Mexico and South America to make coins and chains.

Review and Assess

1. Write a sentence for each vocabulary word.
   conquistador   tribute

2. How did Doña Marina help Cortés to defeat the Aztec?

3. How did the arrival of the Spanish change life for Native Americans?

4. Why did Aztec **culture** and Spanish **culture** come into conflict?

5. What were the **causes** of the Spanish expeditions to the Americas? What were the **effects** of these expeditions?

Look at the map on page 129. Write a few sentences explaining why the location of Tenochtitlán made it difficult to capture.

Suppose that you are Doña Marina. **Write** a speech persuading other Indians to join Cortés against the Aztec.

Using Historical Maps

In 1519, a Portuguese sea captain named Ferdinand Magellan set off to find a sea route to Asia. His expedition included 250 men and five ships. Magellan himself was killed along with several members of his crew in the Philippine Islands.

The map on this page traces Magellan's journey. His route was not useful for trade, but he had proved that a ship could sail around the world.

> **VOCABULARY**
>
> historical map
> map key

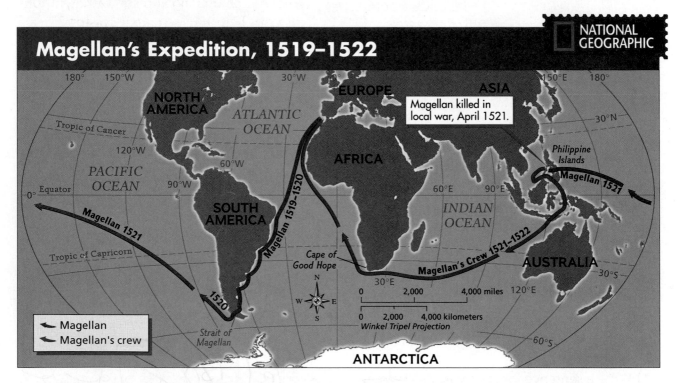

Magellan's Expedition, 1519–1522

NATIONAL GEOGRAPHIC

Magellan killed in local war, April 1521.

- ← Magellan
- ← Magellan's crew

LEARN THE SKILL

One way to study historical events is to look at a **historical map**. This kind of map shows where past events took place. The map above has several features that tell you this is a historical map. It helps to ask questions, such as the following:

1. **Identify the title of the map.**
   Magellan's Expedition, 1519–1522

2. **Find the dates of the map.**
   1519, 1520, 1521, 1522

3. **Look for symbols and a map key.**
   A red arrow shows the part of the voyage that Magellan made before he was killed. The purple arrow shows the part completed by his crew. A **map key**, or legend, can help you to understand the symbols.

TRY THE SKILL

Now try reading this historical map. It shows the Spanish conquest of the Inca Empire. You read about the defeat of the Inca leader, Atahualpa, in the last lesson. This map gives you more information. Use the map to answer the questions.

1. What are the map's title and dates?

2. In which direction did Atahualpa's troops travel?

3. Where were the major battles of the conquest?

4. What are some ways that historical maps can help you learn?

EXTEND THE SKILL

You can learn many facts about history by comparing and contrasting historical maps. The map below shows the west coast of South America before the Inca Empire was formed.

- Name some of the Indian groups that lived in Peru before the Inca Empire expanded.

- In what direction did the Inca troops go to conquer the Chimu people?

- What can comparing and contrasting historical maps help you learn about history?

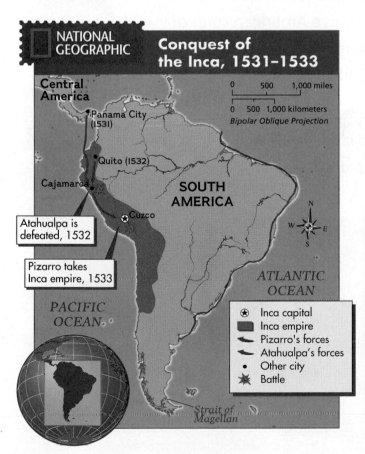

NATIONAL GEOGRAPHIC

Conquest of the Inca, 1531–1533

Central America

Panama City (1531)

Quito (1532)

Cajamarca

SOUTH AMERICA

Cuzco

Atahualpa is defeated, 1532

Pizarro takes Inca empire, 1533

PACIFIC OCEAN

ATLANTIC OCEAN

Strait of Magellan

0   500   1,000 miles
0   500   1,000 kilometers
Bipolar Oblique Projection

⊛ Inca capital
▮ Inca empire
↙ Pizarro's forces
↖ Atahualpa's forces
• Other city
✸ Battle

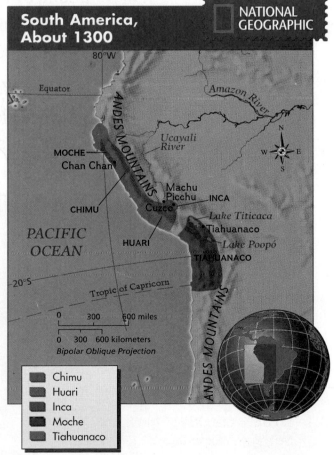

South America, About 1300

NATIONAL GEOGRAPHIC

80°W

Equator

ANDES MOUNTAINS

Amazon River

Ucayali River

MOCHE
Chan Chan

Machu Picchu
Cuzco   INCA

CHIMU

Lake Titicaca
Tiahuanaco
Lake Poopó

PACIFIC OCEAN

HUARI

TIAHUANACO

20°S

Tropic of Capricorn

ANDES MOUNTAINS

0   300   600 miles
0   300   600 kilometers
Bipolar Oblique Projection

▮ Chimu
▮ Huari
▮ Inca
▮ Moche
▮ Tiahuanaco

The Spanish Build an Empire

What was life like for people in New Spain?

Lesson Outline
- Spain's Empire Grows
- Forced Labor
- Colonial Cities

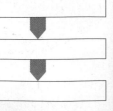

BUILD BACKGROUND

The Spanish conquistadors had conquered the powerful Aztec and Inca Empires. Difficult years followed for the Indians of the new Spanish colonies. Many Indians had reason to remember a song by a Native American ruler of the 1500s named Nezahualcoyotl (NAYZ uh wahl koy oh tuhl):

Even jade is shattered,
Even gold is crushed,
Even quetzal plumes are torn . . .

SPAIN'S EMPIRE GROWS

After Spain's defeat of the Aztec and Inca Empires, other conquistadors spread through much of North America and South America. They hoped to win more land and find more riches for Spain. As they traveled to the north and south, the Spanish brought more Indian cities and villages into their empire.

Coronado Searches for Gold

An African scout named Estevanico (ays tay VAN nee koh) and a Spanish priest called Fray Marcos de Niza had heard stories about seven fabulous cities built entirely of gold. Before they could investigate the stories, Estevanico was killed.

Fray Marcos lived to tell about the Seven Cities of Gold. Later, in 1540, Francisco Coronado, a young conquistador, led a group of Spaniards, Africans, and Indians on a search for the Seven Cities in what is now the southwestern United States. For two years Coronado looked for the cities, but he did not find them. The Seven Cities of Gold did not exist. Coronado wrote a report to the Spanish governor in which he said:

". . . I can assure you that he [Fray Marcos] has not told the truth in a single thing he said, but everything is the opposite . . . the Seven Cities are seven little villages."

Statue of Diego de Mazariegos, a conqueror of southern Mexico

Although Coronado found no cities of gold, he and his expedition were the first explorers to see the Grand Canyon. Coronado's expedition also gave Spain its claim to a large area of the Southwest of the United States.

READING CHECK How did Coronado's expedition prove valuable to Spain?

Exploring

ECONOMICS

The Value of Gold

Gold has been valued since early times for its beauty, its usefulness, and its *scarcity*, or limited supply. Gold will not rust, and it can easily be made into different shapes.

The Spanish made Aztec and Inca gold into coins called *pieces of eight*. These coins could be cut into eight pie-shaped wedges, called *bits*. The United States modeled the silver dollar after the Spanish coin. Eight bits equaled a dollar. Two bits equaled a quarter of a dollar.

Activity

Research the history of United States coins. Make a chart showing the coin, its value, and how it got its name.

FORCED LABOR

Life became very harsh for the Indians of New Spain. Spain began to settle its new colonies by granting **encomiendas** (en koh mee EN dahs) to new colonists. An encomienda was a large area of land that included Indian villages. The Native Americans on the land had to work for the new owner, and the colonist agreed to house and feed them. The system was like slavery, but there were differences. The colonists had to promise to teach the Native Americans new skills and to tell them about Christianity.

Indians worked from dawn to dusk. Sometimes they were harshly treated and could even be whipped. Often, they were hungry. When the Spanish found silver in the mountains of northern Mexico, Indians were forced to work in these mines. The silver helped to make Spain one of the richest and most powerful countries in Europe.

De las Casas

One defender of Indian rights was a Catholic priest named **Bartolomé de las Casas.** He came to the island of Hispaniola in 1513 to run an encomienda, and to be a **missionary**. A missionary is a person who teaches his or her religion to others who have different beliefs. De las Casas treated the Native Americans on his encomienda well. However, he saw the Indians on other encomiendas dying of disease and overwork.

De las Casas Protests

De las Casas gave up his encomienda in 1514. He devoted the rest of his life to ending the system of encomiendas. De las Casas became known as the "Protector of the Indians." Partly due to his efforts, Spain passed a law in 1542 requiring that Indians be paid for their work. Read the excerpt below to find out why he believed the Indians should rule themselves.

Primary Source:

excerpt from **History of the Indies**
— *completed by Bartolomé de las Casas in 1563*

*[Not] only have [the Indians] shown themselves to be very wise peoples and possessed of lively and **marked** understanding, **prudently** governing and providing for their nations . . . and making them prosper in justice, they have equaled many diverse nations of the world, past and present, that have been praised . . . and exceed the wisest of these.*

Why did De las Casas think that the Indians should rule themselves?

marked: obvious, very noticeable
prudently: wisely

Slavery in New Spain

Scholars disagree about the number of Indians in Mexico in 1519. Their estimates range from about 8 to 30 million. By 1568, the population had dropped to less than 3 million. Much of this tragedy was due to new diseases from Europe. However, many of the deaths were caused by overwork. The Spaniards found a cruel solution. They looked to Africa for new slaves.

African captives had been in New Spain since its earliest days. However, enslaved Africans were not brought to New Spain in large numbers until there were no longer enough Indians to work for the Spanish. By 1570, over 200,000 Africans had been taken to New Spain. Most were brought to the Caribbean islands of Cuba and Hispaniola to grow sugar cane.

Enslaved Africans also worked in the mines. At the ports of Veracruz and Acapulco in Mexico, they loaded silver and other goods onto the treasure ships bound for Spain.

Slave Revolts

Under Spanish law, the enslaved Africans could earn money in their spare time. They could use this money to buy their freedom, but some enslaved people were not willing to wait. In the 1560s and 1570s, Africans and Indians began to rebel against the Spanish. Others managed to escape.

In 1609, about 600 Spanish soldiers marched to the mountains around Veracruz on Mexico's gulf coast. They were to recapture an elderly enslaved African named Yanga and 80 of his followers. Thirty years later, the Africans had still not been captured. The Spanish government gave up. Yanga and his followers later built a town called San Lorenzo de los Negros.

READING CHECK How did Spanish colonists find workers for New Spain?

Paintings by Diego Rivera, a Mexican artist, show the harshness with which the Indians and poor Mexican workers were treated.

Growth of the Spanish Empire

During the 1500s, people in many parts of the world found their lives changing in many important ways. This was especially true in the Americas. Study the graphics on these pages. Then answer the questions below.

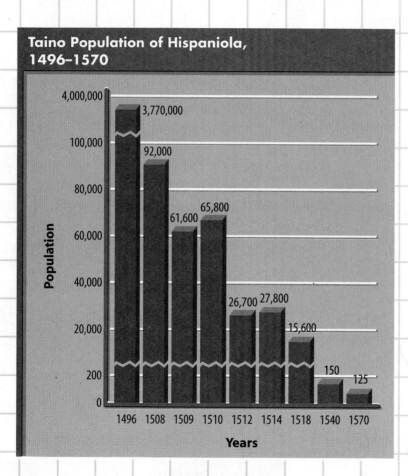

Taino Population of Hispaniola, 1496–1570

Population vs Years

- 1496: 3,770,000
- 1508: 92,000
- 1509: 61,600
- 1510: 65,800
- 1512: 26,700
- 1514: 27,800
- 1518: 15,600
- 1540: 150
- 1570: 125

FRANCISCO CORONADO
He explored much of the American Southwest in search of the rumored Cities of Gold.

ALVAR NUÑEZ CABEZA DE VACA
Shipwrecked in the Gulf of Mexico, he became the first Spaniard to explore Texas.

HERNANDO CORTÉS
He led an expedition from Cuba to Tenochtitlán that ended with the conquest of the Aztec.

QUESTIONS:

1. Which lands in the Western Hemisphere were the first claimed by Spain? Which lands were the last?

2. How did the population of Hispaniola change from 1540 to 1570?

3. What do you think was happening at this time to Indian populations in other Spanish colonies?

THE SPANISH EMPIRE, 1513–1575

NATIONAL GEOGRAPHIC

NORTH AMERICA

ATLANTIC OCEAN

30°N

NEW SPAIN

Gulf of Mexico

Tropic of Cancer

Mexico City

Cuba

Hispaniola

20°N

Jamaica

Puerto Rico

Central America

Caribbean Sea

Equator

Quito

Amazon River

SOUTH AMERICA

PACIFIC OCEAN

PERU

Cuzco

ANDES MOUNTAINS

Tropic of Capricorn

Asunción

Santiago

Valdivia

90°W

60°W

	Lands claimed by Spain in 1513
	Lands claimed by Spain in 1536
	Lands claimed by Spain in 1575

Routes of Exploration

- Ponce de León 1513
- Balboa 1513
- Cortés 1519–21
- Cabeza de Vaca 1529–36
- Pizarro 1531–33
- DeSoto 1539–42
- Coronado 1540–42

| 0 | 500 | 1,000 miles |
| 0 | 500 | 1,000 kilometers |

Mercator Projection

HERNANDO DE SOTO
He explored the American Southeast, and was the first European to see the Mississippi River.

JUAN PONCE DE LEÓN
Stories of a Fountain of Youth led him to explore Florida.

VASCO NÚÑEZ DE BALBOA
He traveled across Central America to become the first European to see the Pacific Ocean.

FRANCISCO PIZARRO
His forces climbed the Andes and conquered the Inca Empire of Peru.

To learn more, visit our Web site:
www.mhschool.com

143

Aztec ruins as well as Spanish colonial and modern buildings can be seen at the Square of Three Cultures in Mexico City.

COLONIAL CITIES

In addition to working on farms and ranches and in mines, Indians were also forced to build New Spain's capital, Mexico City. Hernando Cortés decided in 1522 that "it was well to rebuild" Tenochtitlán. The city had suffered during the Spanish attack and the destruction of its temples. However, the rebuilding would destroy almost all remains of the Aztec city.

Cortés wanted Mexico City to look like a Spanish city. Most cities in Spain had a cathedral, or huge church, and government buildings around a central plaza. Where the Great Temple of the Aztec gods had stood, Cortés began building a cathedral. He planned wide streets leading out of the square. By 1554, Mexico City had many features of a large European city.

Other Colonial Cities

The Spanish built other cities in their new colonies. Almost all of them had the same central square and other European features. In 1534, Pizarro laid out the city of Lima, Peru. Like Cortés, he laid out his city around a central plaza, called the Plaza de Armas. Like Cortés's Mexico City, the main square of Lima is dominated by a great cathedral in which the conquistador was buried. He also built a palace on this square and many of the other buildings of his city had beautiful, carved wooden balconies like those in the cities of southern Spain.

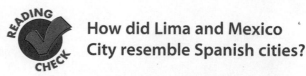

How did Lima and Mexico City resemble Spanish cities?

144

PUTTING IT TOGETHER

In the 1500s, the Spanish Empire expanded to include the Caribbean Islands, Mexico, Central America, Peru, and parts of the southwestern and southeastern United States.

The Spaniards used forced labor to build their empire. Bartolomé de las Casas worked to end the enslavement of Native Americans. Instead, thousands of African captives were brought to New Spain to work.

Spanish colonial cities, such as Mexico City and Lima, Peru, were built to look like cities in Spain.

Spanish conquistadors wore armor like this, which protected them from Indian arrows and stone weapons.

Review and Assess

1. Write one sentence for each vocabulary word.

   encomienda   missionary

2. Why were enslaved Africans brought to the Americas?

3. Describe life in a Spanish colony for: the owner of an encomienda, a Native American, an enslaved African.

4. What were the three cultures that mixed to form the **culture** of Spain's colonial empire?

5. What were some of the **effects** of the Spanish conquest of Central and South America?

Look at a map on page 143. Write directions for Pizarro to travel from the Caribbean to Peru.

Suppose that you wanted to help Bartolomé de las Casas. **Write** a petition to the king of Spain explaining why Indian enslavement must be ended.

VOCABULARY REVIEW

Number a sheet of paper from 1 to 5. Beside each number write the word or term from the list below that matches the description.

colony	encomienda
Columbian Exchange	missionary
conquistador	

1. A person who teaches his or her religion to others who have different beliefs

2. An area, often including Indian villages, that Spain gave to the colonists

3. The movement of people, plants, animals, technology, and diseases across the Atlantic after Christopher Columbus arrived in the Americas

4. A settlement ruled by another country

5. A Spanish soldier who conquered lands for Spain

CHAPTER COMPREHENSION

6. Who were the Taino?

7. How did Christopher Columbus get the money he needed for his journey?

8. What was a good effect of the Columbian Exchange for peoples of the Americas? What was a bad effect?

9. What mistake did Moctezuma make when the Spanish arrived in Mexico in 1519?

10. What lands made up New Spain?

11. Why did Bartolomé de las Casas come to New Spain? What did he do there?

12. Who was Yanga?

13. **Write** a journal entry from the perspective of an Aztec or Spanish soldier in the battle for Tenochtitlán.

SKILL REVIEW

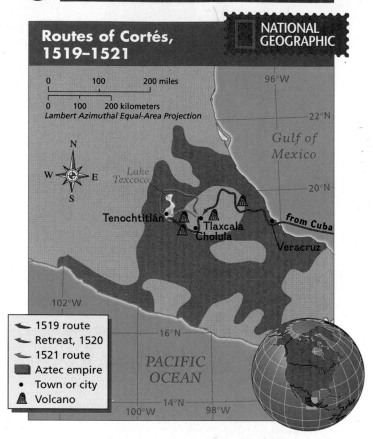

Routes of Cortés, 1519–1521

NATIONAL GEOGRAPHIC

14. **Geography Skill** In which general direction did Cortés travel on the 1519 route? How do you know?

15. **Geography Skill** Near which lake was Tenochtitlán located?

16. **Geography Skill** Which body of water did Cortés take as he traveled from Cuba to reach land?

17. **Geography Skill** To which route does the blue line refer?

18. **Geography Skill** Did Cortés reach Cholula before or after reaching Tenochtitlán?

USING A TIME LINE

1490	1500	1510	1520	1530	1540	1550	1560	1570	1580

1492
Columbus reaches the Americas

1502
Moctezuma II becomes ruler of the Aztec

1521
Tenochtitlán falls to Cortés

1533
Pizarro conquers the Inca

1546
The Spanish conquer the Maya

1570
New Spain has more than 200,000 enslaved Africans

19. Did the Spanish conquer the Maya before or after they conquered the Inca?

20. Choose the event on the time line that you think had the greatest effect on New Spain's economy. Explain your choice.

Writing **About Culture** Suppose you and your community are living on an island in the year 3000. Your people have had no contact with other people for nearly 1,000 years. One day, you see a fleet of ships on the horizon. What good things could happen in your own culture from meeting another culture?

Foldables

Use your Foldable to review what you have learned about Europeans coming to the Americas to explore and conquer. As you look at the front of your Foldable, mentally recall the events that occurred before, during, and after the Spanish began to colonize the Americas. Review your notes on the inside of your Foldable to check your responses. Record any questions that you have. Then discuss them with classmates or review the chapter to find answers.

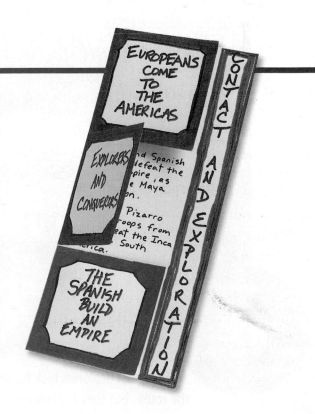

THE Big IDEAS ABOUT...

The Settlement of North America

The wealth of the Spanish colonies attracted other European countries. The French, the Dutch, and the English claimed lands in North America. They hoped to produce wealth from their colonies. The French colonies grew slowly because most French colonists were fur traders or missionaries. The English colonies grew more rapidly because English settlers wanted to establish new homes and new lives.

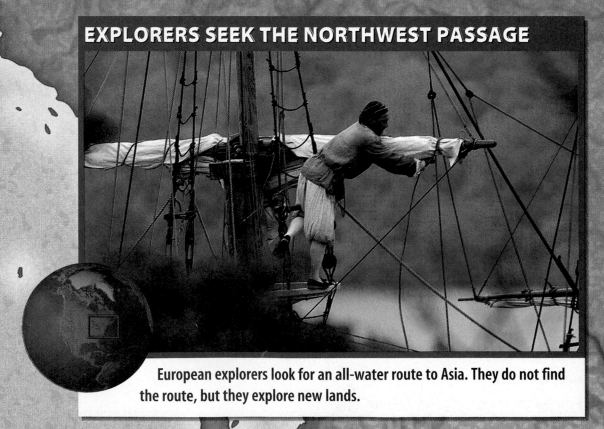

EXPLORERS SEEK THE NORTHWEST PASSAGE

European explorers look for an all-water route to Asia. They do not find the route, but they explore new lands.

THE FIRST ENGLISH COLONIES

The first English colony is on Roanoke Island. The colonists disappear, leaving only the word "Croatoan" carved on a tree. The first successful English colony starts in Jamestown, Virginia.

THE PILGRIMS TRAVEL TO A NEW LAND

The Pilgrims come to North America to find religious freedom. Their first winter is very hard, but neighboring Indians help them to survive.

Foldables

Make this Foldable study guide and use it to record what you learn about "The Settlement of North America."

1. Fold a sheet of 8 1/2" x 11" paper in half like a hamburger, but leave one side 1" longer than the other.

2. On the short side, make two cuts equal distances apart, forming three tabs.

3. Label the three tabs with the lesson titles. Label the 1" tab with the chapter title.

The Search for a Northwest Passage

Find Out!

Why did Europeans search for the Northwest Passage?

Lesson Outline

• A New Route to Asia
• Dutch and French Voyages
• New France's Slow Start

VOCABULARY

Northwest Passage
profit
portage

PEOPLE

John Cabot
Giovanni da Verrazano
Henry Hudson
Jacques Cartier
Samuel de Champlain
Jacques Marquette
Louis Jolliet

READING STRATEGY

Make a chart like this one. Write events from the lesson in the order in which they happened.

BUILD BACKGROUND

The voyages of Columbus thrilled Europe. The riches of Asia seemed to lie at the end of a westward voyage—if only the ships could sail around the lands of the Americas. Spanish explorers had found no sea route across Central or South America. So, other explorers began to look for a water route through North America to Asia.

The Mariners' Museum

European explorers of the 1400s used caravels for long ocean voyages.

1500   1550   1600   1650   1700

You Are Here
1497 – 1673

A NEW ROUTE TO ASIA

Explorers were looking for a **Northwest Passage**, a water route through North America to Asia. Only kings and queens could afford to pay for these expensive voyages. However, Dutch merchants soon found a new way to pay for them. A group of Dutch merchants formed the Dutch East India Company to trade with Asia. The merchants combined their money to pay for each expedition. In return they would receive shares of the **profit** if the expedition was a success. Profit is the amount of money that remains after the costs of a business have been paid.

John Cabot leaves England to search for the **Northwest Passage**.

Early Explorers

In 1497, an Italian named **John Cabot** was sent by the king of England to find the Northwest Passage. His tiny ship, *Matthew*, landed on an island off the coast of Canada. Cabot believed that he had reached Asia. Although he found no treasures of gold or silver, Cabot did discover the valuable fishing area now called the **Grand Banks**. Fish were so plentiful in this part of the Atlantic Ocean that they could be caught simply by dropping a basket into the sea.

Another Italian, **Giovanni da Verrazano** (joh VAHN ee dah vehr uh SAH noh) searched for the Northwest Passage for the king of France. In 1524, Verrazano sailed to North America and explored the Atlantic Coast from the Carolinas to Canada. He did not find the Northwest Passage either, but the entrance to New York Harbor is now named after him.

Why did Europeans send expeditions to North America?

151

DUTCH AND FRENCH VOYAGES

In 1609 the Dutch East India Company hired Henry Hudson, an English captain, to search for a Northwest Passage to Asia. All summer Hudson and his crew sailed his ship, the *Half Moon*, along the coast of North America. They traveled north from present-day South Carolina to Maine. In August, Hudson saw Chesapeake Bay and then Delaware Bay. Continuing north, the little ship reached what is today New York Harbor. Was this the sea route to Asia?

Hudson mapped the harbor. He also traded with Native Americans of the area, the Mannahata. "They go in deerskins loose, well dressed," wrote a crew member. "They have a great store [supply] of maize or Indian wheat, whereof they make good bread."

"Great River of the Mountains"

In September, Hudson sailed north up what is today called the Hudson River. Hudson called it "Great River of the Mountains," and he was sure it was the Northwest Passage. The river narrowed and grew shallow about 150 miles north, near what is today Albany, New York. It was the home of a large settlement of Delaware people. Hudson was amazed at the amount of surplus corn and beans the Delaware were preparing to store. There was "enough to load three ships," he wrote. However, he realized he had not found the Northwest Passage.

On a later voyage in 1611, Hudson's crew, who wanted to return home, took over his ship. Hudson, his son, and loyal members of his crew were set adrift near the Arctic Circle. They were never heard from again.

Hudson's *Half Moon*, as shown in this modern replica, was the most up-to-date exploration ship of its time.

France Looks for Wealth

While Spain was busy building colonies in Mexico and the Caribbean islands in the early 1500s, France was claiming land in North America. French explorers such as **Jacques Cartier** (ZHAHK kahr TYAY) first came to North America in search of the Northwest Passage. In 1534 the French reached what is now **Canada** and claimed the land along the **St. Lawrence River**. The French called it Canada, after the Huron word *kanata*, which means "village." This colony was later called **New France**.

The French did little with their new colonies for more than 60 years. France was involved in long and costly religious wars between Roman Catholics and Protestants in Europe. However, some French did begin fishing off the coast of New France. They also began a fur trade with the Native Americans. This fur trade would soon bring wealth to France.

The Huron and the French

Europeans wore furs to keep warm in their harsh winters. Fur-bearing animals filled the forests of New France. In 1608 a French geographer and explorer who was named **Samuel de Champlain** (duh sham PLAYN) founded a trading post called **Quebec** (kwih BEK) on the St. Lawrence River. It was the first permanent French settlement in North America.

Champlain made friends with the Huron, a group of Native Americans living near Quebec. He learned their language and respected their ways. Champlain

realized that France needed friendly Native American trading partners.

READING CHECK What did the French get from the colonies in North America?

Samuel de Champlain

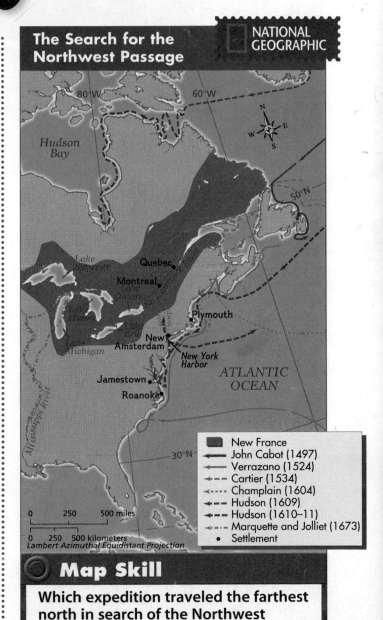

The Search for the Northwest Passage

NATIONAL GEOGRAPHIC

Hudson Bay

80°W   60°W

50°N

Lake Superior

Quebec

Montreal

Lake Ontario

Lake Huron

Lake Erie

Plymouth

Lake Michigan

New Amsterdam

New York Harbor

ATLANTIC OCEAN

Jamestown

Roanoke

Mississippi River

30°N

0   250   500 miles

0   250   500 kilometers
Lambert Azimuthal Equidistant Projection

New France
◀— John Cabot (1497)
◀— Verrazano (1524)
◀--- Cartier (1534)
◀···· Champlain (1604)
◀—— Hudson (1609)
◀— Hudson (1610–11)
◀-·-· Marquette and Jolliet (1673)
• Settlement

Map Skill

Which expedition traveled the farthest north in search of the Northwest Passage? The farthest south?

153

Marquette said that he saw the Mississippi for the first time, "with a joy I cannot express."

NEW FRANCE'S SLOW START

French missionaries also came to North America. These missionaries lived in Huron villages while they tried to convert Native Americans to the Roman Catholic religion.

In 1609 the Huron asked Champlain for help against their rivals, the Iroquois. In return, the Huron would help the French increase their fur-trading business. Champlain agreed, and the Huron remained French allies for many years. The Iroquois, however, remembered their defeat and waited for revenge.

Few Colonists

Not many French colonists came to New France during the 1600s. Colonists could not own land, and Canada's cold climate made farming difficult. Moreover, only Roman Catholics were allowed to settle in New France. As a result, there were fewer than 3,000 French fur traders and missionaries living in Canada in 1660.

Marquette and Jolliet

Champlain traveled in eastern Canada, but he never found a Northwest Passage. Other French explorers also tried to find it, including the priest **Jacques Marquette** (ZHAHK mahr KET). While working as a missionary in what is today Michigan, Marquette heard about a mighty river to the west. Could this river be the long sought Northwest Passage?

Marquette and a former fur trader, **Louis Jolliet** (LOO ee joh lee AY), set out together in 1673 to find this river—the Mississippi. When the explorers reached the Arkansas River, they saw that the Mississippi flowed south. Marquette and Jolliet realized it could not be a Northwest Passage because it did not flow west to the Pacific. They decided to turn back. On their return voyage, they used a **portage** from the Mississippi River to the Great Lakes. A portage is a land route from one body of water to another.

Why did Marquette and Jolliet explore the Mississippi River?

PUTTING IT TOGETHER

Europeans believed that there was a water route through North America to Asia. Many explorers looked for this Northwest Passage and failed, but many discoveries came from their voyages.

John Cabot found a rich Atlantic fishing region. Giovanni da Verrazano explored lower New York Harbor. Henry Hudson found both the river in New York and the bay in Canada that carry his name today.

To finance these expeditions, the Dutch invented a new kind of company. Many merchants combined their money to pay for an expedition and then divided the profits at the end of the voyage.

Review and Assess

1. Write one sentence for each vocabulary term.

   Northwest Passage   portage   profit

2. Why did Europeans want to find a Northwest Passage?

3. What did the Europeans learn from their search for a Northwest Passage?

4. Why were Europeans willing to pay for expensive voyages to find a Northwest Passage?

5. How did the Dutch **solve the problem** of paying for expensive voyages of discovery?

Look at the map on page 153. Make a chart. List the name of the explorer and the discoveries he made.

Start a journal on Henry Hudson's voyage up the Hudson River. **Write** a diary entry for each day until you discover that the river is not the Northwest Passage.

Decision Making

Every day, you make many **decisions**, or choices. You decided whether to go to a basketball game with some friends, or to watch one of your favorite programs on TV.

Whichever activity you choose, you will be engaging in **decision making**. Decision making is choosing from a number of **alternatives** to achieve your goal. An alternative is another way of doing something.

LEARN THE SKILL

1. **Identify a goal.**
   Carla wants to get a good score on the math exam next week, so she'll have to study every night. However, Carla is part of the gymnastic team, which meets two nights a week.

2. **Gather information.**
   Carla asks the gymnastics coach what the team will practice on the days before the test. Will something new be taught? Will her absence have a bad effect on the other members of the team? Carla also looks up her old math scores to see what would happen to her math grade if she doesn't get a good score this time. She asks her parents if they want her to make this decision.

3. **Identify the options.**
   Consider each alternative against values. If Carla studies math every night, she will get a good test score. If she goes to gymnastics, she will stay a strong part of the team.

4. **Predict the consequences of each option.**
   If Carla studies, she may not do as well in gymnastics. If she goes to gymnastics to practice, Carla will not get as good a mark on the math test.

5. **Make a decision that best helps you to reach your goal. Check your decision with your parents, teacher, or other adult.**
   Carla's goal is to do well on the math exam. She decides to study every night.

TRY THE SKILL

John Li is a fifth grader at Benton Elementary School. On Wednesday, he must decide whom to vote for in a student election. Two candidates are running for president. John wants a president who will work well with students and teachers. He also wants a president who will help students take part in his community. John will use what he knows about each candidate's leadership ability and character.

Look at the posters. Then answer the questions.

1. What is John's goal?

2. What information can help John make a decision?

3. What are the options?

4. What are the consequences?

5. What do you think is the best choice for John and why? Talk with your parents, teacher, or other adult about your decision.

EXTEND THE SKILL

Understanding what's involved in making decisions can also help you understand history. People you read about in history all had to make decisions. The choices may have been different, but the process was the same. In the last lesson, you read about the explorers who tried to find a Northwest Passage to Asia. Look back in this lesson to answer these questions.

- What decision did Henry Hudson make after he arrived near Albany, New York?

- What consequences resulted from the decisions of John Cabot and Giovanni da Verrazano to try to find a Northwest Passage?

- How can understanding the decision-making process help you to better understand history?

Roanoke and Jamestown

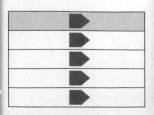
How did England found colonies in North America?

Lesson Outline
• The Lost Colony
• A Permanent Colony
• Jamestown Begins to Grow

BUILD BACKGROUND

One well-known unsolved mystery of American history is the disappearance of the first English colony in North America. More than 100 men, women, and children founded the colony on Roanoke Island, off the coast of North Carolina, in 1585. Three years later, no one was there. The only clue was the word CROATOAN (kroh uh TOH un) carved on a tree. No trace of the colony or the colonists has ever been found.

This reconstruction of Jamestown shows what it looked like almost 400 years ago.

THE LOST COLONY

By the late 1500s Spain's American colonies had made it the wealthiest country in Europe. To share in these riches, the English decided to challenge Spain. They claimed a region north of Florida, a Spanish area. They called their colony **Virginia** in honor of **Queen Elizabeth I**, known as the "Virgin Queen." She is shown to the right.

Sir Walter Raleigh was Queen Elizabeth's trusted adviser. He told her she should begin a colony in North America. Elizabeth granted Raleigh a **charter** to establish a colony in Virginia. A charter was a document permitting colonists to settle land claimed by their ruler.

Roanoke

Roanoke, an Algonkian word, comes from the Roanoac (ROH uh noh uk) people, who built their villages along the streams and rivers of the Atlantic Coast. In 1585 the first English people came to Roanoke Island. They stayed about one year and then returned to England.

In 1587 Raleigh again sent colonists to Roanoke. **John White** was the colony's leader. The colonists asked White to return to England for more food and tools. He did so. After his return, the war between England and Spain began.

Spain sent an **armada**, or large fleet of ships, to invade England. England's small navy defeated the powerful Spanish navy, but the battle delayed White's return.

In 1590, White finally returned to Roanoke, but the colony had vanished! The only clue was the word CROATOAN carved on the trunk of a tree. Croatoan was the name of an island and of a group of Native Americans. What the word meant, we do not know. No trace of the "lost colonists" was ever found.

READING CHECK

What is "the Lost Colony"?

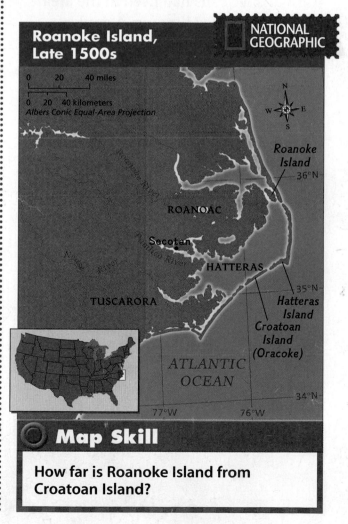

Roanoke Island, Late 1500s

NATIONAL GEOGRAPHIC

0   20   40 miles
0   20   40 kilometers
Albers Conic Equal-Area Projection

Roanoke Island
36°N
ROANOAC
Secotan
HATTERAS
35°N
TUSCARORA
Hatteras Island
Croatoan Island (Oracoke)
ATLANTIC OCEAN
34°N
77°W   76°W

Map Skill

How far is Roanoke Island from Croatoan Island?

A PERMANENT COLONY

In 1606 a group of London merchants asked King James I for a charter for a new company. The merchants sold shares of ownership, or **stock**, in the company. They planned to start a colony in Virginia. Any profits from the colony would be divided among those who bought stock.

The English planned to settle near **Chesapeake Bay**, in eastern Virginia. Native Americans who lived there called their homeland **Tsenacomacoh** (sen uh KAHM uh koh). At first the English and the Native Americans found a way to live together. That soon changed.

The Powhatan

For more than one thousand years Native Americans had lived in the area the English called Virginia. Algonkian-speaking peoples had united to form the Powhatan chiefdom. This was a group

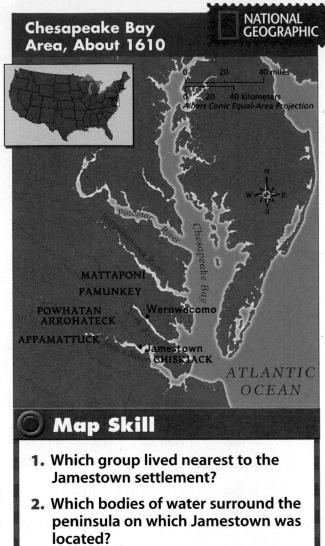

Chesapeake Bay Area, About 1610

NATIONAL GEOGRAPHIC

0   20   40 miles
0   20   40 kilometers
Albers Conic Equal-Area Projection

Potomac River
Rappahannock River
Chesapeake Bay
MATTAPONI
PAMUNKEY
POWHATAN
ARROHATECK
Werowocomo
York River
APPAMATTUCK
James River
Jamestown
CHISKIACK
ATLANTIC OCEAN

Map Skill

1. **Which group lived nearest to the Jamestown settlement?**

2. **Which bodies of water surround the peninsula on which Jamestown was located?**

of Native Americans, including the Powhatan, who united under one main chief. The chief was known as the Powhatan, but the English also gave this name to all the peoples the chief ruled.

Chief Powhatan was a respected Native American leader. Wahunsonacock (wah hun SAHN uh kahk), as his people called him, ruled hundreds of villages. They paid him tribute in deerskins, pearls, corn, and other valuables.

Ashmolean Museum, Oxford

This deerskin cloak was sent to England in 1608. It is called Powhatan's mantle (cloak).

By the early 1600s the Powhatan chiefdom included many Native Americans besides the Powhatan people. Each town and village had its own chief, or leader. Men or women could become a village chief, or even the Chief Powhatan.

The Jamestown Colony

In 1607 the Virginia Company sent its first colonists to Virginia. The settlers, all wealthy men or boys, landed near a large river. They called it the James River after England's **King James I**. They built houses, a church, and a fort. They named their settlement **Jamestown**.

Captain John Smith

Jamestown sat on a swampy peninsula on Chesapeake Bay. The water was salty and dangerous to drink. The swampy land held another danger—disease-carrying mosquitoes. That summer almost half of the colonists died.

John Smith Takes Charge

All of the colonists might have died without **Captain John Smith**. Smith had been sent to protect the settlers. He often told wild tales of his adventures. But he was the strong leader that Jamestown needed.

The colonists spent their time looking for gold instead of planting crops. Smith grew disgusted. So he announced, "He that will not work shall not eat."

Smith forced colonists to build houses and plant crops. Most Jamestown settlers had never worked before. They were not used to such tasks. His orders made him unpopular, but Smith kept the colonists alive.

Trading with the Powhatan

Often the colonists and the Powhatan people fought one another. Yet, the chief often sent them food.

In 1609 Smith had to return to England. The colony again faced hard times. One colonist called the winter of 1609–1610 the starving time. The colony barely survived.

A New Crop

Tobacco is a plant native to the Americas. In 1614 **John Rolfe** harvested his first tobacco crop. People were already smoking tobacco in England. As demand grew, tobacco became a **cash crop**, or a crop that is sold for money.

King James I called tobacco a "stinking weed." But the Virginia Company gave colonists land to grow it. The landowners hoped to become wealthy from tobacco.

What problems faced the new colony at Jamestown?

This portrait of Pocahontas, or Rebecca Rolfe, was painted while she was in England.

JAMESTOWN BEGINS TO GROW

The tobacco farms made settlers rich. They also required many workers. Many people could not afford to pay for their trip. So, the Virginia Company paid for them. These newcomers were **indentured** (ihn DEN churd) **servants**. These servants bound themselves to serve someone for a certain period of time, usually five to seven years, in exchange for something, in this case, land and freedom. In the end, thousands of people came to Virginia as indentured servants.

In 1619 a Dutch ship anchored off Jamestown. Its captain needed supplies. He sent about 20 captive Africans ashore as payment for the supplies. These first Africans in Jamestown were indentured servants. After working for some years, they became farmers and planters. For a few decades, the colony included both free and indentured Africans.

An African named Anthony Johnson arrived in Jamestown in about 1621 and worked there as an indentured servant. After working off his debt, he became a landowner. By 1651 he had more than 250 acres of land on the Pungoteague (PUN goh teeg) River. This area soon became a successful African American community.

By 1661, however, the life of most Africans in Virginia began to change. Great numbers were enslaved and forced to work on large farms.

The Colony Changes

Two other events helped Virginia to grow. As you have read, the first Jamestown colonists were men. In 1619 the Virginia Company sent women to the colony. Men paid for the voyage of their future wives. Jamestown was becoming a place for families to live.

Also in 1619 the **House of Burgesses** met for the first time. The House of Burgesses made laws for the colony. It represented only white men who owned land. It was one of the first steps colonists took toward governing themselves.

The Powhatan and the Colonists Clash

John Rolfe married **Pocahontas**, the daughter of Powhatan, in 1614. She had become a Christian and she took the name Rebecca. The marriage helped keep peace between the English and the Powhatan people for about eight years. In 1617 the Rolfes sailed to England. Sadly, before she could return to Virginia, Pocahontas became ill and died.

Virginia's growth brought problems. Planters were clearing new land for tobacco. They were taking more and more of the Powhatan chiefdom's hunting grounds.

Chief Powhatan's brother, Openchancanough (oh pun CHAN kun awf), became the new Powhatan in 1618. He wanted the English to leave Virginia. In 1622, the forces of the Powhatan chiefdom attacked. They killed about 350 colonists. This was one of the last major battles between Native Americans and the English in Virginia.

A Change of Government

King James I did not like the idea of the colonists governing themselves. In 1624 the king took control of Virginia from the Virginia Company. He named a governor to rule the colony. Later colonists battled with the king's governors. The colonists did not like outside control. They especially resented laws made in far-off England.

What changes took place in the Jamestown colony in 1619?

PUTTING IT TOGETHER

The Jamestown colony in Virginia was founded in 1607. The first permanent English colony in North America, it helped set a pattern for later colonists to follow. Each colony was helped briefly by Native Americans. Then the colonists began taking more and more land for settlement. Conflict between the Native Americans and the colonists soon followed. The colonists also wanted to have more self-government as their colonies grew.

Review and Assess

1. Write one sentence defining each of these vocabulary words or terms.

   cash crop   **indentured servant**
   charter   **stock**
   House of Burgesses

2. Describe Jamestown. What type of settlement was it?

3. Why did the English decide to found colonies in North America?

4. How did tobacco change the **economy** of the Jamestown colony?

5. What was the **cause** of conflict between the English and the Powhatan chiefdom?

Look at the map on page 160. Write a paragraph explaining why Jamestown seems like a good place for a colony.

· ·

Write a story. Tell what might have happened to the settlers of the "Lost Colony." Use details from the lesson to make your story accurate.

The Plymouth Colony

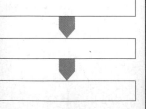

How did the Native Americans help the English at Plymouth?

Lesson Outline
• The Pilgrim Voyage
• A Difficult Winter
• Thanksgiving

VOCABULARY

Mayflower
  Compact
sachem

PEOPLE
Massasoit
Squanto
Samoset
William Bradford
Miles Standish

READING STRATEGY

Make a chart like this one. Write the main events of the lesson in the order in which they happened.

BUILD BACKGROUND

The small English ship *Mayflower* landed at what is now Plymouth, Massachusetts, in December 1620. The one hundred passengers were tired and cold. They faced an uncertain future in that first difficult winter. The struggling colony was saved by the kindness of the nearby Native American people.

Pilgrims at Plymouth

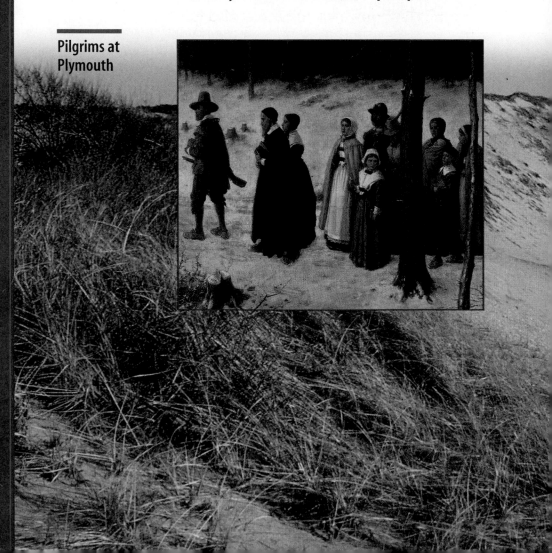

THE PILGRIM VOYAGE

In 1527, King Henry VIII of England left the Roman Catholic Church. He set up the Church of England, and made himself the head of it. Some people thought the king had kept too many Roman Catholic ways and set up their own churches. The government punished many of them.

In the early 1600s one of these groups, called the Pilgrims, moved to the Netherlands. They wanted to worship in peace. However, parents worried that their English children would grow up to be Dutch. King James I allowed the Pilgrims to settle in Virginia. The London Company agreed to pay for the voyage. The Pilgrims would pay the company back in lumber and furs.

On Board the *Mayflower*

The Pilgrims sailed from Plymouth, England, in September 1620 on the *Mayflower*. On board were 100 people. They had barrels of bread and salted beef, pigs, chickens, and goats.

The tiny, crowded ship sailed for 66 days across the stormy Atlantic. Finally in November, a lookout spotted land. The *Mayflower* was far from Virginia. The Pilgrims came ashore on Cape Cod in what is now part of New England.

Why did the Pilgrims come to North America?

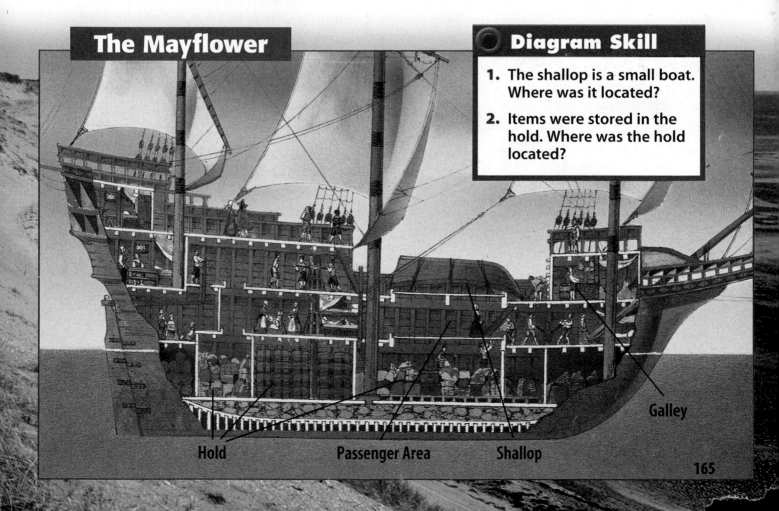

The Mayflower

Diagram Skill

1. The shallop is a small boat. Where was it located?

2. Items were stored in the hold. Where was the hold located?

Hold   Passenger Area   Shallop   Galley

A DIFFICULT WINTER

Before they left the *Mayflower*, the Pilgrims wrote a compact, or agreement. This compact was a form of government for the new colony. In the **Mayflower Compact**, the Pilgrims agreed to obey all the laws of the colony. Only men signed the compact. The Mayflower Compact was one of the first steps to self-government in North America.

Native American Neighbors

Native Americans were already living in the area where the Pilgrims landed. The Wampanoag (wahm puh NOH ahg) had long hunted, farmed, and fished along the coast.

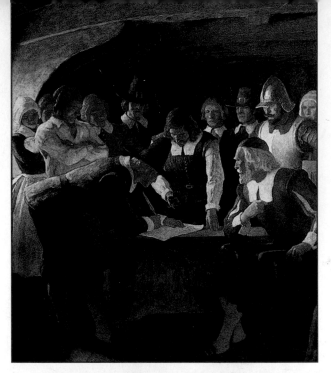

Before leaving the ship, male colonists signed the Mayflower Compact.

The Narragansett, the Pequot (PEE kwaht), and the Mohegan also lived in the area. They spoke forms of the Algonkian language. We use many of their words in English. *Moose, hickory, moccasin,* and *squash* were Algonkian words.

A **sachem** (SAY chum), or leader, headed each group of Native Americans. The sachem of the Wampanoag in the early 1600s was named **Massasoit** (MAS uh soyt). Massasoit knew strange ships were near the New England coast even before the Pilgrims landed.

Squanto was another Wampanoag. English sailors captured Squanto in 1615. Later he was enslaved in Spain. Squanto escaped to England and finally returned to New England in 1619.

A third Native American, a sachem called **Samoset**, had learned some English. These three Native Americans would save the Pilgrims' lives in their first years in New England.

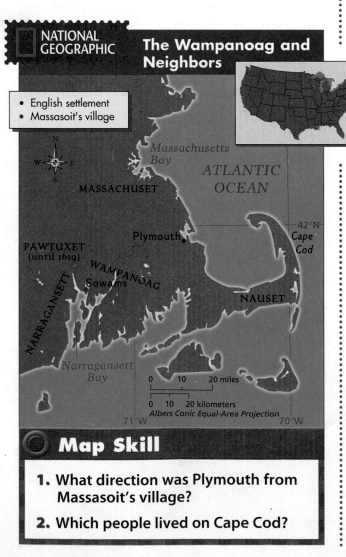

NATIONAL GEOGRAPHIC

The Wampanoag and Neighbors

- English settlement
- Massasoit's village

Massachusetts Bay

ATLANTIC OCEAN

MASSACHUSET

Plymouth

42°N

Cape Cod

PAWTUXET (until 1619)

WAMPANOAG

Sowams

NARRAGANSETT

NAUSET

Narragansett Bay

0   10   20 miles

0   10   20 kilometers
Albers Conic Equal-Area Projection

71°W   70°W

Map Skill

1. **What direction was Plymouth from Massasoit's village?**

2. **Which people lived on Cape Cod?**

The Plymouth Colony

The Pilgrims looked for a place to settle for over a month. They finally chose **Plymouth**. Captain John Smith had named Plymouth Harbor six years earlier.

How did the Pilgrims feel about beginning their life in Plymouth? Read what **William Bradford** wrote.

Primary Source:

excerpt from
Of Plymouth Plantation,
— *written by William Bradford in 1646*

It was winter, and they that know the winters of the country know them to be sharp subject to cruel and fierce storms, dangerous to travel to known places, much more to search an unknown coast . . . .

All things stand upon them with a weather-beaten face, . . . If they looked behind them, there was the mighty ocean which they had passed and was now as a main bar and gulf to separate them from all the **civil** *parts of the world . . . .*

What could now sustain them but the spirit of God and His grace?

civil: social order and organized government

How did William Bradford feel as he looked at the Plymouth colony?

That first New England winter was cold and harsh for the Pilgrims. Without the right kind of food, many died from disease. Everyone was hungry. By spring, only about half of the Pilgrims were still alive. The first governor died, and the Pilgrims elected William Bradford to be their new leader.

Help Arrives

When spring returned, the Pilgrims began to plant crops. One March morning brought a surprise. Samoset entered their settlement. "Welcome, Englishmen!" he greeted them.

Samoset told the surprised Pilgrims how he had learned their language. A few days later, he returned with Massasoit and Squanto. The two sachems worked with the Pilgrim leaders to make a lasting peace agreement.

The Pilgrims had settled on land that was once the home of the Pawtuxet, Squanto's people. Squanto decided to stay with the Pilgrims. He showed them how to plant corn, using fish to fertilize the soil. He also taught the newcomers how to trap rabbits, deer, and other wild animals. With Squanto's help, the Pilgrims began to eat better. Soon, the sickness the Pilgrims had experienced the past winter ended. Squanto was so helpful to the Pilgrims that Bradford called him "a special instrument sent of God for their good."

Why was the first winter in Plymouth so hard on the Pilgrims?

THANKSGIVING

The Pilgrims had built a colony by the autumn of 1621. Besides building homes and planting crops, they had made friends with the Wampanoag.

Governor Bradford noted that "they began now to gather in the small harvest they had, and to fit up their houses and dwellings against winter."

The idea of a harvest festival to give thanks was common to many Indian and European groups. The Pilgrims knew they had good reason to celebrate and to give thanks for their good fortune. They invited Massasoit and 90 of his followers to join them for a great feast. This feast has been called our country's first "thanksgiving."

The Pilgrims celebrated Thanksgiving with the Wampanoag.

A Happy Feast

The English and their Wampanoag guests feasted for three October days. The Indians brought five deer. The Pilgrims added other foods, including wild turkey, goose, and duck.

No one wrote about the foods at that feast, so we can only guess what was served. The Pilgrims had brought seeds from England for cabbage, carrots, turnips, and onions. Lobster, eels, oysters, and fish were plentiful in New England waters. There was also corn for bread and puddings. They may have eaten pumpkin, but not pumpkin pie. Desserts were probably fruits such as plums, gooseberries, and strawberries that had been picked and dried in the spring.

There were different dinner customs for the guests. At mealtime, the Wampanoag sat on the ground. The

Pilgrims probably sat on stools around tables made of wooden planks.

Under the command of **Miles Standish**, men paraded and fired off their guns. There were games, races, and wrestling contests. The Wampanoag showed their skills with bows and arrows. They also performed their own harvest dances. We remember this celebration every November when we have our own Thanksgiving holiday.

READING CHECK Why did the Pilgrims want to hold a Thanksgiving feast?

PUTTING IT TOGETHER

The Wampanoag and Pilgrims were friendly at first. But later the English took more and more land. Soon the New England Native Americans and the English colonists were bitter enemies. Several Wampanoag communities survive today. They preserve their culture through traditional ceremonies.

The Plymouth colony survived and grew. Later, other colonists would seek religious freedom in North America. Among them were the Puritans. Like the Pilgrims, the Puritans suffered for their beliefs in England. They, too, believed in self-government. They hoped they would find a safe home in New England as well.

This statue in Plymouth, Massachusetts, honors Massasoit, a great friend to the Pilgrims.

Review and Assess

1. Write one sentence for each of these vocabulary words.

   Mayflower Compact   sachem

2. Why is the Mayflower Compact an important document?

3. Describe how the Wampanoag helped the Pilgrims.

4. Why did the Pilgrims want to leave Europe?

5. What was the **cause** of Squanto speaking English? What was the **effect**?

Look at the map on page 166. Write directions for Massasoit to reach the colony at Plymouth.

You are a Pilgrim. **Write** a letter to a friend in England. Describe the events of the Thanksgiving feast.

VOCABULARY REVIEW

Number a sheet of paper from 1 to 5. Beside each number write the word or term from the list below that matches the description.

armada   profit

cash crop   sachem

portage

1. A land route from one body of water to another
2. A Native American leader
3. The amount of money remaining after the costs of a business have been paid
4. A large fleet of ships
5. A crop sold for money

CHAPTER COMPREHENSION

6. What was the significance of Samuel de Champlain's founding of Quebec?
7. What was the purpose of Henry Hudson's explorations?
8. Who was Sir Walter Raleigh?
9. Where was Roanoke Island? Why did people from England go there in 1585?
10. What was wrong with the location of Jamestown?
11. How did tobacco play an important role in the development of the Jamestown colony?
12. Why did the Pilgrims want to start a colony in North America?
13. Suppose that you are Pocahontas and are meeting English colonists for the first time. **Write** a diary entry of your thoughts about the meeting.

SKILL REVIEW

Colony	Year Founded	Leader
Roanoke	1585	John White
Jamestown	1607	John Smith
Plymouth	1620	William Bradford

14. **Chart Skill** John Smith was the leader of which colony? What year was this colony founded?
15. **Chart Skill** How many years passed between the founding of Roanoke and of Plymouth?
16. **Reading/Thinking Skill** What is a good first step when making a decision?
17. **Reading/Thinking Skill** Why did explorers Marquette and Jolliet decide to turn back when they reached the Arkansas River?
18. **Reading/Thinking Skill** What led to Queen Elizabeth I's decision to grant a charter to establish a colony in Virginia?

USING A TIME LINE

1580	1585	1590	1595	1600	1605	1610	1615	1620	1625

1585
The first English colony attempted at Roanoke Island

1590
John White returns to Roanoke

1607
Jamestown is founded

1609
Henry Hudson explores coast of North America

1620
The Pilgrims arrive on the *Mayflower*

1621
The Pilgrims and the Wampanoag hold a celebration of Thanksgiving

19. How many years passed from the founding of Jamestown to the Pilgrim celebration of Thanksgiving?

20. Did Henry Hudson explore the coast of North America before or after the first English colony was established in North America?

Activity

Writing **About History** Write about the ways in which the Native Americans and the European colonists cooperated when the first colonies were being established in North America. Then write about why there were clashes between the groups. Think about how these relationships are similar to those of groups of people around the world today and compare them.

Foldables

Use your Foldable flow chart to review what you have learned about the exploration and settling of North America. As you look at each of the four titles on the front of your Foldable, see if you can answer the questions—What? When? Where? Why? Review your notes under the tabs of your Foldable to check your responses. Record any questions that you have. Then discuss them with classmates, or review the chapter to find answers.

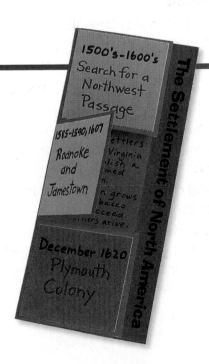

VOCABULARY REVIEW

Number a sheet of paper from 1 to 5. Beside each number write the word or term from the list below that best completes the sentence.

armada   **expedition**

cash crop   **missionary**

colony

1. Tobacco was an important ____ in the Southern colonies.

2. Spain sent an ____ to fight England's fast ships.

3. A ____ taught the Roman Catholic religion in New Spain.

4. The explorer's ____, or journey, took him to distant lands.

5. Sir Walter Raleigh established the first ____ in Virginia.

TECHNOLOGY

For resources to help you learn more about the people and places you studied in this unit visit **www.mhschool.com** and follow the links for Grade 5, Unit 2.

SKILL REVIEW

6. **Reading/Thinking Skill** Why is it important to set a goal when making decisions?

7. **Study Skill** What does a circle graph show you?

8. **Reading/Thinking Skill** How did King Ferdinand and Queen Isabella reach a decision about giving Christopher Columbus money for his expedition?

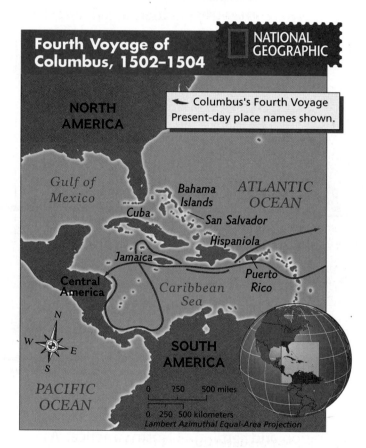

Fourth Voyage of Columbus, 1502–1504

NATIONAL GEOGRAPHIC

← Columbus's Fourth Voyage
Present-day place names shown.

NORTH AMERICA

Gulf of Mexico

Bahama Islands

ATLANTIC OCEAN

Cuba

San Salvador

Hispaniola

Jamaica

Puerto Rico

Central America

Caribbean Sea

SOUTH AMERICA

PACIFIC OCEAN

0   250   500 miles

0   250   500 kilometers
Lambert Azimuthal Equal-Area Projection

9. **Geography Skill** What clues tell you when a map is a historical map?

10. **Geography Skill** About how many miles of the coast of Central and South America did Columbus explore?

1   The Indies were the islands of Southeast Asia. They were a source of gold, jewels, and valuable spices. European traders traveled to the Indies and returned with cargoes that sold for high prices. This made the traders and their countries very rich.

2   Columbus believed the world was round. He decided to sail *west* to reach the Indies. Because it cost less to ship by water, Columbus and his backers would make more money when their cargo was sold.

3   For years, Columbus tried to raise money for an expedition across the Atlantic. In 1486, he traveled to Spain to present his plan to King Ferdinand and Queen Isabella. They discussed his plan with their advisers for six years and finally gave him the money for his expedition in 1492.

1   Why do you think King Ferdinand and Queen Isabella decided to give money to Columbus?

   A   Columbus was a good friend.
   B   They hoped to gain great riches.
   C   They believed Earth was flat.
   D   Columbus knew about spices.

2   The author's purpose in the passage is to—

   A   describe the best route to the Indies
   B   convince the reader that Spain's leaders were wise
   C   explain why Columbus sailed across the Atlantic Ocean
   D   show how to raise money

WRITING ACTIVITIES

Writing to Persuade Suppose you were a spokesperson for the Aztec when Cortés returned to Tenochtitlán. *Write* a speech that tries to persuade Cortés to make peace.

Writing to Inform Suppose you were a colonist in New Spain. *Write* an essay to a local newspaper describing the treatment of Indians and enslaved Africans there.

Writing to Express *Write* about the first meeting between the Wampanoag and the Pilgrims.

The Journal of
Jasper Jonathan Pierce
A Pilgrim Boy

by Ann Rinaldi
illustrated by Larry Reinhart

In this work of historical fiction Jasper Jonathan Pierce is a young servant who is keeping a diary of his life in early Plymouth. His entry for December 9th tells of the arrival of a real ship, the Fortune.

This day as my master and I were repairing some chinks in the house to ready it for winter, an Indian came running into the village. A ship had been spotted off Cape Cod. "A canoe with tall sails," he told us. All went running because at that moment the cannon on Fort Hill boomed. When we arrived there, Captain Standish ordered "every man, **yea**, boy, that can handle a gun to make ready." And we did so. Captain Standish said he feared it was a

A Dear America BOOK
MY NAME IS AMERICA
The Journal of
Jasper Jonathan Pierce

A Pilgrim Boy

Plymouth, 1620

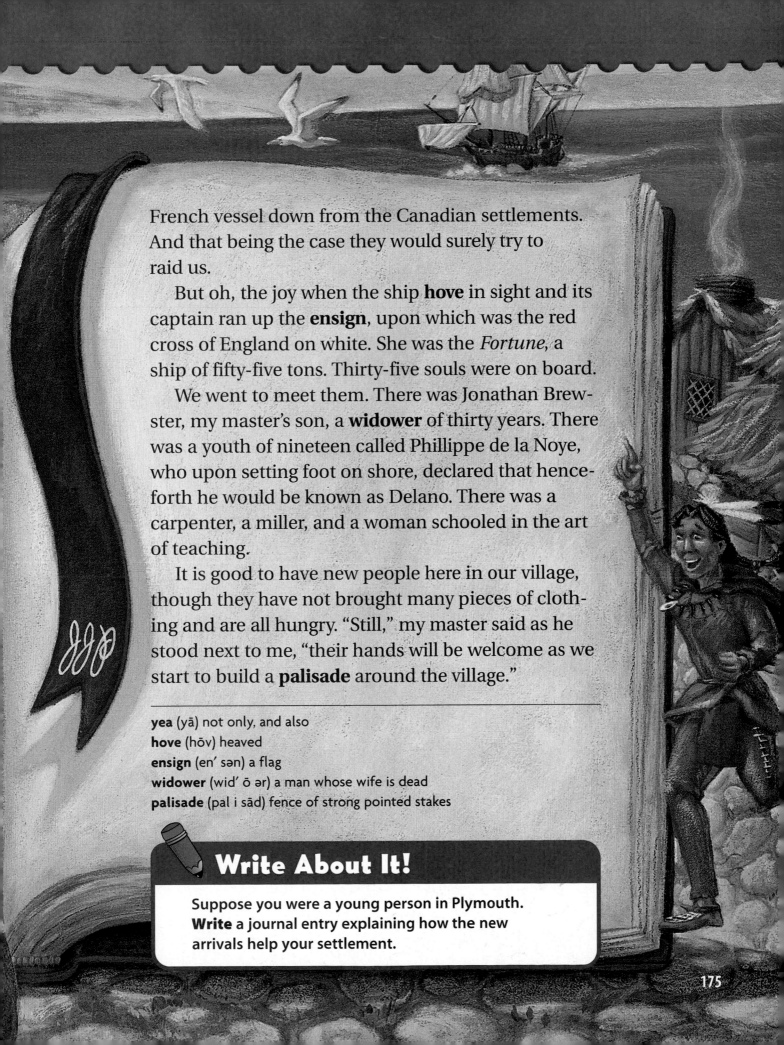

French vessel down from the Canadian settlements. And that being the case they would surely try to raid us.

But oh, the joy when the ship **hove** in sight and its captain ran up the **ensign**, upon which was the red cross of England on white. She was the *Fortune,* a ship of fifty-five tons. Thirty-five souls were on board.

We went to meet them. There was Jonathan Brewster, my master's son, a **widower** of thirty years. There was a youth of nineteen called Phillippe de la Noye, who upon setting foot on shore, declared that henceforth he would be known as Delano. There was a carpenter, a miller, and a woman schooled in the art of teaching.

It is good to have new people here in our village, though they have not brought many pieces of clothing and are all hungry. "Still," my master said as he stood next to me, "their hands will be welcome as we start to build a **palisade** around the village."

yea (yā) not only, and also
hove (hōv) heaved
ensign (en′ sən) a flag
widower (wid′ ō ər) a man whose wife is dead
palisade (pal i sād) fence of strong pointed stakes

Write About It!

Suppose you were a young person in Plymouth. **Write** a journal entry explaining how the new arrivals help your settlement.

Colonization and Conflict

TAKE A LOOK

Why do people leave their homelands?

In the 1770s, 90% of the settlers from England were farmers. Today, only 2% of the workers in the United States are farmers.

For more information about the original 13 colonies, visit our Web site at **www.mhschool.com**

177

THE Big IDEAS ABOUT...

Establishment of the 13 English Colonies

The Puritans' arrival at Massachusetts Bay in 1630 started the settlement that grew into the New England colonies. To the south the natural resources of the Middle and Southern colonies also attracted colonists. All of the colonies were started and paid for by private groups. Some colonists made friends with Native Americans. Others did not. Read on to find out about the first colonists.

THE PURITANS LAND IN NEW ENGLAND

In 1630 John Winthrop leads a group of Puritans to Massachusetts Bay. Religious differences among Puritans lead to the establishment of Rhode Island and Connecticut.

COOPERATION IN THE MIDDLE COLONIES

William Penn, founder of Pennsylvania, and the Lenape sign a Treaty of Friendship. Respect and cooperation among different ethnic groups lead to free trade and economic growth.

GEORGIA IS FOUNDED

James Oglethorpe receives a charter to found Georgia in 1733 and pays Tomochichi for the land on which Georgia's first settlement, Savannah, is started.

Foldables

Make this Foldable study guide and use it to record what you learn about the thirteen colonies.

1. Fold a sheet of paper like a hot dog.

2. On one side of the paper, make two cuts, equal distances apart to form three tabs.

3. Label the tabs with the lesson titles.

New England

What kind of life did the Puritans establish in New England?

Lesson Outline
- Massachusetts Bay
- Puritan Rebels
- Colonial Conflicts

VOCABULARY

covenant
tolerate

PEOPLE

King Charles I
John Winthrop
Roger Williams
Anne Hutchinson
Thomas Hooker
John Mason
Ferdinando
  Gorges
Metacomet

READING STRATEGY

Make a chart like the one below. Use it to compare and contrast the founding of the New England colonies. In each column, name the founder, place, and reason the colony was founded.

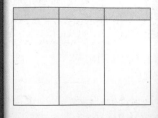

BUILD BACKGROUND

In June 1630 the ship *Arabella* led a fleet into Massachusetts Bay. Aboard the ships were large groups of Puritans. They were Protestants who wanted to reform the Church of England. They felt it followed too many practices of the Roman Catholic Church. After leaving England, the Puritans looked forward to having a home where they could practice their religion in peace.

Pilgrim cradle

MASSACHUSETTS BAY

In England, many Puritans had been jailed because of their religious beliefs. In 1629, a group of wealthy Puritans in England formed the Massachusetts Bay Company. **King Charles I** of England gave the company a charter to settle in North America. The charter was like a permit allowing the Puritans to settle areas claimed by England.

The Puritans brought more than 700 people to North America. They also came with different kinds of equipment, a herd of cows, and about 60 horses. The Puritans founded Massachusetts Bay Colony along the Charles River. The word *Massachusetts* means "at or near the great hill" in Algonkian. They named their first settlement **Boston**.

A City Upon a Hill

John Winthrop was chosen to be the governor of the colony. He wanted to create "a city upon a hill" that would be a model for how God wanted people to live. In the Puritan community, each "free man," as a male colonist was called, signed a **covenant**. A covenant is a special promise between a person and God. In his covenant, a Puritan promised that his family would live by certain rules of the Puritan Church.

Everyone worked hard to build the community. Men, women, and children worked in the fields growing crops and raising cattle, pigs, and sheep. They also helped each other.

In the center of each village was the village common. A common is a grassy area that is shared by everyone in the community. Near the common was the meeting house, which also served as the church. The Puritans also built schools. Free education was unheard of in Europe at the time, but Puritan schools were free.

READING CHECK **How were the Puritans better prepared for settlement than the Pilgrims?**

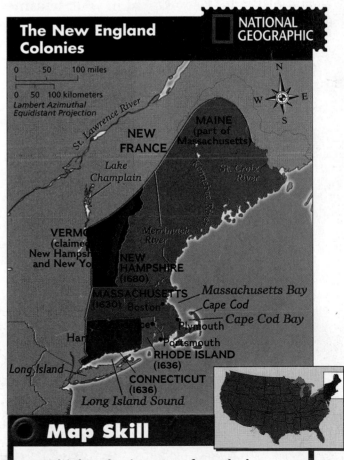

The New England Colonies

NATIONAL GEOGRAPHIC

0   50   100 miles
0   50   100 kilometers
Lambert Azimuthal Equidistant Projection

St. Lawrence River

NEW FRANCE

Lake Champlain

MAINE (part of Massachusetts)

St. Croix River

Kennebec River

VERMONT (claimed by New Hampshire and New York)

Merrimack River

NEW HAMPSHIRE (1680)

MASSACHUSETTS (1630) Boston

Massachusetts Bay
Cape Cod
Cape Cod Bay

Plymouth

Hartford

Portsmouth

RHODE ISLAND (1636)

Long Island

CONNECTICUT (1636)

Long Island Sound

Map Skill

1. Which colonies were founded in 1636?

2. Which land was claimed by both New Hampshire and New York?

PURITAN REBELS

The Puritans started new colonies in the region later named New England. Some of them were started as a result of religious disagreements.

One Puritan who disagreed with Puritan leaders was the minister Roger Williams. He was against colonists taking land that belonged to Native Americans. He also believed the colony should tolerate different religious beliefs. To tolerate means to allow people to have beliefs different from your own.

In 1636, Williams fled Massachusetts. The Narragansett allowed Williams to live on their land. Williams, in turn, paid them for the land. There he founded the settlement of Providence in what became Rhode Island. Rhode Island was the first colony to establish freedom of religion.

Anne Hutchinson was another Puritan who was forced to leave Massachusetts. In 1638 she and her supporters started the settlement of Portsmouth. Her biography is on page 183.

Thomas Hooker was a minister who believed that each church should be independent. In 1636 he and about 100 followers founded the colony of Connecticut.

New Hampshire and Maine

In 1629 present-day Maine and New Hampshire were divided between John Mason and Sir Ferdinando Gorges. Mason named his land New Hampshire. It became a separate colony in 1680. Maine became part of the Massachusetts colony in 1677.

READING CHECK Why did some Puritans rebel against their leaders?

A New England Village

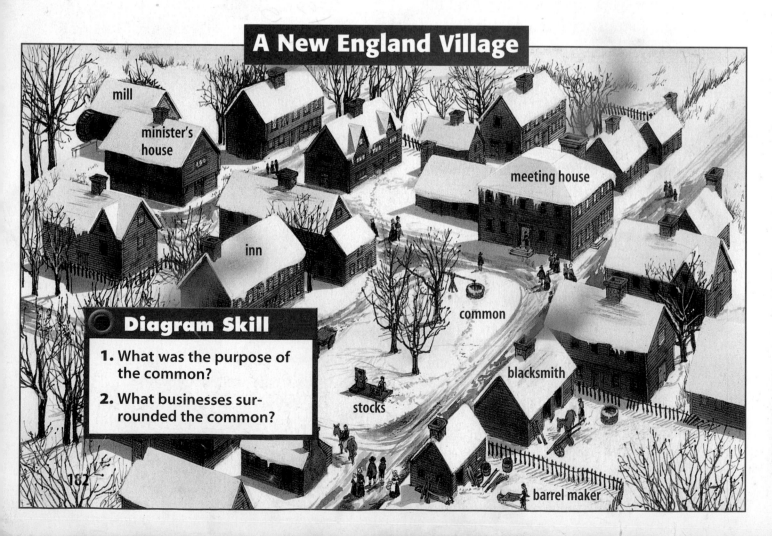

mill

minister's house

inn

meeting house

common

blacksmith

stocks

barrel maker

Diagram Skill

1. What was the purpose of the common?

2. What businesses surrounded the common?

BIOGRAPHY

Focus On: **Courage**

Anne Hutchinson was born in England and grew up to be an independent thinker. She was a deeply religious person who enjoyed the sermons of a Puritan minister, John Cotton. In 1634 Hutchinson and her family followed Cotton to North America.

In the Massachusetts Bay colony, Anne began to meet with other churchgoers in her home to discuss religion. She said to them, "He who has God's grace in his heart cannot go astray." Anne's ideas were different from Puritan beliefs.

In 1637 the Puritans put Hutchinson on trial. During her trial, Hutchinson had the courage to stand by her beliefs. She told the men that only God could be her judge. In the end, Puritan leaders banished her from the colony. She and her followers went to what is now Rhode Island and founded the settlement of Portsmouth. She moved to New York in 1642.

Link to Today Think about a leader of today who has courage. Research this leader, then write a paragraph comparing and contrasting the leader with Anne Hutchinson.

THE LIFE OF ANNE HUTCHINSON	1591 Anne Marbury born in Alford, England	1612 Anne marries William Hutchinson		1634 Anne arrives in Massachusetts Bay		1643 Anne and five of her 14 children are killed
	1590	**1605**	**1620**	**1635**	**1650**	
ELSEWHERE IN THE WORLD		1608 French settlers found Quebec in Canada	1626 Dutch found New Amsterdam (later renamed New York City)		1643 Louis XIV becomes king of France at age 4	1644 Manchus conquer China and rule until 1912

Roger Williams made peace with the Narragansett (right). However, they later followed Metacomet (below) who wanted to force the colonists out of New England.

COLONIAL CONFLICTS

At first the Native Americans helped the colonists. But as the colonies grew, Native Americans lost more land. This led to many disagreements between colonists and Indians. One such disagreement was between the Pequot (PEE kwaht) and colonists in Connecticut. After an English trader was killed, many settlers

demanded that the Pequot be punished. In 1637 colonists surrounded more than 600 Pequot and massacred them. A massacre is a brutal, bloody killing of many people. The colonists won what became known as the Pequot War. They then captured the surviving Pequot and sold them into slavery in the West Indies. After the Pequot War there was no fighting between the colonists and Native Americans for almost 40 years.

By 1675 the Wampanoag had lost so much land that their leader **Metacomet** (met uh KAHM uht), whom the English called King Philip, was preparing to fight the colonists. Even though years earlier Metacomet's father, Massasoit, had helped the Pilgrims, many Native Americans joined Metacomet, including the Narragansett.

King Philip's War, as the struggle was called, was fierce. The conflict killed thousands of people and completely destroyed 12 colonial towns. In 1676 Metacomet was captured and killed. His family was sold into slavery in the West

Indies. This defeat marked the end of strong Native American resistance in New England.

Why did Metacomet fight the colonists?

John Winthrop wanted to create a model for how people should live.

PUTTING IT TOGETHER

Governors such as John Winthrop helped make the New England colonies a success. However, life was not easy for the colonists in New England. Farming was difficult in the thin rocky soil. The colonists fought fierce wars with Native Americans. Still, New England grew rapidly. The area had many natural resources including wild game, berries, and wood. The colonists prospered by working hard and wasting little. They taught their children to read and write and value learning. Their religious beliefs in individual responsibility helped shape our democratic government. Today, some Puritan ideas continue to affect life in the United States. Part of our country's system of public education was modeled after Puritan schools.

Review and Assess

1. Write a sentence for each vocabulary word.

   tolerate   **covenant**

2. Describe the accomplishments of Roger Williams.

3. How did the geography of New England make farming difficult for colonists?

4. What does *Massachusetts* mean and from what language does it come?

5. **Compare** Massasoit's feelings toward the English with those of his son Metacomet. What might have **caused** any differences in how they felt?

Find the map of New England on page 181. What landform would protect ships from rough seas? Draw a picture of the landform with ships in safe waters.

• •

Write a letter to a friend from the point of view of a child in Massachusetts Bay. Describe what your new life is like.

Using Elevation Maps

Much of New England is rocky and mountainous. Colonists were often on the move and it would have helped them to be able to tell how hilly or mountainous an area was. It would have helped colonists to have maps they could use to study the geography of the area.

Today, people use different kinds of maps to find geographical information. The **elevation** of a place, for example, is shown on an elevation map. Elevation is the height of land above sea level.

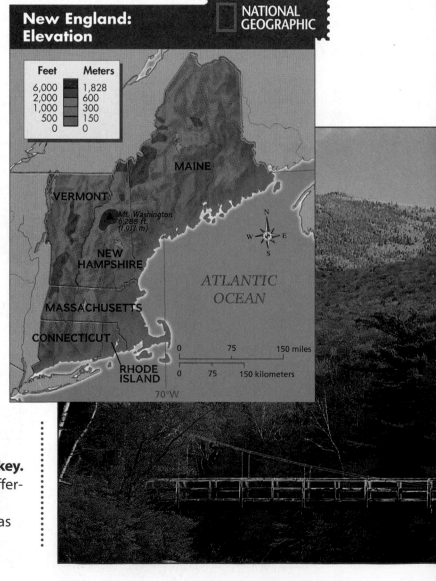

New England: Elevation

NATIONAL GEOGRAPHIC

Feet		Meters
6,000		1,828
2,000		600
1,000		300
500		150
0		0

MAINE

VERMONT

Mt. Washington
6,288 ft.
(1,917 m)

NEW HAMPSHIRE

MASSACHUSETTS

CONNECTICUT

RHODE ISLAND

ATLANTIC OCEAN

0   75   150 miles
0   75   150 kilometers

70°W

LEARN THE SKILL

Follow these steps to better understand how to use elevation maps like the one on this page.

1. **Identify the title of the map.**
   The title of this map is "New England: Elevation."

2. **Look for the elevation key.**
   Elevation is measured in feet or meters above sea level. Sea level is measured as 0 feet or meters around the world.

3. **Identify the ranges of elevation on the key.**
   Elevation maps use color to show the different ranges in elevation. The map on this page used the color red to show the areas with the highest elevation.

TRY THE SKILL

Now try reading the elevation map of New Hampshire. Use the map to answer the following questions. The map can help explain some things about the New England colonies.

1. What is the title of the map?

2. What is the range of elevation in New Hampshire?

3. Where is the lowest elevation found?

4. What did you learn about the elevation of New Hampshire by looking at the map?

5. What are some ways that elevation maps can be useful to you?

EXTEND THE SKILL

You can learn more about the elevation of an area by studying maps with **relief**. Relief is shading that shows the difference in height between land areas. Level, or flat land that stretches for long distances is shown with low or little relief. Land that rises, then drops off within short distances is shown with high, or more, shading. Look at the elevation map of New Hampshire. The heavy shading shows high elevation areas. The light shading shows low elevation.

● Which part of the state has the highest relief?

Now compare the elevation colors and the relief on the map of New Hampshire and of New England.

● **Compare** and **contrast** New Hampshire's elevation with Connecticut's elevation.

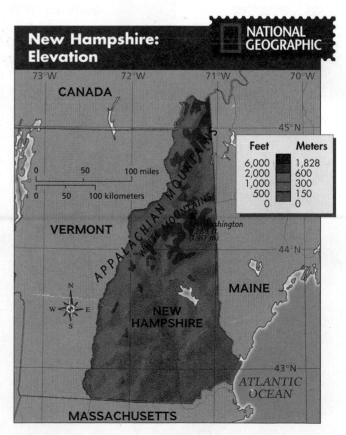

New Hampshire: Elevation

Middle Colonies

What helped the Middle Colonies prosper?

Lesson Outline
- Four New Colonies
- Penn and the Lenape

cooperation

PEOPLE
King Charles II
Peter Stuyvesant
William Penn

READING STRATEGY

Use the chart below to find the main idea and supporting details of this lesson.

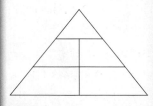

BUILD BACKGROUND

The Dutch began colonizing the area along the Hudson River soon after Henry Hudson explored it in 1609. The colony they called New Netherland grew rapidly. However, New Netherland did not remain a Dutch colony for long. King Charles II of England wanted to control the entire east coast of North America. In 1664, England sent four warships to New Netherland. Peter Stuyvesant, the governor of New Netherland, protested. Still, he was so unpopular that the English were able to take the port and the rest of New Netherland without firing a shot.

You Are Here
1664 – 1704

FOUR NEW COLONIES

The English renamed New Netherland New York in honor of King Charles' brother, the Duke of York. Although New York was now an English colony, many Dutch settlers remained.

In 1664 the Duke of York gave part of New York to two of his friends, Sir George Carteret and Lord John Berkeley. This land became the English colony of New Jersey.

Pennsylvania and Delaware

In 1681 King Charles II of England granted William Penn a charter to start a colony. Penn named it Pennsylvania, which means "Penn's Woods." In 1682 the Duke of York gave William Penn the land that would become Delaware. It was part of Pennsylvania until 1704, when it established its own lawmaking body. Delaware was the last to join what was known as the Middle Colonies.

Quakers

William Penn, a Quaker, wanted his colony to be a place where people could practice their religion freely. The Quakers are a religious group whose nickname comes from their belief that people should "quake

New York (left) was a thriving port in 1679. William Penn (right) is shown with the Pennsylvania charter.

before the power of the Lord." Many Quakers in England had been put in jail because of their religious beliefs.

The Quakers called themselves the Society of Friends. George Fox started The Society of Friends in 1652. Fox told his followers that to know God, they only had to listen to His voice in their heart. They did not need to rely on ministers or churches. They also believed people should "be plain in clothes, furniture, and food."

The Middle Colonies Prosper

Respect and cooperation between the Dutch and English and other immigrant groups helped trade and businesses in the Middle Colonies to prosper.

Cooperation is when two groups work together. Because of this, the population of the colonies grew rapidly and included many different ethnic groups. The Middle Colonies were fortunate to have many deep rivers and ports that they used for sending goods to markets. The rich soil helped farms thrive. Soon people began calling the Middle Colonies the "breadbasket of the colonies."

READING CHECK Why did New York and New Jersey become English colonies?

189

PENN AND THE LENAPE

In 1682 William Penn arrived in North America with about one hundred colonists. His settlement was called Philadelphia. In Greek, the word **Philadelphia** means "brotherly love."

Penn planned for Pennsylvania to be a place of peace where people would treat each other fairly. He believed that the Lenape (LEN nah pee), who were also known as the Delaware, should be included in his plan.

In a letter to the Lenape, Penn wrote that everyone could "live together as neighbors and friends." Unlike most European colonists, Penn paid the Native Americans for their land. Because of Penn's actions, relations between Native Americans and the colonists in Pennsylvania remained peaceful for many years.

READING CHECK Why did the population of the Middle Colonies grow rapidly?

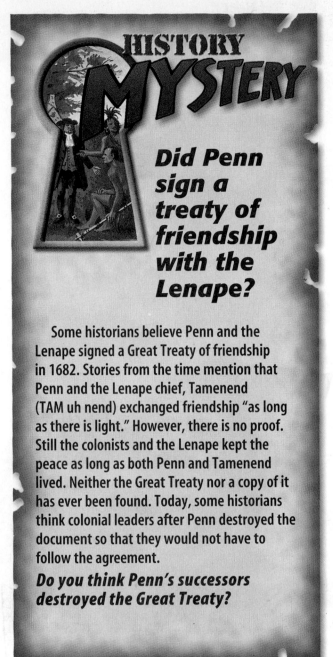

HISTORY MYSTERY

Did Penn sign a treaty of friendship with the Lenape?

Some historians believe Penn and the Lenape signed a Great Treaty of friendship in 1682. Stories from the time mention that Penn and the Lenape chief, Tamenend (TAM uh nend) exchanged friendship "as long as there is light." However, there is no proof. Still the colonists and the Lenape kept the peace as long as both Penn and Tamenend lived. Neither the Great Treaty nor a copy of it has ever been found. Today, some historians think colonial leaders after Penn destroyed the document so that they would not have to follow the agreement.

Do you think Penn's successors destroyed the Great Treaty?

This beautiful pie plate of the 1800s has a design popular with the Pennsylvania colonists. The sampler (right) was embroidered by a Pennsylvania girl.

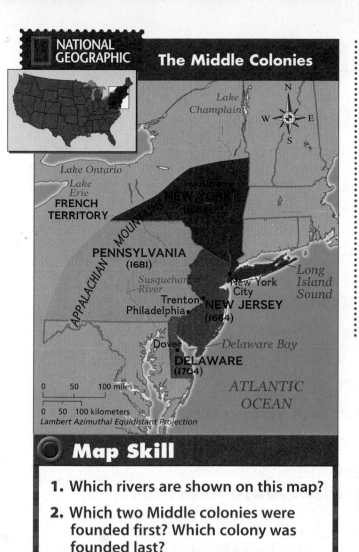

The Middle Colonies

FRENCH TERRITORY

NEW YORK (1664)

PENNSYLVANIA (1681)

Lake Champlain

Lake Ontario

Lake Erie

APPALACHIAN MOUNTAINS

Susquehanna River

Trenton

Philadelphia

New York City

Long Island Sound

NEW JERSEY (1664)

Dover

Delaware Bay

DELAWARE (1704)

ATLANTIC OCEAN

0   50   100 miles

0   50   100 kilometers

Lambert Azimuthal Equidistant Projection

Map Skill

1. Which rivers are shown on this map?

2. Which two Middle colonies were founded first? Which colony was founded last?

PUTTING IT TOGETHER

William Penn began Pennsylvania as a "holy experiment." He offered colonists religious freedom and self-government. He also treated Native Americans as equals and lived with them in peace. Penn's ideas brought many different immigrant groups to live in the Middle Colonies. Respect and cooperation between these groups helped trade and business prosper. The blending of different peoples and cultures that started in the Middle Colonies continues to the present day.

Review and Assess

1. Write a sentence for the vocabulary word.

cooperation

2. Describe the accomplishments of William Penn.

3. How did cooperation and respect between many different immigrant groups affect the economies of the Middle Colonies?

4. What **geographic** features attracted colonists to the Middle Colonies?

5. What were some of the beliefs held by Quakers? What **effect** did these beliefs have on William Penn's colony?

Look at the map of the Middle Colonies on page 191. Research how long it would have taken to travel between New York City and Philadelphia in the early 1700s.

Suppose that you are a Lenape. **Write** a short paragraph that describes what you think about the colonists and their customs.

Southern Colonies

Find Out!

How were the Southern Colonies founded?

Lesson Outline
- Maryland and Carolina
- Georgia

VOCABULARY

proprietor
debtor
confederacy
indigo

PEOPLE

King George II
James Oglethorpe
Tomochichi

READING STRATEGY

Use the chart below to list the causes and effects of the founding of the Southern Colonies.

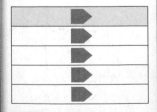

BUILD BACKGROUND

The success and growth of the Virginia colony led the English to allow new colonies to form to its south. In 1634 King Charles I gave Lord Baltimore, a Catholic, a charter to establish the colony of Maryland. The next colony was begun in 1663 when King Charles II gave eight men a charter to found Carolina. Carolina was later divided into North Carolina and South Carolina. In 1732 Georgia was founded. Georgia was the last of the group of settlements that became known as England's Southern Colonies.

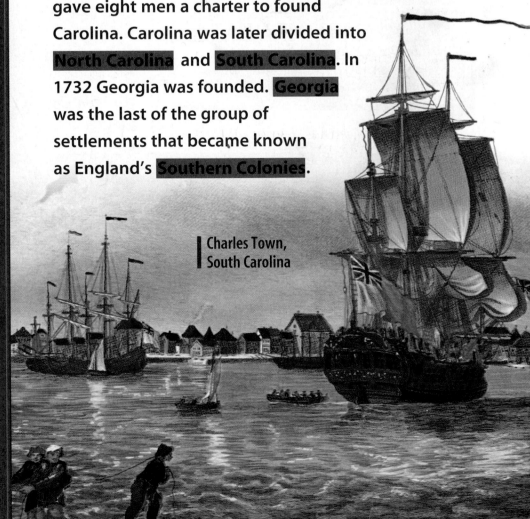

Charles Town, South Carolina

1600	1620	1640	1660	1680	1700	1720	1740	1760

**You Are Here
1634 – 1733**

MARYLAND AND CAROLINA

As you read, in 1634 King Charles I of England gave George Calvert, Lord Baltimore, a charter to start a new colony for Catholics. He called the colony Maryland, after Queen Henrietta Maria of England. Calvert died and his son Cecil, now Lord Baltimore, made plans to make the colony successful. He believed that allowing people of different religions to settle there would aid the colony's growth. In 1649 the colony passed the Maryland Toleration Act. This law said that no Christian should "be in any way troubled [for following] his or her religion."

Carolina

In 1663 King Charles II granted Carolina to eight proprietors. Proprietors were men who owned all the land of the colony. The proprietors divided the land into three counties. In one county, Albemarle, colonists believed the proprietors were more interested in making money than in governing wisely. The colonists, led by John Culpeper, took control of the government. The revolt became known as Culpeper's Rebellion. By 1691 governors were appointed to govern the entire colony with a deputy governor in the North Carolina region. In 1712 North Carolina became a separate colony.

By the early 1700s the Carolinas had become an important economic region.

King George II worried about protecting them. Spain had also claimed the Carolinas and had several settlements to the south of them. To the west, France had a colony.

How was Maryland founded?

George Calvert, Lord Baltimore

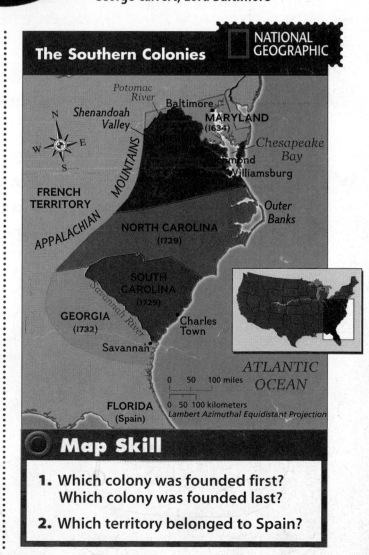

The Southern Colonies

NATIONAL GEOGRAPHIC

Potomac River
Shenandoah Valley
Baltimore
MARYLAND (1634)
VIRGINIA
Chesapeake Bay
Richmond
Williamsburg
FRENCH TERRITORY
APPALACHIAN MOUNTAINS
Outer Banks
NORTH CAROLINA (1729)
SOUTH CAROLINA (1729)
GEORGIA (1732)
Savannah River
Charles Town
Savannah
FLORIDA (Spain)
ATLANTIC OCEAN
0   50   100 miles
0   50   100 kilometers
Lambert Azimuthal Equidistant Projection

● Map Skill

1. **Which colony was founded first? Which colony was founded last?**

2. **Which territory belonged to Spain?**

GEORGIA

In 1732 King George decided his best plan for keeping the Carolinas under English control would be to start a new colony south of the Carolinas. England as well as France and Spain claimed the land south of the Carolinas. King George II wanted a colony there and a military man to found and defend it. He chose General James Oglethorpe for the job.

Oglethorpe wanted to help the debtors in England's prisons. A debtor is a person who owes money. Oglethorpe believed that "England will grow rich by sending her poor abroad." He received a charter to start a colony and named it Georgia after King George II.

The Creek and Oglethorpe

Oglethorpe wanted to make friends with the Native Americans of the area. They included the Muscogee (then called the Creek), Cherokee, Choctaw, and Chickasaw. The most powerful group among them was the Creek Confederacy. A confederacy is a group of countries, states, or people who join for a common purpose. Several independent Creek villages had formed the confederacy to protect their lands.

Tomochichi (toh mah CHEE chee) was the chief of a small Creek group called the Yamacraw. They lived along the Savannah River next to where Oglethorpe planned to settle. Oglethorpe and Chief Tomochichi met. Afterward the Yamacraw agreed to give Oglethorpe land for the settlement later named Savannah.

Even though the area's climate was not suited for it, Oglethorpe gave colonists land for growing grapes and raising silkworms. The following excerpt describes his plan for Georgia.

Primary Source:

excerpt from *Some Account of the Designs of the Trustees for Establishing the Colony of Georgia in America*
— *by James Oglethorpe, 1733*

*The Colony of Georgia lying about the same latitude with part of China, Persia, Palestine, and the **Madeiras**, it is highly probable that when...it shall be...rightly cultivated, England may be supplied...with raw Silk, Wine, Oil, Dyes, Drugs, and many other materials for manufactures, which she is obliged to purchase from Southern countries. As towns are established and grow populous along the rivers Savannah and Alatamaha, they will make such a barrier as will **render** the southern frontier of the British Colonies . . . safe from Indian and other enemies."*

Why did Oglethorpe want to create a barrier of towns?

Madeiras: island off the coast of Morocco
render: cause to be

The Growth of Georgia

Oglethorpe defended Georgia from Spanish attacks. However, his other plans failed. Few debtors came to Georgia. Also, the silkworms died. Colonists who were inland grew crops such as corn and tobacco. Those along the coast grew rice and **indigo** on large farms. Indigo is a plant that produces a blue dye.

Georgia's large farms needed more workers than were available in the colony. Oglethorpe had not allowed slavery. So Georgia colonists pretended to "rent" enslaved Africans from South Carolina. Slavery increased in Georgia. Of the 10,000 people living there in 1760, about 4,000 people were enslaved Africans.

How did Chief Tomochichi help the colonists?

PUTTING IT TOGETHER

The Southern Colonies were started for many reasons. Founders of Virginia and the Carolinas hoped to make money. Maryland was founded as a refuge for Catholics. Georgia began as a place where debtors could make a new start. In the end, most people came to the Southern Colonies to farm the rich, fertile land.

Virginia was the first of the 13 English colonies in 1607. In 1732 Georgia became the last. In less than 50 more years the 13 English colonies would become the United States of America.

Indigo

Review and Assess

1. Write three sentences using each of the vocabulary words.

   debtor
   indigo
   proprietor

2. What was the Maryland Toleration Act?

3. Why did King George II want a colony established south of the Carolinas?

4. What was the government of the Creek called? What was its main purpose?

5. **Predict** what would have happened to Georgia if the English had not settled it.

Identify the major waterways shown on the map on page 193. Make a chart showing how these waterways would be helpful to colonists.

 Suppose you were chosen to establish the colony of Georgia. **Write** a short paragraph describing what you would do.

VOCABULARY REVIEW

Number a sheet of paper from 1 to 5. Beside each number write the word from the list below that matches the description.

cooperation   indigo

covenant   proprietor

debtor

1. When two groups work together
2. A person who owes money
3. A plant that produces a blue dye
4. A person who owned all of the land in a colony
5. Special promise or agreement

CHAPTER COMPREHENSION

6. How did the Puritan colonists provide for education in a way that no European country had done before?
7. Why did Roger Williams leave the Massachusetts Bay Colony?
8. Who was Metacomet?
9. Why did the Quakers come to North America? In which colony did they settle?
10. What different groups of people lived in the Middle Colonies?
11. Who founded the colony of Maryland? What religious group settled there?
12. What role did Native Americans play in the founding of Georgia?
13. **Write** a dialogue in which you present the first meeting between General James Oglethorpe and Chief Tomochichi.

Do not do

SKILL REVIEW

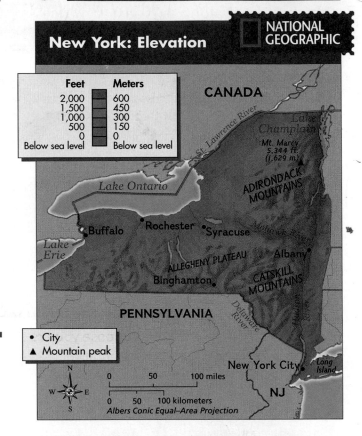

New York: Elevation

 NATIONAL GEOGRAPHIC

Feet	Meters
2,000	600
1,500	450
1,000	300
500	150
0	0
Below sea level	Below sea level

- City
- ▲ Mountain peak

14. **Geography Skill** What is elevation? What does an elevation map tell you?
15. **Geography Skill** What is the highest point in New York?
16. **Geography Skill** What is the elevation of the city of Albany?
17. **Geography Skill** Which New York city has a higher elevation—Buffalo or Rochester?
18. **Geography Skill** If you were the leader of a colony and were searching for a good spot to build a settlement, how might a map showing elevation help you?

USING A TIME LINE

1630	1634	1638	1662	1666	1670	1674	1678	1682	1732

1630
The Puritans found the Massachusetts Bay Colony

1634
Maryland is founded

1637
Anne Hutchinson founds Portsmouth, Rhode Island; Pequot War

1664
New Netherland becomes New York; New Jersey is founded

1675
King Philip's War

1682
William Penn founds Pennsylvania

1732
James Oglethorpe establishes Georgia

19. Which colony was founded last?

20. Which event on the time line had the greatest impact on the Native Americans in New England? Explain.

Writing **About Resources** Suppose you are a young child from one of the 13 English colonies. A friend of yours from England has written to you asking about life in North America. Explain to your friend how your community was able to use the land and resources that they found in order to build a colony.

Use your Foldable to review what you have learned about the original Thirteen Colonies. As you look at the front of your Foldable, make a mental picture of the East Coast of the United States and recall what you learned about the colonization of this area. How were the three regions similar politically, economically, and socially? How did they differ? Review your notes under the tabs to check your memory and responses. Record any questions that you have, and discuss them with classmates or review the chapter to find answers.

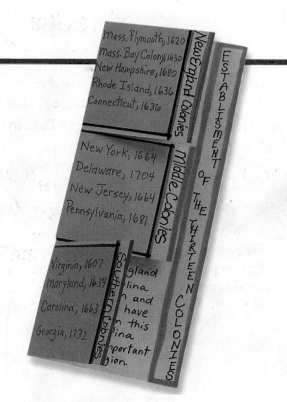

New England Colonies
Mass. Plymouth, 1620
Mass. Bay Colony, 1630
New Hampshire, 1680
Rhode Island, 1636
Connecticut, 1636

Middle Colonies
New York, 1664
Delaware, 1704
New Jersey, 1664
Pennsylvania, 1681

Southern Colonies
Virginia, 1607
Maryland, 1634
Carolina, 1663
Georgia, 1732

ESTABLISHMENT OF THE THIRTEEN COLONIES

Sentence sumery
main ideas

THE Big IDEAS ABOUT...

Life in the Colonies

In the 1700s more people came to the 13 colonies. Some were wealthy. Most were not. Some came as indentured servants. Others were enslaved captives who came against their will. Read on to find out about the people of the English colonies and how they lived.

EUROPEANS RUSH TO THE COLONIES

The promise of cheap land, greater opportunity to earn a living, and religious freedom led many in Europe to leave their homes and live in the English colonies.

DIFFERENT WAYS OF LIFE DEVELOP

Most colonists made their own clothes, grew their own food, and built their own homes.

SLAVERY IN THE COLONIES

African captives were brought to the colonies. Soon enslaved Africans became the main workers on the large farms in the Southern colonies.

THE COLONIAL ECONOMY

As the New England, Middle, and Southern Colonies grew wealthy, their overseas trade increased.

COLONIAL GOVERNMENTS

By 1760, every colony had some form of representative government. While England paid little attention to these governments, feelings of independence grew among the colonists.

Foldables

Make this Foldable study guide and use it to record what you learn about "Life in the English Colonies."

1. Fold a large sheet of paper like a hamburger.

2. Fold the hamburger in half like a hamburger, forming four rectangles.

3. Write the titles of the chapter on the front. Write the titles of the five lessons on the inside.

The Colonists and Why They Came

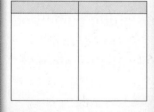

Who came to the colonies in the early 1700s and why?

Lesson Outline
• Colony Fever
• The Slave Trade

BUILD BACKGROUND

By the 1700s many people were coming to the colonies. "You would do well to advise all poor people to take courage and come to this country," said one colonist in a letter to his cousin in Scotland. During this time, wars and poor harvests had weakened many economies in Europe. Not all people came under their own free will. Some poor people and prisoners came to America as indentured servants. Africans came as captives.

Most people who came to the colonies worked hard to build new lives.

You Are Here
1700 –1750

COLONY FEVER

The 13 colonies usually offered a better way of life for the Europeans who chose to come. The promise of cheap land, greater opportunity to earn a living, and religious freedom led many in Europe to leave their homes.

Hard times caused so many people to leave that by 1760 England was said to have "colony fever." The English government began passing laws forbidding people to leave the country. However, many continued to leave seeking a better life in the colonies.

The Voyage West

The voyage to the colonies was dangerous and uncomfortable. It lasted four long months and even people who traveled in the best quarters suffered hardships. Most passengers were crowded between the two decks of the ship. Inside there was little air or light. The ceiling was only 4 $\frac{1}{2}$ feet in height. The food was no better. One passenger wrote that the "meat was old and tainted, the bread mouldy or wormy, the water smelt very bad." The crowded conditions caused illnesses to spread quickly from one person to another. Many people did not survive the trip.

Indentured Servants

To pay the price of their passage to the colonies, many Europeans became indentured servants. In 1700, four out of every five immigrants in Maryland and Virginia were indentured servants. Some

of them had hard lives with little food and harsh treatment. They often ran away from their employers to escape such treatment. One indentured servant wrote, "there [is] nothing to be gotten here but sickness and death. I find [myself in] great grief and misery."

Between 1630 and 1700 half of all the immigrants who came to the colonies were indentured servants. Some were debtors and convicts. Most were young men between the ages of 15 and 25 seeking a better life. The largest group of newcomers who worked as servants in the colonies came from England, Scotland, Wales, and Germany.

 Why did so many Europeans make the voyage to North America?

Posters in London and other cities advertised for colonists.

THE SLAVE TRADE

In the 1600s, Europeans began setting up trading posts in Africa. Rum, cloth, guns, and other goods were brought to them and traded for captives. The **slave trade**, or the business of buying and selling people for profit, destroyed families, villages, and even towns in much of West Africa. In East Africa, Arabs also traded in captives.

Raids for Captives

Families were taken from their homes in raids or taken prisoner in wars Africans fought to gain captives. Most of them were then forced to walk hundreds of miles to forts on the coast. There, captives were sold and placed on ships. One out of seven captives did not survive the ocean voyage. Those captives who did survive the voyage were usually taken to the West Indies, where they were sold to slave owners throughout the colonies. Many ended up as enslaved workers on the large farms of the Southern colonies.

The following excerpt from the **autobiography** of **Olaudah Equiano** (AHL uh dah ih kwee AH nah), describes the horrible conditions on the slave ships. An autobiography is the story of a person's life, written by that person.

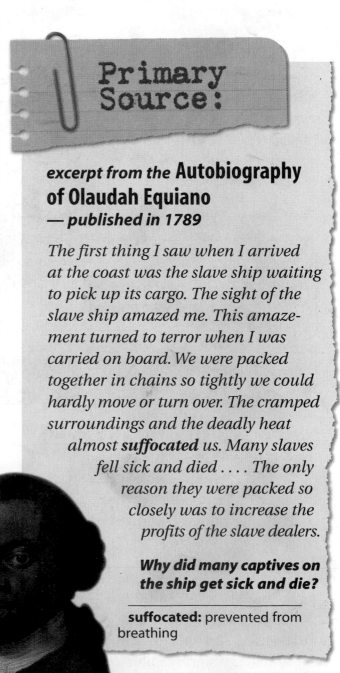

Primary Source:

excerpt from the **Autobiography of Olaudah Equiano** — *published in 1789*

*The first thing I saw when I arrived at the coast was the slave ship waiting to pick up its cargo. The sight of the slave ship amazed me. This amazement turned to terror when I was carried on board. We were packed together in chains so tightly we could hardly move or turn over. The cramped surroundings and the deadly heat almost **suffocated** us. Many slaves fell sick and died . . . . The only reason they were packed so closely was to increase the profits of the slave dealers.*

Why did many captives on the ship get sick and die?

---

suffocated: prevented from breathing

A Mystery

Equiano was a West African who was enslaved in 1756 when he was 11 years old. However, some historians think Equiano was born in South Carolina. It could be that Equiano heard the Story of the Middle Passage from others.

What effect did the slave trade have on West Africa?

This model of a slave ship (right) shows the conditions under which hundreds of slaves were crowded on deck (left).

PUTTING IT TOGETHER

People came to the British colonies for many reasons. Some came for religious freedom. Others came to earn a living. To pay for the price of their voyage, many poor people became indentured servants. Captives from Africa came against their will.

Most of the people who came to the colonies during the 1700s played an important role in the development of the English colonies. They built cities, towns, and farms. They started small businesses. This tradition of people coming to our country to seek a better life continues to this day.

Review and Assess

1. Write one sentence for each vocabulary term.

   autobiography   **slave trade**

2. What was traded for human beings held captive in Africa?

3. For what reasons did people make the voyage to North America?

4. What European ethnic groups came to North America in the 1700s?

5. **Compare** the voyage of indentured servants to that of African captives. What was similar? What was different?

Activities

Find Africa on the Atlas map on page R–6. Research from which areas of Africa people were kidnapped and sold into slavery.

· ·

Suppose you are a European who wants to become an indentured servant to pay for the voyage to the colonies. **Write** a letter explaining your reason to a friend or relative.

The Colonial Way of Life

Find Out!

What was life like for the different groups in the colonies?

Lesson Outline
- Life in the Colonies
- Colonial Cities
- The Frontier

VOCABULARY

frontier
apprentice
backcountry

PEOPLE
Benjamin Franklin

READING STRATEGY

Make a chart like the one below. Use it to compare and contrast the similarities and differences between two port cities in this lesson.

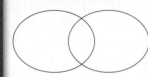

BUILD BACKGROUND

Before 1700 eight out of ten colonists were English or had English parents. However, during the 1700s, large numbers of Germans, Irish, Scotch-Irish, Scots, French, and captive Africans came to the colonies. They brought many different customs and religious beliefs to each of the 13 colonies. This diversity has lasted to the present day.

By 1750 one million people lived in the colonies. The population doubled to more than two million during the next 20 years. As the population increased the **frontier** began to move westward. A frontier is the far edge of a country, where people are just beginning to settle.

You Are Here
1700 – 1790

LIFE IN THE COLONIES

Outside the cities, life in the colonies was simple. Since agriculture was the main way of earning a living, most people lived and worked on a farm. "We are all tillers of the soil," wrote a member of the Pennsylvania legislature. In most of the colonies there were not enough people to do all the work. Most families were large, and every member of the family had to help out.

Some public schools were established. However, many parents taught their children at home. Colonists who wished to learn a skill or craft became **apprentices**. An apprentice is a person who works for a skilled laborer to learn a trade or art. Even doctors learned medicine by apprenticing.

Combining Work with Play

Most colonists made their own clothes, grew their own food, and built their own homes. They also helped their neighbors build barns and houses. Because there was so much work to do, colonists often combined work with play. There were plowing and corn husking competitions, quilting bees, and foot races. The sports of the day included horse racing, bowling, hunting, and fishing.

Many colonists also made their own furniture or did without. At the time, it was slow and expensive to carry anything across land. Only wealthy colonists could afford to buy goods on the ships from London that were loaded with manufactured goods such as clothing, books, and furniture. Many of the large farms in the Southern colonies had their own docks. Wealthy Virginians, for example, depended on England for almost everything. Most ships leaving Virginia docks were headed to London.

 READING CHECK **What was the main way people earned a living in the colonies?**

Colonists used the spinning wheel to make yarn (left). During a reenactment at Williamsburg a barrel maker teaches an apprentice his craft (above).

COLONIAL CITIES

Colonial settlements with good harbors grew rapidly. Warehouses, trading companies, and other small business in these areas prospered. Soon small port towns became cities.

Philadelphia

Philadelphia was the largest of these port cities. In 1723 it had only 10,000 people. By 1775 the population had grown to 35,000. Philadelphia was also a city of many ethnic and religious groups. Doctors, lawyers, business owners, silversmiths, and craftsworkers lived in Philadelphia.

Many religious groups from Europe found tolerance in the city. It was home to the colonies' few Roman Catholic churches. The Moravians (maw RAH vee unz), a Protestant religious group from what is now the Czech Republic, also established a church in Philadelphia.

Exploring TECHNOLOGY

The Lightning Rod

Ben Franklin's experiments with electricity led to his invention of the lightning rod. The rod works by attracting lightning and forcing its electricity into the ground. Lightning rods stop buildings from being hit by lightning. Before the lightning rod, homes, barns, and windmills caught fire as a result of being hit. In fact, Franklin's lightning rod was a good example of one of his famous sayings, "An ounce of prevention is worth a pound of cure."

How do lightning rods prevent fires?

Benjamin Franklin, p........ ......el-phia's best-known citizen, ...o help the city grow. He ....lped est.....sh the first fire departme..t, police force, public library and, in 1740, the city's first college. It later became the University of Pennsylvania. In the late 1700s he also helped start a school for African Americans. As you will read in his biography Benjamin Franklin was also a scientist.

Other Port Cities

By 1720 Boston was a thriving town of about 12,000. Although founded by the Puritans, Boston became a town with people of many political and religious beliefs. Boston was the first colonial city to publish a regular newspaper in 1704, the *Boston News-Letter*.

By 1750 the city of New York had a population of 13,000. Streets were busy all day with people and carriages on their way to shops or inns. Most shop owners worked and lived in their houses.

Charles Town in South Carolina was the busiest city of the Southern colonies. In 1775 Charles Town (renamed Charleston in 1783) was the fourth largest city in the colonies with a population of 12,000. The city had many businesses. It also had more wealthy people for its size than any other city in the colonies. Its wealth came from its exports of indigo and rice. Charles Town was also a center for the arts. In 1750 the first orchestra in the colonies was formed in Charles Town.

READING CHECK

Why did many different religious groups settle in Philadelphia?

BIOGRAPHY

Focus On: Responsibility

Benjamin Franklin was born in Boston in 1706. He was interested in books at an early age. By the time he was 12, Franklin began working as an apprentice in his brother's printing shop. Later he moved to Philadelphia, where he published the *Pennsylvania Gazette* and in 1732, *Poor Richard's Almanack*.

Franklin cared deeply for the American people and helped them in many ways. His kite-flying experiment in 1752 proved that lightning was electricity. He was responsible for helping colonists declare independence from England and plan their new government. Franklin also represented the United States in Europe. Just two months before his death, Franklin signed a request to Congress urging an end to slavery.

Link to Today Think about an American whose actions or ideas have improved people's lives. Research this person, then write a paragraph comparing and contrasting the person with Benjamin Franklin.

THE LIFE OF BEN FRANKLIN	1706 Born in Boston, Massachusetts, January 17	1729 Publishes the Pennsylvania Gazette	1752 Kite experiment; founds first American fire insurance company	1776 Signs the Declaration of Independence	1790 Franklin dies
1700	**1725**	**1750**	**1775**	**1800**	
LIFE AROUND THE WORLD	1700 A great change in technology begins in Europe	1730 More than 50,000 captive Africans begin being shipped each year to the Americas		1769 James Watt improves the steam engine	1789 The French rebel, storming Bastille fortress

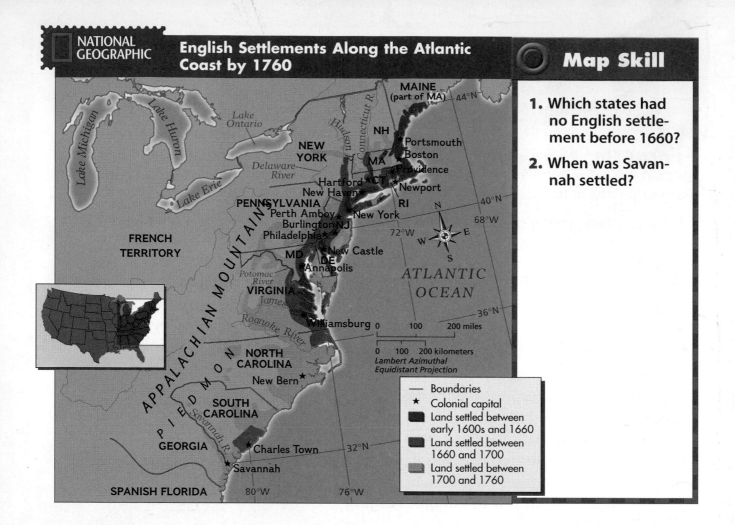

MAINE
(part of MA) 44°N

NH

NEW YORK

Portsmouth
Boston
Providence

MA

Hartford ★ CT
New Haven

Newport

RI

PENNSYLVANIA

Perth Amboy ★
Burlington NJ
Philadelphia ★

New York

40°N
68°W
72°W

FRENCH TERRITORY

MD

New Castle
DE
Annapolis

ATLANTIC OCEAN

Potomac River

VIRGINIA
James

Roanoke River

Williamsburg

36°N

0   100   200 miles

0   100   200 kilometers
Lambert Azimuthal
Equidistant Projection

NORTH CAROLINA

New Bern ★

SOUTH CAROLINA

GEORGIA

Charles Town   32°N

Savannah

SPANISH FLORIDA   80°W   76°W

Lake Michigan
Lake Huron
Lake Ontario
Lake Erie
Delaware River
Hudson
Connecticut R.
Savannah R.

APPALACHIAN MOUNTAINS

PIEDMONT

Boundaries
★ Colonial capital
▮ Land settled between early 1600s and 1660
▮ Land settled between 1660 and 1700
▮ Land settled between 1700 and 1760

1. Which states had no English settlement before 1660?

2. When was Savannah settled?

THE FRONTIER

The large number of Europeans who came to the colonies caused the land along the Atlantic coast to become crowded. You can see this on the map on this page. By the middle 1700s, the land had become too costly for many people to buy. Newcomers who wanted more space began moving west to the area they called the **backcountry**. The backcountry is the name colonists gave to the foothills, or Piedmont, between the Appalachian Mountains and the Atlantic Coastal Plain.

Most people who settled in the backcountry were poor. A Scottish immigrant named Alexander MacAllister told relatives that a person "might make it rich very fast" in the North Carolina back-country. It was a place where people could "breathe the air of liberty."

Life was hard for settlers of the backcountry. The rocky uneven land made farming difficult. There were few large waterways on which to transport goods. The Piedmont couldn't be reached by water, and colonists had to travel by land following trails made by the Native Americans.

Most people who settled the backcountry made houses from roughly cut logs. Many men and women carried rifles wherever they went and spent most of the day hunting. While life was hard, there were families who became wealthy. Two United States Presidents came from families that settled the backcountry.

Yamasee War

Many Native Americans were living in the backcountry. Trade between these Native Americans and colonists helped keep peace although problems still arose. Other colonists used unfair trading practices to capture and enslave Native Americans as payment for debt. In the Yamasee War of 1715, fighting broke out between the colonists of North Carolina and the Yamasee, Muscogee, and Choctaw. Native Americans almost defeated the colonists, but finally had to surrender. The Cherokee had joined the side of the colonists in exchange for trade goods, and fought against the Yamasee.

Why did people settle in the backcountry?

Many colonists built homes like this log cabin in West Virginia.

PUTTING IT TOGETHER

Benjamin Franklin once said, "No gains without pains." This was certainly true of colonists during the 1700s. Through hard work many colonists became successful. By the late 1700s, many colonists enjoyed living conditions equal to those of Europe.

Many colonists also became even more tolerant of different religions. In the 1730s a religious movement called the Great Awakening taught about the importance of religious experience. It changed some practices and stirred feelings of independence.

Review and Assess

1. Write one sentence for each vocabulary word.

   apprentice   backcountry   frontier

2. Which colonial city published the first regular newspaper?

3. Why did many different religious groups choose to live in Philadelphia?

4. How did the lightning rod improve people's lives?

5. What **caused** the price of land to increase along the coastal plain? What **effect** did it have?

Look at the map on page 208 of English settlements along the Atlantic coast by 1760. Use it to write an ad to attract Europeans to come to the colonies. Include information on the map in your ad.

Suppose you lived in the backcountry during the early 1700s. **Write** a journal entry describing your way of life.

Slavery in the Colonies

Find Out!

How did slavery grow in the colonies?

VOCABULARY

plantation
slave codes
overseer

PEOPLE

John Punch
John Woolman
Robert Carter III

READING STRATEGY

Use the sequence of events chart below to show how slavery grew in the colonies.

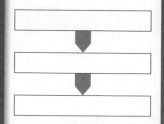

Lesson Outline

• From Indentured Servant to Slave
• Growth of Slavery
• Rebellions

BUILD BACKGROUND

Slavery has been practiced for thousands of years and in many parts of the world. Native Americans as well as people in Europe, Africa, and Asia forced people to work as slaves. Before the 1500s, however, enslaved people were mainly war prisoners. Slavery practiced by Europeans in the Americas was different because it was often based on skin color. Slavery became the main way to get workers for the large farms in the Southern colonies. These large farms were called **plantations** (plan TAY shunz).

FROM INDENTURED SERVANT TO SLAVE

In the early 1600s black and white indentured servants worked in the colonies in fields side by side. Those who broke indenture agreements were punished equally. They also had rights. Black and white servants could protest to the courts if they were mistreated.

When indentured servants finished their time of service, they were supposed to be paid "freedom dues." These dues were usually a piece of land. However, replacing these freed servants was costly. In time, servants received less money or smaller pieces of land. By the late 1600s freedom dues were so small that indentured servants began to protest. In Virginia, the burning of Jamestown in 1676 by freed indentured servants made slavery more attractive to plantation owners.

In 1640 John Punch was the only known enslaved African in the English colonies. He had been an indentured servant. However, he was enslaved when he tried to escape. In 1641 Massachusetts was the first colony to make slavery legal. Soon other colonies passed slave laws. In 1667 Virginia passed a law allowing the enslavement of Africans or Indians even if they were Christians. In 1682 Virginia passed another law that said indentured servants were to be white and slaves were to be black.

Slave Codes

It wasn't until Virginia passed the slave codes of 1705 that the captive

The first slave auction took place in 1655 in New York City.

Africans were caught in a system from which few escaped. Slave codes were rules to keep the enslaved workers under control. They took from the captives most of the rights that people in the colonies enjoyed. Under the slave codes, for example, enslaved people were not allowed to practice their own religion, learn to read, marry, or own property.

The slave codes said that slaveholders who killed an enslaved person would not be punished. The law also made it unlawful to help an escaped slave. These codes soon spread throughout the South.

Why were slave codes passed?

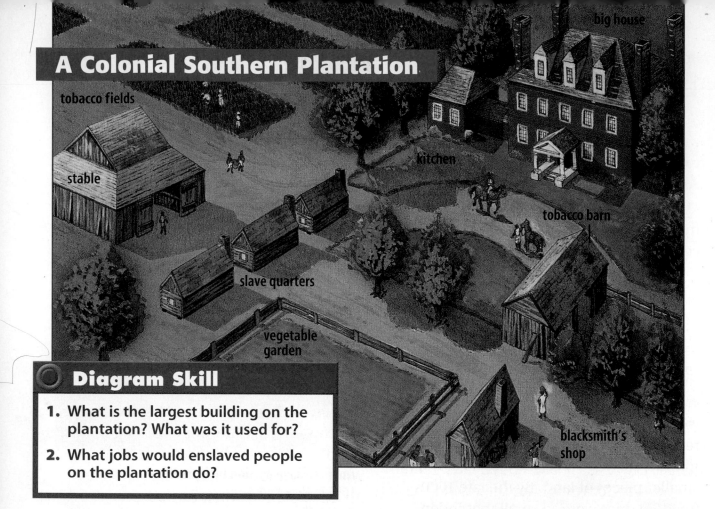

A Colonial Southern Plantation

tobacco fields

stable

slave quarters

vegetable garden

big house

kitchen

tobacco barn

blacksmith's shop

Diagram Skill

1. **What is the largest building on the plantation? What was it used for?**

2. **What jobs would enslaved people on the plantation do?**

GROWTH OF SLAVERY

Slavery grew in the English colonies during the 1600s. By 1671, for example, there were 2,000 enslaved people in Virginia.

Slavery in the North

By 1708 the number of enslaved people in the colonies reached 12,000. The population of enslaved people in the North, however, remained small. Most farms in New England and the Middle Colonies were not very large. Without a lot of land, farmers did not need many workers to run their farms.

Most Africans who were enslaved in the North became servants or skilled workers. They often worked side by side with their owner and learned their owner's trade.

Slavery in the South

Small farms and plantations made up the largest part of the economy in the Southern colonies. While enslaved men, women, and children worked on both types of farms, the greatest number of them worked on large plantations.

Most of the enslaved workers were brought from the present-day countries of Ghana and Nigeria in West Africa. They spoke different languages and had different cultures. The major ethnic groups from Nigeria were the Hausa (HOW sah) and Yoruba (YOH ru bah). The Ashanti (uh SHAHN tee) and the Fante (FAHN tee) came from Ghana.

To keep the captives from communicating with each other, slave traders and slave holders separated those who spoke the same language. Captain William

Smith wrote in 1744, "By having some of every sort on board, there will be no more likelihood of their succeeding in a plot." Enslaved people still found ways to communicate. Not only did they learn words from other languages, some African words, such as banana and boss, became part of the English language.

Plantations

Plantations were like small villages. The center of the plantation was called the "big house," where the planter and the planter's family lived. Many enslaved people worked in the big house as "house slaves." The captives lived in small, often poorly made cabins near the crop fields.

The Overseer

For enslaved people on a plantation, the day began early and ended late. There was no time for rest under the rule of the overseer. The overseer was the boss of the plantation. He told the enslaved Africans where to work and what to do. He also punished them.

The overseer was often an indentured servant or even an enslaved person who sometimes got a share of the plantation's profits. He, therefore, pushed the "field slaves" to work hard from sunrise to sundown. When there was a full moon, some even worked at night.

In the fields, Africans did the dirty, backbreaking work of planting and harvesting tobacco, rice, and indigo. They also took care of animals, cooked, cleaned, and repaired tools.

Many Africans were skilled workers who made furniture, tools, leather goods, or glass. Some of these skills the Africans had learned in their homeland. These skilled workers built many beautiful churches and other buildings. They also helped to build towns and cities.

Family

Family played a key role in helping Africans survive the brutality of slavery. Family members tried to keep in contact with one another, even when they were separated. On the one day that they did not have to work, usually Sunday, enslaved parents often visited their children, who had been sold away from them.

When families were together they talked, told stories, and sang songs. Story-telling has a long tradition in Africa. Most stories were used mainly to teach values and beliefs. While they worked, some of the slaves' songs were used to secretly pass on information. Sometimes it was to signal when and where to meet after work. At some secret meetings enslaved Africans planned their escape.

Even though it was against the rules of the slave codes, some enslaved Africans also secretly learned to read.

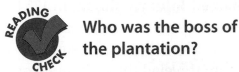

READING CHECK

Who was the boss of the plantation?

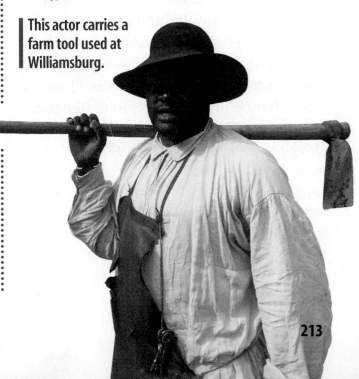

This actor carries a farm tool used at Williamsburg.

213

REBELLIONS

As the enslaved population continued to grow, so did the fear of a revolt. The New York Slave Codes were seen as the cause of the Revolt of 1712. Enslaved Africans and Native Americans set out to burn and destroy homes in New York City. Nine whites were killed in the revolt. After the revolt, no more than two or three enslaved people were allowed to meet. They also had to be off the streets by a certain time.

Some captives were willing to die for their freedom. In the Stono Rebellion of 1739, a captive named Cato led a rebellion in which 30 colonists of South Carolina were killed. What may have caused the rebellion was the Security Act, which had been passed a month earlier. The law made all white men carry firearms to church on Sunday. At the time, whites usually didn't carry weapons.

John Woolman

One of the few European colonists who spoke out against slavery in the 1700s was a Quaker named **John Woolman**. In 1754 he wrote, "the color of a man [means] nothing in matters of right and [equality]." Woolman traveled through much of the Southern colonies and gained first-hand knowledge about slavery.

Woolman also asked slave-holding Quakers to release their captives. Quakers and other colonists did begin to free their slaves. In 1791 the Virginia planter and slave owner **Robert Carter III** said that slavery was against "the true principles of religion and justice." He began freeing the 500 enslaved people on his plantation.

Haverford College

Why did some enslaved people and Quakers fight against slavery? How do you know?

PUTTING IT TOGETHER

Profits from slavery helped the Southern colonies become wealthy. Slave labor played a large part in building much of the South and some of the North. While the plantation system made the planters wealthy, it denied freedom to enslaved Africans. People like John Woolman and Robert Carter III had the courage to speak out against a system that denied people rights and equality. Soon many others would join them in the fight to end slavery.

Carter's Grove slave quarters (above) in Colonial Williamsburg. John Woolman (left) was a New Jersey Quaker who spoke out against slavery.

Review and Assess

1. Write one sentence for each vocabulary word.

   plantation   overseer   slave codes

2. What was the Security Act?

3. What was life like for enslaved people on Southern plantations?

4. How did Woolman and Carter fight for equal rights?

5. What **effect** did slave codes have on slavery in the colonies?

Make a chart listing at least three geographical reasons why the plantation system was more successful in the South than in the North.

Write a paragraph explaining why you think the Stono Rebellion happened.

The Colonial Economies

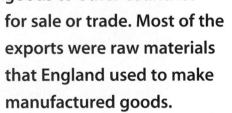

VOCABULARY

export
agriculture
industry
free enterprise
triangular trade
Middle Passage

PEOPLE

Eliza Lucas
   Pinckney

READING STRATEGY

Use the sequence of events chart below to show the steps in the triangular trade.

Lesson Outline

• Regional Economies
• Colonial Trade and Industry
• Triangular Trade

BUILD BACKGROUND

"[T]heir economies scarcely drew them together. If an American raised tobacco or rice he shipped it overseas; if he raised grain or milled flour or baked bread he often dealt in local markets." This is how historian Robert Middlekauff described the colonial economy. Some colonial products could only be **exported** to England. To export means to send goods to other countries for sale or trade. Most of the exports were raw materials that England used to make manufactured goods.

REGIONAL ECONOMIES

As more people arrived in the English colonies, the colonial economies grew. Each was influenced by the region's geography and natural resources. In New England, thick forests, good natural harbors, and an abundance of seafood were the basis of the fishing and shipbuilding industries. The rich soil of the Middle Colonies grew so much wheat and corn that people called their region the "breadbasket of the colonies." The climate of the Southern Colonies was ideal for growing tobacco, rice, and indigo.

New England Agriculture

In the early 1700s, agriculture, or the business of farming, was the way of life for most people. Even in the rocky soil of New England, most farmers produced enough crops to feed their families with extra crops to sell. The Middle Colonies not only exported surplus grain, but also exported pork and beef to Europe and the West Indies. Because the West Indies used most of their land to grow cash crops such as sugar, they imported meat and grain.

The Plantation Economy

Tobacco was the main export of Virginia and Maryland, but the price constantly rose and fell. This change in the price was due to *supply* and *demand*. *Supply* is the amount of goods available at a given price at any

time. *Demand* is how many consumers desire the goods that are in supply and will buy them. In the case of tobacco, when the demand for tobacco was high the price of tobacco rose and the supply increased. In 1681 the governor of Virginia said:

> "... there is no remedy; the market is overstocked ... there is tobacco enough now in London to last all England for five years."

Because of unstable tobacco prices, Maryland and Virginia farmers began growing corn and wheat for export.

Indigo plants were another cash crop of the Southern colonies. In 1739 Eliza Lucas Pinckney began experimenting with indigo, a plant used to make blue dye. She was successful in greatly increasing the production of indigo, making it the second largest cash crop in the South.

Much of the tobacco grown in Virginia (above) was shipped from the port of Jamestown (left).

READING CHECK

What influenced the regional economies of the colonies?

COLONIAL TRADE AND INDUSTRY

The English had established the colonies to provide raw materials for English manufactured goods. Much of the lumber produced by the colonies was exported to England. The colonists used the rest to make houses, furniture, barrels, and boats.

Shipbuilding

In time, the colonies started several **industries** to compete with the English. An industry is all the businesses that make one kind of product or provide one kind of service.

Shipbuilding was one of these industries. It became important in New England where demand for fishing boats and merchant ships was high. Shipbuilding worried the English who wanted the colonists to produce products only for them. By building their own ships the colonists took a step toward having a **free enterprise** economy. In a free enterprise system, people can start any business they want. They decide what to make, how much to produce, and what price to charge. By 1741 New England had more than 800 fishing boats.

The shipbuilding industry was also important in Virginia and the Carolinas where live oak trees provided excellent timber. Shipbuilding helped create other industries. Ships needed ropes, sails, and other equipment, too.

Iron Making

The iron-making industry came from the ore deposits found in most of the colonies. In almost every village blacksmiths hammered out iron nails, axes, kettles, and other metal products.

READING CHECK Why didn't the English want New England to have its own shipbuilding industry?

The Mariners' Museum

Shipbuilders in Philadelphia used the divider (left) to measure.

Rice and the Colonial Economy

During the early 1700s, each colonial region developed its own economy. Shipbuilding and fishing industries, rather than farming, developed in New England. In the South, however, most crops were grown for export. Study the graphics on this page, and then answer the questions below.

NATIONAL GEOGRAPHIC

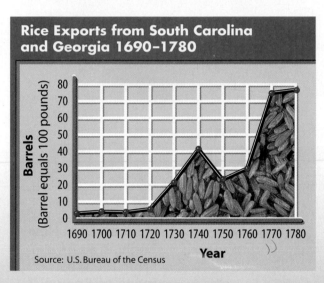

Rice Exports from South Carolina and Georgia 1690–1780

Barrels (Barrel equals 100 pounds)

Year

Source: U.S. Bureau of the Census

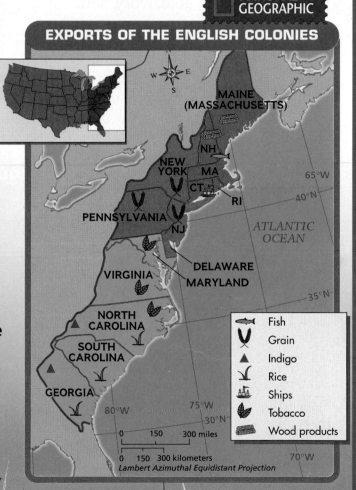

EXPORTS OF THE ENGLISH COLONIES

MAINE (MASSACHUSETTS)

NH

NEW YORK

MA

CT

RI

65°W

40°N

PENNSYLVANIA

NJ

ATLANTIC OCEAN

DELAWARE

MARYLAND

VIRGINIA

35°N

NORTH CAROLINA

SOUTH CAROLINA

GEORGIA

80°W

75°W

30°N

70°W

0   150   300 miles

0   150   300 kilometers
Lambert Azimuthal Equidistant Projection

Fish
Grain
Indigo
Rice
Ships
Tobacco
Wood products

QUESTIONS:

1 Look at the map. Which products were exported from the Southern colonies?

2 Look at the graph. During which period did rice exports show the greatest increase?

3 What conclusions can you draw about the importance of rice in the economy of the 13 colonies?

To learn more, visit our Website:
www.mhschool.com

TRIANGULAR TRADE

English laws controlled trade with its colonies. However, many merchants began to ignore English law. Instead of exporting all their goods to England, they traded with southern Europe, the West Indies, and Africa. The three-cornered route of these voyages became known as triangular trade. The triangle started at such ports as Boston and New York. Traders sailed from these ports to the coast of West Africa, where they traded rum and guns for gold, ivory, and captive Africans.

The second leg of the triangle began in Africa and went to the West Indies. This part of the voyage was called the Middle Passage because it was the mid-dle part of the triangular trade route. Thousands of Africans died on the voyage to the Americas, which lasted from six to eight weeks.

In the West Indies the sea captains traded Africans for molasses, a thick syrup made from sugar cane. Then they returned to New England, where the molasses was made into rum. This was the last leg of the triangular trade route. Port cities such as Boston grew very quickly on the money earned in the triangular trade.

What is triangular trade?

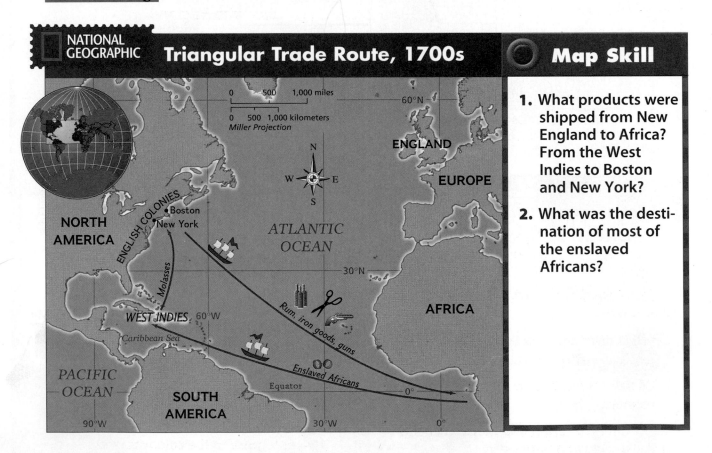

NATIONAL GEOGRAPHIC
Triangular Trade Route, 1700s

Map Skill

0   500   1,000 miles
0   500 1,000 kilometers
Miller Projection

60°N

ENGLAND

EUROPE

NORTH AMERICA

ENGLISH COLONIES

• Boston
• New York

ATLANTIC OCEAN

Molasses

30°N

WEST INDIES   60°W

Caribbean Sea

Rum, iron goods, guns

AFRICA

PACIFIC OCEAN

Enslaved Africans

Equator   0°

90°W

SOUTH AMERICA

30°W   0°

1. **What products were shipped from New England to Africa? From the West Indies to Boston and New York?**

2. **What was the destination of most of the enslaved Africans?**

Colonial Businesses

Colonists could not afford to import all the goods and services they needed from England. Also, the distance between England and the colonies made it impossible to get goods quickly. As a result, colonists started businesses such as brickmaking, glassmaking, papermaking, and ropemaking.

Activity

Research colonial businesses. In one column, make a list of businesses that provided goods. List businesses that provided services in another column.

The Corning Museum of Glass

PUTTING IT TOGETHER

By the middle of the 1700s, the colonists had begun to develop a free enterprise economy. Farming, fishing, shipbuilding, and trading were only a few of the colonial industries. As the colonial economy grew, more colonists were able to support themselves without importing goods from England. Over time the colonists became unhappy with the English laws that controlled trade. The trade laws took money out of the colonies and sometimes caused colonial businesses to go into debt. The colonists began to trade their goods with other nations. The colonists' desire to run their own economy eventually led to conflict with England.

Colonial hand-blown glass bottles

Review and Assess

1. Write one sentence for each vocabulary word.

   **free enterprise   triangular trade
   industry**

2. What kinds of resources did the New England colonies have?

3. Why did the economy of the English colonies grow?

4. Explain how supply and demand affects consumers and businesses.

5. What **caused** English colonists to begin looking for new places to trade their goods? What were some **effects** of the new trade?

Look at the map of Triangular Trade on page 220. Research other triangular trade routes that the colonies had with other countries.

Write a paragraph on the benefits of free enterprise to the colonists who started businesses and to the colonists who bought their goods.

Summarizing

You are watching the news on television; the broadcaster is describing a fire that took place earlier that day. The broadcaster's report takes 30 seconds. Yet you know that the fire department's effort to put out the fire took much longer than 30 seconds. What the broadcaster presented was a **summary** of the event. A summary is a brief way of telling the main points of an event or an idea in your own words. Being able to summarize is a useful skill in remembering what happened in history.

New England needed ships for fishing. However, English ships were too expensive for the colonists to buy. So workers began cutting down trees from New England's large forests to build their own ships. By 1741, New England had a fleet of more than 800 fishing boats. New England ships were built so well that soon the English companies were buying them.

LEARN THE SKILL

Read the above paragraph from your social studies textbook, then follow the steps to create a summary.

1. **Identify the topic.**
   As you read, look for the topic of a paragraph or section. In the paragraph above, the topic is the first sentence. It reads, "New England needed ships for fishing."

2. **Choose supporting information.**
   Look for facts that support the topic. In the paragraph above, supporting information includes: "So workers began cutting down trees from New England's large forests to build their own ships" and "By 1741, New England had a fleet of more than 800 fishing boats."

3. **Organize information.**
   Choose only the facts that support the main idea. In the paragraph above, the last sentence, "New England ships were built so well that soon the English companies were buying them," is extra information that you do not have to include in your summary.

4. **Write the summary in your own words.**
   The summary should be brief. If possible, state it in one sentence. Here is one possible summary of the paragraph:

"New England needed fishing ships, so it began building its own fleet from the trees of its forests. By 1741, it had a very large fleet."

TRY THE SKILL

Read the following paragraph about tobacco.

During the late 1600s, tobacco was exported from the Southern Colonies more than any other product. The demand for tobacco made Virginia the richest of the colonies. Tobacco grew wild in Virginia's moist, warm climate. It even grew in the streets and cemeteries of Jamestown. People built huge plantations for the purpose of raising tobacco. Because harvesting it was backbreaking work, more and more enslaved African Americans were brought into the colony. During the harvest season, even household servants were made to pick in the great fields of tobacco.

Write a brief summary of this article. Answering these questions will help you write the summary:

1. What is the topic?

2. What is the most important information?

3. What facts can you omit from the summary?

4. How can the summary help you understand how the practice of slavery grew in the south?

EXTEND THE SKILL

Knowing how to summarize is a skill you can often use outside of school. Here is a way to practice the summarizing skill. In a newspaper, read an article about a game that was played yesterday. Then, pretending you are a TV sports broadcaster, write out a summary of the game and read it before a pretend TV camera. To improve your skill, try the same procedure with articles on topics like local events or politics. Your summary should answer the following questions:

• What is the topic?

• What are the article's facts?

• How can writing a summary help you find the main idea when you read?

Colonial Governments

Find Out!
How did the colonies govern themselves?

Lesson Outline
• Governing the Colonies
• Governors and Assemblies
• Spirit of Freedom

VOCABULARY

assembly
legislation
militia
delegate
constable
treason

PEOPLE

Richard Henry Lee
John Locke
John Peter Zenger
Phillis Wheatley

READING STRATEGY

Make a chart like the one below to list the main idea and supporting details of this lesson.

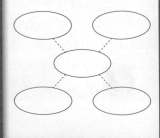

BUILD BACKGROUND

By the 1700s, the colonies had gained experience in governing themselves. England, busy with wars and other troubles at home, often paid little attention to the colonies. There were thousands of miles between the two continents, and mail delivery across the ocean was slow. The result was that the feeling of independence in the colonies grew.

GOVERNING THE COLONIES

As you read in Chapter 5, the first meeting of Virginia's **assembly**, the House of Burgesses, took place in 1619. An assembly is a lawmaking body. By 1760, every colony had elected an assembly like the House of Burgesses. Most made laws that were based on English law such as "innocent until proven guilty."

The colonies were formed for different reasons and were not all governed in the same way. Royal governors, who were appointed by the king of England, ruled eight of the 13 colonies. In proprietary colonies, the proprietor named the governor. Voters in Connecticut and Rhode Island elected the governor.

Colonial Assemblies

After the House of Burgesses was formed, most colonists believed that they had a right to take part in their own government. Many of the charters stated that laws should be made with "the consent of the freemen." At the time only men who owned property could vote or take part in government. Colonial assemblies decided how tax money would be spent and even wrote **legislation**. Legislation is the making or passing of laws.

Laws passed by assemblies had to be approved by the British government. Governors saw to it that the colony obeyed British laws. Sometimes the governor and the assembly disagreed on which laws had to be obeyed. In some colonies, if the governor found the

The British Parliament tried to control colonial assemblies such as the House of Burgesses, which met in Williamsburg's capitol building (left).

assembly unwilling to support him, he could dissolve, or shut down, the colonial assembly.

Assembly members could, in return, refuse to vote for money for the governor's plans. "Let us keep the dogs poor and we'll make them do what we please," one New Jersey assembly member said of the governors. Benjamin Franklin called this practice "the purchase of good laws."

READING CHECK How did assemblies try to control colonial governors?

225

Strong opinions about government were debated at town meetings.

GOVERNORS AND ASSEMBLIES

England had a hard time governing New England. Many New Englanders ignored English laws they did not agree with. They thought that it was more important to "obey God rather than man." Angered by the leaders of the Massachusetts Bay Colony, King Charles II decided to make it a royal colony. But even with a royal governor in charge, the New Englanders remained independent.

In 1741 members of the Massachusetts assembly tried to remove the governor. The governor complained "that they are as big as the Parliament of Great Britain!" England became part of Great Britain in 1707. Parliament is Britain's lawmaking body.

Local Governments

Most of the colonial local governments were much like the county and town governments in England. In New England, the town meeting was the earliest form of local government. The town meeting was a group of male colonists who got together to solve local problems. During a town meeting citizens voted on local laws and on town officials. Today many New England towns still hold town meetings.

In some other colonies, the governor formed a county court to make sure the colonists obeyed the law. The court tried the different cases brought before it. It also was responsible for road construction, ferry service, and the **militia**. A colonial militia was a military force made up of volunteers. It was similar to today's National Guard.

Voting

Not everyone could vote for assembly members, and each colony had its own conditions. On the whole, only adult white males who owned property were allowed to vote. In most of the colonies women, African Americans, Catholics, Jews, Native Americans and the poor could not vote. Also, in most colonies a voter had to belong to a certain church. In the royal colonies, only members of the Church of England could vote. In New England, only members of the Congregational Church could vote. The Pilgrims started the Congregational Church.

Most of the **delegates**, or members of the assembly, were wealthy landowners, lawyers, or merchants. They were most often elected to office because voters believed these men had the time, education, and experience for public office.

Most of the burgesses were wealthy planters. George Washington and **Richard Henry Lee** served as burgesses. They felt it was their duty to help govern the colony. But sometimes the assembly could try their patience. Lee admitted to his brother his disappointment about not getting much work done:

> *I find the attendance on Assemblies so expensive, and the power of doing good so rarely occurring, that I am determined to quit it.*

Elections

Elections were held at the county court house or village common. They were noisy, social occasions. One Virginia colonist wrote that an election "caused a Hubbub for a week or so." He explained that to Virginians used to "dull barbecues and yet duller dances," an election was an exciting event.

On Election Day candidates gave voters punch, cookies, and cakes. George Washington provided similar food and drink during his first election to the Virginia House of Burgesses in 1758.

Unlike today's secret voting, each voter spoke his choice in front of a large crowd. Loud cheers or boos followed each vote. The candidates often personally thanked a voter for his vote.

Law Enforcement

In the 1600s and 1700s **constables** and sheriffs were responsible for making people obey the law and keep the peace.

A constable was a town officer in charge of keeping order.

People accused of serious crimes could lose their lives. Serious crimes were armed robbery, counterfeiting or printing money illegally, murder, piracy, or **treason**. Treason is the betrayal of one's country by giving help to an enemy.

People accused of less serious charges such as swearing, theft, or misbehaving on Sundays were often made to suffer in public. Often the guilty person was placed on a ducking stool or in a pillory. The ducking stool was a chair fastened to the end of a long plank extended from the bank of a pond or stream. The person found guilty was tied to the chair and ducked or plunged into the water several times. The pillory was a wooden structure with holes for the neck and wrists. A person could be locked in the pillory for hours or even days.

READING CHECK

Who was allowed to vote in the colonies?

This pillory was at Boston Town House Square.

227

SPIRIT OF FREEDOM

Many of the colonists had definite ideas about the responsibilities of government and the rights of citizens. Some of those ideas came from John Locke. He was an English philosopher who believed that government was responsible for protecting people's natural rights. Natural rights are the rights all people are born with. Locke also wrote that if a government does not protect the rights of its citizens, citizens have the right to find other rulers. Locke's ideas grew increasingly popular in the colonies.

Freedom of the Press

In 1734 John Peter Zenger, a German immigrant, was put in jail for publishing stories in the *New York Weekly Journal*. The stories accused New York's royal governor, William Cosby, of being dishonest.

Zenger's trial established an important right, freedom of the press.

The governor accused Zenger of printing remarks attacking the government. A lawyer named Andrew Hamilton defended Zenger at his trial in 1735. Hamilton argued that Zenger should not be punished for printing stories that are true even if they are about a government official. Every person had the right to "publicly [oppose] the abuses of power . . . of men in authority."

The jury agreed with Hamilton and found Zenger not guilty. Zenger's victory helped establish an important right, freedom of the press. This meant that the colonists could speak or print the truth without fear of being put in jail.

Phillis Wheatley

Enslaved African Americans took special note of the growing calls for freedom. One of them, Phillis Wheatley, was the first important African American poet. Born in what is now Senegal in West Africa, she was kidnapped and brought to

the colonies at the age of eight. Wheatley was then sold to John Wheatley in Boston. It was common for enslaved people to be given the last name of their owner.

Mr. and Mrs. Wheatley taught young Phillis to read and write English. In 1773 she published a book of poetry called *Poems on Various Subjects: Religious and Moral*. In one poem, Wheatley contrasts her status as a slave with the colonists' desire for independence. "In every human . . . God has implanted a principle, which we call love of freedom," she wrote. "The same principle lives in us."

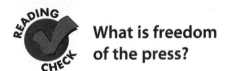

What is freedom of the press?

PUTTING IT TOGETHER

With the English government thousands of miles away, colonists needed to establish laws that would meet their needs. People in the 13 colonies held town meetings, elected assemblies, and created laws to govern themselves. These laws showed the colonists' desire to be free to live as they chose. These strong beliefs in the right to freedom and self-government would grow and later shape the new government of the United States.

Phillis Wheatley wrote of liberty and the hope that slavery would end.

Review and Assess

1. Write one sentence for each vocabulary word.

   assembly   legislation   militia

2. Who elected the governor in Connecticut and Rhode Island?

3. What were the major duties of the colonial assemblies?

4. Identify some ways you think the rights of the colonists were different from the rights of citizens today.

5. How do you think John Zenger made his **decision** to print stories criticizing New York's governor?

Look at the world map on page 220. What is the distance between England and the United States? How do you think this distance affected how colonies were governed by England?

Write a short speech that a British colonist might have written in support of self-government for the colonies.

VOCABULARY REVIEW

Number a sheet of paper from 1 to 5. Beside each number write the word or term from the list below that matches the description.

frontier	slave codes
industry	slave trade
legislation	

1. The making or passing of laws
2. A word used by colonists to describe the far edge of their settlements
3. The business of buying and selling captive people for profit
4. All the businesses that make one kind of product or provide one kind of service
5. Rules to keep enslaved workers under control

CHAPTER COMPREHENSION

6. What was the voyage to the American colonies like for both Europeans and African captives?
7. Why was the Yamasee War fought?
8. How was the family important to enslaved Africans?
9. What was the Middle Passage?
10. Why was New England the most difficult region for England to control?
11. How did the colonists begin to create a free enterprise system?
12. How did the trial of John Peter Zenger become important to the colonists?
13. Suppose you are a young person who wants to become an indentured servant to pay for your passage to the colonies. **Write** a letter to your parents explaining your reasons.

SKILL REVIEW

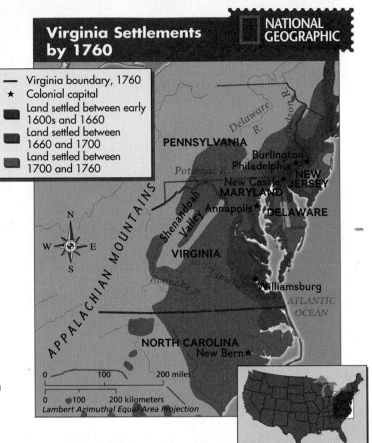

Virginia Settlements by 1760

NATIONAL GEOGRAPHIC

— Virginia boundary, 1760
★ Colonial capital
■ Land settled between early 1600s and 1660
■ Land settled between 1660 and 1700
■ Land settled between 1700 and 1760

0   100   200 miles
0   100   200 kilometers
Lambert Azimuthal Equal-Area Projection

14. **Geography Skill** Which city was settled earlier—Annapolis or Williamsburg?
15. **Geography Skill** When was the Shenandoah Valley settled?
16. **Study Skill** What is a good first step in writing a summary?
17. **Study Skill** What can help you find the most important information when choosing facts for your summary?
18. **Study Skill** What facts should you leave out when writing a summary?

USING A TIME LINE

1725	1730	1735	1740	1745	1750	1755	1760	1765	1770

1729
Benjamin Franklin founds Philadelphia's first newspaper

1735
Trial of John Peter Zenger

1739
Stono slave rebellion in South Carolina

1744
Eliza Lucas Pinckney successfully grows indigo

1750
The colonies have 250,000 enslaved persons

1760
More Europeans arrive in the colonies

1775
Philadelphia is the largest colonial city

19. Which of the events shown would have been the first item to be covered in Benjamin Franklin's newspaper?

20. How many years passed between the Stono slave rebellion and the slave population in the colonies reaching 250,000?

Writing **About Early Communities** Suppose you could travel back in time to the mid-seventeenth century, when the 13 colonies were first being settled. What advice would you offer to the colonists? What do you know now that would help them in their attempts to build an economy and a community?

Foldables

Use your Foldable to review what you have learned about life in the English colonies. As you look at your journal, mentally recall the events that brought colonists to America and the reasons they stayed. Differentiate between those who came to America willingly and those who came against their will. Review your notes under the lesson titles on your Foldable to check your memory and responses. Record any questions that you have. Then discuss them with classmates or review the chapter to find answers.

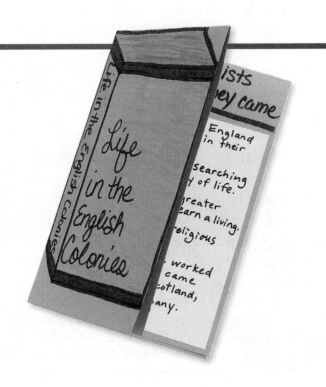

THE Big IDEAS ABOUT...

European Rivalries in North America

As you read in Unit 2, the English were only one of the European powers in North America. The French and Spanish also claimed lands that had long been home to Native Americans. Read on to find out how the Spanish controlled much of the West and Southwest and how the French controlled much of what is now the Middle West and Canada.

SPANISH SETTLEMENTS SPREAD NORTH

To protect their northern border from the French and English and to teach Native Americans about Christianity, Spain builds settlements in what they called New Mexico.

NEW FRANCE EXPANDS

In the 1700s fur traders build a network of trading posts throughout North America.

THE FRENCH AND INDIAN WAR

As the French and English colonies expand, conflicts over land grow. This leads to what the English called the French and Indian War.

Foldables

Make this Foldable study guide and use it to record what you learn about "European Rivalries in North America."

1. Fold a sheet of paper like a hamburger, but make one side 1" longer than the other.
2. Make one cut in the middle of the short side, dividing it into two equal sections.
3. Write the title of the chapter on the 1" tab.

Spanish Settlements Spread North

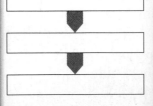

Why did Spaniards settle in the Southwest and California?

VOCABULARY

mission
convert
presidio

PEOPLE

Don Juan de
  Oñate
Antonio de
  Otermín
Popé
Diego de Vargas
Junípero Serra

READING STRATEGY

Make a chart like this one. In each box write down the sequence of events for this lesson in the order they happened.

Lesson Outline

- The Spanish in
  New Mexico
- Pueblo Revolt
- Spanish Texas and
  California

BUILD BACKGROUND

In the late 1500s and during the 1600s, the Spanish began to settle land to the north of Mexico. Some went north to search for gold. Others went to teach Christianity to the Native Americans. In 1565, Spain founded St. Augustine in Florida. It was the first permanent European settlement in what is now the United States.

THE SPANISH IN NEW MEXICO

In 1595 King Philip III of Spain gave the Spanish conquistador **Don Juan de Oñate** (HWAHN DE oh NYAH tay) permission to build a settlement in the lands the Spanish called **New Mexico**. Oñate was a Spaniard who was born in Mexico.

San Gabriel Settlement

In July 1598 Don Juan de Oñate and more than 400 colonists began to build a Spanish settlement in New Mexico. It was San Gabriel, on the west bank of the Rio Grande. Two years later Oñate, now governor, made San Gabriel the capital of New Mexico. Oñate believed that "Spanish rule of Native Americans would bring them peace, justice, salvation, orderliness, and protection." But Oñate spent more time searching for silver than being governor. In 1608 he was removed and in 1609 a new governor was appointed to New Mexico. The capital moved 30 miles south to **Santa Fe**.

Missions

Between 1609 and 1770 the Spanish built hundreds of settlements in North America. Many of them were **missions**. A mission is a religious settlement where missionaries

live and work. The purpose of the Spanish missions was to **convert** the Pueblo and other Native Americans to the Roman Catholic religion. To convert means to cause a person to change a belief.

Many Pueblo became a part of mission life. They accepted the food, clothing, and shelter the missions gave them. However, many of the Pueblo began to suffer from hunger. It is their custom to give part of their crops to help the needy. Now they had to give part of their crops to the Spanish. Some also were forced to work for the Spanish without pay.

The Roman Catholic Church was the center of the mission. Missions also had farms, ranches, orchards, workshops, and sleeping quarters. The Pueblo in the mission were not allowed to speak their own languages or practice their religion. They went to religious services and received religious instruction in the morning. During the rest of the day, the Pueblo worked in the mission.

READING CHECK What was the purpose of the Spanish missions?

St. Augustine is on the left. The statue above is of Don Juan de Oñate.

235

A Spanish Mission

Diagram Skill

1. What buildings do you see?

2. Which do you think is the most important building in the mission?

tanning hides

living quarters

church

blacksmith shop

236

PUEBLO REVOLT

By 1640, thousands of Native Americans had died as a result of disease and drought. Because of this, many Native Americans in the Southwest began practicing both Christianity and their traditional religions again. This angered Spanish religious leaders who had forbidden them to do so. Also, the food the Pueblo gave the Spanish as taxes drained the Pueblo food supply. Hundreds died from starvation.

The Revolt of 1680

In 1675 the Spanish governor, **Antonio de Otermín** (ahn TOH nee oh day oh ter MEEN), jailed 47 Pueblo religious leaders. One of them was a medicine man named **Popé** (Poh PAY). The Pueblo threatened to leave the mission, and the Spanish set free the religious leaders. Popé then began planning a rebellion.

Popé convinced the Pueblo communities to unite to force the Spanish to leave. He was also able to get them to work with the Apache.

Before the revolt was to take place, runners brought knotted cords to each Pueblo village. The knots showed how many days were left before the revolt. On August 10, 1680, the Pueblo attacked "with shamelessness and daring," Otermín wrote. The revolt lasted nine days. The Spanish survivors were forced to flee New Mexico.

Diego de Vargas

New Spain was troubled by the loss of New Mexico to the Pueblo. They needed it to protect their northern border. In 1691 **Diego de Vargas** (dee AYE goh day VAHR gus) was selected to take back

General Diego de Vargas retook land in New Mexico without firing a shot.

New Mexico. The next year, Vargas set out with about 200 troops to convince Pueblo communities that the Spanish would not punish them. In the 12 years since the revolt, Popé and other Pueblo leaders had died and the Pueblo communities were no longer united under one leader. Vargas was able to convince 23 communities to accept the friendship of Spain. Vargas agreed to allow the Pueblo to live in their own communities apart from the Spanish and to practice their traditional religion.

 Why did the Pueblo revolt against the Spanish?

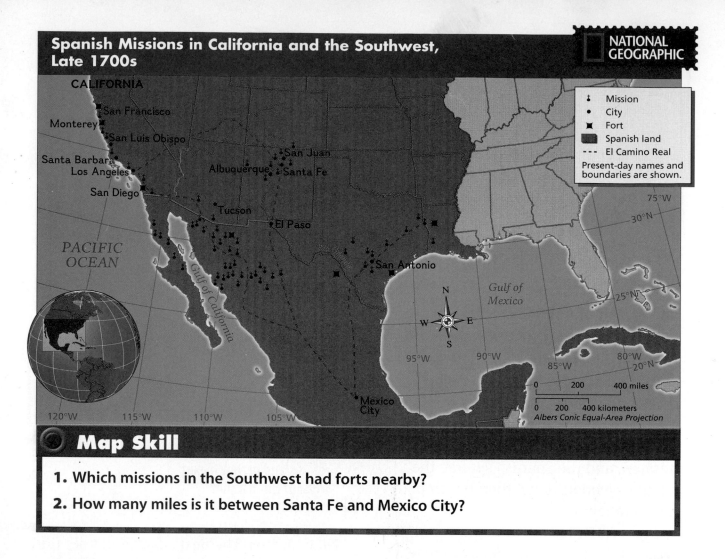

CALIFORNIA

San Francisco
Monterey
San Luis Obispo
Santa Barbara
Los Angeles
San Diego

San Juan
Albuquerque
Santa Fe

Tucson

El Paso

PACIFIC OCEAN

Gulf of California

San Antonio

Gulf of Mexico

Mexico City

Mission
City
Fort
Spanish land
El Camino Real
Present-day names and boundaries are shown.

75°W
30°N
25°N
20°N
95°W 90°W 85°W 80°W
120°W 115°W 110°W 105°W

0   200   400 miles
0   200   400 kilometers
Albers Conic Equal-Area Projection

Map Skill

1. Which missions in the Southwest had forts nearby?
2. How many miles is it between Santa Fe and Mexico City?

SPANISH TEXAS AND CALIFORNIA

In the 1680s, the Spanish began building settlements in the area that is now **Texas**. They were built to keep French explorers and traders out of the area. In 1682 they established the first mission in Texas, the mission of Corpus Christi de la Isleta. In 1718, they founded a mission, San Antonio de Valero (day vah LAIR oh). The mission's church later became known as the Alamo. Four other missions and a **presidio** were later built in the area. A presidio is a military fort where soldiers live. The missions the Spanish built around what is today **San Antonio** became known as the Alamo chain.

California Missions

By the 1760s Russian hunters and fishing ships had already visited the coast north of **California**. Spain feared that if they didn't settle California, Russia or England would. In 1769 a Spanish missionary named Father **Junípero Serra** (hoo NEE pair roh SEH rah) led an expedition that was divided into five groups. Two traveled by land and three by sea. They planned to meet at **San Diego**, a good harbor on the California coast that had first been explored by Juan Rodríguez Cabrillo in 1542. Despite a crippled leg, Father Serra walked for six weeks to reach San Diego. On July 16, the first California mission was founded, Mission San Diego de Alcalá near a Kumeyaay (Koom e YAY) village. By 1823 there were 21 missions in California. As you can see from the map on page 238, these missions stretched as far north as present-day **San Francisco**. California was the last part of New Spain to be settled.

El Camino Real (el kah MEE noh re AHL) connected the Spanish missions in the Southwest to Mexico. El Camino Real or "royal road" was the first road to stretch from Santa Fe to Mexico City in 1581. Later, the El Camino Real expanded to Texas, Arizona, and California.

Why did the Spanish build settlements in California?

PUTTING IT TOGETHER

The Pueblo Revolt and the regaining of some rights by the Pueblo did not stop the growth of Spanish settlements in North America. By 1800 the Spanish controlled much of the land in what is now the United States.

Today, the influence of Native Americans and the Spanish can still be seen. Many cities like Taos, New Mexico, have Pueblo names. Others, like San Antonio, Texas, have Spanish names. Herders throughout the region follow the methods of herding cattle on horseback developed in Spain and Mexico.

Review and Assess

1. Write one sentence for each vocabulary word.

   convert   mission   presidio

2. What did Oñate believe Spanish rule would bring to Native Americans?

3. Why did the Spanish settle the Southwest and California?

4. Why were the Pueblo able to continue practicing some of their traditional ways of life after the revolt?

5. What **alternatives** could the Pueblo or the Spanish have chosen to prevent the Pueblo revolt of 1680? **Decide** which alternative you think would have worked best.

Activities

Look at the map of Spanish missions on page 238. Plan a car trip on the El Camino Real. Choose the cities you would like to visit.

Write a diary entry about working in a mission from the point of view of a Pueblo. Include details shown in the diagram on page 236.

New France Expands

Why did France expand its colonies in North America?

Lesson Outline
• The Fur Trade
• French Louisiana

VOCABULARY

voyageur
coureurs de bois

PEOPLE
Jean Baptiste
  Point du Sable
René Robert La
  Salle
Pierre Le Moyne
  d'Iberville
Jean-Baptiste Le
  Moyne de
  Bienville

READING STRATEGY

Make a chart like this one. Use it to compare and contrast New France with the 13 colonies.

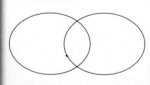

BUILD BACKGROUND

As you read in Chapter 5, France did not attempt to settle New France in the same way as the English. Only Catholics were allowed to settle and French colonists could not own land. Also, France was divided by religious wars between Catholics and Protestants. As a result, by 1660 only 3,000 colonists lived in New France. Most were fur traders and missionaries. By the 1700s fur traders had built a network of trading posts throughout North America.

Many French trappers learned about the fur trade from Native Americans.

THE FUR TRADE

The fur trade was the major economic activity in New France. Fur traders bought furs at trading posts. The furs were then transported to Quebec by **voyageurs** (vwah yah ZHURZ). Voyageurs were people who carried furs and other goods by canoe. In 1701 the French built a trading post which became the city of **Detroit**.

In the 1770s a Haitian fur trader named **Jean Baptiste Point du Sable** (ZHAHN bap TEEST PWAN doo SAH bluh) built a trading post off Lake Michigan. It grew to become the city of **Chicago**.

Native American Relations

France granted few people the right to trap and trade in its American colonies. As a result, many trappers became **coureurs de bois** (KUR rer duh BWAH), or "woods runners" in French. The coureur de bois trapped furs without permission from France. Many trappers became friends with Native Americans, learning their languages and customs.

READING CHECK

Why did many trappers learn Native American languages and customs?

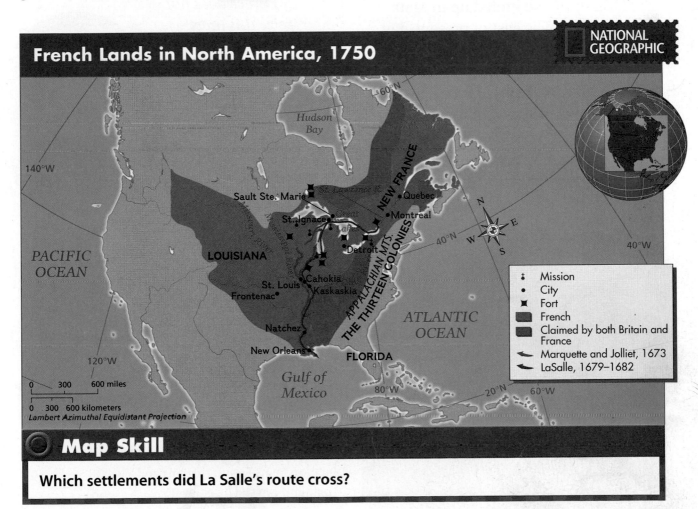

French Lands in North America, 1750

NATIONAL GEOGRAPHIC

Hudson Bay

140°W

160°N

NEW FRANCE

Sault Ste. Marie

St. Ignace

Great Lakes

Quebec

Montreal

PACIFIC OCEAN

LOUISIANA

Detroit

St. Louis
Frontenac

Cahokia
Kaskaskia

APPALACHIAN MTS.

THE THIRTEEN COLONIES

ATLANTIC OCEAN

40°W

Natchez

New Orleans

FLORIDA

Gulf of Mexico

120°W

80°W

20°N

60°W

40°N

	Mission
	City
	Fort
	French
	Claimed by both Britain and France
	Marquette and Jolliet, 1673
	LaSalle, 1679–1682

0   300   600 miles
0   300   600 kilometers
Lambert Azimuthal Equidistant Projection

Map Skill

Which settlements did La Salle's route cross?

FRENCH LOUISIANA

As you read in Chapter 5, Louis Jolliet and Jacques Marquette explored the Mississippi River in search of the Northwest Passage. In 1682 French explorer René Robert La Salle (lah SAHL) followed the Mississippi to the Gulf of Mexico and claimed the entire Mississippi Valley for France. He named it Louisiana after Louis XIV. He was given rights to "build forts at the places where he may consider them necessary" in the area between Florida and Mexico. Find Louisiana on the map on page 241.

La Salle's Attempt Fails

In 1684 La Salle left France with 300 colonists headed for the mouth of the Mississippi. However, La Salle sailed past the Mississippi and ended up in Matagorda Bay, 80 miles east of present-day Corpus Christi. Many of the colonists died from disease. One ship returned to France, while another was lost at sea. By 1687 only 36 colonists remained.

Settlements in Louisiana

In 1698 Pierre Le Moyne d'Iberville (PE air LA moyn DI ber VIL) argued for a French settlement at the mouth of the Mississippi. The following excerpt explains why Iberville wanted to settle Louisiana:

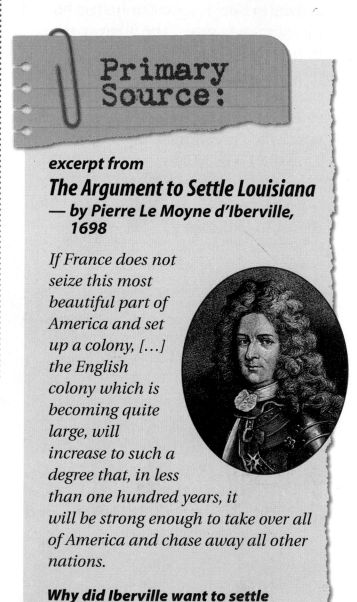

Primary Source:

excerpt from

The Argument to Settle Louisiana
— by Pierre Le Moyne d'Iberville, 1698

If France does not seize this most beautiful part of America and set up a colony, [...] the English colony which is becoming quite large, will increase to such a degree that, in less than one hundred years, it will be strong enough to take over all of America and chase away all other nations.

Why did Iberville want to settle Louisiana?

Today, in New Orleans' French Quarter, many French customs and traditions can still be enjoyed.

Fort Maurepas and New Orleans

In 1699 Iberville, and his brother, **Jean-Baptiste Le Moyne de Bienville** (JON bab teest LA moyn duh BE yen VIL) established the first French settlement in Louisiana, Fort Maurepas, in what is today Ocean Springs, Mississippi.

During the early 1700s, the French built forts, missions, and other settlements in Louisiana. In 1718 Bienville founded **New Orleans** which became the capital of Louisiana in 1722.

The establishment of Louisiana to the west of the 13 colonies stopped the English from expanding.

What stopped La Salle from settling the Mississippi Valley?

PUTTING IT TOGETHER

By the middle of the 1700s, the French had built settlements throughout New France. As a result, they had surrounded the growing 13 colonies. The French also had won many Native American friends. The voyageurs and coureurs de bois helped to form strong partnerships with them. In the next lesson you will see how the French, English, and Native Americans fought to control much of North America.

French fur traders used Dixie money. The word *dix* means "10" in French.

Review and Assess

1. Write one sentence for each vocabulary term.

   coureurs de bois   voyageur

2. How did Native Americans help the French?

3. What did the French do to stop England from taking over all of North America?

4. How did the fur trade shape the growth of New France?

5. **Compare** and **contrast** the French and the English colonies of North America.

Look at the map of New France on page 241. Research the names of each waterway LaSalle used between 1679 and 1682.

Write a paragraph about what you might have seen while traveling between Detroit and Quebec in 1750.

Making Generalizations

In Unit 2, you read about a number of explorers who claimed land in North America for France. At first, it might seem that men as different as Samuel de Champlain, Jacques Marquette, and René Robert La Salle had little in common. However, if you look closer, you might see some similarities. From them you might be able to make a broad statement about what makes an explorer successful. A statement that shows how facts, items, or events that seem different have some things in common is a **generalization**.

By reading about Champlain, Marquette, and La Salle, you discover they all knew how to lead others. They also liked to explore the unknown.

> **VOCABULARY**
>
> generalization

Jacques Marquette

Samuel de Champlain

La Salle

LEARN THE SKILL

Follow these steps to make a generalization about the French in North America.

1. **Identify the topic.**
   You must decide what you want to make the generalization about. Here you want to make a generalization about the French in North America.

2. **Gather examples.**
   Next, gather examples about your topic. In the last lesson, you learned about the explorers, what they did, and the effect this had on others.

3. **Examine the examples for similarities.**
   What is alike about the examples, and what is different? Do they have anything in common?

4. Make the generalization.

Form a generalization that is true about the French in North America: Although the French claimed a large part of North America, they did not settle in large numbers.

TRY THE SKILL

Try making a generalization about another topic in history you've studied recently, such as governments in the 13 colonies. Only some colonies had royal governors, but all colonies had assemblies. Eligible colonists voted for members of the assemblies. Use this information to answer the following questions.

To help you make the generalization, follow these steps:

1. What is a generalization?

2. What generalizations can you make about colonial governments?

3. What steps did you take to make your generalization?

4. Why is it important to have several examples to make a generalization?

EXTEND THE SKILL

Understanding how to make generalizations can help you better understand the world today. It can help you see how different facts and events are related. For example, the right to vote is an important right for all Americans. However, the equipment used for voting is not the same in all states. Some states use voting machines, others use paper ballots. Some ballots, or the paper used in voting machines, are hard to read. Use this information to help you answer the following questions:

- What generalization can you make about voting in the United States?

- How does making generalizations help you understand events that happen today?

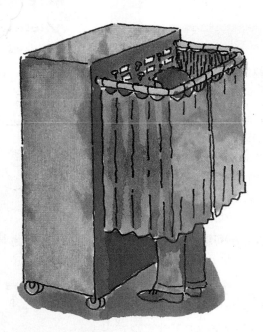

The French and Indian War

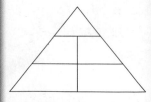
What were the results of the French and Indian War?

VOCABULARY

French and
   Indian War
Treaty of Paris
Proclamation of
   1763

PEOPLE

George
   Washington
William Pitt
Pontiac

READING STRATEGY

Make a chart like this one. Use it to draw conclusions about how the outcome of the French and Indian War affected the 13 colonies.

BUILD BACKGROUND

During the 1700s, the French and British had fought three wars. The fourth conflict began in 1754 when British colonists moved into North American lands claimed by France. This conflict is called the French and Indian War because the British were fighting the French and their Native American allies.

You Are Here
1754 – 1763

FRANCE AND ENGLAND GO TO WAR

Britain and France both claimed the land in the Ohio River valley. The Ohio River valley lies between the Appalachian Mountains and the Mississippi River. For the first half of the 1700s, Native Americans of the area were successful in keeping both the French and British colonists from settling there. Then some Iroquois began to sell their land to British colonists. France feared the British would take over the region. Britain saw the forts the French were building as a threat to the British settlers in the area.

Early French Victories

The first battle came in 1754 at Fort Duquesne (doo KAIN). The lieutenant governor of Virginia sent a young George Washington to lead a small group of troops to force the French out of the Ohio River valley.

When Washington arrived, his troops attacked and defeated a small force of French soldiers in the woods near the fort. "I heard the bullets whistle; and believe me, there is something charming in the sound," wrote Washington.

Washington's troops quickly built a temporary fort out of logs and called it Fort Necessity. Soon a larger French army attacked the fort, and Washington's men were defeated.

George Washington (above) was 21 years old when he fought in the French and Indian War (left).

Many of France's early victories were due to the help they received from their longtime ally, the Huron, and other Native American groups. Soon the French mastered the Native American method of warfare. They made surprise attacks on the British from behind trees and large rocks or anywhere they could hide. In contrast, the British marched in the open battlefield in long rows. This made them an easy target for the enemy.

Why did the British colonists want control of the Ohio River valley?

247

TURNING POINT OF THE WAR

In 1757 the British leader, William Pitt, believed that the British could win their power struggle with the French in North America. He began to pour more money, troops, and equipment into the effort there. The result was an immediate turn in the war. In 1758 British troops took Fort Duquesne and renamed it Fort Pitt. Fort Pitt is where the city of Pittsburgh stands today. Britain then tried to convince Native Americans in the area to side with the British. At first the Iroquois refused, "You have disregarded us, thrown us behind your back," said Tiyanoga (tih an OH guh), a Mohawk leader.

In 1759 the Iroquois decided to join the British against their old enemies, the Huron and the French. In return the British promised to keep the colonists away from Iroquois lands. Later that year, Britain captured the capital of New France, Quebec. Montreal surrendered in 1760.

In 1762, as the war was ending, France gave Spain much of Louisiana to keep it out of Britain's hands. By the terms of the Treaty of Paris, signed in 1763, Great Britain gained all of France's lands in the

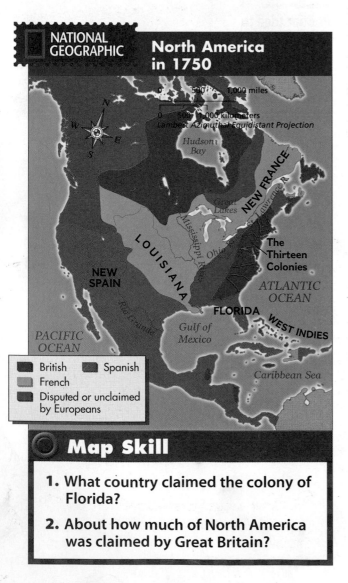

NATIONAL GEOGRAPHIC

North America in 1750

0 500 1,000 miles
0 500 1,000 kilometers
Lambert Azimuthal Equidistant Projection

Hudson Bay

NEW FRANCE

Great Lakes

St. Lawrence R.

Mississippi River

Ohio

LOUISIANA

NEW SPAIN

The Thirteen Colonies

ATLANTIC OCEAN

FLORIDA

WEST INDIES

Rio Grande

Gulf of Mexico

PACIFIC OCEAN

Caribbean Sea

■ British ■ Spanish
■ French
■ Disputed or unclaimed by Europeans

Map Skill

1. What country claimed the colony of Florida?

2. About how much of North America was claimed by Great Britain?

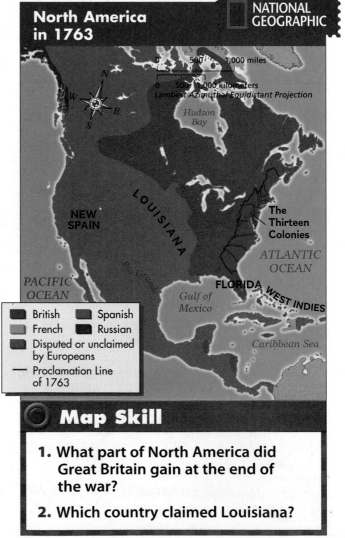

North America in 1763

NATIONAL GEOGRAPHIC

0 500 1,000 miles
0 500 1,000 kilometers
Lambert Azimuthal Equidistant Projection

Hudson Bay

Great Lakes

LOUISIANA

NEW SPAIN

Rio Grande

PACIFIC OCEAN

The Thirteen Colonies

ATLANTIC OCEAN

FLORIDA

WEST INDIES

Gulf of Mexico

Caribbean Sea

■ British ■ Spanish
■ French ■ Russian
■ Disputed or unclaimed by Europeans
— Proclamation Line of 1763

Map Skill

1. What part of North America did Great Britain gain at the end of the war?

2. Which country claimed Louisiana?

Ohio River valley and Canada. Britain also gained the Spanish colony of Florida.

After the War

Soon after the war ended, British colonists again began moving west into the Ohio River valley. To preserve Indian hunting grounds, an Ottawa chief, **Pontiac** (PAHN tee ak), urged the Native Americans there to "drive off your land those who will do you nothing but harm." In 1763 they captured and burned British settlements but were soon defeated by the British army. Britain feared a long and costly war. To prevent another revolt, Britain issued the **Proclamation of 1763**. This proclamation, or official announcement, set aside all British land west of the Appalachians for Native Americans. Its goal was to protect the fur trade and draw new settlers to Canada or other British colonies. To prevent colonists from moving into the region, Britain sent soldiers

to the frontier. The colonists were angered by being kept out of western lands and the fur trade.

 What resources helped Britain win the war?

PUTTING IT TOGETHER

The French and Indian War changed the way colonists saw themselves and Britain. Colonists had fought against a common enemy and won. Soon they would unite again to fight Great Britain for their independence.

Pontiac tried to unite the tribes of the Great Lakes area and Ohio and Mississippi valleys.

Review and Assess

1. Write one sentence for each vocabulary term.

   **French and Indian War   Treaty of Paris
   Proclamation of 1763**

2. Who was Chief Pontiac and what did he do?

3. How did North America change as a result of the French and Indian War?

4. Why did the British issue the Proclamation of 1763?

5. Based upon the maps shown on page 248, what **conclusions** can you make about France's influence in North America?

Look at the maps on page 248. What was the major change between 1750 and 1763? Draw a flag that represents what the U.S. would be today if these changes had not occurred.

Write a letter to a relative from the point of view of a British colonist in 1754. Explain how the French and Indian War is affecting your life.

Being a Good Citizen
Work Together to Work Things Out

"Anyone can do it and everyone should," Alexandra Cerda says about a program called AIM, Amigos in Mediation. *Amigos* is Spanish for "friends" or "partners." "Kids become mediators," says Alan Galvez, age 10, "when they help other kids work out their problems on their own."

Both Alexandra and Alan are fifth graders at Scobee Elementary School in San Antonio, Texas. Every year about 40 students volunteer for this program

"Honesty is very important."

and agree to come to a one-hour training session every day after school for two weeks. School counselors Chris Christensen and Abby Kelly say that training teaches students the rules for mediation.

Students asking for mediation must agree to tell the truth, not to interrupt, and not to make faces or use bad language during their meeting. "Honesty is very important," says Alexandra. "If kids don't tell the truth about what they did or how they feel about what happened, it will be very hard to help them work out their problems."

In their training session, volunteers practice their new skills in pretend mediations. "Sometimes," says

"…help other kids work out their problems."

250

Alan, "a teacher sends two students who are fighting to us, but most of the time, kids come on their own. They know that they might end up getting in worse trouble if we don't help them."

Causes of problems include pushing, shoving, name-calling, and doing things out of turn. The mediations take place in the counselors' office. "Our job is to stay calm and be patient," says Alexandra. "We have to listen to each person's side of the story. We can't take sides. Sometimes the hardest part is keeping the two kids from interrupting each other."

Alexandra and Alan like being mediators. "It feels good," says Alan, "to help someone else with their problems. I'm glad we're helping kids get along with each other."

San Antonio, Texas

Be a Good Citizen

Making Connections

- **What are some causes of conflicts at your school? What guidelines, or rules, do students use to solve conflicts?**

- **What are some jobs for adults that are similar to being a conflict mediator?**

Talk About It!

- **Why is honesty so important during the process of mediation?**

- **What skills might make a good mediator? What might be the hardest part of this job?**

Act On It

In the Classroom

Identify a recent problem involving your classmates. How was the problem settled? Write a list of suggestions that would have helped to mediate the problem peacefully.

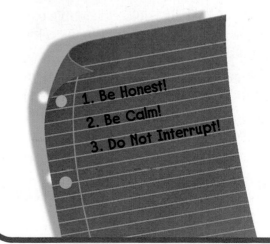

1. Be Honest!
2. Be Calm!
3. Do Not Interrupt!

Chapter 8 REVIEW

VOCABULARY REVIEW

Number a sheet of paper from 1 to 5. Beside each number write the word or term from the list below that matches the description.

mission	**Treaty of Paris**
presidio	**voyageur**
Proclamation of 1763	

1. A person who carried furs and other goods by canoe

2. A religious settlement where missionaries live and work

3. A Spanish military fort where soldiers live

4. An official announcement that set aside all British land west of the Appalachians for Native Americans

5. A document that gave Britain all of France's lands in the Ohio River valley and Canada

CHAPTER COMPREHENSION

6. What agreement did Diego de Vargas make with the Pueblo people?

7. What route connected Spain's colonies in the Southwest to Mexico?

8. What was the most important economic activity of the French in New France?

9. Why were the 13 colonies unable to expand after settlements were built in Louisiana?

10. What method of warfare did the French use during the French and Indian War?

11. How did William Pitt contribute to the change in the French and Indian War?

12. **Write** a newspaper article that reports on one event that occurred during the French and Indian War.

SKILL REVIEW

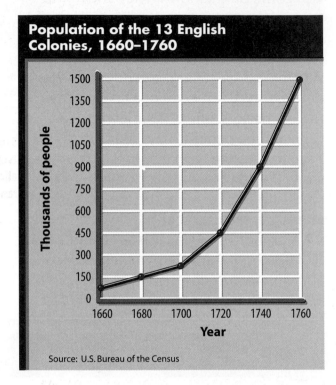

Population of the 13 English Colonies, 1660–1760

Source: U.S. Bureau of the Census

13. **Reading/Thinking Skill** What is a generalization?

14. **Reading/Thinking Skill** What steps do you follow in making a generalization?

15. **Reading/Thinking Skill** What generalizations can you make about the population of the 13 colonies at the time of the French and Indian War?

16. **Reading/Thinking Skill** Why is comparing important in making generalizations?

17. **Reading/Thinking Skill** Is the statement "Native Americans were sometimes on the side of the French during the French and Indian War" a generalization? Why or why not?

18. **Reading/Thinking Skill** Suppose you made the statement: "To win a war you must have Native Americans on your side." Is this generalization true? Explain.

USING A TIME LINE

| 1590 | 1610 | 1630 | 1650 | 1670 | 1690 | 1710 | 1730 | 1750 | 1770 |

1565
The Spanish found St. Augustine

1598
The first Spanish settlement of New Mexico is founded

1642
French missionaries found Montreal

1663
New France becomes a colony

1682
René Robert La Salle claims the Mississippi River valley for France

1692
The Spanish regain control of New Mexico

1763
French and Indian War ends; Pontiac's Rebellion; Proclamation of 1763

1769
Father Junípero Serra begins to build missions in California

19. Look at the events that took place in 1763. How were they related?

20. Was Montreal founded before or after New France became a colony?

Writing **About Culture** Think about the Spanish and French who settled in different parts of North America. What are some ways their culture became a part of the culture of the United States over time? Use some examples from the present day.

Use your Foldable to review what you have learned about the rivalry between Spain and France in the Americas. As you look at the front of your Foldable, mentally recall ways in which these countries have influenced America—past and present. Review your notes under the tabs of your Foldable to check your memory and responses. Record any questions that you have. Then discuss them with classmates or review the chapter to find answers.

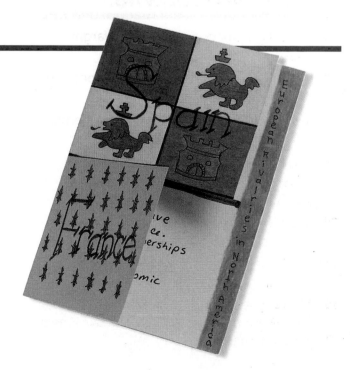

VOCABULARY REVIEW

Number a sheet of paper from 1 to 5. Beside each number write the word or term from the list below that best completes the sentence.

cooperation   **legislation**

covenant   **Treaty of Paris**

frontier

1. The ___ officially ended the French and Indian War in 1763.

2. A ___ is a special promise or agreement.

3. The making or passing of laws is known as ___.

4. Trade prospered in the colonies, with ___ between the Dutch and English groups.

5. A ___ is a term colonists used for land at the edge of their settlements.

TECHNOLOGY

For resources to help you learn more about the people and places you studied in this unit, visit **www.mhschool.com** and follow the links for Grade 5, Unit 3.

⬤ SKILL REVIEW

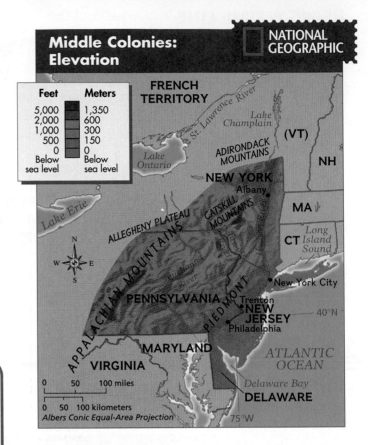

Middle Colonies: Elevation

NATIONAL GEOGRAPHIC

Feet	Meters
5,000	1,350
2,000	600
1,000	300
500	150
0	0
Below sea level	Below sea level

FRENCH TERRITORY
St. Lawrence River
Lake Champlain
(VT)
NH
Lake Ontario
ADIRONDACK MOUNTAINS
NEW YORK
Albany
MA
Lake Erie
ALLEGHENY PLATEAU
CATSKILL MOUNTAINS
CT
Long Island Sound
APPALACHIAN MOUNTAINS
Hudson River
PENNSYLVANIA
PIEDMONT
New York City
Trenton
NEW JERSEY
Philadelphia
40°N
MARYLAND
VIRGINIA
ATLANTIC OCEAN
Delaware Bay
DELAWARE
75°W

0 50 100 miles
0 50 100 kilometers
Albers Conic Equal-Area Projection

6. **Reading/Thinking Skill** What is a generalization?

7. **Study Skill** How is writing a summary different from rewriting something in your own words?

8. **Study Skill** When might writing a summary be helpful to you?

9. **Geography Skill** What is the highest elevation in the Catskill Mountains?

10. **Geography Skill** Is the elevation of Trenton higher than sea level?

1   The large number of Europeans who came to the colonies caused the land along the Atlantic coast to become crowded . . . . Newcomers who wanted more space began moving west to the area they called the backcountry.

2   Most people who settled in the backcountry were poor. A Scottish immigrant named Alexander MacAllister told relatives that a person "might make it rich very fast" in the North Carolina backcountry.

3   Life was hard for settlers of the backcountry. The rocky uneven land made farming difficult . . . . The [area] couldn't be reached by water and colonists had to travel by land following trails made by Native Americans.

1   Based on the paragraphs, which of these generalizations is true?

   A   The Scottish made up the population in the backcountry.

   B   Even poor colonists could afford land in the backcountry.

   C   All of the people in the backcountry overcame their hardships.

   D   Farming was impossible.

2   Which is the best summary of this passage?

   A   The backcountry was a difficult place to live in, but people made a life for themselves there.

   B   Some people became rich there.

   C   Newcomers who wanted space moved to the backcountry.

   D   People in the backcountry traveled along Native American trails.

WRITING ACTIVITIES

Writing to Persuade Suppose that William Penn has asked you to help him bring people to his colony. *Write* an advertisement in which to persuade people to settle there.

Writing to Inform *Write* an essay about the triangular trade. Identify the goods and people involved as well as the routes that the trade followed.

Writing to Express Suppose that you are a soldier defending Fort Duquesne or Fort Necessity during the French and Indian War. *Write* a letter describing your experience.

LITERATURE

PAUL REVERE'S
Ride

Selections from the poem by
Henry Wadsworth Longfellow
Illustrated by Keith Garletts

Paul Revere was a hero who, with two other Patriots,
rode across the countryside to warn of a British attack.
This celebrated poem commemorated the ride.

Listen, my children, and you shall hear
Of the midnight ride of Paul Revere,
On the eighteenth of April, in Seventy-five;
Hardly a man is now alive
Who remembers that famous day and year.

He said to his friend, "If the British march
By land or sea from the town to-night,
Hang a lantern aloft in the **belfry** arch
Of the North Church tower as a signal light,—
One if by land, and two if by sea:
And I on the opposite shore will be,
Ready to ride and spread the alarm
Through every Middlesex village and farm,
For the country folk to be up and to arm."
Then he said, "Good-night!" and with
muffled oar

---

belfry (bel'fre') a room in a tower where bells are hung
muffled (muf'əld) deadened or softened (sound)

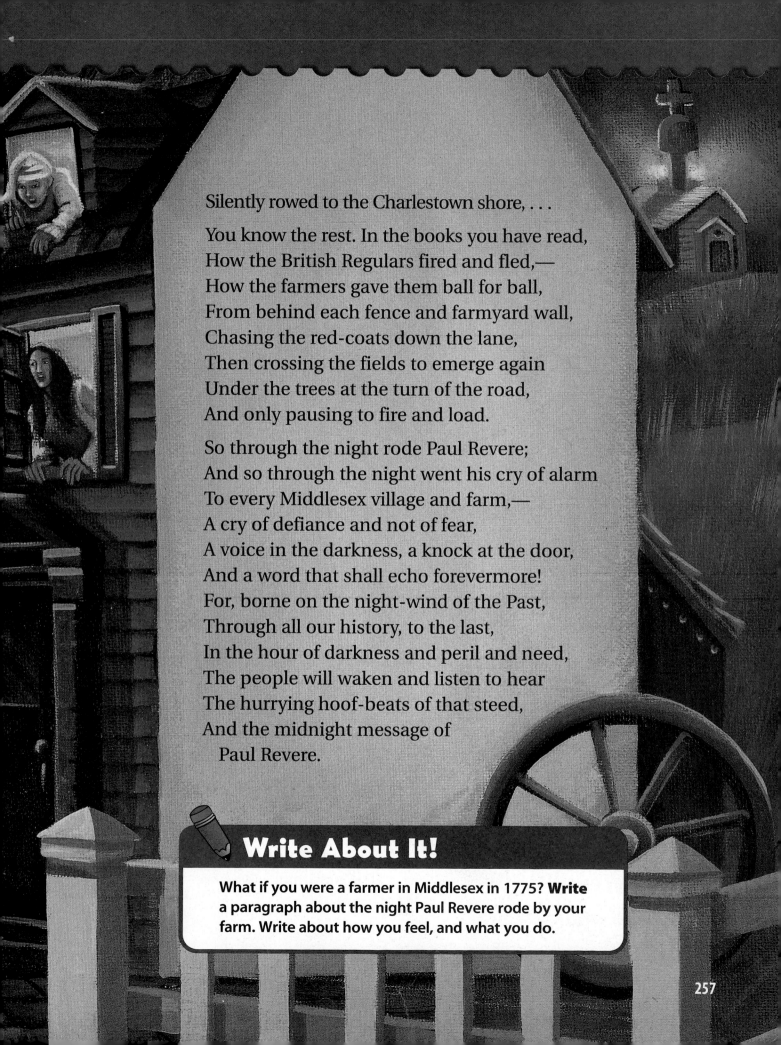

Silently rowed to the Charlestown shore, . . .

You know the rest. In the books you have read,
How the British Regulars fired and fled,—
How the farmers gave them ball for ball,
From behind each fence and farmyard wall,
Chasing the red-coats down the lane,
Then crossing the fields to emerge again
Under the trees at the turn of the road,
And only pausing to fire and load.

So through the night rode Paul Revere;
And so through the night went his cry of alarm
To every Middlesex village and farm,—
A cry of defiance and not of fear,
A voice in the darkness, a knock at the door,
And a word that shall echo forevermore!
For, borne on the night-wind of the Past,
Through all our history, to the last,
In the hour of darkness and peril and need,
The people will waken and listen to hear
The hurrying hoof-beats of that steed,
And the midnight message of
    Paul Revere.

Write About It!

What if you were a farmer in Middlesex in 1775? **Write**
a paragraph about the night Paul Revere rode by your
farm. Write about how you feel, and what you do.

4

The Fight for Independence

TAKE A LOOK

How did people travel during the Revolutionary War?

People had few choices when it came to transportation during the Revolutionary War. Today, people travel by trains, planes, and automobiles.

For more information about the fight for independence, visit our Web site at www.mhschool.com

THE Big IDEAS ABOUT...

Breaking Ties with Great Britain

In 1765 Great Britain began to pass several unpopular tax laws. This sparked a rebellion among colonists. They organized to protest the unfair taxation and attempts by the British to limit their rights. Finally, the colonists declared themselves independent. Read on to find out how the English colonists moved toward independence from Great Britain.

TAXATION WITHOUT REPRESENTATION

The Sons and Daughters of Liberty organize protests against the new British taxes.

FIRST BATTLES OF THE AMERICAN REVOLUTION

Paul Revere rides to Lexington, Massachusetts, warning minutemen that British troops are headed for Concord.

THE DECLARATION OF INDEPENDENCE

Ben Franklin, John Adams, and Thomas Jefferson work on the Declaration of Independence, which explains why the colonies ought to be free from England.

Foldables

Make this Foldable study guide and use it to record what you learn about "Breaking Ties with Great Britain."

1. Fold a sheet of paper like a hot dog. Cut the hot dog in half along the fold line.

2. Tape the short ends of the two section halves together to make one long strip of paper.

3. Fold the strip in half and then into thirds. Refold to make a six-tab accordion time line. Use this time line with chapters 9 and 10.

The Colonists Protest British Rule

 **What led the colonies to break away from Britain?**

Lesson Outline
- Unfair Laws
- Unrest Increases
- The First Continental Congress

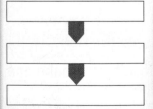
BUILD BACKGROUND

In the 1760s unrest swept through the colonies. Their assemblies had become responsible for many of their own taxes. Now Great Britain was raising taxes on colonial imports. After the French and Indian War, Britain needed to raise money to pay for the war. Colonists wanted their own assemblies to decide what their taxes should be. The British had no right to tax colonists since colonists had no representation in the British government, a right all Englishmen had long had. Cries of "Taxation without representation is tyranny" filled the streets.

UNFAIR LAWS

Until 1763 taxes on colonial trade had been thought of as a way to control trade, not to raise money. The Molasses Act of 1733 had been passed to limit the amount of molasses and sugar colonists bought from parts of the West Indies not under British control. However, most colonists ignored the law. It was repealed, or canceled, in 1764.

That same year the British passed the Sugar Act of 1764, which taxed sugar. In violation of the rights the colonists had as English, it allowed those accused of breaking this law to be tried without a jury of their peers. Also it permitted English officials to sell seized cargoes and ships and to keep part of the money from their sale.

The Stamp Act

Another unpopular tax was the Stamp Act of 1765. It forced colonists to pay a tax every time they bought a newspaper or pamphlet or signed a legal document. The profits from this tax were the first to be sent directly to England.

Another measure, the Quartering Act, forced colonists to provide British soldiers stationed in America with a place to live, food, drink, and candles. This denied colonists their right as English not to have a standing army in peacetime without their consent.

The Sons of Liberty held rallies to protest the Stamp Act (left) and other British laws (above).

Riots and angry speeches became frequent. Patrick Henry, a member of the House of Burgesses, argued that only the Virginia assembly could tax Virginians. The British accused him of treason, the betrayal of one's country. "If this be treason," Henry replied, "make the most of it."

Sons of Liberty

To fight the hated Stamp Act, some colonists formed the Sons of Liberty. Liberty means freedom. These colonists organized protests against the taxes. These protests forced some stamp-tax agents to quit their jobs. One member, Samuel Adams, wrote newspaper articles attacking the Stamp Act.

READING CHECK

Why did the new taxes anger colonists? How do you know?

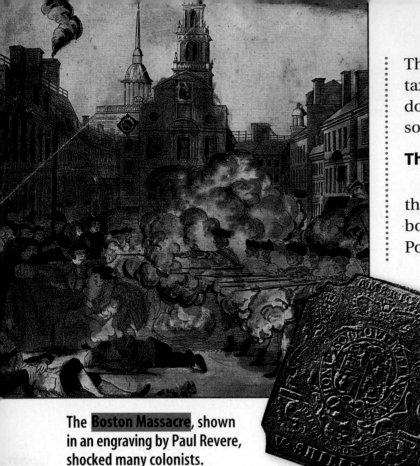

The **Boston Massacre**, shown in an engraving by Paul Revere, shocked many colonists.

UNREST INCREASES

In October 1765 delegates from nine colonies attended a Stamp Act Congress. They decided that Parliament, the British lawmaking body, could not tax the colonies without their consent. They demanded that the Stamp Act be repealed, or canceled. A year later, Great Britain repealed the Stamp Act.

Townshend Acts

Many members of the British government disliked giving in to the rebellious colonists. They also needed to raise money. In 1767 Charles Townshend (TOWN shund), the treasurer of the British government, called for new taxes. One of the Townshend Acts taxed tea, paper, glass, lead, and paint imported from Britain. Colonists in Boston held a town meeting to protest the new taxes.

They decided to **boycott**, or not buy, the taxed goods. Boycott means to refuse to do business or have contact with a person, group, or country.

The Daughters of Liberty

In 1767 women formed groups called the Daughters of Liberty to support the boycott against the Townshend Acts. Poet and playwright Mercy Otis Warren encouraged women to give up teas and other goods from Britain. "We'll quit the useless vanities [luxuries] of life," she wrote.

The Daughters of Liberty held "spinning bees" to spin thread so that they would not have to import clothes from Britain. Read more about boycotts in Exploring Economics on page 267.

The Boston Massacre

Unrest in Boston soon grew worse. The people of Boston grew angry when British troops entered the city in October 1768. This was the first time the British sent soldiers to control the colonists. Some colonists picked fights with the British. Young boys threw snowballs at soldiers and called them "lobsters" because of their red uniforms.

On March 6, 1770, church bells rang as a large group of colonists met outside the Customs House. **Crispus Attucks**, a former slave, yelled to the crowd, "The way to get rid of these soldiers is to attack the main guard." In the confusion that followed, the British soldiers fired. Five men were killed, including Attucks.

The people of Boston were horrified at the killings. Many people spread news of the **Boston Massacre** to turn public opinion against the British.

Boston Forms a Committee

In October 1772 Samuel Adams asked the members of a Boston town meeting to form a committee "to state the rights of the colonists." The committee was soon formed. By 1774 all of the colonies except Pennsylvania had formed Committees of Correspondence. The committees of each colony wrote to each other to inform colonists about important political events in the colonies.

Read the excerpt from *The Rights of the Colonists.*

Primary Source:

excerpt from
The Rights of the Colonists
— The Report of the Committee of Correspondence to the Boston Town Meeting, November 20, 1772

Among the natural rights of the Colonists are these: First, a right to life; Secondly, to liberty; Thirdly, to property; together with the right to support and defend them in the best manner they can.

All men have a right . . . in case of **intolerable oppression,** *civil or religious, to leave the society they belong to, and enter into another.*

What rights did the committee believe the colonists had?

intolerable: unbearable
oppression: to control by cruel and unjust means

The Tea Act

Great Britain repealed the Townshend Acts but kept a tax on tea. They thought that if they lowered its price below the price of smuggled tea, the colonists would buy it. In 1773 ships carrying thousands of pounds of tea sailed across the Atlantic Ocean to Boston and other colonial ports.

In early December, Abigail Adams, wife of John Adams, reported that the colonists were preparing a protest: "The flame is kindled [lit] and like Lightning it catches from Soul to Soul."

On December 16, 1773, a group of colonists disguised as Mohawks crept toward Boston Harbor. "Boston will be a teapot tonight!" they shouted. They then boarded a ship and dumped 342 chests of valuable tea into the harbor.

When King George III learned of the "tea party" he demanded that the colonists of Boston be punished. Parliament decided to close the port of Boston until the colonists paid for the tea. Town meetings were banned. Colonists called Parliament's actions the Intolerable Acts.

READING CHECK **What was the main purpose of the Sons of Liberty?**

Colonial teapot with a protest to the Stamp Act

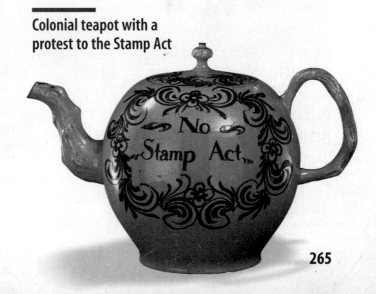

THE FIRST CONTINENTAL CONGRESS

On September 5, 1774, delegates from every colony except Georgia met at Carpenter's Hall in Philadelphia. This was the First Continental Congress. The delegates discussed how they would respond to the Intolerable Acts. They decided to send a petition to King George III asking for the repeal of the acts. A petition is a written request signed by many people.

To fight the Intolerable Acts, the delegates agreed to stop trade with Britain. Fearing that they would have to defend their liberty in battle, the Congress also asked the colonists to gather **minutemen** to defend the cities. Minutemen had to be ready for battle at a minute's notice.

By 1775 able-bodied men in every colonial town had to join the **militia**. A colonial militia was a military force made up of volunteers. Most militia members were farmers, craftworkers, business owners, and wealthy men. At first some militias allowed both free and enslaved African Americans to join. Later most colonial militias refused to accept any African Americans.

The First Continental Congress also decided that if the British did not change its policies at the end of one year it would stop all exports to Britain. They also agreed to meet in May 1775 if Britain refused their demands.

READING CHECK ✓ **What did the First Continental Congress do to fight the Intolerable Acts?**

Carpenter's Hall in Philadelphia, where the First Continental Congress met, has more than 150,000 visitors each year.

PUTTING IT TOGETHER

The Sugar Act of 1764 was the first of several laws that took away the rights of the colonists as Englishmen. These included the right to be considered innocent until proven guilty and the right of trial by jury.

Members of the Committees of Correspondence found that by writing and organizing they could make Britain repeal some of its laws. In this way they would move the colonies closer to liberty.

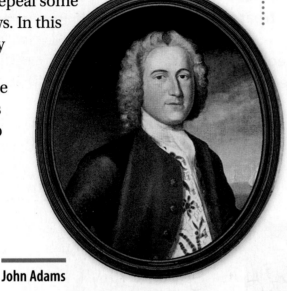

John Adams

ECONOMICS

The Power of Boycotts

The Daughters of Liberty were successful in their boycott of British imports. British merchants, hurt by the boycott, convinced the government to repeal the Townshend Acts.

Today boycotts are a powerful way to force a company to change its policies. If consumers refuse to buy a company's product or service, the company will not make a profit. This will force the company to either change its policy or go out of business.

Activity

Think of a product or service you use every day. Then write an essay explaining how you would replace that product or service if it were boycotted.

Review and Assess

1. Write one sentence for each of the vocabulary terms.

   boycott   militia   Stamp Act

2. Why did many colonists oppose the Stamp Act?

3. What acts of the British Parliament caused the colonists to rebel?

4. How did the British **government** respond to the Boston Tea Party?

5. What **effects** did the Committees of Correspondence have? Explain your answer.

Make a chart of the laws that were passed by Parliament between 1763 and 1774. Next to each law list the rights the colonists had as English that were ignored.

Suppose you were a member of the Massachusetts Committee of Correspondence. **Write** a letter describing the Boston Tea Party and the Intolerable Acts.

Reading Political Cartoons

Have you ever drawn a picture to express how you feel about someone or some event? That is what a **political cartoon** does. A political cartoon is a drawing that expresses a cartoonist's opinion about people, political events, or newsworthy issues. Political cartoons deal with very serious issues. Yet cartoonists often treat these issues in a humorous way.

Political cartoons are one way that people in the 13 colonies expressed their opinions. These were printed in newspapers and pamphlets.

VOCABULARY
political cartoon
symbol

The horse AMERICA throwing his Master

LEARN THE SKILL

Look at the cartoon on this page as you follow these steps.

1. Identify symbols.
Political cartoons often contain **symbols** that help get their message across to readers. A symbol is something that stands for something else. You know, for example, that the 50 stars of the United States flag stand for the 50 states.

Symbols can be hard to understand, especially in cartoons from the past. The British cartoon above, published in 1779, is predicting the outcome of the Revolutionary War. The kicking horse is a symbol for the 13 colonies. Notice the rider, Great Britain, is shown as backwards. The riding crop Great Britain is carrying has various weapons of war at the end and is a symbol for the war. The man to the right is carrying a French flag and represents France, an ally of the colonies in the war.

2. Look for other clues.

Some cartoonists use captions or labels or a title. The title of the cartoon on page 268 is, "The horse AMERICA throwing his Master." Other cartoonists use dialogue (DI uh lahg) in order to express their opinions in words. Dialogue is conversation. The cartoon does not have any dialogue. If there is dialogue, try to figure out who is speaking.

TRY THE SKILL

Look at the cartoon below. It was drawn in 2001.

1. What is this cartoon about?

2. Who is speaking in this cartoon?

3. What point is this cartoonist trying to make?

4. Is this cartoonist finding fault with or praising something?

EXTEND THE SKILL

Reading political cartoons can help you learn about important issues of today, both in your city and country. Political cartoons give readers something to think about, or sometimes something to laugh about.

Create your own political cartoon. The subject matter can be your school or town, or can be about something happening in a far-away country.

- What is the subject matter of your political cartoon?

- Did you use any symbols?

- What feeling is your cartoon expressing?

- How do political cartoons help you understand issues important to you or your community?

The Revolution Begins

Find Out! *What were the first battles of the American Revolution?*

Lesson Outline
- First Battle of the American Revolution
- The Conflict Spreads
- Patriots and Loyalists

VOCABULARY

Loyalists
Patriots

PEOPLE

John Hancock
Thomas Gage
Paul Revere
William Dawes
John Parker
Ethan Allen
Benedict Arnold

READING STRATEGY

Use a word map like the one below. Write "American Revolution" in the center and names, places, and terms linked with the war in the outer circles.

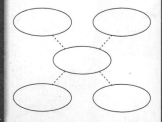

BUILD BACKGROUND

The actions of the colonists angered George III, the King of England. However, he was sure he could make the rebels obey. Soon colonists heard the rumor that the British were going to arrest Sam Adams and John Hancock, a leading Boston supporter of liberty. Next the British would march to Concord to capture weapons the militia had stored there. The militias near Lexington were given orders "to be ready at the beat of the drum."

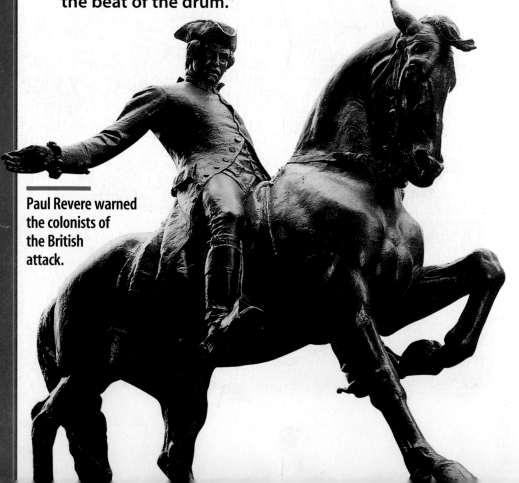

Paul Revere warned the colonists of the British attack.

FIRST BATTLE OF THE AMERICAN REVOLUTION

In February 1775 Parliament declared that the Massachusetts colonists were in rebellion. General **Thomas Gage**, commander of British forces in North America, decided to take the arms and gunpowder in Concord. On the night of April 18, about 700 British soldiers left Boston.

Paul Revere's Ride

A silversmith named **Paul Revere** learned that the British were headed for Concord. He rode to Lexington to warn Adams and Hancock. Revere's friend **William Dawes**, a shoemaker, joined him on the way. Their routes are shown on the map below. A doctor named Samuel Prescott soon joined them.

Revere's ride alerted the minutemen, who galloped from Lexington. The militia captain, **John Parker**, assembled about 70 men on the Lexington common. "Stand your ground!" he ordered. "Don't fire unless fired upon, but if they mean to have war, let it begin here." No one knows who fired the first shot, but as the British advanced, someone fired. In the battle that followed, eight militia were killed and ten wounded.

READING CHECK Why did General Gage decide to go to Concord?

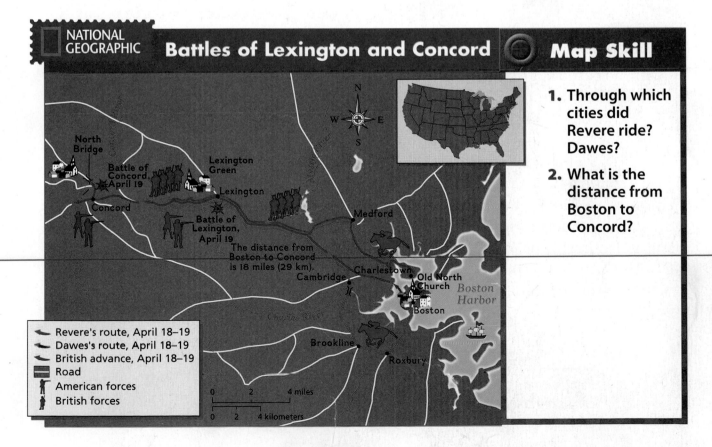

NATIONAL GEOGRAPHIC **Battles of Lexington and Concord** **Map Skill**

North Bridge
Battle of Concord, April 19
Concord
Lexington Green
Lexington
Battle of Lexington, April 19
The distance from Boston to Concord is 18 miles (29 km).
Medford
Charlestown
Cambridge
Old North Church
Boston
Boston Harbor
Brookline
Roxbury

Revere's route, April 18–19
Dawes's route, April 18–19
British advance, April 18–19
Road
American forces
British forces

0   2   4 miles
0   2   4 kilometers

1. Through which cities did Revere ride? Dawes?

2. What is the distance from Boston to Concord?

Muskets

The **Militiaman's Fowler**, used by the colonists, was usually made out of parts from older, worn-out weapons. The musket was a firearm that was used before the invention of the rifle. They were six or seven feet long, and weighed up to 40 pounds. They worked very simply. The trigger created a spark that lit gunpowder which exploded, forcing the bullet out of the gun.

Muskets often could not hit a target at more than 100 yards. Their bullets had no spiral so they left the gun more like a shot-put than a football. Because muskets need a spark to fire, they often didn't work at all in the rain.

Why was it difficult for a musket to hit targets far away? In what situations did muskets not work at all?

Concord Museum

Knowing that they were badly outnumbered, the 250 militiamen waited for reinforcements from nearby towns. After a brief clash between a group of Redcoats and minutemen at North Bridge, the British began to return to Boston. By now the countryside was swarming with angry colonists. Minutemen shot musket balls at the British from behind trees and stone fences. "Heavy fire from all sides," reported one British officer, "from walls, fences, houses, trees, and barns." More than 90 British soldiers were killed and 174 wounded. Read more about muskets in Exploring Technology to the left.

Patrick Henry

On March 23, 1775, Patrick Henry argued before the members of the Virginia House of Burgesses that the British troops were in Boston to take away the

THE CONFLICT SPREADS

After the battle at Lexington, the British then marched five miles to Concord. There, they searched for arms and gunpowder. The women of Concord kept the soldiers from finding most of the weapons. They had hidden them under straw in barns and in freshly plowed fields. The British only managed to destroy a cannon and a small amount of ammunition.

Patrick Henry's speech convinced colonists to organize a militia.

colonists' rights. "Gentlemen may cry peace, peace!" he said. "But there is no peace. The war is actually begun!" His voice rising, Patrick Henry said:

> Is life so dear, or peace so sweet, as to be purchased at the price of chains and slavery? Forbid it, almighty God! I know not what course others may take; but as for me, give me liberty or give me death.

Patrick Henry's speech inspired colonists to break with Great Britain. As a result, the House of Burgesses voted to organize a militia.

The militia captured cannons like this one at Fort Ticonderoga.

Fort Ticonderoga Falls

While minutemen took positions around Boston, a militia leader from Vermont named Ethan Allen and a New Englander named Benedict Arnold decided to try and take Fort Ticonderoga. This fort on Lake Champlain was a main supply post for the British army. Allen led a group called the Green Mountain Boys. They were mostly farmers and included both blacks and whites.

Near dawn on May 10, 1775, the Green Mountain Boys crept past soldiers on duty at the fort. Allen woke the commander and demanded his surrender. "Come out of there, you old rat," he shouted. Without any bloodshed, the Americans had captured British cannons and cut off British support from Canada.

Battle of Bunker Hill

Some 1,200 militia around Boston were sent across the bay to Charlestown in June. The colonists knew that whoever controlled the hills around Charlestown would be able to fire cannons on Boston.

During the night the colonists quickly dug out a rough fort near Breed's Hill. At dawn a British ship in the harbor began to fire its cannons at the tired men.

After noon British troops marched on the fort. To conserve ammunition, a militia officer ordered, "Don't fire till you see the whites of their eyes." No one knows whether it was Colonel William Prescott or General Israel Putnam. The colonists bravely fought off two charges before they ran out of ammunition. A third charge forced them to retreat to nearby Bunker Hill. The British commander Colonel Pitcairn leaped upon a wall of the fort to claim victory. Peter Salem, a former slave, killed him with a single shot.

This conflict was later called the Battle of Bunker Hill. The British "victory" cost the lives of more than 1,000 British soldiers and 400 colonists.

Why did the House of Burgesses want a militia?

After the Battle of Bunker Hill (shown above) many colonists had to decide whether to be **Patriot** or **Loyalist**.

PATRIOTS AND LOYALISTS

Benjamin Franklin, who you read about in Chapter 7, had hoped that Britain and the colonies would make peace. However, after the Battle of Bunker Hill, Franklin wrote to a friend who was a member of Parliament, "You have begun to burn our towns, and murder our people. Look upon your Hands! They are stained with the blood of your Relations! You and I were long Friends: You are now my Enemy, and I am, Yours."

Choosing Sides

Not all Americans were ready to completely break from Britain in 1775. Most colonists spoke English, shared English customs and laws, and had relatives in Britain. The British were the colonists' major trading partner. British ships protected colonial trade routes.

About one out of three of the colonists were **Loyalists**. Loyalists were people who remained loyal to Britain. Another third supported the fight for independence. These Americans were known as **Patriots**. The remaining one-third did not take sides. This group included many Quakers, who oppose all wars.

Loyalists, like the Patriots, were against many British policies but favored peaceful forms of protest. They believed that independence would mean the loss of economic benefits of trade with Britain. Some Loyalists believed the Patriots were bringing about change for their own personal gain.

King George III did not think much of the colonists' will to fight. He continued to think that once the colonists "have felt a small blow, they will submit." But by 1776 more and more colonists wanted to declare independence.

 **Why were Loyalists against independence from Britain? How do you know?**

PUTTING IT TOGETHER

In the First Continental Congress the colonists gained experience in forming a government for a new country. In the first battles between colonists and British troops, the colonial militias learned some of the skills they would need in the American Revolution.

Some colonists still hoped the British would repeal the Intolerable Acts and restore peace. However, after the Battle of Bunker Hill, many colonists joined the Patriot side. Colonial unity and military readiness were the beginning of a new country— a country separate from Britain.

Colonial soldiers carried a flask, spoon, and a plate for meals, and a lantern (left) for sending messages.

Review and Assess

1. Write one sentence for each vocabulary word.

   Loyalists   Patriots

2. Why was the capture of Fort Ticonderoga important?

3. What happened at the battles of Lexington and Concord?

4. What did the Virginia House of Burgesses do after hearing Patrick Henry's speech?

5. List in **sequence** the events leading to the first shot in Lexington, or the "shot heard round the world."

Activities

Look at the map on page 271. Starting with Revere's ride, draw a time line that shows the events of the battles of Lexington and Concord.

Write a short speech to the House of Burgesses that would inspire the members to take action. Be sure to include supporting details in your verbal communication.

275

The Declaration of Independence

find out!

What was the purpose of the Declaration of Independence?

VOCABULARY

Continental army
traitor
Declaration of Independence

PEOPLE

Thomas Jefferson
Henry Knox
William Howe
Thomas Paine

READING STRATEGY

Using a main idea chart like the one below, list the supporting details behind the Principles of the Declaration.

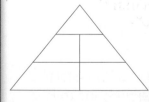

Lesson Outline
• War Draws Near
• Declaration of Independence
• Principles of the Declaration
• Birth of a Nation

BUILD BACKGROUND

In May 1775, the Second Continental Congress met in Philadelphia. They had to decide what to do after the battles of Lexington and Concord. The delegates did not agree on what path to take. They did agree they had to take steps to protect the colonies. John Adams suggested that the Congress form a "Grand American army," with troops from every colony.

You Are Here
1775 – 1776

WAR DRAWS NEAR

In June 1775, John Adams nominated George Washington to be commander in chief of the new Continental army. He praised Washington as "a gentleman whose skill as an officer . . . would command the respect of America."

The Second Continental Congress also formed a post office so that all the colonies could share news. The Congress also began to ask European countries for their support.

Olive Branch Petition

"The war is now heartily entered into," wrote Thomas Jefferson of Virginia, a delegate to the Congress. Many agreed with him, including John Hancock. Hancock, a new delegate from Massachusetts, was serving as president of the Congress.

In July 1775 the Congress tried one last time to make peace with Britain. The delegates sent what they called the "Olive Branch Petition" to King George. The olive branch is a symbol of peace. The petition stated that Americans were loyal to Britain. In addition, it asked the king to repeal the Intolerable Acts and end the fighting. King George refused to even read the petition from what he called an "illegal congress." He threatened to "bring the traitors to justice." A traitor is someone who turns against his or her country.

Ticonderoga Museum

Washington Retakes Boston

Washington began to make plans to drive the British from Boston. He sent Henry Knox, a former bookseller, to Fort Ticonderoga. Knox and his men dragged cannons from the New York fort more than 250 miles over frozen rivers and snowy hills to Boston. When the British, led by British General William Howe awoke on March 5, 1776, they saw the cannons aimed at them. Washington told his brother that the British soldiers and Loyalists fled "in a shameful and precipitate [hurried] manner." The colonists took Boston.

The paintings "Spirit of '76" (left) and of the cannon being dragged from Fort Ticonderoga (above) show the determination of the Patriots to win independence.

READING CHECK

Identify three accomplishments of the Second Continental Congress.

DECLARATION OF INDEPENDENCE

In January 1776 <mark>Thomas Paine</mark>, an Englishman who had settled in Pennsylvania, published a pamphlet called *Common Sense*. In it Paine argued that the colonists owed no loyalty to an unjust ruler. Paine used language most people could easily understand. In three months, more than 100,000 copies of his pamphlet were sold. "I find *Common Sense* is working a powerful change in the minds of many," said George Washington.

In June 1776 Richard Henry Lee of Virginia proposed "that these united colonies are, and of right ought to be, free and independent states." Many colonists agreed. The Second Continental Congress named a committee to write a statement of independence.

The committee asked John Adams, Benjamin Franklin, Thomas Jefferson, Roger Sherman, and Robert Livingston to prepare a <mark>Declaration of Independence</mark>. Adams convinced Jefferson to write it. "You can write ten times better than I can," Adams argued. Jefferson was only 33 years old at the time.

Jefferson was well prepared when he sat down to write the Declaration. As a law student at the College of William and Mary in Virginia he had heard Patrick Henry speak against the Stamp Act. He had also read Thomas Paine's *Common Sense* and studied the ideas of John Locke. Locke believed that all people are born with certain rights, including life, liberty, and the right to own property. It was the responsibility of government to protect these rights.

Jefferson wrote the Declaration in two weeks, then showed it to Franklin and John Adams. They made a few changes,

1 April 19, 1775: First battles of Revolution at Lexington and Concord.

6 July 2, 1776: Debate on the Declaration of Independence begins.

7 July 4, 1776: The Declaration is approved.

8 July 8, 1776: The Declaration is read to a large crowd.

Steps to the Declaration of Independence

but agreed the Declaration was ready to be shown to the Congress. Jefferson wrote in clear, simple English. He wanted "to place before mankind the common sense of the subject, in terms so plain and firm as to command their assent [consent] . . . it was intended to be an expression of the American mind . . . ."

The Debate

On a hot July day the Congress began debating the content of the Declaration. For three days Jefferson sat silently listening to the delegates as they made changes in his work. Adams defended the Declaration. Franklin whispered reassuring words to Jefferson.

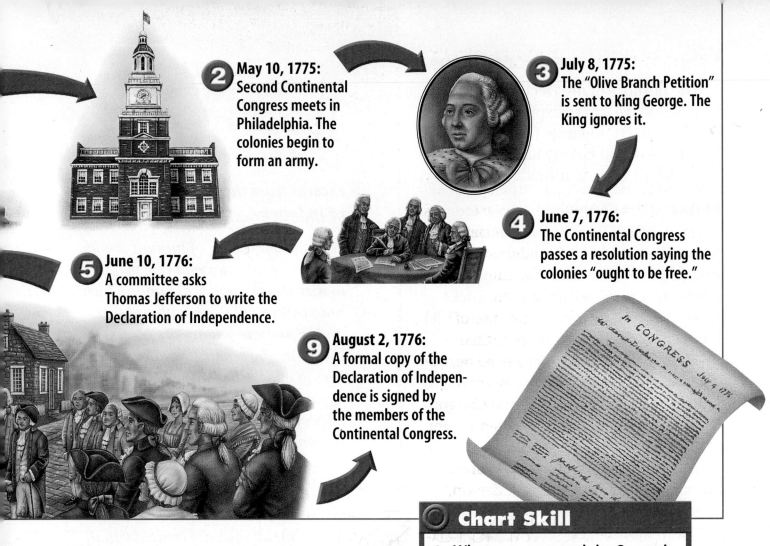

2 May 10, 1775:
Second Continental Congress meets in Philadelphia. The colonies begin to form an army.

3 July 8, 1775:
The "Olive Branch Petition" is sent to King George. The King ignores it.

4 June 7, 1776:
The Continental Congress passes a resolution saying the colonies "ought to be free."

5 June 10, 1776:
A committee asks Thomas Jefferson to write the Declaration of Independence.

9 August 2, 1776:
A formal copy of the Declaration of Independence is signed by the members of the Continental Congress.

Chart Skill

1. **What event caused the Second Continental Congress to meet?**

2. **What happened on July 2, 1776? Why was it important?**

The delegates made some of Jefferson's attacks against King George and Parliament less angry. Some of the colonies were against describing slavery as a "cruel war against human nature." Congress then took these words out of the document. After the Declaration was approved, Richard Henry Lee told Jefferson that although the delegates had changed some of what he wrote, "the [Declaration] in its nature is so good that no cookery can spoil the dish."

Signing the Declaration

On July 4, 1776, the Continental Congress approved the Declaration of Independence. John Hancock was the first to sign it. He wrote his name in large letters, "so the king doesn't have to put on his glasses," he is supposed to have said. Today a person's signature is sometimes called a "John Hancock."

Signing the document took courage. Each man who signed it knew that Britain would now consider him a traitor. "We must all hang together," Benjamin Franklin half-joked, "or [else] we shall all hang separately." Today the original copy of the Declaration is in the National Archives Building in Washington, D.C.

READING CHECK **Why was the Declaration of Independence created?**

PRINCIPLES OF THE DECLARATION

The purpose of the Declaration of Independence was to explain why the colonies had to separate from Great Britain. No other colony had ever before done this in writing. It was a bold step.

Rights of the People

After explaining why the Declaration was written, Jefferson listed the rights that all people should have. They were the same as those given by John Locke. Instead of the "right to own property," Jefferson wrote "the pursuit of happiness."

The second truth is that people establish governments in order to "secure [protect] these rights." The governments get their power, or authority, from "the consent of the governed," or all of the people.

Jefferson then listed the colonists' complaints against King George. The King had, for example, forbidden the colonial assemblies to meet, kept soldiers in the colonies without colonial consent, deprived colonists of the right of trial by jury, and taxed the colonies without their consent.

To conclude, Jefferson echoed the words of Richard Henry Lee. It was time, he argued, for the colonists to declare "that these United Colonies are, and of Right ought to be, Free and Independent States."

The following excerpt is from the beginning of the Declaration of Independence.

READING CHECK

What were some of the complaints Jefferson listed? How do you know?

Primary Source:

excerpt from the Declaration of Independence, 1776

*When in the course of human events, it becomes necessary for one people to **dissolve** the political bands which have connected them with another, and to **assume** among the powers of the earth, the separate and equal station to which the Laws of Nature and of Nature's God **entitle** them, a decent respect to the opinions of mankind requires that they should declare the causes which **impel** them to the separation.*

*We hold these truths to be self-evident, that all men are created equal, that they are **endowed** by their Creator with certain **unalienable** Rights, that among these are Life, Liberty, and the pursuit of Happiness.*

According to the Declaration of Independence, why did the colonies seek independence?

dissolve: to bring to an end
assume: take on
entitle: have as a right
impel: inspire
endowed: given
unalienable: cannot be taken away

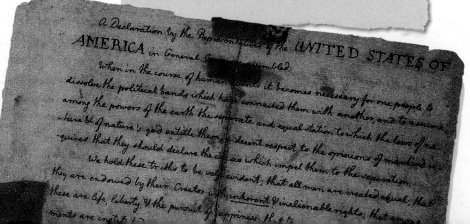

BIOGRAPHY

Focus On: **Responsibility**

THOMAS JEFFERSON held many offices, including that of President of the United States. Today he is also remembered for the way in which he carried out his responsibility to write a Declaration of Independence from England. He also helped create the government that the United States has today.

Thomas Jefferson was born in Virginia on April 13, 1743. He practiced law and became a member of the Continental Congress in 1775. A firm believer in protecting the basic rights of people, he said: "A Bill of Rights is what the people are entitled to against every government on Earth . . . . "

After he left the Presidency in 1809, Jefferson retired to Virginia where he became an inventor and followed interests, such as architecture and natural history. He died on July 4, 1826, on the 50th anniversary of the signing of the Declaration of Independence.

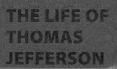 **Think about a leader of today who showed responsibility. Then write a paragraph comparing this person's actions to those of Jefferson.**

THE LIFE OF THOMAS JEFFERSON	1772 Jefferson marries Martha Wayles Skelton	1779 Jefferson is elected Governor of Virginia	1784 Jefferson becomes Minister to France	1801 Jefferson is elected third President of the United States

1770	1780	1790	1800	1810

LIFE AROUND THE WORLD	1774 Louis XVI becomes King of France	1791 Mozart's opera *The Magic Flute* opens in Vienna, Austria	1804 Napoleon crowns himself Emperor of France	

BIRTH OF A NATION

The purpose of the Declaration of Independence was to explain to the world why the colonies had to separate from Great Britain. The colonies had taken a bold step. No other colony had declared independence from its ruling country in writing before. As one President said many years later, the Declaration gave "hope to the world, for all future time."

After the Declaration was approved, copies were sent immediately to the Continental army and to cities and towns throughout the colonies. Bells rang, cannons roared, and colonists cheered when the Declaration was read. Today we celebrate Independence Day, July 4, as the birth of our nation. Abigail Adams wrote to her husband John about the celebration that was held in Boston in 1776:

> *After dinner the King's [coat of] Arms were taken down from the State House and every [symbol] of him from every place in which it appeared [was] burnt ... Thus ends royal Authority in this State.*

What did colonists end by approving the Declaration of Independence?

The reading of the Declaration of Independence drew large crowds in Philadelphia.

HISTORY MYSTERY

Why is our flag red, white, and blue?

In 1776, the Continental Congress decided the United States needed its own flag with 13 stars and 13 stripes for the 13 colonies.

The flag was red, white, and blue, but the First Continental Congress never explained why those colors were chosen. In 1782, Congress declared that the color red stands for bravery, white for purity, and blue for justice. However, this referred to the Great Seal of the United States, not the flag.

What else might the colors have stood for?

PUTTING IT TOGETHER

The Declaration of Independence was one of the most important documents in human history. It was the first to set out the rights and responsibilities of people in a democracy. Although in 1776 only white male property owners were allowed to vote, over time the phrase "all men are created equal" has been expanded to include all people.

People of other countries have also looked to the Declaration of Independence to help them express their desire for self-government and freedom. Over the years peoples of Europe, Asia, Africa, Central America, and South America have used it as a model for their own statements of independence.

Review and Assess

1. Write one sentence for each vocabulary term.

   Continental army   traitor

2. What was the United States army originally known as?

3. What was Thomas Jefferson's purpose in writing the Declaration of Independence?

4. What act did the Second Continental Congress make in 1775? In 1776?

5. Read the excerpt from the Declaration of Independence on page 280. Whose **point of view** does this document represent?

Activities

Use the Atlas map on pages R16–R17 to locate Fort Ticonderoga by using latitude and longitude. The approximate latitude and longitude of Fort Ticonderoga is 45°N and 74°W. Then use the scale of miles/kilometers to measure the distance between Fort Ticonderoga and Boston.

Write a pamphlet like *Common Sense* on a subject you would like to inspire others about.

VOCABULARY REVIEW

Number a sheet of paper from 1 to 5. Beside each number write the word or term from the list below that matches the description.

boycott	Stamp Act
Loyalists	traitor
Patriots	

1. Someone who turns against his or her country
2. People who supported the fight for independence
3. To refuse to do business or have contact with a person, group, or country
4. People who were loyal to Britain
5. Something that required colonists to pay a tax every time they bought a newspaper or pamphlet or signed a legal document

CHAPTER COMPREHENSION

6. Describe the role Samuel Adams played during the conflict between Britain and the English colonies.
7. What were the Townshend Acts?
8. Why did the colonists object to the new British taxes?
9. What was unusual about the capture of Fort Ticonderoga?
10. What did the Battle of Bunker Hill accomplish?
11. Why was *Common Sense* important to the cause of independence?
12. What was the purpose of the Declaration of Independence?
13. **Write** a dialogue in which a Loyalist and a Patriot discuss their opinions about the American Revolution.

SKILL REVIEW

14. **Study Skill** What is a political cartoon?
15. **Study Skill** What symbols does the cartoonist use in the cartoon above? What do they mean?
16. **Study Skill** What is the caption of the cartoon? How does this help you to understand the drawing?
17. **Study Skill** How do you think this cartoon might have influenced a colonial reader?
18. **Study Skill** Do political cartoons express feelings?

USING A TIME LINE

1766	1767	1768	1769	1770	1771	1772	1773	1774	1775

1765
Stamp Act
is passed

1767
Townshend
Acts

1769
Thomas Jefferson
is elected to
Virginia House
of Burgesses

1770
Boston
Massacre

1773
Boston
Tea Party

1774
Intolerable
Acts; First
Continental
Congress
meets

1776
Thomas Paine
publishes
*Common
Sense;*
Declaration of
Independence
is written

19. Study the dates for the Boston Tea Party and the Intolerable Acts. Which was a cause of the other? Which was an effect?

20. How many years passed between Thomas Jefferson getting elected to the Virginia House of Burgesses and his drafting the Declaration of Independence?

Writing **About Independence** Suppose you were from a small colony that had just gained independence from a larger country. A neighboring colony is considering asking for their independence too. Would you recommend they follow your example? If not, why? If so, how would you explain the benefits of being an independent nation?

Foldables

Use your Foldable to review what you have learned about the colonists and their fight for independence. As you look at the first three sections of your Foldable time line, mentally recall the events that led up to the revolution and the drafting of the Declaration of Independence. Review your time line notes to check your memory and responses. Look at the blank time line section, and use what you know and what you have learned to predict what you will study in Chapter 10.

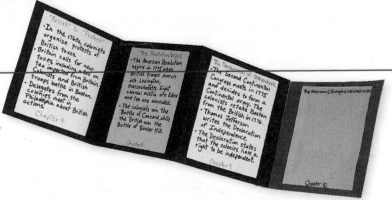

THE Big IDEAS ABOUT...

The American Revolution

After the signing of the Declaration of Independence, the British colonists fought to win independence from Great Britain. Both sides thought the war would end quickly. In the winter of 1776, the Patriots were already losing hope. However, the war went on for eight years. In addition, the Patriots were able to win the friendship of France and Spain. Read on to find out about events in the colonies during the Revolutionary War and how the war was finally won.

THE CONTINENTAL ARMY

The leadership of George Washington is one of the most important advantages that the Patriots have over the Redcoats.

TURNING POINTS

Many battles are fought in the first three years of the war. The Patriots win important victories in Trenton and Saratoga, but Philadelphia is lost.

INDEPENDENCE IS WON

The Battle of Yorktown is the last major battle of the Revolutionary War. The British surrender to George Washington on October 19, 1781. The colonists win.

Foldables

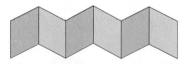

Use the Foldable time line you made in Chapter 9 to record what you learn about "The American Revolution."

1. Write the titles of the three lessons of this chapter, in order, on the three remaining sections of the Chapter 9 time line.

2. Draw six key events that occurred during the American Revolution, in order of their occurrence, on the back of your time line.

3. Write a caption for each illustration.

287

American Strengths and Weaknesses

How did the Continental army differ from the British army?

Lesson Outline
- **Redcoats and Continentals**
- **Washington Leads the Army**
- **African American Soldiers and Patriot Spies**

VOCABULARY

mercenary

surveyor

PEOPLE

Martha Washington

Mary Ludwig Hays

Margaret Corbin

Ester DeBerdt Reed

READING STRATEGY

Create a two-columned chart like the one below. In the first column, list the names of people or groups who helped the Patriots. In the second column, explain how they helped.

BUILD BACKGROUND

The Americans and British both expected the war to end quickly. Instead it took eight years. During that time, the Continental army suffered great hardships. People's lives changed. Merchants, farmers, and craftworkers left their families to join the army. Women kept farms and businesses running. Some colonists joined the army as cooks and servants. Others raised money, sewed clothes for the soldiers, and nursed the wounded. This quiet work often made the difference between victory and defeat.

George Washington (right). Today people wear Patriot uniforms (above, right) to reenact Revolutionary War battles.

REDCOATS AND CONTINENTALS

In 1776, Great Britain had the most powerful navy in the world. They also had well trained and highly disciplined soldiers. In August 1776, the British captured Long Island near New York City. They did it because they had the money to hire German **mercenaries**. A mercenary is a soldier paid to fight for another country. These mercenaries were called Hessians because they came from the German state of Hesse-Kassel.

The British did have some disadvantages. First, the war was not popular in Great Britain. Many of the people in Britain didn't want to pay the taxes needed to fight the war. Second, it was slow and costly for Britain to fight a war thousands of miles away across the Atlantic Ocean.

The Patriots

In contrast to the British army, the colonies entered the war without an army or a navy. Getting men to serve in the newly formed Continental army was difficult. Most colonists preferred to be volunteers in the local militias. Keeping soldiers was also a problem. Many quit the army because they often went without pay, food, uniforms, and weapons.

The American army, however, had some strengths. The Continental soldiers were defending their homes, which gave them the will to keep on fighting. Unlike the British who were new to the colonies, the Americans knew the land. They used this knowledge for planning attacks.

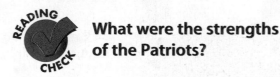 **What were the strengths of the Patriots?**

WASHINGTON LEADS THE ARMY

Another advantage the Patriots had was the strong leadership of George Washington. During the French and Indian War, Washington had been commander of the Virginia militia. Now he faced a much greater responsibility. He was in charge of getting an untrained army ready to fight against a major world power.

Washington's Early Years

In 1732, George Washington was born in Westmoreland County, Virginia. His parents were not among Virginia's wealthiest, but they were landowners. Washington was good at mathematics, but never went to college.

At the age of 16, Washington landed his first job, as a surveyor. A **surveyor** is a person who measures land. In the middle of the 1700s many colonists were moving west and needed his services. His work paid well, and he was able to buy land.

The young Washington joined the Virginia militia in 1752. He hoped a military career would bring him honor. When he learned that soldiers from the colonies were paid less to fight for the British than soldiers in the regular British army, he became angry. Then, during the French and Indian War, the British lowered Colonel Washington's rank because they did not want colonists to rise above captain. Washington left the militia in protest. He later returned when the governor of Virginia restored his original rank.

Mount Vernon
Potomac River
Office
Stables
Kitchen
Bowling Green
Workshops, Storage, Spinning House, and Icehouse
Gardens

Diagram Skill

1. Where on the house is the cupola located?

2. Which area was located farthest from the house?

Mount Vernon (From the Rear)

Cupola
Mrs. Washington's Bedroom
General Washington's Bedroom
Parlor
Dining Room

While still in the military, Washington was elected to the House of Burgesses in 1758. There he met Thomas Jefferson and Patrick Henry, and later joined colonial protests against the British.

In 1759, Washington retired from military life to manage his land. By then, he had become the most famous American in the military. That same year, he married a wealthy widow named Martha Custis. George and Martha Washington moved to Mount Vernon, the plantation he owned on the Potomac River in Virginia. Martha Washington supported the Patriots. During the American Revolution, she helped her husband with his paperwork. She also sewed socks and cooked soup for the soldiers.

Support for the Soldiers

Fortunately, there were many Americans who helped the Continental army. Many women supported their husbands in battles and some even fought when their husbands were wounded or killed. Mary Ludwig Hays carried water for the soldiers in the battle of Monmouth, earning her the nickname Molly Pitcher. Upon the death of her husband in the attack on Fort Washington, Margaret Corbin took over his cannon and fought the British until she was wounded. Some

women, like Deborah Sampson, disguised themselves as men and fought as soldiers. Ester DeBerdt Reed formed a committee to go door-to-door asking women to contribute money for the soldiers. Eventually her committee became the Ladies Association, the first women's organization in North America.

READING CHECK How did women help the Continental army?

George and Martha Washington are shown above. Molly Pitcher helps at the Battle of Monmouth, New Jersey (below).

AFRICAN AMERICAN SOLDIERS AND PATRIOT SPIES

In 1775, the Americans debated whether to allow enslaved men to be soldiers. Many were afraid that enslaved African Americans might rebel if given guns. Washington agreed not to allow any more African Americans to join the army. He himself owned slaves, which his wife's family had given him. In 1776, however, Washington changed his mind. Britain had won the support of many enslaved people by promising them their freedom.

How could the colonies continue to enslave African Americans when they were willing to fight and die for the freedom of all Americans? Some states began to answer that question. In 1780, Pennsylvania adopted a plan for abolishing, or ending, slavery. Many northern states soon followed. In other states, such as Virginia, enslaved African Americans who fought with the Patriots were freed.

A Patriot Spy

Washington was very clever when it came to spying on the British. One London newspaper said, "Washington did not really outfight the British, he simply outspied us." Washington's spies used code numbers instead of names, sent coded messages, and risked death if caught.

One of the spy rings was called the Mulligan spy ring. The businessman Haym Salomon (HI am SAL uh mun) was a member when the British captured New York City. A Jew who had fled Poland after Russia's invasion, Salomon believed strongly in the cause of independence and freedom. He spoke several languages including German. Salomon spoke with German soldiers, urging them to leave the British army. He was caught by the British, but he escaped. Later Salomon raised

This painting by David Wagner shows the bravery of African American soldiers at the Battle of Rhode Island.

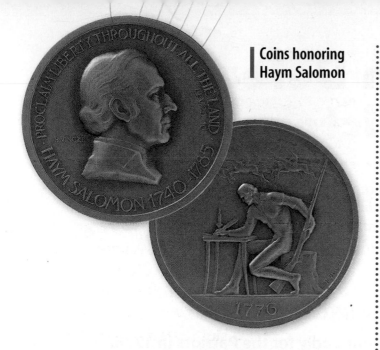

PUTTING IT TOGETHER

The colonies entered the Revolutionary War without an army or a navy. Soon George Washington took charge of the newly formed Continental army. His experience and leadership would prove valuable to the outcome of the war.

Although Washington first agreed not to allow African Americans to join the Continental army, in 1776 he changed his mind. This decision had great effects on how slavery was viewed. Although it would take over 85 more years before slavery would end in the United States, Washington's decision was a small step in the fight against slavery. One of the plantation owners who freed his slaves after the war ended was George Washington.

money for the Continental Army. Salomon gave so much of his own money to the Patriots he died penniless in 1785.

What did both the British and Patriots promise African Americans for their support in the war?

Review and Assess

1. Write a sentence using the vocabulary word.
   mercenary

2. What was George Washington's first job? What did it allow him to do?

3. What were the strengths and weaknesses of the British and American forces at the start of the Revolution?

4. What caused some states to consider ending slavery?

5. Why did Washington **decide** to leave the militia during the French and Indian War?

Look at the physical map of the United States on page R18-R19. Find the Potomac River. Then look at the United States map on page R16-R17. What city is located on the Potomac River?

Research George Washington's early years. Then **write** an essay on the traits he showed as a young man that would help him become a strong leader later in life.

From Defeat to Victory

What was the turning point of the American Revolution?

Lesson Outline
• Battle of Trenton
• Victory at Saratoga
• The Americans Gain

VOCABULARY

Treaty of Alliance

PEOPLE

Nathan Hale

John Burgoyne

Thaddeus Kosciuszko

Benedict Arnold

Marquis de Lafayette

Friedrich von Steuben

George Rogers Clark

John Paul Jones

READING STRATEGY

Using a cause and effect chart like the one below, write the causes of the battles described in the lesson and their outcomes.

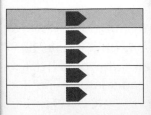

BUILD BACKGROUND

The war went badly for the Patriots in 1776. Nathan Hale was a 21-year-old Patriot spy in New York. He drew plans of troop positions but he was captured. As he walked to the gallows he said, "I only regret that I have but one life to lose for my country."

That winter, Washington and his small army stood between the British and Philadelphia. The winter winds chilled them to the bone. Food and ammunition were in short supply. "I think the game is pretty near up," the tired commander wrote.

BATTLE OF TRENTON

After British General William Howe won control of New York and New Jersey, he ordered his troops into winter quarters in Trenton, Princeton, and other New Jersey towns. Washington knew that the British would not fight again until the spring. Therefore, he planned a surprise attack. After nightfall on Christmas Day, December 25, 1776, Washington and his troops crossed the Delaware River into New Jersey. The next morning, they surprised the Hessians and took more than 900 prisoners. "This is a glorious day for our country," said Washington.

A week later, British troops advanced toward Trenton to retake it. However, during the night of January 2, 1777, Washington's troops silently marched past British forces. The next morning, they took Princeton in a brilliant victory over the Redcoats.

Washington now had control of almost all of New Jersey. He moved his troops to winter quarters near Morristown. There he began to rebuild his army. With the successes at Trenton and Princeton, Washington was hopeful of the future.

Philadelphia

By the spring of 1777, Washington had received weapons from France and rebuilt his army. Howe wanted to take the Patriots' capital, Philadelphia. Washington placed his troops between Philadelphia and Howe's forces when they were marching toward Chesapeake Bay. In a surprise move, the British army swung around the Continental army and attacked from behind. The Patriots had to retreat. The British took Philadelphia on September 26. The Continental Congress fled to York, Pennsylvania.

Why was Washington successful at the Battle of Trenton?

The Continental Army braved the cold at Valley Forge (left). Nathan Hale told the British that his country was worth dying for (above).

295

VICTORY AT SARATOGA

The British planned to cut New England and New York off from the rest of the colonies. British general **John Burgoyne** (bur GOYN) decided the best way to do this was to capture the Hudson River Valley.

Burgoyne's troops were stationed in Canada. Their march south toward Albany, New York, was not easy. Along the way, groups of Patriots attacked from the woods. Burgoyne's troops had to cut roads through thick forests and swamps. It took them all day to travel one mile.

Meanwhile the American forces near Albany began to prepare for the British. **Thaddeus Kosciuszko** (THA dee us kahs ee US koh), a Polish engineer serving with the Americans, had placed cannons on a high cliff overlooking the road to Albany. Local farmers, many with excellent shooting skills, came to the aid of the Continental army. They fortified an area approximately 40 miles north of Albany called **Freeman's Farm**. By the time Burgoyne reached **Saratoga**, New York, on September 19, 1777, the Americans greatly outnumbered the British. "American militia," the general wrote, "swarmed around . . . like birds of prey." The Patriots won what became known as the First Battle of Freeman's Farm.

Burgoyne did not retreat to Canada. On October 7, 1777, Burgoyne attacked again. This time a general named **Benedict Arnold** won the Second Battle of Freeman's Farm. Soon the British found themselves surrounded by Patriot

The Continental Army camped in New York in preparation for battle with the British.

forces. Burgoyne surrendered on October 17, 1777. Patriots took nearly 6,000 prisoners and a large supply of arms.

The victory at Saratoga was a turning point for the Patriots. It showed that Americans could defeat a large British force. It also convinced France to openly support the Americans by signing the Treaty of Alliance.

Marquis de Lafayette

The Marquis de Lafayette (mahr KEE de laf ee ET) was a wealthy French nobleman. His father had died fighting the British when Lafayette was a child.

In July 1777, when he was 19, Lafayette wrote to John Hancock. He asked for two things. The first was to serve at his own expense. The second was to begin his service as a volunteer. Hancock made Lafayette a major general on George Washington's staff. He and Washington became like a father and son.

Valley Forge

After the British took Philadelphia, Washington moved his troops to their winter camp at Valley Forge near Philadelphia. Supplies were dangerously low. Most of the troops survived by eating firecakes, a thin bread of flour and water cooked over an open fire. At least 2,500 died of disease. Many soldiers left and went home. Martha Washington, the wife of George Washington, helped comfort and nurse the sick. One out of three soldiers had no shoes at all. George Washington noted bitterly that

Baron von Steuben joins Washington at Valley Forge.

"you might have tracked the army . . . by the blood of their feet" upon the snow.

In February 1778, Friedrich von Steuben (FREED rihk vahn STOO bun) a soldier from the German state of Prussia, arrived at Valley Forge. He helped train the ragged Continental troops. Von Steuben taught them to be on time. Even rags, he told them, could be kept clean. Von Steuben also taught the troops the fighting methods that the Europeans were using. Under his careful training, a group of colonial storekeepers, farmers, and other citizens was turned into a powerful army.

READING CHECK

Why do you think the Battle of Saratoga was considered a turning point for the Patriots?

THE AMERICANS GAIN

In 1778, **George Rogers Clark** decided to try and drive out the British from the Ohio River valley. Clark captured several forts including **Fort Vincennes** (vihn SENZ). The British soon retook the fort, but Clark refused to give up. In February 1779, Clark's men marched to the fort, wading waist-deep through icy swampland. He tricked the British into believing he had a large army by having his men yell and scream as they attacked the fort. The British quickly surrendered. Americans now controlled the Ohio River valley.

Fighting at Sea

For the most part, the few ships in the American navy had little effect on the outcome of the war. However, in April 1778, Captain **John Paul Jones** raided England's coast. The next year, Jones's battleship, the *Bonhomme Richard*, faced the British battleship *Serapis*. The British pounded the *Bonhomme Richard* with cannon fire, leaving it badly damaged. When the British captain asked Jones if he was ready to surrender, Jones yelled back, "I have not yet begun to fight." In the end, the *Serapis* surrendered.

To lift their spirits, colonists often quoted heroes like John Paul Jones. They also sang favorite songs like "Yankee Doodle."

READING CHECK How did George Rogers Clark recapture Fort Vincennes?

Primary Source:

"Yankee Doodle"
— *A Patriot song*

*Father and I went down to camp,
Along with Captain Gooding;
And there we saw the men and boys,
As thick as* **hasty pudding**.

*(chorus)
Yankee doodle, keep it up,
Yankee doodle dandy;
Mind the music and the step,
And with the girls be handy.*

*There was Captain Washington
Upon a slapping stallion,
A-giving orders to his men,
I guess there was a million.*

And then they had a **swamping** *gun,
As big as a log of maple
On a* **deuced** *little cart,
A load for father's cattle.*

What is Captain Washington doing in the song?

_____

hasty pudding: a thick corn meal mush
swamping: big or heavy
deuced: darned

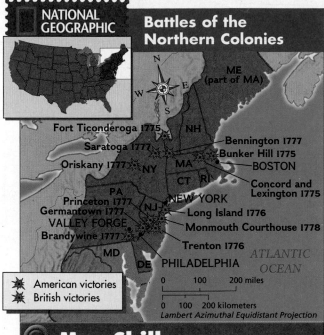

Battles of the Northern Colonies

ME (part of MA)

Fort Ticonderoga 1775
NH
Bennington 1777
Saratoga 1777
Bunker Hill 1775
Oriskany 1777
NY
MA
BOSTON
CT RI
Concord and
Lexington 1775
PA
Princeton 1777
NJ
NEW YORK
Germantown 1777
Long Island 1776
VALLEY FORGE
Monmouth Courthouse 1778
Brandywine 1777
MD
Trenton 1776
DE
PHILADELPHIA
ATLANTIC
OCEAN

0   100   200 miles

0   100   200 kilometers
Lambert Azimuthal Equidistant Projection

✷ American victories
✷ British victories

Map Skill

1. In which year did the greatest number of battles take place?

2. How many victories does the map show that America had between 1775 and 1778? The British?

3. Where in Pennsylvania did battles take place?

PUTTING IT TOGETHER

With his success at Fort Ticonderoga and Saratoga, many considered Benedict Arnold "the very genius of war." However, Arnold was also criticized for living beyond his means.

In 1780, Washington gave Arnold command of West Point, a key fort in New York. Arnold planned to tell the British about West Point's defenses. When the Americans found out, Arnold escaped and joined the British army. Today, "Benedict Arnold" has come to mean a traitor to one's country.

Review and Assess

1. Write one sentence using the vocabulary term.

   Treaty of Alliance

2. How did the capture of Fort Vincennes help the Americans?

3. How did the Patriots defeat the British in the Battle at Saratoga?

4. How did **geography** and climate play a role in the outcome of the battles discussed in this lesson?

5. Based on the events in this lesson, what **predictions** would you make about the rest of the war? Explain your answer.

The Patriots made several gains in their battles in the North. Draw a large map highlighting the battles they won. Under each, write a caption giving the main reason why they won.

Suppose you were at Valley Forge. **Write** a letter home about the conditions, your feelings, and what you are doing.

Lesson 3

The War Ends

Find Out! *What ended the Revolutionary War?*

Lesson Outline

- British Advance in the South
- Victory at Yorktown
- Treaty of Paris

VOCABULARY

Treaty of Paris

Second Treaty of Fort Stanwix

PEOPLE

Francis Marion

Nathanael Greene

Charles Cornwallis

James Armistead

Joseph Brant

READING STRATEGY

Using a sequence of events chart like the one below, explain the steps that led to the end of the American Revolution. Start with the British capture of Charles Town.

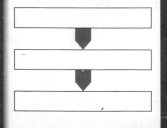

BUILD BACKGROUND

In 1779, Spain joined the war on the Patriots' side. Spanish Louisiana's governor, Bernardo de Gálvez (ber NAHR doh DE GAHL vez), opened up the port of New Orleans to American ships and ended trade with Britain. De Gálvez also sent money and supplies to George Rogers Clark to keep the British from moving west. After losing at Saratoga, the British tried to take control of the South.

BRITISH ADVANCE IN THE SOUTH

In 1780, British forces landed near Charles Town, South Carolina. They slowly closed in on the city, trapping the 5,500 Patriot defenders. Almost the entire Southern army was lost.

Captain **Francis Marion** led a small band of Patriot soldiers in the South Carolina countryside. They made quick attacks on the British and hid in the Carolina swamps. Marion became know as the "Swamp Fox." Years later the poet William Cullen Bryant wrote:

> *Our band is few, but true and tried,*
> *Our leader frank and bold;*
> *The British soldier trembles*
> *When Marion's name is told.*

Marion's men also fought in North Carolina under General **Nathanael Greene**. Greene's approach was: "We fight, we get beat, rise and fight again." Between 1778 and 1781, the greatly outnumbered and poorly equipped Patriots were defeated at Savannah, Charles Town, and Camden.

Cornwallis surrendered to Washington at Yorktown (left). Francis Marion's band (above) crossed the Pee Dee River to attack the British.

By the spring of 1781, British commander **Charles Cornwallis** declared he was "quite tired of marching about the country" chasing Greene.

Guilford Court House

In March 1781, a bloody exchange at Guilford Court House, North Carolina, cost Cornwallis one-fourth of his men. The British were able to claim victory because they drove Greene from the battlefield. "Another such victory," one British officer said, "would destroy the British army." Cornwallis left the Carolinas with his forces greatly weakened and in need of supplies.

READING CHECK **Why did the British put so much effort into fighting in the South?**

James Armistead (on the right) spied on Cornwallis during the war.

VICTORY AT YORKTOWN

When General Cornwallis marched north, he got as far as Yorktown, Virginia. There a huge force faced him. This was to be the last stand for the British.

Cornwallis Surrenders

When General Cornwallis asked his servant James Armistead to spy on the Americans, he did not know that Armistead was already spying *for* them. Armistead told Lafayette about Cornwallis's plans. He also gave Cornwallis false information about the Americans.

Washington was therefore able to trick Cornwallis into thinking he was going to attack New York. Instead more than 17,000 American and French soldiers surrounded Yorktown. French warships blocked the harbor and prevented the British from retreating. The

map on page 307 shows the routes each side took and the positions of their troops.

In late September, American and French troops closed in on the British at Chesapeake Bay, preventing escape by sea. Cornwallis surrendered to Washington and the French on October 19, 1781. One person described the sadness of the event.

Which ally helped Washington win at Yorktown?

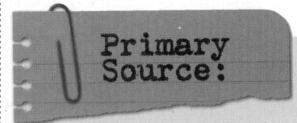

Primary Source:

excerpt from **Witness to the British surrender at Yorktown**
— *Sarah Osborn's declaration to the Court of Common Pleas in Wayne County, Pennsylvania, November 20, 1837*

*The officers rode on in front of the army, who marched out beating and playing a melancholy [sad] tune, their drums covered with black handkerchiefs and their **fifes** with black ribbons tied around them. They marched on to an old field and there each soldier grounded their arms. They then marched back into town to await their destiny.*

Why did the British cover their drums with black handkerchiefs?

fife: A flute-like musical instrument

France and the American War for Independence

France was eager to help the Patriots. However, the French did not send troops until after the Patriots won the Battle of Saratoga in 1777. Study the graph and text on this page. Then answer the questions below.

French Troops in the American Revolution

In February 1778, France entered into an alliance with the 13 colonies. It would take many months, however, before the French could ready a force and get it to America. Then, only two-thirds of the troops that France had promised to send to the United States made it to American shores. France aided the American war effort by fighting the English on the seas as well. As a result, England could not send as many troops to North America.

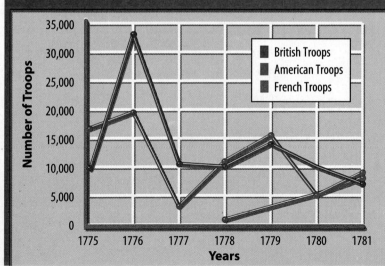

Troops in American Revolutionary War

Number of Troops: 35,000 / 30,000 / 25,000 / 20,000 / 15,000 / 10,000 / 5,000 / 0

Years: 1775 / 1776 / 1777 / 1778 / 1779 / 1780 / 1781

- British Troops
- American Troops
- French Troops

QUESTIONS:

1. In which four years did American troops outnumber English troops?

2. What percentage of the promised French troops arrived in the United States?

3. What can you infer about how France helped America win the war?

To learn more, visit our Web site: **www.mhschool.com**

TREATY OF PARIS

Although the war dragged on for two more years with minor skirmishes, the Battle of Yorktown was the last major battle of the war. King George III wanted to continue to fight, but the British people did not support the war. Britain also feared losing other parts of the British Empire. With a change in the British government in 1782, peace talks with the Americans began.

At the peace talks between the British and the Americans in Paris, Benjamin Franklin, John Adams, and John Jay represented the United States. The Treaty of Paris was signed on September 3, 1783. It recognized the independence of the United States. The land west of the Appalachians became part of the United States. Florida, which had come under British control, was returned to Spain.

Loyalists Flee

After the war, nearly 100,000 Loyalists fled the United States for Canada and Europe. Most were wealthy merchants. Their leaving opened up many opportunities for the Americans to start businesses. However, not all Loyalists could afford to leave. Those who stayed faced open dislike and were treated badly.

The Iroquois Confederacy

Both the Americans and British tried to win the support of the Native Americans during the Revolution. In the Iroquois Confederacy, the Tuscarora and Oneida, who valued the colonists' trade, decided to help the Patriots. The Mohawk, Cayuga, Seneca, and Onondaga fought with the British. Their leader, Joseph Brant, hoped that the British would protect Iroquois lands from settlement by the colonists.

By choosing the losing side in the war, the Iroquois lost much of their land. In the Second Treaty of Fort Stanwix of 1784, the Iroquois Confederacy lost their

The French rejoice at the end of the Revolutionary War (below). Joseph Brant (above right) fought with the British.

land in the Ohio River Valley. The Oneida and Tuscarora, who sided with the Patriots, were forced to smaller lands east and north. Many Iroquois chose to leave the United States for Canada.

What is the Treaty of Paris?

PUTTING IT TOGETHER

Years after the American Revolution, John Adams was asked about the meaning of the war. He said that there had been two revolutions. One was the war itself. The other "was in the minds and hearts of the people."

The United States had won their freedom from Britain. More united than ever before, the American people now had to sit down and form a new government. What kind of government would they form? In the next chapter, you will read about how this was done.

The Purple Heart was the first American military medal.

Review and Assess

1. Write a sentence using the vocabulary term.
   Treaty of Paris

2. What happened to the Iroquois after the war?

3. Why was Cornwallis's defeat at Yorktown important?

4. How did the departure of the Loyalist merchants create opportunities for Americans?

5. What were the goals of France and Spain in **deciding** to help the Patriots? Explain your answer.

Look at the map of the Battle of Yorktown on page 307. Make a chart with two columns. In one column list the major physical features around Yorktown. In the other column explain how the Patriots and their friends used those features to their advantage. Why was it a good location to trap Cornwallis?

Suppose you are a Loyalist living in the colonies after the war. **Write** a letter to your family in Britain telling them you'll be moving to Canada. Explain why.

Comparing Maps at Different Scales

Major battles of the American Revolution were fought in almost all of the 13 colonies. The map on this page shows the battles in just three colonies—New Jersey, Pennsylvania, and Virginia. Maps of such large areas help to locate battles.

Yet sometimes you may want to find more detailed information. Suppose you want to know the route the army took in a battle. Then you would need a map that showed a smaller area in greater detail.

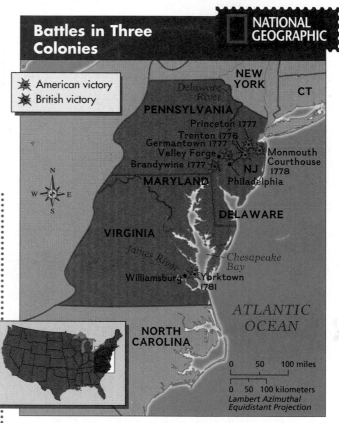

Battles in Three Colonies

NATIONAL GEOGRAPHIC

★ American victory
★ British victory

NEW YORK
CT
Delaware River
PENNSYLVANIA
Princeton 1777
Trenton 1776
Germantown 1777
Valley Forge
Brandywine 1777
NJ
Monmouth Courthouse 1778
MARYLAND
Philadelphia
DELAWARE
VIRGINIA
James River
Chesapeake Bay
Williamsburg
Yorktown 1781
ATLANTIC OCEAN
NORTH CAROLINA

0   50   100 miles
0   50   100 kilometers
Lambert Azimuthal Equidistant Projection

LEARN THE SKILL

Look at the maps on these pages as you follow the steps.

1. **Find the map scale.**
    No map can be as large as the part of Earth it shows. So all maps are drawn to scale. A map scale uses a unit of measurement, such as an inch, to represent a real distance on Earth. Each map has its own scale depending on the size of the area and the amount of information that needs to be shown.

2. **Identify which type of map you need.**
    Decide which map scale would best give you the information you want to find. A large-scale map, like the one you would need to show a specific battle, shows a smaller area in greater detail. A large-scale map helps make some information easier to read and interpret. A small-scale map, like the map of major battles, shows a large area, but not much detail.

3. **Compare the map scales.**
    Look at the map on this page. In order to locate each of the battles in the three colonies, the map has to show a large area in the middle of the Atlantic coast. Using the map scale you can figure out the distance an army had to travel between the battle of Princeton and Trenton. But it does not show the exact route the army took because it is a small-scale map. You need a larger scale map that shows more detail.

4. Compare the details.
If you have a hard time identifying large and small-scale maps, look for details such as routes and army camps.

TRY THE SKILL

Now compare the map of battles in New Jersey, Pennsylvania, and Virginia to the map of the Battle of Yorktown on this page.

1. Which map scale is larger?

2. Which of the two maps is a small-scale map?

3. Which map shows more detail?

4. How does comparing maps at different scales help you to better understand history?

EXTEND THE SKILL

Create two maps. On the first, draw a map of your county or city. Label this map with the names of towns within the county, and indicate which town is yours. On the second, map your own town. Include some streets, parks, or recognizable landmarks. Indicate the location of your home. Both should include a map scale.

- Which map is large scale and which is small scale?

- What information can you see in the map of your town that you can't see in the map of your county?

- How can maps at different scales help you **compare** and **contrast** information?

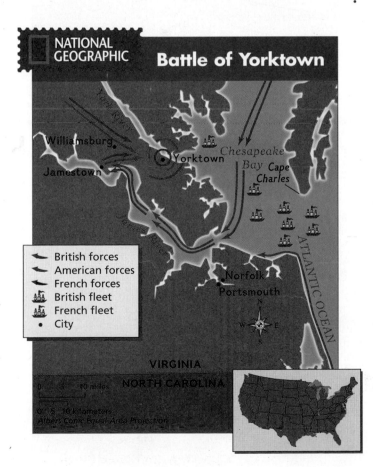

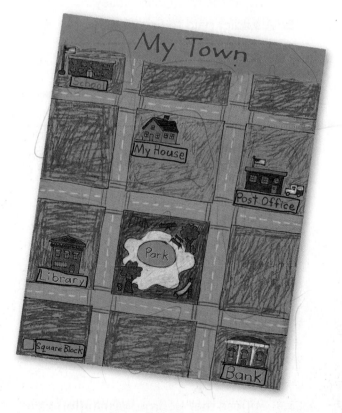

VOCABULARY REVIEW

Number a sheet of paper from 1 to 5. Beside each number write the word or term from the list below that matches the description.

mercenary   **surveyor**

Second Treaty of Fort Stanwix   **Treaty of Alliance**

Treaty of Paris

1. A treaty signed by France in support of the Americans in their fight against the British

2. A person who measures land

3. This ended the war between the United States and Great Britain

4. A treaty in which the Iroquois lost their land in the Ohio River valley

5. A soldier paid to fight for another country

CHAPTER COMPREHENSION

6. What were some of the disadvantages the British had in the American Revolution?

7. How did the French support the Patriots during the war?

8. What was it like for the soldiers during the winter of 1777 at Valley Forge?

9. Why was Benedict Arnold considered a traitor to the Patriots?

10. What did George Rogers Clark and John Paul Jones have in common?

11. How did Bernardo de Gálvez help the Patriot cause?

12. What were the terms of the Treaty of Paris?

13. Suppose that George Washington has asked you to help him inspire his troops during their winter at Valley Forge. **Write** a speech for him to give to his soldiers.

SKILL REVIEW

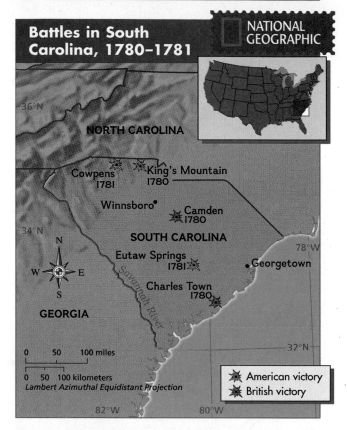

Battles in South Carolina, 1780–1781

NATIONAL GEOGRAPHIC

NORTH CAROLINA

Cowpens 1781   King's Mountain 1780

Winnsboro   Camden 1780

SOUTH CAROLINA

Eutaw Springs 1781   Georgetown

Charles Town 1780

GEORGIA

0 50 100 miles
0 50 100 kilometers
Lambert Azimuthal Equidistant Projection

American victory
British victory

14. **Geography Skill** What is a map scale?

15. **Geography Skill** What is the difference between a large-scale map and a small-scale map?

16. **Geography Skill** How do you decide whether to use a large-scale map or small-scale map?

17. **Geography Skill** What is the distance between Charles Town and Camden?

18. **Geography Skill** What kind of information could you see on a large-scale map of Charles Town that is not on this map?

USING A TIME LINE

| 1775 | 1776 | 1777 | 1778 | 1779 | 1780 | 1781 | 1782 | 1783 | 1784 |

1777
Battle of Saratoga; Continental army winters at Valley Forge

1779
Clark retakes Fort Vincennes; *Bonhomme Richard* defeats British ship *Serapis*

1781
American victory at the Battle of Yorktown

1783
The Treaty of Paris ends the war

19. Compare and contrast the events that occurred in 1777 with those of 1779.

20. Which event on the time line had the greatest impact on the Treaty of Paris of 1783? Explain.

Writing **About Patriotism** Think about what it means to be a patriot. Would you fight for your country? Write song lyrics or a speech about the United States. Explain what it is like to be an American and how you feel about your country.

Use your Foldable time line to review what you have learned about events and beliefs before, during and after the American Revolution. Open your time line and look at the illustrations on the back of each of the sections as you mentally recall what you learned about the war for independence. Review your notes on the front of your Foldable time line to check your memory and responses. Record any questions that you have on your Foldable. Then discuss them with classmates or review the chapter to find answers.

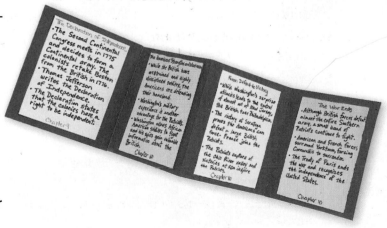

The Constitution of the United States

After winning the War for Independence the states were faced with creating

a government for their new country. Because of their experience with Great

Britain most Americans did not want a powerful central government. The

result was that the new government was too weak to be effective.

THE ARTICLES OF CONFEDERATION

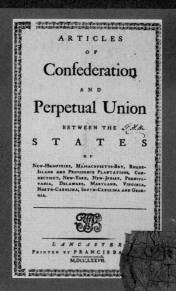

One success of the Articles of Confederation is the Northwest Ordinance. It provides a way for new territories to become states.

THE CONSTITUTIONAL CONVENTION

James Madison believes Americans should form a new central government.

THE CONSTITUTION

The United States Constitution is the world's oldest written plan of government still in use.

RATIFYING THE CONSTITUTION

The Constitution has to be approved by the states. Alexander Hamilton writes newspaper articles to win support for the Constitution.

Foldables

Make this Foldable study guide and use it to record what you learn about "The Constitution of the United States."

1. Fold an 8 ½" x 11" piece of paper in half like a hamburger, leaving one side 1" longer than the other.

2. Make 3 cuts, equal distance apart, on the short side of paper, forming four tabs.

3. Write the chapter title on the 1" tab, and the following dates on the front of the four tabs: 1781, 1787, 1788, 1791.

The Articles of Confederation

What effect did the Articles of Confederation have on the United States?

Lesson Outline
• Our First Government
• A Plan for New States

VOCABULARY

Articles of Confederation
Shays's Rebellion
Northwest Ordinance
territories
statehood

PEOPLE

Daniel Shays
Richard Allen

READING STRATEGY

Use a cause-and-effect table like the one below to list some effects the Articles of Confederation had on the United States.

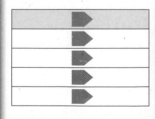

BUILD BACKGROUND

The United States was free from Great Britain. Now it was time to form a new government.

George Washington worried about quarrels between states. "We are apt to run from one extreme into another," he wrote.

Abigail Adams wrote to her husband, John Adams, "I desire that you would remember the ladies. We will not hold ourselves bound to obey laws in which we have no voice or representation."

OUR FIRST GOVERNMENT

Years of living under British rule made many Americans distrust a strong central government. So in 1777 the Second Continental Congress adopted the **Articles of Confederation**. The Articles of Confederation left the central government weak and gave most of the power to the states.

Conflicts between the states increased. Under the Articles of Confederation, Congress could do little to settle these quarrels. It had no power to enforce the laws it passed. Most people thought of themselves only as citizens of the states in which they lived and not as citizens of the United States. Under the Articles of Confederation, each state made its own laws, collected its own taxes, and printed its own money. Money printed in one state, however, was not accepted in another.

Shays's Rebellion

Because Congress had no power to raise money to pay soldiers who had fought in the Revolution, many soldiers were unable to pay their debts. This caused serious problems in Massachusetts.

Massachusetts charged heavy taxes on land. Many soldiers had returned to farming. When their farmers were unable to pay the taxes, courts began jailing farmers and taking their land. Congress owed many of these farmers money.

In 1786 **Daniel Shays**, a Massachusetts farmer, organized over a thousand farmers to protest against the taxes. When the local militia was called in, the protest turned bloody. The uprising, called **Shays's Rebellion**, left eight men dead.

Many blamed the Articles of Confederation for the rebellion. "Our body politic is dangerously sick," concluded Patrick Henry. George Washington added that things would never improve under the "half-starved, limping government."

Abigail Adams (left) advised her husband John Adams in her letters. Daniel Shays (above) protests high taxes.

READING CHECK Why did many blame the Articles of Confederation for Shays's Rebellion?

A PLAN FOR NEW STATES

The central government was weak, but it did pass some important laws. One of them was the Northwest Ordinance, passed in 1787. This law set out a plan for new territories to become states. A territory is an area of land that belongs to a government. In 1783 the Treaty of Paris gave the United States most of the land from the Atlantic Ocean to the Mississippi River. This land included a region called the Northwest Territory, which included land that would become the states of Indiana, Ohio, Wisconsin, Michigan, and Illinois.

The Northwest Ordinance divided this huge territory into smaller territories. Within each territory land was divided into townships of six square miles each. Each township became a self-governing part of the territory. People who settled the territories had the same rights as citizens of the 13 states. The ordinance also prohibited slavery.

The Free African Society

That same year, 1787, some African Americans began to demand more rights. Richard Allen, a former slave, started the Free African Society in that year. This was the first organized movement for rights by African Americans in North America.

Settling the New Territories

Thousands of people from the United States began moving into the Northwest Territory. Many came for the promise of land. Once the population of a territory reached 60,000, the territory could apply for statehood. Statehood means to become a state.

The territories all set aside land for schools. The Land Ordinance of 1785 had been passed requiring this because leaders of the new government believed people had to be educated to govern themselves.

What did new territories have to do to become states?

The Northwest Territory, 1787

NATIONAL GEOGRAPHIC

Legend:
- United States
- Northwest Territory
- Present-day state boundary

CANADA (GREAT BRITAIN)

LOUISIANA (SPAIN)

WISCONSIN

MICHIGAN

Lake Superior

Lake Michigan

Lake Huron

Lake Ontario

Lake Erie

Mississippi River

ILLINOIS   IN   OHIO

NEW YORK

PA

MD

VIRGINIA

(Claimed by VA)

(Claimed by NC)

NORTH CAROLINA

SOUTH CAROLINA

GEORGIA

(Claimed by GA)

0   150   300 miles

0   150   300 kilometers
Albers Equal-Area Projection

Map Skill

What landforms form the borders of some of the states in the Northwest Territory?

PUTTING IT TOGETHER

Although the nation became a single country after the Revolution, many people still thought of themselves as citizens of only their home states. After years of British rule, many Americans were afraid of a strong central government. Still, many saw that the Articles of Confederation wasn't working. They called for a stronger central government.

The Congress of the Confederation did pass one important law–that was the Northwest Ordinance. It would serve as a model for creating new territories for more than one hundred years.

Americans moved west in Conestoga wagons (left) and invented national symbols such as the first flag (above), and state seals (right).

Review and Assess

1. Write two sentences using each of the vocabulary terms.

   Articles of Confederation
   Northwest Ordinance

2. Why did the Articles of Confederation give most powers to the states?

3. How did the Articles of Confederation change the colonists' minds about the role of a central government?

4. Why might a small-scale map have been more useful than a large-scale map for settlers who were planning a route to a place located in the Northwest Territory?

5. Identify the **cause** of Shays's Rebellion. What **effect** did it have on Congress?

Look at the map on page 314. Research when states in the Northwest Territory became states. Make a map of the region with the state's name, year it became a state, and its capital.

• •

Write a journal entry from the point of view of a farmer in Massachusetts during Shays's Rebellion. It should describe how you felt.

315

The Constitutional Convention of 1787

VOCABULARY

Virginia Plan
legislative branch
executive branch
judicial branch
Supreme Court
New Jersey Plan
Great
Compromise

PEOPLE

Alexander
Hamilton
Gouverneur
Morris
James Madison
Roger Sherman

READING STRATEGY

Use a chart like the one below. In each column, list the responsibilities of the three branches of government.

Find Out!

How was the Constitution of the United States created?

Lesson Outline
• The Delegates Gather
• Father of the Constitution
• More Compromises

BUILD BACKGROUND

To address the growing problems between the states, the Congress met in Annapolis, Maryland. They agreed a convention should be held to fix the Articles of Confederation. Alexander Hamilton wrote letters inviting delegates to what became known as the Constitutional Convention.

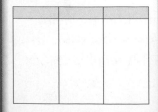

Independence Hall (left), in Philadelphia and George Washington (right) acting as president of the Convention.

THE DELEGATES GATHER

On May 25, 1787, the Constitutional Convention opened in Independence Hall, Philadelphia. Twelve of the 13 states sent delegates. Rhode Island refused to attend because it didn't want the national government to interfere with its affairs.

The Delegates

All 55 delegates were white men who owned property. More than half were lawyers. Most had fought in the Revolution. The delegates included George Washington and George Mason of Virginia and **Gouverneur Morris** of New York. It was Morris who actually wrote the Constitution by putting together the resolutions and decisions of the Convention. Washington came although he had retired from public life in 1782. He felt his country needed him. At the age of 81,

Benjamin Franklin was the oldest delegate. One newspaper called the delegates the "wisdom of the continent." Thomas Jefferson and John Adams, however, were unable to attend because they were abroad serving as ambassadors. An ambassador is an official representative sent to another country.

Soon after the Convention began, George Washington was elected as its president. He insisted that what went on in the meeting be kept a secret. So he had the windows shut and the doors closed. It would be easier to work without problems if there were no pressure from the public.

READING CHECK Why did George Washington insist that what was discussed at the meeting be kept a secret?

James Madison's plan helped the delegates at the Convention form a new government.

FATHER OF THE CONSTITUTION

One delegate, **James Madison**, came to the Convention 11 days early. Long before the meeting, he had asked his friend Thomas Jefferson for books about the government of other countries. Jefferson sent back trunk loads of books from his library in Paris, France. Madison spent all of his daylight hours reading. Delegate William Pierce of Georgia wrote that Madison was "the best informed man on any point in the debate."

Because Madison took notes of everything that happened, we know what happened on each day of the Convention. "This was a task," he said, that ". . . nearly killed me." He also wrote, "I was not absent a single day, nor more than a fraction of an hour in any day."

Madison's Plan of Government

When the Constitutional Convention opened, James Madison immediately put forth a plan of government he had already worked out. That's when the meeting became known as the Constitutional Convention. Later Madison became known as the "Father of the Constitution."

Madison's plan was presented by Virginia's popular governor, Edmund Randolph. The plan came to be called the **Virginia Plan**. Madison made sure that his plan was the first one discussed at the convention.

The Virginia Plan said that the central government should have three branches, or parts. A **legislative** (LEJ his lay tihv) **branch**, or law-making body, called the Congress, would make laws for the country and raise money for the central government.

A President would head the **executive** (eg ZEK yuh tihv) **branch**. The role of the President would be to carry out the laws made by Congress. The third was a **judicial** (joo DIHSH ul) **branch** that would decide the meaning of laws. A body of judges, called the **Supreme Court**, would head the judicial branch. Most states had already adopted this three-part model of government for their state governments. This model was based on the British government.

It was important to Madison that the delegates consider the Virginia Plan before they spent time changing the Articles of Confederation. On May 30, just five days from the start of the Convention, the delegates voted to accept part of the Virginia Plan. They were going to form a new government.

The Debate

The Virginia Plan called for two houses of Congress that would be based on population. This brought a heated debate between delegates from large states and small states. Large states liked the plan because it would give them more representatives than the smaller states. Small states did not like the plan. If they had fewer representatives than the large states, they would have less power and little influence in Congress.

Under the Articles of Confederation, all of the states had equal power. The small states wanted to keep it that way. They presented the **New Jersey Plan**, which gave all states the same number of representatives. As the graph below shows, Virginia, with a population of more than 700,000 would have the same number of representatives as the state of Delaware, which had a population of about 59,000.

The debate between large states and small states threatened to end the Convention. Some delegates talked of going home. The delegates then decided to set up a committee to work out a compromise. As you read in Chapter 2, a compromise is when each side gives up something it wants in order to reach an agreement. It took the delegates two months to reach an agreement.

Roger Sherman's Plan

Roger Sherman, a judge from Connecticut, saved the Convention. Thomas Jefferson claimed Sherman, who was known for his clear thinking, had "never said a foolish thing in his life." Sherman proposed a plan that became known as the **Great Compromise**.

In the Great Compromise the new Congress would have two separate houses. In the House of Representatives, the number of each state's representatives would be based on population, which favored the large states. In the Senate, each state would have two representatives, which favored the small states.

 READING CHECK

What contribution did Roger Sherman make to the Constitution?

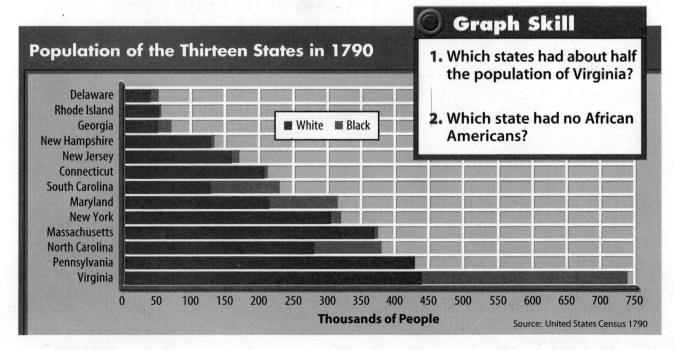

Population of the Thirteen States in 1790

■ White ■ Black

Thousands of People

Source: United States Census 1790

Graph Skill

1. **Which states had about half the population of Virginia?**

2. **Which state had no African Americans?**

MORE COMPROMISES

The delegates also had to work out other compromises. These debates were heated as well.

Electoral College

Some delegates felt that only members of Congress should vote for the President of the United States. They worried that everyday citizens could be fooled into voting for an unacceptable candidate. Others argued that all citizens should vote for the President. They finally reached an agreement that was acceptable to both sides and created the Electoral College. In the Electoral College, each state has as many votes as the state's number of senators and representatives in Congress. State committees select the members of the Electoral College.

The Question of Slavery

Because the Constitution says that the number of each state's representatives would be based on population, the issue of slavery arose. Should enslaved people be counted in a state's population? Many northern states wanted to end slavery. Most southern states, which had many enslaved Africans, wanted slavery to continue.

Finally, a compromise was reached. Every five enslaved people would be counted as three citizens. In addition, the delegates agreed not to end slave trading with other countries before 1808. Many delegates were unhappy with this compromise. Without it, however, the southern states might have left the Convention. There would have been no Constitution.

The delegates to the Constitutional Convention signed the Constitution of the United States on September 17, 1787. Now they could open the doors and windows. However, they would have to carry the Constitution back to their states for

Smithsonian Institution

This painting of the signing of the Constitution is in the Capitol, Washington, D.C. The trunk (left) held the papers from the Constitutional Convention.

approval. Before the Constitution was approved, the states discovered they would have to debate yet another compromise, one that added protection for individual rights.

What is the Electoral College?

PUTTING IT TOGETHER

When Ben Franklin came out of the convention hall for the last time, Eliza Powel stopped him. She asked him what kind of government the country would have. "A republic if you can keep it," he told her.

The hard job of keeping the republic alive still lay ahead, and it continues today. Writing the Constitution was a struggle that involved many compromises. People with different points of view often have to compromise in order to reach an agreement.

Franklin, Madison, and the other delegates had done something few had done before. They had created a complex written plan of government. You can read the Constitution on page R26 in the back of this book.

Eliza Powel of Philadephia (above left) helped to welcome the delegates.

Review and Assess

1. Write three sentences using each vocabulary term:

   Great Compromise   **Supreme Court**
   New Jersey Plan

2. How did James Madison prepare for the Constitutional Convention?

3. On what issues did the delegates compromise in order to get the Constitution signed?

4. What did the Virginia Plan propose?

5. **Compare** the New Jersey Plan to the Virginia Plan. Who favored each plan? Why?

Look at the chart of population of the 13 states on page 319. Determine the total population of the New England, Middle, and Southern colonies.

Write a script for a film about the Constitutional Convention. Focus on the debate about the Great Compromise.

Recognizing Points of View

People often disagree because they have different **points of view**. A point of view is the position from which a person looks at something.

Suppose, for example, you and your parents disagree on what you should do on Sunday afternoon. You want to go to soccer practice with your friends. It's important to you to play well and not to disappoint your friends. Your parents want you to visit your grandparents with them. They think family members should get together often. You and your parents have different points of view.

> **VOCABULARY**
>
> point of view

LEARN THE SKILL

Follow these steps to recognize a point of view.

1. **Identify a person's position.**
   A person's position is their view. How do they feel about the issue? Look at the excerpt to the right written by Alexander Hamilton. As you learned, he had the idea for the Constitutional Convention. Hamilton was a supporter of the Constitution. He wanted the states to unify under one government. Hamilton's statement reflects the point of view of the Federalists.

2. **Identify which words or statements are used to explain the point of view.**
   Hamilton used the words *in my opinion* and *should* which are clues that he was expressing an opinion. He was giving his view of what was the "right" thing to do.

> *The confederation in my opinion should give Congress complete sovereignty; except as to that part of internal police, which relates to the rights of property and life among individuals and to raising money by internal taxes. It is necessary, that every thing, belonging to this, should be regulated by the state legislatures. [In virtually all else] Congress should have complete sovereignty.*
>
> *– Alexander Hamilton*

TRY THE SKILL

Now try identifying the point of view of Patrick Henry, who was not present during the Constitutional Convention. He turned down his invitation. Here is what Henry said about the discussion of a Constitution and the unification of the states:

> Is this ... an association of a number of independent states, each of which retains its individual sovereignty? It is not a democracy, wherein the people retain all their rights securely.... The rights of conscience, trial by jury, liberty of the press ... all **pretensions** to human rights and privileges, are **rendered** insecure, if not lost, by this change ... liberty ought to be the direct end of your government.
>
> —Patrick Henry
>
> **pretensions:** false acts or beliefs
> **rendered:** made

In other words, according to Henry, the Constitution could possibly create a government too powerful, like that of Britain, and could take away the rights people just finished fighting for.

1. What position did Henry support in his statement?

2. What words or phrases tell you about Henry's point of view?

3. How does recognizing a person's point of view help you understand accounts of what happened in the past?

EXTEND THE SKILL

Public figures today often express their points of view in newspapers, on television, and in debates.

Suppose you and a partner are public officials. Choose an issue of importance to you about which you have different points of view. Explain your point of view, using fact and opinion.

- What issue did you choose?

- Do you think your life experience helped to shape your point of view? Analyze how.

Today politicians express their different points of view during televised debates.

The Constitution

What kind of government did the United States Constitution create?

Lesson Outline
- A Federal System
- A Balance of Power

READING STRATEGY

Using a Venn diagram like the one below, compare and contrast federal and state powers.

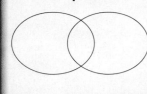

BUILD BACKGROUND

The United States Constitution is the world's oldest written plan of government. It is still in use partly because its framers made sure that it could change with the needs of a growing country. They provided for **amendments**, or additions, to the Constitution. "In framing a system which we wish to last for ages, we should not lose sight of the changes which ages will produce," wrote James Madison, "Every word [of the Constitution] decides a question between power and liberty." The Constitution had to protect the rights of both individuals and states.

Members of Congress meet to discuss and vote on proposed laws in the Capitol Building.

A FEDERAL SYSTEM

The government under the Articles of Confederation had been weak. Yet the framers of the Constitution did not want a powerful central government. So they worked for a balance.

The Preamble

"We the people of the United States," begins the **Preamble** (PREE am bul), or introduction to the Constitution. The authors wanted to show that the people held the power in this country—that it was a **democracy**. It is also a democratic **republic**. A republic is a system of government in which the people choose representatives to make the laws and run the government. The Preamble to the Constitution lists its most important goals.

Division of Powers

The Constitution divided the power of government between the states and the central government. This is called a **federal system** of government. Only the federal government was given the power to declare war, coin money, make treaties with other countries, run the post office, and settle disputes between states.

However, the three main branches of government—legislative, executive, and judicial—have to answer to the people and no one else. The states have power to set up public schools and local governments and run elections. Both state and federal governments have the right to collect taxes and to pass laws. They too have to answer to the people.

 **What is a federal system of government?**

 Primary Source:

Preamble to the Constitution of the United States
— approved by the states in 1788

*We the People of the United States, in Order to form a more perfect Union, establish Justice, insure **domestic Tranquility**, provide for the common Defense, promote the general Welfare, and secure the blessings of Liberty to ourselves and our **Posterity**, do **ordain** and establish this Constitution for the United States of America.*

What goals does the Preamble list giving power to the people?

domestic tranquility: peace within the country
posterity: future generation
ordain: make legal

A BALANCE OF POWER

The framers of the Constitution drew from their past experience as British colonists. The authors knew that when one branch of government has too much power, the government would not work well. So they set up a system of **checks and balances**. In this system, the powers of one branch of government are balanced by the powers of another. Each branch can check, or stop, another branch. If one branch tried to use its powers wrongly, the other two could keep it under control. Look at the flowchart below to see how the system of checks and balances works.

Cooperation Between Branches

The system of checks and balances makes it impossible for one branch of the federal government to act without the cooperation of another branch. For example, the President orders the army into

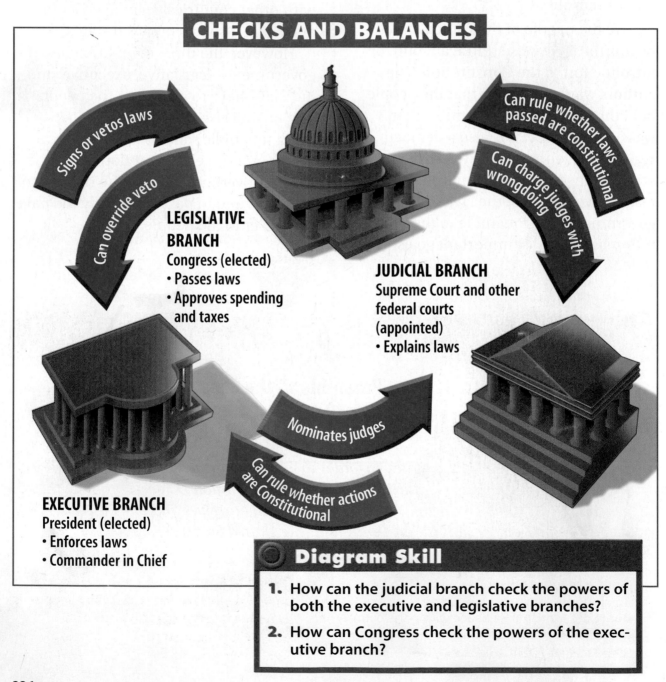

CHECKS AND BALANCES

Signs or vetos laws

Can override veto

Can rule whether laws passed are constitutional

Can charge judges with wrongdoing

LEGISLATIVE BRANCH
Congress (elected)
• Passes laws
• Approves spending and taxes

JUDICIAL BRANCH
Supreme Court and other federal courts (appointed)
• Explains laws

Nominates judges

Can rule whether actions are Constitutional

EXECUTIVE BRANCH
President (elected)
• Enforces laws
• Commander in Chief

Diagram Skill

1. How can the judicial branch check the powers of both the executive and legislative branches?

2. How can Congress check the powers of the executive branch?

326

battle. Yet only Congress can declare war. So Congress has a check on the President's powers.

Congress may pass any law. However, the President can **veto**, or refuse to approve, that law. The system of checks and balances does not end there. If two-thirds of the members of both houses of Congress agree, Congress can override, or cancel, a veto. In this way, Congress can pass a law the President has vetoed.

The Supreme Court can put a stop to any law passed by Congress or signed by the President that it decides is not allowed by the Constitution. However, the Supreme Court did not gain this right until 1803.

How does the system of checks and balances work?

PUTTING IT TOGETHER

The Constitution balances freedom and power by creating a federal system of government. That government unites the states while sharing power with them. The people of each state elect representatives to run the state and federal governments. When new needs arise, the people can amend, or change, the Constitution. This ability to pass and change laws is an important right of the people. The Constitution has worked for more than 200 years because of the system of checks and balances, and rules for adding amendments.

The Supreme Court met in the Capitol Building until this marble building was completed in 1935.

Review and Assess

1. Write four sentences using each of the vocabulary terms.

   amendment   **federal system**
   democracy   **republic**

2. What unique powers is the President allowed under the Constitution?

3. How does the system of checks and balances keep one branch of government from gaining too much power?

4. What are some of the powers that the federal **government** and the states have?

5. How does the Constitution **compare** with the Articles of Confederation?

Look at the Division of Powers section on page 325. Make a three-column chart showing the powers of the executive, judicial, and legislative branches of the federal government.

Write a description of how a law vetoed by the President can still become a law. Include the role of the judicial branch in your answer.

327

Lesson 4

Ratifying the Constitution

Find Out!

How was the Constitution adopted by the states?

Lesson Outline
• Debates over the Constitution
• Adding a Bill of Rights
• The First Political Parties

VOCABULARY

ratify
Federalist
Antifederalist
Bill of Rights
secretary
Cabinet
political party

PEOPLE

George Mason
George Washington

READING STRATEGY

Create a word map like the one below. Place the Constitution in the center. Use the bubbles to name some of the ways the Constitution benefited the country.

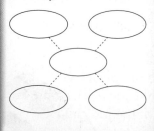

BUILD BACKGROUND

To become law, the Constitution needed approval from nine of the 13 states. Each state held a convention to debate whether or not to **ratify**, or officially approve, the Constitution in 1787. Feelings ran high in the states. Some states saw a vote for the Constitution as "a vote for clarity and sense." However, many other state leaders feared the kind of government that would result. They thought the states would lose their rights. The debate over ratifying the Constitution had begun.

DEBATES OVER THE CONSTITUTION

Newspapers in many states published the Constitution. Soon after, leaders in the 13 states wrote newspaper articles explaining their positions. They also gave speeches and published pamphlets.

On December 7, 1787, Delaware became the first state to ratify the Constitution. But it would take nine months before the Constitution would be approved by two-thirds of the states. During this time, there was fierce debate.

Supporters of the Constitution were called **Federalists** because the Constitution called for a federal system of government. Opponents of the Constitution, like Virginia's Patrick Henry, were called **Antifederalists**. Henry was afraid the states would lose their freedom under the Constitution. "Liberty," Henry said, "give us that precious jewel, and you may take everything else!"

"There is no quarrel between government and liberty," said Edmund Pendleton of Virginia. Yet Antifederalists, like the Massachusetts writer Mercy Otis Warren, were not convinced. Warren saw efforts to ratify the Constitution as "dark, secret"

plots of men who were "growing rich" while "lovers of freedom" suffered.

James Madison, Alexander Hamilton, and John Jay, a lawyer from New York, built a strong case for the Constitution in *The Federalist Papers*. *The Federalist Papers* were a series of 85 articles published in New York newspapers. It argued that a weak government actually threatened people's freedoms. Only the strong government provided by the Constitution could protect the rights of all.

Patrick Henry (above) led the opposition to the Constitution, which Alexander Hamilton (right) strongly supported.

Why were *The Federalist Papers* written?

329

ADDING A BILL OF RIGHTS

In 1788, a debate over protecting citizen's rights slowed the ratification of the Constitution. Some critics of the Constitution were upset that it had no **Bill of Rights**. A Bill of Rights is a document that describes the basic rights of the people. Antifederalists believed it would help keep the federal government from becoming too powerful. Also, almost every state constitution included a bill of rights.

In 1776, **George Mason** had written *The Demand for Rights*, this country's first Bill of Rights, as part of Virginia's constitution. He based it partly on an English bill of rights written almost 100 years earlier. Mason felt strongly that the Constitution should also have a bill of rights. Therefore he refused to sign the Constitution.

By January 9, 1788, five states—Delaware, Pennsylvania, New Jersey, Georgia, and Connecticut—had ratified the Constitution. The Federalists needed four more states before the Constitution would become law.

The Debate in Massachusetts

Federalists argued that Massachusetts already had a bill of rights in its state's constitution. Antifederalists echoed Mason's cry. They wanted a bill of rights added to the United States Constitution.

John Hancock, now the governor of Massachusetts, told the delegates that a bill of rights could be added to the Constitution as amendments. Massachusetts delegates then ratified the Constitution.

Adding the Bill of Rights to the Constitution was possible because the Constitution provided for amendments. George Mason realized that people might want to change the Constitution. "It will be better to provide for [amendments] . . . than to trust to chance and violence," he said.

On June 21, 1788, New Hampshire became the ninth state to ratify the document. Now the Constitution was law. Rhode Island was the last state to ratify it on May 29, 1790.

George Washington was cheered as he rode to his inauguration in New York City.

Amending the Constitution

The framers of the Constitution allowed for amendments. However, they did not want people to change it without serious debate. As a result, they made changing the Constitution a long, slow process. Before the states can vote on an amendment, two-thirds of both the Senate and the House of Representatives must approve it. Another way to start the process is to have two-thirds of the states ask Congress to call a special convention. Then, three-quarters of all the states must ratify the amendment. If this happens, the amendment becomes part of the Constitution. Since the Bill of Rights was added in 1791, some 10,000 amendments have been proposed. Only 17 have been added.

The First Government

The Electoral College would never again so easily reach a decision as they did in 1789 when George Washington received every vote to be president of the United States.

On April 14, 1789, Washington set out from Mount Vernon for the country's temporary capital, New York City. Every city along the way held a celebration.

On April 30 Washington walked out onto a balcony at Federal Hall. He placed his left hand on an open Bible and took the President's oath of office. He swore to "preserve, protect, and defend the Constitution of the United States," and added the words, "So help me God!"

Washington took the oath of office at Federal Hall. Many Americans collected election buttons.

Smithsonian Institution

The Cabinet

To help the President run the government, Congress set up three government departments. An official, called a secretary, headed each office.

The Secretary of the Treasury, Alexander Hamilton, formed a plan for the economy of the country. The Secretary of State, Thomas Jefferson, handled the country's dealings with other countries. The Secretary of War, Henry Knox, took charge of the country's defense. The Attorney General made sure that the country's laws were obeyed. The heads of the three departments and the Attorney General formed the Cabinet.

READING CHECK

What were the tasks of the first Cabinet members?

331

LITERATURE

BIG MEN, BIG COUNTRY:
Davy Crockett Teaches the Steamboat a Leetle Patriotism

Selections by Paul Robert Walker
Illustrated by Thomas Buchs

Storytelling on the frontier was an art. With each new telling, stories became bigger and better, and became known as tall tales. The characters were often fictional, but some, like Davy Crockett, were real heroes.

Back in the early days of our country, when pioneers were settling the wilderness between the Appalachian Mountains and the Mississippi River, there was a half-horse, half-alligator, half-snapping turtle kind of man called a ring-tailed roarer. The ring-tailed roarers were bigger, stronger, and smarter than the average pioneer. . . . And the biggest, strongest, smartest . . . ring-tailed roarer of the whole bunch was Davy Crockett.

Davy lived in a log cabin deep in the wilderness of Tennessee. . . . Davy's best friend was a bear named Death Hug. . . .

Davy was usually a pretty happy ring-tailed roarer, but one morning he woke up in a terrible mood. "Death Hug," he growled . . . "What say we wander over to the Big Muddy and ride on one of them loco-motive river towns they call a steamboat?". . .

A few minutes later, the steamboat arrived. . . . But when they got to the front of the line, the captain shook

PAUL ROBERT WALKER

BIG MEN, BIG COUNTRY

JAMES BERNARDIN

his head and closed the gate. "No bears allowed," he said.

"You panther pup!" Davy cried. "My bear travels where I travel."

"I'm sorry sir," said the captain politely. "It's company policy.". . .

Davy roared. "Maybe you ain't heard that this here is the United States of America, where every citizen, human or bearlike, has the right to ride in a steamboat."

The captain's face turned crimson and his voice got a **mite** less polite. "Maybe you ain't heard that this is the finest steamboat on the Big Muddy," he said. "She can pass any boat on the water and leave it behind like a tree on the shore.". . .

Davy stormed down the gangplank and into the forest. He found a hollow gum tree and chopped it down with a flash of lightning from his eyes. Then he hacked it open on one side, so it looked like a long, narrow canoe. . . .

Things went a little slow at first, but . . . the hollow gum tree passed that unpatriotic steamboat. . . .

Davy Crockett stood in the hollow gum tree and doffed his coonskin hat to the Stars and Stripes. "Well, boys, he said, "I guess we taught that locomotive river town a leetle bit of patriotism."

---

mite (mīt) little bit

Write About It!

Write a few sentences explaining why you think the tall tale became important to pioneers struggling with their environment.

A New Nation

TAKE A LOOK

Why did the United States grow and prosper after 1800?

In the 1800s, wagon trains moved at about two miles per hour. Today, the fastest trains in the United States travel at about 150 miles per hour.

For more information about early
U.S. history, visit our Web site at
www.mhschool.com

THE Big IDEAS ABOUT...

The Young United States

Having defeated the British army, the United States established itself as a new, independent country. Now, it would begin to grow. Pioneers would move west and settle there.

By 1812, however, the United States would find itself involved in yet another war. Read on to learn about this war.

BEYOND THE APPALACHIANS

Daniel Boone is an early trail-blazer in the West. He creates several roads that later explorers will use on their journeys.

THE WAR OF 1812

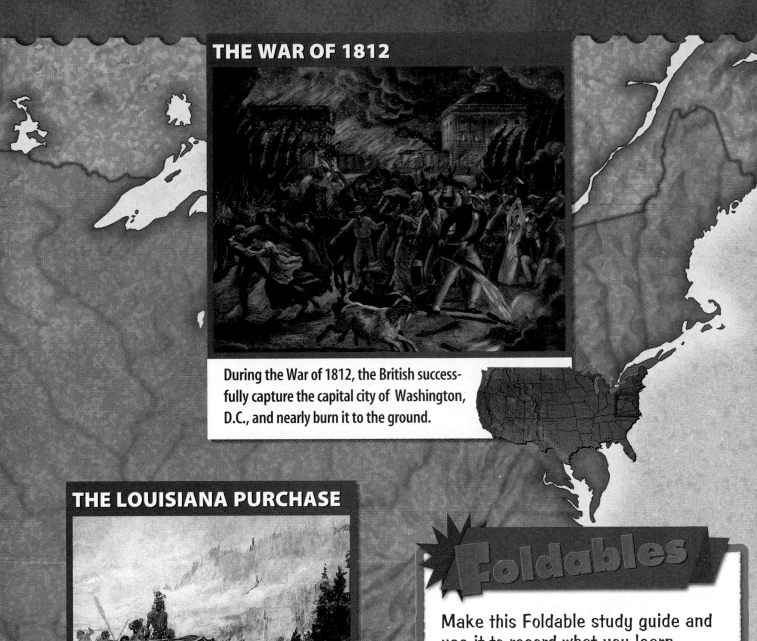

During the War of 1812, the British successfully capture the capital city of Washington, D.C., and nearly burn it to the ground.

THE LOUISIANA PURCHASE

President Jefferson more than doubles the size of the United States with the Louisiana Purchase. He sends explorers Lewis and Clark to explore and map the area.

Foldables

Make this Foldable study guide and use it to record what you learn about "The Young United States."

1. Fold a large sheet of paper into a shutter fold.
2. Sketch the Appalachian Mountains along the right edge, the Mississippi River down the middle, and label the left side of your Foldable, "West."
3. Label the three inside sections with lesson titles.

Beyond the Appalachians

What challenges did new settlers face as they moved west?

Lesson Outline
• An Expanding Nation
• Daniel Boone

VOCABULARY

pioneer

PEOPLE
Daniel Boone
John Findley

READING STRATEGY

Use the chart below to find the main idea and supporting details. In the center of the map write "trailblazers." In the blank spaces write the areas that the trailblazers explored as they moved west.

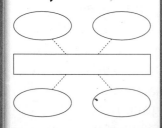

BUILD BACKGROUND

In the late eighteenth century, a great spirit of adventure captured many Americans. Even as the American Revolution was being fought in the colonies, courageous settlers were beginning to explore lands far to the west, across the Appalachian Mountains. After the war, the population of the new nation began to grow rapidly, as did the cost of land. Westbound settlers followed paths worn by Native Americans and blazed new trails to Kentucky, Mississippi, and Indiana Territories.

You Are Here
1769 – 1800

AN EXPANDING NATION

The borders of the United States in 1800 stretched from the Atlantic Coast to the Mississippi River. The United States was bordered by British Canada to the north and Spanish Louisiana and Spanish Florida, which is present-day western Florida, to the south. To the west, across the Mississippi, lay French Louisiana.

By this time, the population of the United States had grown to nearly four million people. English, Scots-Irish, and Germans continued to leave their homelands to seek freedom and new opportunities in the young United States.

Inexpensive farmland was becoming scarce in the states. When prices rose as high as $50 per acre, people began moving west to find cheaper lands to settle. The people who led the way west were called **pioneers**.

The main way west at this time was across the Appalachians. Beyond the mountains to the west lay the Central Plains, filled with rich soil ideal for farming. The woodlands and prairies provided shelter for deer and gophers. South of the Central Plains was the Gulf Coastal Plain. Its dense forests, grassy marshes, and swamps were filled with such wildlife as opossums and muskrats.

Native Americans had long farmed these lands. The Miami had been growing corn in the fertile Ohio River valley for hundreds of years. Along the Gulf Coast were many Choctaw villages. The Shawnee and Cherokee lived in the land that would become the state of Kentucky. These lands were also important hunting grounds for these tribes.

READING CHECK

Why did the lands west of the Appalachians draw pioneers?

NATIONAL GEOGRAPHIC

The United States, 1800

VT 1791
ME (part of MA)
L. Superior
L. Ontario
NH
MA
NY
RI
CT
CENTRAL PLAINS
Terr. NW of Ohio R.
PA
NJ
DE
MD
Indiana Territory
L. Michigan
Huron
Susque...
Missouri R.
KY 1792
VA
APPALACHIAN MOUNTAINS
TN 1796
NC
SC
GA
ATLANTIC COASTAL PLAIN
ATLANTIC OCEAN
Terr. South of Ohio R.
Mississippi Territory
GULF COASTAL PLAIN
Gulf of Mexico

States
Territories

0   200   400 miles
0   200   400 kilometers
Albers Conic Equal-Area Projection

Map Skill

1. What could make it difficult to reach the Mississippi?

2. Which areas were not states?

DANIEL BOONE

Finding the way west across the peaks and thick forests of the Appalachians was not easy. The trails that the pioneers followed began as Native American paths. Trailblazers cut their way through the forests, making paths wider.

Daniel Boone, a famous trailblazer, explored, hunted, and trapped in the Appalachians. Asked if he had ever been lost, Boone replied, "No, but I was bewildered [confused] once for three days." Because of his skill at finding trails, Boone was called "the pathfinder."

A trader named John Findley told Boone about a "gap," or narrow valley, that Native Americans used. In 1773 Boone led five families across the gap, now known as the Cumberland Gap, to settle in Kentucky. That October, a group of Delaware, Shawnee, and Cherokee were returning from a meeting discussing the settlers on their lands. They found Boone's group and attacked them, killing Boone's son James and three others. The group decided to leave Kentucky.

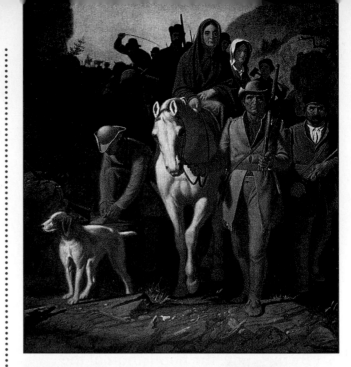

This painting shows Boone leading pioneers across the Cumberland Gap. In Kentucky, settlers worked hard to clear the land for farming (below).

Two years later, Boone helped persuade the Cherokee to sell much of their land in Kentucky. Boone then expanded two Native American trails that led to the Cumberland Gap. These trails became the Wilderness Road.

By 1776 about 200 people were living in Boonesborough, the new settlement founded by Boone and his men. By 1792 enough people were living in Kentucky for it to become our fifteenth state.

READING CHECK Why did the pioneers first settle Kentucky?

348

Wilderness Road, 1770s

Great Trading Path
Occaneechi Path
Warrior's Path
Wilderness Road
)(Gap

N W E S

Ohio R.

Lexington
Boonesborough
Harrod's
Town
KENTUCKY

Kentucky R.
Cumberland Gap

Cumberland R.

VIRGINIA

APPALACHIAN MOUNTAINS

NORTH CAROLINA

SOUTH CAROLINA

0 100 200 miles
0 100 200 kilometers
Lambert Azimuthal Equidistant Projection

ATLANTIC OCEAN

Map Skill

1. **Which route went through the Cumberland Gap?**

2. **Which routes would a pioneer from Virginia take to reach the Ohio River?**

PUTTING IT TOGETHER

By 1800, farmland in the United States was becoming scarce and expensive. In search of more land, pioneers traveled beyond the Appalachian Mountains. Thanks to them, our nation continued expanding. It stretched from the Atlantic Coast to the Mississippi River.

Daniel Boone was one of the first pioneers. He widened Native American trails to create roads. One such road, the Wilderness Road, cut through the Cumberland Gap to Kentucky.

Farmers on the frontier used a walking plow like this one to till the soil.

Review and Assess

1. Write one sentence for the vocabulary word below.

   pioneer

2. Why did the pioneers move west in the late 1700s and early 1800s?

3. What were some of the difficulties new travelers faced as they traveled west?

4. What effect did Daniel Boone have on the expansion of U.S. borders?

5. **Compare** the viewpoint of pioneers about the Wilderness Road with the viewpoint of Native Americans in Kentucky.

Look at the map of the Wilderness Road in the 1770s above. Suppose you lived in South Carolina and wanted to visit Lexington, Kentucky. Describe the routes you would take to get there.

 Write a diary entry describing what your life is like as a 10-year-old pioneer in Kentucky.

349

The Louisiana Purchase

What did Thomas Jefferson accomplish as President?

Lesson Outline
- President Thomas Jefferson
- The Louisiana Purchase
- The Corps of Discovery

VOCABULARY

Louisiana Purchase

PEOPLE
Benjamin Banneker

Pierre L'Enfant

Thomas Jefferson

Napoleon Bonaparte

Meriwether Lewis

William Clark

Sacagawea

York

READING STRATEGY

Use the sequence of events chart below to list the events that led to the Louisiana Purchase. Start with "Spain returns land to France."

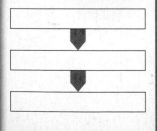

BUILD BACKGROUND

In 1791, President George Washington hired **Benjamin Banneker** to help lay out our national capital, the city of Washington, D.C. An African American, Banneker began with plans already laid out by French architect **Pierre L'Enfant** (pee AIR LAHN fahn).

When President John Adams spent his first night in the White House, in 1800, he said, "May none but wise and honest men ever rule under this roof."

Benjamin Banneker

Black Heritage USA 15c

Smithsonian Institution

You Are Here
1791 – 1806

PRESIDENT THOMAS JEFFERSON

Thomas Jefferson became the third President of the United States in 1801. A Democratic Republican, he believed in the rights of the states to make many of their decisions. The nation now had 16 states.

Fear of France

A few months after he was elected, Jefferson avoided a costly war with France over the vast lands west of the Mississippi. René Robert La Salle had first claimed this territory for France in 1682. In 1762 France gave it to Spain. Spain returned the land to France in 1800.

About this time General Napoleon Bonaparte (nuh POH lee un BOH nuh pahrt) ruled France and was fighting with Great Britain and other European countries. He had already taken over much of Europe. Jefferson feared that

Napoleon wanted to expand the French Empire in the Americas. The French territory of Louisiana was already equal in size to the United States. President Jefferson was worried that France might block, or close, the port at New Orleans in Louisiana. Many farmers east of the Mississippi shipped their goods down the river to this busy port city. Jefferson said that whoever blocked the Mississippi, stopping both trade and westward-bound settlers, was "our natural enemy." He decided to explore purchasing New Orleans from France.

READING CHECK **Why did Jefferson want to purchase New Orleans from France?**

President Thomas Jefferson (above) hoped that the ambitious leader, Napoleon Bonaparte (right, center of picture), would sell New Orleans to the United States.

Native Americans helped Lewis and Clark along their way.

THE LOUISIANA PURCHASE

In 1803, Jefferson sent James Monroe to Paris with an offer to purchase New Orleans. Monroe was surprised to learn that France wanted to sell not just New Orleans, but the whole territory of Louisiana to pay for its war with Britain. The United States agreed to a purchase price of $15 million, or about four cents per acre. Doubling the size of the United States, the **Louisiana Purchase** included land west of New Orleans to present-day Idaho and north to Canada.

Few Americans knew anything about this huge territory. Jefferson asked his assistant **Meriwether Lewis** to lead an expedition to explore Louisiana and the Missouri River, and to find a safe route to the Pacific Ocean. Lewis had been an army officer in the Northwest Territory. **William Clark**, a fellow army officer and friend of Lewis, agreed to join him. Jefferson told Lewis to write down everything he saw. A young Shoshone woman named **Sacagawea** (sah kah jah WEE uh) became the translator for the expedition.

READING CHECK

What was the Louisiana Purchase?

NATIONAL GEOGRAPHIC

The Louisiana Purchase, 1803

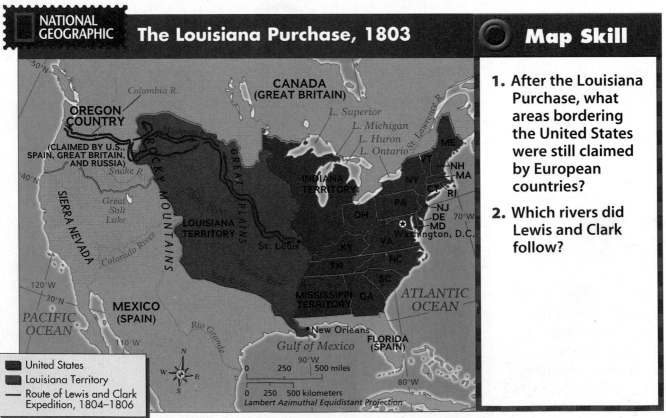

Map Skill

1. After the Louisiana Purchase, what areas bordering the United States were still claimed by European countries?

2. Which rivers did Lewis and Clark follow?

Legend:
- United States
- Louisiana Territory
- Route of Lewis and Clark Expedition, 1804–1806

BIOGRAPHY

Focus On: Responsibility

Sacagawea was born around 1787 in a Shoshone village in what is now eastern Idaho. At age 11, she was kidnapped and brought to the Missouri River Mandans. Later, she married a French fur trapper, Toussaint Charbonneau (too SAHN SHAHR buh noh).

Sacagawea and her husband joined the Lewis and Clark expedition in 1804. She took on many responsibilities and quickly earned the respect of Lewis and Clark. Once she rescued important papers from the Missouri River when Lewis and Clark's canoe capsized. She also gave birth to a son, Jean Baptiste, while journeying.

In one story, Sacagawea's brother, a Shoshone chief, did not want to help the explorers continue their trip until Sacagawea convinced him to.

Sacagawea and her husband returned to Fort Mandan in 1806.

Link to Today Think about someone who has handled many responsibilities. Research and write a paragraph about the person.

THE LIFE OF SACAGAWEA	**1787** Sacagawea is born in a Shoshone village	**1804** Sacagawea meets Lewis and Clark at Fort Mandan	**1805** Sacagawea leads Lewis and Clark to her brother's tribe	**1806** Sacagawea and her husband return home
	1780	**1790** **1800**	**1810**	**1820**
LIFE AROUND THE WORLD	**1789** French Revolution begins	**1800** British convicts are sent to Australia	**1801** United Kingdom is formed	**1804** Haiti gains independence from France

353

THE CORPS OF DISCOVERY

The Lewis and Clark Expedition was called the "Corps of Discovery." It included 42 men, about half of whom were soldiers. One of them was an enslaved African American named York. The rest were trappers and scouts.

On May 14, 1804, the Corps set out from St. Louis in three boats. They slowly moved west along the Missouri River. Lewis had spent $2,500 for supplies, including eyeglasses, mirrors, fishhooks, and shirts to be used as gifts for Native Americans they would meet.

The Corps of Discovery spent its first winter in a Mandan village in present-day North Dakota. There, Sacagawea and her husband agreed to join the expedition as translators. They set out across the Great Plains to the Rocky Mountains. Lewis and Clark kept journals to record what they saw.

Lewis and Clark traveled up the Missouri River in a keelboat named *Discovery*. A modern-day replica of the boat is shown. Clark described the keelboat in his journal (right).

From the Rockies, the expedition followed the Snake River and then the Columbia River to the Pacific Ocean. In November 1805, 18 months after the

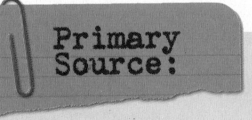

Primary Source:

excerpt from **The Journal of Captain Meriwether Lewis**
—written on May 29, 1805

*Great abundance of the Argalia or big-horned animals in the high country through which this river passes. Captain Clark, who **ascended** this river much higher than I did, has call[ed] it Judith's River [a section of the Missouri River in Montana]. The bottoms of this stream, as far as I could see, were wider and contained more timber than the Missouri. Here I saw some box alder intermixed with the cottonwood willow; rosebushes and honeysuckle, with some red willow, **constitute** the undergrowth.*

What did Lewis see west of the Missouri River?

ascend: to climb; to go higher
constitute: to make up the majority of a whole

354

PUTTING IT TOGETHER

With the Louisiana Purchase completed by President Thomas Jefferson, the United States doubled its land. Lewis and Clark explored 3,000 miles of territory. Meanwhile in 1803, the powers of the branches of government were becoming more defined. In a Supreme Court case, *Marbury versus Madison,* William Marbury demanded that Secretary of State James Madison appoint him justice of the peace in the District of Columbia.

The previous President, John Adams, made the appointment, but his term ended before Marbury took office. The Supreme Court decided that it could not rule on the appointment because the 1789 federal law giving the Supreme Court power to do so was unconstitutional. By this case, the Court showed it had the right to review whether laws passed by Congress are allowed by the Constitution.

expedition began, they arrived at what a Shoshone chief had called the "great shining lake." By the end of the return journey, the Corps of Discovery had mapped more than 8,000 miles.

READING CHECK What part of America did Lewis and Clark explore? How do you know?

Review and Assess

1. Write a sentence for the vocabulary term below.

   Louisiana Purchase

2. What goals did Lewis and Clark have for their expedition?

3. How did the United States grow while Jefferson was President?

4. Why was President Jefferson able to make the Louisiana Purchase so easlly?

5. **Analyze** the many ways in which Sacagawea helped Lewis and Clark.

Look at the map on page 352. Outline the path that the Corps of Discovery took on their journeys west. Then add physical features to your map from the map on pages R18–R19.

Write a letter that Meriwether Lewis or William Clark might have written to President Jefferson about the expedition's progress.

Comparing Maps

In this chapter you have used maps to find historical information. The maps you have used are called historical maps. In this textbook you have also used maps that communicate other kinds of information. For example, a **political map** shows the boundaries of states or countries. Elevation maps show the shape of the land and how high it is. Sometimes you need information that cannot be obtained from one map alone. In this case you need to compare different kinds of maps.

VOCABULARY

political map

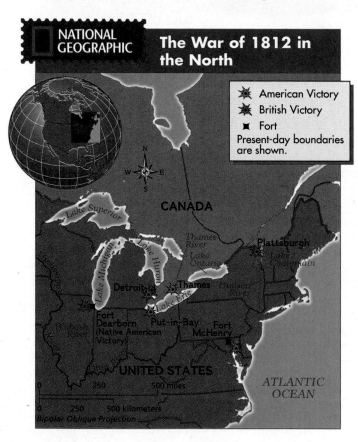

NATIONAL GEOGRAPHIC

The War of 1812 in the North

American Victory
British Victory
Fort
Present-day boundaries are shown.

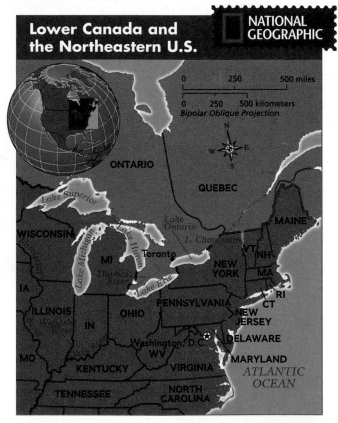

Lower Canada and the Northeastern U.S.

NATIONAL GEOGRAPHIC

LEARN THE SKILL

Follow these steps to compare maps.

1. **Identify what type of information you need.**
   Does your question require more than one map? For example, you will be studying the

War of 1812. Suppose you need to know where a battle took place during the war. A historical map will show you where it occurred, but it may not offer present-day state boundaries. A political map will show you state boundaries of today, but it will not indicate historic battle scenes.

2. **Identify what type of maps you have.**
The first map on page 356 shows the War of 1812 in the North. It is a historical map. The map to its right shows state boundaries for the Northeastern United States and Southeastern Canada. It is a political map. Alone, neither map can answer your question. Used together, they can.

3. **Identify areas you need to study.**
You would like to locate the battles of Put-in-Bay, which took place on Lake Erie, and Fort Dearborn; and the Battle of the Thames. You know you need to study the Great Lakes area and nearby Canada on the map of the War of 1812. Use the legend box to find symbols you need to locate the battles.

4. **Use landmarks to compare the maps.**
Now find Mississippi in the same area on the political map. Use landmarks such as the Thames River and Lake Erie. You will find that Fort Dearborn is in present-day Illinois. The Battle of Put-in-Bay occurred on the Lake Erie border of Ohio. The Battle of the Thames was fought in present-day Ontario, Canada.

TRY THE SKILL

The map of the War of 1812 shows several kinds of information about that time. By comparing the two maps, you can learn some of the ways the United States has changed since then.

1. What information do you need?

2. How will the types of maps on page 356 help you find the information you need?

3. Which areas on the maps will you compare?

4. Which landmarks will you look at?

5. Why do people often need more than one map to obtain information?

EXTEND THE SKILL

Suppose you want to find out which groups of Native Americans lived in your state in the 1600s and which live there today. Research this information. Then decide which kinds of maps would best present these facts. Draw the two maps, including labels, key, and any other information you think would be helpful.

If your state has no large groups of Native Americans today, you may draw a map of the state with a label explaining this. Another choice would be to draw a map of another time period in which Native Americans lived in your state.

● How can comparing and contrasting maps help you learn more about the geography and history of your state?

The War of 1812

What did President Madison do to protect the young United States?

Find Out!

Lesson Outline
- The War at Sea
- The War on Land
- Era of Good Feelings

VOCABULARY

neutral
War Hawks
War of 1812
Battle of New Orleans
Era of Good Feelings
Monroe Doctrine

PEOPLE

James Madison
Tecumseh
Henry Clay
Oliver H. Perry
Andrew Jackson
Dolley Madison
Francis Scott Key
James Monroe
Absalom Jones

READING STRATEGY

Use the chart below to organize causes of the Era of Good Feelings.

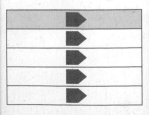

BUILD BACKGROUND

When **James Madison** became President of the United States in 1809, Americans were angered by the growing conflict with Native Americans in the Ohio River valley. A Shawnee chief named **Tecumseh** had begun organizing Native Americans to force the settlers to leave the area.

Many Americans thought that the British were helping the Native Americans. The angry Americans wanted to force the British out of Canada and the Spanish out of Florida as well. Senator **Henry Clay** of Kentucky urged the United States to "take the whole continent."

Library of Congress

THE WAR AT SEA

While conflict spread through the Ohio River valley, Great Britain and France were fighting. President Madison tried to keep the United States **neutral** (NOO trul), which means not taking sides. However, both countries began taking American ships by force. The British even impressed American sailors, or took them off American ships and forced them to serve in the British navy.

"Free trade and seamen's rights!" cried Senator Henry Clay. He led the **War Hawks**, members of Congress who wanted to declare war against Great Britain. The War Hawks pressed Congress to declare war on Britain in June 1812. It became known as the **War of 1812**.

"Old Ironsides"

Despite the power of the British navy, the United States enjoyed some early victories at sea. On August 19, 1812, just off the coast of Nova Scotia in Canada, the USS *Constitution* sank the *Guerrière* (ger ee YAIR), one of Britain's finest warships. Sailors nicknamed the *Constitution* "Old Ironsides." Cannonballs seemed to bounce off its tough oak sides.

In 1813 Commodore **Oliver H. Perry** fought the British navy on Lake Erie. His ship's flag read, "Don't give up the ship." Perry kept fighting until most of his crew lay wounded or dead. Perry and a few men then rowed out under heavy fire to a second ship and went on to defeat the British.

READING CHECK Who were the War Hawks?

The USS *Constitution* (left) won an important U.S. victory at sea, as did Commodore Perry (right) on Lake Erie (far right)

THE WAR ON LAND

The war on land was difficult. Many Native Americans continued to side with the British. Tecumseh was urging Native Americans not to sell their land to new settlers. "Why not sell the air, the clouds, and the great sea?" he asked. He and the British won several victories near the Great Lakes. In 1813 Tecumseh was killed in a battle near Detroit.

In Tennessee, American commander **Andrew Jackson** defeated the Muscogee (Creek). Having lost their land to the United States, many Muscogee fled to Florida and joined Native Americans there.

This portrait (left) is thought to be of Tecumseh. First Lady Dolley Madison (below) was in the White House when Washington was invaded.

The New York Historical Society

Exploring
ECONOMICS

War and the Economy

War affects a nation's economy. In their long war, Britain and France each tried to damage the other's foreign trade. However, ships of neutral nations could enter European ports. The United States, a neutral nation, benefited.

Then Britain and France decided to limit trade by neutral nations. The United States reacted by ending trade with Europe. This hurt the British and the American economies. Our nation needed the money it earned by trading overseas. When President Madison reopened trade in 1810, British ships stopped U.S. ships at sea. Angry Americans demanded that we declare war on Britain.

Research and list ways in which wars with other nations affect our nation's economy.

The Burning of Washington

In 1814, British troops surrounded American ports. They also landed at Chesapeake Bay and moved west toward Washington, D.C. First Lady **Dolley Madison** wrote, "Will you believe it? Here I am within sound of the cannon!" She raced through the White House, saving important state papers and a famous painting of George Washington.

The British burned the capital city, then moved on to Baltimore and attacked Fort McHenry. After watching an all-night battle there, **Francis Scott Key**, a lawyer, wrote the poem that in 1931 became the lyrics to our country's national anthem, "The Star-Spangled Banner." A national anthem is a song of praise for a country.

Why was the war on land difficult for the United States?

The Star-Spangled Banner

Music attributed to J. S. Smith

Words by Francis Scott Key

Oh, __ say! can you see, by the dawn's ear-ly light,

What so proud-ly we hailed at the twi-light's last gleam-ing?

Whose broad stripes and bright stars, through the per-il-ous fight,

O'er the ram-parts we watched were so gal-lant-ly stream-ing?

And the rock-ets' red glare, the bombs burst-ing in air,

Gave proof through the night that our flag was still there.

O, say does that __ Star-Span-gled Ban-ner __ yet __ wave __

O'er the land __ of the free and the home of the brave?

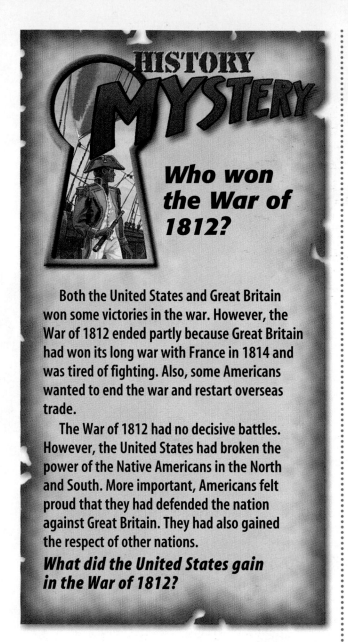

HISTORY MYSTERY

Who won the War of 1812?

Both the United States and Great Britain won some victories in the war. However, the War of 1812 ended partly because Great Britain had won its long war with France in 1814 and was tired of fighting. Also, some Americans wanted to end the war and restart overseas trade.

The War of 1812 had no decisive battles. However, the United States had broken the power of the Native Americans in the North and South. More important, Americans felt proud that they had defended the nation against Great Britain. They had also gained the respect of other nations.

What did the United States gain in the War of 1812?

ERA OF GOOD FEELINGS

A peace treaty ending the War of 1812 had been signed in 1814. However, Andrew Jackson, now a general, did not know this. In 1815 he led Americans to a victory over the British in the Battle of New Orleans. While 50 of Jackson's troops were killed, the British lost 2,000.

After the war, the United States began a time of peace and prosperity. The Democratic-Republicans became the sole political power. This brief one-party era became known as the Era of Good

Feelings. American citizens supported the government and were more united than ever before. The people were "one great family with a common interest," said James Monroe, the new President.

The A.M.E. Church

Among the Americans who enjoyed better times after the War of 1812 were free African Americans. In 1816 Absalom Jones and Richard Allen, both ministers, founded the African Methodist Episcopal (A.M.E.) Church in Philadelphia. It was the first official church for African Americans. It welcomed all people.

National Portrait Gallery/Smithsonian Institution ▶

Richard Allen (above right), a founder of the First A.M.E. Church in Philadelphia (above), worked to improve life for African Americans.

The Monroe Doctrine

James Monroe was reelected in 1820. He soon became concerned about European involvement in the Western Hemisphere. All of Spain's Latin American colonies except for Puerto Rico and Cuba had become independent. Monroe worried that Spain would try to regain its colonies.

In 1823 Monroe gave a speech warning Europe against this. This announcement was called the **Monroe Doctrine**. It said that the United States opposed "future colonization by any European powers" in the area and promised that the United States would not take part in any European wars.

What important events occurred during the Era of Good Feelings?

National Portrait Gallery/Smithsonian Institution

PUTTING IT TOGETHER

Although the United States attempted to remain neutral in European conflicts, it eventually went to war with Britain. In the War of 1812, Commodore Perry defeated the British on Lake Erie. However, the United States lost several land battles. The British even burned Washington, D.C.

After the war, the President issued his Monroe Doctrine, warning European nations to stay out of affairs in the Western Hemisphere.

The promise made by James Monroe (above) that the United States would not take part in any European wars lasted until 1917.

Review and Assess

1. Write one sentence for each of the vocabulary terms below.

   Battle of New Orleans
   Monroe Doctrine
   neutral
   War of 1812

2. What did the United States gain from the War of 1812?

3. How did the Monroe Doctrine protect the United States?

4. Explain how war can affect a country's **economy**.

5. What was Tecumseh's **point of view** on the War of 1812? What might have led him to look at the war in this way?

In 1815 news of the peace treaty reached Andrew Jackson too late to stop the Battle of New Orleans. Trace the map on page 364. Then plot a route on the map showing how news of the treaty might have reached Jackson and his troops.

Write a poem about the scene Francis Scott Key saw that inspired him to write "The Star-Spangled Banner."

Chapter 12 REVIEW

VOCABULARY REVIEW

Number a sheet of paper from 1 to 5. Beside each number write the word or term from the list below that matches the description.

Louisiana Purchase

Monroe Doctrine

neutral

pioneer

War Hawks

1. A person who leads the way, usually to make a new home and become a settler
2. The territory purchased by the United States from France in 1803
3. Not taking sides
4. Members of Congress who wanted to fight Great Britain
5. A declaration that opposed European colonization or interference in the Western Hemisphere

CHAPTER COMPREHENSION

6. Who was Daniel Boone?
7. What was the Cumberland Gap?
8. What was the goal of Lewis and Clark?
9. How did the War of 1812 end?
10. What was the Era of Good Feelings?
11. Why did President James Monroe issue the Monroe Doctrine? What did it say?
12. Suppose you are one of the first pioneers to settle in Boonesborough. **Write** a diary entry describing the first day in your new home on the frontier.
13. What is a national anthem?

SKILL REVIEW

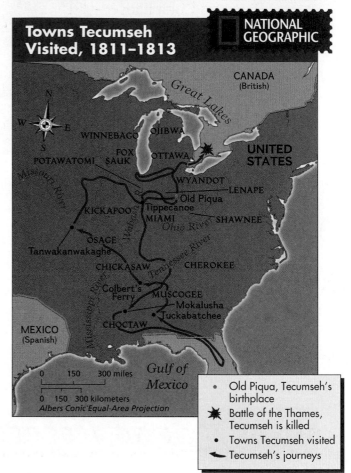

Towns Tecumseh Visited, 1811–1813

NATIONAL GEOGRAPHIC

- Old Piqua, Tecumseh's birthplace
- Battle of the Thames, Tecumseh is killed
- Towns Tecumseh visited
- Tecumseh's journeys

14. **Geography Skill** What kind of map is this? What other kinds of maps do you know how to read?
15. **Geography Skill** What are some of the steps involved in comparing maps?
16. **Geography Skill** In what present-day state did the Ojibwa live? Compare this map to the map on pages R8–R9 to determine the answer.
17. **Geography Skill** In what present-day state did the Kickapoo live? Compare this map to the map on pages R16–R17 to determine the answer.
18. **Geography Skill** Why is it helpful to compare maps?

USING A TIME LINE

1770	1775	1780	1785	1790	1795	1800	1805	1810	1815

1770
Population of 13 colonies reaches 2 million

1773
Daniel Boone leads pioneers through Cumberland Gap

1790
Population of the United States reaches 4 million

1801
Thomas Jefferson becomes President

1803
Louisiana Purchase

1806
Lewis and Clark return from expedition to the West

1812
War with Great Britain begins

19. What information can you find on the time line about the population of the United States?

20. Which event on the time line was a cause of Lewis and Clark's expedition? Explain.

Writing **About Geography** Suppose your family heard about some exciting opportunities in a city or town that they had never been to before. Would you encourage them to move there? What questions would you have about the place? What are some things that would keep your family from moving? What would convince them to move?

Foldables

Use your Foldable to review what you have learned about how and why the young United States more than doubled in size at the beginning of the 1800s. As you look at the front of your Foldable, mentally sequence the key events that contributed to this land expansion. Look at your notes on the inside of your Foldable to check your memory and responses. Record any questions that you have. Then discuss them with classmates or review the chapter to find answers.

THE **Big** IDEAS ABOUT...

The Nation Grows

Many changes are taking place in the United States in the early 1800s. Factories turn out new products. Trains with steam engines carry goods and passengers across the nation. Thousands of people go west after the discovery of gold in California. A war with Mexico ends with the United States gaining the area that is now the Southwest. Read on to learn how these events affect life in the United States.

THE PRESIDENCY OF ANDREW JACKSON

Andrew Jackson is the first person from the West elected President. A "man of the people," he offers new ideas about what a President should be.

THE INDUSTRIAL REVOLUTION

The first factories in the United States are built in New England. Soon cities become centers of manufacturing. Canals and railroads change the way people in our nation travel.

MOVING WEST

People from the East Coast and new immigrants head west on routes such as the Oregon Trail. Some are looking for land to settle. Others are hoping to "strike it rich."

TEXAS AND THE WAR WITH MEXICO

American settlers in Mexican Texas create a Texas republic. After Texas becomes a state in 1845, the United States and Mexico fight a war.

Foldables

Make this Foldable study guide and use it to record what you learn about "The Nation Grows."

1. On a large sheet of paper, draw a line from the top corner of one edge to the middle of the other. Cut off the resulting triangle.

2. Fold the paper into fourths. Accordion the fold.

3. Write the chapter title on the front. Open and label the four columns with lesson titles.

The Industrial Revolution

How did the Industrial Revolution change life in the United States?

VOCABULARY

Industrial Revolution
cotton gin
interchangeable parts
reaper
steam engine
canal

PEOPLE

Samuel Slater
Eli Whitney
Francis C. Lowell
Cyrus McCormick
John Deere
Robert Fulton
DeWitt Clinton
Peter Cooper

READING STRATEGY

Make a chart like this one to list inventions in one column and inventors in the other.

BUILD BACKGROUND

The Spinning Jenny is a large wooden machine that twists fiber into thread. It was the first machine used in a new kind of manufacturing. Before 1800, everything was made by individual workers in shops or homes using hand tools. After 1800 machines began to replace hand workers in many industries. This dramatic change from making goods by hand at home to making them with machines in factories is called the **Industrial Revolution**.

THE FIRST AMERICAN FACTORY

The Industrial Revolution began in Britain in the late 1700s in the textile, or cloth-making, industry. The first machines used waterpower to produce cloth cheaply. The British passed laws to prevent the export of machines or plans for machines. British businesses wanted to keep the new technology a secret.

American Free Enterprise

In the United States, businesses could decide for themselves how best to use their resources. American businesses wanted to start their own factories to make cloth. An Englishman named Samuel Slater heard that business owners in the United States would pay well for the new technology. Slater memorized the plans of the British spinning machines.

In 1789, Slater slipped out of Britain. A Rhode Island merchant hired him to build spinning machines. By 1790 Slater had built the first American cotton-spinning machines.

The price of cotton was high for the new factory. On cotton plantations, enslaved workers pulled cotton seeds from the fibers by hand. It was a slow and difficult task. In 1793 Eli Whitney invented the cotton gin, a machine that removes cotton seeds. The gin,

Samuel Slater's factory (left) In Rhode Island; the spinning frame invention (right), which made a very strong cotton thread, was the prototype for many factory machines.

which is short for "engine," could clean up to 50 times more cotton than workers could by hand.

The cotton gin changed the economy of the South. It made cotton and slavery profitable. Many planters were now determined to protect slavery.

READING CHECK Why did Slater come to the United States?

Exploring
TECHNOLOGY

Power for Machines

The Industrial Revolution began with inventions in the textile industry. Machines were developed to spin and weave cloth quickly. The biggest technological change was the source of power for these machines—water.

A factory, a large building housing many machines, was built near a swift river or stream. The rushing water turned a large wheel in the factory, which powered many machines.

Factory work had many effects. Workers had to come to the factory instead of working at home. They worked long hours, but they were paid more money than farm workers. Soon, factory villages became cities as people came to find work.

Science Museum, London

Explain why factories were built near rivers or streams with swift-moving water.

Lowell, Massachusetts, in 1830

Textile mill

Dock to unload cotton

Boarding house

Merrimack River

Church

Boarding house

Diagram Skill

1. Why was the mill located near the river?

2. What is the machine used by the woman at the right?

MACHINES CHANGE OUR NATION

In 1798, Eli Whitney came up with a new way to manufacture products. He agreed to make 10,000 guns, called muskets, for the U.S. army. He created tools to make each part of every musket the same, or standard. These **interchangeable parts** were made to fit any of the muskets. Manufacturing time and costs dropped.

The Factory System

After visiting factories in Britain, **Francis C. Lowell** and his partners built a textile factory in Waltham, Massachusetts, in 1813. All the steps of cloth-making took place in their factory from making thread to weaving cloth.

In 1817, a factory town, **Lowell, Massachusetts**, was built. It was the first planned town for workers in the United States. "Mill girls," the young women who worked at Lowell, lived in boarding houses and worked 12- to 14-hour days for six days a week. The wages were higher than on local farms.

Machines for Farming

In 1832, **Cyrus McCormick** built an improved **reaper**, a machine with sharp blades to cut grain. It could cut up to four times as much grain as hand workers.

In 1837, an Illinois blacksmith named **John Deere** improved the plow so it would cut through the tough roots of prairie grass. He fashioned a steel saw into a plow shape.

READING CHECK

Explain how machines changed the American way of life.

Transportation in 1860

Industry grew in the United States throughout the 1800s. New factories opened where there was water, and later coal for steam, to power the machines. Study the graphics on this page. Then answer the questions.

NATIONAL GEOGRAPHIC

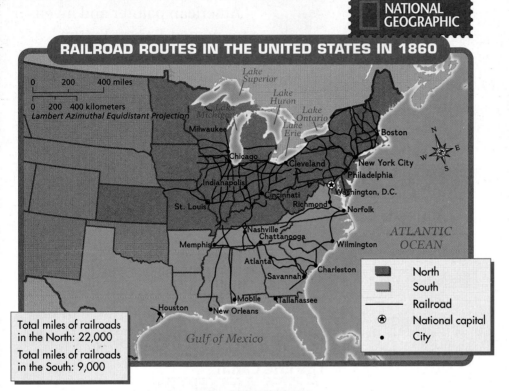

RAILROAD ROUTES IN THE UNITED STATES IN 1860

Total miles of railroads in the North: 22,000

Total miles of railroads in the South: 9,000

Legend:
- North
- South
- Railroad
- ⊛ National capital
- • City

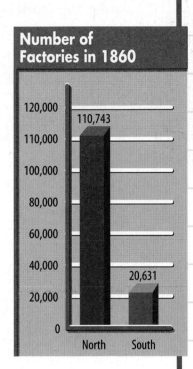

Number of Factories in 1860

- North: 110,743
- South: 20,631

QUESTIONS:

1. Did the North or South have greater industrial production?
2. How did industrial production affect the miles of railroad?
3. Look at both graphics. Make a generalization about industry in the North and South.

To learn more, visit our Web site: **www.mhschool.com**

NEW WAYS TO TRAVEL

In 1800, public transportation was slow and uncomfortable. Most roads were narrow dirt trails filled with potholes and tree stumps. When it rained, these roads became muddy swamps. Even on a good journey, travel on these roads was painfully slow. It took four days, for example, for a stagecoach to make the 215-mile trip from Boston to New York. A stagecoach is a large, horse-drawn carriage for passengers, baggage, and mail.

In 1811, the federal government started building the **National Road** from Cumberland, Maryland, to Vandalia, Illinois. This stone and gravel road linked the East with what was then the Western frontier. This road was a great improvement in transportation.

Transportation improved even more after the invention of the **steam engine**. A steam engine uses the energy from steam to power its engine. It can produce much greater power than a team of horses, so it can pull heavier loads.

Robert Fulton

Steam Power

Until the early 1800s, the easiest way to travel was on America's rivers. Most people and products traveled on rafts or flat-bottomed boats. The crews of these boats used long poles to push them downstream with the current. It was a much harder task to push the boat upstream against the current. An American painter and inventor named **Robert Fulton** learned of a steam engine developed in Scotland. Fulton thought that this steam engine could be used to power a boat upstream.

Fulton worked for years on his design. In August 1807, Fulton's steamboat, the *Clermont*, was ready to run up the Hudson River from New York City to Albany. Fulton's boat was powered by two large paddle wheels connected to a steam engine. Some people called the boat "Fulton's Folly," but the 150-mile trip took just 32 hours. Other boats took from 8 to 11 days for the same trip.

The Erie Canal

In October 1825, the governor of New York, **DeWitt Clinton**, stood on the deck of a small boat bobbing on the waves of New York Harbor. He poured a bucket of water from Lake Erie into the Hudson River. The ceremony, called the "Wedding of the Waters," marked the opening of a human-built waterway, or **canal**.

If a stagecoach got stuck on a muddy road, the passengers had to get out and push.

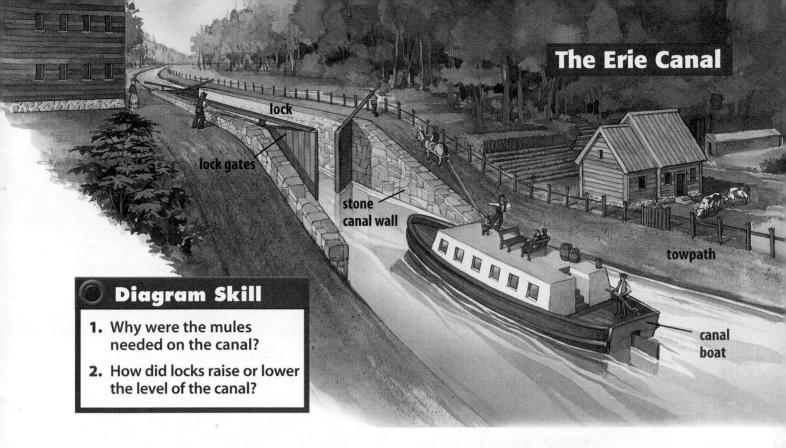

lock

lock gates

stone canal wall

towpath

canal boat

Diagram Skill

1. Why were the mules needed on the canal?

2. How did locks raise or lower the level of the canal?

"Clinton's Ditch"

The **Erie Canal** connected the port of New York with the Great Lakes. Governor DeWitt Clinton's critics called it "Clinton's Ditch." They thought his idea of a 350-mile man-made waterway was impossible.

It also seemed impossible to raise the $7 million cost of the canal. The governor asked European investors to buy shares. An investor is a person who puts money into a project to make a profit. By July 4, 1817, Clinton had raised the money and work began on his "Grand Canal."

From the very beginning, the Erie Canal was a big job. It was not easy to find enough people to do the digging. The first workers were local farmers, but there weren't enough farmers and they had to take care of their crops. They could work only part of the year. This problem was solved by hiring immigrants from Europe.

Another problem quickly became obvious. Land along Lake Erie was 565 feet higher than land along the Hudson River. That meant the canal had to drop more than 500 feet from west to east. The solution was a series of locks. A lock on a canal is like an elevator. It uses water to lift or lower boats to the next level on the canal.

Canal Fever

In spite of these problems, the Erie Canal opened in 1825 with a great celebration. Governor Clinton rode the first boat from Lake Erie to New York Harbor.

The Erie Canal was an instant success. Farmers from Ohio, Illinois, and Indiana were able to ship their crops quickly and cheaply to the East. Factories in the East were able to ship their products to the Midwest. Trade boomed and New York City became the largest city in the country and a center for shipping and trade.

READING CHECK

What developments made it easier to travel by 1840?

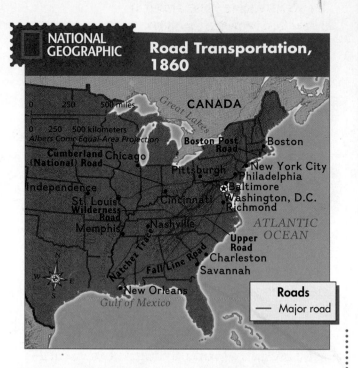

NATIONAL GEOGRAPHIC

Road Transportation, 1860

CANADA

Great Lakes

Boston Post Road
Boston

Cumberland (National) Road
Chicago

Pittsburgh

New York City
Philadelphia

Independence

Baltimore
Washington, D.C.
Richmond

St. Louis
Cincinnati

Wilderness Road

Nashville

ATLANTIC OCEAN

Memphis

Natchez Trace

Upper Road

Fall Line Road

Charleston
Savannah

New Orleans

Gulf of Mexico

0 250 500 miles
0 250 500 kilometers
Albers Conic Equal-Area Projection

Roads
— Major road

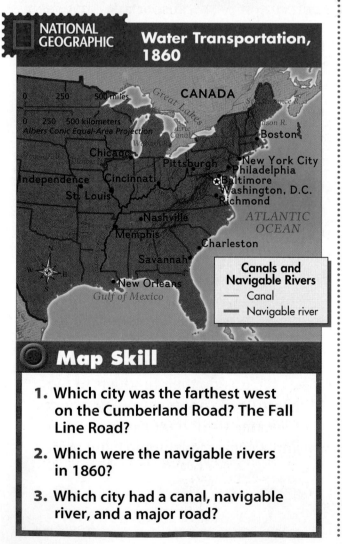

NATIONAL GEOGRAPHIC

Water Transportation, 1860

CANADA

Great Lakes

St. Lawrence R.

Hudson R.

Erie Canal

Wabash R.

Boston

Chicago

Pittsburgh

New York City
Philadelphia

Independence

Cincinnati

Baltimore
Washington, D.C.
Richmond

St. Louis

Nashville

ATLANTIC OCEAN

Memphis

Charleston

Savannah

New Orleans

Gulf of Mexico

0 250 500 miles
0 250 500 kilometers
Albers Conic Equal-Area Projection

Canals and Navigable Rivers
— Canal
— Navigable river

Map Skill

1. Which city was the farthest west on the Cumberland Road? The Fall Line Road?

2. Which were the navigable rivers in 1860?

3. Which city had a canal, navigable river, and a major road?

STEAM LOCOMOTIVES

Canal fever gripped the United States. Hundred of miles of canals were in use by the 1830s. There were plans for many more. However, these canals would soon be replaced by a brand new invention—the railroad.

The first "rail roads" had been coaches set on iron rails and pulled by horses. In 1829, an English inventor replaced the horse with a locomotive, a rail car powered by a steam engine. This was the same kind of steam engine used by Fulton on the *Clermont*.

In 1830, **Peter Cooper**, a New York businessman, brought this English "iron horse" to America. Cooper convinced the Baltimore and Ohio Railroad Company to replace its horses with steam locomotives. He built a small locomotive and named it *Tom Thumb*, after the tiny character in the children's story.

Few people believed *Tom Thumb* could actually move. A Baltimore stagecoach company challenged the little locomotive to a race. *Tom Thumb* was doing quite well until something went wrong

with one of its parts. Although the little engine lost the race, it led the way for the railroads that crisscrossed the United States in the next one hundred years.

How did the railroad change travel in the United States?

PUTTING IT TOGETHER

The Industrial Revolution changed technology in the United States. It also brought new and great wealth to some entrepreneurs (ahn truh pruh NOOR). An **entrepreneur** is a person who organizes and runs a new business. The Industrial Revolution also brought changes to ordinary people's lives and to different regions of our nation. People paid less for some products, but the workers in the new factories worked long hours in difficult conditions. Transportation between regions improved. However, the new technology created differences between the North and the South.

Review and Assess

1. Write one sentence for each vocabulary term.

   cotton gin   **reaper**
   Industrial Revolution   **steam engine**
   interchangeable parts

2. Why did most people and products travel on America's rivers?

3. Identify changes in the United States caused by the Industrial Revolution.

4. How did the Erie Canal make New York City into a center of trade and shipping?

5. Plantation owners were excited about the invention of the cotton gin. How might their **point of view** differ from that of an enslaved person?

Look at the maps on page 374. Draw a map showing how a farmer would get wheat from a farm in Michigan to a market in New York City.

Write a poem or letter describing the workday that a mill girl in Lowell might have written to a friend or relative. Use details from the lesson to make your writing realistic.

The Presidency of Andrew Jackson

Find Out! How did the United States change under President Andrew Jackson?

Lesson Outline
- Jackson Becomes President
- Jackson Makes Changes
- The Trail of Tears

VOCABULARY

Bank of the
  United States
Indian Removal
  Act
Trail of Tears

PEOPLE

John Quincy
  Adams
Andrew Jackson
Sequoyah
John Ross
Osceola

READING STRATEGY

Make a chart like this one. Write the main idea of the lesson in the top space. Write supporting details in the spaces below.

BUILD BACKGROUND

In 1824, President **John Quincy Adams** told Americans that "... a population of four millions has expanded to twelve. A territory bounded [ended] by the Mississippi River has been extended from sea to sea. New states have been admitted to the Union ...."

A new kind of nation was emerging as President Adams spoke. Soon the people in the frontier states would vote for a new kind of leader to represent them.

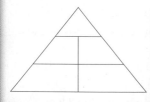

JACKSON BECOMES PRESIDENT

Between 1812 and 1821, six new states joined the Union. These states allowed all white men older than 21 to vote. These new voters helped elect **Andrew Jackson**. He had little formal education and came from a state west of the Appalachians.

The new President was a hero of the War of 1812. He was also a self-taught lawyer and a judge. He owned a large plantation in Tennessee, but in spite of his wealth and success, he frightened wealthy political leaders. They worried about what he would do as President.

Lively posters helped elect Jackson, seen here with Justice John Marshall. His statue (left) is in Washington, D.C.

New York Historical Society

Election of "Old Hickory"

Jackson's military victories had made him famous, but his triumph at New Orleans almost did not take place. His troops were marching to protect the city from a British attack during the War of 1812 when Jackson received an order to disband the army at once. His troops grumbled that they had marched a long way for nothing. Jackson agreed and refused to obey the order. His troops easily defeated a well-trained British army. "He's tough," one soldier said, "tough as hickory," a tree that has very hard wood. After that Jackson became known as "Old Hickory."

When he ran for President in 1828 he was seen as the candidate of "the common man." Jackson won by a landslide. A landslide election happens when one candidate wins a large majority of the votes.

A huge crowd gathered in Washington to watch Jackson's inauguration in 1829. Everyone was invited to the White House to celebrate after the ceremony. People stood on chairs to see Jackson, even overturning tables. Jackson barely managed to escape out a back door. A new kind of presidency began that day.

READING CHECK

How was Jackson different from Presidents before him?

377

JACKSON MAKES CHANGES

President Jackson believed in "protecting all and granting favors to none." He favored no groups. During his time as president, Jackson worked hard to protect the rights of American farmers, new settlers on the frontier, and working people. His particular enemy was the **Bank of the United States**.

In 1816, this bank was given control of the money supply of the United States. This meant that its decisions affected every person in the United States.

Jackson was convinced that the charter of the Bank of the United States was unconstitutional. He also believed that the bank was an enemy of democracy.

In 1836, Jackson removed all the federal government's money from the Bank of the United States. This greatly reduced the bank's power. Jackson ordered the federal money to be put into state and local banks. There were no controls on these banks and many of them invested unwisely in land. When the economy

Cherokee dancers used this Eagle Dance wand in ceremonies for peace and war. Sequoyah is shown below with his Cherokee alphabet, called "talking leaves."

weakened in 1837, there was no way to get back this money. Hard times followed for many Americans. This was the first great economic downturn in American history.

Trouble in South Carolina

In 1832, Congress passed a new tax on imported goods. The law protected new American industries, but it made imported items very expensive. Southern states had few local industries, so they had to import many products.

People in South Carolina were particularly angry about the new law. South Carolina's leaders said the law was unconstitutional and threatened to leave the Union if the tax was collected in their state.

Jackson reacted quickly. He sent troops and warships to South Carolina to collect the tax. The crisis passed when a compromise was reached. However, the issue of a state's right to leave the Union remained to be settled.

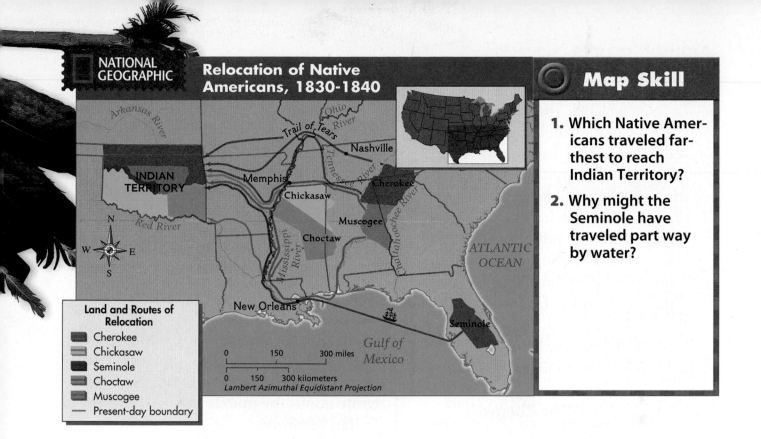

Map Skill

1. Which Native Americans traveled farthest to reach Indian Territory?

2. Why might the Seminole have traveled part way by water?

Land and Routes of Relocation
- Cherokee
- Chickasaw
- Seminole
- Choctaw
- Muscogee
- Present-day boundary

0   150   300 miles

0   150   300 kilometers
Lambert Azimuthal Equidistant Projection

Bad Times for Native Americans

Some Native American communities were doing well in the early 1800s. These groups were located in the Southeast and included the Cherokee, Choctaw, Chickasaw, Muscogee, and Seminole. They had signed treaties with the federal government that gave them control of their lands and protection from new settlers.

The Native Americans developed schools and local governments. One of the achievements of this period was the development, by the Cherokee, of the first written Native American alphabet. **Sequoyah**, a Cherokee silversmith, worked for 12 years to create an alphabet. His writing system used Greek, Hebrew, and English symbols for Cherokee sounds. His newspaper, the *Cherokee Phoenix*, is still printed today.

Conflict over land rights led to almost constant problems with the settlers. The problem grew worse in 1830 when gold was discovered on Cherokee lands within the state of Georgia.

As a general, Andrew Jackson had fought several wars with Native Americans. He was convinced that they were a threat to the growth of the United States. He wanted to move all Native Americans to lands west of the Mississippi. He thought this would end the trouble.

Jackson urged Congress to act. In 1830, the **Indian Removal Act** was passed. This law allowed the President to remove Native Americans from their homelands and relocate them to the **Indian Territory**, which is now the state of Oklahoma. The Indians were forced to sign agreements with the federal government. They gave up their lands in the East and moved to new homes across the Mississippi River.

Why were there conflicts between Native Americans and settlers in the Southeast?

THE TRAIL OF TEARS

In 1831, the United States government began forcing Native Americans to leave their homes. In Alabama, some who refused to leave were forced into slavery. White settlers in Georgia held a lottery to see who would get Cherokee farms. But the Cherokee boldly refused to leave.

Led by their chief, John Ross, the Cherokee went to the Supreme Court. In 1832 the Court ruled that Georgia could not force the Cherokee from their land. "Well, [Chief Justice] John Marshall has made his decision, now let him enforce it," Jackson is believed to have said. The President refused to obey the Court's decision. He ordered the Cherokee removed along with the others.

In 1838, United States soldiers rounded up the Cherokee, burned their houses, and forced them to begin the eight-hundred-mile march to Indian Territory. In their own language, the Cherokee called this forced march "the place where they cried." Later it became known as the Trail of Tears.

The march took more than a year. About 4,000 out of 15,000 Cherokee people died along the way. Among them was Quatie, the wife of Chief John Ross. She had given her only blanket to a sick child. John Burnett, a young soldier from Tennessee who had grown up among the Cherokee, served as interpreter. He later wrote about the march west to the Indian Territory.

Native Americans on the Trail of Tears.

excerpt from An Account,
—by John G. Burnett,
published in 1890

"[In] May 1838, . . . I saw helpless Cherokees arrested and dragged from their homes . . . I saw them loaded like cattle or sheep into six hundred and forty-five wagons and started toward the west . . . [When] the bugle sounded and the wagons started rolling many of the children rose to their feet and waved their little hands good-by to their mountain homes, knowing they were leaving them forever. Many of . . .them had been driven from home barefooted."

How did Burnett feel about the way the Native Americans were removed?

Native Americans were also removed from Florida. One group, the Seminole, resisted. Their chief, Osceola, organized an army that fought against United States soldiers. Osceola was captured in 1837 and died in prison. Many Seminole retreated into Florida's swamps. A few remained in Florida while others left.

What was the effect of the Indian Removal Act of 1830?

PUTTING IT TOGETHER

The election of Andrew Jackson was the first election of a President who had not been born wealthy and in which voting was not limited to property owners. However, his presidency had mixed results. He supported farmers, working people, and new settlers in the West, but his treatment of Native Americans cast a cloud over the country.

Review and Assess

1. Write one sentence for each vocabulary term.

   Bank of the United States
   Indian Removal Act
   Trail of Tears

2. How had voting laws changed by 1828? How did this affect elections?

3. What changes occurred in the United States while Andrew Jackson was President?

4. Why did manufacturers support the tax on imported products and farmers resist it?

5. Compare the **point of view** of a Cherokee and a settler about the Indian Removal Act .

Look at the map on page 379. Make a chart of the Native American groups who were moved west. Write the names of the groups and where they lived before they moved to the Indian Territory.

Write an editorial for a newspaper in 1831. Your editorial should agree or disagree with the Indian Removal Act. Include reasons that support your opinion.

Being a Good Citizen
Saving Our Canal

As you read in Lesson 2, John Ross showed loyalty to the Cherokee by going to the Supreme Court. Students in Hocking County, Ohio, showed their loyalty by working to preserve the heritage of their state.

"It took ten years and a special Ohio birthday," says Sandra Starner, "but in 2000 my students helped save a part of Ohio history." In 1990, Starner was teaching at Rockbridge Elementary, in rural Hocking County, Ohio. Near the school was Lock Number 12, part of the Hocking Canal built in 1843. This canal was part of the Ohio-Erie Canal system. Mules pulled canal boats carrying coal, iron ore, and farm products from Rockbridge to cities on the Great Lakes.

Mrs. Starner's class often took trips to the lock, where they talked about local history. One day the students learned that the lock had been sold. The new owner planned to take it apart, selling the old stone blocks and filling in the canal. "When students heard the news, they decided to try to save the lock." The class wrote letters to the governor and other officials and historical societies, begging them to take over the property, but nothing happened.

Ten years passed. Ohio was preparing for the 200th anniversary of its statehood in 2003. The state wanted to preserve historic sites. A mother of one of the students remembered their letter-writing campaign. She told state officials to contact Mrs. Starner. The class of 2000 went to work.

"We filled out applications, and wrote letters to the state officials planning the birthday celebration, explaining why the lock should be an official historic site," says Adam Stohs. A new owner agreed to donate the site to the state. Local businesses helped students raise

"We set out to make a difference and we did."

money for the official historic bronze marker. Darrin Hacquard and other students removed a sofa, some old tires, other trash, and brush from the lock.

On June 2, 2000, ten years after they began the campaign, Mrs. Starner and many students from her 1990 class attended a special ceremony. Lock Number 12 of the Hocking Canal became an official Ohio historical site.

Adam and Darrin represented the class of 2000. Darrin recalls, "My older brother was in Mrs. Starner's class ten years ago. We set out to make a difference and we did . . . Generations from now people will come to this site and say this is the way it was in the 1840s."

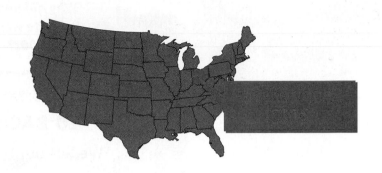

Be a Good Citizen

Making Connections

- What are some historical landmarks in your community or state?

- What are some ways Americans show respect for their local history?

Talk About It!

- What steps did Mrs. Starner and her class take to preserve the lock site?

- What event or events helped the students to save the canal lock?

Act On It

In the Community

Plan a walking tour of historic landmarks in your area. If one is related to someone who showed loyalty to the community or country, write a paragraph describing how.

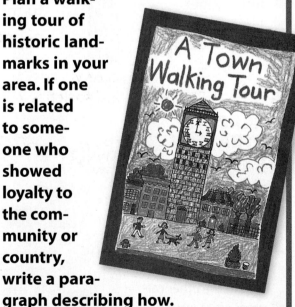

In the Classroom

As a class, discuss historical landmarks in your area. Choose one to learn more about. Write a paragraph about the landmark. Do research and learn its history.

Moving West

Why did people migrate west in the 1800s?

Lesson Outline
- The Trip West
- Why They Went
- The Gold Rush

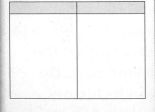
BUILD BACKGROUND

"We left our home in Iowa with three wagons drawn by seven yoke [pairs] of oxen, it was thought that horses were not suitable to draw wagons across the Rocky Mountains . . . . Two of the wagons were loaded with provisions [supplies] and the third a light wagon carried the small children and some beds."

This is how John Breen recalled his family's move to the West in 1846. Breen was one of thousands of people who traveled to the West to begin a new life.

THE TRIP WEST

People had many reasons for traveling west of the Mississippi River. Some hoped for religious freedom. Others hoped to discover gold or silver and make a fortune. Still others came for cheap land.

The journey west took between four and five months. A family had to take all the supplies they would need, not only for the journey, but also to set up house when they arrived. Their wagons carried flour, water, dried meat, seeds for planting, weapons and bullets, farm tools, and pots and pans for cooking. This didn't leave much room for family treasures.

Travelers left in spring to get across the Rocky Mountains before snow blocked the passes. These large groups of wagons were called **wagon trains**. As long as the settlers kept moving west, Native Americans left them alone. Some Indians even supplied travelers with vegetables and buffalo meat.

Western Trails

One route to the West was called the Santa Fe Trail. It crossed New Mexico and Arizona before following an old Spanish road to Los Angeles. However, most travelers took the **Oregon Trail** to the **Oregon Territory**. More than 300,000 people followed the Oregon Trail west. So many wagons crossed on the Oregon Trail that some of the deep ruts of their wheels are still visible today.

READING CHECK What made traveling west in the 1800s a challenge?

NATIONAL GEOGRAPHIC

Trails to the West, 1840–1860

Map Skill

1. Which trails led into California?

2. Which trail began at the Mississippi River?

Legend:
- • City
- ⊁ Fort
-)(Mountain pass
- — Trail

Whitman Mission
Ft. Vancouver
Ft. Walla Walla
Bozeman Trail
Oregon Trail
Ft. Boise
California Trail
Ft. Hall
Split Rock
Independence Rock
Red Buttes
Ft. Laramie
Soda Springs
South Pass
Platte River
Mormon Trail
Nauvoo
Donner Pass
Salt Lake City
Ft. Bridger
Chimney Rock
Omaha
St. Louis
Sacramento
San Francisco
Sutter's Fort
Castle Rock
Oregon Trail
Independence
Old Spanish Trail
PACIFIC OCEAN
Los Angeles
Santa Fe Trail
Santa Fe
Red River
El Camino Real (from Mexico)
El Paso
Gulf of Mexico

0 250 500 miles
0 250 500 kilometers
Lambert Azimuthal Equidistant Projection

130°W 120°W 110°W 100°W 90°W
40°N 30°N

WHY THEY WENT

Two early travelers on the Oregon Trail, **Marcus Whitman** and his wife, **Narcissa Whitman**, were missionaries. They set out in 1836 and traveled for about six months. Their mission near the Columbia River in the Oregon Territory became a resting place for travelers.

The Northwest was a region of rich forests with many fur-bearing animals. Fur trappers had crossed the mountains for years. Later travelers saw other possibilities. In letters to her family, Narcissa Whitman described the rich farmland, dense woodlands, and snow-capped mountains. "It is indeed, a lovely situation," Whitman wrote. Her letters were published and encouraged other Americans to settle in Oregon.

The Mormon Migration

Early in 1847, more than 14,000 travelers left Nauvoo, Illinois, along a route called the **Mormon Trail**. The travelers were part of a religious group called the Church of Jesus Christ of Latter-day Saints, or Mormons. The Mormons had been badly treated in the East because of their beliefs. They hoped to find a safe place to settle in the West.

Brigham Young led the Mormons on their long march. Their wagons crossed ice-covered rivers as they followed the Oregon Trail. Near Fort Bridger, in what is now Colorado, the group left the trail and headed south into lands claimed by Mexico. In July 1847, the first Mormons reached a large lake now known as the **Great Salt Lake**. The present-day state of **Utah** got its name from the Ute (YOOT) people who shared this area with the Shoshone people.

At first, it did not seem like a good place to settle. "Everything looked gloomy, and I felt heartsick," wrote a Mormon traveler named Harriet Young. However, the soil was rich, and the Mormons used irrigation to grow crops. **Salt Lake City**, one of the first Mormon settlements, grew rapidly. By 1850 it had about 5,000 Mormons.

Stopping Off

Many of the wagon trails had been Native American trails that were developed in the early 1800s by fur trappers. By 1859, these trails were crowded with wagon trains and pioneers on foot.

Because they lived in the western mountains, fur trappers were called **Mountain Men**. In 1843 a Mountain Man named **Jim Bridger** had established a fort in Wyoming. Soon travelers along the Mormon Trail and the **California Trail** used this fort as a rest stop. Fort Bridger was also a place for trading goods and repairing wagons.

Pioneers took only a few treasures to the West.

The Oakland Museum

Another famous Mountain Man was **James Beckwourth**, a runaway slave who was hired as a trader by the American Fur Company. In 1859 he reached a gap, now called Beckwourth Pass, in the northern Sierra Nevadas. He got along so well with Native Americans that he was made a chief of the Crow people and was buried on their land.

Lightening the Load

One of the landmarks pioneers looked for on the Oregon Trail was **Chimney Rock**. This famous rock formation is located near present-day Bayard, Nebraska. It marked the spot where supplies usually began to run low. The oxen

James Beckwourth

pulling the wagon would be getting weaker by this point as well. To lighten their wagons and help the oxen, pioneers would often toss out furniture and other heavy possessions. For many years, both sides of the Oregon Trail were littered with these household goods.

The westward journey was frightening, difficult, and long, but there were many who had happy memories. Read what Octavius T. Howe wrote about his journey west.

READING CHECK

What groups of people moved to the West?

Primary Source:

excerpt from
Argonauts of '49
— by Octavius T. Howe, pioneer

" . . . *Those who crossed the plains . . . never forgot the . . . thirst, the intense heat and bitter cold, the* **craving** *hunger and the* **utter** *physical exhaustion of the trail . . . . Neither would they ever forget the level prairie, . . . the glorious sunrise in the mountains . . . and the pure sweet air of the desert . . . .*"

What did Howe remember about the journey west?

craving: deep
utter: total

THE GOLD RUSH

A group of men had gathered to work at a mill on the American River in California in 1848. James Marshall, an engineer, woke the others one morning by pounding on the boards of the mill. James Brown, one of the men he awakened, takes up the story.

"Who is that pounding so early?" Some one of the party looked out and said it was Marshall shutting the gates . . . . This brought to my mind what he had said the evening before about finding gold, and I said, "Oh, he is going to find a gold mine this morning."

Brown's joke turned out to be a fantastic prediction. Marshall did find gold that morning and soon people were racing across the continent along the California Trail.

Gold was discovered first at Sutter's Mill, the mill that Marshall had been building. So many people arrived seeking

People from many countries panned for gold in California.

a fortune that this migration became known as the California Gold Rush. Ulysses S. Grant, later the commander of Union armies in the Civil War, was a young lieutenant in California at the time. "All thought that fortunes were to be picked up, without effort, in the gold fields on the Pacific," Grant later wrote.

"Gold fever" struck thousands of would-be miners. Because they reached California in 1849, these fortune-hunters called themselves forty-niners. A few lucky ones struck it rich. For the rest, the long days of wading in streams or bending over gravel beds led to exhaustion and disappointment. Many lived in wooden huts or canvas tents.

Supplies from the East had to travel around Cape Horn, south of Chile and Argentina. It was a long and dangerous voyage. As more and more miners came to California, the price of food and supplies skyrocketed. Even an ounce of gold, which was worth about $16 at the time, would not go far when flour cost 25 cents a pound and potatoes were 16 cents apiece.

The Golden State

In 1847 San Francisco had only 800 people. By December 1849 the population had climbed to 25,000. Many Californians wanted statehood. They believed that California needed courts of law and elected officials to keep order in the fast-growing region.

Because they did not like the California constitution, others

opposed California's statehood. For example, it gave married women in California the right to own property. The property of married women in the East belonged to their husbands. Also, California had outlawed slavery, and Southerners did not like this. In spite of these arguments, California became a state in September 1850.

How did the discovery of gold affect life in California?

PUTTING IT TOGETHER

In the 1800s, thousands of people traveled to the West seeking a better life. They followed the Oregon Trail, the Mormon Trail, the California Trail, and other trails first established by Native Americans and by Mountain Men.

The 1849 Gold Rush attracted thousands of people from the United States and all over the world to areas around Sutter's Mill, California. This helped to make the 1840s to 1860s one of the great periods of movement in the history of the United States.

People eagerly read ads for travel to California, where they hoped to find gold (above right).

Review and Assess

1. Write one sentence for each vocabulary word.

   forty-niners   **Mountain Men**
   Gold Rush

2. Why were Mountain Men important in the history of the West?

3. What were some reasons people settled the West in the 1800s?

4. Why did prices rise in California after gold was discovered?

5. How might the **point of view** of a Mexican landowner, a Native American, and a settler from the East have been different when California became a state?

Look at the map on page 385. Make a map showing what trail you would take traveling west.

. . . .

Write a letter to a friend in the East describing your daily life as a miner looking for gold in California. Include what you do, what you eat, prices, and the things you see.

Distinguishing Fact From Opinion

In the last lesson, Octavius T. Howe wrote about the hunger, thirst, heat, and cold during the journey to the West. These are **facts**, statements that can be checked and proved true. He also wrote about the beauty of a sunrise and the pure air of the desert. These are Howe's **opinions**, his personal beliefs or views.

LEARN THE SKILL

Use the excerpt below as you follow the steps to distinguish facts from opinions. It was written by a Californian named Tallman Rolfe who visited a town called Rough and Ready in 1849. The letter was to a friend.

> ...Children are not numerous in California. The birth of a child is an inspiration for celebrating. I happened to pass through Rough and Ready late in '49 and experienced the excitement due to the arrival of a daughter at the home of Henry Sales, who was probably the most prosperous and popular resident of that lively district .... The Sales were very happy for the time ... rich ground was discovered on one of their claims by one ... who saw gold shining in a pool as he stooped to get a drink of water.

To help you distinguish facts from opinions, try the following:

1. **Identify the statements that you think are facts.**
   Letters and other accounts can prove that he visited Rough and Ready in 1849 and visited the Sales. The discovery of gold on their claim can also be checked.

2. **Identify parts of the letter as opinions.**
   It is Rolfe's opinion that Sales was the most popular man in the district. We have no way to check this opinion. It is also his opinion that the Sales were very happy.

3. **Check for clue words showing opinions.**
   Words such as *I think, I feel, it seems,* or *was probably* are based on feelings or personal likings and cannot be proved. Some sentences use descriptive words such as *good, best,* or *wonderful.* They express beliefs and cannot be proved.

TRY THE SKILL

Now read the excerpt from this letter from a California pioneer woman. Then answer the questions that follow.

I determined to set up a rival hotel. So I bought two boards from a man who was building the second wooden house in town. With my own hands, I chopped stakes, drove them into the ground, and set up my table. I bought provisions at a neighboring store, and when my husband came back at night he found, mid the weird light of the pine torches, twenty miners eating at my table. Each man as he rose put a dollar in my hand and said I might count him as a permanent customer. I called my hotel 'El Dorado.'

From the first day, it was well patronized, ...

1. How can you identify the facts?

2. Which parts of the excerpt are possible opinions?

3. Which clue word shows an opinion?

4. Why is it important to distinguish facts from opinion?

EXTEND THE SKILL

Read your local newspaper and a magazine. Find an example of a fact and an example of an opinion in the newspaper and magazine. Explain your choices in a brief paragraph for each example.

- What parts of a newspaper are most likely to contain opinions? Was it easy to distinguish fact from opinion in the magazine? Explain.

- How can distinguishing facts from opinions help you better understand history?

Texas and the War with Mexico

Lesson Outline
- Texas and Mexico
- Conflict Leads to War
- Statehood and War
- The War Ends

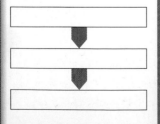 *How did Texas become a state?*

VOCABULARY

Treaty of
  Guadalupe
  Hidalgo

manifest destiny

PEOPLE

Stephen F. Austin

Antonio López
  de Santa Anna

David Crockett

Jim Bowie

William Travis

Suzanna
  Dickenson

Sam Houston

Lorenzo
  de Zavala

James K. Polk

Zachary Taylor

**READING
STRATEGY**

Make a chart like this
one to list lesson
events in order.

BUILD BACKGROUND

"I think I derived [got] more satisfaction from the view of flourishing farms springing up in this wilderness than military or political chieftains do from the retrospect [memory] of their victorious campaigns. My object is to build up for the present as well as for future generations . . . ."

Stephen Austin wrote these words as he thought back on his early years in Texas.

TEXAS AND MEXICO

For years Spaniards in Mexico heard stories of "the great kingdom of the Tejas (TAY hahs)." In the stories, Native American people called the Caddo referred to themselves as tejas, or "friends." As a result, the Spanish called the entire region Texas.

Under Spain, Texas was included in the colony of Mexico. After ten years of war, Mexico won its independence from Spain in 1821. Texas then became part of the new Mexican Republic.

Mexican leaders worried because few people lived in Texas. Mexicans also feared that the United States would settle Texas. Mexico's rulers offered land to Mexicans to encourage settlement in Texas.

"Gone to Texas"

Mexico gave Missouri merchant Moses Austin permission to bring American settlers to Texas in 1821 if they agreed to become Mexican citizens. Austin died, and his son, Stephen F. Austin, completed his plan in 1822. He brought about 300 families to Texas. These settlers came to be known as "The Old 300."

In the 1820s and 1830s, land in Texas was cheaper than land in the United States. In fact, it was often free. "Texas fever" soon swept the United States. Mary Austin Holley, an American, was impressed by the Texas soil. In 1831 she wrote, "The

newcomer has but to plant his seeds in the ground, and the increase is astonishing."

Sources of Conflict

Slavery was illegal under Mexican law, but Mexican leaders allowed slavery in Texas to encourage American immigration. Even so, the Mexican government required settlers in Texas to become Mexican citizens, join the Roman Catholic Church, and learn Spanish. However, most Americans did not learn Spanish or change their religion. They also ignored the laws because the government of Mexico was too far away to enforce them.

The Alamo (left) is in San Antonio, Texas. The painting above is of Stephen Austin.

READING CHECK

What were the problems between the Mexican government and the American settlers?

CONFLICT LEADS TO WAR

Mexico's leaders began to worry that they would lose Texas. By 1830 Americans in Texas outnumbered Mexican residents, or Tejanos, by three to one. Mexican leaders decided to stop immigration from the United States. This decision angered many Americans living in Texas.

Mexico outlawed slavery in Texas in 1829. Many planters complained that they could not grow cotton without slave labor. A planter named John Durst wrote to Stephen F. Austin, "We are ruined forever."

In 1833 a number of Texans asked Austin to go to Mexico City to explain why Texans were against the new laws. They hoped that the Mexican government would agree to make Texas a separate Mexican state. Instead, Austin was arrested for trying to start a rebellion and was put in jail for more than a year.

Texas Revolts

Mexico's president, **Antonio López de Santa Anna** (ahn TOH nee oh LOH pes DE SAHN tah AH nah) sent about 1,400 Mexican troops into Texas in 1835. Santa Anna had seized power in Mexico the year before. He had thrown out Mexico's constitution and made himself president for life. Now Santa Anna planned to end the arguments with Texas.

Santa Anna was disliked by many Texans—Tejanos and Americans alike. They opposed his takeover of the Mexican government, and they joined together to fight Santa Anna's troops. A Tejano leader, Juan Seguín (HWAHN se GHEEN), organized volunteers into a Texas army.

Volunteers also arrived from the United States. **David Crockett**, a former United States Congressman from Tennessee, joined the fight. **Jim Bowie**, also from Tennessee, led a volunteer force. **William Travis**, a lawyer from Alabama, had been appointed commander of the Texas army.

Texas State Library

David Crockett (right) and Juan Seguín (center) died at the Alamo during the Mexican attack led by Santa Anna (left).

Re-enactments of Mexican troops charging the Alamo can be seen today.

Remember the Alamo!

The Texas army took control of the **Alamo**, a Spanish mission in San Antonio that was changed into a fort. Between 187 and 257 Texas rebels, wives, and children, camped inside. More than 4,000 of Santa Anna's troops surrounded the fort.

On February 23, 1836, the Mexican troops attacked the Alamo. After almost two weeks of fighting the Texans, Mexican soldiers broke through their defenses on March 6. In hand-to-hand fighting, most of the Alamo's defenders were killed. More than 1,000 Mexican soldiers died as well.

Alamo survivors, mostly women and children, met Santa Anna. He ordered **Suzanna Dickenson**, whose husband was one of the dead, to carry the news of the Texans' defeat. She took a letter from Santa Anna to the headquarters of **Sam Houston**. Houston, born in Virginia, was a general in the Texas army.

During the battle of the Alamo, 59 Texas delegates met in Washington-on-the-Brazos and approved a Declaration of Independence on March 2, 1836. It proclaimed the new Republic of Texas.

The outnumbered Texas army was defeated on March 19. More than 350 prisoners were marched to a fort at **Goliad** (GOH lee ad). Against the advice of his officers, Santa Anna had all the prisoners executed. This act shocked Texas.

Texas Becomes Independent

In April, Houston's troops surprised Santa Anna near the **San Jacinto** (sahn hah SEEN toh) **River**. Shouting "Remember the Alamo!" and "Remember Goliad!" the Texans defeated the Mexican army on April 21.

The battle was over in 18 minutes. Santa Anna was captured. He agreed to ask Mexico to grant independence to Texas in exchange for his freedom.

Why did settlers want Texas to leave the Mexican Republic?

Star of the Republic Museum

STATEHOOD AND WAR

Sam Houston was elected the first president of the Republic of Texas. **Lorenzo de Zavala** (loh REN soh DEH sah VAH lah), a Tejano officer, became the first vice president. The Texans chose a flag with a single white star. The young republic was nicknamed "the Lone Star" republic. Its capital was **Houston**.

The Lone Star Republic

In 1836 Sam Houston asked President Andrew Jackson to make the Republic of Texas a state. Mexico threatened to go to war if Texas became a state. Jackson knew that Texas would allow slavery. He did not want to lose the support of Northern leaders who opposed slavery. Jackson turned down Houston's request.

By 1844 political leaders had changed their minds. **James K. Polk** promised the American people "all of Texas," and was elected President. Texas entered the Union in 1845.

War with Mexico

In 1845 President Polk sent an official to Mexico to settle the border dispute between Texas and Mexico at the **Rio Grande**. He also offered to buy the Mexican territories of California and New Mexico for $30 million. Mexico angrily refused the offer.

President Polk ordered General **Zachary Taylor** and his troops in Texas to march to the Rio Grande in April 1846. They made it across the Rio Grande and captured several Mexican cities. Taylor's forces defeated Santa Anna's army at the Battle of Buena Vista in 1847.

The war spread quickly. California was part of Mexico at the time, but Americans there declared an independent republic, called the "Bear Flag Republic" in June 1846. The United States navy arrived soon after and claimed California.

At the same time, Stephen Kearny and his troops captured New Mexico's capital at Santa Fe. They then marched to California. After several battles, Mexico's troops surrendered in January 1847.

READING CHECK

Why did Texas statehood lead to war with Mexico?

The earliest Texas flags had the lone star design (above) created by Lorenzo de Zavala.

San Jacinto Museum of History

BIOGRAPHY

Focus On: Loyalty

Sam Houston lived in Virginia and Tennessee before spending several years living with the Cherokee. He admired the Cherokee, but he also hoped to organize them into an army to free Texas from Mexico. Houston wanted Texas to be part of the United States.

Being loyal to Texas, he became head of the Texas army and later the first President of Texas in 1836. In 1846, he went to Washington as a Texas Senator. Loyal also to the Cherokee, he fought in the Senate for Native American rights. In 1859, he was elected governor of Texas. He showed his loyalty to the Union in 1861 by refusing to take Texas out of the Union when it seceded. The Confederate government then removed him from office. He retired from public life.

Link to Today **What is loyalty? Choose someone alive today. Make a class presentation to show how this person has been loyal in his or her life.**

THE LIFE OF SAM HOUSTON	1793 Sam Houston is born	1836 Houston defeats Santa Anna; becomes first President of Texas	1845 Houston elected U.S. Senator	1863 Houston dies in Texas
	1800	1815	1830	1845	1860

LIFE AROUND THE WORLD	1822 Liberia is founded in West Africa	1824 South Americans win independence from Spain	1853 Matthew Perry opens Japan to trade

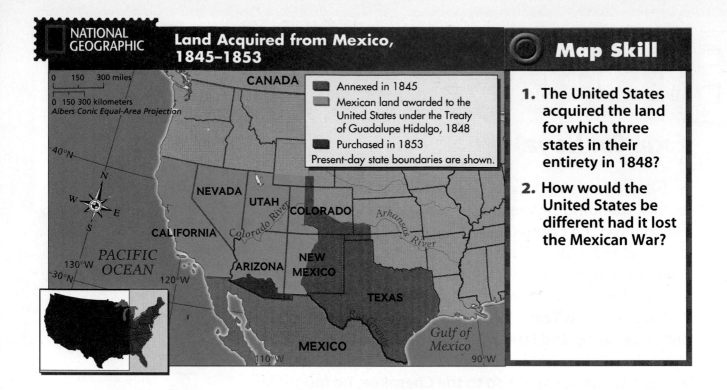

0 150 300 miles
0 150 300 kilometers
Albers Conic Equal-Area Projection

CANADA

Annexed in 1845
Mexican land awarded to the United States under the Treaty of Guadalupe Hidalgo, 1848
Purchased in 1853
Present-day state boundaries are shown.

40°N

130°W

30°N

120°W

110°W

90°W

NEVADA

UTAH

COLORADO

Arkansas River

CALIFORNIA

Colorado River

PACIFIC OCEAN

ARIZONA

NEW MEXICO

TEXAS

MEXICO

Gulf of Mexico

1. **The United States acquired the land for which three states in their entirety in 1848?**

2. **How would the United States be different had it lost the Mexican War?**

THE WAR ENDS

An American army led by General Winfield Scott landed on the coast of Mexico in 1847, and headed inland toward Mexico City. The fortress guarding the Mexican capital was called **Chapultepec** (chuh POOL tuh pek). Scott's troops attacked the fortress in September 1847. Inside were fewer than 1,100 Mexican troops, including *Los Niños,* a group of young military cadets. After a fierce battle, Americans captured the fortress.

The Peace Treaty

In 1848 the signing of the **Treaty of Guadalupe Hidalgo** (gwah dah LOO pay hih DAL goh), ended the war. Mexico accepted the Rio Grande as its border with Texas. Mexico also gave up half of its territory to the United States, which agreed to pay $15 million to Mexico for the lands, shown on the map above.

The 80,000 Mexicans living in Mexico's former lands had to choose between Mexican and American citizenship. Only 2,000 chose to remain Mexican. The new citizens were guaranteed the same rights as other Americans, yet many of them lost their lands because they were unfamiliar with the English language and with American courts of law.

_____

These fifty-dollar notes called "redbacks" were printed by the Republic of Texas.

Archives Division–Texas State Library

398

A New Idea

Jane Cazneau was a journalist who wrote an editorial about Texas in 1845. She was the first person to state the idea that it was the **manifest destiny** of the United States to occupy land from the Atlantic to the Pacific. Manifest destiny was a belief in the right of the United States to expand its borders and to claim new lands. This belief continued to play a key role in the settlement of western lands.

"Old Rough and Ready" – Zachary Taylor

What were the results of the Mexican War?

PUTTING IT TOGETHER

The United States gained a vast territory as a result of the Mexican War. General **Zachary Taylor** used his fame as a commander in the Mexican War to help him become the twelfth President of the United States in 1849. The officers of the United States army who fought in the war gained valuable battlefield experience. In less than 20 years, these same veterans would be fighting again—often against each other—on United States soil.

Review and Assess

1. Write one sentence for each vocabulary term.

   manifest destiny
   Treaty of Guadalupe Hidalgo

2. What was the importance of the Battle of San Jacinto?

3. What events caused Texas to change from a Mexican territory to the twenty-eighth state of the United States?

4. Why might Mexicans living in the lands lost to the United States have agreed to become United States citizens?

5. Identify some **facts** and some **opinions** that led to the Texas Revolution.

Look at the map on page 398. What states contain land that was once part of Mexico? Research the area of each state and figure out the total number of square miles the United States gained.

Write an editorial expressing your opinion about the war with Mexico. It should be from the point of view of a reporter in 1846 and should include both opinions and facts.

VOCABULARY REVIEW

Number a sheet of paper from 1 to 5. Beside each number write the word or term from the list below that matches the description.

cotton gin

reaper

forty-niners

Trail of Tears

manifest destiny

1. A belief in the right of the United States to expand its borders and claim new lands

2. Fortune hunters who came to California in 1849

3. A machine that uses sharp blades to cut grain

4. A machine that removes cotton seeds

5. The forced march of Cherokee in 1838 from their homes in Georgia to the Indian Territory

CHAPTER COMPREHENSION

6. What was the Industrial Revolution?

7. How did the invention of interchangeable parts change American manufacturing?

8. How did the National Road improve transportation in the United States?

9. How did the Indian Removal Act of 1830 affect Native Americans?

10. What were some of the reasons people moved to the West in the early 1800s?

11. Why did President Jackson turn down Texas' request to join the United States?

12. What were the terms of the Treaty of Guadalupe Hidalgo in 1848?

13. **Write** an advertisement for one of the inventions you read about in the chapter. Be sure to describe how the invention is useful.

 SKILL REVIEW

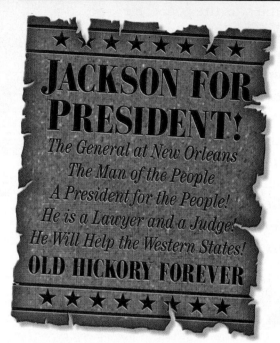

14. **Reading/Thinking Skill** Look at the poster. Which statements are facts? Explain your choices.

15. **Reading/Thinking Skill** Which statements are opinions? How do you know?

16. **Reading/Thinking Skill** Which of the following is a fact?

    a. The steam engine produces much greater power than a team of horses.

    b. Andrew Jackson was known as "Old Hickory."

    c. United States soldiers wanted the Cherokee lands.

17. **Reading/Thinking Skill** Why is it important to be able to distinguish fact from opinion?

18. **Reading/Thinking Skill** Write a letter to a friend during the election of 1828. In your letter explain why you do or do not support Andrew Jackson. Include facts and opinions in your letter.

USING A TIME LINE

1790	1800	1810	1820	1830	1840	1850

1790
Samuel Slater builds first spinning machines in Rhode Island

1807
Steamboat *Clermont* makes trial run

1821
Mexico wins independence from Spain

1825
Erie Canal is completed

1830
Tom Thumb makes its first run

1836
Battle of the Alamo; Republic of Texas established

1846
The Mexican War begins

1848
The Mexican War ends; gold discovered in California

19. What event helps explain why canals were important for only a short time?

20. How many years passed between Mexican independence from Spain and the end of the Mexican War?

***Writing* About Historical Events** Think of an event you read about in this chapter: the Industrial Revolution, the settlement of the West, or Texas and the Mexican War. Write about how the event changed the United States. How would your life be different if this historical event had not taken place?

Use your Foldable to review what you have learned about the expansion of the nation. As you will notice, your Foldable increases in size from east to west. Mentally review what you learned about industrialization and westward expansion. Look at your notes in the columns of your Foldable to check your memory and responses. Record any questions that you have. Then discuss them with classmates or review the chapter to find answers.

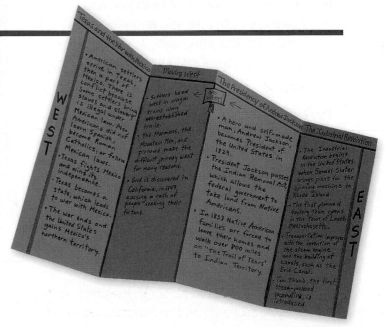

VOCABULARY REVIEW

Number a sheet of paper from 1 to 5. Beside each number write the term from the list below that best completes the sentence.

forty-niners	**neutral**
Louisiana Purchase	**Trail of Tears**
Monroe Doctrine	

1. The ____ is also known by the Cherokee as "the place where they cried".

2. The ____ opposed European colonization in the Western Hemisphere.

3. President Madison tried to keep the United States ____ during European conflicts.

4. The ____ came to California in search of gold.

5. President Thomas Jefferson arranged the ____, which doubled the size of the United States.

TECHNOLOGY

For more resources to help you learn more about the people and places you studied in this unit, visit **www.mhschool.com** and follow the links for Grade 5, Unit 5.

● SKILL REVIEW

6. **Geography Skill** How is a historical map different from a political map?

7. **Geography Skill** How could you find out which present-day states Lewis and Clark traveled through?

8. **Study Skill** What are the clue words that help you know that something is an opinion?

9. **Study Skill** Is the following statement a fact or an opinion?
   Sam Houston was the first president of the Republic of Texas.

10. **Study Skill** What is one way to check the statement above?

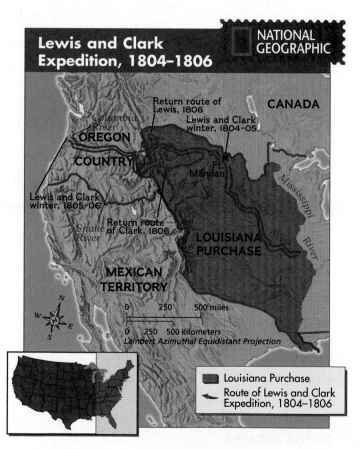

Lewis and Clark Expedition, 1804–1806

1   The Texas army took control of the Alamo. . . . Texas rebels, some with wives and children, camped inside. More than 4,000 of Santa Anna's troops surrounded the fort.

2   On February 23, 1836, Mexican troops attacked the Alamo. After almost two weeks of fighting the Texans, Mexican soldiers broke through their defenses on March 6. In hand-to-hand fighting, most of the Alamo's defenders were killed. More than 1,000 Mexican soldiers died as well.

3   . . . The outnumbered Texas army was defeated on March 19. More than 350 prisoners were marched to a fort at Goliad. . . . Against advice, Santa Anna had all the prisoners

executed. This act shocked Texas.

1 Which of these sentences from the paragraphs is an opinion?

  A   On February 23, 1836, Mexican troops attacked the Alamo.

  B   In hand-to-hand fighting, most of the Alamo's defenders died.

  C   More than 1,000 Mexican soldiers died as well.

  D   This act shocked Texas.

2 Which sentence would not belong in an outline of this passage?

  A   Texas rebels camped inside.

  B   More than 4,000 Mexican soldiers surrounded the Alamo.

  C   All Texans were angry when they heard about the Alamo.

  D   Santa Anna was captured.

WRITING ACTIVITIES

Writing to Persuade Suppose that you are a member of Congress in 1811. *Write* a speech that explains your point of view about going to war with Great Britain. Try to persuade other members to support your point of view.

Writing to Inform Suppose you are a newspaper reporter assigned to cover the race between *Tom Thumb* and the horse-drawn coach. *Write* an article about the race and include people's reactions to the new steam locomotive.

Writing to Express *Write* about the battles Texas fought to gain its independence.

NORTH STAR TO FREEDOM:

The Story of the Underground Railroad

Selections by Gena K. Gorrell
Illustrated by Mark Schroder

When slavery became illegal in the North many enslaved African Americans ran away from the South. Some were helped by a secret network of people known as the Underground Railroad.

It's the middle of the night, and you're suddenly wide awake. What was that noise?

"Hush . . . don't wake the others! Just lie still and don't make a sound!"

It's your mother—but what's she doing at this hour? The sky is black, and you can see stars through the cracks in the shed roof. The boards beneath you are hard, and a splinter is digging into your back, but you try not to move. As the cold night wind blows through the walls, you pull your thin jacket closer around you . . . .

"Get up and slip out the door. Don't take anything—just creep out quiet as a mouse!"

As you tiptoe through the half-open door, she's right behind you, carrying a bundle. She takes your hand and hurries you down the cattlepath. It's hard to walk in the dark with bare feet; you can't see where the stones are and you stub your toes.

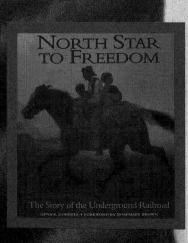

NORTH STAR TO FREEDOM

The Story of the Underground Railroad
GENA K. GORRELL • FOREWORD BY ROSEMARY BROWN

"Are we going to Papa?"

"No. Papa's gone, child, I told you that. They sent him away and I got no idea where to find him."

Even in her whisper, you can hear her voice tremble.

"Then where are we going?"

"Not so loud! We're going to Canada."

"Where's Can—"

"Don't ask me where it is, or how far! All I know is, we walk toward the North Star and pray God will take care of us. All I know is, we can't stay here no more! They took away your papa, they took away your brother, and I'm not waiting till they take you too!"

She's walking so fast that it's hard to keep up with her, but at least you don't feel cold anymore. You're just trying to sort things out in your mind when she speaks again, this time more calmly, but so seriously that your stomach turns right over.

"We're going together, child, and I pray the Lord will get us both to Canada. But if anything happens to me, don't you stop—just keep following that star. Because beginning tonight—beginning the minute we walked out of that shed back there—we're free. And we're not ever going to be slaves again."

Write About It!

Suppose you were traveling on the Underground Railroad. **Write** a journal entry describing some of your experiences.

Unit 6

Slavery and Emancipation

TAKE A LOOK

How did slavery and states' rights lead to the Civil War?

Mounted soldiers were valued for their speed and power for over 2,000 years. Today soldiers depend on armored vehicles, missiles, and aircraft.

U.S. Army Center of Military History

For more information about the Civil War, visit our Web site at **www.mhschool.com**

Slavery Divides the Nation

By the 1850s differences between the North and the South had created two distinct ways of life in the United States. The deepest division between the states was over the expansion of slavery. This and other differences between the states would cause the Southern states to break from the United States and try to form their own country. Read on to find out about the events that led to one of the bloodiest periods in the history of the United States, the American Civil War.

SLAVERY DIVIDES THE COUNTRY

Slavery is part of a larger issue—the economy. The South uses slave labor to help grow most of the crops they sell. The work in Northern factories is done largely by immigrants.

THE ABOLITION MOVEMENT

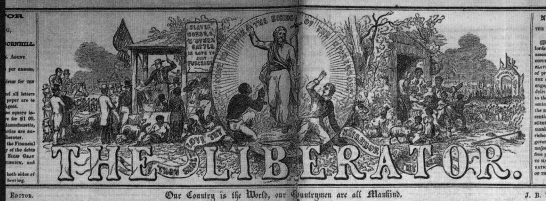

Newspapers and books play an important role in getting people to join the movement to end slavery. Yet their fight is not easy.

THE ELECTION OF 1860

Abraham Lincoln promises to end the spread of slavery. When Lincoln wins the election of 1860, one by one Southern states gradually leave the Union to form their own country, the Confederate States of America.

Foldables

Make this Foldable study guide and use it to record what you learn about "Slavery Divides the Nation."

1. Fold an 8 ½" x 11" sheet of paper in half like a hamburger, leaving a 1" tab.

2. Make two cuts on the short side forming three tabs.

3. Write the chapter title on the 1" tab and lesson titles on the 3 tabs. Draw frames around all titles. Draw lines connecting all lesson frames to the chapter frame.

"King Cotton" and the Spread of Slavery

VOCABULARY

prejudice

PEOPLE

Nat Turner

Frederick Douglass

Elizabeth Jennings

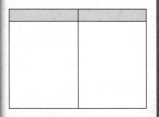

What major differences divided the North and the South in the 1850s?

Lesson Outline
- Two Different Ways of Life
- Opposing Slavery
- Free African Americans

READING STRATEGY

Copy the chart below. Then use it to compare and contrast how the North was different from the South.

BUILD BACKGROUND

"Why am I a slave? I will run away. I will not stand it. Get caught or get clear. I'll try it . . . . It cannot be that I shall live and die a slave." Many enslaved Africans in the South during the 1840s and 1850s knew these words from "The Fugitive's Song." Yet only about 1,000 a year were able to escape. Most continued to live without freedom or rights, and under terrible hardships. Their work was needed to keep the economy of the South prosperous. At the same time, slavery was dividing the United States.

1800	1810	1820	1830	1840	1850	1860	1870	1880

You Are Here
1831–1860

TWO DIFFERENT WAYS OF LIFE

By 1850 two distinct ways of life existed in the United States—one Northern and one Southern. Their economies affected their views about slavery. Although most people in both the North and the South were farmers, manufacturing was becoming much more important in the North. Immigrant men and women worked in Northern factories. In 1854 there were more than 400,000 immigrants in the United States. The largest number came from Ireland and Germany. They were fleeing political and economic problems in their homelands.

Although many immigrants came to the United States to be farmers, many found work in the large cities of the North.

"King Cotton"

Most Southerners owned small farms but did not have slaves. It was cotton grown on large plantations that produced most of the South's wealth. By 1860 the South produced about two-thirds of the world's supply of this valuable crop. "Cotton is king," went the old saying.

Some supporters of slavery argued that enslaved people in the South were better off than immigrants and other workers in the North. George Fitzhugh, a Virginia lawyer said, "The free laborer must work or starve. He is more of a slave than the [N]egro, because he works longer and

By 1860 about 4 million enslaved African Americans picked and cleaned cotton on Southern plantations.

Exploring ECONOMICS

Cotton Production

In the early 1800s, the South became the world's largest producer of cotton. In 1817, the South produced 461,000 bales. As demand for cotton grew, so did supply. By 1840 production soared to 1.35 million bales. As demand for cotton increased, so did the need for workers to harvest it. This caused slavery to expand into new territories. Between 1815 and 1860 cotton made up more than half of American exports. This economic growth also helped the North, where merchants made money shipping cotton. The North also used it to make clothes.

Draw a chart showing the effects that increased demands for cotton had on the economy.

harder for less allowance [reward] than the slave. . . ."

Many, however, saw slavery as unjust and cruel. In 1839, a member of the American Anti-Slavery Society said:

Slaveholders talk of treating men well, and yet not only rob them of all they get, . . . but rob them of THEMSELVES, . . . hands and feet, all their muscles, and limbs, and senses, their bodies and mind, their time and liberty.

Where did the North get most of its labor?

OPPOSING SLAVERY

Slavery had gradually ended in the North after the American Revolution. In 1808, Congress had made it illegal to import slaves from Africa. Still the number of enslaved African Americans in the nation grew. Many of them were born to parents who were enslaved. Others were brought into the country illegally.

Nat Turner's Rebellion

The number of slave rebellions also grew. One of the most serious took place on August 21, 1831. Nat Turner led a small band of enslaved people in Southampton County, Virginia. For two days, they went from farm to farm and killed nearly 60 men, women, and children from slave-holding families. Turner hid in the woods for six weeks before he was caught. All the rebels were hanged.

After Turner's rebellion, many slave owners feared for their lives. As one planter said, "I have not slept without [worry] in three months." Terrified whites in the South killed more than 100 innocent enslaved and free blacks in 1831. Some states passed laws forbidding African Americans from gathering in public places and holding religious services. In Virginia speaking against slavery became a crime in 1832.

Frederick Douglass

One of the people who spoke out against slavery was Frederick Douglass. Read the following excerpt from a speech he gave at an Independence Day picnic.

READING CHECK Why did the number of enslaved African Americans grow rapidly after 1808?

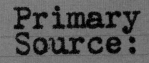

Primary Source:

excerpt from **a speech by Frederick Douglass**
— in Rochester, New York, July 4, 1852

*Fellow citizens, . . . why am I called upon to speak here today? . . . Are the great principles of political freedom and of natural justice, **embodied** in that Declaration of Independence, extended to us? . . . This Fourth of July is yours, not mine . . . There are seventy-two crimes in the state of Virginia which, if committed by a black man . . ., subject him to the punishment of death; while only two of the same crimes will subject a white man to the like punishment . . . am I to argue that it is wrong to make men **brutes**, to rob them of their liberty, to work them without wage, to keep them ignorant of their relations to their fellow men, to beat them with sticks, to **flay** their flesh with the lash, to load their limbs with irons, to hunt them with dogs, to sell them at auction, to **sunder** their families, . . . ?*

What does the celebration of the Declaration of Independence mean to Douglass?

---

embodied: contained
brutes: animals

flay: strip away
sunder: break apart

BIOGRAPHY

Focus On: **Courage**

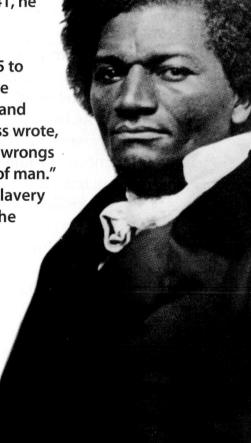

FREDERICK DOUGLASS was born into slavery in 1818. For 20 years he endured cruel treatment. In 1838 Douglass courageously disguised himself as a sailor and boarded a ship for New York. In 1841, he became a lecturer for the Massachusetts Anti-Slavery Society. He gave speeches about his experiences as an enslaved person. From 1845 to 1847, Douglass went to Great Britain, where he spoke against slavery and for women's rights and free public school education. In 1846, Douglass wrote, "I cannot allow myself to be insensitive to the wrongs and sufferings of any part of the great family of man."

Douglass began publishing his own anti-slavery newspaper, *The North Star*, in 1847. During the Civil War, Douglass served as an adviser to President Lincoln. Today, Douglass is remembered for his courage in speaking out for the rights of all Americans.

Link to Today

Think about a leader in the 1900s who had the courage to speak out for people's rights. Then write a paragraph comparing and contrasting this leader to Douglass.

THE LIFE OF FREDERICK DOUGLASS	**1818** Douglass born in Maryland	**1838** Douglass escapes slavery	**1845** Douglass publishes his autobiography	**1847** Douglass publishes *The North Star*	**1889** Douglass becomes U.S. minister to Haiti	**1895** Douglass dies

1820	**1840**	**1860**	**1880**	**1900**

LIFE AROUND THE WORLD	**1822** Liberia is founded	**1842** China opens its ports to Western traders	**1861** Serfdom is abolished in Russia	**1895** The radio and film projector are invented in Europe

FREE AFRICAN AMERICANS

There were free African Americans in both the North and the South, especially in the cities where there were more chances of finding work. However, most of them lived in the North. By 1850 more than 430,000 free African Americans lived in our country. Some had been freed by their owners. Others bought their freedom.

Prejudice

Life for free African Americans was difficult. In the South they had to carry certificates of freedom, register with the police, and sometimes pay a tax. As in the South, many places in the North barred African Americans from lecture halls, hotels, and restaurants. They were forced to sit in separate sections in white churches. And they were still denied equal legal and voting rights. Because of **prejudice** most skilled jobs were closed to them. Prejudice is a negative opinion formed without proof.

Free African Americans fought prejudice in different ways. On July 16, 1854, 24-year-old schoolteacher, **Elizabeth Jennings** climbed aboard a "whites only" streetcar in New York. She refused to leave. After a struggle, a police officer removed her. Jennings went to court to fight the company's policy. Her lawyer was Chester A. Arthur, a future President of the United States. In 1855 the judge ruled, "Colored persons . . . had the same rights as others and could neither be excluded by any rules of the company, nor by force or violence."

Neighborhoods

Many African Americans had been freed when the northern states ended slavery. They set up organizations to meet their needs. African American Baptist and Methodist church groups ran many of them. They established schools, held social events, and helped escaping slaves. By 1846 the African Methodist Episcopal Church had nearly 300 branches.

In the early 1800s, New York became a center for the movement to end slavery. African Americans in the city also started communities as a response to prejudice. By 1825 **Seneca Village** was a fairly large community of African American property owners. **Weeksville** was established in Brooklyn in 1838, as a home to ministers, teachers, and other African American professionals. In Virginia, **Umbler** was a community of free African Americans that had existed since the 1700s.

 How was life difficult for free African Americans?

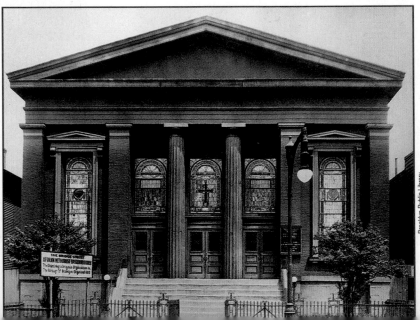

This African American Methodist Episcopal Church in Brooklyn, New York, was founded in 1818.

414

United States Population, 1860

The North

Immigrants
3,543,847

Other Americans
15,092,263

The South

Immigrants
480,032

Other Americans
7,752,043

Enslaved People
3,950,521

Source: United States Census, 1860

Graph Skill

1. **What was the South's total population?**

2. **How many more people lived in the North than in the South?**

PUTTING IT TOGETHER

By 1850 the North and South had different ways of life. Their populations were made up of different groups of people whose views did not agree. The divisions between the North and South grew wider because of slavery. Northern political leaders were still careful about attacking slavery in the South. They feared that a struggle over slavery would destroy the country. Yet it was a struggle that would not be avoided for long. "On the subject of slavery," said one South Carolina newspaper, "the North and South . . . are not only two Peoples, but they are rival, hostile Peoples."

Review and Assess

1. Write a sentence for the vocabulary word.
   prejudice

2. Describe the different ways in which Frederick Douglass resisted slavery.

3. Summarize the major differences between the North and the South in 1860.

4. How was the **economy** of the North different from that of the South?

5. **Compare and contrast** the views of slavery given by George Fitzhugh on page 411 and Frederick Douglass on page 412.

Look at the graphs above. In which region were there more immigrants? How many more immigrants were there in that region than the other region?

Write a speech that Frederick Douglass might have given about prejudice against African Americans in the North.

Speaking Out Against Slavery

Find Out!

Who fought for abolition and women's rights in the early 1800s?

Lesson Outline
- The Abolition Movement
- Escaping Slavery
- Abolition and Women's Rights

VOCABULARY

abolitionist

Underground Railroad

Seneca Falls Convention

PEOPLE

William Lloyd Garrison

Harriet B. Stowe

Angelina Grimké

Sara Grimké

Levi Coffin

Harriet Tubman

Lucretia Mott

Elizabeth Cady Stanton

Sojourner Truth

READING STRATEGY

Use a chart like the one below to list similarities between the abolition and women's movements.

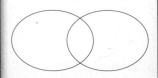

BUILD BACKGROUND

As the practice of slavery grew during the 1800s, more and more people spoke out against it. In 1831 William Lloyd Garrison began a newspaper in Boston called *The Liberator*. Its strong words against slavery caused a stir throughout the United States. "On this subject I do not wish to think, or speak, or write with moderation . . . AND I WILL BE HEARD."

THE NORTH STAR.
VOL. I. NO. 31. ROCHESTER, N. Y., FRIDAY, JULY 28, 1848. WHOLE NO.—81.

UNCLE TOM'S CABIN

UNCLE TOM LEAVING HOME

Harriet Beecher Stowe Center

National Park Service, Frederick Douglass NHS

THE ABOLITION MOVEMENT

People who spoke out against slavery were called **abolitionists**. An abolitionist was someone who wanted to abolish, or end, slavery in the United States.

Spreading the Word

The printed word played an important role in getting people to join the abolitionist movement. By 1860 about 17 African American newspapers alone were printed in the United States. People who opposed, or were against, the abolitionists tried to stop these and other abolitionist newspapers. In some places copies of *The Liberator* were burned and mail carriers refused to deliver it.

The Liberator also upset some Northerners. Garrison demanded that blacks have the same rights as whites. Although Northerners did not own slaves, many of them did not believe in equal rights for blacks and whites.

The most famous abolitionist newspaper grew to be *The North Star*, started by Frederick Douglass in 1847. The others included the *Freeman's Advocate*, *Freedom's Journal*, and *The Mirror of Liberty*.

Uncle Tom's Cabin

One of the most popular statements against slavery in the United States was made in 1852 by an abolitionist in Massachusetts. **Harriet Beecher Stowe** wrote a novel called *Uncle Tom's Cabin*. It described the lives of the enslaved. One character, Eliza Harris, escaped to prevent her young son from being sold away from her. Another, Uncle Tom, died under the whip of the cruel overseer Simon Legree. The book sold more than 300,000 copies within its first year of publication.

Southern Abolitionists

A number of Southern whites fought for the abolition of slavery. Among them were **Angelina Grimké** and **Sara Grimké**, daughters of a wealthy South Carolina judge and plantation owner. They had seen the evils of slavery firsthand. Sara "believed their bondage [slavery] inconsistent with justice and humanity." Eventually, the two sisters moved to the North where they worked openly for the end of slavery. There they were among the first women to speak publicly for abolition.

READING CHECK **How did *Uncle Tom's Cabin* support abolition?**

Uncle Tom's Cabin by Harriet Beecher Stowe (left) and the newspaper *The North Star* (far left) spoke out against slavery.

417

ESCAPING SLAVERY

Like Frederick Douglass, many African Americans risked their lives to escape to the free Northern states. They also went to the Western Territories, Canada, Mexico, and the Caribbean Islands. Many traveled for weeks or months crossing hundreds of miles almost entirely at night. During the day they hid from slave catchers roaming the fields and forests searching for escaped slaves.

The Underground Railroad

Some abolitionists worked to end slavery legally. Others took direct action to help those who were enslaved. One way was through the **Underground Railroad**. Neither underground nor a railroad, the Underground Railroad was a system of secret routes that escaping captives followed to freedom. The escaping slaves and those who helped them used railroad terms as code words. Those who guided and transported escaping slaves were called "conductors." The slaves were called "passengers." The places where slaves hid along the way were called "stations." People who fed and sheltered them were "station masters."

Songs were often used to signal their plan to escape. The song on page 419, "Follow the Drinking Gourd," gave directions for escaping north in code. Each of the rivers in the song was an actual river. For example, the "great big river" was the Ohio River. The "drinking gourd" was the

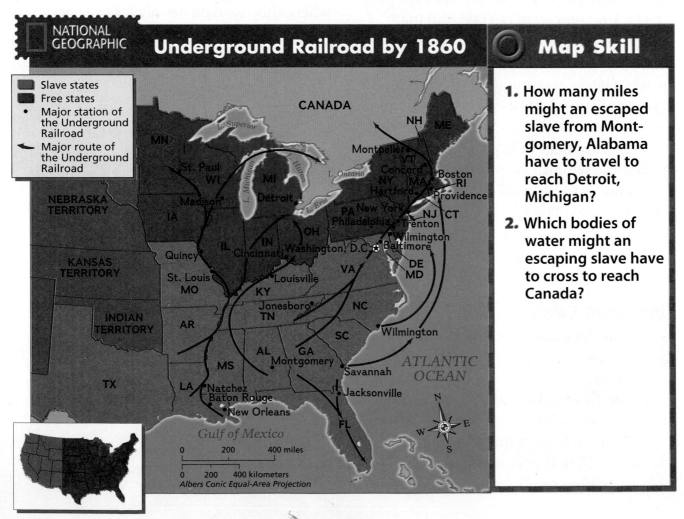

NATIONAL GEOGRAPHIC

Underground Railroad by 1860

Map Skill

Legend:
- Slave states
- Free states
- • Major station of the Underground Railroad
- ← Major route of the Underground Railroad

CANADA

L. Superior

L. Michigan

L. Huron

L. Ontario

L. Erie

MN

St. Paul
WI
MI
Madison
Detroit

NEBRASKA TERRITORY

IA

IL
Quincy
Cincinnati
IN
OH

KANSAS TERRITORY

St. Louis
MO
KY
Louisville

INDIAN TERRITORY

AR

Jonesboro
TN

TX

LA
Natchez
Baton Rouge
New Orleans

MS

AL
Montgomery

GA

NC

SC
Wilmington

Savannah

Jacksonville

FL

NH
ME

Montpelier
VT
Concord
NY
MA
Boston
RI
Hartford
Providence
PA
New York
NJ CT
Philadelphia
Trenton
Wilmington
Washington, D.C.
Baltimore
DE
MD
VA

ATLANTIC OCEAN

Gulf of Mexico

0   200   400 miles

0   200   400 kilometers
Albers Conic Equal-Area Projection

N
W   E
S

1. How many miles might an escaped slave from Montgomery, Alabama have to travel to reach Detroit, Michigan?

2. Which bodies of water might an escaping slave have to cross to reach Canada?

418

Little Dipper. One of the stars in the Little Dipper is the North Star, which escaping slaves used to guide them north.

*The river ends between
    two hills,*
*Follow the drinking
    gourd.*
*There's another river on
    the other side,*
Follow the drinking gourd.
*When the great big river
    meets the little river,*
Follow the drinking gourd.
*For the old man is a-waiting for
    to carry you to freedom*
If you follow the drinking gourd.

A Quaker from Indiana, Levi Coffin, was known as the "president of the Underground Railroad." His home was along one of the major transportation routes. His wife Catherine Coffin fed, clothed, and hid more than 3,000 slaves in their home.

Most of the volunteers on the Underground Railroad were African American. Some of them were still enslaved.

Harriet Tubman

One of the best known volunteers on the Underground Railroad was Harriet Tubman. In 1849 Tubman heard that she and other slaves on her Maryland plantation were to be sold farther south. Tubman knew that life was harder there. She told her husband, John, "There's two things I've a right to: death or liberty. One or the other I mean to have. No one will take me back alive."

Although her husband refused to join her, Tubman fled from the plantation in the middle of the night. She headed for the house of a white woman known to help those escaping slavery. The woman gave her two slips of paper with the names of families on the route north who would help her. Tubman traveled at night, mostly through swamps and woodlands. After traveling 90 miles, she reached the free soil of Pennsylvania. She later said,

"I looked at my hands, to see if I was the same person now that I was free . . . I felt like I was in heaven."

Tubman returned 19 times to guide her family and many others to freedom. She was given the nickname "Moses," after the Hebrew prophet who led his people out of slavery in Egypt. "I never run my train off the track, and I never lost a passenger," said Tubman. More than 300 slaves owed their freedom to her. Southern slave owners offered $40,000 reward for her capture. William Still, secretary of the Underground Railroad in Philadelphia, said of Tubman "in point of courage . . . she was without equal."

Harriet Tubman

READING CHECK **How did the Underground Railroad help Harriet Tubman?**

ABOLITION AND WOMEN'S RIGHTS

Women in the early 1800s also had very few rights. As the abolition movement strengthened, so did the fight for women's rights. In 1837 Angelina Grimké wrote: "The discussion of the rights of the slave has opened the way for the discussion of other rights." She meant the rights of women.

The Seneca Falls Convention

In 1840 a World Antislavery Convention was held in London. It refused to allow women to take part. This angered two of its delegates, **Lucretia Mott** and **Elizabeth Cady Stanton**. They decided to organize their own convention to discuss women's rights. It would be held in **Seneca Falls**, New York.

On July 19, 1848, more than 240 people attended the **Seneca Falls Convention**.

After two days of debate, the convention approved a "Declaration of Rights and Sentiments." It began with the statement "All men and women are created equal." It went on to say "The history of mankind is a history of repeated injuries . . . on the part of man toward women." Then it listed 18 rights they believed women should have. These included the rights to vote, to higher education, to own property if married, and to have equal rights with men. These became known as equal rights.

Sojourner Truth

Throughout the 1840s and 1850s **Sojourner Truth** gave speeches around the country about abolition and women's rights. Born into slavery in New York around 1797, she was freed in 1827. At the age of 46, she began speaking out about the evils of slavery and women's rights. Read the excerpt below.

Primary Source:

excerpt from **a speech by Sojourner Truth**
— *at the Women's Rights Convention in Akron, Ohio, 1851*

I have heard about the sexes being equal. I can carry as much as any man, and can eat as much too, if I can get it. I am as strong as any man that is now. As for intellect, all I can say is, if a woman have a pint, and a man a quart—why can't she have her little pint full? You need not be afraid to give us our rights for fear we will take too much, for we can't take more than our pint'll hold . . . .

What do you think Truth is calling for when she asked, "why can't she have her little pint full?"

These statues in Seneca Falls honor the early leaders of the women's rights movement.

PUTTING IT TOGETHER

Many people found that the abolition and the women's rights movements together made both movements stronger. "I am for any movement whenever and wherever there is a good cause to promote, a right to assert [defend], a chain to be broken, a burden to be removed, or a wrong to be redressed [corrected]," said Frederick Douglass at the Seneca Falls Convention. But as both movements gained strength, the United States became even more divided than it already was. Some feared a division between the states would soon lead to war.

In 1851 Truth had attended the Women's Rights Convention in Akron, Ohio. She had listened as men spoke about how a woman's place was in the home and how women were weaker than men. Then Truth went up to the platform and asked simply, "May I say a few words?" Her few words are still quoted today.

How did the women's movement grow out of the abolition movement?

Review and Assess

1. Write one sentence for each vocabulary term.

   abolitionist
   Seneca Falls Convention
   Underground Railroad

2. In the early 1800s, what rights did women not have?

3. Who were the leaders of the abolition and women's rights movements?

4. How would the Declaration of Rights and Sentiments affect citizens' rights?

5. **Predict** what effects conflict over slavery would have on the movement for women's rights.

Look at the map on page 418. Use it to write directions for slaves escaping from Louisiana and heading to Minnesota.

Write a poem about one of the people discussed in this lesson.

Analyzing the News

In the nineteenth century people's main source of news was from newspapers. Today, people can also get news from television, radio, and the Internet.

In order to analyze the news, you must understand the different kinds of articles in the news. For example, local, state, national, and international news in newspapers and on television and radio all have articles of recent events, articles on topics they think may be of interest to readers, and many special features.

LEARN THE SKILL

Follow these steps to analyze articles in the news.

1. **Identify the kind of article you are reading or listening to.**
   A **news article**, or story, describes an important event that has recently taken place.

   Many news organizations offer **feature articles**. Feature articles are detailed reports on a person, an issue, or an event. An article on the history of the Olympics, for example, is a feature article.

   Some news organizations also offer **editorials**. An editorial is an article in which an editor, or a person who runs a news organization, gives his or her opinions on important issues. Many newspapers also contain letters to the editor from readers who give their opinions on issues.

2. **Determine the writer's point of view.**
   Ask yourself if the writer, newspaper, or television station has a point of view. News arti-

cles are supposed to be objective, or without a point of view. Editorials and feature articles express points of view more freely.

3. **Identify facts and opinion.**
   Check to see if the news mainly answers the questions *Who? What? When? Where?* and *Why?* If the article expresses feelings and uses words such as *I*, *my*, or *we*, it mainly expresses opinions.

4. **Compare the news sources with other papers or television stations to see if they agree.**
   If two or three news sources agree, the information is more likely to be accurate.

TRY THE SKILL

The Examiner

WOMEN'S CONVENTION HELD

Seneca Falls, New York, Thursday, July 20, 1848. Yesterday, in the Wesleyan Chapel in Seneca Falls, a convention was held. A group of five local women organized the meeting to discuss the rights of women. The convention opened at 11:00 A.M. to an audience of over one hundred gentlemen and ladies. The first session, called to order by Mr. James Mott, opened with an address by Mrs. Elizabeth Cady Stanton. Mrs. Stanton declared the goal of the meeting was "to discuss our rights and wrongs, civil and political." She then read a document titled "The Declaration of Rights and Sentiments." A spirited debate followed in which both the ladies and gentlemen present participated.

Now try identifying what the news story above is about and what media it is from.

1. What kind of article is it?

2. What is the writer's point of view?

3. Does the article have mainly facts or opinion?

4. How does analyzing the news help you to understand what you are reading or listening to?

EXTEND THE SKILL

Today people write news stories for newspapers, television, radio, and the Internet. Suppose you were a news writer, reporter, or editor. Choose an issue of importance to you and write a news story, feature, or editorial about that issue in the media of your choice.

● What issue did you choose?

● Did you write a news story, feature, or editorial?

● How does the ability to understand the news help you to gain accurate information?

Heading Toward War

Lesson Outline
• A Nation Divided
• The Conflict Spreads
• Election of 1860

VOCABULARY

Missouri Compromise

Compromise of 1850

Fugitive Slave Law

Kansas-Nebraska Act

Dred Scott Decision

secede

Confederacy

states' rights

PEOPLE

Henry Clay

Abraham Lincoln

John Brown

Jefferson Davis

READING STRATEGY

Use a chart like the one below to list the sequence of events leading to secession.

BUILD BACKGROUND

In 1820 Congress tried to end the quarrels over slavery by passing the Missouri Compromise. The compromise created an imaginary line through the Louisiana Territory. Except for Missouri, states north of the line would be free states. States to its south would allow slavery. This compromise worked until 1850, when California asked to join the United States. A new compromise was made, but the conflict over slavery grew. In 1858, Abraham Lincoln, then a candidate for the Senate said, "A house divided against itself cannot stand. I believe this government cannot endure half slave and half free."

You Are Here
1820 – 1860

A NATION DIVIDED

The compromise over which states did and did not allow slavery worked as long as the balance between them held. In 1850 the United States had 15 slave states and 15 free states. Then California asked to join the United States as a free state. This would tip the balance in Congress in favor of the free states and might cause the United States to break apart.

Senator **Henry Clay** of Kentucky was a slave holder but believed strongly in the Union. He came up with a solution, known as the **Compromise of 1850**. It allowed California into the Union as a free state. In return, the North agreed to allow the territories of New Mexico and Utah to decide for themselves whether or not to allow slavery. The North also agreed to the **Fugitive Slave Law** of 1850, which required police in free states to help capture escaping African Americans.

 READING CHECK What was the Fugitive Slave Law of 1850?

The painting on page 424 shows the Senate debating the **Compromise of 1850**.

The Missouri Compromise, 1820

NATIONAL GEOGRAPHIC

CANADA (Britain)

OREGON COUNTRY (Claimed by U.S. and Britain)

UNORGANIZED TERRITORY

MICHIGAN TERRITORY

VT ME
NH
MA
NY RI
CT
PA NJ
OH DE
IL IN
VA MD
MO
KY

PACIFIC OCEAN

ATLANTIC OCEAN

MEXICO (Spain)

ARKANSAS TERRITORY

TN
NC
SC
MS AL GA
LA

FLORIDA TERRITORY

Gulf of Mexico

0   250   500 miles
0   250   500 kilometers
Albers Conic Equal-Area Projection

Free state
Free territory
Slave state
Slave territory
— Missouri Compromise Line

Map Skill

How many states were free states? Slave states?

THE CONFLICT SPREADS

Many people were against the Compromise of 1850. Among them were abolitionists. They argued that the Fugitive Slave Law clashed with the Bill of Rights. Under the law, a free African American could be captured and sold into slavery.

Kansas-Nebraska Act

In 1854 Congress passed the Kansas-Nebraska Act. This law allowed the Kansas and Nebraska territories to decide for themselves whether to allow slavery. The act angered abolitionist groups because both territories were north of the Missouri Compromise Line. Groups were afraid planters would win enough votes for the territories to allow slavery to begin

moving into the territories. People who were committed to making the territories free were called "free soilers."

In 1856, violence broke out between supporters of slavery and the "free soilers." Hundreds of people were killed. The newspapers referred to the territory as "Bleeding Kansas."

A New Political Party

A new political party, the Republican Party, took a stand on the slavery issue. Republicans opposed allowing slavery in the territories. One member of the new party was Abraham Lincoln, a lawyer from Illinois. Morally opposed to slavery, he also was firmly against the extension of slavery into the territories.

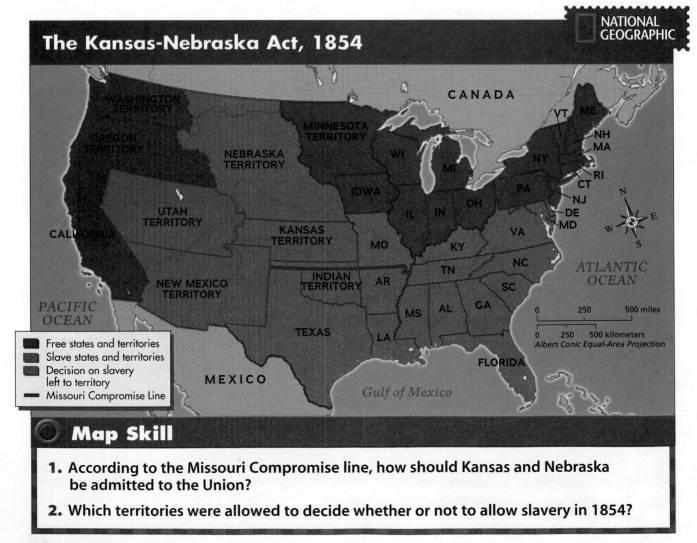

The Kansas-Nebraska Act, 1854

NATIONAL GEOGRAPHIC

Free states and territories
Slave states and territories
Decision on slavery left to territory
Missouri Compromise Line

Map Skill

1. According to the Missouri Compromise line, how should Kansas and Nebraska be admitted to the Union?

2. Which territories were allowed to decide whether or not to allow slavery in 1854?

Dred Scott

In 1857 the Supreme Court added to the conflict over slavery when it made its Dred Scott Decision. Dred Scott, an enslaved man, had asked the Court for his freedom because he had lived with his owner in a free territory. The Supreme Court ruled against Scott. The decision stated that enslaved people were property. The Constitution protects the right of citizens in our nation to take their property anywhere. The Supreme Court also said that the Missouri Compromise had not been constitutional. Congress did not have the right to make certain territories "free" because that would keep slave holders from moving their property.

Several Northern state legislatures passed resolutions stating that the Dred Scott Decision "was not binding in law and conscience." Some leaders, including Abraham Lincoln, said that the Dred Scott Decision did not have to be obeyed. The other branches of government had not supported the Court's decision.

John Brown's Raid

An abolitionist named John Brown and his followers hoped to start a rebellion that would end slavery. At dawn on October 16, 1859, they took control of a building in Harpers Ferry, Virginia, where the federal government stored weapons. Brown and his men were arrested.

John Brown's raid added to Southerners' fears that Northerners would stop at nothing to abolish slavery. Northerners were divided. Abolitionist Theodore Parker called Brown "a saint." *The Liberator* called Brown's plan "insane."

Abraham Lincoln

In 1858 Abraham Lincoln ran for senator as a member of the Republican Party. His opponent was the author of the Kansas-Nebraska Act, Senator Stephen A. Douglas, a Democrat. Douglas was known as the "Little Giant." Although short, he was a powerful speaker. During the campaign, Lincoln was firmly against slavery spreading to any new territories. Douglas, on the other hand, supported popular sovereignty. He believed each territory should be allowed to make its own decision about issues such as slavery. Lincoln lost the election, but the debate over slavery made him well-known across the country.

READING CHECK Which issues worsened the division between the North and South from 1854 to 1859?

ELECTION OF 1860

In 1860 Lincoln faced three candidates in the race for the Presidency. One of them was Douglas. Of the four, Lincoln was the only candidate firmly against the spread of slavery.

To preserve the Union, Lincoln said he would leave slavery alone where it already existed. However, if no new slave states were admitted to the Union, the free states would keep their majority in Congress, and the South could never gain political power. Some Southern states talked about **seceding** if Lincoln were elected.

To secede meant that the states would leave the Union. Lincoln called talk of leaving the Union "humbug."

The First State Secedes

Lincoln won the election. Would some of the Southern states leave the Union? In December 1860, the state of South Carolina voted to secede. By the following March, Mississippi, Florida, Alabama, Georgia, Louisiana, Texas, and South Carolina had formed a new country, the Confererate States of America, or **Confederacy**. They drafted a constitution and named a president. They chose **Jefferson Davis**, a

After Lincoln won the election of 1860 (below), Southern states chose Jefferson Davis (above) to be their president.

United States Senator from Mississippi and a planter who had fought in the Mexican War. The Union was now split.

Why did Southern states secede from the Union?

Dred Scott (left) was denied his freedom by the Supreme Court.

PUTTING IT TOGETHER

The Dred Scott Decision, the Kansas-Nebraska Act of 1854, and John Brown's raid in 1859 deepened conflicts between the states. During his presidential campaign, Abraham Lincoln did not oppose slavery where it existed, but he did oppose its spread to other states. Southerners supported **states' rights**. They believed each state should be allowed to make its own decisions about most issues. For many Southerners, the only course of action left seemed to be to secede. To Lincoln, seceding from the Union was illegal because the Constitution divided power between the federal government and the states. A state that seceded was claiming to have supreme authority. The conflict between North and South was about to become a war.

Review and Assess

1. Write one sentence for each vocabulary term.

   Dred Scott Decision
   Kansas-Nebraska Act
   secede

2. How did the Southern states respond to Lincoln's election?

3. What events of the 1850s caused the country to pull apart?

4. What two **government** actions undid the Missouri Compromise?

5. **Compare** the various opinions about John Brown's raid.

Look at the maps on pages 425 and 426. Describe how the United States changed between 1820 and 1854. Then prepare an outline for a documentary on the changes.

• •

Write an editorial in a Northern newspaper protesting the Dred Scott Decision.

VOCABULARY REVIEW

Number a sheet of paper from 1 to 5. Beside each number write the word or term from the list below that matches the description.

abolitionist   prejudice

Dred Scott   Underground
Decision   Railroad

Kansas-Nebraska
Act

1. A negative opinion formed without proof

2. An 1854 law that allowed the Kansas and Nebraska territories to decide whether to be free or slave states

3. A person who wanted to end slavery in the United States

4. A system of secret routes used by escaping slaves to reach freedom

5. An 1857 Supreme Court decision that said slaves were private property

CHAPTER COMPREHENSION

6. What were some results of Nat Turner's rebellion?

7. What was Umbler?

8. How was *The Liberator* important to the abolitionist movement?

9. What was Levi Coffin called?

10. Who was Sojourner Truth?

11. What was the Compromise of 1850?

12. What was Abraham Lincoln's position on slavery during the election of 1860?

13. Suppose that you are an observer at the Seneca Falls Convention of 1848. **Write** a letter describing the event.

SKILLS REVIEW

The National Era

A NEW STORY

by Mrs. Stowe

Washington, D.C., May 8, 1851.
Week after next we propose to commence [start] in the *Era*, the publication of a new story by Mrs. H. B. Stowe, the title of which will be, "UNCLE TOM'S CABIN, OR THE MAN THAT WAS A THING." Mrs. Stowe is one of the most gifted and popular of American writers. We announce her story in advance, that none of our subscribers may lose the beginning of it, and that those who desire to read the production as it may appear in successive numbers of the *Era*, may send us their names in season.

14. **Study Skill** What are three different types of articles that can be found in a newspaper?

15. **Study Skill** What appears on the editorial page of a newspaper?

16. **Study Skill** What is the writer's point of view for the article above?

17. **Study Skill** Answer the questions *Who? What? When?* and *Where?* and *Why?* for the article above.

18. **Study Skill** Why is knowing how to analyze the news an important skill?

USING A TIME LINE

1830	1835	1840	1845	1850	1855	1860	1865	1870	1875

1831
Nat Turner's rebellion; William Lloyd Garrison publishes *The Liberator*

1845
Frederick Douglass publishes his autobiography

1848
Seneca Falls Convention

1852
Harriet Beecher Stowe publishes *Uncle Tom's Cabin*

1857
The Dred Scott Decision

1860
Lincoln is elected President

1861
Confederate States of America is formed

19. How are the events listed on the time line for 1860 and 1861 related?

20. In what years on the time line were abolitionist writings published? What were they?

Writing **About Beliefs** Why do you think people have different beliefs? Where do you think beliefs come from? Think about some of the advantages of having a country made up of people with different beliefs. Then think of some disadvantages of this. How can differences in beliefs lead to war?

Use your Foldable to review what you have learned about slavery in America. As you look at the concept map on the front of your Foldable, mentally review how and why slavery divided the nation. Look at your notes under the tabs of your Foldable to check your memory and responses. Record any questions that you have. Then discuss them with classmates or review the chapter to find answers.

THE Big IDEAS ABOUT...

The Civil War and Reconstruction

Many Northerners and Southerners wanted to avoid a war between the states. However, when the Confederacy attacked a fort in South Carolina, it led to a war that divided our nation and cost the lives of many thousands of people. Read on to find out about the time when Americans fought Americans and how after the war, Northerners and Southerners began the work of reuniting the country.

THE WAR BEGINS

President Lincoln vows not to let Union property be taken by Confederate troops. Fort Sumter in South Carolina is Union property, and Confederate takeover of the fort makes armed conflict a certainty.

EMANCIPATION PROCLAMATION

President Abraham Lincoln issues the Emancipation Proclamation, which ends slavery in the Confederacy.

SURRENDER AT APPOMATTOX

On April 9, 1865, Confederate General Robert E. Lee surrenders to Union General Ulysess S. Grant, ending the Civil War. Five days later, President Lincoln is shot.

RECONSTRUCTION

During Reconstruction the nation is reunited and three amendments are added to the Constitution.

Foldables

Make this Foldable study guide and use it to record what you learn about "The Civil War and Reconstruction."

1. Fold a large sheet of paper into a shutter fold.
2. Fold the shutter fold in half like a hot dog.
3. Form four tabs, by cutting along the fold lines in the middle of the two long tabs.
4. Label the four tabs with lesson titles.

The Nation Divided by War

Find Out! *How did the Civil War begin?*

Lesson Outline
• North versus South
• Battle of Bull Run
• The First Modern War

VOCABULARY

Civil War
Anaconda Plan
blockade
total war
civilian

PEOPLE

Robert E. Lee
Winfield Scott
Thomas "Stonewall" Jackson

READING STRATEGY

Copy the chart below. Then compare and contrast the advantages of the North and the South during the Civil War.

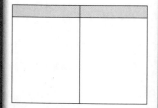

BUILD BACKGROUND

When President Lincoln took office on March 4, 1861, he promised to "hold, occupy, and possess" all federal property in the Southern states. This included the military post of Fort Sumter in Charleston, South Carolina. Angry at Union troops for occupying what they considered Confederate land, the Confederate army fired on Fort Sumter. The Union troops surrendered the next day.

NORTH VERSUS SOUTH

Fort Sumter was the first battle of the Civil War. A civil war is a war between two groups of citizens of the same country. No one was killed at Fort Sumter. However, the battle shook the nation. After the battle, Virginia, North Carolina, Arkansas, and Tennessee left the Union. With 11 states, the Confederacy thought it would win a quick victory.

Strengths of the Confederacy ①

Both the North and the South thought the war would be over in months. Both sides also believed they had the advantage. The South's greatest strength was its army. Southern boys grew up riding horses and using guns to hunt. The South also had many well-trained officers. Among them was Robert E. Lee of Virginia. Lee graduated from the United States Military Academy at West Point and had served in the military for more than 30 years. When the war began, Lincoln asked Lee to command the Union army. Lee did not like slavery. However, Lee's loyalty to Virginia was important to him, "I cannot fight against my birthplace." Lee soon became commander of the Confederate army.

Only about one-fourth of Southerners owned slaves. Yet many Southerners who did not own slaves volunteered to fight. They believed they were fighting to protect their way of life.

After the Battle of Fort Sumter (left), Robert E. Lee (above) became commander of the Confederate army.

Strengths of the Union ②

The North had a larger population and more resources than the Confederacy. This made it possible for the North to build and supply a larger army.

You can see from the graph on page 451 that most of the country's people and factories were in the North. The factories would be used to make weapons and uniforms for the Union army. In addition, the North was better able to feed a large army. Although the South was a farming area, the North grew most of the country's food. Finally, the North had most of the country's railroads, which could be used for moving soldiers and supplies.

READING CHECK

What were the strengths of the North? What were the strengths of the South?

General Winfield Scott's Anaconda Plan

1 In the first step, the North would use its navy to block off, or **blockade**, Southern ports. Without trade the South would be unable to buy the weapons and supplies it needed.

2 In the next step, the North would take control of the Mississippi River. This would cause the South to be split into two parts. Also the South would not be able to use the river to move supplies.

3 Finally, Union troops would invade from both east and west.

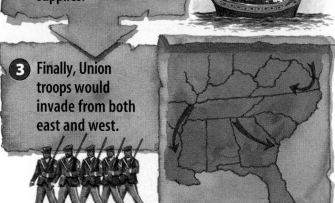

Chart Skill

1. What did the first step of the Anaconda Plan hope to accomplish?

2. Why do you think General Scott thought his plan would succeed?

BATTLE OF BULL RUN

Citizens of both the Union and the Confederacy thought of the war as a short, glorious struggle. However, the commander of the Union army knew that he had to plan carefully.

A Plan for Victory

To defeat the Confederacy, President Lincoln and General **Winfield Scott** had made a plan for winning the war. Scott called it the **Anaconda Plan**, after the anaconda snake, which squeezed its prey to death. The flowchart on the left shows how the plan would work.

Scott's plan was not popular at first. Many Northerners thought that if the Union army could capture the Confederate capital of Richmond, Virginia, the war would be over quickly. Only later would people realize the importance of the Anaconda Plan.

Cotton Diplomacy (4)

Jefferson Davis, President of the Confederate States of America, knew that a Union blockade of major Southern ports could be very damaging to the Confederacy. Davis hoped that Great Britain and France, whose industry depended on Southern cotton, would come to the aid of the Confederacy. This diplomatic effort came to be known as "cotton diplomacy." Britain and France did give the Confederacy several armed warships, but that was all. The South would have to fight alone.

Northern diplomats were successful in convincing Europeans not to recognize the Confederacy as an independent nation. Perhaps most important of all, Britain and France would not fight for the South unless the Confederacy could show that it might win the war.

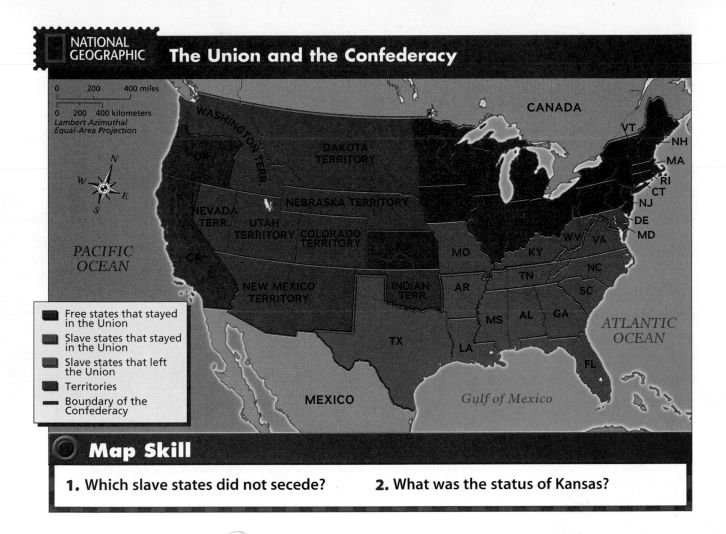

0   200   400 miles

0   200   400 kilometers
Lambert Azimuthal
Equal-Area Projection

CANADA

PACIFIC OCEAN

ATLANTIC OCEAN

MEXICO

Gulf of Mexico

- ■ Free states that stayed in the Union
- ■ Slave states that stayed in the Union
- ■ Slave states that left the Union
- ■ Territories
- — Boundary of the Confederacy

Map Skill

1. Which slave states did not secede?   **2.** What was the status of Kansas?

The First Major Battle ⑤

On July 21, 1861, the Union army fought Confederate troops at a stream in Manassas, Virginia, called **Bull Run**. At first, the Union army appeared to be winning. As some Confederates began to flee, an officer noticed that Confederate General T. J. Jackson was standing firm with his troops. "There stands Jackson like a stone wall!" he cried. Jackson soon was known as **Thomas "Stonewall" Jackson**.

The Confederates regrouped around Jackson in what came to be known as the First Battle of Bull Run. Soon, frightened Northern troops began running away in panic. The Union troops retreated to Washington, D.C. The war's first major battle ended with a victory for the South.

Why was the Union's plan for victory called the Anaconda?

This Confederate soldier had his photograph taken wearing full battle uniform.

437

THE FIRST MODERN WAR

The Civil War has been called the first modern war because it changed the way wars were fought. New technology made the war more deadly than earlier wars. The Gatling machine gun could fire 250 bullets in a minute. Iron-covered battleships, called ironclads, made wooden ships seem outdated overnight.

Total War

The Civil War was a total war. A total war is when each side not only strikes against one another's soldiers, but against civilians and the economic system of the enemy. A civilian is a person not in the armed forces.

Each side used all of the resources available to them. The war introduced the use of ironclad ships, mines, and submarines. Railroads and telegraphs changed how generals made battlefield decisions.

Building New Ships

By 1864 almost 700 ships were in the Union navy. In contrast, the South had few ships. So it decided to improve the ships they had. The Confederates raised a sunken Union ship named the *Merrimack* and covered it with thick metal plates. On March 8, 1862, the *Merrimack*, now renamed the *Virginia*, sank two Northern ships and defeated three others near Hampton Roads, Virginia.

The next day a strange looking Union ship appeared in the harbor. It was the *Monitor*, an ironclad Union ship. For

The Merrimack (C.S.S. Virginia)

Flagpole

Gun crew

Bow gun

Iron plating

Cast iron ram

Diagram Skill

1. How were the sailors firing the cannon protected?

2. How many cannons did the *Virginia* have?

Exploring TECHNOLOGY

The Telegraph

In the 1830s, Samuel Morse invented a device to send messages by electricity. It was called the telegraph. It sent a message using a series of clicks, or sounds. Morse also developed the Morse Code—an alphabet of long and short bursts of electricity that stood for letters and numbers.

Before the telegraph, it could take weeks for a letter to arrive. With the telegraph, a message was received in minutes. Soon, telegraph wires and offices sprang up all over the country. By 1861, the Western Union Company had installed 67,000 miles of telegraph lines across the country.

Why did the telegraph become popular so quickly?

Charles Harrington, Cornell University

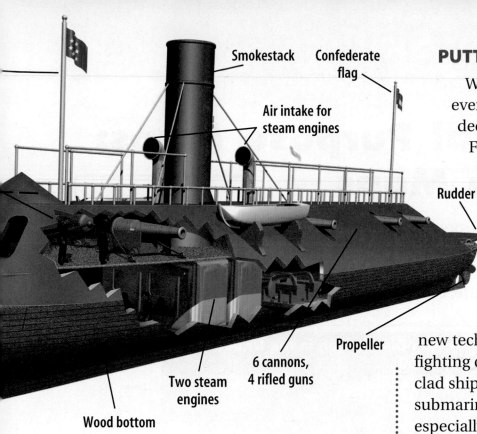

Smokestack   Confederate
flag

Air intake for
steam engines

Rudder

Propeller

6 cannons,
4 rifled guns

Two steam
engines

Wood bottom

PUTTING IT TOGETHER

When the Civil War began, almost everyone thought the war would be decided quickly. However, after the First Battle of Bull Run, people realized the war could last for years. Although the North had more soldiers, resources, factories, and railroads, the South had more experienced soldiers and military leaders.

The first modern war saw new technology that made long-range fighting common and more deadly. Iron-clad ships, mines, machine guns, and submarines caused vast destruction, especially in the South. Other countries were beginning to realize the growing military power of the United States.

more than four hours the *Monitor* and the *Virginia* battled. In the end, neither one could damage the other.

How did new technology change the way war was fought?

Review and Assess

1. Write one sentence for each vocabulary word.

    blockade   civilian   total war

2. Describe the Anaconda Plan and how it was supposed to work.

3. How did the Civil War begin?

4. How did new **technology** change how wars were fought?

5. Choose the **point of view** of either the North or the South. Tell why your side expects to win.

Using the Atlas map on page R16, draw your own map showing General Scott's Anaconda Plan. Which Confederate cities were ports? How would these cities be affected by Scott's Plan?

Write a speech that Lincoln might have given explaining why the Confederate attack on Fort Sumter meant war.

Using Special Purpose Maps: Distribution Maps

VOCABULARY
distribution map

The map below is a special purpose map called a **distribution map**. Distribution maps show how something is spread out over an area. Some of the things distribution maps can feature include language, climate, and products.

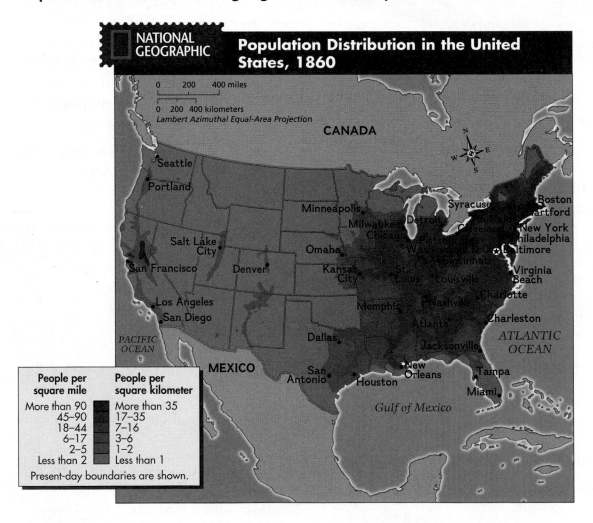

NATIONAL GEOGRAPHIC

Population Distribution in the United States, 1860

0   200   400 miles

0   200 400 kilometers
Lambert Azimuthal Equal-Area Projection

CANADA

Seattle
Portland

Minneapolis
Milwaukee
Chicago
Detroit
Syracuse
Buffalo
Cleveland
Boston
Hartford
New York
Philadelphia
Baltimore
Pittsburgh
Washington, D.C.
Cincinnati

Salt Lake City
Omaha
San Francisco
Denver
Kansas City
St. Louis
Louisville
Virginia Beach
Charlotte

Los Angeles
San Diego
Memphis
Nashville
Charleston
Atlanta

PACIFIC OCEAN

MEXICO
San Antonio
Dallas
Houston
New Orleans
Jacksonville
Tampa
Miami

ATLANTIC OCEAN

Gulf of Mexico

People per square mile	People per square kilometer
More than 90	More than 35
45–90	17–35
18–44	7–16
6–17	3–6
2–5	1–2
Less than 2	Less than 1
Present-day boundaries are shown.	

LEARN THE SKILL

Study the map on this page as you follow the steps to learn about distribution maps.

1. **Identify the title of the map.**
   The title of this map is "Population Distribu-tion in the United States, 1860." The map shows how people were spread across the United States in 1860.

2. **Study the map key.**
   The map is shaded in six different colors. Each color represents the population den-

sity, or how many people live per square mile or kilometer.

3. **Look carefully at the symbols on the map.**
Use the map key as you examine the map to determine where few people lived. Now find out where most of the people lived.

TRY THE SKILL

Use the population distribution map of the southeastern United States today to answer the following questions:

1. Which state has the most areas with less than 10 people per square mile? Which state has no areas with more than 250 people per square mile?

2. Why are many large cities located near rivers, lakes, and oceans?

3. **Compare and contrast** coastal Louisiana with coastal North Carolina. How is the population distribution of these areas alike?

4. How can distribution maps help you better understand where people live?

EXTEND THE SKILL

Compare the population map of the Southeast with the land use of the Southeast. Then answer the questions below:

● Do more people live in farm communities or urban areas?

● Do more people live in forest land or farmland?

● How can comparing distribution maps help you understand the world today?

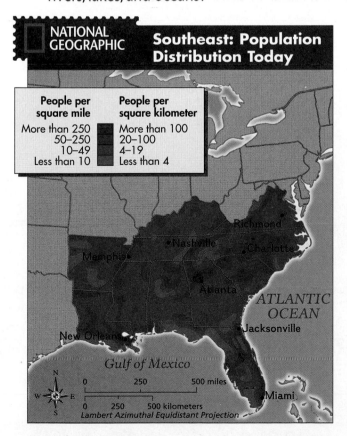

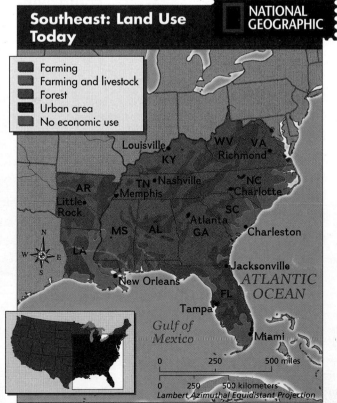

The Union Moves Toward Victory

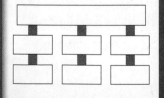

How did the Union finally begin to win the war?

Lesson Outline
- Antietam and the End of Slavery
- The Death Toll Rises
- Gettysburg

VOCABULARY

Emancipation Proclamation

Gettysburg Address

PEOPLE

Mary Ann Bickerdayke

Clara Barton

Sally Tompkins

Ulysses S. Grant

George Meade

George Pickett

READING STRATEGY

Copy the word map below. Write the main idea of this lesson in the top box. Write in the factors that support this idea in the boxes below.

BUILD BACKGROUND

In the autumn of 1862, Northern support for the war was starting to weaken. Union troops were making little progress. Southerners too were suffering. One Confederate soldier wrote, "Day after day and night after night did we tramp along the rough and dusty roads." Both Union and Confederate troops were losing heart. Neither side was sure that it could win.

ANTIETAM AND THE END OF SLAVERY

In the spring of 1862, Union soldiers marched into Virginia. They were soon beaten back by Robert E. Lee. For the next few months, Confederate generals fought their way into Maryland. It appeared that the Confederacy was about to win their independence. That hope faded when Confederate troops met Union forces at **Antietam** (an TEE tum), Maryland, on September 17, 1862. The Confederacy retreated after one of the bloodiest battles in United States history.

The Emancipation Proclamation ⑧

Five days after the Battle of Antietam, President Lincoln changed the way people thought of the war. He issued the Emancipation Proclamation. To emancipate means to free someone. The proclamation said that as of January 1, 1863, "all persons held as slaves within any state . . . in rebellion against the United States, shall be then, henceforth, and forever free." The Emancipation Proclamation ended slavery in the Confederacy. However, it did not end slavery in the slave states that stayed in the Union. What had been a struggle to preserve

More than 23,000 troops were killed or wounded at Antietam, Maryland (far left). Soon after the battle, President Lincoln (above) issued the **Emancipation Proclamation**.

the Union was now also a battle to end slavery.

Juneteenth ⑨

On January 1, 1863, when the Emancipation Proclamation went into effect, African Americans greeted the day with joy. However, it took years for the Union army to put the Emancipation Proclamation into effect throughout the Confederacy. The news did not reach African Americans in Texas until June 19, 1865. June 19, often called "Juneteenth," is still celebrated in African American communities in Texas and other areas as the day slavery ended.

READING CHECK

What is the Emancipation Proclamation?

443

THE DEATH TOLL RISES

The number of dead and injured soldiers rose steadily in 1862. Men of all ages served. In both the North and the South, boys as young as 14 joined the fighting by pretending to be 18. The oldest man to serve in the war was an 80-year-old grandfather from Iowa.

The 54th Regiment

While African Americans had been serving in the Union navy long before the war began, they were prohibited from serving in the army. The Emancipation Proclamation changed all that.

One of the first African American troops to fight for the Union army was the 54th Massachusetts Colored Regiment. A regiment is a group of at least one thousand soldiers. Two sons of Frederick Douglass served in the all-volunteer regiment.

On July 18, 1863, the 54th Regiment attacked Fort Wagner in Charleston, South Carolina. Almost half of its members were killed, wounded, or captured in the Southern victory. Their bravery changed public opinion in the North to accept African American troops.

African American Soldiers in the South

Not all African Americans served on the Union side. On March 13, 1865, General Lee convinced the Confederate Congress to allow African Americans to fight for the South. These African Americans were promised freedom.

On March 19, in Richmond, Virginia, a new Confederate unit, which included African American hospital workers, marched up Main Street. None had uni-

Among African Americans who fought in the Union army was this soldier (right) and the 54th Regiment (below), which stormed Fort Wagner in 1863.

forms, but they began training in Capitol Square. The war ended before they had a chance to fight.

Women and the War ⑫

Women were not allowed in either the Union or the Confederate armies. Yet they contributed to the war effort in many ways. The war forced many women to work outside the home for the first time. Others, like Malinda Blalock of North Carolina, disguised themselves as men to fight on the battlefield.

Many women in the North worked in factories and stores while the men were away at war. More than 3,000 Northern women worked as army nurses. Mary Ann Bickerdayke, for example, served the Union in 19 battles. She performed medical operations and passed out food and supplies.

Clara Barton from Massachusetts also began her war work passing out food and supplies to Union troops in Virginia. Later she assisted with hundreds of operations, even digging bullets out of soldiers' wounds with her penknife. Union general George McClellan called Barton "the true heroine of the age, the angel of the battlefield." After the war Barton founded the American Red Cross in 1881.

Like women in the North, women in the South helped in the war. Many ran their family businesses, farms, and plantations. Sally Tompkins ran a private hospital in Richmond, which treated more than 1,300 soldiers. Her hospital saved all but 73 of them. This was the best record of any war hospital North or South. When Jefferson Davis placed all Southern hospitals under the control of the military, Sally Tompkins was made a captain. Tompkins

Many women, including Clara Barton, worked as army nurses, caring for the wounded.

was the only woman to hold a military rank in the Confederate army.

The Battle of Vicksburg ⑬

By the spring of 1863, the Anaconda Plan was close to achieving its goal. In the West Ulysses S. Grant had won some important Union campaigns at Fort Donelson and Shiloh, Tennessee.

Vicksburg, Mississippi, was a key city guarding the Mississippi River between Memphis and New Orleans. Grant tried to capture the city from the north, but a steep hill protected the northern edge of the city. Grant realized that getting over the hill would be too difficult, and so he attacked from the southern side.

Grant trapped the Confederates in the city. The attack continued for 48 days. On July 3, 1863, lacking supplies, the Confederates surrendered. Later, Grant said, "The fate of the Confederacy was sealed when Vicksburg fell."

READING CHECK **How did African Americans and women help the Union army?**

445

GETTYSBURG

14

While Grant pounded Vicksburg, General Lee's men faced Union troops under General **George Meade** in Gettysburg, Pennsylvania. On July 3, General **George Pickett** was ordered to charge the center of the Union lines across a great open field. The Confederate army made what came to be known as Pickett's Charge and the Union troops fired. Lee's army had to retreat. More than 28,000 Confederate soldiers were killed or wounded.

The Union victories at both Vicksburg and Gettysburg had changed the course of the war in favor of the North.

Months later President Lincoln came to Gettysburg to declare the battlefield a national cemetery. Read the **Gettysburg Address** he made there.

Primary Source:

The Gettysburg Address
— delivered by President Abraham Lincoln on November 19, 1863

*Four **score** and seven years ago our **fathers** brought forth, upon this continent, a new nation, **conceived** in Liberty, and dedicated to the **proposition** that all men are created equal.*

Now we are engaged in a great civil war, testing whether that nation, or any nation, so conceived, and so dedicated, can long endure. We are met here on a great battlefield of that war. We have come to dedicate a portion of it as a final resting place for those who here gave their lives that that nation might live. It is altogether fitting and proper that we should do this.

*But in a larger sense we cannot dedicate—we can not **consecrate**—we can not **hallow** this ground. The brave men, living and dead, who struggled, here, have consecrated it far above our poor power to add or **detract**. The world will little note, nor long remember, what we say here, but can never forget what they did here. It is for us, the living, rather to be dedicated here to the unfinished work which they have, thus far, so nobly carried on.*

It is rather for us to be here dedicated to the great task remaining before us—that from these honored dead we take increased devotion to that cause for which they here gave the last full measure of devotion—that we here highly resolve that these dead shall not have died in vain; that this nation, under God, shall have a new birth of freedom; and that this government of the people, by the people, for the people, shall not perish from the earth.

What was the main message of the speech?

___

score: times twenty
fathers: forefathers or ancestors
conceived: formed
proposition: intention or plan

consecrate: set apart as holy
hallow: consider holy
detract: take away

The Gettysburg Address lasted only two minutes. When President Linoln finished speaking, the audience was silent. Lincoln thought his speech was a failure. However, it became one of the greatest speeches ever given. The President's words inspired the war-weary Union not to give up on the war. He made it clear that democracy, a united country, and the abolition of slavery were causes worth fighting for to the bitter end.

 Which side won the Battle of Gettysburg?

Ulysses S. Grant cut the Confederacy in two when he won the Battle of Vicksburg.

PUTTING IT TOGETHER

After the Emancipation Proclamation, the war was fought not only to unite the country but also to end slavery. In the South the proclamation would end an entire way of life that the Confederate army was fighting to preserve. By the summer of 1863, however, Southern defeats by Generals Grant and Meade were crushing the Confederate army. One soldier wrote, "It seems incredible that human power could effect such a change in so brief a space. Yesterday, we rode on the pinnacle [brink] of success—today absolute ruin seems to be our portion."

Review and Assess

1. Write one sentence for each vocabulary term.

   Emancipation Proclamation
   Gettysburg Address

2. Why did President Lincoln come to Gettysburg months after the battle?

3. What events helped to turn the war in favor of the Union?

4. Why did Lincoln announce the Emancipation Proclamation *after* the Battle of Antietam?

5. **Compare** reactions to the Emancipation Proclamation from the point of view of Southern slave owners, Northern abolitionists, other Northerners, and newly freed slaves.

Draw a map locating the battles of Antietam, Vicksburg, and Gettysburg. Then illustrate it to show why these battlers were important.

Write a newspaper article about one of the events in this lesson.

The War Ends

Find Out!

How did the Civil War end?

Lesson Outline
- Battle for the South
- The Election of 1864
- Surrender at Appomattox

VOCABULARY

draft
Thirteenth
Amendment

PEOPLE

William Tecumseh
Sherman

READING STRATEGY

Copy the chart below. Then write down the cause and effect of the final events of the Civil War.

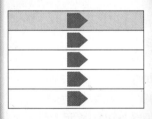

BUILD BACKGROUND

"I'm a tired man," President Lincoln said about the hardships of the war. By 1864 nearly everyone had suffered some kind of loss as a result of the Civil War. In the South the Union blockade of Southern ports made food and supplies scarce. In the North riots against the **draft** broke out in New York and other Northern cities. A draft is the selection of men who have to serve in the military. All men between the age of 20 and 45 were drafted into the Union army. One newspaper wrote, "Our bleeding, bankrupt, almost dying country longs for peace [and] shudders at the prospect . . . of new rivers of human blood."

BATTLE FOR THE SOUTH

Grant's success in 1863 convinced Lincoln to put him in charge of the Union army. Grant's plan was to fight until he wore out the Confederate army. Grant ordered General William Tecumseh Sherman, now in charge of forces in the West, into Georgia to do the same.

Sherman Burns the South 15

In September 1864 Sherman captured and burned Atlanta, Georgia, one of the South's largest cities. Sherman's troops destroyed nearly everything in their path.

His troops then marched to Savannah, Georgia. His 60,000 men cut a 300-mile path of destruction across Georgia. In December 1864, Sherman captured Savannah.

From Savannah Sherman marched into South Carolina. As they marched, the Union troops destroyed or burned down nearly every building in their path.

Grant and Lee Standoff 16

Meanwhile, Grant planned to capture Richmond. His troops slowly moved south toward the Confederate capital. Lee kept one step ahead of him. In the first month Grant lost about 2,000 men each day. Unable to break Lee's army, Grant moved his army south of Rich-

Sherman's march to the sea destroyed the Confederacy's last source of supplies for its armies.

mond, near Petersburg. There the two forces fought a standoff that would last well into 1865.

READING CHECK What was General Grant's plan for ending the war?

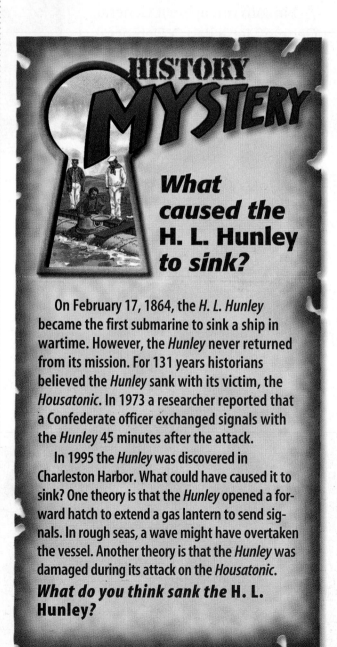

HISTORY MYSTERY

What caused the H. L. Hunley to sink?

On February 17, 1864, the *H. L. Hunley* became the first submarine to sink a ship in wartime. However, the *Hunley* never returned from its mission. For 131 years historians believed the *Hunley* sank with its victim, the *Housatonic*. In 1973 a researcher reported that a Confederate officer exchanged signals with the *Hunley* 45 minutes after the attack.

In 1995 the *Hunley* was discovered in Charleston Harbor. What could have caused it to sink? One theory is that the *Hunley* opened a forward hatch to extend a gas lantern to send signals. In rough seas, a wave might have overtaken the vessel. Another theory is that the *Hunley* was damaged during its attack on the *Housatonic*.

What do you think sank the H. L. Hunley?

THE ELECTION OF 1864

While Grant and Sherman waged war in the South, President Lincoln had to fight for his re-election in 1864. As the election approached, many believed Lincoln would lose. The nation was tired of war and some called for peace talks.

Tide Turns for Lincoln

Lincoln ran against General George McClellan, a Democrat whose party called for a cease-fire. Many believe it was Sherman's capture of Atlanta that changed the mood in the North. Voters began to rally around Lincoln. Even McClellan changed his position on a cease-fire. In the Electoral College, Lincoln won every state except Delaware, Kentucky, and New Jersey. In the popular vote, Lincoln won with 55 percent against McClellan's 45 percent.

Lincoln's victory showed that voters not only approved of his policies during the war but also approved of his call to end slavery. Now it was time for the abolition of slavery to be added to the United States Constitution.

In February 1865, Congress voted to pass the **Thirteenth Amendment** to the Constitution. It was ratified by the states and became law on December 6, 1865. It read:

Neither slavery nor involuntary servitude, except as a punishment for crime whereof the party shall have been duly convicted, shall exist within the United States, or any place subject to their jurisdiction.

Although the Thirteenth Amendment settled the issue of slavery in the United States, the place of African Americans in American society remained unclear.

READING CHECK How did Lincoln know that voters supported his call to end slavery?

Lincoln's supporters used badges (above center), flags, and even lanterns during his 1864 campaign.

450

Civil War Battles and Resources

The Civil War began on April 12, 1861. Both the North and the South expected to win. Study the map and graph and then answer the questions.

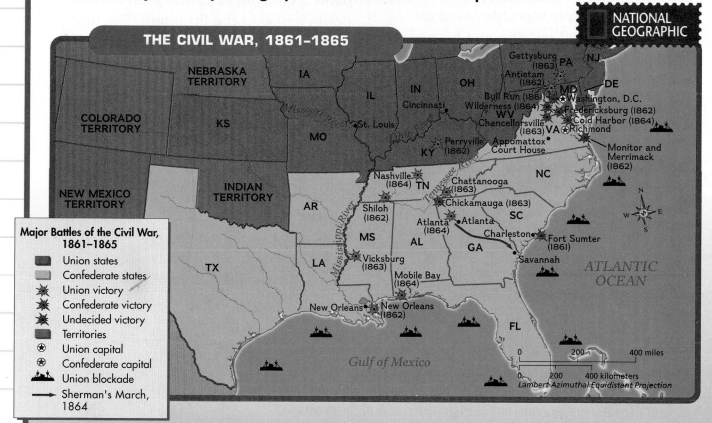

THE CIVIL WAR, 1861–1865

NATIONAL GEOGRAPHIC

Major Battles of the Civil War, 1861–1865
- Union states
- Confederate states
- Union victory
- Confederate victory
- Undecided victory
- Territories
- Union capital
- Confederate capital
- Union blockade
- Sherman's March, 1864

Lambert Azimuthal Equidistant Projection

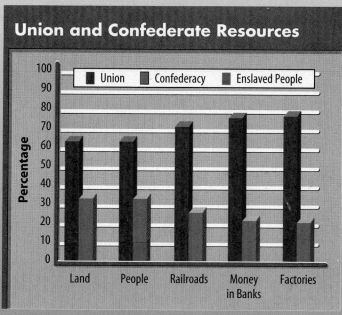

Union and Confederate Resources

Percentage

■ Union   ■ Confederacy   ■ Enslaved People

Land   People   Railroads   Money in Banks   Factories

QUESTIONS:

1. Which Union states had battles?
2. What percentage of the total railroads were in the Confederacy?
3. What might have happened if the Confederates had won at Gettysburg?

To learn more, visit our Web site:
www.mhschool.com

451

SURRENDER AT APPOMATTOX 18

Nine months after the battle at Petersburg began, Grant's 125,000 men were closing in on Lee's starving army of 35,000. Finally, on April 2, 1865, Lee took his army west, hoping to find food and to gather more Confederate troops. In response to Lee's actions, Union forces entered Petersburg and Richmond.

The Union army was able to cut off Lee's supplies and put him and his army in danger of being surrounded, "There is nothing left for me to do, but go to General Grant," Lee said. The Confederate army was ready to surrender.

On April 9, 1865, Grant and Lee met in Appomattox Court House, Virginia. Lee wore a crisp grey uniform. "I have to look my best," he said. "I may be Grant's prisoner." Grant did not take any prisoners. Instead, Grant said, "Each . . . man will be allowed to return to his home, ..."

After Lee's surrender, Jefferson Davis fled westward, where he hoped to keep the Confederacy alive. On May 10, 1865, he was captured. Davis was imprisoned for two years at Fort Monroe in Virginia.

Lincoln Is Shot 19

Five days after Grant and Lee agreed to the terms of surrender, President and Mrs. Lincoln were watching a play at Ford's Theater in Washington, D.C. Suddenly a gunshot rang out. John Wilkes Booth had shot the President. The next morning, April 15, 1865, President Lincoln died. The poet Walt Whitman expressed the country's sadness:

> O Captain! My Captain, our fearful trip is done,
> The ship has weather'd every storm, the prize we sought is won.

Whitman's "prize" was many things. It was an end to the war, an end to slavery, and a new beginning for the United States, which was united once again.

Mourners (below) follow Lincoln's funeral car (lower right) and procession down Broadway in New York City. The hat Lincoln wore at Ford's Theater (upper right) and the fan with scenes of the events there (far upper right) are tragic reminders of the President's death.

Smithsonian Institution

Troops Return Home 20

For soldiers returning home in the South, the destruction of war was overwhelming. Few farms were in working condition. However, property was not the only thing that had been destroyed in the Southern states. A way of life had ended forever. One Confederate soldier returning home to Richmond wrote, "I shall not attempt to describe my feelings. The city [is] in ruins . . . . With a raging headache and a swelling heart I reach my home, and here the curtain falls."

In the North, upon seeing his family's farm in Indiana, a Union soldier said, "a feeling of profound contentment . . . too deep to be expressed by mere words." The next day he put on old clothes and went to work in his father's cornfield.

Why did General Lee surrender? Explain your answer.

Smithsonian Institution

PUTTING IT TOGETHER

After four long years, our nation's most destructive war was finally over. The Union had survived, but the cost of war was huge. About 620,000 people had died. The South lay in ruins. About two-thirds of its wealth had been lost. About one of every ten Southern white men had been killed.

While tensions between the North and the South remained, the task of rebuilding the country still lay ahead.

Review and Assess

1. Write a sentence for each of the following vocabulary words.

   draft   Thirteenth Amendment

2. How did total war help the Union defeat the Confederacy?

3. What key events and battles helped end the Civil War?

4. What were the terms of Lee's surrender?

5. What **generalizations** can you make about the costs of the Civil War for both the North and the South?

Look at the map on page 451. List the battles that ended in victory for the Confederacy in one column. In the other, list the victories for the Union.

Write a news article that describes the end of the Civil War.

Drawing Inferences

Suppose you are invited to a party. When you arrive, you see one of your friends dressed as a robot. Another friend is dressed as a scarecrow. What's wrong? Based on the clues, you figure out that you are at a costume party.

Sometimes meanings or connections are not always clear. It can be helpful to draw **inferences** when you read or study. An inference is something you figure out based on clues and information that you already know. Making inferences can help you better understand what you read. It can also help you make sense of new information.

| **VOCABULARY** |
| inference |

LEARN THE SKILL

Follow the steps below to draw an inference.

1. **Identify clues.**
   Suppose you have just arrived at summer camp. When you go over to introduce yourself to those sharing your cabin, you find them putting away their things. One of them has brought a tennis racquet, another has a basketball, and the third has a baseball glove. One of the cabin mates tells you that there is a basketball hoop near the lake. They ask if you would like to play sometime.

2. **Compare the clues to information you already have.**
   You know that a tennis racket, basketball, and baseball gloves are all sports equipment. You also know that people often own items based on their interests.

3. **Make an inference.**
   You figure out that your cabin mates enjoy playing sports. To make this inference, you put the clues together with the information you already had. Drawing inferences is like "reading between the lines."

TRY THE SKILL

In the last lesson, you read how the United States ratified the Thirteenth Amendment. Read the following passage. Then answer the questions below.

> *Although the Thirteenth Amendment settled the issue of slavery in the United States, the place of African Americans in American society remained unclear.*

1. What clues does the above passage have about African Americans after the Thirteenth Amendment?

2. How do the clues compare to the information you have about the lives of African Americans before the Thirteenth Amendment?

3. What inference did you make?

4. How can drawing inferences help you better understand what you read?

EXTEND THE SKILL

Knowing how to draw inferences can also help you understand history. It helps connect facts and events from the past. Read the following passage about Lee's surrender to Grant. Then make an inference and answer the questions below.

> *On April 9, 1865, Grant and Lee met in Appomattox Court House, Virginia. Lee wore a crisp grey uniform. "I have to look my best," he said. "I may be Grant's prisoner." Grant did not take any prisoners. Instead, Grant said, "Each ... man will be allowed to return to his home ..."*

- What inference can you make about Lee's surrender to Grant?

- What inference can you make about Grant's decision not to take prisoners?

- How can drawing inferences help you better understand history?

Reconstruction and After

 What happened in the South after the Civil War?

Lesson Outline
• Plans for Reconstruction
• Freedmen's Bureau
• Violence in the South

VOCABULARY

Reconstruction
black codes
Fourteenth Amendment
Freedmen's Bureau
sharecropping
impeach
Fifteenth Amendment
Jim Crow laws
segregation

PEOPLE

Andrew Johnson
Hiram R. Revels

READING STRATEGY

Copy the chart below. Compare and contrast what helped and hurt African Americans after the war.

BUILD BACKGROUND

After the Civil War, the South was in ruins. Soon a national debate began over whether Congress or the President should make decisions on rebuilding the South, or Reconstruction. Before his death, President Lincoln announced his plan for Reconstruction. Lincoln had encouraged Americans to put away their malice, or bad feelings, about the war, "with malice toward none, with charity for all . . . let us strive on to finish the work we are in."

© The Museum of the Confederacy

PLANS FOR RECONSTRUCTION

After Lincoln's death Vice President Andrew Johnson, a Democrat from Tennessee became President. Johnson soon announced his own plan for Reconstruction. The defeated Southern states had to pledge their loyalty to the Union and abolish slavery. By the fall of 1865, every Confederate state but Texas had followed these steps to rejoin the Union.

Black Codes 21

Members of Congress did not want state governments set up under Johnson's plan. Many of the South's newly elected officials were the same people who had led the Confederacy. Congress pointed out that under the leadership of all-white legislatures, very little was likely to change for blacks.

Across the South the new state governments had passed laws called black codes. The black codes described the rights and duties of the freed African Americans. They made it unlawful for African American to live in certain areas and to hold certain jobs. The black codes also said that African Americans without jobs could be arrested and forced to work in order to pay their fines.

Members of Congress voted not to admit the newly elected Southern lead-

Richmond, Virginia (left), lay in ruins after the war. Andrew Johnson (above) became President after Lincoln's death.

ers to Congress. Instead, the Congress began to develop its own plan for Reconstruction.

The Fourteenth Amendment 22

Congress said the Thirteenth Amendment did not go far enough to improve the lives of African Americans. Not one Southern state allowed blacks the same rights as whites. In 1866 Congress proposed a Fourteenth Amendment. This amendment made blacks citizens of the United States and guaranteed them the same legal rights as whites. President Johnson tried to prevent the Fourteenth Amendment from passing, but it became part of the Constitution in 1868.

READING CHECK Why did Congress develop its own plan for Reconstruction?

FREEDMEN'S BUREAU

23

As Congress worked on its own plan for Reconstruction, millions of newly freed African Americans, or "freedmen," faced an uncertain future. For freed people without jobs or land, emancipation meant hunger and homelessness. In order to help freed people build new lives, Congress created the **Freedmen's Bureau** in March 1865. The Bureau provided food, clothing, shelter, medical care, jobs, and legal help to both blacks and whites. The Bureau also set up more than 4,000 schools for newly freed people.

African Americans also provided their own schooling. By 1870 they spent more than $1 million on education. In time, black colleges and universities were started in the South. Among them were Fisk University in Tennessee and Morehouse and Spelman Colleges in Georgia.

The **Freedmen's Bureau** set up schools in the South for African Americans who had been freed.

From Slavery to Sharecropper

24

The Civil War and the falling price of cotton left most landowners with little or no money to pay the freed people to work the land. To survive, the freed people needed to earn a living. In order to make money from their fields, white landowners began to rent their land to blacks and poor whites. The landowners usually accepted part of the crop grown on their land as rent. Often the landowner's share was as much as one-half of the crop. This system of renting land and promising to pay with a share of the crop raised on it is called **sharecropping**. The people who rent the land are called sharecroppers.

Low cotton prices made it hard for sharecroppers to earn enough money to survive. Many sharecroppers had to borrow food and supplies from local stores, creating debts that grew larger every year. Some landowners cheated sharecroppers by selling them supplies at high prices. Every year most sharecroppers slipped deeper into debt.

© Cook Collection Valentine Museum

Sharecroppers (left) worked the cotton fields after slavery ended. Hiram Revels (below), was the first African American Senator.

Congress Takes Control 25

In 1867 Congress announced its plan for Reconstruction in the First Reconstruction Act. Under Congress's plan, the new leaders would be blacks and whites loyal to the Union. As a result, 600 African Americans were elected to state office. Sixteen African Americans were elected to Congress, including Blanche K. Bruce. Hiram R. Revels from Mississippi was the first African American elected to the Senate.

Congress's plan also called for the Union army to rule the South until new state governments were formed. With the troops came many Northerners who planned to start businesses. They were called carpetbaggers because many of them traveled with suitcases made of carpeting. Southerners believed carpetbaggers were looking to profit from the South's suffering. Most carpetbaggers were former Union officers and Freedmen's Bureau officials.

Johnson Impeached 26

At the same time, Congress passed laws limiting the President's power. In 1868 the House of Representatives voted to impeach President Johnson because he refused to obey these new laws. To impeach means to charge a government official with wrongdoing. Under the Constitution, if two-thirds of the Senate find a President guilty, the President is removed from office. President Johnson was saved by just one vote, that of Senator Edmund Ross of Kansas. Johnson stayed in office, but had lost his fight to control Reconstruction.

Why did most sharecroppers slip into debt?

VIOLENCE IN THE SOUTH

The new state governments controlled by Northerners angered many Southern whites. New state leaders had raised taxes sharply to pay for new schools and roads although Southerners could not vote until their states had been readmitted to the Union. Seeing blacks holding public office also angered many whites.

Some Southerners turned to violence to frighten African Americans and their white supporters. In 1866 six former Confederate officers formed the Ku Klux Klan. Disguised in white robes and hoods, its members terrorized African Americans. "The Ku Klux Klan [is] riding nightly over the country . . . robbing, whipping, . . . and killing our people," said a petition to Congress by black citizens of Kentucky in 1871.

The Fifteenth Amendment 27

Some white Southerners tried to prevent blacks from voting. Sometimes whites kept the voting places secret from black voters. In 1870 the **Fifteenth Amendment** was passed. It said states could not deny male citizens the right to vote "on account of race or color."

This poster shows how African American communities organized for the passage of the Fourteenth Amendment.

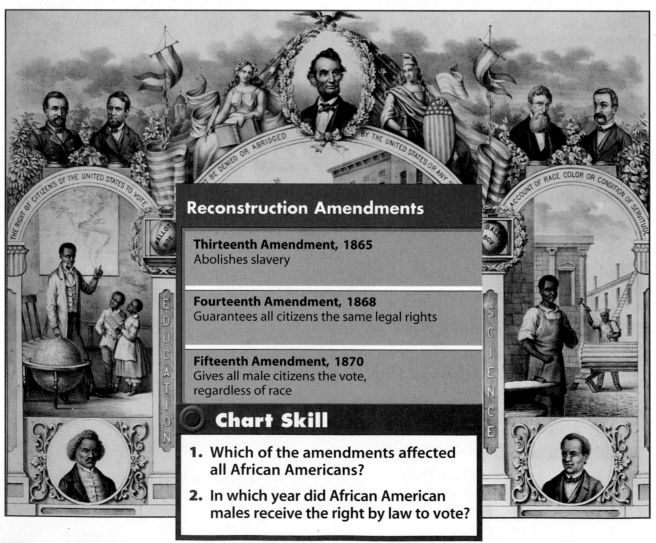

Reconstruction Amendments

Thirteenth Amendment, 1865
Abolishes slavery

Fourteenth Amendment, 1868
Guarantees all citizens the same legal rights

Fifteenth Amendment, 1870
Gives all male citizens the vote, regardless of race

Chart Skill

1. Which of the amendments affected all African Americans?

2. In which year did African American males receive the right by law to vote?

460

Reconstruction Ends 28

The presidential election of 1876 brought about the end of Reconstruction. Republican Rutherford B. Hayes lost the popular vote, but the electoral vote was in question. Votes in some Southern states seemed to be inaccurate. To settle the argument Hayes promised to remove Union troops from all Southern states. In exchange, Democrats would allow Hayes to become President. By 1877 the last Union soldiers had left the South.

After Reconstruction, the Southern states quickly passed Jim Crow laws. Jim Crow laws made the separation of white and black people legal. Another name for the separation of people by race is segregation. Under Jim Crow laws, blacks and whites could not use the same schools, restaurants, trains, hotels, or parks. Frederick Douglass said in 1883, "Thus in all the relations of life and death we are met by the color line."

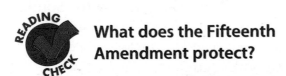
What does the Fifteenth Amendment protect?

This political cartoon was drawn in 1875 to support equal rights.

PUTTING IT TOGETHER

While Reconstruction gave African Americans citizenship, it did not solve the economic problems of the South. As during slavery, most blacks picked cotton on land that was owned by whites. After Reconstruction, Jim Crow laws made segregation legal and denied African Americans equal rights. Not until the Civil Rights movement of the 1950s and 1960s would African Americans gain the rights guaranteed to all citizens by the Thirteenth, Fourteenth, and Fifteenth Amendments to the Constitution.

Review and Assess

1. Write one sentence for each vocabulary term.

   black codes   **Reconstruction**
   Freedmen's Bureau

2. Explain why the Thirteenth, Fourteenth, and Fifteenth amendments were passed.

3. How did Reconstruction change the South?

4. What economic effects did sharecropping have?

5. **Analyze** the effects groups like the Ku Klux Klan had on Reconstruction.

Look at the chart on page 460. Write about how life should have changed for African Americans after the Thirteenth, Fourteenth, and Fifteenth Amendments were passed.

Write an editorial against the Jim Crow laws.

461

Points of View
How Did Lincoln's Death Affect Reconstruction?

Historians disagree about how Lincoln's death affected Reconstruction. Some think African Americans would still have had to fight for equality. Others disagree. Read the three different points of view, then answer the questions that follow.

ROBERT F. ENGS
Professor of History, University of Pennsylvania
Excerpt from an interview, 2001

"Lincoln could have pushed the nation toward more certain guarantees of black liberty and might have gotten some land for freed slaves in the South. A less violently hostile white South, however, may have meant that Lincoln and Congress would not have had the support needed to pass the Fourteenth and Fifteenth Amendments.**"**

REBECCA PLANT
Associate Professor of History, Vanderbilt University
Excerpt from an interview, 2001

"At the war's end, few Northerners favored giving the vote to blacks. . . . if Lincoln had lived, the end result would probably have been the same. Southern whites were determined to put a system in place that kept freedmen and women down. Under Lincoln, they would simply have achieved this goal more quickly . . . his main concern was to restore the Union. . . .**"**

CATHY NELSON

State Coordinator, Ohio Underground Railroad Association

Excerpt from an interview, 2001

❝Lincoln ... believed slavery was morally wrong ... If he had lived, Reconstruction would have been a period that brought the country and blacks and whites together. He would have worked gradually to see that blacks were treated fairly and given their civil rights. His goal was to restore power to the South.... Reconstruction under Johnson was a move back towards slavery.**❞**

Thinking About the Points of View

1. What does Robert Engs think Lincoln's goals for Reconstruction might have been? Why does he think Lincoln's plans might have weakened support for the Fourteenth and Fifteenth Amendments?

2. Why does Rebecca Plant think African Americans would have had less political power if Lincoln had lived? In what ways does she agree with Professor Engs?

3. How does Cathy Nelson think Andrew Johnson's goals for Reconstruction differed from Lincoln's? How does her opinion disagree with the others?

4. What other points of view might people have on this issue?

 Building Citizenship

Courage

What risks did African Americans take by demanding their rights during Reconstruction?

Why did it take courage for African Americans to vote?

 Write About It!

Write a paragraph describing a problem in your school or neighborhood. Explain how you or someone else acted with courage to solve the problem.

LITERATURE

Kiansis

Illustrated by Raul Colón

*The first American cowboys were the vaqueros.
Two hundred years before people from the United
States arrived in Texas, the vaqueros rode the open
range of the Southwest. "Kiansis" is typical of the songs,
called* corridos, *that vaqueros sang as they sat at their
campfires. The Country Western music of today has its
roots in the singing vaqueros.*

Cuando salimos **pa'** Kiansis con una grande partida, ¡ah, qué camino tan largo! no contaba con mi vida.	When we left for Kansas with a great herd of cattle, Ah, what a long trail it was! I was not sure I would survive.
Nos decía el **caporal**, como queriendo llorar: —Allá va la novillada, no me la dejan pasar.	The **caporal** would tell us, as if he were going to cry, "Watch out for that bunch of steers; Don't let them get past you.
¡Ah, qué caballo tan bueno! todo se le iba en correr, ¡y, ah, qué fuerre aguacerazo! no contabe yo en volver . . .	Ah, what a good horse I had! He did nothing but gallop And, ah, what a violent cloudburst! I was not sure I would come back . . .

---

pa' (pä) para
caporal (kä pö räl') el que esta al mando del ganado

---

caporal (kä pö räl') trail boss

llegamos al Río Salado
y nos tiramos a nado,
decía un americano:
—Esos hombres ya se ahogaron

Pues qué pensaría ese hombre
que venimos a **esp'rimentar**
si somos del Río Grande,
de los Buenos pa'nadar

Y le dimos vista a Kiansis,
y nos dice el caporal:
—**Ora** sí somos de vida,
ya vamos a hacer corral.

Y de vuelta en San Antonio
compramos buenos sombreros
y aquí se acaban cantando
versos de los aventureros.

We got to the Salado River,
and we swam our horses across;
An American was saying,
"Those men are as good as drowned."

I wonder what the man thought,
that we came to learn, perhaps
why, we're from the Rio Grande,
where the good swimmers are from.

And then Kansas came in sight,
and the caporal tells us,
"We have finally made it,
we'll soon have them in the corral."

Back again in San Antonio,
we all bought ourselves good hats,
And this is the end of the singing
of the stanzas about the trail drivers.

---

esp'rimentar (esp rĕ men tär′) experimentar
ora (ô rä′) ahora

Write About It!

Vaqueros worked around the clock and were completely isolated for long periods of time. Read the lyrics to the song again. **Write** a paragraph on why the singer was not sure he would survive.

The Nation Changes

TAKE A LOOK

How did the move west and industrialization change the nation?

Before the railroad, it took 7 months to cross North America. Trains shortened the trip to about a week. Today a plane crosses the continent in 5 hours.

For more information about the changing west and industrialization, visit our Web site at **www.mhschool.com**

THE Big IDEAS ABOUT...

The Changing West

As the Civil War came to an end, people were ready to explore the western territories of the United States. A new railroad that stretched cross-country made it easy to do so. Immigrants, African Americans, and citizens in many eastern states looked to the Great Plains for a new beginning.

But what effect would this have on the Native Americans who had long made their homes on the Great Plains? Read on to find out how their lives would change forever.

THE TRANSCONTINENTAL RAILROAD

The completion of the transcontinental railroad shortens the time it takes to travel from coast to coast.

THE CATTLE KINGDOM

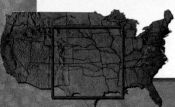

Cowhands usually wait until spring to begin their long and difficult cattle drive north.

HOMESTEADING ON THE PLAINS

Settlers often find the Great Plains environment harsh. One described it as "just sky and grass and grass and sky."

THE PLAINS WARS

After many years of war, most Native Americans are forced to leave their natural homelands and live on reservations.

Foldables

Make this Foldable study guide and use it to record what you learn about "The Changing West."

1. Fold an 8 ½" x 11" piece of paper in half like a hot dog, leaving one side 1" longer than the other.

2. Make 3 cuts, equal distance apart, on the short side of paper, forming four tabs.

3. Write the chapter title on the 1" tab, and the lesson titles on the four small tabs.

The Transcontinental Railroad

How did the transcontinental railroad help our country grow?

Lesson Outline
• Demands for a Railroad
• A Tremendous Task
• Competing to Win

VOCABULARY

transcontinental railroad
Pacific Railroad Act

PEOPLE

Grenville Dodge
Charles Crocker

READING STRATEGY

Use a sequence-of-events chart like the one below to list the steps that led to the building of the transcontinental railroad.

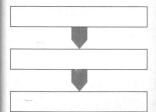

BUILD BACKGROUND

At the end of the Civil War, most of the country's railroad tracks were east of the Mississippi River. To get to the West Coast, people traveled by boat, (which took months), or wagon trains (which took many weeks). Both journeys were dangerous. A **transcontinental railroad**, some said, was needed. A transcontinental railroad is one that crosses an entire continent.

A transcontinental railroad would have to cross mountains, deserts, and vast plains.

DEMANDS FOR A RAILROAD

Many people wanted to go west in the 1860s. They did not do so unless they had good reason. In 1838 the people of the Iowa Territory asked Congress for help building a transcontinental railroad. Congress denied the petition, saying it would be like trying "to build a railroad to the moon."

Railroad builders thought a transcontinental railroad was risky. They worried about conflicts with the many Native Americans who lived in the West. The railroad would cut across their lands. The geography of the West also discouraged the builders. How would they build a railroad across the vast Great Plains, the snow-covered Rocky Mountains, the deserts of the Great Basin, and the rugged Sierra Nevadas of California?

The Government Acts

After the California gold rush in 1849, demand for a transcontinental railroad increased. Finally, in July 1862, Congress passed the **Pacific Railroad Act**. This act offered two companies government loans and free land to build the railroad. President Lincoln hoped that a transcontinental railroad would help the Union during the Civil War.

The two companies decided to build from opposite directions and meet somewhere in the middle. Thomas Durant headed the Union Pacific Railroad. Under the leadership of **Grenville Dodge**, the Union Pacific would lay track westward

Exploring
TECHNOLOGY

Steam-powered Trains

Richard Trevithick, an Englishman, built the first steam-powered railroad engine in 1804. It pulled ten tons of cargo at a top speed of five miles per hour.

In 1829, George Stephenson made an engine he called the *Rocket* that reached speeds of 30 miles per hour. It used small tubes that ran through the boiler and produced steam quickly.

Now that railroad engines could travel faster than horse-drawn vehicles, they became the most popular form of transportation in the nation. Over the next few decades, better wheels, brakes, and other improvements allowed the locomotive to reach speeds of up to 50 miles per hour.

Activity

How do you think today's trains are improvements over trains in the 1800s?

from Omaha, Nebraska. The second company, Central Pacific Railroad, was headed by Leland Stanford. A merchant named **Charles Crocker** would lead the Central Pacific eastward from Sacramento, California.

What was the Pacific Railroad Act?

475

A TREMENDOUS TASK

Building the transcontinental railroad was costly and involved thousands of workers, many of whom were injured. Because of the Civil War, supplies were often hard to get. Both companies needed iron rails, but they were made on the East Coast. Central Pacific had to ship the iron rails by sea around South America, which was costly and took months. Union Pacific shipped the rails by steamboat on the Missouri River. Thus, by 1865, more than three years after they started, neither railroad company had lain more than 50 miles of track.

Workers on the Central Pacific

Finding workers to lay the track was another problem. Many men were still serving in the Union and Confederate armies. Because of the recent gold rush, the Central Pacific had trouble keeping its

Many immigrants helped with the difficult task of building the railroad.

workers from taking better paying jobs or quitting to look for gold and silver. To get workers, Crocker began hiring Chinese immigrants in 1865. The Chinese were paid the same as other workers but they provided their own food and shelter. By 1867, Chinese workers made up nine out of ten workers.

Accidents and deaths were common, especially for the Central Pacific workers. The most dangerous work was often given to Chinese or Irish immigrants. To blast roadbeds through the Sierra Nevadas, for example, they used a method developed in China. By lowering themselves down the mountains in baskets, workers were able to drill holes in the hard granite rock. Then, they filled the holes with gunpowder. Thousands of workers died doing this.

Workers on the Union Pacific

At first, the Union Pacific hired former Civil War soldiers and free African Americans to work on the railroad. Later, Grenville Dodge hired mostly Irish and German immigrants. They were paid low wages, even for the times—about $2.50 to $4 a day. However, Dodge provided food and housing.

The song on the next page was sung by Union Pacific workers. Some say it was adapted from an Irish hymn, and others from African Americans who lived in Louisiana.

READING CHECK Why did both railroad companies prefer using immigrant labor?

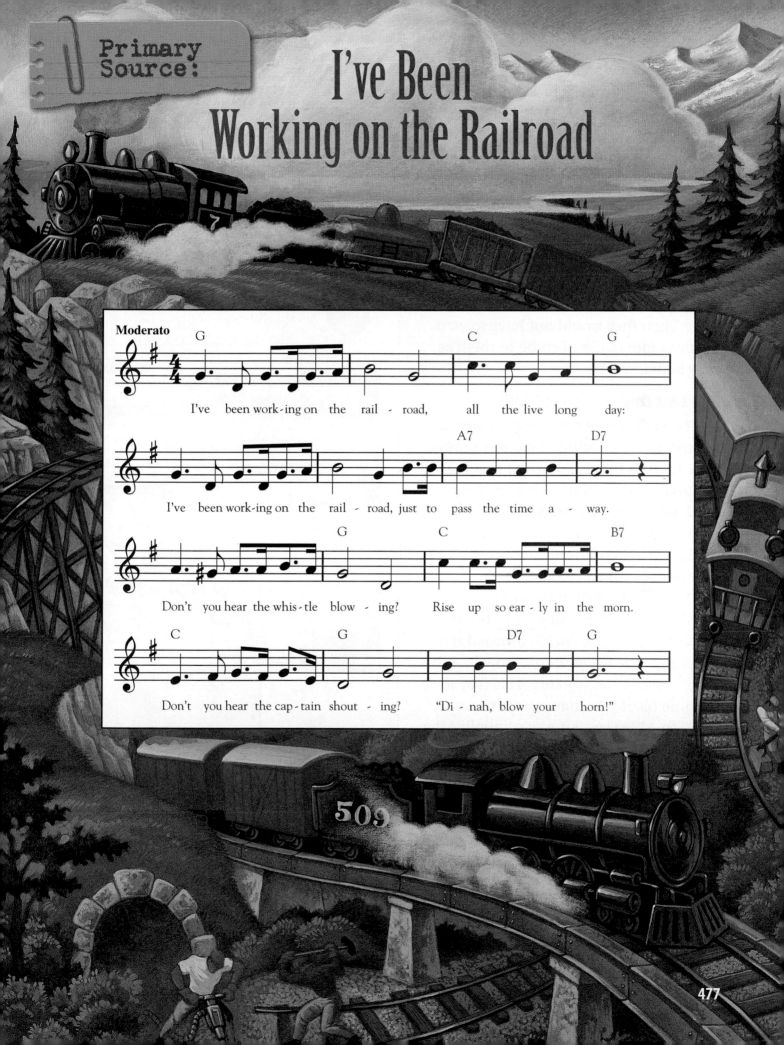

COMPETING TO WIN

Amendments were added to the Pacific Railroad Act to speed up the building of the railroad. They offered more money and land for every mile of completed track. The Union Pacific quickly took the lead. Dodge's crew had the advantage of laying track on the flat land of the Great Plains. Crocker's men, on the other hand, had to cross over or blast through mountains. His workers began transporting supplies over the mountains before the crew. Then they would not have to wait for the supply train to come to them as they laid new track.

The Last Day

The race between the two companies heated up as the railroad neared completion. Charles Crocker learned that the Union Pacific had finished six miles of track in one day. He made a $10,000 bet with Thomas Durant, head of the Union Pacific, that the Central Pacific could lay ten miles of track in a day.

On April 28, 1869, only 16 miles separated the two companies. In 12 hours the crew of the Central Pacific finished ten miles plus a few feet more. Crowds gathered to watch the workers. This feat set an all-time record for many years to come. The Ten-Mile Day came to symbolize the hard work of the thousands of men who worked on the railroad.

The Golden Spike

For six years, railroad workers had worked constantly, laying more than 1,700 miles of track. On May 10, 1869, the two railroads met at Promontory Point, Utah. On this day, a crowd of railroad workers, reporters, and soldiers gathered at Promontory Point to watch the last spikes being hammered into the tracks by Chinese workers.

At the finish, Central Pacific's Leland Stanford held a railroad spike made of pure gold. When the golden spike was hammered in, a simple message was telegraphed across the country: "Done."

Cannons roared, bells rang, and fireworks exploded to celebrate the completion of the transcontinental railroad.

READING CHECK **Which railroad leader won the $10,000 bet?**

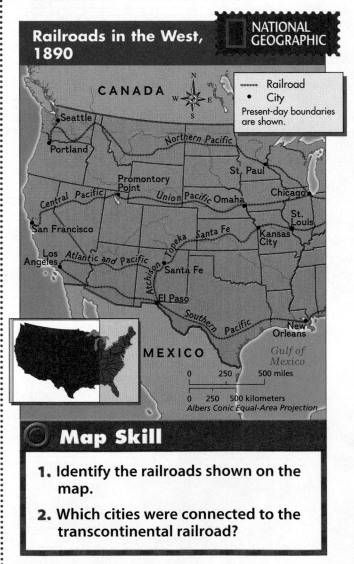

Railroads in the West, 1890

NATIONAL GEOGRAPHIC

CANADA

Seattle
Portland
Northern Pacific
St. Paul
Promontory Point
Central Pacific
Union Pacific Omaha
Chicago
San Francisco
St. Louis
Los Angeles
Atlantic and Pacific
Topeka
Atchison
Santa Fe
Santa Fe
Kansas City
El Paso
Southern Pacific
New Orleans
MEXICO
Gulf of Mexico

Railroad
• City
Present-day boundaries are shown.

0   250   500 miles
0   250   500 kilometers
Albers Conic Equal-Area Projection

Map Skill

1. Identify the railroads shown on the map.

2. Which cities were connected to the transcontinental railroad?

The golden spike (left) was used at the completion of the transcontinental railroad. The spike reads, "May God continue the unity of our Country as the Railroad united two great Oceans of the world."

PUTTING IT TOGETHER

Service on the transcontinental railroad began immediately. It cost first-class passengers $100 to travel between Omaha and Sacramento. Passengers riding coach paid $75. The trip was noisy and uncomfortable and the food was bad.

Even so, many people thought of it as a miracle. Thinking of the early European explorers, one writer said, "Having never found a Northwest Passage, Americans had fashioned one instead." Soon people and products were traveling from New York to San Francisco in about a week.

Review and Assess

1. Write a sentence for each of the following vocabulary terms.

   Pacific Railroad Act
   transcontinental railroad

2. What was the Ten-Mile Day?

3. How did the transcontinental railroad affect the settling of the West?

4. What were some of the reasons the United States Congress passed the Pacific Railroad Act?

5. **Predict** the effects that the transcontinental railroad would have on the ways of life of the Native Americans.

Use the map on page 478 and the Atlas map on pages R18–R19 to identify the landforms the transcontinental railroad had to cross. Then organize a debate on the topic "which landform caused the most difficulty?"

Write a journal entry describing a typical work day that you would have had as a railroad worker for one of the two companies that built the transcontinental railroad. What new sights did you see? How did you feel?

Reading A Time Zone Map

In the late 1800s, railroads made it easier for people to cross the country. The fact that every town had a different time troubled the people who set the train schedules.

To solve this problem, **time zones** were set up in 1884. The world was divided into 24 different time zones—one for each hour in a day. Starting from the prime meridian at Greenwich, England, the time zones were laid out at every 15 degrees of longitude.

VOCABULARY

time zone

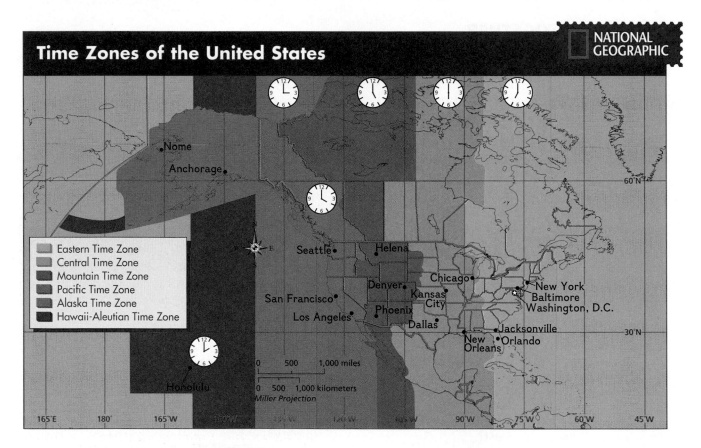

Time Zones of the United States

NATIONAL GEOGRAPHIC

Legend:
- Eastern Time Zone
- Central Time Zone
- Mountain Time Zone
- Pacific Time Zone
- Alaska Time Zone
- Hawaii-Aleutian Time Zone

Cities: Nome, Anchorage, Seattle, Helena, Chicago, New York, Baltimore, Washington, D.C., Denver, Kansas City, San Francisco, Phoenix, Los Angeles, Dallas, Jacksonville, New Orleans, Orlando, Honolulu

0   500   1,000 miles
0   500   1,000 kilometers
Miller Projection

165°E   180°   165°W   ...W   ...W   120°W   ...W   90°W   75°W   60°W   45°W
60°N
30°N

LEARN THE SKILL

Follow these steps to better understand how to use time zone maps.

1. **Identify the time zones on the map.**
   As you can see from the map, the United

States has six time zones. The map shows that the borders of the time zones no longer follow longitude lines exactly. They take into account national and state borders.

2. **Find your starting point on the map.**
   Suppose you are in Dallas, Texas, and want

to know what time it is in San Francisco, California. Find Dallas on the map and notice that it is six o'clock. Then find San Francisco and find the time there.

3. Add or subtract an hour for each time zone that is crossed.
The time in any zone east of you is always later than it is in your zone. As you move to the east, add one hour for each time zone you cross. As you move west, subtract one hour for each time zone you cross.

TRY THE SKILL

Now look at the time zone map to answer the following questions.

1. What time zone is to the west of Denver, Colorado?

2. What time zone is to the east?

3. If it is 5:00 P.M. in Denver, what time is it in New York?

4. If the President planned to broadcast a live speech from Denver at 5:00 P.M., what time would the broadcast air in Seattle, Washington? How did you calculate the time?

5. How can reading a time zone map help you when taking a trip?

EXTEND THE SKILL

Compare the map on page 480 to the map on page 478. When the railroad was completed, celebrations were held in Chicago, New York, and Sacramento.

● The golden spike was hammered in at 12:47 P.M. central daylight time. What time was it in Sacramento? Chicago? New York?

● How can using time zone maps help you understand conflicts in dates in history?

VOL. XXIX.....NO. 8,764.

THE PACIFIC RAILROAD.

THE OFFICIAL ANNOUNCEMENT OF ITS COMPLETION.

To the Associated Press.

PROMONTORY SUMMIT, Utah, May 10.—The last rail is laid! The last spike driven! The Pacific Railroad is completed!

The point of junction is 1,086 miles west of the Missouri River, and 690 miles east of Sacramento City.　　　　LELAND STANFORD,
　　　　　　　　　　　　Central Pacific Railroad.

T. C. DURANT,
SIDNEY DILLON, } Union Pacific Railroad.
JOHN DAFF.

INTERESTING PROCEEDINGS IN THE WASH-INGTON TELEGRAPH OFFICE.
[BY TELEGRAPH TO THE TRIBUNE.]

WASHINGTON, May 10.—The announcement having been made here about noon to-day that the driving of the spikes in the last rail which would complete the line of railroad between the Atlantic and Pacific Oceans would be communicated to all the telegraph offices in the country the instant the work was done,

The Cattle Kingdom

Find Out!

How did railroads change the cattle industry?

Lesson Outline
• Cowboys on the Trail
• The Cattle Industry

VOCABULARY

cattle drive
railhead
stockyards
cowtowns

PEOPLE

Nat Love
Joseph McCoy

READING STRATEGY

Use a two-column chart like the one below to compare. In one column, list what life was like in the West before the transcontinental railroad. In the other, list what life was like after the railroad.

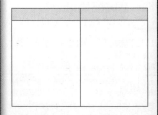

BUILD BACKGROUND

"I'm an old cowhand from the Rio Grande" is from a famous song. Cowboys, or cowhands, have lived and worked in the United States since the Spanish brought cattle and horses to North America in the 1500s. Unlike the romantic hero shown in the movies, cowboys lived a hard and dangerous life. By the mid-1800s, Texas ranchers were raising millions of longhorn cattle, which thrived on the open ranges of the state. In 1866, a steer, or male cow, could be purchased for about $5 in Texas. In the North, where cattle were scarce, a steer was worth $40. The problem for ranchers was to get their cattle north.

COWBOYS ON THE TRAIL

Texans realized that if they could get their cattle to the railroads, they could ship them east and sell them for more money. Thus began the time of the **cattle drives**. A cattle drive was a long journey taken by cowboys to herd, or drive, cattle from ranches in Texas north on trails leading to the railroads.

The cowboys of the mid-1800s came from many backgrounds. Most of the white cowboys had fought for the Confederacy during the Civil War. Another one-quarter to one-third were African American or Mexican American. In fact, Mexican and Native American vaqueros, or cowboys, started many of the cattle ranching practices that are used in the United States today.

Nat Love, an African American who was once enslaved, wrote about the code that cowboys lived by:

"There's a man's work was to be done, and a man's life to be lived, and when death was to be met, he met it like a man."

Love became the champion roper of the Western cattle country.

Thousands of cattle were driven north from Texas by cowboys.

Life on the Trail

Life on the cattle drive was hard, unending work. It began in spring. Leading the way was the trail boss in the chuck wagon, which also carried food and supplies. The cattle drive often had 2,000 to 3,000 longhorn cattle. Between 8 and 20 cowboys tended the herd.

Cowboys faced many dangers on the trail. These included thieves and Native Americans who did not want the herds trampling their land. The most dangerous part of the drive was usually controlling the herd. Anything, even lightning streaking across the sky, could scare a herd into stampeding. Once a stampede started, the cattle could trample anything in their path. To keep the herd calm, cowboys often sang to them. Cattle drives could last around 100 days.

READING CHECK

What danger did cowboys face on a cattle drive?

483

THE CATTLE INDUSTRY

Once cowboys carved out a path they liked, they tended to continue using it on their cattle drives. One of the most famous of the trails was the Chisholm Trail. The Chisholm Trail ran all the way from San Antonio, Texas, to Abilene, Kansas.

Railheads and Cowtowns

Towns soon developed near the new railroad tracks. In Kansas, Abilene and Dodge City were both such towns. These towns were called railheads. The people of Kansas realized that they could make money from the cattle trade as well as from the railroads.

In 1867, a rancher named Joseph McCoy built stockyards, or cattle pens, in Abilene. He set the stockyards right next to the railroad tracks. McCoy charged cowboys to house their longhorns while waiting for the next train east. He soon set up a hotel for tired cowboys to rest before they began the journey home.

Stores, restaurants, and other businesses sprang up at points along the trails. Eventually, entire towns developed for cowboys passing through. These towns were called cowtowns.

Railheads such as Abilene and Dodge City became centers from where cattle were shipped to meat-packing plants in Chicago. By 1870, Chicago was the world's largest supplier of fresh beef and had grown into a major city.

The new railroads helped the cattle industry to grow. However, they also caused the end of the cattle drives. Early railroads in the West ran between the East and the West. When railroads stretched south into Texas, cattle drives faded.

READING CHECK

What was the difference between a cowtown and a railhead?

Dodge City, Kansas, was one of the busiest railheads in the late 1800s.

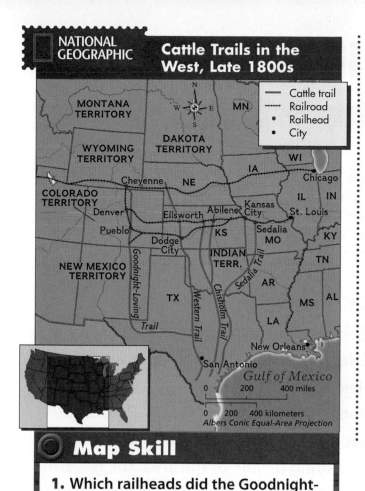

NATIONAL GEOGRAPHIC

Cattle Trails in the West, Late 1800s

Legend:
— Cattle trail
····· Railroad
• Railhead
● City

MONTANA TERRITORY
WYOMING TERRITORY
DAKOTA TERRITORY
MN
WI
IA
Cheyenne
NE
Chicago
COLORADO TERRITORY
Denver
Ellsworth
Abilene
Kansas City
St. Louis
IL
IN
Pueblo
Dodge City
KS
Sedalia
MO
KY
Goodnight-Loving Trail
INDIAN TERR.
Sedalia Trail
TN
NEW MEXICO TERRITORY
AR
TX
Western Trail
Chisholm Trail
MS
AL
LA
New Orleans
San Antonio
Gulf of Mexico

0   200   400 miles
0   200   400 kilometers
Albers Conic Equal-Area Projection

Map Skill

1. Which railheads did the Goodnight-Loving trail meet?

2. Which trail started in San Antonio?

PUTTING IT TOGETHER

The transcontinental railroad offered Texas ranchers an opportunity to make larger profits from their cattle. Once they started driving their cattle north, a new industry developed. The life of the cowboy became the subject of many movies and stories. The songs cowboys sang on their drives became part of our popular culture. Today, the cattle industry remains an important part of our economy. Cowboys still work on ranches, but they use modern technology.

_____

Cowboys of the past as well as today rely on well-made saddles and lassos.

Review and Assess

1. Write one sentence for each of the vocabulary terms:

   cattle drive   **railhead**
   cowtowns   **stockyards**

2. Near what city did the Chisholm Trail begin? In what city did it end?

3. What effect did the transcontinental railroad have on the West?

4. How did the railroad change the **economy** of cattle ranching?

5. **Compare** some of the dangers cowboys faced on the cattle drive with the dangers a cowhand might face today. How are they the same? How are they different?

Use the map above to make a list of the important cattle trails and the railheads where they ended. Use the map scale to figure out which trail was longest.

· ·

Write a song about your life as a cowhand on the cattle drive. Include an event that might have occurred and how you felt about life as a cowhand.

485

Lesson 3

Settling on the Plains

How did the settlers of the Great Plains use their environment?

Lesson Outline
- The Homestead Act
- The Settlers Arrive
- Exodusters

VOCABULARY

Homestead Act
homesteader
sodbusters
soddies
exodusters

PEOPLE

James Oliver
Joseph Glidden
Henry Adams

READING STRATEGY

Use a word map like the one below. Placing Great Plains in the center, summarize words that you associate with its climate.

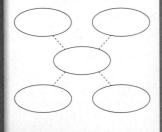

BUILD BACKGROUND

Early settlers heading west wrote of crossing miles and miles of dry grassland in the center of the country. Some called it the "Great American Desert." After the completion of the transcontinental railroad, settlers continued to the West Coast and avoided the Great Plains. To bring people to the area, the government and the railroad companies offered many acres of this land for sale at low prices. Starting in 1862, the United States government sold or gave away almost two hundred million acres of land.

You Are Here
1862 – 1879

THE HOMESTEAD ACT

Ads throughout the nation announced "cheap, fertile land," and "low prices!" Yet few people believed that they could farm the dry, treeless Great Plains. Then in 1862 President Lincoln signed the **Homestead Act**. The act gave 160 acres, or one quarter square mile, of public land to adult men 21 years of age, widows, or heads of a family. All the settlers had to do was pay a small fee of $1.25 an acre, farm the land, and live on it for five years. The people who claimed land under this act were called **homesteaders**.

Hopes for Settlement

President Lincoln hoped that the Homestead Act would draw farmers to the Great Plains. He also believed that the nation's economy would grow once the new transcontinental railroad was built.

People who lived in the East, African Americans from the South, and immigrants from Denmark, France, Norway, Russia, and Sweden eagerly sought to become homesteaders. The promise of building better lives for themselves and their families gave them hope. Most claimed land in Kansas, Nebraska, and the Dakota Territory. This area, although dry, was not a desert. It was on the dry side of the line separating Humid America and Arid America.

 READING CHECK **Why did railroad companies want to bring settlers to the Great Plains?**

These Kansas **homesteaders** were among the more than 400,000 people who paid as little as $12 for their land.

THE SETTLERS ARRIVE

The homesteaders set out for the prairie in many ways—bouncing stagecoaches, railroads, and crowded Conestoga wagons. When they arrived, the flat, windy land seemed strange and lonely. It was "just sky and grass and grass and sky," wrote Kansas homesteader Lydia Toothaker. Most of the settlers had never seen the Great Plains. They soon found that the lack of trees and water and the harsh climate made farming difficult on the Plains. Yet through hard work and with the help of new technology, many homesteaders succeeded in building farms.

Sodbusters

The endless acres of tall buffalo grass were both a blessing and a curse to the new settlers. The thick, tangled roots of the grass filled the top three inches of the soil. This "sod" was so matted and tough that it broke most iron plows. Because they had to "bust" through the thick sod to plant their crops, the new settlers earned the nickname sodbusters.

Sodbusters who could afford it used a new tool to turn the sod over. James Oliver invented a new type of steel plow in South Bend, Indiana, in 1877. His plow was able to cleanly slice through the sod without getting stuck. He called it the chilled-steel plow.

The sodbusters also found a use for the tough prairie sod. They used it as building material. Settlers cut thick brick-shaped slabs of sod and piled it in layers to make the walls and roofs of their homes. Houses made from sod were called soddies. As the following excerpt from a Kansas homesteader describes, the soddies were often dark and uncomfortable.

excerpt from a letter by Emma Brown — written in 1870

The roof . . . was of Kansas dirt, and when the rains came proved unsatisfactory indeed. We moved into this house about the first of August, 1870, and I felt as happy as a Queen. But a rainy time set in and continued. . . . It was two weeks I was left alone with the children. And the roof leaked!

Finally, when nearly everything in the house was soaked and the fuel gone I went to a neighbor's and found **haven** *in their* **dugout**. *But before morning there was six inches of water in it, so we had to make another move. The next shelter was under some boards stood up against a stone wall, [and we remained] there a day and a night.*

Why were sodhouses unsatisfactory?

haven: shelter
dugout: underground house

Life on the Plains

Homesteaders faced other hardships, such as prairie fires, unpredictable weather, and insects. The dry prairie grass caught fire and easily spread. The new settlers learned to dig trenches around homes and fields to slow the spread.

Weather on the Plains was also hard to bear. In winter, blizzards began so suddenly that a person could get lost between the house and barn and freeze

Many sodbusters build thriving farms in spite of tough prairie grass and frequent tornados.

to death. A Dakota schoolboy described an oncoming blizzard in 1888:

> *Suddenly we looked up and saw something coming rolling toward us with great fury from the northwest, and making a loud noise.*

The summer had different problems. Tornados, or swirling funnels of dust traveling at high speeds, could materialize suddenly, and lift homes right off the ground. They were capable of destroying everything in their path.

Insects were another problem. In 1874, called the "Great Grasshopper Year," millions of grasshoppers swarmed over the Plains. The hungry insects, piled 6 inches deep, could eat 100 acres of corn in a few hours. Many settlers on the Plains had to give up their farms.

New Technology on the Plains

For every homesteader who left the Plains, more arrived. Technology soon made life a little easier. Windmills made it possible to draw up water from underground. Powered by the constant prairie winds, windmills pumped underground water to the surface. Farmers then dug irrigation ditches to water crops.

In 1874 Russian settlers introduced a kind of wheat that could survive on the Plains. The same year, Joseph Glidden invented barbed wire. He twisted two wires together, then wrapped sharp barbs around them. By 1880 he had sold 80 million pounds of wire. Settlers used it for fences to keep cattle out of their fields.

READING CHECK Why was the chilled-steel plow important to the Plains?

EXODUSTERS

Thousands of African Americans also traveled to the Great Plains. They hoped to find freedom from violence and unfair treatment. The best-known town they settled was **Nicodemus**, Kansas. It was founded by settlers from Kentucky.

At first, many African Americans worked as farmhands to earn the money to pay the fee for a homestead. They faced difficult years when their supplies ran low and cattle trampled their crops. Even so, Nicodemus grew.

Leaving for Kansas

In the 1870s, **Henry Adams**, a former Civil War soldier, made speeches encouraging other African Americans to leave the South. "We lost all hopes," said Adams. "The whole South—every state in the South—had got into the hands of the very men who held us as slaves."

In 1879, thousands of African Americans lined the banks of the Mississippi River, waiting to sail to Kansas. This period became known as the "Kansas Fever Exodus." An exodus is a journey to freedom. According to the Bible, Moses helped the Israelites escape slavery in Egypt to reach the Promised Land.

Like the sodbuster, many freed slaves believed Kansas could be a kind of Promised Land. During 1879 alone, 20,000 African Americans left the South for Kansas. They were called **exodusters**.

Many exodusters sang along their journey to Kansas. In one song, "The Land That Gives Birth to Our Freedom," the exodusters sang of what they hoped to find in Kansas:

We wanted peaceful and quiet firesides;
No one to disturb us or turn us out.
Marching along, yes we are marching along,
To Kansas City we are bound.

The Kansas Fever Exodus did not last for long. Although African Americans

Exodusters lined the shores of the Mississippi River in hopes of leaving the South.

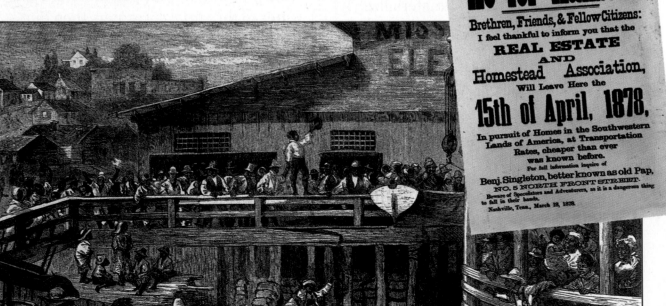

Kansas State Historical Society

Kansas State Historical Society

This exoduster family settled in Kansas.

PUTTING IT TOGETHER

Farmers faced many hardships as they settled the land in the Plains. While they were going through difficult times, industry and business was growing. Some farmers felt that the federal government did not support the farming industry. They organized the Populist Party in 1892 in order to have a voice in government.

One writer of the time, Mark Twain, criticized unfair business and government practices. In his 1873 book, *The Gilded Age,* he wrote, "There is no country in the world…that pursues corruption as inveterately [continually] as we do."

were legally free, some white Southerners unfairly jailed or refused to let black passengers onto boats leaving the South. However, many exodusters succeeded in getting to Kansas where they left a legacy of successful farming communities.

African Americans also settled in other parts of the West, such as California, Oregon, and Washington. A homesteader named George Washington founded the town of Centralia, Washington, in 1872.

How did African American settlers earn the name "exodusters"?

Review and Assess

1. Write a sentence for each of the following vocabulary terms.

   **exodusters   sodbusters
   homesteader**

2. What was the Homestead Act?

3. How did settlers on the Great Plains use its resources to survive?

4. Explain how new **technology** made farming life slightly easier for the settlers.

5. **Compare** the reasons that both white and black homesteaders left their homes to settle on the Great Plains.

Activities

Compare the Atlas maps on pages R16 and R19. List the present-day states that are on the Great Plains.

Write a letter as a sodbuster or exoduster to a friend back home. In one paragraph, describe the best thing about life on the Great Plains. In another paragraph, describe the hardest part of life there.

491

Reading and Thinking Skills

Identifying Frame of Reference

In this lesson, you learned about life on the Plains. From the point of view of the homesteaders, the Plains were a dry land with unpredictable weather that made it difficult to survive. However, Native Americans believed that the land was an ideal location for hunting. Both groups believed they were correct about the Plains.

In order to understand how such different statements can both be true, you need to understand their frame of reference. A **frame of reference** is the basis a person uses when forming a point of view. It can be influenced by many aspects of a person's background, including his or her cultural, economic, or geographical background, knowledge, and experiences.

LEARN THE SKILL

Follow the steps below to determine frame of reference.

1. **Research the backgrounds of the people involved.**
   Knowing the background will help you see what each person has experienced and considers important. The Native Americans had lived on the Plains for many years and knew how to hunt buffalo and build appropriate shelter on the grasslands. Also, buffalo thrived on the Plains grasses. The settlers were used to the East Coast, with its forests, rivers, and plentiful resources.

2. **Identify points of view.**
   Identify how both parties feel about the subject at hand. The Native Americans felt that the prairie was an ideal place for living. The homesteaders, on the other hand, felt life there was extremely difficult.

3. **Compare the event being discussed with each person's background.**
   Establishing a frame of reference for a person will help you better understand his or her view. This will help you to assess what a person says or writes about an issue.

492

TRY THE SKILL

Emma grew up on a small farm in western Pennsylvania. She has rarely traveled outside of her area. Jocelyn is from Pittsburgh, Pennsylvania. She lives in an apartment building where several of her classmates also live. Here's what Emma, then Jocelyn had to say about a county fair they attended:

Emma: *"The crowd was wonderful. I met many people from far away! I can't imagine how they'll clean up that mess though—there was litter all over."*

Jocelyn: *"The country was so clean and beautiful. But even this far from the city, there were far too many people. Waiting on lines took forever."*

1. What is the background of Jocelyn? Of Emma?

2. What are the points of view of Jocelyn and Emma?

3. How does knowing each frame of reference help you understand their points of view?

4. How does knowing frame of reference help you understand people's opinions?

EXTEND THE SKILL

Many magazines and television stations interview people about events, especially events such as elections, sports games, or natural disasters. Choose an event you are interested in and research interviews given by the people involved. Then, identify how the frame of reference of all the people who were interviewed affected the viewpoints given.

- What experiences in their backgrounds might account for each frame of reference?

- How did each person's frame of reference differ?

- How can learning frame of reference help you see things from someone else's point of view?

493

What caused the Plains Wars?

The Plains Wars

Lesson Outline
- Native American Homelands
- Wars Break Out
- Native American Losses

VOCABULARY

property rights
reservation
Custer's Last
   Stand

PEOPLE

Crazy Horse
George Custer
Sitting Bull
Chief Joseph
Helen Hunt
   Jackson

READING STRATEGY

Using a main idea chart like the one below, list the reasons Plains Native Americans and the United States battled in the Plains Wars.

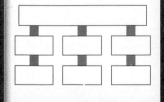

BUILD BACKGROUND

Since the 1860s, the Native Americans of the Great Plains watched their homelands slowly being destroyed. Railroads steamed through, bringing hunters who shot buffalo by the hundreds. By 1890 the number of buffalo had shrunk from several million to less than 1,000. Soon homesteaders started farms and towns. Having lost both their land and the buffalo that were their main source of food, shelter, and clothing, the Native Americans fought back. They hoped to keep their last hunting grounds.

Library of Congress/Denver Public Library

NATIVE AMERICAN HOMELANDS

The Homestead Act offered new settlers **property rights** to the land they settled and a chance to improve their fortunes. Property rights are the rights to own or use something—land, for example. People could buy or sell land. The Native Americans viewed land differently. Most did not believe that anyone could sell land. "One does not sell the earth upon which the people walk," explained **Crazy Horse**, a Lakota chief. That did not mean that Native American groups did not fight over hunting grounds.

Life on the Reservation

Since the early 1800s the United States government had been breaking treaties made with the Native Americans of the Plains. Although the government promised not to take over these lands, it sometimes offered them to homesteaders.

Then the government decided to move the Native Americans to **reservations**. A reservation is a territory set aside for Native Americans. This would make more land available to new settlers. Government leaders also thought they could turn Native Americans into farmers.

However, most Native Americans of the Plains did not want to live on reservations. They were used to riding over hundreds of miles of prairie tracking buffalo. They had learned to survive the unpredictable seasons by moving their camps. Ten Bears, a Comanche (kuh MAN chee) leader, explained why he and many other Native Americans did not want to give up their way of life:

> *I was born upon the prairie where the wind blew free and there was nothing to break the light of the sun. I was born where there were no enclosures [fences or walls] . . . I want to die there and not within walls.*

Why did the government want to move Native Americans to reservations?

When the Native Americans were forced to live on reservations (left), few buffalo remained to roam the Plains.

495

Chief Sitting Bull (left) defeated the cavalry under Colonel George Custer at the Little Bighorn River.

WARS BREAK OUT

During the middle 1800s, Native Americans regularly clashed with settlers and soldiers on the Plains. This period of conflict is often called the Plains Wars. The Native Americans lost most of these battles. Native Americans of the Plains were skilled warriors. Still, they could not compete with the weapons of the new settlers or their growing numbers. Between 1850 and 1870, the white population of the West grew from 200,000 to 1,400,000.

A Broken Treaty

In the Treaty of 1868, the United States had agreed that the territory around the Black Hills belonged to the Lakota. The Black Hills are located in what are today South Dakota and Wyoming.

The peace was shattered in 1874. That year, Colonel George Custer escorted a survey group of miners, journalists, and photographers. The group found gold near present-day Custer, South Dakota. Word of the gold strike spread quickly. Soon, 15,000 miners rushed to Lakota lands to find gold.

The Battle of Little Bighorn

At first, the government offered to buy the Black Hills for $6 million. When the Lakota refused, they were ordered to leave their land and settle on reservations. Led by the Lakota chiefs Sitting Bull and Crazy Horse, many Lakota set up camps on the Little Bighorn River. The Lakota also united with the neighboring Cheyenne and Arapaho to fight. General George Crook and 1,300 troops battled 1,500 Plains Indians at Rosebud Creek on June 17, 1876. They fought to a stalemate.

Colonel Custer and 600 of the Seventh Cavalry soldiers camped nearby. Cavalry are soldiers who fight on horseback. Custer did not know that his men were outnumbered. On June 25, 1876, Custer led his group to attack the Native Americans' camp from the northeast. Major Marcus A. Reno led a second group from the west side of the river. Captain Fred Benteen led the attack from the south.

Reno's men reached the camp, but almost 1,000 Native Americans quickly defeated his small force. When Benteen heard about the numbers of Native Americans, he rushed to tell Custer. However, it was too late. Custer and his men were attacked from all sides. Colonel Custer died, along with more than 200 soldiers.

The Battle of the Little Bighorn is also known as Custer's Last Stand. It was to be the last major Native American victory on the Plains. The United States reacted by sending more soldiers to the Plains. After years of losing many battles, the last Native Americans of the Plains were moved to reservations beside the Missouri River in 1877.

The Nez Percé

At about the same time the Nez Percé (nez PURS) began fighting to keep their lands along the Wallowa River in Oregon.

In 1876, to make room for settlers, the United States demanded that the Nez Percé move to a reservation in the Idaho Territory. Chief Joseph of the Nez Percé refused. Fighting broke out, and the Nez Percé chiefs realized that they would soon be forced out of their homes. They decided to flee to Canada in late June of 1877.

The Nez Percé began their 1,200-mile march to Canada with about 700 men,

women, and children. They were 40 miles from Canada when American soldiers caught up to them. Chief Joseph surrendered to General Nelson Miles on October 5, 1877. In a speech Chief Joseph explained why he would fight no more.

READING CHECK Why did wars break out on the Plains?

Primary Source:

excerpt from **Chief Joseph's speech**
— **as reported by Lieutenant C.E.S. Wood in 1877**

Tell General Howard . . . I am tired of fighting. Our chiefs are killed. . . . The old men are all dead. . . . It is cold and we have no blankets. The little children are freezing to death. My people, some of them, have run away to the hills, and have no blankets, no food; no one knows where they are— perhaps freezing to death. I want to . . . look for my children. . . . Maybe I shall find them among the dead. Hear me, my chiefs. I am tired; my heart is sick and sad. From where the sun now stands I will fight no more . . . .

What concerns did Chief Joseph have for his people?

Native American Reservations, 2000

Reservations managed by the federal government

Map Skill

1. Which states east of the Mississippi River have reservations?

2. Why do you think most reservations are located in the western United States?

NATIVE AMERICAN LOSSES

After their surrender, the Nez Percé were taken to a fort in Kansas. Far from their homeland and without freedom, many died. Many other Native Americans faced similar losses. As you can see from the map on this page, few lands belong to the Native Americans today.

Helen Hunt Jackson

Many Americans felt regret and shame about the way the United States treated the Native Americans. Many religious leaders or writers spoke or wrote of it. Among them was **Helen Hunt Jackson** of Massa-

Helen Hunt Jackson

chusetts. She described these feelings in her book, *A Century of Dishonor*. In 1881 she wrote:

> *My object . . . has been to simply show our causes for national shame in the matter of our treatment of the Indians . . . for the American people, as a people, are not at heart unjust.*

The government later asked Jackson to report on the treatment of California's Native Americans.

READING CHECK

Why do you think many Native Americans were taken far from their homelands?

498

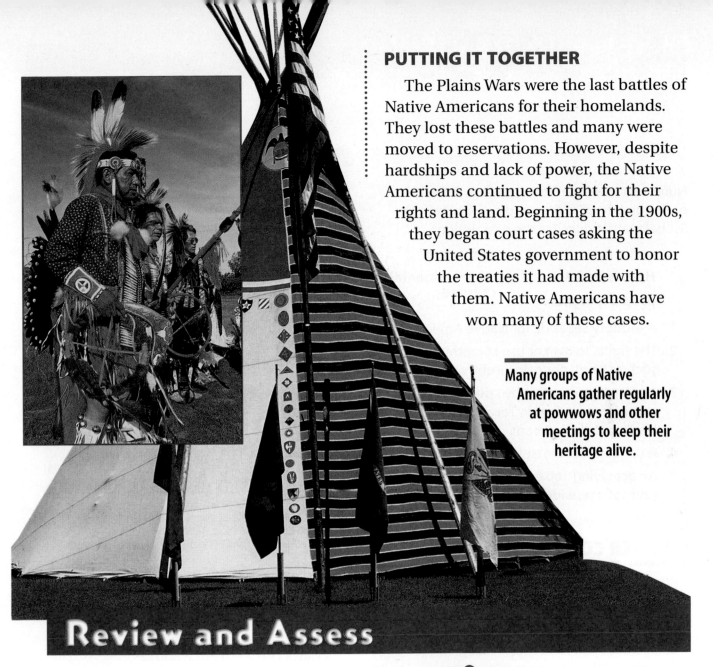

PUTTING IT TOGETHER

The Plains Wars were the last battles of Native Americans for their homelands. They lost these battles and many were moved to reservations. However, despite hardships and lack of power, the Native Americans continued to fight for their rights and land. Beginning in the 1900s, they began court cases asking the United States government to honor the treaties it had made with them. Native Americans have won many of these cases.

Many groups of Native Americans gather regularly at powwows and other meetings to keep their heritage alive.

Review and Assess

1. Write a sentence using the following terms:
   property rights   reservation

2. Who was Chief Joseph?

3. What were some of the causes of the Plains Wars of the middle and late 1800s?

4. Explain why newcomers to the West changed the way of life of the Native Americans on the Plains.

5. **Predict** how things might have been different on the Great Plains if no railroads had been built there.

Study the map on page 498. Then compare it with the physical map of the United States on pages R18–R19. Identify the kinds of land that the states with the greatest number of reservations have.

Write a paragraph from the point of view of a Native American heading for the Little Bighorn River. The paragraph should express why his or her action is so important.

499

VOCABULARY REVIEW

Number a sheet of paper from 1 to 5. Beside each number write the word or term from the list below that matches the description.

cattle drive   reservation

Homestead Act   transcontinental
                                          railroad
property rights

1. A territory set aside for Native Americans

2. The rights to own or use something—such as land—for gain, profit, or sale

3. A long journey taken by cowboys to drive cattle from ranches in Texas north on trails leading to the railroads

4. A railroad that crosses an entire continent

5. An act giving 160 acres of land to men 21 years of age, widows, or heads of family

CHAPTER COMPREHENSION

6. Who worked on the transcontinental railroad? What was the work like?

7. What were the soddies?

8. In what ways were the cowboys in the mid-1800s a diverse group?

9. How did the growth of the railroads change the cowboys' way of life?

10. What hardships did the homesteaders face? How did they meet the challenges?

11. How did the railroads affect Native Americans of the Great Plains?

12. In what ways did Native Americans resist the end of their way of life? What was the result of their efforts?

13. **Write** a news story about the completion of the transcontinental railroad. Include details about the railroad and the celebrations.

SKILL REVIEW

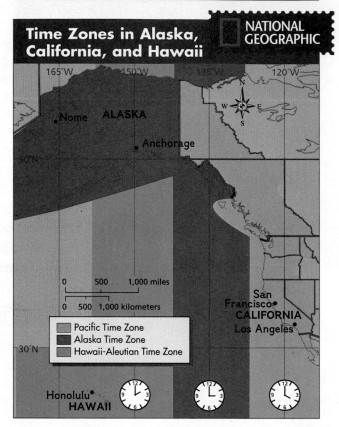

Time Zones in Alaska, California, and Hawaii

NATIONAL GEOGRAPHIC

Pacific Time Zone
Alaska Time Zone
Hawaii-Aleutian Time Zone

14. **Geography Skill** What time zone is Hawaii in? Alaska? California?

15. **Geography Skill** Is the time zone east of you later or earlier than the time in your zone?

16. **Geography Skill** If you are in Los Angeles and need to call someone in Honolulu at 6 P.M., at what time in your zone do you need to make the call?

17. **Reading/Thinking Skill** Many homesteaders found the prairie strange and lonely when they arrived. What was their frame of reference?

18. **Reading/Thinking Skill** Why is it important to know a person's frame of reference when considering his or her point of view?

USING A TIME LINE

1860	1865	1870	1875	1880	1885	1890	1895

1862
Pacific Railroad Act; Homestead Act

1869
Transcontinental railroad is completed

1876
Battle of the Little Bighorn

1877
James Oliver invents steel plow; Chief Joseph surrenders

1879
Kansas Fever Exodus

1890
Number of buffalo falls below 1,000

1895
Number of homesteaders reaches 430,000

19. How are the last two events on the time line related?

20. How many years passed between the completion of the transcontinental railroad and the Kansas Fever Exodus?

***Writing* About Culture** How does your environment affect your way of life? How would changes to the environment affect you? What if a new railroad were built right in the middle of your neighborhood? Write about the ways in which your way of life is dependent on your surroundings and how your life would change if your surroundings changed.

Use your Foldable to review what you have learned about the changing American West. Look on the front of your Foldable and mentally review the causes of the changes and their effects on the American West. Look at your notes under the tabs of your Foldable to check your memory and responses. Record any questions that you have. Then discuss them with classmates or review the chapter to find answers.

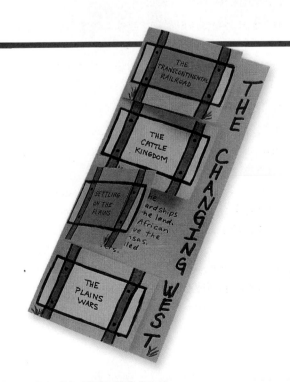

The Nation Is Industrialized

The United States changed rapidly in the late 1800s and early 1900s. New industries developed and new products spread across the nation. Millions of immigrants poured into the growing cities of the Middle West and the East. As the United States became stronger and richer, it began to play a larger role in world events. It fought a war with Spain and dug the Panama Canal, linking the Atlantic and Pacific oceans. Read on to learn about the role the United States began to take in the world.

BIG BUSINESS

Putnam County Historical Society

The Industrial Revolution causes American business to grow rapidly. Some business leaders become very rich, while workers begin to demand better working conditions.

GROWTH OF CITIES

The nation's cities become centers of industry. New factories attract millions of immigrants who are eager to settle in the United States.

HAWAII, ALASKA, AND THE SPANISH-AMERICAN WAR

The United States gains respect from other nations of the world. A war with Spain gives the United States territories abroad.

THEODORE ROOSEVELT

FOR PRESIDENT: THEO. ROOSEVELT.

FOR VICE-PRESIDENT: CHAS. W. FAIRBANKS.

REPUBLICAN   CANDIDATES.

Theodore Roosevelt passes laws that give government more control over some business practices. He also leads a movement to protect the nation's natural wonders.

Foldables

Make this Foldable study guide and use it to record what you learn about "The Nation is Industrialized."

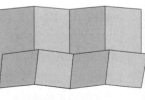

1. Fold about a three-inch tab along the long edge of a sheet of large paper.
2. Fold the paper in half like a hot dog, and then in half again to form four pockets.
3. Place glue on the fold lines and ends of the short pocket tab.
4. Glue to long side to form four pockets. Allow it to dry before using.

Big Business

Lesson Outline
- America—Invention Capital of the World
- Industrial Leaders
- The Rise of Unions

VOCABULARY

monopoly
corporation
sweatshop
labor union
strike

PEOPLE

Andrew Carnegie
Thomas A. Edison
Alexander G. Bell
Lewis Latimer
Elijah McCoy
John D. Rockefeller
Samuel Gompers
Mary Harris Jones

READING STRATEGY

Make a chart like this one to summarize lesson facts. Write the names of people from the lesson in one column and what they did in the other column.

BUILD BACKGROUND

In 1848 a boy from Scotland came to the United States with his family. They settled in Pittsburgh and he went to work in a cotton mill at the age of 13. He was paid $1.25 a week. The boy was ambitious. He taught himself to read and learned from borrowed books. He saved his money and invested in new companies. When Andrew Carnegie retired at the age of 65, he had $400 million. His was just one of the great fortunes made during this era of big business.

Andrew Carnegie used some of his wealth to improve the world.

AMERICA—INVENTION CAPITAL OF THE WORLD

The last half of the 1800s was a period of new inventions in the United States. In fact, the United States was soon called "the invention capital of the world."

The Great Inventors

Two inventors led the way to the modern world. They were Thomas Alva Edison and Alexander Graham Bell.

In his workshop in Menlo Park, New Jersey, Thomas Edison produced more than 1,000 inventions. He began to study ways to change electric current into light in 1878. He experimented with materials for the wire in his light bulb and settled on cotton thread. Later, Lewis Latimer found a way to make this wire, or filament, out of carbon, which lasted longer.

Alexander Graham Bell was a teacher of the deaf. He wanted to help his students by inventing a machine that could transmit the human voice. Latimer drew the plans for Bell.

On March 10, 1876, Bell set up part of his invention in one room and part in another room. Wires connected the two parts. Bell used his invention to call his assistant in the other room, "Mr. Watson—Come here—I want to see you." Watson had received the first telephone message.

READING CHECK Why were Edison's and Bell's inventions important?

Thomas Edison produced more than 1,000 inventions.

U.S. Inventors, 1801–1943

Inventor	Invention
Alexander G. Bell 1847—1922	telephone (1876)
Gail Borden 1801—1874	condensed milk (1856) concentrated fruit juice (1862)
George Washington Carver 1864—1943	uses for peanuts and sweet potatoes (1918)
Thomas Alva Edison 1847—1931	inventions included the phonograph (1877) and the light bulb (1879)
Lewis Latimer 1848—1928	process for making carbon for electric lamps
Elisha Graves Otis 1811—1861	elevator with emergency brake (1852)
Nikolai Tesla 1856—1943	radio and electric currents (1892)
George Westinghouse, Jr. 1846—1914	air brake for locomotive (1868)

Chart Skill

Which industries did the inventions create or affect?

505

Rockefeller and Standard Oil

1 In 1858, at the age of 19, Rockefeller begins his own oil-purchasing business. He realizes that refineries control the oil business. Five years later he buys his first refinery.

2 By 1870, Rockefeller owns many refineries. He forms the Standard Oil Company to control all oil production, from drilling to selling gasoline and kerosene. He sells his products cheaper than his competitors.

4 The first anti-monopoly laws in 1890 and a book criticizing Standard Oil's business practices cause public opinion to turn against Rockefeller. In 1911, a Federal court orders that Standard Oil be broken up into 7 smaller companies.

3 In 1871, Standard Oil demands railroads ship its oil at cheaper prices than those paid by competitors. This forces many out of business. Rockefeller owns 90% of all refineries by 1878.

Chart Skill

1. How long was Standard Oil in business?

2. How did Rockefeller gain control of the oil industry?

INDUSTRIAL LEADERS

Elijah McCoy was another inventor. His "oil cup," invented in 1872, poured oil onto the moving parts of locomotives and other machines while they were running. McCoy's product was so good that people insisted on buying only the "real McCoy."

New companies were started to make use of the new technologies and to make a profit. McCoy founded McCoy Manufacturing Company. Edison's invention led to the General Electric Company, and Bell's to the Bell Telephone Company. These made the United States a leading industrial nation by the late 1800s.

Carnegie and Steel

One of the industries that changed our nation in the 1800s was steel making. People had known how to make steel for cen-turies, but it was a very expensive process. That is why most machines were made of iron even though steel is a stronger metal.

In the 1850s, the Bessemer Process, a cheaper method of making steel, was discovered. Andrew Carnegie, a young businessman at the time, saw how important this new and cheaper method could be. In 1873 he put it to work in a new steel mill near Pittsburgh, Pennsylvania.

Steel production in the United States rose from 68,000 tons in 1870 to 10 million tons in 1900. The Carnegie Steel Company was producing much of the new steel.

By 1900 Carnegie was one of the richest men in the world. Carnegie retired in 1901 and spent the rest of his life helping the world. Carnegie said, "The man who dies rich dies disgraced." He built universities, libraries, museums, and concert halls.

Oil Changes the Nation

In the 1860s Americans began to drill for petroleum (pih TROH lee um), a fossil fuel in the earth. John D. Rockefeller was born to a poor family. He learned that a way had been found to make kerosene (KER uh seen), a type of fuel oil, from petroleum. Rockefeller believed kerosene would replace animal fat as fuel. In 1865 he went into the oil-refining business.

Competition encourages new technology and ways of thinking. Competition in the oil business was so fierce that Rockefeller decided to make his refineries the most productive in the industry. His company, Standard Oil, controlled 90 percent of the oil business in the United States by 1878. Standard Oil had become a monopoly, a company that controls an entire industry. A monopoly may charge higher prices because it has little or no

---

Early oil wells in Pennsylvania

Exploring ECONOMICS

Many Companies, Lower Prices

Before the light bulb, people lit their homes with kerosene lamps or natural gas. However, these forms of lighting were dirty, dangerous, and expensive.

Thomas Edison began to experiment with electric light in 1878. He found a way to create a better filament that would last for 100 hours.

The first light bulbs were expensive because they had to be made by hand. Edison built a factory to produce his light bulbs, and the price of the bulbs continued to drop.

Other companies entered the market. Their competition forced the price of light bulbs down even lower. Soon, light bulbs were affordable for most Americans.

Activity

Make a list of all the ways you use electricity during a typical day.

competition. In free enterprise customers have a choice; they can buy the goods at higher prices or do without them.

A New Kind of Company

Many new businesses became corporations. A corporation is a large business that is owned by people who own shares of the company. Some corporations, such as Standard Oil, became large and powerful.

READING CHECK How did monopolies and corporations affect the way business was done in America?

507

THE RISE OF UNIONS

Some workers continued to work in small businesses. However, many went to work in **sweatshops**, small factories in unsafe buildings with unhealthy working conditions. By the late 1800s, many others worked in large factories or mines run by corporations.

Many of these workers in the new industries and corporations were immigrants. Having come from countries where it is cheaper to live, they often accepted lower wages than native-born Americans. They accepted lower wages in order to survive.

Working Conditions in Factories

Laborers in the factories worked 12–14 hour days, six days a week. There were few holidays and no vacations. Workers were exposed to harmful fumes and dangerous conditions.

In 1911 a fire in the Triangle Shirtwaist factory in New York City took the lives of 146 women and girls. This sweatshop had flimsy fire escapes and its doors were kept locked. When a fire broke out, many of the workers fell to their deaths while trying to escape through the windows.

Children, some ten years old or younger, worked long hours in coal mines and other businesses. They rarely went to school. Many women also had to work. However, their wages were only about half as much as men.

The Birth of Unions

Workers, including women and children, had worked hard for centuries on farms and in small shops. Now, hundreds of people were crowded together in sweatshops and factories. Workers formed organizations called **labor unions** to fight for better conditions. Workers who joined a labor union had a greater chance of gaining better wages and working conditions.

Most business owners fought these unions. People who joined unions were often fired. One union weapon was the **strike**. In a strike, all the workers in a business refuse to work until the owners meet their demands. When unions organized a strike, owners hired strikebreakers, or nonunion workers who replaced the striking workers.

The Movement Grows

A cigar maker named **Samuel Gompers** founded the American Federa-

Children, some as young as nine, worked long hours in factories.

tion of Labor, or AFL, in 1886. A federation is an organization made up of several groups with a common goal.

The AFL helped to get laws passed that shortened work hours, ended child labor, and required employers to pay workers for injuries received on the job. Gompers believed that the strike was a powerful weapon in the struggle for workers' rights.

 How did labor unions improve working conditions in American factories?

PUTTING IT TOGETHER

Corporations and industries changed the way people around the world did business. As corporations and industry grew, more people had jobs and overall their wages were higher. Meanwhile, workers in these new industries wanted better work conditions and organized into unions.

Mary Harris Jones was a famous labor union leader. In 1900 Pennsylvania coal miners went on strike, and "Mother" Jones organized women to drive away strikebreakers. In 1903 she led a children's march to protest child labor. Because of her efforts, the Pennsylvania legislature passed a law in 1905 forbidding children to work until they were 14 years old.

Review and Assess

1. Write one sentence for each vocabulary word.

   **corporation   monopoly   sweatshop
   labor union   strike**

2. How did Rockefeller change the oil industry?

3. How did new inventions and technologies change life in the United States?

4. How does a monopoly change the **economy** of a country?

5. How did the immigrants' **frame of reference** allow them to accept lower wages?

Create a poster praising the improvements in shipping and railroads that helped to make large businesses in the United States profitable.

Choose an inventor or an invention from the 1800s. **Write** a paragraph describing your choice and explaining why it or its inventor is important.

Lesson 2

The Growth of Cities

Find Out!

What were cities like in the United States in the late 1800s?

Lesson Outline
• Industrial Cities
• The New Immigrants
• Helping the Immigrants

VOCABULARY

slum
tenement
Great Chicago
  Fire
settlement house

PEOPLE

Jane Addams

READING STRATEGY

Make a chart like this one to recognize the main idea. In the center circle, write the main idea of the lesson. Write supporting details in the circles around the main idea.

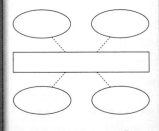

BUILD BACKGROUND

Here at our sea-washed, sunset gates shall stand
A mighty woman with a torch, whose flame
Is the imprisoned lightning, and her name
Mother of Exiles. From her beacon-hand
Glows world-wide welcome.

Emma Lazarus's poem describes the Statue of Liberty in New York Harbor. It was the first sight many immigrants had of their new country.

The Brooklyn Bridge opened in 1883.

You Are Here
1870 – 1924

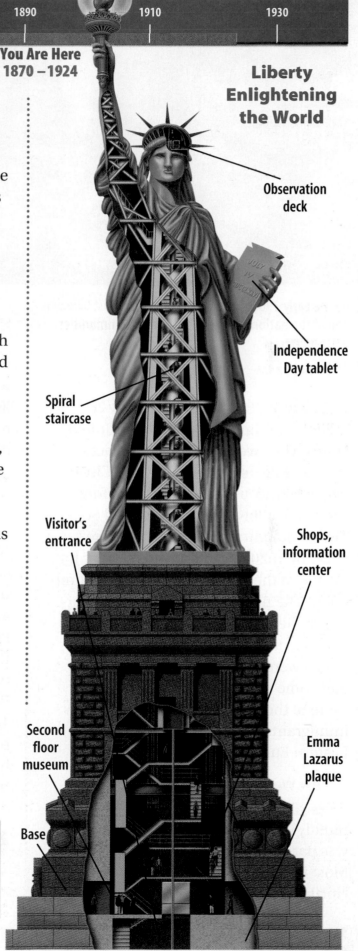

Liberty
Enlightening
the World

Observation
deck

Independence
Day tablet

Spiral
staircase

Visitor's
entrance

Shops,
information
center

Second
floor
museum

Emma
Lazarus
plaque

Base

INDUSTRIAL CITIES

The growth of new industries led to a rapid increase in the size of cities in the United States. Only one in six Americans lived in a city in 1850. By 1900, one in three Americans was living in a city. Some cities began to specialize in certain industries. Chicago was a meat-packing center, Cleveland was an oil-refining center, and Pittsburgh was the capital of steel.

City Life Changes

In the cities dirt streets were paved with asphalt. Water was brought to houses and factories in pipes. Most important for health, sewers were built to carry the waste products away.

The way city people traveled changed, too. In 1887, Richmond, Virginia, became the first American city to have electric streetcars. Boston followed in 1897 with the nation's first subway. New rail systems allowed people to live in the suburbs.

One of America's most famous inventions – the skyscraper – was the product of two new technologies. One of them was cheaper steel. The other was the elevator. It moved people upward quickly and easily. Buildings began to reach higher than five floors.

READING CHECK

How did inventions change cities?

◉ Diagram Skill

1. Where is the observation deck?

2. Where is the staircase located?

By the early 1900s New York City's Lower East Side was one of the nation's largest immigrant communities.

THE NEW IMMIGRANTS

Between 1870 and 1924 nearly 26 million immigrants entered the United States. They were examined at places such as Ellis Island in New York City or Angel Island in San Francisco before they were allowed into the United States. Those thought to be unhealthy were sent back. By 1920 about one out of every four people in the United States was an immigrant. The new immigrants faced different challenges from those immigrants who had arrived earlier. The new immigrants were different from those who had come earlier. First, there were far more of them. Second, most of the new immigrants were from Southern and Eastern Europe.

A New Way of Life

As you have read, American cities grew rapidly after the Civil War. This increase was partly due to arriving immigrants. Most headed directly for cities in the Northeast, where jobs were plentiful. In these cities they formed their own communities where they could live with others who spoke their language and followed their traditions.

The vast number of immigrants created a housing shortage. As a result, immigrants often wound up in slums. A slum is a poor, crowded section of a city with run-down and unsafe housing. Often immigrants were crowded together in tenements. A tenement is a building that is carved up into small apartments.

Some tenements lacked heat and hot water. Bathrooms were often in the hallway and shared by several families. Families of six or seven people lived together in one or two rooms. Under these crowded conditions diseases spread rapidly.

The Great Chicago Fire

Chicago was one of the cities that had grown quickly. It had many immigrants who lived in small wooden buildings that caught fire easily. No one is sure what happened in 1871. One story says that a Mrs. O'Leary's cow knocked over a kerosene lamp. Whatever the cause, the result was a terrible fire that spread quickly through the wooden buildings. By the time it died out 24 hours later, the Great Chicago Fire had killed hundreds of people. Nearly 100,000 people were left homeless. A third of the city of Chicago had been destroyed.

What were some of the challenges immigrants in the cities faced in the late 1800s?

Immigration to the United States 1870–1924

In the 50 years between 1870 and 1920, about 28 million immigrants entered the United States. Use the map and the graph to answer the questions.

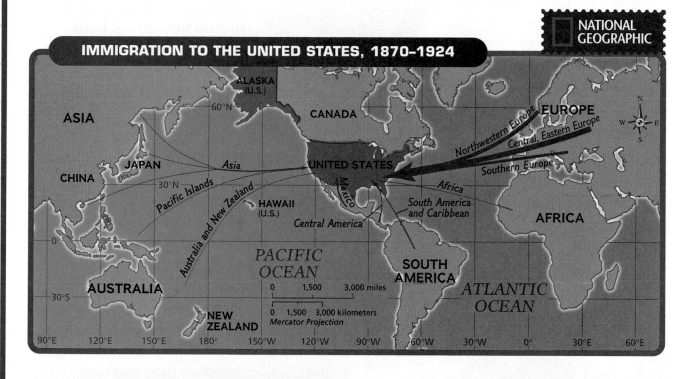

IMMIGRATION TO THE UNITED STATES, 1870–1924

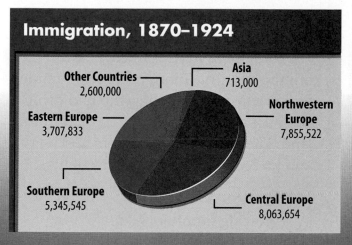

Immigration, 1870–1924

Other Countries
2,600,000

Asia
713,000

Northwestern Europe
7,855,522

Eastern Europe
3,707,833

Southern Europe
5,345,545

Central Europe
8,063,654

QUESTIONS:

1. What are the "other countries" listed on the circle graph?

2. Most Asian immigrants were coming from which two countries?

3. Why do you think most immigrants landed on the East Coast of the United States during these years?

To learn more, visit our Web site:
www.mhschool.com

HELPING THE IMMIGRANTS

Most of the immigrants to the United States before the Civil War had an easier time fitting in. The Irish, for example, already spoke English. Many Germans had money to buy land or start businesses. The new immigrants, on the other hand, were poor and few spoke English. Their languages, religions, and other traditions seemed strange to many Americans.

Like many immigrants in the late 1800s, Michael Markiw came to the United States from eastern Europe. He left Ukraine, then a part of Russia, in 1907.

In June 1907, I came to Pittsburgh, Pennsylvania, USA, to my friend, who

Jane Addams

was a choir leader at St. John Baptist Church, South Side, Pittsburgh. The next day, I got a job at Boyers Pipe Mill in Pitt. At 10 cents an hour. . . . As a boarder, two of us slept in one room at $3 a month and in one year's time, I saved $200.

Community Centers

Jane Addams, a young Chicago woman decided to share her knowledge of art and literature with the poor. In 1889 she and a friend moved into an old house once owned by Charles Hull. At Hull House they held readings, slide shows, and teas for the neighborhood women. They quickly realized that their neighbors had more important needs.

Hull House was the country's first settlement house. A settlement house is a community center that provides child care, education, and other services to the poor. Jane Addams soon organized classes on a variety of subjects at Hull House. It helped immigrants learn English, find jobs, and become American citizens.

Hull House also sponsored lending libraries, summer camps, and playgrounds. Settlement houses quickly caught on. By 1900 there were more than 100 settlement houses in cities throughout the country. Immigrants also founded organizations for people who had come from the same community in their homeland. They helped newcomers find work and understand their new way of life.

Immigration Ends

A growing number of Americans wanted the flood of immigrants stopped. Some Americans believed that immi-

Immigrants who arrived in the United States in the early 1900s (bottom far left) often could only afford to live in **tenements** (near left).

grants were taking jobs away from native-born citizens. After 1882 a law kept Chinese immigrants from entering the United States until 1943. Congress passed a law in 1924 that limited the number of immigrants from Europe. After 300 years, the law ended free immigration from Europe. The number of immigrants dropped to a trickle.

How did Jane Addams help immigrants?

PUTTING IT TOGETHER

After the Civil War, cities in our nation grew rapidly as they became centers of industry. They attracted people from all over the world seeking equality of opportunity.

The immigrants faced many challenges. They lived in crowded buildings and were often forced to take dangerous jobs. Many did not speak English or did not understand the new country they had entered. Settlement houses opened to help immigrants adjust to their new lives. In spite of great difficulties, many immigrants not only improved their lives, but their sons and daughters have become leaders in every walk of life.

Review and Assess

1. Write one sentence for each vocabulary word.

   Great Chicago Fire   **slum**
   settlement house   **tenement**

2. Why did immigrants come to the United States during this period?

3. How did American cities change in the late 1800s?

4. How did settlement houses help immigrants fit into the American **culture**?

5. How might an immigrant's **frame of reference** make it difficult to understand the culture of the United States?

Look at the map and graph on page 513. Make a bar graph to show the same information. You may change the categories. For example, you may wish to put all immigrants from Europe into one group.

Write about the services you would offer if you were setting up a settlement house in a United States city in 1900. Explain how each service will help immigrants adjust to life in the United States.

Using Primary and Secondary Sources

In Lesson 2, you read about Jane Addams and Hull House. If you want to learn more about this subject, you can look at two kinds of sources.

The first is a **primary source**. Primary sources are accounts by people involved in the events being written about. They provide firsthand details that give you an idea of how people of the time thought and felt. Items such as letters, diaries, newspaper stories, speeches, official documents, auto-biographies, photographs, and paintings are primary sources.

The second kind is called a **secondary source**. Secondary sources are written by people who were not there. Secondary sources often provide useful summaries of historical events. This textbook is an example of a secondary source.

LEARN THE SKILL

Read the excerpt on this page. Then follow the steps to learn more about primary and secondary sources.

The dozens of younger children who first came to Hull House were organized into groups which were not quite classes and not quite clubs.... The public schools then contained little hand work of any sort, so that naturally any instruction which we provided for the children took the direction of this ... work. But it required a constant effort that the pressure of poverty itself should not defeat the educational aim. The girls in the sewing classes would count the day lost when they could not carry home a garment, and the insistence that it should be neatly made seemed [strange] to those in dire need of clothing.

1. **Identify whether the source is a personal or eyewitness account.**
    In primary sources, the account expresses the view of only one person. In the passage to the left, Jane Addams tells her opinions.

2. **Identify whether the source helps you understand what the time was like.**
    The passage describes a time when immi-

The children at Hull House in Chicago were taught many skills.

grants needed to gain an education, and to learn a trade at which they could earn a living.

3. **Identify if the source is primary or secondary.**

In this case, the passage is a primary source because it gives a personal eyewitness account and helps us understand what the time it describes was like.

TRY THE SKILL

Study the excerpt below. Use it to answer the following questions.

> ... one part of Chicago that dramatized all its problems more than any other, ... was the five miles of Halsted Street from the Chicago River to the stockyards ... It was to Halsted Street that Jane Addams came, ... to [start] what was to be a great experiment in social service....
>
> They thought of it as a simple matter of neighborliness. "It is natural to feed the hungry and care for the sick," wrote Jane Addams.... That is what they proposed to do and that is what they did.

1. Is the passage a personal account or was it written by someone who was not there?

2. Does the passage include more than one point of view?

3. Is the passage a primary source or a secondary source?

4. How can using primary and secondary sources help you to better understand history?

EXTEND THE SKILL

Identifying primary and secondary sources can also help you understand information you read in magazines and newspapers. Look in magazines and newspapers for articles on a topic you are interested in. Try to find articles by someone who saw what they wrote about. Also look for articles that are secondary sources that summarize something, giving a broader picture. Next, write a paragraph explaining how these primary and secondary sources are different.

● What do the primary sources tell you?

● How are the primary sources different from the secondary sources?

● How do primary and secondary sources help you to understand what you read?

Both Posters: Library of Congress

The United States Gains Territories

How did the United States gain new territories in the late 1800s?

Lesson Outline
- The United States Expands
- War with Spain

VOCABULARY

Rough Riders
Buffalo Soldiers
Spanish-
  American War

PEOPLE

James Cook

Queen
  Liliuokalani

William McKinley

George Dewey

Theodore
  Roosevelt

READING STRATEGY

Make a chart like this one to recognize sequence of events. Head the columns Alaska, Hawaii, Guam. Write events from the lesson in the correct columns.

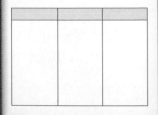

BUILD BACKGROUND

". . . when the explosion came. It was a bursting, rending, and crashing roar of immense volume . . . . The situation could not be mistaken. The Maine *was blown up and sinking."*

Captain Charles Sigsbee described his experience when the battleship USS *Maine* exploded and sank in the harbor of Havana, Cuba, in 1898. The war that followed made the United States into a world power.

The USS *Maine* explodes in Havana harbor.

518

THE UNITED STATES EXPANDS

After the Civil War, the United States gained the territories of **Alaska** and **Hawaii**. For the first time, the United States acquired land beyond its borders. Soon other overseas territories would follow.

"Seward's Ice Box"

Russia had colonized Alaska in the eighteenth century. It was a vast land of more than 500,000 square miles. Its people, especially the Inuit, have lived there for thousands of years. In 1867 Russia offered to sell its colony to the United States. American Secretary of State William Seward said the government would pay $7.2 million for Alaska, or about 2 cents an acre. Some Americans thought the deal was foolish and referred to Alaska as "Seward's ice box" or "Seward's folly."

How wrong they were quickly became apparent! In the 1880s gold was discovered in the area that is now Juneau, Alaska's state capital. Alaska's plentiful resources also include fish, lumber, and oil.

The Kingdom of Hawaii

The United States gained Hawaii in a different way. The Pacific islands of Hawaii have been inhabited since the first people reached them between A.D. 600 and A.D. 1000. In 1778 an English sea captain named **James Cook** landed in Hawaii and opened the way for Christian missionaries, who arrived in Hawaii in the 1820s.

This wooden church was built by Russian colonists in the Pribilof Islands, Alaska.

By the 1890s Americans had migrated there. Some had become wealthy by building large pineapple and sugar cane plantations. **Queen Liliuokalani** (lee lee oo woh kah LAH nee), Hawaii's ruler, wanted to restore power to native-born Hawaiians. In 1893 the American planters revolted and overthrew the queen. Then they asked that Hawaii join the United States. At first, President Grover Cleveland refused, but in 1898, Hawaii became a United States possession.

In 1959 Alaska became the forty-ninth state and Hawaii became the fiftieth.

How did Hawaii and Alaska become United States territories?

519

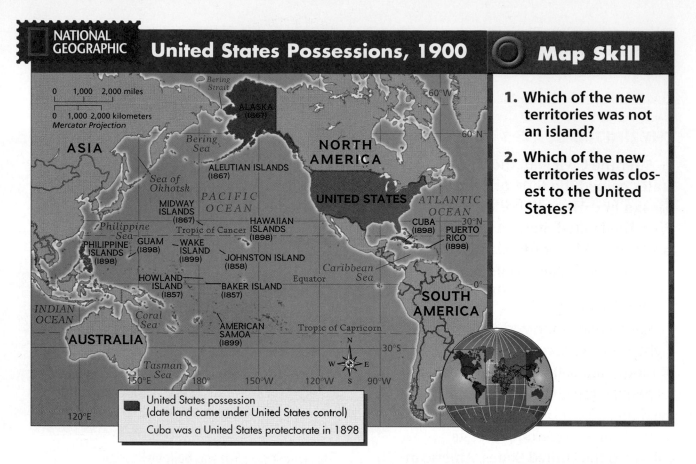

1. Which of the new territories was not an island?

2. Which of the new territories was closest to the United States?

WAR WITH SPAIN

Spain had lost all but two colonies in the Western Hemisphere—the Caribbean islands of **Puerto Rico** and **Cuba**. In 1895 the people of Cuba began a revolt against their Spanish colonial government. Thousands of Cubans were jailed or killed by Spanish troops.

"Remember the *Maine*"

President **William McKinley** sent the battleship USS *Maine* to Havana in January 1898 to protect Americans in Cuba. On February 15, the *Maine* exploded, killing 260 United States sailors.

Two New York City newspapers happened to be competing for readers at the time. Their news stories made the Spanish seem cruel and unjust. One paper, *The Journal*, said the *Maine* was destroyed by Spanish agents. There was no proof that Spain had anything to do

with the explosion, but our country rallied to the cry "Remember the *Maine*." On April 25, 1898, Congress declared war.

The United States decided to attack other Spanish possessions in addition to Cuba and Puerto Rico. Battleships under Admiral **George Dewey** sailed to the **Philippines**, a Spanish colony in the Pacific. Dewey told a ship's captain, "You may fire when you are ready, Gridley." The battle destroyed Spain's Pacific fleet.

The Rough Riders

The Assistant Secretary of the Navy, **Theodore Roosevelt**, quit his job and called on friends and volunteers to go with him to Cuba. His group, called the **Rough Riders**, included cowhands from the West, Harvard students, and Western sheriffs.

On July 1, 1898, the Rough Riders attacked Spanish positions at the Battle of San Juan Hill. They were joined by African

American cavalries known as the "Buffalo Soldiers" who had defended new settlers during the Plains Wars. Roosevelt led a sweeping charge up the hill which instantly made him an American hero.

The Spanish-American War ended in August 1898. The peace treaty made Cuba independent. The United States gained Puerto Rico, Guam, and the Philippines.

Philippine rebels had been battling the Spanish when the United States took control of the Philippines. Under Emilio Aguinaldo (ah gwee NAHL doh), Filipinos fought for independence until 1901. In 1946, the Philippines gained independence. However, both Guam and Puerto Rico have chosen to remain part of the United States, and their people are United States citizens.

Queen Liliuokalani was the last queen of Hawaii. Hawaii's state flower is the hibiscus.

What caused the Spanish-American War?

PUTTING IT TOGETHER

After the Civil War, Americans became interested in gaining new territory abroad, including Alaska and Hawaii. In the Spanish-American War of 1898, the United States gained Puerto Rico, Guam, and the Philippines. As a result of the war, the United States was recognized as a world power, a role that continues to this day.

Review and Assess

1. Write one sentence for each vocabulary word.

   **Buffalo Soldiers   Spanish-American War
   Rough Riders**

2. Which two United States territories later became states?

3. What territories did the United States gain as a result of the war with Spain?

4. How might the possession of overseas territories have changed United States **culture**?

5. How might the Spanish **point of view** about the Spanish-American War be different from that of the United States?

Study the map on page 520. Then make a two-column chart. List the territories gained in 1898 in one column. Then list the territories gained in other years in the second column, with the dates they came under the control of the United States.

Write a letter to the editor of a newspaper supposing you had just heard about the explosion of the USS *Maine*. Express your opinion.

The Rough Rider President

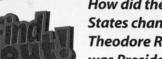

How did the United States change while Theodore Roosevelt was President?

VOCABULARY

reform
trust
assembly line
conservationist
national park

PEOPLE

Upton Sinclair
Ida Tarbell
William Gorgas
Orville Wright
Wilbur Wright
Henry Ford
John Muir

READING STRATEGY

Use a chart like this one to write the main idea of the lesson. Fill in the circles with supporting details from the lesson.

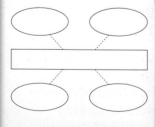

BUILD BACKGROUND

President Theodore Roosevelt often quoted an African proverb, "Speak softly and carry a big stick; you will go far." President Roosevelt's presidency was a time of change in the United States and in the rest of the world. As American power increased, other countries began to look on the United States with a new respect.

ROOSEVELT AND REFORM

Theodore Roosevelt was elected Vice President in 1900. Less than a year later, President William McKinley was assassinated, or murdered, for political reasons. Theodore Roosevelt became President at the age of 42, the youngest person to take the office of President up to that time.

Roosevelt became President when large corporations were making some people very rich. Meanwhile, others were living in poverty. Many Americans began to demand reform, or changes to make things better. Roosevelt and the reformers thought that the way to do this was to pass laws that gave government more control over some business practices. Roosevelt was determined to see that "every man has a square deal."

The Trust Buster

Writers known as "muckrakers" brought attention to dishonest business practices. One of these muckrakers, Upton Sinclair, wrote a novel about the meat-packing industry. *The Jungle* described how unhealthy and dirty meat was sold to unknowing customers. "There was never the least attention paid to what was cut up for sausage," he wrote. Roosevelt read the book and pushed Congress to pass the Pure Food & Drug Act and the Meat Inspection Act in 1906. These laws set up government testing to be sure that medicines and food were safe.

A muckraking reporter named Ida Tarbell published a series of magazine

President Theodore Roosevelt (far left, center) is carved on Mount Rushmore, South Dakota. He and muckrakers like Ida Tarbell (above) helped reform unfair business practices.

articles in 1903. She described the dishonest business practices of the Standard Oil Company. Tarbell wrote about Standard Oil, "… they had never played fair, and that ruined their greatness for me."

Another unfair business practice was the trust. A trust is an organization formed by leading companies in an industry to direct their activities. Roosevelt believed that big business was important to the economy, but he thought that the government should break up "bad" trusts. When Roosevelt left office 25 trusts had been divided into smaller companies. This earned him the nickname of "the trust buster."

How did Roosevelt try to give every American a "square deal?"

523

BIOGRAPHY

Focus On: **Leadership**

Jovita Idar was born in Laredo, Texas, in 1885, one of eight children. In 1903, she joined two of her brothers at their family's newspaper, *La Crónica*. Its purpose was to inform readers about discrimination against Mexican Americans, their poor economic conditions, and the loss of Mexican culture in the United States.

Idar's two main interests were women and education. "Educate a woman," she said, "and you educate a family." In 1911, she became the first president of a league of Mexican women to improve education for poor children.

Idar married in 1917 and moved to San Antonio, where she opened a free kindergarten for poor children. She also translated for Spanish-speaking patients in a county hospital. She died in San Antonio, Texas, in 1946.

Link to Today **Think about a person today who is helping immigrants to the United States. Write a paragraph comparing the person to Jovita Idar.**

The UT Institute of Texan Cultures at San Antonio

THE LIFE OF JOVITA IDAR	1885 Idar is born in Laredo, Texas	1903 Idar receives her teaching certificate	1911 Idar serves as president of the League of Mexican Women	1914 Idar takes over the family newspaper when her father dies	1946 Idar dies in San Antonio

1885   **1900**   **1915**   **1930**   **1945**

LIFE AROUND THE WORLD	1899 Boer War begins in Africa	1910 Chinese Republic is founded	1914 World War I breaks out	1917 The Mexican Revolution ends with a new constitution	1939 World War II starts in Europe

THE PANAMA CANAL

President Roosevelt wanted the country to "dare mighty things." One of them was the digging of a canal.

Need for a New Canal

At the beginning of the Spanish-American War, the battleship *Oregon* had sailed from San Francisco for Cuba. It circled South America and arrived in Cuba a month later. Roosevelt realized that a canal in Central America would cut 7,000 miles off this trip.

The **Isthmus** (IS mus) **of Panama** connects North and South America. An isthmus is a narrow strip of land that connects two larger landmasses. With American help, Panama gained independence from Colombia, South America, in 1903.

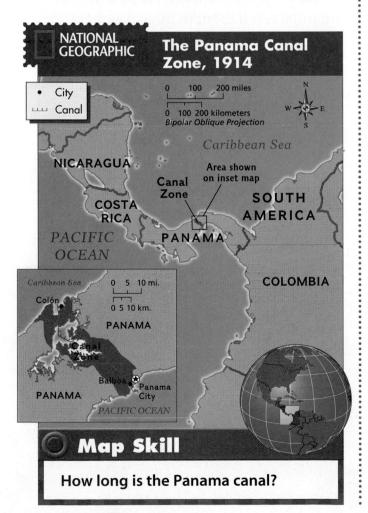

NATIONAL GEOGRAPHIC

The Panama Canal Zone, 1914

- City
- Canal

0   100   200 miles

0 100 200 kilometers
Bipolar Oblique Projection

Caribbean Sea

NICARAGUA

Canal Zone

Area shown on inset map

COSTA RICA

SOUTH AMERICA

PACIFIC OCEAN

PANAMA

COLOMBIA

Caribbean Sea

0 5 10 mi.

Colón

0 5 10 km.

PANAMA

Canal Zone

Balboa

Panama City

PANAMA

PACIFIC OCEAN

Map Skill

How long is the Panama canal?

Roosevelt's visit to Panama is the first time a President traveled out of the United States.

The United States then purchased a ten-mile wide strip of land from Panama. The **Panama Canal** was to be built on this strip, known as the Canal Zone. Roosevelt gave orders to "make the dirt fly in Panama."

A Dangerous Project

Before the project could begin, the danger of diseases in the area such as malaria and yellow fever had to be addressed. Both were carried by mosquitoes.

Roosevelt gave the task of battling the mosquitoes to Colonel **William Gorgas**. Gorgas was a doctor who had ended yellow fever in Cuba after the Spanish-American War. In Panama he spread oil over the pools of water where the insects laid their eggs. By 1906 the area was safe.

For seven years, more than 40,000 men worked on the canal. It succeeded, but even with new technologies, 5,609 lives were lost due to disease and accidents.

READING CHECK

What helped the United States complete the Panama Canal?

NEW INVENTIONS

The late 1800s and early 1900s were a time of many new inventions to improve the way people lived. It was also a time when Americans, led by President Roosevelt, began to protect the natural wonders of our nation.

The First Flight

For centuries, people had dreamed about flying machines. Two American brothers, **Orville** and **Wilbur Wright**, made the dream come true. For years, the Wright brothers had read anything they could find about flight. Then, in the fall of 1900, they went to the beach at **Kitty Hawk**, North Carolina, to experiment with gliders. By 1902 their glider flew a distance of more than 600 feet.

In 1903 they were ready to add an engine to their aircraft. On the morning of December 17, the brothers moved their airplane onto the beach. Orville climbed aboard, and they started the engine. The airplane ran along the sand for about 40 feet—then lifted up into the sky. It flew more than 100 feet before landing. Orville wrote later that the flight with a person on board was a "first in the history of the world."

The Model T

Automobiles were first built in Europe in the late 1800s. By the 1890s, Americans were also making automobiles, but they were handmade and very expensive. **Henry Ford**, an early automobile manufacturer, found a faster and cheaper way in 1913. He used an **assembly line**, a moving belt that carried the automobiles past the workers. At each work area, a worker fitted one part to the car as it moved past. To lower costs, Ford decided to specialize, or build only one model of car. He made all parts for the car interchangeable and manufactured them in huge numbers.

The assembly line method cut the price of Ford's car, the Model T, from $850 in 1908 to $300 in 1925. By 1923 one out of every two cars sold in the United States was a Model T.

The Wright Brothers flew 120 feet in 12 seconds on December 17, 1903. This Model T (right) is from 1922.

Saving the Land

In 1903 President Theodore Roosevelt visited **Yosemite National Park** with **John Muir**. Muir was one of the country's first **conservationists**, or people who work to preserve the wilderness. Muir and the President felt strongly about the need to protect our wilderness.

President Roosevelt created new **national parks**, areas set aside for their natural beauty. He also made the Grand Canyon and other natural wonders into national monuments to protect them. He had about 150 million acres of land set aside as national forests.

Roosevelt also created wildlife refuges, natural environments where animals are protected from hunters. Roosevelt saved a small bear that was being chased for sport. A cartoonist heard the story and drew a cartoon of the bear. "Teddy bears," based on the cartoon, soon became popular.

How did transportation and conservation change in the early 1900s?

PUTTING IT TOGETHER

To many people, Theodore Roosevelt reflected the ideas Americans have about progress. The Panama Canal improved transportation and trade which helped the economic development of our country. Henry Ford's decision to specialize in the Model-T and to mass produce it were important in our nation's industrial development. Moreover, affordable automobiles and the invention of the airplane affected the lives of people around the world.

Campaign buttons for the election of Theodore Roosevelt as President showed him as a reform candidate.

Review and Assess

1. Write one sentence for each vocabulary word below.

   assembly line   **reform**
   conservationist

2. Describe the economic impact of mass production and specialization.

3. What were some of the changes that took place while Roosevelt was President?

4. Explain how American ideas about progress helped the **economic** development and growth of the United States.

5. Write a letter to the editor **analyzing** the importance of building the Panama Canal.

Look at the map on page 525. Plan a tour for a cruise going through the Panama Canal. List the places the ship will stop.

Write a poster to persuade people to take a trip by airplane, to buy a Model T, or to take a trip to the West Coast by ship through the Panama Canal.

Points of View
When Should the Government Break Up Monopolies?

In the early 1900s, not all Americans agreed with President Theodore Roosevelt's decision to take government action against monopolies. Read and think about three different points of view, then answer the questions that follow.

KATHLEEN DUROUSSEAU
Lawyer, San Francisco, California
Excerpt from an interview, 2001

66The federal government should think about many factors in deciding how to treat a monopoly. If a company is ... charging very high prices ... to maintain its power, the government should step in ... the government must be careful not to stifle [destroy] innovation in new technology. It must not ... prevent them from investing in new products and services that will benefit consumers.99

SCOTT PERWIN
Lawyer, Professor of anti-trust law, Miami, Florida
Excerpt from an interview, 2001

66U.S. anti-trust laws state that monopolies are something to avoid and competition is something to encourage .... Sometimes companies become monopolies because ... they are the only company selling a certain product ... generally the government doesn't try to break up a monopoly unless it does something ... such as trying to exclude [shut out] competitors in unfair ways.99

SETH COTLAR
Professor of History, Williamette University
Salem, Oregon
Excerpt from an interview, 2001

66The government should always break up monopolies ... The benefit of the free market is competition. If there is monopoly, there is no competition. Monopolies reward those who already have power and harm those who do not have economic power. By regulating [controlling] monopolies, the government protects the weak from the strong ... The job of a democratic government is to protect the majority of the people who often have fewer resources than a very powerful minority. **99**

Thinking About the Points of View

1. What factors does Kathleen DuRousseau think are important in deciding when the government should act against a monopoly?

2. According to Scott Perwin, when does the law allow the courts to try to break up a monopoly?

3. What does Seth Cotlar think should be done with monopolies? How does Cotlar's viewpoint differ from the viewpoints of Perwin and DuRousseau?

4. What other points of view might people have on this issue?

 Building Citizenship

Justice

The American legal system is based on justice. Justice requires fairness to the company and to the consumer. Discuss how justice might allow some monopolies to continue but end others.

 Write About It!

Suppose you were a student in the early 1900s. Write a letter to your local newspaper. Explain your opinion of monopolies and what you think the government should do about them.

Chapter 17 REVIEW

VOCABULARY REVIEW

Number a sheet of paper from 1 to 5. Beside each number write the word or term from the list below that matches the description.

conservationist	settlement house
reform	strike
Rough Riders	

1. A community center that provides child care, education, and other services to the poor
2. Changes designed to make things better
3. The refusal of workers in a business to work until owners meet their demands
4. A group of volunteers, including Western cowhands and sheriffs, who joined Theodore Roosevelt to fight the Spanish-American War
5. A person who works to preserve the wilderness

CHAPTER COMPREHENSION

6. What was the AFL? What did it it do for workers?
7. Why did some Americans want to keep immigrants from entering the United States?
8. Why was the USS *Maine* important?
9. What were the results of the Spanish-American War?
10. What is a trust buster? A muckraker?
11. Who was Ida Tarbell?
12. Why did Theodore Roosevelt create national parks?
13. Suppose that you are the director of a settlement house. **Write** a daily schedule of events that you have planned for one day.

SKILL REVIEW

You made me glad when you ... assented [agreed] to my request to write an article for the American Federationist on some phase [part] of the meaning of the new uprising of women workers ...

— excerpt from a letter written by Samuel Gompers to Ida Tarbell, February 3, 1910

14. **Study Skill** What is a primary source? What is a secondary source?
15. **Study Skill** What is the difference between a primary and a secondary source?
16. **Study Skill** What kind of source is this textbook?
17. **Study Skill** Is the excerpt above an example of a primary or secondary source? How do you know?
18. **Study Skill** **Write** a paragraph explaining why historians should use both primary and secondary sources.

USING A TIME LINE

1870	1880	1890	1900	1910	1920	1930

1872
Elijah McCoy invents oil cup

1873
Carnegie builds steel mill

1876
First telephone conversation

1878
Edison begins work on electric light bulb

1898
Spanish-American War

1901
Theodore Roosevelt becomes President

1903
Wright Brothers make first airplane flight

1914
Panama Canal is completed; Ford begins his assembly line

1924
Congress limits immigration

19. What new technologies were developed in the years of this time line?

20. How many years passed between the Spanish-American War and the opening of the Panama Canal to shipping?

***Writing* About Culture** Imagine a conversation between two immigrants. One is an Irish immigrant who came to the United States in 1850. The other is an Italian immigrant who arrived in the United States in 1900. Write a conversation between the two immigrants. Their conversation should tell how their experiences were the same and different. They might also talk about what they have contributed to life in the United States.

Foldables

Use your Foldable to review what you have learned about the industrialization of the United States. As you look at the lesson titles on the pockets of your Foldable, mentally review the events that led to the United States becoming one of the world's largest industrialized nations. Look at your note cards in each pocket to check your memory and responses. Record any questions that you have. Then discuss them with classmates or review the chapter to find answers.

VOCABULARY REVIEW

Number a sheet of paper from 1 to 5. Beside each number write the term from the list below that best completes the sentence.

cattle drive   **Rough Riders**

conservationist   **settlement house**

reservation

1. A ____ is a territory set aside for Native Americans by the United States government.

2. Hull House was the country's first ____.

3. During a ____, cowboys journeyed from ranches in Texas to the railroads.

4. Theodore Roosevelt was part of the ____, who fought in Cuba during the Spanish-American War.

5. John Muir was a ____ who worked to protect the country's wilderness.

TECHNOLOGY

For more resources to help you learn more about the people and places you studied in this unit, visit **www.mhschool.com** and follow the links for Grade 5, Unit 7.

SKILL REVIEW

The Spanish were outnumbered . . . on San Juan Hill 16 to 1. But before the day was over, it was clear that the American army had underestimated the military skill of the Spanish soldiers . . . [It] was Theodore Roosevelt's recklessly brave antics that captured the imagination of the American public . . . . Despite these heroics, General Shafter [an American general] was horrified by the casualties [among the American soldiers].

6. **Geography Skill** Why were time zones set up in 1884?

7. **Geography Skill** Look at the map on page 480. If it is 7:00 p.m. in Boston, what time is it in Minneapolis?

8. **Study Skill** Is the excerpt above a primary or secondary source? How can you tell?

9. **Study Skill** Is an encyclopedia a primary source or a secondary source? Which kind of source is a photograph?

10. **Reading/Thinking Skill** Why is frame of reference an important skill to learn when studying history?

Read the passage and the questions that follow. Write the best answers to the questions on a piece of paper.

1   The roof . . . was of Kansas dirt, and when the rains came proved unsatisfactory indeed. We moved into this house about the first of August, 1870, and I felt as happy as a Queen. But a rainy time set in and continued. . . . It was two weeks I was left alone with the children. And the roof leaked!

2   I was born upon the prairie where the wind blew free and there was nothing to break the light of the sun. I was born where there were no enclosures. . . . I want to die there and not within walls.

1 Compared to the speaker in Passage 1, the speaker in Passage 2 is more likely to—

  A enjoy having lots of neighbors
  B complain about the weather
  C talk about the beauty of the prairie
  D decide to move to a town

2 What is the main issue on which the two speakers disagree?

  A the benefits of prairie life
  B the way people spend their time
  C the importance of friends and family
  D the need to care for the earth

WRITING ACTIVITIES

Writing to Persuade Suppose you have been hired to persuade African Americans in the South to move to the Great Plains in the 1870s. *Write* a brochure that will persuade them to start a new life in the West.

Writing to Inform Read the song "Kiansis" on pages 468 and 469. Write an explanation of how the song reflects the times in which it was created.

Writing to Express *Write* a verse of a poem or song that describes what it was like to work on the railroad.

LITERATURE

Through My Eyes

Selections by Ruby Bridges
Illustrated by Anthony Carabucci

Ruby Bridges was six years old in November 1960 when she walked through an angry crowd into an all-white school. Ruby's words tell an amazing story of bravery.

When we finally got into the building, my new teacher was there to meet us. Her name was Mrs. Henry. She was young and white. I had not spent time with a white person before, so I was uneasy at first. Mrs. Henry led us upstairs to the second floor. As we went up, we hardly saw anyone else in the building. The white students were not coming to class. The halls were so quiet, I could hear the noise the marshals' shoes made on the shiny hardwood floors.

Mrs. Henry took us into a classroom and said to have a seat. When I looked around, the room was empty. There were rows of desks, but no children. I thought we were too early, but Mrs. Henry said we were right on time. My mother sat down at the back of the room. I took a seat up front, and Mrs. Henry began to teach.

THROUGH MY EYES

RUBY BRIDGES

I spent the whole first day with Mrs. Henry in the classroom. I wasn't allowed to have lunch in the cafeteria or go outside for recess, so we just stayed in our room. The marshals sat outside. If I had to go to the bathroom, the marshals walked me down the hall.

My mother sat in the classroom that day, but not the next. When the marshals came to the house on Wednesday morning, my mother said, "Ruby, I can't go to school with you today, but don't be afraid. The marshals will take care of you. Be good now, and don't cry."

I started to cry anyway, but before I knew it, I was off to school by myself.

Write About It!

Why do you think Ruby's right to an equal education was important not only to her, but to children of all racial backgrounds?

Unit 8

The Modern Era

TAKE A LOOK

Our nation faced which challenges in the 1900s and early 2000s?

The Space Shuttle reenters Earth's atmosphere at 17,000 miles per hour, becoming so hot it would melt without its covering of heat-proof tiles.

For more information about the Modern Era, visit our Web site at **www.mhschool.com**

THE Big IDEAS ABOUT...

Good Times and Hard Times

The last 100 years were a time of great change in the United States. The United States entered World War I and came out as one of the world's leading nations. A stock market crash in 1929 and World War II brought hard times. However, by the end of the twentieth century the United States becomes the leading nation in the world. Read on to find out more about these events.

The United States enters World War I in 1917, and the war ends in 1918.

The 1920s bring prosperity. Most Americans enjoy better times. New technology changes the way Americans live.

THE GREAT DEPRESSION

The good times stop when the stock market crashes in 1929. Franklin Roosevelt becomes President and tries to get Americans back to work.

WORLD WAR II

Another world war begins in 1939. The United States joins the war after Japan attacks our naval base at Pearl Harbor.

THE COLD WAR

The United States and the Soviet Union face an uneasy peace in 1945. The two great powers begin a period of tension called the Cold War.

Foldables

Make this Foldable study guide and use it to record what you learn about "Good Times and Hard Times."

1. Place three sheets of paper one inch apart, forming one-inch tabs along the short side of the paper.

2. Roll the bottoms of the three sheets up to make five tabs the same size. Fold and staple.

3. Write the title of the chapter on the large tab, and the lesson titles on the five equal-sized tabs.

World War I

What effect did World War I have on the United States?

Find out!

Lesson Outline
• The War Begins
• American Forces in Europe
• Fighting Discrimination

VOCABULARY

World War I
Allied Powers
Central Powers
Treaty of Versailles
League of Nations
Great Migration
discrimination
NAACP

PEOPLE

Woodrow Wilson
Booker T. Washington
W.E.B. Du Bois
Ida Wells-Barnett

READING STRATEGY

Use the chart to compare and contrast the positive and negative effects of World War I on the nation.

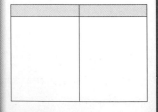

BUILD BACKGROUND

In August 1914, a bloody struggle among many of the European nations broke out. Americans were eager to stay out of a conflict far away, but would eventually be drawn in. The war would last more than four years and would cost millions of lives. The whole world seemed involved in a war like no one had seen before, earning it the title World War I.

THE WAR BEGINS

World War I began in 1914 after a Serbian student assassinated Archduke Francis Ferdinand of Austria. The archduke was the heir to the throne of Austria-Hungary. Before this time, unrest in Europe had led many of its nations to form alliances. An alliance is a treaty of friendship between nations who promise to defend each other if any are attacked. Austria-Hungary and its ally, Germany, declared war on Serbia. Serbia was helped by its ally, Russia, who had alliances with France and Britain.

Soon Europe was divided into two groups. On one side were the Allied Powers, which included Britain, France, Russia, Belgium, and later Italy. On the other side were the Central Powers, led by Germany, Austria-Hungary, and Turkey.

The War at Sea

Each country wanted control of the seas during World War I so that it could prevent war supplies from being shipped to its enemies. In the Atlantic Ocean, the Germans were feared for their new and deadly submarines called U-boats. The U-boat could sneak up on enemy ships, rise to the surface, and sink them without any warning.

On May 1, 1915, a British passenger ship called the *Lusitania* left New York. Its cargo included weapons for the British.

The sinking of the *Lusitania* angered many Americans. After several attacks on American ships, the United States sent soldiers to Europe to help fight World War I (far left).

A German U-boat sank the *Lusitania* near Ireland. Among the 1,198 people drowned were 128 United States citizens. Americans were angry.

War Is Declared

From January to March 1917, the Germans sank eight American ships. In response, President Woodrow Wilson asked Congress on April 2, 1917 to declare war on the Central Powers. Four days later, Congress passed the War Resolution. The United States was at war.

READING CHECK How did the sinking of the *Lusitania* change American attitudes about the war?

AMERICAN FORCES IN EUROPE

On April 6, 1917, the United States declared war on Germany. Soon, thousands of American troops were rushed to Europe.

The Front Line

In just a year, almost 250,000 American soldiers had crossed the Atlantic. Upon arrival, they discovered that this was a new kind of war. Advances in technology had made combat more destructive. Bullets from one machine gun could hit dozens of soldiers at a time. Tanks rumbled across the battlefield. Airplanes attacked from above. The Germans used poison gas.

Back Home

On the "home front," Americans made many contributions to the war effort. The government requested "Wheatless Mondays" and "Meatless Tuesdays" so more would be available for troops. The army also needed supplies such as weapons, food, clothing, and fuel. Factories worked overtime. Ten million Americans worked in the war industries. With so many men fighting in the war, jobs that had been closed to women and African Americans became available to them. Over 100,000

Victory is a Question of Stamina
Send – the Wheat
Meat · Fats · Sugar
the fuel for Fighters
UNITED STATES FOOD ADMINISTRATION

women went to work for the first time—in weapons factories.

Peace

The constant arrival of American troops, money, and supplies weakened the Central Powers. On November 11, 1918, they surrendered. Today, we celebrate this day as Veterans Day.

The "war to end all wars" was over, but at least ten million soldiers had been killed, including 100,000 American soldiers.

In 1919, representatives of the Allied Powers met at **Versailles** (vair SI), near Paris, France. They created a peace agreement that placed full responsibility for the war on Germany. The **Treaty of Versailles** took away Germany's colonies and redrew its borders. It also demanded that Germany pay heavy fines to the Allied Powers.

The destruction during World War I inspired President Wilson to suggest the **League of Nations**, the first organization designed to prevent future wars.

The League began meeting in 1920. Worried that membership in the League would involve the nation in future wars, Congress vetoed plans to join the League.

READING CHECK

How did citizens help the war effort?

Posters (above) urged Americans to support the troops while women worked in factories so men could join the army.

World War I

More than ten million soldiers were killed during World War I. Study the graphics. Then answer the questions.

QUESTIONS:

1 Who had fewer soldiers: the Allied or Central Powers?

2 Which countries were part of the Allied Powers?

3 Which Allied country shared the largest border with Germany?

Total Number of Armed Forces in World War I

Country	Soldiers
Russia	12,000,000
Germany	11,000,000
Great Britian	8,904,467
France	8,410,000
Austria-Hungary	7,800,000
Italy	5,615,000
United States	4,355,000

= 1 Million
■ Central Powers
■ Allies

Number of Soldiers (in millions)

To learn more, visit our Web site:
www.mhschool.com

NATIONAL GEOGRAPHIC

ALLIED POWERS IN EUROPE

☐ Allied countries

SWEDEN
North Sea
DENMARK
UNITED KINGDOM
NETHERLANDS
RUSSIA
GERMANY
BELGIUM
ATLANTIC OCEAN
FRANCE
SWITZERLAND
AUSTRIA-HUNGARY
ROMANIA
Black Sea
ITALY
PORTUGAL
SPAIN
SERBIA
BULGARIA
MONTENEGRO
ALBANIA
GREECE
OTTOMAN EMPIRE (TURKEY)
Mediterranean Sea

0   250   500 miles
0   250   500 kilometers

543

FIGHTING DISCRIMINATION

The war effort created thousands of jobs that had not been available to women and African Americans. Limited resources made jobs in the South scarce and low-paying. Many African Americans struggled to make a living. When news of war jobs in the Northeast and Middle West reached them, African Americans left the South. Historians call this period the Great Migration.

In Chicago, the African American population nearly tripled in the years 1910 to 1920. About 500,000 African Americans went north during the war years seeking opportunity and equality.

A Continuing Struggle

Most African Americans moved north to escape discrimination and poverty. Discrimination is an unfair difference in the treatment of people. People in both the North and the South had been taking steps to fight discrimination and to educate African Americans in the skills they would need to get better jobs.

In 1881 a former slave named Booker T. Washington had founded the Tuskegee Institute in Alabama. Tuskegee was a school specifically for African Americans. They were taught skills such as printing, bricklaying, and teaching.

By 1909, the National Association for the Advancement of Colored People, or NAACP, was founded by both blacks and whites to fight discrimination. By 1920 the NAACP had 90,000 members. W.E.B. Du Bois (doo BOYS), one of its founders, wrote that an African American wished to keep from "having the doors of opportunity closed roughly in his face." Du Bois was one of the first leaders to urge African Americans to join together to fight prejudice.

Ida Wells-Barnett was another founder of the NAACP. Wells-Barnett was a former slave who became a reporter and part owner of *Free Speech*, a newspaper in Memphis, Tennessee. Author of many articles about violence toward

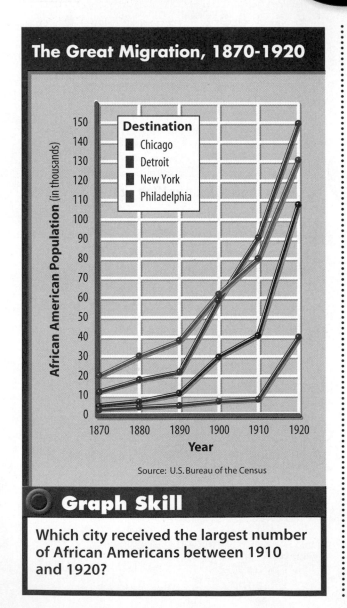

The Great Migration, 1870-1920

Destination
- ■ Chicago
- ■ Detroit
- ■ New York
- ■ Philadelphia

African American Population (in thousands)

150 140 130 120 110 100 90 80 70 60 50 40 30 20 10 0

1870 1880 1890 1900 1910 1920

Year

Source: U.S. Bureau of the Census

Graph Skill

Which city received the largest number of African Americans between 1910 and 1920?

NAACP leaders W.E.B. Du Bois (far left) and Charles Evers, shown here at a meeting in Mississippi in 1963, worked to end discrimination.

PUTTING IT TOGETHER

World War I strengthened the role of the United States in world events. It also produced hardship, and many young men lost their lives. When the war ended, Americans looked forward to more peaceful times.

African Americans, she hoped her work would inspire others to work to end the violence. "Can you remain silent," she wrote ". . . when [African Americans are being killed] in our own community and country?"

The Great Migration provided better lives for many African Americans. It also provided workers to factories in the North and this helped expand our economy. This economic expansion allowed the United States to grow. It also helped set the stage for the economic boom of the 1920s.

Why did African Americans begin moving to the North?

Review and Assess

1. Write one sentence for each vocabulary term.

   **discrimination   Treaty of Versailles
   NAACP**

2. Why did the United States enter World War I?

3. How did World War I affect the United States?

4. What technological advances made World War I more destructive than earlier wars?

5. Name one **cause** and one **effect** of the Great Migration. Give reasons for your choice.

Make a chart showing the effects of the Great Migration. Include the limited resources of the South and the economic development and growth of the United States in the chart.

Write a newspaper editorial in support of or against membership in the League of Nations.

545

Good Times

Why are the 1920s known as the "Roaring Twenties"?

Lesson Outline
- The Roaring Twenties
- Technology Boom
- Suffrage and Women at Work
- Free Enterprise at Work

VOCABULARY

Roaring Twenties
jazz
suffrage
media
Nineteenth
  Amendment
League of
  Women Voters

PEOPLE

Duke Ellington
F. Scott Fitzgerald
Dorothy Parker
Langston Hughes
Charles
  Lindbergh
Amelia Earhart
Susan B. Anthony

READING STRATEGY

Use a cause and effect chart. Write the effects of the new technology of the 1920s.

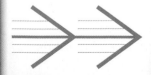

BUILD BACKGROUND

After World War I, the United States enjoyed a time of prosperity for about ten years. A growing number of people made fortunes in the stock market. Some people were still struggling, but they earned more and they had more free time. Labor unions fought for a shorter workday. In 1923 United States Steel Corporation was one of the first companies to change to an eight-hour workday. New technology, such as the washing machine and vacuum cleaner, made chores easier and quicker to do. The excitement of the decade led to the nickname the "Roaring Twenties."

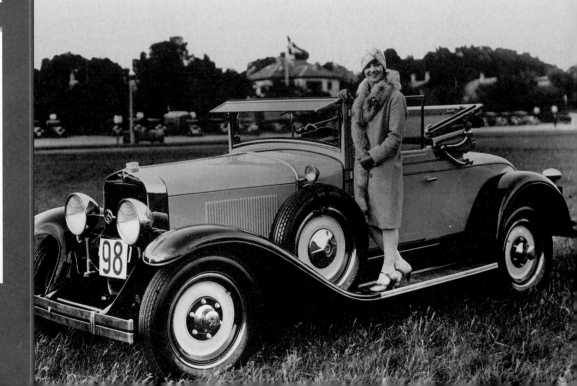

THE ROARING TWENTIES

With the horrors of World War I behind them, Americans were eager to enjoy themselves. Especially popular was the music that African Americans who had migrated to the North and Midwest introduced there. Across the country, people couldn't get enough of **jazz**. Jazz was one of the first forms of music in the United States to make the rhythms of the bass instruments as important as the melody. **Duke Ellington** was one of the more famous jazz composers of the decade. His music, considered classic jazz today, gave rise to another nickname for the 1920s, "the Jazz Age."

Years of Creativity

One place where people went to hear jazz was in Harlem, a New York City neighborhood where many African Americans live. A cultural movement called the Harlem Renaissance began there in the 1920s. A poet who lived in Harlem, **Langston Hughes**, described his feelings about the 1920s in "Harlem Night Song."

> *Night-sky is blue.*
> *Stars are great drops*
> *Of golden dew.*
> *In the cabaret [nightclub]*
> *The jazz-band's playing . . .*

Other writers in the United States also tried to capture the magic of the Roaring Twenties. One of them, **F. Scott Fitzgerald**, author of *The Great Gatsby*, once described the 1920s as "the greatest, gaudiest spree

Flappers (left) danced to the jazz music of musicians like Duke Ellington (above), at the piano.

[lively party] in history." Other well-known writers of the period are Ernest Hemingway, William Faulkner, and **Dorothy Parker**. Parker wrote poetry, short stories, and reviews of books and plays. She wrote about the flapper, a woman who expressed her freedom by wearing short skirts and hair, and dancing.

Prohibition

In 1919 the Eighteenth Amendment to the Constitution made it illegal to make or sell alcoholic beverages. The Prohibition amendment was unpopular and was repealed, or voted out of law, in 1933.

READING CHECK **Why were the 1920s called the "Roaring Twenties"?**

547

TECHNOLOGY BOOM

Advances in technology helped shape the Roaring Twenties. Electricity put entertainment at people's fingertips, and allowed them to learn about what was happening in other parts of the country. The automobile brought people closer together. Indeed, the automobile changed life in the United States and around the world.

During the 1920s, many people owned automobiles for the first time. By the end of the decade, there was one car on the road for every five people. The first shopping center with a parking lot opened in Kansas City, Missouri, in 1924. In fact, the word motel—meaning a hotel for motorists—first appeared in 1925.

Entertainment and Heroes

Electricity brought entertainment to anyone who could afford a radio. The first radio station started broadcasting in 1920. By 1940, people were listening to the radio for about four and a half hours every day. They listened to music, news, sporting events, comedy shows, and the first "soap operas."

Another invention that changed American life was Thomas Edison's "moving pictures." Hollywood, California, became the center of production for these "silent films". In 1927, films took a new step when the Al Jolson movie *The Jazz Singer* appeared in theatres. This "talking picture" ended silent film production almost overnight. Within five years, more than 80 million Americans were going to movie theaters every week.

The new technology created many new heroes. Americans were eager to read about film stars such as Charlie Chaplin and Mary Pickford. Newspapers and magazines made people famous.

The greatest of all the heroes of the 1920s was Charles Lindbergh, an airplane pilot who flew across the Atlantic alone in 1927. He flew from New York to Paris, France, in about 33 1/2 hours. In 1928 Amelia Earhart and a team of two others flew across the Atlantic on the twenty-fifth anniversary of the Wright Brothers' first flight ever in 1903. In 1937, Earhart disappeared over the Pacific Ocean attempting to fly around the world.

HISTORY MYSTERY

What Happened to Amelia Earhart?

Amelia Earhart held many flying records. In 1932 she became the first person to fly alone across the Atlantic Ocean. In 1935 she became the first woman to fly across the Pacific Ocean.

In 1937 Earhart began an attempt to fly around the world. She had completed two-thirds of the flight when her plane disappeared near Howland Island in the South Pacific. She was never seen again. Some people say that Earhart was a spy who was captured by the Japanese. Others believe that she simply crashed into the Pacific Ocean. For now, Earhart's disappearance remains a mystery.

What do you think happened to Amelia Earhart?

Suffragists in 1915 hold a banner urging a New York senator to support the Nineteenth Amendment.

SUFFRAGE AND WOMEN AT WORK

After more than 50 years of struggle and hard work, women finally won the right to vote in national elections in 1920.

Suffrage for Women

The fight for suffrage, or the right to vote, began with the Seneca Falls Convention in 1848. As Susan B. Anthony argued, suffrage was "the pivotal right, the one that underlies all other rights." Suffragist leaders gained strength in 1870 when the Fifteenth Amendment granted African American men the right to vote. In 1872, Anthony and a group of women marched into a polling place in Rochester, New York, and cast their votes in a presidential election. The women were arrested and fined. Finally, six years later, in 1878, a women's suffrage amendment was introduced in Congress.

Fighting for the Vote

Congress did not pass the women's suffrage amendment in 1878. Still, the amendment was reintroduced in every session of Congress for the next 40 years.

Many suffragist leaders, such as Carrie Chapman Catt, traveled across the country giving speeches and organizing workers. She led a "suffrage army" of one million volunteers. She used the media to spread her arguments. The media is any method of communication that reaches large numbers of people. Radio and newspapers are forms of media.

In 1920 these efforts paid off. Congress passed the Nineteenth Amendment, which guaranteed every adult woman the right to vote. On August 26, 1920, the states approved this amendment.

Women at Work

In the 1920s and 1930s, women went to work in greater numbers than ever before. Women worked in factories, businesses, and in other jobs that only men had once done. In 1930, the U.S. Census reported that women worked as everything from lawyers to house painters.

 READING CHECK How did women's lives change in the 1920s?

BIOGRAPHY

Focus On: Courage

State Historical Society of Wisconsin

Carrie Chapman Catt was born Carrie Lane in Ripon, Wisconsin, in 1859. After college, she became a teacher in Mason City, Iowa, and then the superintendent of schools in 1883. Around that time, Catt became involved in fighting for the right to vote.

Over time, Catt supervised thousands of volunteers and gave hundreds of speeches in favor of women's right to vote. She was elected president of the National American Woman Suffrage Association from 1900 to 1904, and again from 1915 to 1920.

Catt worked against great odds but held firm to her beliefs. "There will never be a true democracy until every responsible and law-abiding adult in it, has his or her own voice in government." When American women won the right to vote in 1920, it was largely because of Catt's work.

That year, Catt founded the **League of Women Voters**, which still exists today. She also founded the National Committee on the Cause and Cure of War in 1925. She died in 1947.

Link to Today Think about a leader of the 1900s who works for people's rights. Write a paragraph comparing this person to Carrie Chapman Catt.

THE LIFE OF CARRIE CHAPMAN CATT	1859 Carrie Lane is born in Ripon, Wisconsin	1883 Catt becomes superintendent of schools in Mason City, Iowa	1900 Catt is president of National American Woman Suffrage Association	1920 Catt founds League of Women Voters
	1860	1875	1890	1905	1920
LIFE AROUND THE WORLD		1876 Alexander Graham Bell invents the telephone		1914 World War I begins; the Panama Canal opens	1918 World War I ends

FREE ENTERPRISE AT WORK

The freedom and excitement of the 1920s was also felt by the businesses of the time. New businesses and industries were created and more businesses became specialized.

Mostly, the government left business alone. More businesses issued stock to help themselves grow, and more people than before chose to invest in stocks. One result was that these producers could take risks to make products they thought would sell. Those who made their products efficiently made more profit. Consumers felt free to spend their money as they wished. In this way millions of producers and consumers made economic decisions that determined how scarce resources would be used.

How did the free enterprise system help producers and consumers in the 1920s?

PUTTING IT TOGETHER

The Roaring Twenties was an exciting time for many in the United States. However, the decade did not bring good times for everyone. Veterans returning from World War I believed that jobs should go to people born in the United States, making it harder for immigrants to find jobs. African Americans also faced difficult times. They struggled even more as hate groups such as the Ku Klux Klan gained new strength.

The Roaring Twenties would not last forever. Hard times were ahead for practically all Americans.

Women's fashions in the Roaring Twenties included brightly colored high-heel shoes.

Kent State University Museum

Review and Assess

1. Write one sentence for each vocabulary term.

   jazz   media   suffrage

2. What was the Harlem Renaissance?

3. How did the Roaring Twenties earn its nickname?

4. How did the automobile change Americans' shopping and traveling habits?

5. **Analyze** how some businesses made more profit during the 1920s than before.

Once the automobile became common, people from cities could take day trips into the country. Use a map of a city in your area. Make a road map of towns and sights nearby that you could visit on a day trip.

Write a newspaper article in favor of the Nineteenth Amendment. Clearly state the reasons you support this new amendment to the United States Constitution.

The Great Depression

Find Out!

How did the Great Depression affect the United States?

Lesson Outline
- The Good Times End
- A New President
- New Programs at Work

VOCABULARY

Stock Exchange
Great Depression
Dust Bowl
New Deal
unemployment
hydroelectricity

PEOPLE

Herbert Hoover
Franklin Delano
  Roosevelt
Eleanor
  Roosevelt

READING STRATEGY

Make a chart like this one to show cause and effect. In one column, write an event. In the other column, write an effect that the event caused.

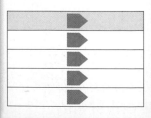

BUILD BACKGROUND

"So, first of all, let me assert [tell] my firm belief that the only thing we have to fear is fear itself— nameless, unreasoning, unjustified terror which paralyzes needed efforts . . . ."

President Franklin Roosevelt tried to calm Americans' fears about the economy in 1933. Millions of people were without jobs or hope. His words helped to restore confidence in the American system.

THE GOOD TIMES END

In the 1920s many people bought stocks. However, prosperity vanished overnight with the crash of the New York Stock Exchange in 1929. A stock exchange is a special market where shares of stock are bought and sold. Stock prices began to drop in September of 1929. Many investors, afraid of losing money, tried to sell their stocks. This caused stock prices to fall faster. Investors panicked. Everyone wanted to sell. Soon many stocks were worthless.

Also at this time, the government was supporting businesses and farms in producing a lot of goods and crops. By the late 1920s the producers made too much to sell. Many businesses and farms failed. Thousands of people lost their jobs and savings. Banks failed. This led to a time of widespread economic hardships in the 1930s called the Great Depression.

The Dust Bowl

Years of drought in the 1930s made the Great Depression even worse for farmers. Many farmers in the Great Plains watched their crops die. Up to 150,000 square miles of the Great Plains were turned into dust. This area was called the "Dust Bowl." High winds that blew across the region kicked up the dry dirt. The dust storms blotted out the sun and buried farmhouses up to the window-

sills. A woman named Mary Owsley recalled, "you had to clean house from attic to ground. Everything was covered in sand."

Thousands of farmers lost their farms. More than half the population of the Dust Bowl left the region. Many went to California where they hoped to find work, but jobs were scarce in California, too.

Why did the Great Depression cause hard times?

The Dust Bowl, 1935–1940

NATIONAL GEOGRAPHIC

ID   WYOMING   SD

■ Dust Bowl

NE

UTAH   COLORADO

KANSAS   MO

AZ   NEW MEXICO

OKLAHOMA   AR

TEXAS   LA

MEXICO

0   200   400 miles
0   200   400 kilometers
Albers Conic Equal-Area Projection

N W–E S

Gulf of Mexico

Map Skill

Which six states were part of the Dust Bowl?

Worried investors (left) gather in front of the New York Stock Exchange in 1929.

A NEW PRESIDENT

By 1932 more than 5,000 banks had failed, and 32,000 companies and stores had closed. More than 12 million Americans—one of every four adults—could not find work. Many families lost their homes, and some communities had to close schools because no one could pay taxes.

President Herbert Hoover, like many Americans, believed that the economy would soon recover. However, the hard times got harder. Many Americans wanted the government to do more. Therefore, they voted for a leader who promised to end the economic crisis.

Franklin Delano Roosevelt

Franklin Delano Roosevelt was a cousin of Theodore Roosevelt. He was born in 1882 and had entered politics as a young man. In 1921 a disease called polio took away the use of his legs. Over the next few years, he worked hard to recover. His wife, Eleanor Roosevelt, encouraged him to return to politics. Widely known by his initials, FDR was elected governor of New York in 1928.

One year after the Depression hit, Roosevelt spoke of new solutions. "The country," he said, "demands bold, persistent [steady] experimentation." Statements like this made people think that FDR might have the solution to the nation's problems. In 1932 he was elected President.

The new President faced a difficult task. The country's confidence had disappeared along with the good times. In his first inaugural address FDR promised to fight the Depression with all the powers of the federal government.

Primary Source:

excerpt from

the First Inaugural Address
—by President Franklin Delano Roosevelt, March 4, 1933

*Our greatest primary task is to put people to work. This is no unsolvable problem if we face it wisely and courageously. It can be accomplished in part by direct **recruiting** by the Government itself, treating the task as we would treat the emergency of a war . . . the task can be helped by definite efforts to raise the values of agricultural products . . . it can be helped by preventing . . . the loss . . . of small homes and farms . . . It can be helped by the unifying of relief activities . . . It can be helped by national planning . . . There are many ways in which it can be helped, but it can never be helped merely by talking about it. We must act and act quickly.*

What solutions does President Roosevelt suggest to deal with the Great Depression?

recruiting: hiring, employment

The New Deal

Roosevelt thought that the government could help to end the Great Depression. He called his program the New Deal. He included many original ideas to help businesses, farmers, and the unemployed recover from the Depression.

The New Deal began by closing the nation's banks. Each bank was investigated during this "bank holiday." Those that were run properly reopened under government supervision. Farms and businesses in danger of going bankrupt received low interest loans. A system was developed to control the ways that stocks were bought and sold. People regained their trust in the economy.

One of the most important laws of the New Deal was the Social Security Act of 1935. It gave financial help to retired or disabled Americans and helped the jobless. By 1940 the government had provided $16 billion to help the unemployed.

The New Deal also helped people who had jobs. Congress passed the Wagner Act

In Chicago, 1930, hungry men wait for food in a soup kitchen line.

in 1935. This law recognized the right of workers to form labor unions. Years later another law set a minimum wage for all Americans and made the standard work week 40 hours long.

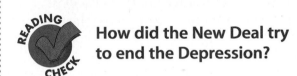

READING CHECK How did the New Deal try to end the Depression?

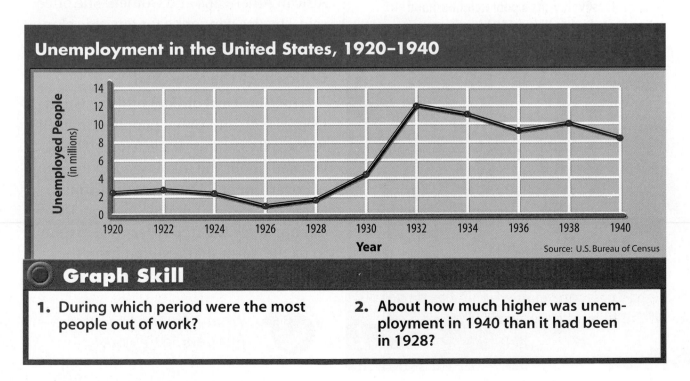

Unemployment in the United States, 1920–1940

Unemployed People (in millions)

Year

Source: U.S. Bureau of Census

Graph Skill

1. During which period were the most people out of work?

2. About how much higher was unemployment in 1940 than it had been in 1928?

555

NEW PROGRAMS AT WORK

The New Deal was designed to put Americans to work. It saved existing jobs, and it helped people without jobs. Throughout the 1930s, **unemployment**, or the number of workers without jobs, remained high. To fight unemployment, FDR created programs that he thought would create jobs.

"Alphabet Soup"

Many New Deal programs were identified by their initials. Some people jokingly called the New Deal programs "alphabet soup." The FERA, or Federal Emergency Relief Administration, helped local relief organizations. It put people to work on public projects. The WPA, or Works Progress Administration, hired jobless people to build schools, libraries, playgrounds, and hospitals. The WPA also paid artists, teachers, and musicians to work on WPA projects. The CCC, or Civil-

Eleanor Roosevelt visits a poor neighborhood in San Juan, Puerto Rico, in 1934.

ian Conservation Corps, hired young men to maintain many of the nation's forests.

The PWA, or Public Works Association, built dams on the Columbia River. Another New Deal program was the Tennessee Valley Authority (TVA). The TVA built bridges, roads, and dams along the Tennessee River. These dams helped irrigate the soil and prevented flooding. They also produced **hydroelectricity** for people in rural areas. Hydroelectricity is electricity produced by the force of running water.

An Active First Lady

First Lady Eleanor Roosevelt played a key role in helping FDR meet the challenge of the Depression. She was the first President's wife to be so active. She traveled constantly, inspecting soup kitchens and visiting the jobless and reporting on what she had seen and heard. FDR called his wife an extra set of "eyes and ears."

Eleanor Roosevelt strongly supported equal rights of all citizens, especially for African Americans and women. She once said, "Justice cannot be for one side alone, but must be for both."

Criticism of the New Deal

The New Deal did not end the Great Depression, and many people criticized Roosevelt's economic decisions. They worried about the increased involvement of government in business decisions. Some businesses felt that such decisions did not allow the free enterprise system to fix the harm that resulted from the crash of the stock market.

What New Deal programs put people to work?

PUTTING IT TOGETHER

The Great Depression was the worst economic crisis in our nation's history. Franklin Roosevelt's New Deal could not end the Great Depression, but it gave work and hope to millions of Americans. New Deal ideas, such as Social Security, remain in effect today.

The New Deal increased the role that government played in people's lives. TVA projects continue today to provide low-cost electricity. Bank accounts continue to be protected by the Federal Deposit Insurance Corporation. Some leaders argue about whether or not these programs are still useful. They also argue that the federal government has become too big and takes actions that are really the responsibilities of the states or private individuals.

In 1939 this family of Oklahoma farm workers took to the road to find work.

Review and Assess

1. Write one sentence for each vocabulary term.

   Great Depression   **Stock Exchange**
   hydroelectricity   **unemployment**
   New Deal

2. How were New Deal programs helpful to the economy? What were some concerns about the New Deal programs?

3. What did some New Deal programs do to help people during the Depression?

4. Why did the stock market crash of 1929 cause a problem for the American **economy**?

5. What were some **causes** and **effects** of Franklin Roosevelt's New Deal?

Research the percentage of unemployed people in the United States between 1980 and 2000. Then make a line graph like the one on page 555.

• •

Newspaper reporters liked to accompany Eleanor Roosevelt on her travels. **Write** a newspaper article about a trip the First Lady might have taken to a Dust Bowl community. Describe the conditions you see and the reactions of the people to the First Lady's visit.

World War II

How did the United States enter and win World War II?

Lesson Outline
• Steps to War
• The War Abroad and at Home
• A Global War
• The War Ends

VOCABULARY

dictator
Axis
Allies
World War II
communism
internment camp
concentration camp
Holocaust

PEOPLE

Benito Mussolini
Adolf Hitler
Josef Stalin
Dwight D. Eisenhower
Harry S. Truman

BUILD BACKGROUND

"Yesterday, December 7, 1941—a date that will live in infamy [shame]—the United States of America was suddenly and deliberately attacked by naval and air forces of the Empire of Japan.... As Commander-in-Chief of the Army and the Navy, I have directed that all measures be taken for our defense."

President Franklin D. Roosevelt was telling Congress about the Japanese surprise attack at **Pearl Harbor** in Hawaii. The United States was about to enter World War II.

READING STRATEGY

Make a sequence of events chart to write important lesson events in the order in which they happened.

STEPS TO WAR

Many countries besides the United States experienced the Great Depression. The hard times made it easy for **dictators** to take control in several countries. A dictator is a leader with complete authority over the government. **Benito Mussolini** (be NEE toh mus oh LEE nee) made himself dictator of Italy. **Adolf Hitler** and his Nazi (NAH tsee) Party took over Germany. A group of military officers directed the government of Japan. In 1936 these three countries signed a treaty of friendship. They called themselves the **Axis** countries.

During the 1930s the Axis countries invaded their neighbors. Japan conquered a region of China called Manchuria. Italy invaded Ethiopia in East Africa. Germany took over Austria and Czechoslovakia. Americans hoped the United States could stay out of the war.

The War Begins

On September 1, 1939, Hitler invaded Poland. Great Britain and France, who called themselves the **Allies**, declared war on the Axis. **World War II** had begun.

In 1940 Hitler's armies invaded Denmark, Norway, the Netherlands, Belgium, and France. Only Britain remained free to fight the Nazis.

Pearl Harbor

By 1941 the Japanese were taking over islands in the Pacific Ocean. On December 7, the Japanese made a surprise attack on Pearl Harbor, the American naval base in Hawaii. Japanese bombs

Dictators Benito Mussolini and Adolf Hitler appeared together in Munich, Germany.

destroyed ships, planes, and military supplies. They also killed 2,403 Americans. John Garcia, a Hawaiian civilian who was then only 16 years old, helped rescue American sailors:

Some were unconscious, some were dead. So I spent the rest of the day swimming inside the harbor along with some other Hawaiians. I brought out I don't know how many bodies.

President Roosevelt went to Congress the next day and asked it to declare war on Japan. Three days later Germany and Italy declared war on the United States.

How did the Axis dictators cause World War II?

THE WAR ABROAD AND AT HOME

In June of 1941, Hitler's armies invaded the Soviet Union. The largest country in the Soviet Union was Russia. It had been controlled by a communist government since a revolution in 1917. **Communism** is an economic and political system in which the government owns all property.

Since the 1920s the Soviet Union had been ruled by a dictator named **Josef Stalin**. Stalin had made a deal with Hitler to keep the two countries from fighting each other. When Hitler broke the deal, the Soviet Union joined the Allies against Germany.

A Global War

The war took place on two fronts, or areas of fighting. On the Pacific front the Allies fought the Japanese in China and on the Pacific islands. On the other front, stretching across Africa and Europe, Allied soldiers faced Germany and Italy.

Over the next four years, more than 15 million Americans served in the military. Our armed forces were still segregated as they had been in World War I. However, women were allowed to join the military services for the first time. By 1943 every branch of the United States military had units for women. More than 270,000 women signed up for the Women's Army Corps, or WACs. Women pilots also flew supply planes across the Atlantic.

Industry Prepares for War

President Roosevelt declared that the United States must become "the arsenal of democracy." An arsenal is a place where weapons are made or stored. Across the nation, factories worked overtime to supply materials for war.

One German general was not impressed by American industry. "The Americans can't build planes, only electric iceboxes and razor blades," he said, but he was wrong. American factories quickly converted their production from consumer products to war materials. By 1944 factories produced about 263 planes a day! By the end of the war, more than 70,000 ships and 3 million machine guns rolled out of American factories.

Library of Congress

While men risked their lives in World War II, women supported the war effort by working in factories.

On the Home Front

Many of the workers in these factories were women. As men entered the armed forces women took their places in factories and on other jobs. The employment of women nearly doubled during World War II. By the end of 1943, more than 300,000 women worked in the aircraft industry alone.

As in World War I, Americans were asked to conserve materials. Children collected scrap metal, bottle caps, and rubber bands, which were recycled into military products. People cut down on their use of gasoline, aluminum foil, meat, and other items. The government issued ration books to help conserve food needed by the military. Each book had coupons that consumers had to use to purchase scarce products such as coffee, sugar, and tires. Many Americans grew victory gardens to help the war effort.

Japanese Americans and the War

The Japanese attack on Pearl Harbor made some people worry that the large number of Japanese Americans living on the West Coast might want to help the Japanese. These fears proved to be entirely groundless. No Japanese Americans were found guilty of treason.

However, the government made more than 100,000 Japanese Americans leave their homes on the West Coast in 1942. They were moved to hastily built **internment camps** inland. An internment camp is a place where people are imprisoned during wartime. Jeanne Wakatsuki Houston was seven years old when her family was sent to the Manzanar internment camp in California. She later remembered her life in the camp.

Primary Source:

excerpt from
"Farewell to Manzanar"
—by Jeanne Wakatsuki Houston

[We] *"were able to take a **desolate** stretch of wasteland and gradually make it livable. But the situation there—especially in the beginning— the packed sleeping quarters, the **communal** mess halls, the open toilets—all this was an open insult."*

What was life like in an internment camp?

desolate: empty
communal: shared

Many Japanese Americans joined the Armed forces. One army unit made up entirely of Japanese Americans received 900 Purple Heart medals for bravery. Other Japanese Americans served as pilots, bombers, and interpreters.

During the war and long afterward, people protested against relocation camps. Finally, in 1988, the United States government apologized for its actions.

READING CHECK How did Americans at home help in the war effort?

A GLOBAL WAR

World War II was truly a world war. By 1943 the war had reached a turning point. Soviet forces delivered a massive defeat to Axis armies in Stalingrad, a city in the Soviet Union. By 1944 the Allies had begun to push their enemies back.

The Normandy Invasion

In 1944 the Allies prepared to invade Europe. The leader of the Allies' military forces in Europe, General **Dwight D. Eisenhower**, began planning the massive invasion. It took place on June 6, or "D-Day." Several hundred thousand Allied troops landed on beaches in Normandy, France. Find Normandy on the map.

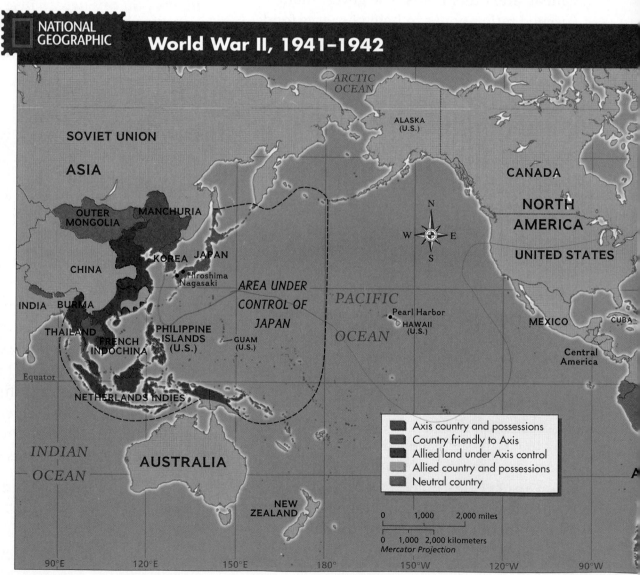

NATIONAL GEOGRAPHIC

World War II, 1941–1942

ARCTIC OCEAN

ALASKA (U.S.)

SOVIET UNION

ASIA

CANADA

NORTH AMERICA

OUTER MONGOLIA

MANCHURIA

UNITED STATES

CHINA

KOREA   JAPAN

Hiroshima
Nagasaki

AREA UNDER CONTROL OF JAPAN

PACIFIC OCEAN

INDIA   BURMA

Pearl Harbor

HAWAII (U.S.)

MEXICO

CUBA

THAILAND

FRENCH INDOCHINA

PHILIPPINE ISLANDS (U.S.)

GUAM (U.S.)

Central America

Equator

NETHERLANDS INDIES

INDIAN OCEAN

AUSTRALIA

Axis country and possessions
Country friendly to Axis
Allied land under Axis control
Allied country and possessions
Neutral country

NEW ZEALAND

0   1,000   2,000 miles

0   1,000   2,000 kilometers
Mercator Projection

90°E   120°E   150°E   180°   150°W   120°W   90°W

Allied soldiers on the Normandy beaches (left) in 1944. Soviet soldiers captured Berlin (below) in 1945.

Thousands of Allied soldiers were killed, but they took Normandy. The Allies freed France, Belgium, and Luxembourg by September. Allied troops next pushed toward Germany.

Meanwhile the Soviet army was pushing west. After their defeat at Stalingrad, Hitler's forces retreated toward Germany. On April 16, 1945, the German capital, Berlin, fell to Soviet forces. Germany surrendered on May 7. The war in Europe was over.

READING CHECK How did the Allies defeat Hitler's forces?

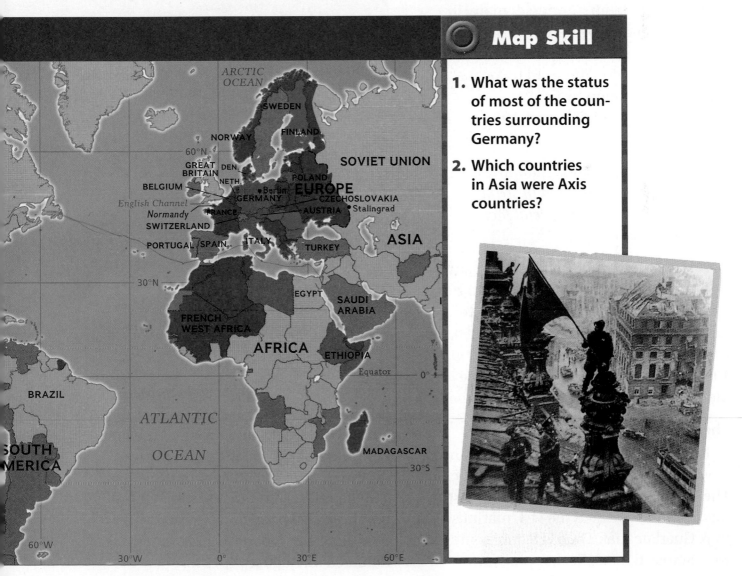

Map Skill

1. What was the status of most of the countries surrounding Germany?

2. Which countries in Asia were Axis countries?

THE WAR ENDS

Some of the worst destruction of the war took place off the battlefield. The Allies discovered concentration camps as they advanced in 1944. These prison camps were used by the Nazis to enslave or murder people they regarded as their enemies.

Death Camps

As many as 12 million men, women, and children died at the hands of Nazi Germany. About half of the victims were Jews. Unfairly blaming Jews for Germany's defeat in World War I, as well as for other problems, Hitler singled them out for destruction. By the end of the war 6 million Jews had been murdered, many in gas chambers. This attempt to destroy the Jewish people is known as the Holocaust (HAHL uh kawst). The word holocaust means "destruction by fire."

Leon Bass, a soldier in an African American unit, described one camp:

I saw human beings... standing there, skin and bones, dressed in striped pajamas. They had skeletal faces with deep-set eyes.

Nonmilitary groups, or civilians, suffered in Asia as well. Japan had used force and terror to control its conquered territories. In China, for example, over 200,000 civilians were massacred in Nanjing in 1937. Many prisoners of the Japanese died in concentration camps.

The War on Japan

Beginning in 1942 the Japanese advanced toward Australia and east across the Pacific. The United States was determined to stop this advance. In 1943 the U.S. marines took Guadalcanal. Then U.S. forces moved west across the Pacific, hopping from

island to island. They freed the Gilbert, Mariana, Philippine, and other islands.

In 1945, American forces had attacked Japan and captured two islands, Iwo Jima and Okinawa. Over 75,000 Allied soldiers were killed or wounded.

President Roosevelt died suddenly in April 1945. The new President, Harry S. Truman, faced a difficult decision. Should he order an invasion of Japan? Truman decided that the United States must spare the lives of those who would die in an invasion of Japan. He ordered the use of the atomic bomb, an extremely destructive new weapon.

On August 6, 1945, a single airplane, the *Enola Gay*, flew over the Japanese city of Hiroshima and dropped the first atomic bomb. In seconds, the city was destroyed, and 100,000 people died. Japan still did not surrender. A second atomic bomb was dropped on Nagasaki three days later. The Japanese government surrendered on August 14, 1945.

While there was joy that the the war was over, there was also sadness at the destruction and death that World War II caused in Europe, Asia, and elsewhere.

 How was Japan defeated in 1945?

PUTTING IT TOGETHER

The dictators had caused World War II. Though at first successful, they were finally defeated by the Allies at a terrible cost. The war made the United States the most powerful country in the world. The United States also was the only nation with the atomic bomb. Albert Einstein, the scientist whose ideas had helped develop the bomb, said, "The unleashed power of the atom has changed everything . . ."

Over 50 million soldiers and civilians had lost their lives during World War II. Much of Europe and Asia lay in ruins, and people were homeless and starving. The United States would face many challenges as it worked to help the world rebuild. The task was made more difficult by the growing suspicions of the Soviet Union.

Nazi soldiers round up Polish Jews to be sent to a concentration camp.

Review and Assess

1. Write one sentence for each vocabulary word.

   communism   dictator   Holocaust

2. How did World War II change life for Americans?

3. How did the United States join the Allies and help to win World War II?

4. What did American women do to help the Allies win World War II?

5. What **point of view** is shown by the German general who said that Americans could build only ice boxes and razor blades?

Look at the map on pages 562 and 563. Make a chart listing Allied countries in one column, neutral nations in another column, and Axis nations in the third column.

• •

Write an ad for the American war effort. It should encourage Americans to save and recycle important materials. Make your ad into a poster. You may choose to draw a picture for your poster.

565

The Postwar Years

How did the Cold War affect life in the United States?

Lesson Outline
- The Cold War
- The United States and the Cold War
- Two Hot Spots

READING STRATEGY

Make a chart to list the lesson's main idea and supporting details.

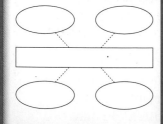

BUILD BACKGROUND

"It is my duty . . . to place before you certain facts about . . . Europe. From . . . the Baltic to . . . the Adriatic an iron curtain has descended across the Continent."

With this famous phrase, the **Iron Curtain**, British Prime Minister Winston Churchill described the invisible line separating the communist countries of Europe from the noncommunist ones. He was also calling attention to a new period in history—one in which the United States would play a large part.

Barbed wire divides Cold War Berlin.

THE COLD WAR

In April 1945, delegates from 50 countries came to San Francisco for the first meeting of a new organization. The **United Nations** was an international organization working for world peace. The meeting was the largest gathering of leaders in history.

Harry S. Truman

Postwar Tensions

President Truman faced problems with the Soviet Union. Differences between the two countries had been set aside during the war, but now they appeared again. The **Cold War**, a rivalry between the United States and the Soviet Union, was developing. It was fought with ideas, words, money, and sometimes force.

In 1945, Soviet troops had occupied the countries of Eastern Europe and brought them under Soviet rule. The map below shows which countries became communist after World War II.

World leaders in the West feared the spread of communism. In 1949 the United States and the countries of Western Europe formed an alliance called the North Atlantic Treaty Organization (NATO) to fight the spread of communism.

What was the Cold War?

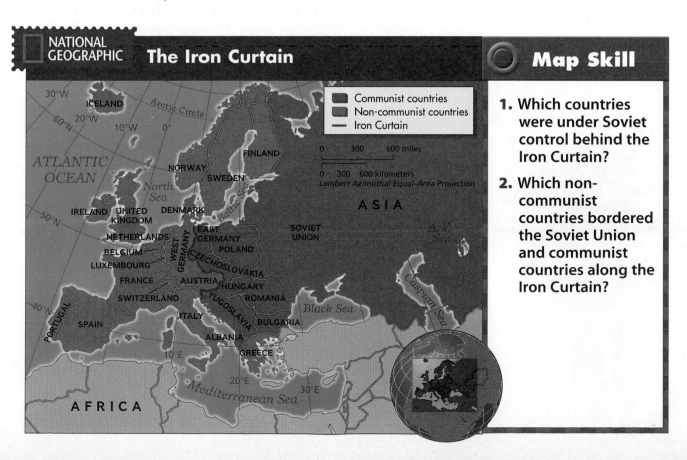

NATIONAL GEOGRAPHIC **The Iron Curtain**

Legend:
- Communist countries
- Non-communist countries
- Iron Curtain

0   300   600 miles
0   300   600 kilometers
Lambert Azimuthal Equal-Area Projection

Map Skill

1. **Which countries were under Soviet control behind the Iron Curtain?**

2. **Which non-communist countries bordered the Soviet Union and communist countries along the Iron Curtain?**

THE UNITED STATES AND THE COLD WAR

President Truman sponsored a program to provide $13 billion in food and goods to help Western Europe recover from World War II. Called the Marshall Plan, the program provided food and materials that European countries needed to rebuild their economies. The plan also helped prevent the spread of communism to Western Europe.

The Cold War Heats Up

The Korean peninsula had been divided into two countries in 1945. South Korea became a republic. North Korea had a communist government. On June 25, 1950, North Korean troops led a surprise attack on South Korea to unite the two countries by force. This was the beginning of the Korean War.

The United States rushed troops to aid South Korea. The United Nations also sent soldiers from 16 countries there.

United Nations forces, most of which were American troops, stopped the North Koreans and freed Seoul (SOHL), the capital city of South Korea. UN troops then moved into North Korea. China, which had been a communist country since 1949, sent its armed forces to aid North Korea. The war continued with neither side able to defeat the other. Finally, a settlement was reached in July 1953.

A Time of Tensions

In the early 1950s, the United States and the Soviet Union began an arms race. Each nation worked to build more atomic weapons than the other, thinking that these powerful weapons would keep each side from attacking the other. Many people feared a war involving atomic weapons. Some families even built bomb shelters in their backyards. Mistrust of the Soviet Union and its goals increased.

Joseph McCarthy, a United States senator, claimed that Communists were working to overthrow American democracy. He made many claims about the influence of these Communists, but he was unable to prove any of his charges. Between 1950 and 1954 many people were called before McCarthy's Senate committee. Some lost their jobs after being called before McCarthy's committee. The word McCarthyism is used today to describe false accusations made to damage people because of their political beliefs.

UN troops pass refugees fleeing the fighting in Korea.

The Eisenhower Years

Dwight D. Eisenhower became President in 1953. His quiet manner reassured Americans. So did the economic prosperity that began in the 1950s.

After the decade of the Great Depression and the hard wartime years, Americans wanted consumer products and family life. American industries expanded and began to produce more and better peacetime products. Many Americans bought the new cars and household appliances that the factories turned out. Others were eager to travel in new airplanes.

Special loans from the federal government helped millions of war veterans and their families to buy new homes. Most of these people wanted to live in the suburbs so they could have space for their children to play. Builders rushed to put up instant suburbs of mass-produced houses to meet the demand. Many Americans began to commute, or travel to work, each day.

New Inventions

Many new inventions changed the way Americans lived in the 1950s. It seemed that there was an endless supply of new products to save labor in the home, improve the quality of life, or to entertain the entire family.

The invention that brought one of the greatest changes was the television. In 1950 only one out of ten American families owned a television set. By the early 1960s the number had jumped to nine out of ten.

Most television programs were thought of as entertainment. However, the evening news on television grew to be as

Eisenhower's campaign button captures his popularity.

popular as other programs. Newspapers declined in popularity as people realized they could see the day's events on their television. Soon, the ability to watch events as they happened would help Americans to understand events around the world.

The Space Program

In 1957 the nation was stunned when Soviet scientists launched the first artificial satellite into space. A satellite is an object in space that circles a larger object such as Earth. The satellite, *Sputnik*, drew an immediate response from the United States. On January 31, 1958, an American satellite was launched successfully and the nation entered a new contest with the Soviet Union, the space race. This was a competition to gain control of space.

READING CHECK

How did American life change in the 1950s?

TWO HOT SPOTS

In 1961 John F. Kennedy became President of the United States. At 43, he was the youngest elected President in United States history. Almost immediately, Kennedy faced crises in Berlin and Cuba.

The Berlin Wall

Germany had been divided after World War II. The Soviet Union occupied the eastern part of the defeated nation. France, Britain, and the United States occupied the western section. Although the capital, Berlin, lay inside the Soviet zone, the city was divided between the former Allies.

Soviet control tightened in the area it occupied, and many East Germans tried to flee to the West to find a better life. In spite of attack dogs and guards, many of these escapes were successful. The East German government decided to end the problem.

First the East Germans closed the border between East Berlin and West Berlin in August 1961. Then they began to build a wall to separate the two halves of the city. The concrete wall divided the city, its neighborhoods, and, in some cases, even its streets. The Berlin Wall was an ugly symbol of the Cold War.

The Cuban Missile Crisis

On New Year's Day in 1959 Fidel Castro seized power in Cuba. At first, he was very popular because his forces had overthrown a corrupt dictator. However, Castro began to seize property belonging to foreigners as well as Cuban professionals and businesspeople. Cubans began to flee to the United States.

In 1960 Castro declared he was a Communist and formed close ties with the Soviet Union. Financial aid and special advisers were sent from Moscow to help Castro control Cuba.

The American government began to train refugees to return to Cuba and overthrow Castro. In 1961 a force of about 1,000 Cubans landed at a place called the Bay of Pigs. The small force was quickly defeated by Castro's troops, and the United States was widely criticized for its failure to support the invasion.

In 1962 a new Cuban crisis developed. The United States announced that the Soviet Union was building military bases on the island. They were

President Kennedy met Soviet leader, Khrushchev, in Vienna, Austria, in 1961.

also installing missiles that were aimed at the United States.

President Kennedy declared a blockade of Cuba. No ships were allowed in or out. Soviet ships were approaching the island with missiles on board. Breaking the American blockade would mean war, probably nuclear war.

Fear increased as the world watched the Cuban Missile Crisis unfold. Finally the Soviet leader, Nikita Khrushchev, ordered his ships to turn around. The world breathed a sigh of relief. However, many Americans continued to wonder how the United States would be affected by a communist nation only 90 miles from Florida.

Which two events in the early 1960s almost led to war?

PUTTING IT TOGETHER

The Cold War conflicts between the United States and the Soviet Union influenced events around the world for more than 40 years. In Korea, the struggle led to actual war. In Cuba and Berlin, fighting was prevented.

During the postwar years, the United States economy grew. New inventions and technology, such as television caused American life to change. Many Americans moved to the suburbs as the nation's industries expanded and people found work easily.

Review and Assess

1. Write one sentence for each vocabulary term.

   arms race   **satellite**
   Iron Curtain

2. How did the United States take part in the Korean War?

3. How did the Cold War affect the way Americans acted during the 1950s?

4. How did the expanding **economy** improve life for most Americans?

5. What was the **cause** of the Soviet construction of an Iron Curtain? What was the **effect** of the Iron Curtain?

Activities

Make a map of the Soviet Union. Then research which countries were formed after the fall of the Soviet Union and add them to your map.

....

Write a paragraph describing an event from the Cold War and how it ended. Explain the cause or causes of the event as well as its effect on Americans during the Cold War.

Drawing Conclusions

The Cuban Missile Crisis began when an American plane photographed unusual activity in Cuba. When the photos were shown to President John Kennedy, he realized what they meant. President Kennedy looked at the photographs and drew the **conclusion** that the Russians were planning to put missiles in Cuba. Whenever you reach an opinion after looking at evidence, you draw a conclusion.

An American plane took this photograph of a missile site being built in Cuba in 1962.

LEARN THE SKILL

Follow these steps to draw a conclusion.

1. **Gather information.**
   President Kennedy needed to know whether the photographs really showed unusual activity in Cuba. He probably asked for photographs of the military bases in the past.

2. **Identify the subject.**
   The subject is the Cuban military bases. Past photos showed no unusual activities. The current photographs showed construction activity at the bases. Other photos showed Soviet ships bringing missiles to Cuba.

3. **Look for connections between the pieces of information.**
   Kennedy and his advisers saw the connection between the photos. There were photos of military bases in Cuba. There were photos of missiles on Soviet ships heading to Cuba. The missiles and the bases were connected.

4. **Draw a conclusion.**
   Kennedy and his advisers drew the conclusion that the Russians were planning to put the missiles on Cuban bases. This would enable the Russians to use the Cuban missile bases to threaten the United States.

TRY THE SKILL

Now try reading the text of President Kennedy's television speech to the American people. Follow the steps and draw a conclusion from the information in the text.

"... Each of these missiles, in short, is capable of striking ... any ... city in the southeastern part of the United States, in Central America, or in the Caribbean area.

Additional sites not yet completed appear to be designed for intermediate ... missiles capable of traveling more than twice as far—and thus capable of striking most of the major cities in the Western Hemisphere. ... In addition, jet bombers, capable of carrying nuclear weapons, are now being uncrated and assembled in Cuba, while the necessary air bases are being prepared."

1. What is the subject of the information in the speech?

2. What connection is there between the pieces of information?

3. What conclusion can you draw from the information President Kennedy gives in his speech?

4. How can drawing conclusions help you to make sense out of the different pieces of information?

EXTEND THE SKILL

You draw conclusions every day. For example, you see an ad for a new movie starring your favorite actor. You draw the conclusion that you will probably like the new movie. You read about an event in the newspaper and reach a conclusion from the information that is given to you.

Think of a newspaper or television news story that you have learned about recently.

Do some research to find out more information about the event.

Write a brief outline of the event. Include the subject of the event. List the important information you have found. State the conclusion you drew from the information.

- What was the subject of the event you chose?

- What information did you use to draw a conclusion?

- How does drawing conclusions help you to understand events in history?

VOCABULARY REVIEW

Number a sheet of paper from 1 to 5. Beside each number write the word or term from the list below that matches the description.

arms race   **suffrage**

communism   **unemployment**

Great Migration

1. The number of workers without jobs
2. The right to vote
3. The movement of many African Americans from rural areas in the Southeast to urban areas in the Northeast and Middle West beginning in the 1890s
4. An economic and political system in which all property is owned by the government
5. Competition between the superpowers to build the most powerful weapons

CHAPTER COMPREHENSION

6. What event set off World War I?
7. What were the terms of the Treaty of Versailles?
8. Name two American writers of the 1920s.
9. How did the Dust Bowl affect farmers?
10. What decision did President Truman make about ending the war with Japan?
11. What was the Cold War?
12. Why did the Cuban Missile Crisis cause great fear all over the world?
13. Suppose that you are Charles Lindbergh or Amelia Earhart flying across the Atlantic Ocean for the first time. **Write** a description of what you see looking down at the world from the air.

SKILL REVIEW

14. **Reading/Thinking Skill** What is a conclusion?
15. **Reading/Thinking Skill** After you identify the subject of the information, what is the next step in drawing a conclusion?
16. **Reading/Thinking Skill** Suppose that you see everyone on your street carrying umbrellas. What conclusion would you draw about the weather forecast?
17. **Reading/Thinking Skill** What conclusion can you draw about Eleanor Roosevelt's role as First Lady from the photograph above? What evidence leads you to this conclusion?
18. **Reading/Thinking Skill** Why is it important to draw conclusions about the information you read?

USING A TIME LINE

1910	1920	1930	1940	1950	1960	1970

1917
United States enters World War I

1920
19th Amendment gives women the vote

1929
Great Depression begins

1939
World War II begins in Europe

1945
Allies win World War II

1950
Three-year Korean War begins

1962
Cuban Missile Crisis

19. Which events on the time line happened during the Cold War?

20. How many years did World War II last?

Writing **About Economics** Suppose you lived during the Roaring Twenties. Think about a new product that people might want to buy to improve their everyday lives. Write a description of your new product. Explain how you would manufacture the product and how your idea would help the economy grow.

Use your Foldable to review what you have learned about the modern era of United States history. As you look at the three tabs of your Foldable, mentally review what you learned about the good times, hard times, and wars during the first half of the twentieth century. Review your notes on the inside of your Foldable to check your memory and responses. Record any questions that you have. Then discuss them with classmates or review the chapter to find answers.

THE Big IDEAS ABOUT...

A Changing World

After World War II, the United States enjoyed a period of economic prosperity.

However, not all Americans enjoyed the benefits of the country's new wealth.

African Americans and others suffered from prejudice and discrimination.

In the 1960s the civil rights movement brought great changes that inspired

many Americans to demand justice and equality. Read on to find out how

America faced the challenges of the late twentieth century.

THE CIVIL RIGHTS MOVEMENT

Martin Luther King, Jr., is arrested for his involvement in the civil rights movement. His leadership leads to the movement's successes.

THE GREAT SOCIETY

Signing the Civil Rights Bill into law is one of President Lyndon Baines Johnson's "Great Society" measures.

END OF THE COLD WAR

The Cold War buildup of nuclear weapons by the United States and the Soviet Union causes fear in many people. They are relieved when the Cold War finally ends.

THE SPACE RACE

Cold War competition with the Soviet Union leads to technological advances for both the Soviet Union and the United States.

Foldables

Make this Foldable study guide and use it to record what you learn about "A Changing World."

1. Fold a sheet of notebook paper in half like a hot dog.
2. On one side only, cut along every third line to make 10 or more tabs.
3. Fold a sheet of construction paper in half like a hot dog, and store your vocabulary Foldable inside.
4. Write the chapter title on the construction paper cover.

The Civil Rights Movement

Find Out!

What was the result of the Civil Rights Movement?

VOCABULARY

activists
integrate
Civil Rights Act
Voting Rights Act

PEOPLE

Thurgood Marshall

Rosa Parks

Martin Luther King, Jr.

John F. Kennedy

Lyndon Baines Johnson

READING STRATEGY

Make a chart like this one. On the left, write causes of the civil rights movement. On the right, write its effects.

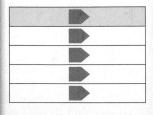

Lesson Outline

• Fighting Segregation
• Civil Rights and Voting Rights

BUILD BACKGROUND

"When we let freedom ring . . . we will be able to speed up that day when all of God's children . . . will be able to join hands and sing . . . 'Free at last! free at last! thank God Almighty, we are free at last!'"

In his famous 1963 speech, Martin Luther King, Jr., asked for a law to protect the rights given all citizens by the Fourteenth Amendment. At this time segregation was widespread, especially in the South. Also, many rights were still being denied to African Americans.

You Are Here
1954 – 1968

FIGHTING SEGREGATION

In 1892 Homer Plessy, an African American, refused to sit in a segregated railroad car. When the Supreme Court heard his case, *Plessy versus Ferguson*, it upheld the idea of "separate but equal" facilities for blacks and whites.

For almost 60 years, under *Plessy versus Ferguson*, facilities and services for blacks and whites were separate. However, they were not equal in quality. For example, many state governments spent less money on schools for African Americans. Black students often had no books and studied in run-down buildings.

The Brown Decision

Thurgood Marshall was a lawyer with the NAACP who wanted to overturn *Plessy versus Ferguson*. He hoped to show that "separate but equal" was not legal under the Fourteenth Amendment. It says, "No state can deny to any person . . . the equal protection of the laws."

Marshall got his chance when the parents of Linda Brown sued the Board of Education of Topeka, Kansas, because their daughter was being poorly educated in a segregated school. Marshall argued the case *Brown versus the Board of Education of Topeka, Kansas* before the Supreme Court. On May 17, 1954, the Court ruled that segregation in public schools was unconstitutional.

Segregated Buses

On December 1, 1955, Rosa Parks boarded a bus in Montgomery, Alabama.

On this day, the white section of the bus filled up, and the driver ordered Parks to give up her seat. When Parks refused she was arrested and jailed.

News of Parks's arrest spread, and soon a boycott was organized in protest. Martin Luther King, Jr., was a boycott organizer. Hundreds of African Americans refused to ride Montgomery's buses. Bus companies began to lose money.

White people tried to scare the boycotters but the boycott continued. The Supreme Court heard Rosa Parks's case, and in December 1956 ordered Montgomery to end segregation on its buses.

READING CHECK

Who fought to end segregation in the 1950s?

Rosa Parks's actions led many people to join the fight against segregation.

CIVIL RIGHTS AND VOTING RIGHTS

In the 1960s the civil rights movement grew. Americans fought for laws that would protect civil rights, ensure voting rights, and end segregation.

Sit-Ins

On February 1, 1960, four African American college students sat down at the "whites only" Woolworth's lunch counter in Greensboro, North Carolina. The next day the four students returned with 19 other protesters. In a week there were 400 black and white protesters. By summer Greensboro and other cities had integrated their lunch counters.

Freedom Riders

In 1961 "Freedom Rides" on public buses brought attention to segregation in public buses and stations. The freedom riders were groups of citizens, mainly college students, who tried to help poor African Americans. These activists, people who take action for political goals, also helped in other ways. For example, they went door-to-door to register African American voters in Mississippi.

Birmingham and Washington

In May of 1963 Birmingham, Alabama, was still a segregated city. The Southern Christian Leadership Conference (SCLC), with Martin Luther King, Jr., as its president, organized boycotts and protest marches to bring attention to Birmingham. King was arrested and jailed for three days. Arrests of adults and children caught the attention of the public. President John F. Kennedy ordered 3,000 troops to the city to protect the protesters. Birmingham was forced to integrate, or to bring blacks and whites together.

In June 1963 King and other leaders called for a march on Washington, D.C., to persuade the federal government to pass a new civil rights law. The March on Washington was a great success. More than 250,000 Americans gathered on August 28, 1963, to hear speeches, songs, and prayers. King gave this now-famous speech.

Primary Source:

excerpt from

"I Have a Dream" speech
— by Martin Luther King, Jr.

*I have a dream that one day this nation will rise up and live out the true meaning of its **creed**: "We hold these truths to be self-evident that all men are created equal . . ."*

I have a dream that my four little children will one day live in a nation where they will not be judged by the color of their skin but by the content of their character. . . .

I Have A Dream... ONE AMERICA

Smithsonian Institution

This will be the day when all of God's children will be able to sing with a new meaning, "My country, 'tis of thee, sweet land of liberty, of thee I sing. Land where my fathers died, land of the pilgrim's pride, from every mountainside, let freedom ring."

What was King's dream?

---

creed: stated belief

The Civil Rights Act of 1964

In 1964 President **Lyndon Baines Johnson** promised to support a new civil rights law. Within months he signed the **Civil Rights Act** of 1964. This law made segregation illegal in public places, including hotels, theaters, playgrounds, and libraries.

Violence in Selma

The Civil Rights Act was law. However, unfair voting practices such as literacy tests, taxes at polling places where elections were held, and a requirement to own property still kept many African Americans from voting in some parts of the country.

Protesters planned to march from Selma to Montgomery, Alabama. On March 7, 1965, they left Selma, but they were forced back by law enforcement officials. Many were hurt. The violence led to March 7 being known as "Bloody Sunday." Marchers were told they needed a court order to continue their march.

On March 21 the marchers reached Montgomery, Alabama's capital. Shock over the march's violence speeded the passage of the **Voting Rights Act** of 1965. By 1968, African Americans were being elected to government offices.

READING CHECK **Which two new laws resulted from civil rights activities?**

The civil rights movement included sit-ins like the one in Greensboro (left) and protest marches from cities such as Selma to Montgomery (below).

BIOGRAPHY

Focus On: **Justice**

Dr. Martin Luther King, Jr., inspired people from all walks of life to protest racial discrimination, poverty, and war. A believer in nonviolent resistance, in 1964 he became the youngest person ever awarded the Nobel Peace Prize.

While at Crozier Theological Seminary, King became acquainted with Mohandas Gandhi's philosophy of nonviolent social protest. Later, King wrote, "I came to feel that this was the only... sound method open to oppressed people in their struggle for freedom."

King first became widely known for his leadership during the 1956 Montgomery bus boycott. King was assassinated on April 4, 1968, in Memphis, Tennessee. In 1986 a national holiday was established in his honor to be observed on the third Monday in January.

Link to Today Think of a situation in our nation today that seems unfair. Write a paragraph that tells what Dr. King might have done to address the situation.

THE LIFE OF MARTIN LUTHER KING, JR.

1929	1955	1963	1968
Martin Luther King, Jr., is born in Atlanta, Georgia	King joins the Montgomery bus boycott	King leads the March on Washington	On April 4, Martin Luther King, Jr., is assassinated

1930   1940   1950   1960   1970

LIFE AROUND THE WORLD

1931	1939	1945	1956	1964
Japanese occupy Manchuria	Germany invades Poland	World War II ends	Morocco, Tunisia, and Sudan gain independence	Military leaders seize power in Brazil

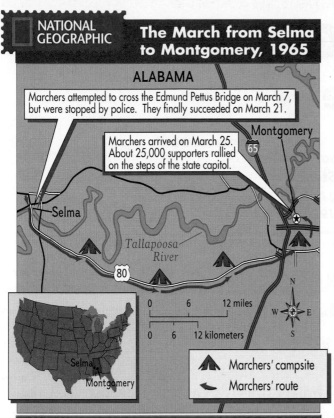

NATIONAL GEOGRAPHIC
The March from Selma to Montgomery, 1965

ALABAMA

Marchers attempted to cross the Edmund Pettus Bridge on March 7, but were stopped by police. They finally succeeded on March 21.

Marchers arrived on March 25. About 25,000 supporters rallied on the steps of the state capitol.

Montgomery

Selma

Tallapoosa River

▲ Marchers' campsite
— Marchers' route

0   6   12 miles
0   6   12 kilometers

Selma
Montgomery

Map Skill

1. In which general direction did the marchers move from Selma to Montgomery?

2. What happened on March 7?

PUTTING IT TOGETHER

Much has changed since the civil rights movement began in the 1950s. Segregation is illegal in all public and most private places. Discrimination still exists, but our country has come closer to the ideal of "liberty and justice for all." Leaders such as Jesse Jackson and Coretta Scott King, Martin Luther King's widow, have carried the legacy of the movement into the new millennium. As you will read, the nonviolent ideas and methods of Martin Luther King, Jr., have inspired other groups to struggle for their rights.

WE MARCH FOR INTEGRATED SCHOOLS NOW!

Signs supporting civil rights were a common sight in the 1960s.

Review and Assess

1. Write one sentence for each vocabulary term.

   **Civil Rights Act   Voting Rights Act
   integrate**

2. What were the goals of the civil rights movement?

3. What difficulties did civil rights workers face?

4. Analyze the events that led to the passage of the Civil Rights Act and the Voting Rights Act.

5. How would you describe King's **frame of reference** for his "I Have a Dream" speech?

Activities

Research a route to the capitol building in your state. Then make a map showing the route.

Write a letter to your newspaper editor in support of the civil rights activists involved in one of the protests you learned about in this lesson. Pretend it is sometime in the 1950s or 1960s.

The Great Society

Find Out!

What two wars did the United States fight during the 1960s and 1970s?

Lesson Outline
• War on Poverty
• The Vietnam War

VOCABULARY

migrant farm
 worker
La Causa
Vietnam War

PEOPLE

Malcolm X
César Chávez
Dolores Huerta
Richard Nixon

READING STRATEGY

Make a chart like this one to list the main ideas and supporting details in this lesson.

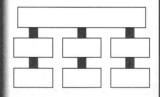

BUILD BACKGROUND

On November 22, 1963, the United States suffered a sudden and great blow. President John F. Kennedy was traveling with First Lady Jacqueline Kennedy in Dallas, Texas. The President's car was open so that the crowds could see him. Then shots were fired at the car, and President Kennedy was killed. Within only a few hours, Vice President Lyndon Baines Johnson was sworn in as the new President. In 1964, Johnson was reelected in a landslide.

WAR ON POVERTY

The Civil Rights Act of 1964 and the Voting Rights Act of 1965 were part of Johnson's "Great Society." This society, Johnson said, "rests on abundance [plenty] and liberty for all. It demands an end to poverty and racial injustice."

Government Programs

In 1964 almost half of all nonwhite Americans were poor, while about two out of ten white Americans were poor. Because of this, on August 20 Johnson signed the Economic Opportunity Act (EOA) into law.

Johnson wanted to help the poor succeed. Programs created under the EOA included Food Stamps, Job Corps, College Work Study, and Head Start.

Another Great Society program was Medicare, which began in 1965. It helps people over the age of 65 pay for their medical care. The Department of Housing and Urban Development was also started in 1965 to provide a "decent, safe, and sanitary [clean] home . . . for every American."

Americans Help Themselves

Nongovernment leaders fought poverty in other ways. Martin Luther King, Jr., began what he called "The Poor People's Campaign" to end poverty. Malcolm X, a leader in the African American community, believed that blacks needed to take control of their own lives. Neither Martin Luther King, Jr., nor Malcolm X lived to see the results of

President Johnson meets with young people at a job opportunity center in Philadelphia.

their struggles. Malcolm X was shot to death while speaking in New York in 1965. King was shot and killed in Memphis, Tennessee, three years later.

Organizing Migrant Workers

Most migrant farm workers suffered discrimination and poverty. A migrant worker moves from farm to farm picking different crops. Their poverty led César Chávez (SE sahr CHAH vez) and Dolores Huerta (WER tah) to found the National Farm Workers Association in 1962 to help migrant workers. The farm workers' struggle for a better life came to be called "La Causa," Spanish for "The Cause."

READING CHECK **In what ways did Americans fight poverty in the 1960s?**

585

THE VIETNAM WAR

Throughout the 1960s a war fought in Asia affected the United States deeply. The country of Vietnam had been divided in 1954. North Vietnam had a communist government supported by the Soviet Union and China. South Vietnam was a republic backed by the United States. A war between the two Vietnams alarmed leaders in the United States. They feared that a North Vietnamese victory would lead to the spread of communism throughout Asia.

"Hawks" and "Doves"

In 1964 the United States became involved in fighting with North Vietnam. Over the next three years, over 500,000 United States soldiers fought in the

More than 500,000 American soldiers fought in Vietnam.

Vietnam War. However, the United States Congress never declared war on North Vietnam as required in the Constitution.

People disagreed about whether the United States should be fighting in Vietnam. The "hawks" believed the United States had to fight North Vietnam to stop communism from spreading. The "doves," on the other hand, believed that the United States should not fight in a war where its own safety was not threatened. The first protest against the war in Vietnam was held on April 17, 1965, in Washington. Millions of Americans from all walks of life were against the war. However, most of the protests were on college campuses. In 1970, at Kent State University in Ohio, four student protestors were shot and killed by the National Guard troops called in to maintain order.

The United States Pulls Out

In 1968 Richard Nixon was elected President. He promised to achieve "peace with honor" in Vietnam. In 1969 he began withdrawing United States troops. However, Nixon continued the bombing of North Vietnam. United States planes also began bombing communist targets in Cambodia, a country west of Vietnam where North Vietnamese had bases. In 1970 the United States sent soldiers to Cambodia as well.

The country remained badly divided over the war. Finally in 1973, the United States signed a treaty to end the fighting. Almost two million people died in the war, including over 57,000 Americans.

What were the views of the "Doves" and the "Hawks" on the Vietnam War?

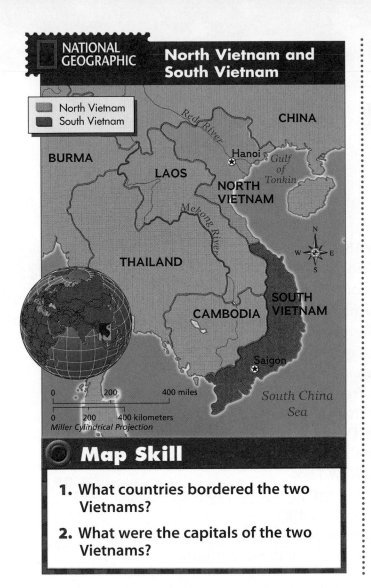

NATIONAL GEOGRAPHIC
North Vietnam and South Vietnam

North Vietnam
South Vietnam

CHINA
BURMA
Red River
Hanoi
Gulf of Tonkin
LAOS
NORTH VIETNAM
Mekong River
THAILAND
SOUTH VIETNAM
CAMBODIA
Saigon
South China Sea

N
W   E
S

0   200   400 miles
0   200   400 kilometers
Miller Cylindrical Projection

Map Skill

1. **What countries bordered the two Vietnams?**

2. **What were the capitals of the two Vietnams?**

PUTTING IT TOGETHER

The fighting continued in Vietnam after the United States troops withdrew. In 1975 North Vietnam conquered South Vietnam. The two parts of Vietnam were reunited under a communist government. Thousands of South Vietnamese fled to the United States.

The fate of American soldiers still missing in action continues to be a source of conflict between the United States and Vietnam. In the early 1990s, the Vietnamese government began releasing information on the missing soldiers. In 1995 the United States reopened trade relations with Vietnam. In 2000, the two countries signed a trade agreement.

Review and Assess

1. Write one sentence for each vocabulary term.

   migrant farm worker   **Vietnam War**

2. What are some of the Great Society programs the United States government started to help the poor?

3. What two wars were fought by the United States in the 1960s and 1970s?

4. How did the Vietnam War affect American society?

5. What **conclusion** can you draw about life in the United States during the middle and late 1960s?

Activities

Research the products Vietnam manufactures today. Then make a map of the route these products would make to reach the United States.

Write a paragraph in which you propose a program like the "Great Society" or "War on Poverty" to Congress. Explain the need for the program and how it will help.

Being a Good Citizen
Finding Common Ground

As you read in Chapter 18, the United States and the Soviet Union had little in common during the Cold War. In the same way, students may think their worlds are very different. However, a sense of compassion can change their opinions about others.

Teenagers Kimberly Trent and Dustin Broglin believed that their lives were very different. Dustin lives on a farm in Holcomb, Missouri. Kimberly lives in a New York City apartment. "We each," said Dustin, "had our ideas about . . . the other place. I thought city people would be kind of stuck up. They would think that life in Holcomb was probably dull."

"...Each group's view of the other group began to change."

Dustin, Kimberly, and 29 other New York and Missouri students created an unusual after-school art project. For six months, they worked on a 35-foot-long mural illustrating their communities.

The two groups used the Internet to send digital images showing the history, geography, and culture of their communities. "Each group's view of the other group began to change," says Sandra Stein, co-director of the project.

"I started to see," says Kimberly, "that no matter where we live, our views, the music and fashions we like, and much else are pretty much the same."

David Loewenstein, the other co-director, helped them choose images for the mural.

To increase a sense of understanding, the New York half of the mural was painted in Missouri, and the Missouri half was done in New York.

"In the center," says Kimberly, "we put the things that brought us together like the computer and paint brushes."

Dustin says the project had a permanent effect on him. "When it came right down to it, we were pretty much the same."

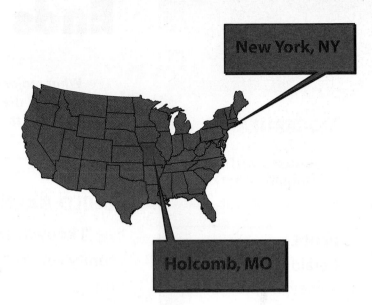

Be a Good Citizen

Making Connections

- **Why is it unjust to form opinions about people without knowing them?**

Talk About It!

- **What do you think the phrase "common ground" means?**

- **How did working on the mural project change the way Dustin thought about people he had never met before? Why?**

Act On It

In the Classroom

Talk to a classmate you do not know well. Discover something that you have in common. Report to the class what you have learned that you share with your partner.

THINGS IN COMMON
MUSIC	folksongs
PETS	nothing in common
FOODS	nothing in common
SCHOOL SUBJECTS	math

The Cold War Ends

Lesson Outline
• Watergate
• Equal Rights
• The Cold War Ends
• War and a New President

VOCABULARY

Americans with Disabilities Act
Persian Gulf War

PEOPLE
Gerald Ford
Shirley Chisholm
Sandra O'Connor
Jimmy Carter
Ronald Reagan
Mikhail Gorbachev
George Bush
Colin Powell
Bill Clinton
Albert Gore, Jr.
George W. Bush

BUILD BACKGROUND

"I know that you are one who sees when an opportunity comes," Richard Nixon said to Mao Zedong (MOU DZE DUNG), the leader of communist China, in 1972. Richard Nixon was the first United States President to visit China. Nixon also became the first President to visit the Soviet Union since World War II. Billions of tax dollars were being spent on the arms race. As more powerful weapons were developed, the world was becoming a more dangerous place.

In 1972 President Nixon and First Lady Pat Nixon meet with Mao Zedong in China.

READING STRATEGY

Make a chart like this one to summarize the main ideas of this lesson.

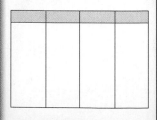

You Are Here
1972 – 2001

WATERGATE

President Nixon's visits to China and the Soviet Union helped to ease Cold War tensions. These visits were important achievements for President Nixon. In 1972 he was reelected by a large majority. Two years later, however, he was forced to leave office because of the Watergate Scandal. A scandal is any action that brings disgrace.

The Watergate Scandal

The Watergate Scandal began with what seemed to be a simple burglary. On June 17, 1972, five men were arrested for breaking into an office in the Watergate building in Washington, D.C. It soon was discovered that the men, who were connected to the President's re-election campaign, had been spying on the headquarters of Nixon's political opponent.

Nixon said he knew nothing about the break-in. Later, White House recordings showed that he was involved in the Watergate Scandal and the efforts to cover it up. Congress prepared to impeach President Nixon for breaking the law. Instead of risking impeachment, Nixon resigned from office on August 9, 1974. He was the first President ever to resign.

President Gerald Ford

Vice President Gerald Ford of Michigan then took office as President. Ford was the first person to serve as Vice President and President without having been elected to either office.

Nixon waves good-bye at the end of his presidency.

Early in his presidency, Ford gave Nixon a pardon. This meant that Nixon would not be punished for any crimes. Ford said that the Watergate Scandal was "an American tragedy . . . which . . . could go on and on and on, or someone must write the end to it."

Many people disagreed with Ford's decision to pardon Nixon. They believed that, if there was evidence of wrongdoing, Nixon should have been brought to trial.

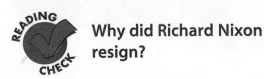

READING CHECK Why did Richard Nixon resign?

591

EQUAL RIGHTS

After the success of the civil rights movement, other groups sought equal protection under the law. Women, older Americans, and the disabled were three of these groups.

The Women's Movement

The first wave of the women's rights movement won women the right to vote in 1920. The United States Constitution, however, does not specifically guarantee women the rights that are guaranteed to men. In 1923, Alice Paul introduced the Equal Rights Amendment.

Throughout the 1900s, professional women such as Amelia Earhart supported the Equal Rights Amendment. Many others opposed it. The 1960s civil rights movement started a second wave of the women's rights movement. In 1966, Betty Friedan founded the National Organization for Women (NOW) to help seek equality for all women.

Shirley Chisholm (below) and (above, left to right) Bella Abzug, Gloria Steinem, Dick Gregory, Betty Friedan, and Elizabeth Holtzmann are among those who supported women's rights to a career outside the home.

However, many women disagreed with NOW. Spokeswomen such as Phyllis Schlafly told Americans that many women believed their most important job was in the home.

The Equal Rights Amendment passed the United States Senate and the House of Representatives on March 22, 1972. Then it was sent to the states for ratification. Congress gave a seven-year deadline for 38 states to approve. However, time ran out with only three states to go.

By the 1960s, women's roles had changed. In 1968 Shirley Chisholm became the first African American woman to win election to the House of Representatives. Ella Grasso was elected governor of Connecticut in 1974. She became the first woman governor in United States history who had not replaced or filled in for her husband. In 1981 Sandra Day O'Connor became the first woman named to the Supreme Court, and in 1993 she was joined by Ruth Bader Ginsberg.

Justice for All

In 1970 Maggie Kuhn became concerned about the older Americans in our country. Kuhn's employers had forced her to retire from her job when she turned 65 years old. Kuhn then helped to found the Gray Panthers. This organization helped get a law passsed making it illegal to force people over 65 years of age to retire.

Another struggle for rights took place at Gallaudet (gawl uh DET) University in Washington, D.C. Gallaudet is a school for the deaf and hearing-impaired. In 1988 the school officials refused to appoint a deaf person to be president of the school. Gallaudet students fought back with boycotts, petitions, and marches. In time the position went to a candidate who was partly deaf.

The Gallaudet protest was part of a larger fight for the rights of people with disabilities. A major gain was made in 1990 when the Americans with Disabilities Act, or ADA, became law. This law made it illegal for employers to discriminate against people with disabilities. It also guaranteed them access to public facilities.

What groups struggled for equal rights in the late 1960s and 1970s?

Sandra Day O'Connor is the first woman appointed as a Supreme Court Justice.

THE COLD WAR ENDS

The United States continued to play a major role in world events in the 1970s. In 1976 <mark>Jimmy Carter</mark>, a former governor of Georgia, was elected President. Carter was interested in strengthening human rights around the world.

World Tensions

Carter helped bring peace to two long-time enemies in the Middle East. In 1979 Egypt's leader Anwar Sadat (AHN wahr sah DAHT) and Israel's leader Menachem Begin (men AH hem BAY gin) signed a peace treaty in Washington, D.C. That same year Carter signed a treaty with Soviet leaders to limit the building of certain nuclear weapons.

In 1980 <mark>Ronald Reagan</mark>, a former California governor, was elected President. Reagan, a leader of the growing conservative movement, believed it was important to strengthen the United States against the Soviet Union.

During the 1980s the United States greatly increased spending on nuclear

Begin, Carter, and Sadat (above, left to right) worked for peace in the Middle East. Reagan and Gorbachev (below) celebrate the signing of a treaty limiting nuclear missiles.

weapons and continued to pay for many other government programs. From 1981 to 1988 the national debt grew. The national debt is the amount of money the government owes. In 1995 the national debt was almost $5 trillion. That amount

was equal to $20,000 for every person in the United States!

The Iron Curtain Is Lifted

Like the United States, the Soviet Union was spending large amounts of money on the arms race. So much money was spent on weapons that the Soviet economy suffered. The great cost of weapons was one factor that helped to bring an end to the Cold War.

Another factor in the Cold War's end was the reform policy of a Soviet leader named **Mikhail Gorbachev** (MIHK ìl GAWR buh chahv), who took office in March 1985. He gave more freedoms to the Soviet people. He also worked to improve relations with the United States. In 1987 Reagan and Gorbachev signed the first arms treaty that called for both superpowers to destroy some nuclear missiles.

People in other communist countries responded to Gorbachev's changes by demanding more freedom for themselves. In 1989 the people of East Germany tore down the Berlin Wall, symbol of the Iron Curtain.

Soon communist governments in East Germany, Poland, Hungary, Czechoslovakia, and Romania were overthrown. Estonia, Latvia, and Lithuania, which were made part of the Soviet Union in 1940, demanded their independence. The Iron Curtain of communism was lifted completely in 1991, when the Soviet Union broke up into 15 independent republics. With the end of the Soviet Union, the Cold War was over. The new republics, however, had to begin searching for ways to make their economies stronger.

With the fall of Soviet-backed governments in 1991, conflicts began to break out between ethnic groups in Eastern Europe. The wars between the Serbs, the Bosnians, the Albanians, and the Croatians in the former country of Yugoslavia were particularly bloody. The armed forces of each side even attacked civilian populations as each group resumed centuries-old conflict. Thousands were killed and hundreds of thousands became refugees. To halt these war crimes, NATO bombed military and civilian targets in Bosnia and Kosovo. Yet, the conflict continues today.

 What brought the Cold War to an end?

This statue of a founder of the Soviet Union's spy system was one of many torn down in Russia at the end of the Cold War.

595

WAR AND A NEW PRESIDENT

The Gulf War

In 1988, near the end of the Cold War, Reagan's Vice President, George Bush of Texas, was elected President. He soon faced a major challenge in the Middle East. In 1990 Iraq invaded the oil-rich country of Kuwait. Within days, the United States demanded that Iraq withdraw from Kuwait. By January 1991, more than half a million troops from the United Stated and its allies were in the Gulf region. On January 16, allied bombing of Iraq began in the Persian Gulf War. A ground war began on February 23. Colin Powell, chairman of the Joint Chiefs of Staff and the highest ranking

President Bush (center), General Powell (right), and other government officials discuss the Gulf War.

American military officer, took command of the military operation. By March 3, Iraq had signed a cease-fire with the United States and the fighting ended.

Clinton Becomes President

During the 1992 presidential campaign Bill Clinton, former governor of Arkansas, focused on the economy. Many people were unemployed, and Clinton was elected by an Electoral College landslide. By the end of his first term, he had cut the budget deficit greatly.

Clinton's economic and foreign policies were successes. However, Clinton spent much of his two terms under investigation for possible illegal actions. In 1998, Clinton became the second President to be impeached by the House of Representatives. However, a Senate trial found him not guilty of the charges.

NATIONAL GEOGRAPHIC

Iraq and Kuwait

- Iraq
- Kuwait
- ★ Capital

TURKEY

SYRIA

LEBANON

IRAQ
Baghdad ⊛

IRAN

ISRAEL

JORDAN

KUWAIT ⊛ Kuwait City

SAUDI ARABIA

BAHRAIN

Persian Gulf

QATAR

Red Sea

0   250   500 miles

0   250   500 kilometers
Lambert Azimuthal Equidistant Projection

Map Skill

What body of water borders both Iraq and Kuwait?

Why did Clinton beat Bush in the 1992 election?

Exploring ECONOMICS

Economic Interdependence

During the 1900s the economy of the United States increasingly became part of the world economy. One way to understand this interdependence is to look at the labels on your sneakers, for example. They may have been made in Thailand with rubber from Vietnam and laces made of cotton grown in Egypt. Countries began to specialize in this way as they looked for ways to use resources to make goods cheaply and then export at low prices. Many countries found it cheaper to import these goods than to manufacture them.

Look for articles on world economic interdependence in newspapers and magazines. Then list the arguments for and against it.

PUTTING IT TOGETHER

In the 2000 election, Clinton's Vice President, **Albert Gore, Jr.**, of Tennessee, faced **George W. Bush**, son of former President George Bush and former First Lady Barbara Bush. The election was one of the closest in U.S. history, with Florida's 25 electoral votes in dispute. Neither Gore nor Bush had enough votes in the Electoral College to win. Both men needed Florida's electoral votes. When the two sides could not agree on how the ballots should be counted, the Supreme Court had to decide. Although Gore had won the popular vote, the Court ruled that George W. Bush had won the Florida electoral votes and the election. He became President in January 2001.

Review and Assess

1. Write one sentence for each vocabulary term.

   Americans with Disabilities Act
   Persian Gulf War

2. Which presidents were threatened by impeachment trials?

3. Identify the major events of the last 30 years of the twentieth century.

4. Identify the accomplishments of Colin Powell in the Gulf War.

5. Identify two **causes** of the end of the Cold War.

Research the Persian Gulf War. Make a chart listing which countries fought against Iraq and which countries supported Iraq. Include a bibliography.

Write a list of your federal and state representatives. Include their political party, number of years in office, previous offices held, and their street or email address.

Using Reference Sources and Databases

You have just read about the last years of the twentieth century. If you wanted to learn more about them, you could look in a **reference source**. A reference source contains basic facts about many different subjects, or many different facts about one subject.

An **encyclopedia** is one type of reference source. Encyclopedias provide general information about many different subjects, arranged in alphabetical order.

Another type of reference source is an **atlas**. An atlas provides maps and other geographical information. A historical atlas tells you how geography has changed over time.

Another way to find information is to use a **database**. A database contains articles, pictures, maps, music, primary sources, and other information that has been stored electronically. Some databases are on **CD-ROM**. A CD-ROM is a computer disk that can store large amounts of information. Other databases are on the Internet. The Internet is a computer network that allows you to reach sources of information such as libraries, schools, or government offices.

VOCABULARY

- reference source
- encyclopedia
- atlas
- database
- CD-ROM
- call number

LEARN THE SKILL

Follow these steps to use reference sources.

1. **Decide what you want to search for.**
   Suppose you are writing a paper on the 2000 election. You decide you want to find a quote from a speech made by George W. Bush.

2. **Decide which database to use.**
   Different databases contain different types of information. To find which sources would have speeches by George W. Bush, you might start with the database in your school or local library. Look for the subject's **call number**, the series of letters and numbers that tell you exactly where to locate it on the shelf. If you can't find what you want in the library, try a CD-ROM or the Internet.

3. **To search on the Internet, identify unique key words or details about your subject.**
   Because a database can store so much

information, it is important to be specific. To find what you need, you might choose the key words "George W. Bush." If the search engine gives you too many results, you may need to use more specific key words, such as "speeches by."

TRY THE SKILL

Now suppose that you want to find information on President Bill Clinton's Middle East policy. Clinton was President from 1993 to 2001.

1. Where might you find information on Bill Clinton's Middle East policy?

2. Which database would you use to search for information on Clinton's Middle East policy?

3. Suppose you want to find more specific information on Clinton, such as a speech he made on the Middle East. What key words would you use?

4. How can using reference sources and databases help you to study history?

EXTEND THE SKILL

Organizing databases can help you work with different information sources at the same time. Organize a database on the Internet as you search for information about a topic such as Muslims in the United States. You might look for information on the following details:

● the number of Muslims living in the U. S.

● neighborhoods where a large population of Muslims live

● how the Muslim culture has enriched a neighborhood

Explain how you organized the databases you used.

● How did using databases help you find the information you needed?

● Why is it helpful to you to know how to use a variety of different reference sources?

New Challenges

What challenges does the United States face today?

Lesson Outline
- Terrorists Strike
- Making a Better World

VOCABULARY

terrorism
gene
DNA

PEOPLE
Neil Armstrong

READING STRATEGY

Use a chart like this one to note the main idea and supporting details of this lesson.

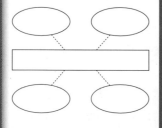

BUILD BACKGROUND

In his inaugural address in 1961, President John F. Kennedy challenged the people of the world: "Together let us explore the stars, conquer the deserts, eradicate [end] disease . . . join in creating . . . a new world of law, where the strong are just and the weak secure and the peace preserved."

The United States became a leader in space exploration and medical research. However, the search for peace became increasingly difficult.

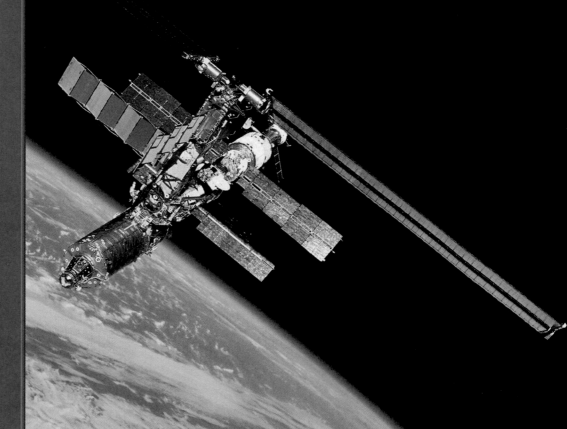

TERRORISTS STRIKE

Ethnic, economic, religious and political unrest made peace seem an impossible goal in the 1990s and early 2000s. Terrorism has increased, and has been aided by technology. Terrorism is the use of fear and violence to gain political goals.

The Attacks Begin

Many nations, especially Israel and Ireland, have lived with terrorism for years. The United States, however, had few terrorist attacks until the 1990s.

On February 26, 1993, a bomb went off in the World Trade Center in New York. The blast killed six people and injured over 1,000 others. Two men, who supported the cause of Palestine, were convicted in the attack.

On April 19, 1995, a federal building in Oklahoma City, Oklahoma, was bombed, killing 168 people. An American political extremist was found guilty of the crime.

Terrorists struck again at the summer Olympic Games in Atlanta, Georgia, in 1996. One person was killed. The bomber was never captured. In August of 1998, bombs destroyed U.S. embassies in Kenya and Tanzania. These attacks, and another on the U.S.S. *Cole* in 2000, were blamed on a network of terrorists based in the Middle East who opposed American policies, culture, and influence.

September 11, 2001

On the morning of September 11, 2001, terrorists hijacked four airliners from Boston, Newark, and Washington, D.C. They crashed the first two planes

Rescue workers raise the American flag over ruins of the World Trade Center in New York City after terrorist attacks.

into the World Trade Center in New York City. Both towers collapsed and 2,830 people were lost. After the attack, transportation in New York ceased, and businesses closed. At the same time, terrorists flew a third plane into the Pentagon, the nation's military headquarters, outside Washington, D.C. Nearly 200 people died and the Pentagon was badly damaged. Passengers on the fourth plane fought the terrorists and the plane crashed in Pennsylvania's woods. September 11 was a devastating day in our nation's history. A total of 3,063 people were lost on this day.

How have terrorists struck the United States?

601

MAKING A BETTER WORLD

After the attacks, stronger security was ordered at airports, train stations, and communications centers. President George W. Bush took steps to calm the nation and fight terrorism.

Meanwhile, the United States and its allies began to seize terrorists' money around the world. In October 2001, they also began bombing targeted areas in Afghanistan.

Evidence pointed to an extremist group of terrorists. Its members were the ones responsible for the attack on our embassies in East Africa. Although the group claimed to be fighting for Islam, President Bush told the world "The enemy is not our many Muslim friends. . . . Our enemy is a radical network of terrorists."

A New Diversity

Muslim Americans were quick to denounce the terrorist attacks. Many Muslim Americans are recent immigrants from Asia and the Middle East. In the 2000 census, there were 28 million foreign-born Americans. Like earlier immigrants, the new immigrants have brought their customs, traditions and religion, and are working hard to be good citizens.

Exploring Space

In 1961, President John F. Kennedy set the goal of "landing a man on the moon . . ." The goal was reached on July 20, 1969, when **Neil Armstrong** walked on the moon.

Later space projects included unmanned exploration of space. Today, 16 nations are contributing their efforts to the International Space Station, a permanent science institution orbiting Earth.

New Frontiers of Health

Scientists are also using new technology to find cures for diseases, such as

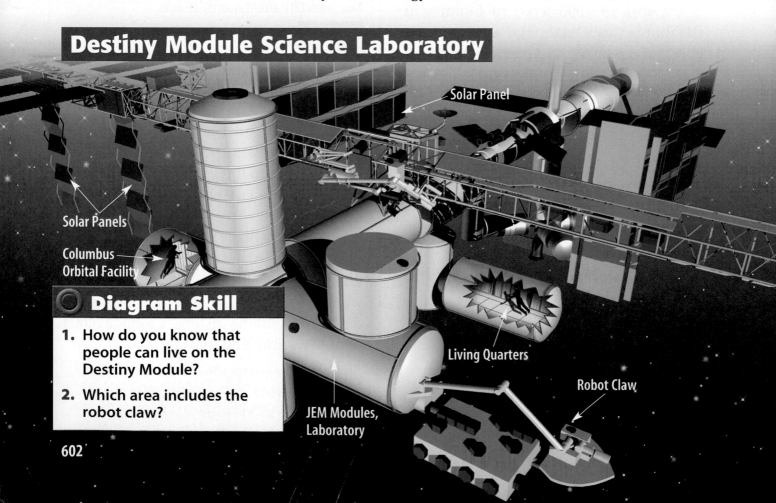

Destiny Module Science Laboratory

Solar Panel

Solar Panels

Columbus Orbital Facility

Living Quarters

Robot Claw

JEM Modules, Laboratory

◉ Diagram Skill

1. How do you know that people can live on the Destiny Module?

2. Which area includes the robot claw?

1   The first wave of the women's rights movement won women the right to vote in 1920. The United States Constitution however, does not specifically guarantee women the rights guaranteed to men. In 1923, Alice Paul introduced the Equal Rights Amendment.

2   In 1966, Betty Friedan founded the National Organization for Women (NOW). However, many women disagreed with NOW.

3   The Equal Rights Amendment passed the United States Senate and the House of Representatives on March 22, 1972. Then it was sent to the states for ratification. Congress gave a seven-year deadline for 38 states to approve. However, time ran out with only three states to go.

1 Based on the paragraphs, the reader can conclude that—

A   Betty Friedan was able to convince many people to support the Equal Rights Amendment

B   Congress supported the Equal Rights Amendment

C   The Equal Rights Amendment became law in 1972

D   Amendments to the Constitution take too much time

2 In the first paragraph, the word <u>wave</u> means—

A   a swell of water in the ocean

B   to gesture a greeting

C   one of a series of actions

D   semi-curly hairstyle

WRITING ACTIVITIES

Writing to Persuade Suppose that you write advertisements in the 1920s. *Write* an advertisement for a new invention, such as radio programs, moving pictures, or an automobile. Use words and ideas that will persuade readers to try the invention.

Writing to Inform *Write* a news story to describe the 1963 March on Washington. Describe what you see and hear during the day. Include quotes from the speech by Martin Luther King, Jr.

Writing to Express *Write* about the ways in which the United States changed during World War II.

In American classrooms, people of different ethnic backgrounds and cultures learn together.

cancer and AIDS (acquired immune deficiency syndrome). Doctors use lasers to perform complex surgery.

Researchers are also trying to identify every human **gene**. A gene contains all the information that gives living things their characteristics. New technology can identify **DNA**, the substance that carries genetic information. DNA is often used to help solve crimes.

READING CHECK How are Americans working to make the world a better and safer place?

PUTTING IT TOGETHER

New technologies have moved humans into space and helped us to explore the worlds around us. Computers have made information more available, and other advances have helped us fight disease.

Americans are working to end terrorism and make the world a safer place. President Bush told the nation, "As long as the United States of America is determined and strong, this will not be an age of terror; this will be an age of liberty, here and across the world."

Review and Assess

1. Write one sentence for each vocabulary word.

   DNA   gene   terrorism

2. How did the United States react to the attacks on the World Trade Center and the Pentagon?

3. **Analyze** some of the ways that advances in technology can help us in the future.

4. How do terrorist attacks affect the United States **economy**?

5. What **inferences** can you draw about the role of technology in modern American life?

Activities

Make a chart. In it explain how scientific discoveries and technological innovations in medicine, communication, and transportation have benefited individuals and society in the United States.

Write a paragraph about what it might be like to work in the International Space Station. Use the illustration of one of the station's science laboratories on page 602.

VOCABULARY REVIEW

Number a sheet of paper from 1 to 5. Beside each number write the word or term from the list below that best completes the sentence.

Civil Rights Act   **suffrage**

communism   **terrorism**

integrate

1. Birmingham was forced to ____ blacks and whites.
2. An economic and political system in which all property is owned by the government is called ____.
3. Violence is used in acts of ____ to cause fear and to gain political goals.
4. American women's fight for ____, or the right to vote, began with the Seneca Falls Convention in 1848.
5. The ____ of 1964 made segregation illegal in public places.

TECHNOLOGY

For more resources to help you learn more about the people and places you studied in this unit, visit **www.mhschool.com** and follow the links for Grade 5, Unit 8.

SKILL REVIEW

Americans evacuate the United States Embassy in Saigon at the end of the Vietnam War.

6. **Study Skill** Where could you find information on the Vietnam War in the library? Which reference source would show you a map of Vietnam today?
7. **Study Skill** Why is it important to know how to use different kinds of reference sources?
8. **Study Skill** What different reference sources can you find through this social studies book?
9. **Reading/Thinking Skill** What conclusion can you make about the fact that the Berlin Wall was torn down in 1989?
10. **Reading/Thinking Skill** If you have many pieces of information about a topic, how do you use them to make a conclusion?

Unit 9

Our Neighbors in the Western Hemisphere

TAKE A LOOK

Who are our neighbors in the Western Hemisphere?

When Mexico City was built in 1535, it had about 30,000 people. Today it is one of the world's largest cities, with a population of about 20 million.

For more information about our neighbors in the Western Hemisphere, visit www.mhschool.com

609

Canada

 *How are the land, history, and culture of Canada special?*

Lesson Outline
- Canada's Land
- Canada's Past
- Canadians Today

VOCABULARY

bilingual

province

North American
    Free Trade
    Agreement

PEOPLE

Jacques Cartier

Samuel de
    Champlain

**READING
STRATEGY**

Using a Venn
diagram like the one
below, compare and
contrast Canada with
the United States.

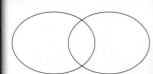

BUILD BACKGROUND

"Oh Canada we stand on guard for thee. God keep our land glorious and free." These words are from Canada's national anthem. Canada, the northernmost country in North America, is glorious in many ways. Snow-capped mountains, dense forests, frozen plains, and shining lakes make Canada a land of beauty. Canada is also a land of diversity. Many ethnic groups came to Canada from Asia, Africa, India, and Europe. Canada's two largest ethnic groups are British Canadians and French Canadians. As a result, Canada is a bilingual country, or a country of two languages.

**You Are Here
1500 – 2000**

CANADA'S LAND

Canada is the largest country in the Western Hemisphere. It is divided into ten **provinces** and three territories. A province is a territory that has its own government, like states in America.

Canada's largest region is the **Canadian Shield** in central Canada. Carved out by glaciers long ago, it divides the eastern and western parts of the country. East of the Canadian Shield are the Appalachian Highlands. This region has wooded hills.

The most populated region is the **Great Lakes—St. Lawrence Lowlands**. Because this area has fertile soil and mild climate, nine out of ten Canadians live here.

West of the Canadian Shield lies the Interior Plains. It has some of the best farmland in Canada. The Western Mountain Region is located between the Interior Plains and the Pacific Ocean. The winters are long and harsh here. North of the Canadian Shield is the frozen Arctic North.

READING CHECK What are Canada's major physical regions?

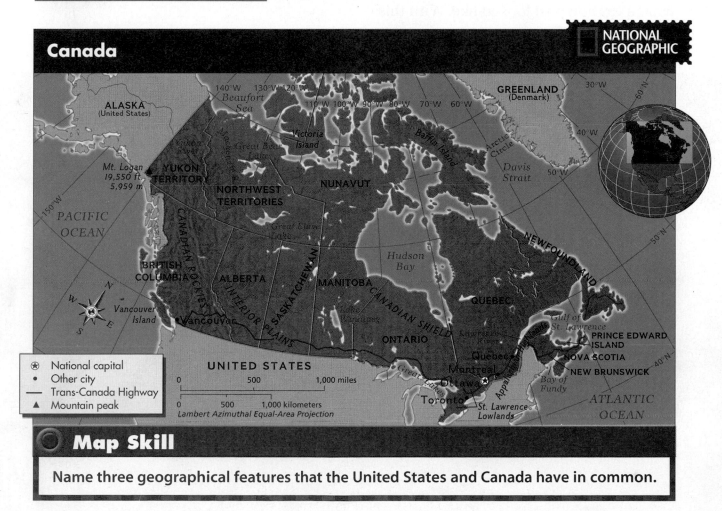

Canada

NATIONAL GEOGRAPHIC

- ✪ National capital
- • Other city
- — Trans-Canada Highway
- ▲ Mountain peak

0   500   1,000 miles
0   500   1,000 kilometers
Lambert Azimuthal Equal-Area Projection

Map Skill

Name three geographical features that the United States and Canada have in common.

CANADA'S PAST

As you read in Chapter 5, the explorer Jacques Cartier first reached Canada in 1534. Cartier was looking for a sea route to Asia. Instead he saw a land that was rich in fish, forests, and fur.

French Canada

In 1608 Samuel de Champlain started the colony of New France in the Great Lakes—St. Lawrence Lowlands. The colony grew wealthy from the fur trade. Most of the traders who ran the Canadian trading posts were French. But soon the British trade began to cut into the market. The traders bought furs from the Indian and European trappers and sent the furs to large settlements on the St. Lawrence River. The diagram on this page shows what a trading post looked like. With this success came conflict with Great Britain's colonies to the south. As you know, France lost all of its land in Canada to Britain when they lost the French and Indian War. However, French colonists in Canada were uneasy with their new rulers. Britain tried to gain their loyalty by letting them keep their language and laws.

After the American Revolution many American Loyalists moved to Canada. Most settled in the Great Lakes-St. Lawrence Lowlands. These English-speaking newcomers did not like living with French Canadians. As a result, Britain divided this region into two new colonies in 1791. The colony of Quebec was mostly French. The colony of Ontario was mostly English.

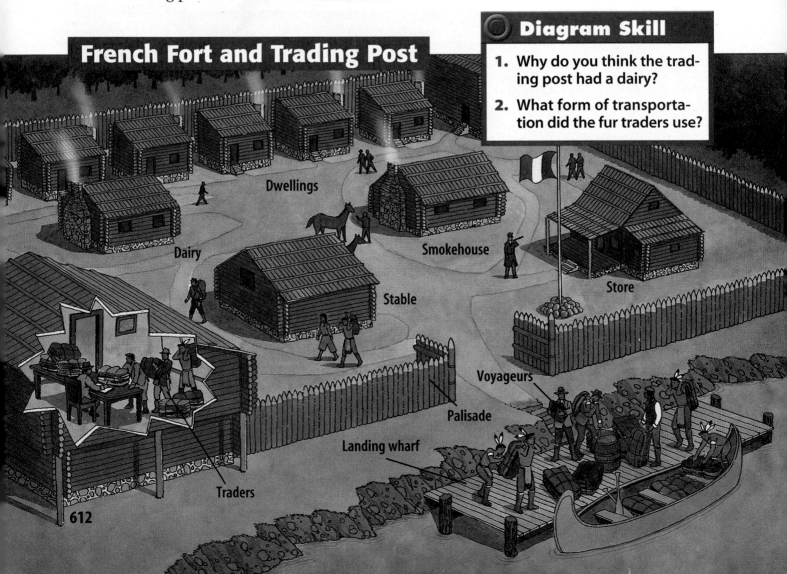

French Fort and Trading Post

Dwellings

Dairy

Smokehouse

Store

Stable

Voyageurs

Palisade

Landing wharf

Traders

Diagram Skill

1. Why do you think the trading post had a dairy?

2. What form of transportation did the fur traders use?

The Canadian Parliament (left) is in Ottawa. These Inuit children (below) live in Nunavut.

Canada, however, remained part of the British Empire. This meant that the king or queen of Britain served as Canada's head of state.

Canada Expands

In order for Canada to expand, the new government had to overcome barriers of distance and geography. As in the United States, Canada decided to build a railroad across the country. The Canadian Pacific Railway was finished in 1885 and helped unite the growing country. Today Canada has ten provinces and three territories. The most recent territory is Nunavut. Its name means "Our Land" in Inuktitut, the language of the Inuit. Carved out of the Northwest Territory in 1999, Nunavut's populaton is 85 percent Inuit.

 READING CHECK **What events helped to unite the people of Canada in the 1800s?**

War of 1812 and Self-Government

During the War of 1812 United States soldiers invaded Canada several times. French and English Canadians fought together to drive them out. Their success gave Canadians a sense of unity and shared identity. If they were capable of defending their land, why couldn't they govern themselves? In 1838, Britain slowly began allowing the Canadian colonies to become self-governing provinces.

In 1867 Britain's parliament approved the Constitution Act of 1867. This law united Ontario, Quebec, New Brunswick, and Nova Scotia into one nation. The city of Ottawa in Ontario was chosen to be their capital.

CANADIANS TODAY

Compared to its size, Canada's population is small—around 30 million people. Over three-fourths of Canada's people live in cities or towns. Montreal and Toronto are Canada's largest urban areas.

Like the United States, Canada is a nation of immigrants. In 1881 thousands of Chinese workers came to Canada to work on the Canadian Pacific Railway. Later many of them settled in the city of Vancouver. Today Vancouver's Chinatown is a favorite attraction among tourists.

The first to settle the Interior Plains were the Mennonites from Russia. Like the Quakers, the Mennonites did not believe in fighting wars. The Mennonites found religious freedom and rich land to farm in Canada. The Mennonites were soon followed by Swedes, Finns, Icelanders, Germans, Italians, Ukrainians, Jews, Poles, Czechs, Slovaks, and others. They filled the Plains with a variety of languages and cultures.

Today most Canadian immigrants are from Asia, Africa, and Latin America. Like earlier immigrants they came to Canada seeking freedom and a better life.

Canada's Native Peoples

The first Canadians were native American peoples such as the Inuit and the Cree. Today, Canada has nearly 550,000 Indians and 36,000 Inuit. Most Inuits live in Nunavut. Most of Canada's Indians belong to one of ten major groups—the Algonkian, Athapaskan, Haida, Iroquoian, Kootenayan, Salish-an, Siouan, Tlingit, Tsimshian, and Wakashan. Most live on one of the 2,200 reserves. A reserve is an area of land in Canada set aside for Indians.

British and French Canadians

The two largest ethnic groups in Canada are the British and French Canadians. They are separated not only by language, but also by religion and geography. Most French Canadians are Roman Catholic and live in Quebec. Most of the British Canadians are Protestant and live in Ontario.

In the 1960s the French in Quebec began what they called a "Quiet Revolution." They demanded the right to preserve their culture and to have more power to control Quebec's economy. Many French Canadians also talked of making Quebec a separate country.

Vancouver's Chinatown was named a historic district in 1971.

In the province of Quebec, which includes the capital, Quebec City, people primarily speak French.

PUTTING IT TOGETHER

President John F. Kennedy once told Canadians, "Geography has made us neighbors. History has made us friends. Economics has made us partners."

Canada and the United States share the world's longest undefended border. Canada is also the largest trading partner of the United States. In 1992 Canada, Mexico, and the United States signed the **North American Free Trade Agreement** (NAFTA) to boost trade among the three neighbors and to bring about greater economic interdependence.

The demands of the French Canadians caused the Canadian Constitution to be changed in 1982. It gave Canada two official languages—English and French. Every province was required to use both languages in schools and courts. Yet the movement to make Quebec a country continued. In 1995, Quebec voted to remain part of Canada.

READING CHECK

Who were the first people to settle the Interior Plains of Canada?

Review and Assess

1. Write one sentence for each vocabulary term.

   bilingual   province   NAFTA

2. How are the British and French Canadians different?

3. What are the major geographic features and ethnic groups in Canada?

4. Why do you think the Constitution of 1982 gave Canada two official languages?

5. **Compare and contrast** the geography of the United States and Canada.

Look at the map of Canada on pages R4–R5. Draw a map showing a possible water route to Asia through Canada if the ice melted in the north.

Write an essay on why you think some people in Quebec want to make it a separate country.

Mexico

Who are the people of Mexico?

Lesson Outline
- Mexico's Land
- Mexico's Past
- Mexico Today

Find out!

VOCABULARY

rain forest
mestizo

PEOPLE

Miguel Hidalgo
Benito Juárez

READING STRATEGY

Use a two column chart like the one below. Compare the different types of land in Mexico, naming each in the first column, and describing it in the second.

BUILD BACKGROUND

Mexico is the southernmost neighbor of the United States. It is also the largest Spanish-speaking country in the world. There, each year, at eleven o'clock on the night of September 15, shouts fill the air of every Mexican city and town. Mexicans are celebrating the "Call of Dolores," a speech made by a Roman Catholic priest named **Miguel Hidalgo** (mee GEL ee DAL goh). This speech inspired Mexicans to fight for independence from Spain. Mexico won its independence in 1821. Today it is a nation rich in cultures and traditions.

MEXICO'S LAND

Mexico shares a 1,900-mile border with the United States. The Rio Grande forms about half of that border.

Mexico's two main mountain ranges are the Western Sierra Madre (see ER rah MAH dre) and the Eastern Sierra Madre. Sierra Madre means "mother mountains" in Spanish. Many of Mexico's mountains are active volcanoes.

The Central Plateau is where most of Mexico's people live and its capital,

Mexico City, is located. Although Mexico City is in the tropics, it has a moderate climate because it is 7,350 feet above sea level.

In contrast, Mexico's lowland coastal plains have a tropical climate. **Rain forests** cover parts of the Yucatán Peninsula. A rain forest is a forest that receives lots of rain year round.

Where do most people in Mexico live?

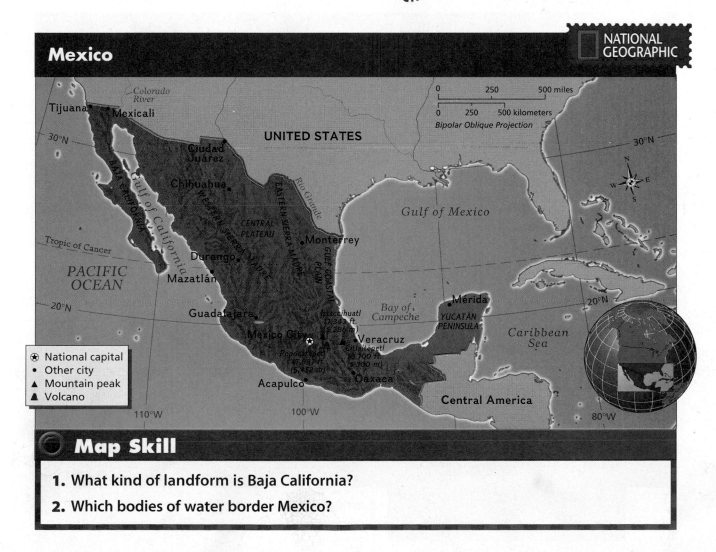

Mexico

NATIONAL GEOGRAPHIC

Legend:
- ⊛ National capital
- • Other city
- ▲ Mountain peak
- ▲ Volcano

Map Skill

1. What kind of landform is Baja California?

2. Which bodies of water border Mexico?

617

MEXICO'S PAST

As you read in Chapter 1, the first people to live in Mexico were Indians. In the Yucatán Peninsula, the Maya built stone temples and wrote books on history, science, and religion about 1,500 years ago. Later, in the 1400s the Aztec Empire spread east and west in the Central Plateau.

In 1519 Hernando Cortés met the Aztec emperor Moctezuma in Tenochtitlán. At first their meeting was friendly. But within two years Cortés and the Spaniards fought the Aztec, Moctezuma was dead, and Tenochtitlán lay in ruins. By the 1520s Spanish troops had conquered all of Mexico and most of Central America.

For the next 300 years Mexico was a Spanish colony. The king of Spain gave large grants of land to Spanish soldiers, colonists, and Catholic priests. He also allowed them to force Indians to work.

From the early days of Spanish rule, there was a mixing of different people in Mexico. Many of Cortés's soldiers married Aztec women. Their children were the first **mestizos** (mes TEE shohs). Today eight out of ten Mexicans are mestizos.

During Spanish rule, however, Indians were never treated as equals. Indians were forced to work for little or no pay. As a result, Mexico was, in the words of Daniel Cosio Villegas, "a powder keg [ready to] explode at any moment."

Archeologists excavated this Aztec sculpture in Mexico City in 1978.

Mexico Resists Spanish Rule

In 1810, that explosion came in the form of a rebellion. In the town of Dolores, a priest named Miguel Hidalgo climbed to the top of the church steps and addressed the Indians and mestizos who had gathered below. Read the excerpt from Hidalgo's famous speech, "Cry of Dolores."

The Sunday market in Tlacolula is known for its traditional Zapotec pottery.

Primary Source:

excerpt from *Cry of Dolores*
— *by Miguel Hidalgo, September 16, 1810*

It is not right that we Mexicans, having a rich and beautiful country, should remain under the rule of the [Spanish]. They treat us as slaves; we cannot speak freely or enjoy the fruits of our soil, for they own everything . . . . We must all unite and run out the [Spanish]. What do you say? Will you take arms and join me? Will you give your life, if necessary, to free your country?

What reasons did Hidalgo give for going to war against Spain?

The war against Spain lasted for 11 years and cost many lives. Finally, in 1821, Mexico won its freedom.

After the war, much of Mexico was in ruins. The country was divided between a few thousand wealthy landowners and millions of poor Indians and mestizos. For the next 100 years Mexico was torn apart by revolutions and civil wars. During that troubled time the nation lost half of its territory to the United States.

A few leaders, like President **Benito Júarez** (Be NEE toh HWAHR es), a Zapotec Indian, worked hard to improve life for all Mexicans in the middle 1800s.

Mexico's last revolution ended in 1917 with a new constitution. Mexico became a federal republic with 31 states. Since then Mexico's leaders have been elected by the people. The president serves only one six-year term.

Who are mestizos?

MEXICO TODAY

Although Mexico is in North America, it is also part of Latin America. The name "Latin America" is given to the lands in the Western Hemisphere that were settled by the Spanish and Portuguese. Latin America includes Mexico, Central America, and South America.

Mexican Culture

Today Mexico is a blend of Indian and Spanish cultures. Although Spanish is the national language, the Aztec language of Nahuatl is spoken by many Mexicans. More than 15 other Indian languages are also spoken.

Daring divers at the La Quebrada cliffs in Acapulco plunge more than 120 feet into the Pacific Ocean.

As you have read, the Spanish brought Christianity to the Indians throughout their colonies in the Americas. Today, most Mexicans are Roman Catholics. Yet many still observe Indian holidays and customs. For example, the Day of the Dead, on which Mexicans honor their dead relatives, was an important Aztec holiday.

Industry

In recent years, large companies from other countries have opened factories called *maquiladoras* (mah kee lah DOHR ahs) in Mexico. Thousands of Mexicans now work in maquiladoras, making cars, textiles, computers, and other products.

Mexico is a leading exporter of manufactured goods, oil and oil products, silver, coffee, and cotton. Nearly 90 percent of its exports go to the United States.

Tourists flock to Mexico to see its ancient Indian cities and Spanish architecture. Many come to lie on the beautiful beaches of resorts such as Acapulco. Many tourists also visit Guadalajara (gwah dah lah HAH rah), Mexico's second largest city. Guadalajara is known for its fine pottery and glassware.

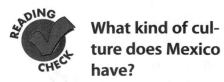

What kind of culture does Mexico have?

PUTTING IT TOGETHER

Many people who live in the Southwest and California have roots in Mexico. As a result, many of the customs and traditions of Mexico are celebrated in this region. Cinco de Mayo celebrates the victory of the Mexican army over the French on May 5, 1862. It is celebrated on a much larger scale in the United States than in Mexico.

Mexico and the United States maintain close economic ties. Since the passing of NAFTA in 1994, trade between the United States and Mexico has doubled.

The Day of the Dead (left) is a holiday that brings together Spanish and Aztec traditions. A mural at Chamizal National Memorial (above) in El Paso, Texas, celebrates the friendship between Mexico and the United States.

Review and Assess

1. Write one sentence for each vocabulary term.

   mestizo   rain forest

2. How many Indian languages are spoken in Mexico?

3. How are the people of Mexico a blend of Indian and Spanish cultures?

4. How has geography affected the **economy** of Mexico?

5. Make **conclusions** about why the Mexicans wanted independence from Spain. Explain your answer.

Look at the map of Mexico on page 617. What kind of map would you compare with this one to find a dry, warm area of Mexico? Research and compare the maps. Choose a place to vacation, then explain why you chose the area you did.

Write a paragraph explaining why you think 90 percent of Mexican exports are shipped to the United States.

621

Central America and the Caribbean

Who are the people of Central America and the Caribbean?

Lesson Outline
- The Land
- Central America and the Caribbean's Past
- Central America and the Caribbean Today

VOCABULARY

hurricane
commonwealth

PEOPLE

Toussaint
  L'Ouverture
Rigoberta
  Menchú

READING STRATEGY

Use the word map below to brainstorm. In the center, write the Caribbean Islands. In each bubble, write down the names of some of the islands that make up the Caribbean, and a fact about each.

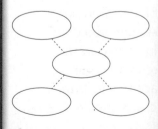

BUILD BACKGROUND

When Christopher Columbus sailed into the Caribbean Sea in 1492, he described the land as "the best and most fertile…in the world." Central America and the Caribbean Islands have a tropical climate. Columbus said it was "a land to be desired, and once seen, never to be left." Today, for many people, there is no lovelier place to live or visit. However, this region has also been rocked with earthquakes, volcanoes, and violent storms that can destroy in minutes what it took a lifetime to build.

Arenal Volcano in Costa Rica is one of several active volcanoes in Central America.

THE LAND

Many of the Caribbean Islands are made of coral reefs. Others are the tops of undersea volcanoes that reach above sea level. Most of these volcanoes are inactive. The largest islands in the Caribbean are Hispaniola, Cuba, Puerto Rico, and Jamaica.

Hurricanes are violent storms with powerful winds and enormous waves. Hurricanes have raced across the Caribbean, and sometimes Central America, destroying everything in their path.

Central America begins at the southern border of Mexico and stretches down to South America. Rugged mountains run through Central America. Large parts of Belize, Guatemala, and Honduras are covered with dense rain forests. Along the Pacific and Caribbean coasts are steamy lowlands.

READING CHECK Coral reefs and volcanoes make up what landform in the Caribbean?

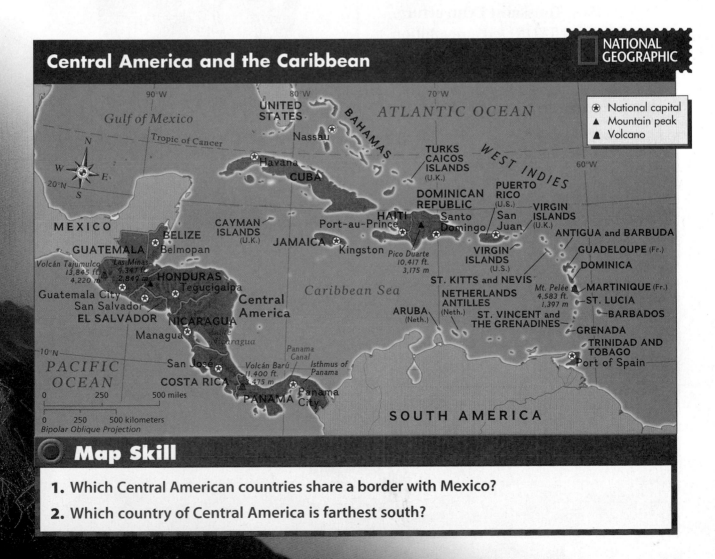

Central America and the Caribbean

NATIONAL GEOGRAPHIC

- ⊛ National capital
- ▲ Mountain peak
- ⚠ Volcano

Map Skill

1. Which Central American countries share a border with Mexico?

2. Which country of Central America is farthest south?

CENTRAL AMERICA AND THE CARIBBEAN'S PAST

Before 1492, both Central America and the Caribbean were home to different native cultures. In northern Central America, descendants of the Maya still farmed fields of corn and beans. In southern Central America many other groups got their food by farming, fishing, and hunting.

As you have read in Chapter 4 Christopher Columbus arrived in 1492. After Columbus's voyage, the Spanish and later the French, British, and Dutch set up colonies here. Planters from these countries brought enslaved people from Africa to work on their large plantations.

In the 1790s, Toussaint L'Ouverture (too SAN loo ver TYUR) led a revolution that ended slavery for Haiti and won Haiti's independence from France. In the early 1800s, slavery was abolished in Central America and the Caribbean. After that the planters brought farmworkers from China, India, and other parts of Asia to work on their plantations.

In 1821 five Central American countries became independent from Spain.

Toussaint L'Ouverture (right) ended slavery in Haiti. El Morro fort (below) guarded the entrance to San Juan Bay, Puerto Rico.

In Central America, coffee is grown on large plantations in the highlands.

Cuba and Puerto Rico were ruled by Spain until the Spanish-American War in 1898.

The British colonies were slower to break their ties with the ruling country. Jamaica was a colony until 1962. The Bahamas became independent in 1973. Belize gained its independence in 1981. The French islands of St. Barthélemy, Martinique, and Guadeloupe are not colonies, but parts of France.

Even after these countries became independent, small groups of landowners continued to control most of the wealth and power. El Salvador, for example, was once owned by 14 families. These families supported military leaders and dictators who controlled the government.

While a few families were very rich, most people were very poor and had little or no land. They survived mainly by working on plantations that grew such crops as sugar, coffee, and bananas.

In the 1980s dictators in Haiti, Panama, El Salvador, and Nicaragua were overthrown. In 1990, Haitians elected Jean-Bertrand Aristide (JAHN BAIR trahnd AH rihs teed) to be their president. Military leaders overthrew him the following year. With the help of the United States, Aristide regained his office in 1994. Today democratic governments in the region continue to gain strength as military leaders and dictators lose power.

READING CHECK Who led a revolution for Haiti's independence from France?

Rigoberta Menchú (below) has led the struggle for democratic rights for Indians in Guatemala (right).

CENTRAL AMERICA AND THE CARIBBEAN TODAY

Today the Caribbean is a blend of Indian, African, Asian, and European cultures. Calypso and reggae music, for example, are Caribbean musical styles that blend Indian, African, and European sounds and instruments. The blending of cultures has also influenced language. For example, the people of Haiti speak Haitian Creole, a mix of French and African languages.

In Central America descendants of the Maya and other Indians live in Central America. The majority of the population of Guatemala is Native American. Many people in the English-speaking country of Belize have African roots, while people in Costa Rica have mainly European roots. In Nicaragua and El Salvador, most people are mestizo.

Industry

Much of Central America and the Caribbean is dependent on agriculture. Cash crops of sugar, coffee, cacao, and cotton are grown for export. Today, many countries are becoming less dependent on agriculture. For example, food processing has become a major industry in Central American countries. Other industries produce clothing, shoes, furniture, paper, and building materials.

Because they have few mineral resources, Caribbean nations have had difficulty establishing industries. One exception, Puerto Rico, has become an important manufacturing center. Its factories produce many products, ranging from clothing to computers.

One of the most valuable industries in the Caribbean is tourism. Thousands of people work in hotels, shops, restaurants, and entertainment spots that have been built especially for tourists.

Fighting for Equal Rights

In many Central American and Caribbean countries, Indians are fighting for equal rights. In the 1970s and 1980s, thousands were killed during a civil war in Guatemala. The victims included the brother, father, and mother of a Quiche (KEE che) Indian woman named **Rigoberta Menchú**. This led Menchú to dedicate her life to helping Indians fight for their rights. For her efforts Menchú won the Nobel Peace Prize.

When she accepted the prize, Menchú said that bringing about peace is very hard work. Today, she promotes better cultural understanding by bringing together people of different ethnic backgrounds.

How has the blending of cultures influenced language in the Caribbean?

PUTTING IT TOGETHER

The United States has many economic interests in Central America and the Caribbean. Many American companies are involved in the agriculture and tourist industries of the region. The Panama Canal, built and then controlled by the United States until 2000, is an important trade route.

As you read in Chapter 17, the United States gained control of Puerto Rico during the Spanish-American War. Today, Puerto Rico is a **commonwealth** of the United States and its people are United States citizens. A commonwealth is a country or state governed by its people. Because of this relationship, many Puerto Ricans now live in the continental United States.

Review and Assess

1. Write a sentence for each vocabulary word.
   commonwealth   hurricane

2. In which countries in Central America and the Caribbean were dictators overthrown in the 1980s?

3. Who are the peoples that make up Central America and the Caribbean Islands?

4. Why do many Caribbean nations have difficulty establishing industries?

5. What **effects** did European colonization have on the peoples of Central America and the Caribbean?

Look at the map of Central America and the Caribbean on page 623. **Compare and contrast** the geography of the Caribbean Islands with the countries of Central America. Make a chart listing their similarities in one column and the way they are different in the other column.

. . . .

Write a paragraph explaining why much of Central America and the Caribbean have had military leaders and dictators.

Part 4

South America

How are the land and cultures of South America special?

Lesson Outline
- South America's Land
- South America's Past
- South America Today

VOCABULARY

favela
inflation

PEOPLE

Simón Bolívar
José de San Martín

READING STRATEGY

Use a sequence of events chart like the one below to show the steps South America took to achieve its independence.

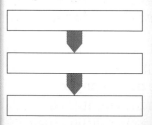

BUILD BACKGROUND

As you read in Chapter 4, Spain claimed much of South America in the 1500s. In 1810 Simón Bolívar of Venezuela began the fight to free South America from Spanish control. "I swear before God and by my honor never to allow my hands to be idle nor my soul to rest until I have broken the chains that bind us to Spain." Bolívar went on to become a hero to the people of South America, who call him "The Liberator."

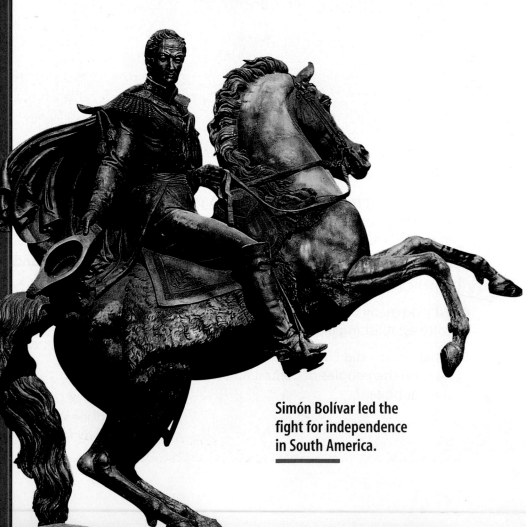

Simón Bolívar led the fight for independence in South America.

SOUTH AMERICA'S LAND

As you can see from the map on this page, South America stretches from the tropical Caribbean Sea to the cold, stormy water off Cape Horn. Much of South America is in the Southern Hemisphere. Its seasons are opposite of ones in the Northern Hemisphere. If you went to Chile (CHEE le) in December, it would be summer. If you went in July, it would be winter.

Much of South America lies in the tropics. Yet temperatures can vary greatly. In lowland areas, it is often hot. In the mountains, it can be bitterly cold.

The world's second longest river, the Amazon, flows east more than 4,000 miles from the Andes Mountains to the Atlantic Ocean. The world's largest rain forest is in Brazil's Amazon Basin.

The **Andes Mountains** stretch more than 4,000 miles along the west coast of South America. The southern plains are like our nation's Great Plains. This region is called the **Pampas**.

READING CHECK What season does Chile have in December?

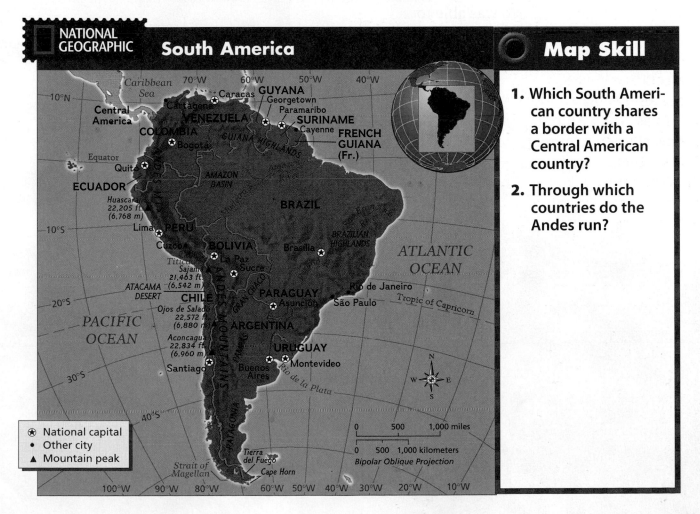

NATIONAL GEOGRAPHIC — South America

Map Skill

1. Which South American country shares a border with a Central American country?

2. Through which countries do the Andes run?

* National capital
* Other city
▲ Mountain peak

629

SOUTH AMERICA'S PAST

The Inca empire was the first great empire in South America. It rose out of a small village called Cuzco (KOOS koh) where the people grew maize and other crops in a fertile valley in what is today Peru. When drought reduced the amount of fertile farmland, the Inca took over their neighbors' land. During the 1300s the Inca ruled most of the Cuzco Valley and demanded tributes from the other people living there. Governors were appointed to each region. People from all corners of the empire were required to do jobs for the government.

Tales of gold brought Spanish conquistadors to South America. In 1531 Francisco Pizarro invaded the land of the Incas. Because there was a civil war among the Incas, Pizarro was able to defeat the Incas with 200 men. The Incan empire became the new Spanish colony of Peru.

Soon conquistadors were moving across South America. Some went north from Peru to conquer Colombia and Venezuela. Others marched south where they founded Chile. A few crossed the Andes and claimed regions that later became the countries of Paraguay, Uruguay, and Argentina.

Portugal, meanwhile, had founded Brazil, the largest colony in South America. North of Brazil, the Netherlands, Great Britain, and France each started a colony in a hot swampy region. The Dutch and British colonies became the nations of Suriname and Guyana. French Guiana today is part of France.

The Fight for Independence

Napoleon Bonaparte, the dictator of France, helped South America decide to declare independence from Spain. In 1808 Napoleon invited the king of Spain and his son to France. When they arrived, Napoleon put them both in jail. He then appointed his brother to be the king of Spain.

Spanish colonists in South America didn't want to take orders from Spanish officials who were taking orders from a French king. In 1810 Simón Bolívar started the fight for independence in Venezuela. He inspired his soldiers with the cry, "Spaniards, you will receive death at our hands! Americans, you will receive life!"

At first Bolívar suffered several defeats. These defeats, however, made him more determined. In 1819 Bolívar's army defeated a larger Spanish army in Colombia. This freed Venezuela and Colombia from Spanish rule.

In the south, **José de San Martín** of Argentina led the

Many of the massive stone walls built by the Incas still stand near Cuzco, Peru, in the Andes (left). José de San Martín (above right) crossed the Andes to defeat the Spanish.

fight. San Martín won several victories in Argentina. Yet he did not stop there. He believed that no part of South America could be free until all of it was free.

In 1817 San Martín led an army of 4,000 men through the icy peaks of the Andes Mountains into Chile. His troops quickly defeated the Spanish forces. Next he went to liberate Peru, but he was unable to break through the Spanish stronghold. Then in 1824 Simón Bolívar marched his forces into Peru and defeated the last Spanish army in South America.

Brazil

In 1822, Brazilians began talking about their own independence. A Portuguese prince named Pedro answered by raising his sword and shouting, "The hour is now! Independence or death!"

Late in 1822 the prince was crowned Dom Pedro I, Emperor of Brazil. Unlike Spain, Portugal did not resist. By 1825 it had recognized Brazil's independence.

 READING CHECK **What brought Spanish conquistadors to South America?**

SOUTH AMERICA TODAY

The Roman Catholic missionaries from Spain who first came to South America converted many of the natives to Christianity. Today most South Americans are Roman Catholics, though many have continued their traditional religious practices.

As elsewhere in Latin America, South America has many mestizos. In many countries, Europeans brought Africans by force to work on plantations. African religious beliefs, music, and dance have enriched the culture of South America.

In the 1800s and 1900s many immigrants from Europe and Asia came to South America for the same reasons they came to North America. A large number of Italians settled in Argentina and Brazil. Brazil has one of the largest Japanese communities to exist outside of Japan.

Today, the mix of cultures has given booming cities like **São Paulo** (SOW POW loh) in Brazil an international flavor. Every year thousands of people move to São Paulo, seeking opportunities.

The rich live alongside the poor people in the **favelas** (fah VAY lahz), or slums.

Economy

South America has plentiful mineral resources. Oil has helped Venezuela prosper. The Amazon rain forest is rich in minerals, timber, and other resources.

Agriculture is also a major part of the economy of South America. Colombia, for example, grows sugar, coffee, cacao, and bananas for export. The cattle industry thrives on the pampas of Argentina. Today, manufacturing and trade are important to the economies of many countries. For example, Buenos Aires (BWAY nohs I rus) in Argentina, is a major port city.

In the future, trade might increase if NAFTA is expanded to include South America. However, many South American countries

Buenos Aires has one of the largest ports in the world.

PUTTING IT TOGETHER

South America faces many challenges in the years to come. One challenge is the clearing of the vast Amazon rain forest. Environmentalists object to the clearing of the rain forest because many plants and animals will become extinct. Some of them play an important role in medical research. Clearing the rain forests is also harmful to the world's ecosystem. However, many Brazilian farmers want to clear the forest so they can farm the land, make money, and have a better life. Many of the products Brazilian farmers produce are sold to consumers in the United States at low prices. Brazil's challenge is to develop its rain forest resources without harming the ecosystem of the rain forest itself and its own economy.

have a problem with **inflation**. Inflation is a rise in the prices of goods and services. Inflation causes the value of the country's money to decline.

READING CHECK

What crops are grown in Colombia?

Tourists take canopy walks over the Brazilian rain forest (above). Soccer is the favorite sport in South America.

Review and Assess

1. Write a sentence for each vocabulary word.
   favela   inflation

2. What countries colonized South America?

3. What geographical features influence the people of South America?

4. Which blend of **cultures** are found in South America?

5. Make an **inference** about why the American Revolution was an inspiration to South American rebels against Spain.

Choose four cities you would like to visit. Then plan a road trip. Determine the distance between each city.

Write a short travel brochure that encourages people from the United States to visit South America.

VOCABULARY REVIEW

Number a sheet of paper from 1 to 5. Beside each number write the word or term from the list below that best completes the sentence.

bilingual   **province**

favela   **rain forest**

hurricane

1. A ____ is a violent storm with powerful winds and enormous waves.

2. A forest that receives lots of rain year round is known as a ____.

3. A country in which two languages are spoken is ____.

4. A ____ has its own government and is similar to a state.

5. A ____ is a South American word that means "slum," or a very poor neighborhood in a big city.

TECHNOLOGY

For more resources to help you learn more about the people and places you studied in this unit, visit **www.mhschool.com** and follow the links for Grade 5, Unit 9.

SKILL REVIEW

6. **Study Skill** Would a photograph of Jean-Bertrand Aristide be a primary or secondary source? How do you know?

7. **Study Skill** If you were to use the World Wide Web to find out what the weather is like in São Paolo, Brazil, in August, what key words would you use to search?

8. **Reading/Thinking Skill** What conclusion can you make about why the Mexicans wanted independence from Spain?

9. **Reading/Thinking Skill** *French Canadians speak a nicer form of French than the people in France do.* Is this statement a fact or opinion? How do you know?

10. **Geography Skill** If it is 6:00 p.m. in Montreal, Canada, what time is it in Mexico City?

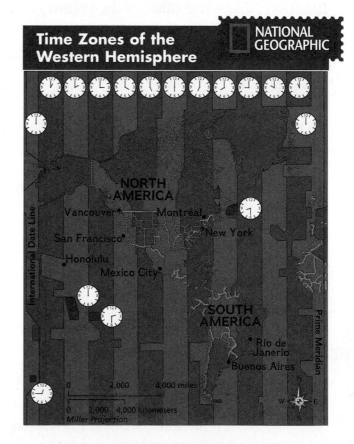

Time Zones of the Western Hemisphere

Art

- Create a travel brochure for one of the countries or regions you learned about in this unit.

- First, choose a region that you would like to focus on. Then do some research on some interesting features or sites in your region. You might choose to research a particular city in your region or a special geographical feature.

- Then fold a sheet of colored paper into three sections. On the outside fold, write the name of the place you are describing. Beneath the name draw a picture of the place.

- On the inside folds, write facts about the subject of your brochure. Explain why visitors would enjoy the place. Include pictures to make the brochure attractive.

Make a Regions Chart of the Western Hemisphere

- Create a chart of the Western Hemisphere with the columns "Region," "Geography/Climate," and "People."

- Fill in each column with as much information as you can from this unit. Also include the United States as one of your regions.

- Then illustrate your chart with drawings or pictures that relate to the information in each column. For Instance, you might want to draw a picture of a volcano when describing the geography of Central America and the Caribbean.

WRITING ACTIVITIES

Writing to Persuade Suppose you are a French-speaking resident of Quebec in 1982. *Write* a speech in which you try to persuade other Canadians that Canada should officially become a bilingual country.

Writing to Inform Suppose you lived in one of the countries described in this unit. *Write* a letter to a pen pal in the United States in which you include details of your daily life.

Writing to Express *Write* a paragraph in which you express your opinion about the North American Free Trade Agreement and the significance of trade between the United States, Canada, and Mexico.

Reference Section

The Reference Section has many parts, each with a different type of information. Use this section to look up people, places, and events as you study.

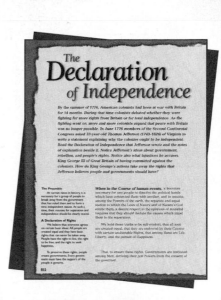

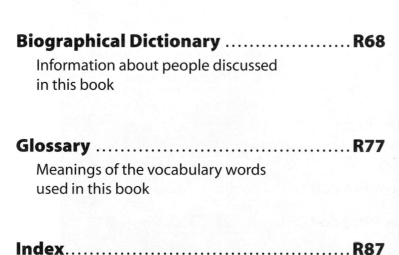

Thomas Jefferson

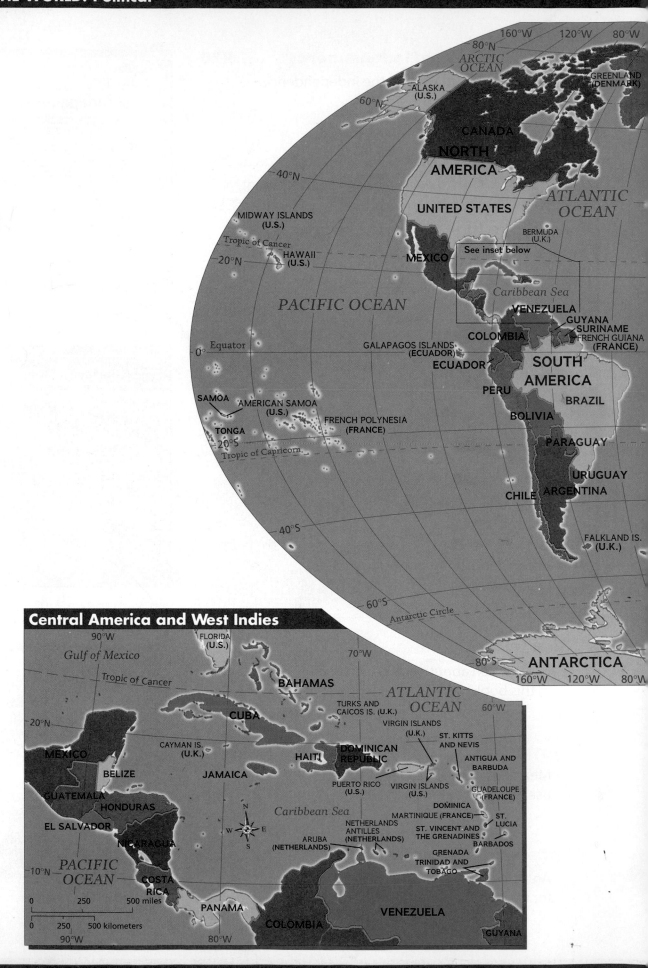

160°W 120°W 80°W
80°N
ARCTIC
OCEAN
GREENLAND
(DENMARK)
ALASKA
(U.S.)
60°N
CANADA
NORTH
AMERICA
40°N
ATLANTIC
OCEAN
UNITED STATES
MIDWAY ISLANDS
(U.S.)
BERMUDA
(U.K.)
Tropic of Cancer
See inset below
20°N
HAWAII
(U.S.)
MEXICO
Caribbean Sea
PACIFIC OCEAN
VENEZUELA
GUYANA
SURINAME
COLOMBIA
FRENCH GUIANA
(FRANCE)
GALAPAGOS ISLANDS
(ECUADOR)
0°
Equator
ECUADOR
SOUTH
AMERICA
PERU
BRAZIL
SAMOA
AMERICAN SAMOA
(U.S.)
BOLIVIA
TONGA
FRENCH POLYNESIA
(FRANCE)
PARAGUAY
20°S
Tropic of Capricorn
URUGUAY
CHILE
ARGENTINA
40°S
FALKLAND IS.
(U.K.)
60°S
Antarctic Circle
80°S
ANTARCTICA
160°W 120°W 80°W

Central America and West Indies

90°W
FLORIDA
(U.S.)
Gulf of Mexico
70°W
ATLANTIC
OCEAN
Tropic of Cancer
BAHAMAS
60°W
20°N
TURKS AND
CAICOS IS. (U.K.)
CUBA
VIRGIN ISLANDS
(U.K.)
ST. KITTS
AND NEVIS
CAYMAN IS.
(U.K.)
DOMINICAN
HAITI REPUBLIC
ANTIGUA AND
BARBUDA
MEXICO
JAMAICA
PUERTO RICO
(U.S.)
VIRGIN ISLANDS
(U.S.)
GUADELOUPE
(FRANCE)
BELIZE
DOMINICA
GUATEMALA
MARTINIQUE (FRANCE)
ST.
LUCIA
HONDURAS
Caribbean Sea
NETHERLANDS
ANTILLES
(NETHERLANDS)
ST. VINCENT AND
THE GRENADINES
EL SALVADOR
N
ARUBA
(NETHERLANDS)
BARBADOS
W E
NICARAGUA
GRENADA
S
TRINIDAD AND
TOBAGO
10°N
PACIFIC
OCEAN
COSTA
RICA
0 250 500 miles
PANAMA
VENEZUELA
0 250 500 kilometers
COLOMBIA
GUYANA
90°W
80°W

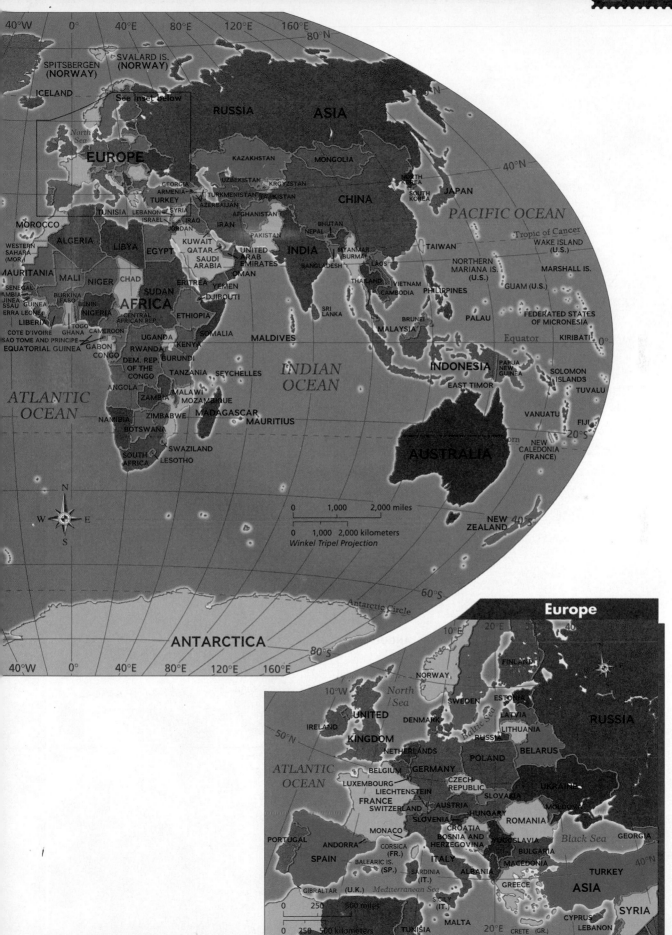

NATIONAL
GEOGRAPHIC

40°W   0°   40°E   80°E   120°E   160°E

80°N

SPITSBERGEN
(NORWAY)

SVALARD IS.
(NORWAY)

ICELAND

See inset below

North Sea

RUSSIA   ASIA

EUROPE

KAZAKHSTAN

MONGOLIA

40°N

GEORGIA
ARMENIA
TURKEY
TUNISIA   LEBANON
ISRAEL   SYRIA
JORDAN
IRAQ

UZBEKISTAN   KRGYZSTAN
TURKMENISTAN   TAJIKISTAN
AZERBAIJAN
AFGHANISTAN

NORTH
KOREA
SOUTH
KOREA

JAPAN

PACIFIC OCEAN

MOROCCO

ALGERIA

LIBYA

EGYPT

IRAN

PAKISTAN

CHINA

INDIA

BHUTAN
NEPAL

MYANMAR
(BURMA)

TAIWAN

Tropic of Cancer

WAKE ISLAND
(U.S.)

WESTERN
SAHARA
(MOR.)

MAURITANIA

MALI

NIGER

CHAD

SUDAN

KUWAIT
QATAR
SAUDI
ARABIA

UNITED
ARAB
EMIRATES

OMAN

YEMEN

BANGLADESH

LAOS

THAILAND

VIETNAM

CAMBODIA

PHILIPPINES

NORTHERN
MARIANA IS.
(U.S.)

GUAM (U.S.)

MARSHALL IS.

SENEGAL
AMBIA
JINEA
SSAU   GUINEA
ERRA LEONE

LIBERIA

BURKINA
FASO

BENIN

NIGERIA

ERITREA

DJIBOUTI

ETHIOPIA

AFRICA

CENTRAL
AFRICAN REP.

SRI
LANKA

MALDIVES

BRUNEI

MALAYSIA

PALAU

FEDERATED STATES
OF MICRONESIA

COTE D'IVOIRE
SAO TOME AND PRINCIPE
EQUATORIAL GUINEA

TOGO
GHANA

CAMEROON

GABON

CONGO

RWANDA
BURUNDI

UGANDA

KENYA

DEM. REP.
OF THE
CONGO

SOMALIA

TANZANIA

SEYCHELLES

Equator

INDONESIA

PAPUA
NEW
GUINEA

KIRIBATI

SOLOMON
ISLANDS

0°

ANGOLA

ZAMBIA

MALAWI
MOZAMBIQUE

INDIAN
OCEAN

EAST TIMOR

TUVALU

ATLANTIC
OCEAN

NAMIBIA

BOTSWANA

ZIMBABWE

MADAGASCAR

MAURITIUS

VANUATU

FIJI

NEW
CALEDONIA
(FRANCE)

20°S

SOUTH
AFRICA

SWAZILAND

LESOTHO

AUSTRALIA

N
W   E
S

0   1,000   2,000 miles

0   1,000   2,000 kilometers
Winkel Tripel Projection

NEW
ZEALAND

40°S

60°S

Antarctic Circle

ANTARCTICA

80°S

40°W   0°   40°E   80°E   120°E   160°E

Europe

10°E   20°E   40°

FINLAND

NORWAY

SWEDEN

ESTONIA

RUSSIA

North
Sea

UNITED
KINGDOM

DENMARK

LATVIA

LITHUANIA

Baltic Sea

RUSSIA

BELARUS

IRELAND

ATLANTIC
OCEAN

50°N

NETHERLANDS

BELGIUM

LUXEMBOURG

GERMANY

POLAND

LIECHTENSTEIN

FRANCE

SWITZERLAND

CZECH
REPUBLIC

SLOVAKIA

AUSTRIA

HUNGARY

SLOVENIA

UKRAINE

MOLDOVA

ROMANIA

MONACO

CROATIA

PORTUGAL

ANDORRA

CORSICA
(FR.)

BOSNIA AND
HERZEGOVINA

YUGOSLAVIA

Black Sea

GEORGIA

BULGARIA

SPAIN

BALEARIC IS.
(SP.)

SARDINIA
(IT.)

ITALY

MACEDONIA

ALBANIA

TURKEY

40°N

GIBRALTAR   (U.K.)   Mediterranean Sea

GREECE

SICILY
(IT.)

ASIA

SYRIA

0   250   500 miles

0   250   500 kilometers

TUNISIA

MALTA

20°E

CRETE
(GR.)

CYPRUS

LEBANON

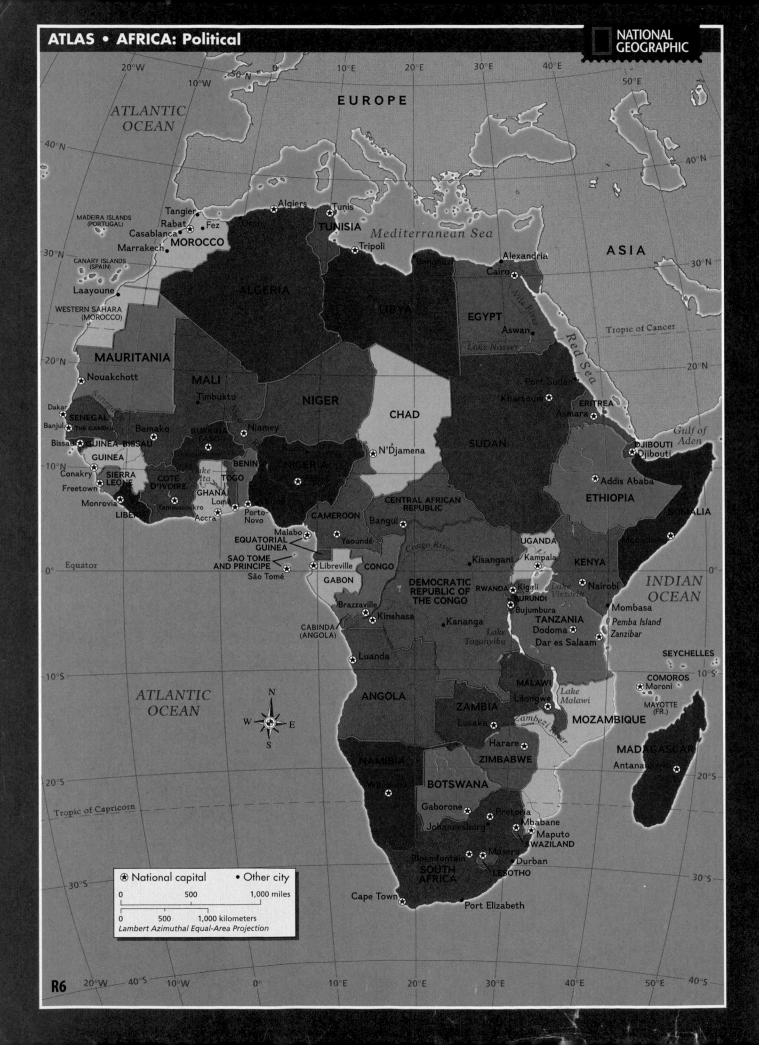

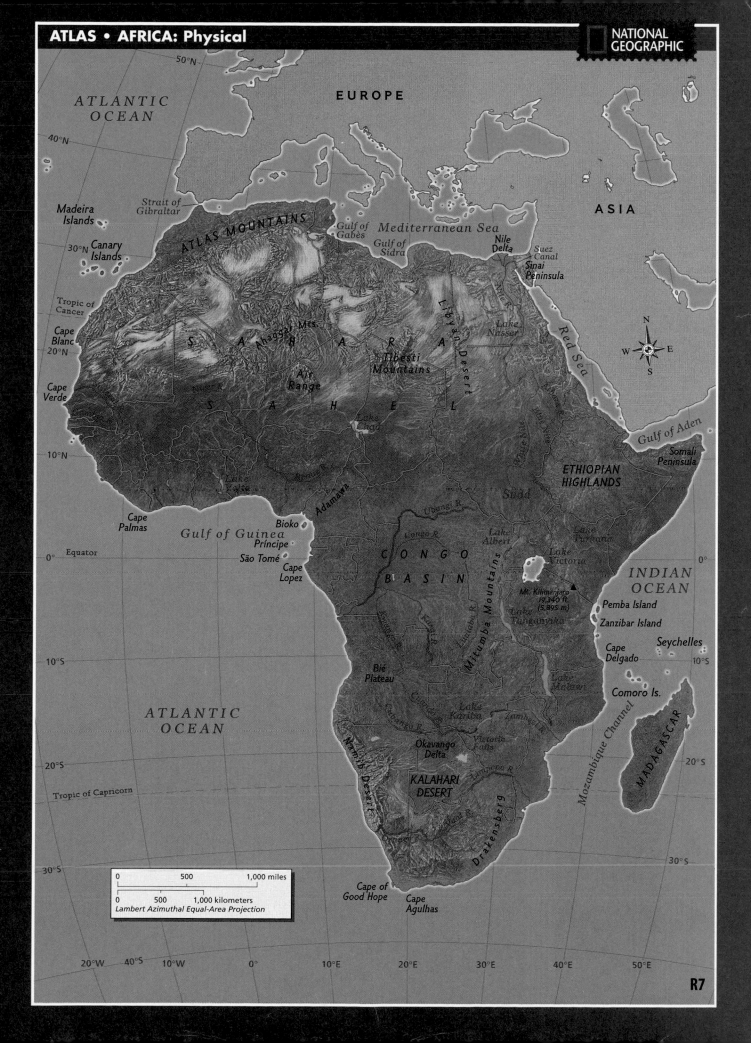

NATIONAL GEOGRAPHIC

EUROPE

ATLANTIC OCEAN

ASIA

Madeira Islands

Strait of Gibraltar

ATLAS MOUNTAINS

Gulf of Gabès

Mediterranean Sea

Nile Delta

Suez Canal

Sinai Peninsula

Canary Islands

Gulf of Sidra

Tropic of Cancer

Cape Blanc

S A H A R A

Ahaggar Mts.

Tibesti Mountains

Libyan Desert

Nile R.

Lake Nasser

Red Sea

N
W E
S

Air Range

Cape Verde

S A H E L

Niger R.

Lake Chad

White Nile

Blue Nile

Gulf of Aden

Somali Peninsula

Cape Palmas

Gulf of Guinea

Bioko

Príncipe

São Tomé

Cape Lopez

Benue R.

Lake Volta

Adamawa

Ubangi R.

Congo R.

Lake Albert

Lake Turkana

ETHIOPIAN HIGHLANDS

Sudd

Equator

C O N G O
B A S I N

Lake Victoria

INDIAN OCEAN

Mitumba Mountains

Mt. Kilimanjaro 19,340 ft (5,895 m)

Pemba Island

Zanzibar Island

Lukuga R.

Lake Tanganyika

Cape Delgado

Seychelles

Kasai R.

Bié Plateau

Cuanza R.

Comoro Is.

ATLANTIC OCEAN

Cuango R.

Cubango R.

Lake Kariba

Zambezi R.

Lake Malawi

MADAGASCAR

Mozambique Channel

Namib Desert

Okavango Delta

Victoria Falls

Limpopo R.

KALAHARI DESERT

Drakensberg

Orange R.

Tropic of Capricorn

Cape of Good Hope

Cape Agulhas

0   500   1,000 miles
0 500 1,000 kilometers
Lambert Azimuthal Equal-Area Projection

NATIONAL
GEOGRAPHIC

1,000 miles
1,000 kilometers
500
500
Two-Point Equidistant Projection

PACIFIC OCEAN

ARCTIC OCEAN

North Pole

ATLANTIC OCEAN

EUROPE

AFRICA

AUSTRALIA

New Guinea

Arafura Sea

INDIAN OCEAN

Equator

Tropic of Cancer

Bering Sea

KAMCHATKA PENINSULA

Kuril Islands

Hokkaido

Honshu

Shikoku
Kyushu

Sea of Okhotsk

Sakhalin

Sea of Japan

SIKHOTE ALIN RANGE

KOLYMA RANGE

CHUKCHI RANGE

Wrangel Island

East Siberian Sea

CHERSKIY RANGE

VERKHOYANSK RANGE

YABLONOVYY RANGE
STANOVOY RANGE

GREATER KHINGAN RANGE

Manchurian Plain

Yellow Sea

East China Sea

Taiwan

Hainan

South China Sea

Gulf of Tonkin

Philippine Islands

Philippine Sea

Celebes Sea

Celebes (Sulawesi)

Borneo

Java Sea

Java

Sumatra

Strait of Malacca

Gulf of Thailand

INDOCHINA PENINSULA

North China Plain

QIN LING

GOBI

Mongolian Plateau

Lake Baikal

ALTAY MOUNTAINS

TIAN SHAN

Turpan Depression
-505 ft
(-154 m)

Tarim Basin

TAKLIMAKAN DESERT

ALTUN SHAN

KUNLUN MOUNTAINS

Plateau of Tibet

HIMALAYA

Mt. Everest
29,028 ft.
(8,848 m)

SIBERIA

CENTRAL SIBERIAN PLATEAU

WEST SIBERIAN PLAIN

Taymyr Peninsula

New Siberian Islands

Laptev Sea

Kara Sea

Yamal Peninsula

Yenisey R.

Angara R.

Ob R.

Irtysh

Lena R.

URAL MOUNTAINS

Ural R.

Kazakh Uplands

KIRGHIZ STEPPE

Lake Balkhash

Aral Sea

Syr Darya

Ustyurt Plateau

HINDU KUSH

Amu Darya

Indus R.

Great Indian Desert

Ganges R.

Brahmaputra R.

Indian Subcontinent

DECCAN PLATEAU

WESTERN GHATS

EASTERN GHATS

Bay of Bengal

Andaman Islands

Andaman Sea

Nicobar Islands

Sri Lanka

Maldive Islands

Lakshadweep

Arabian Sea

Socotra

Gulf of Aden

Gulf of Oman

Persian Gulf

PLATEAU OF IRAN

ZAGROS MOUNTAINS

Tigris R.

Euphrates R.

Mesopotamia

Syrian Desert

Nafud

ARABIAN PENINSULA

Rub al Khali

Red Sea

ANATOLIA (ASIA MINOR)

Bosporus

Black Sea

Sea of Azov

Mediterranean Sea

Caspian Sea

Kura R.

N
E
S
W

R9

ATLANTIC OCEAN

ARCTIC OCEAN

Arctic Circle

Barents Sea

ICELAND
Reykjavik

FAROE ISLANDS (DEN.)

SHETLAND ISLANDS (U.K.)

NORWAY
Bergen
Oslo
Narvik

SWEDEN
Göteborg
Stockholm

FINLAND
Helsinki

RUSSIA
Murmansk
Arkhangelsk
St. Petersburg
Moscow
Kazan
Volga

North Sea

UNITED KINGDOM
Glasgow
Edinburgh
Liverpool
London

IRELAND
Belfast
Dublin

DENMARK
Copenhagen

Baltic Sea

ESTONIA
Tallinn

LATVIA
Riga

LITHUANIA
Vilnius
Kaliningrad

RUSS.

BELARUS
Minsk

POLAND
Warsaw
Lodz
Wroclaw

GERMANY
Hamburg
Berlin
Essen
Cologne
Bonn
Leipzig
Dresden
Munich

NETHERLANDS
Amsterdam

BELGIUM
Brussels

LUXEMBOURG
Luxembourg

FRANCE
Le Havre
Paris
Nantes
Bordeaux
Lyon
Marseille

Bay of Biscay

SPAIN
Bilbao
Madrid
Valencia
Seville
Barcelona
Cartagena

PORTUGAL
Porto
Lisbon

ANDORRA
Andorra la Vella

GIBRALTAR (U.K.)

BALEARIC ISLANDS (SP.)

SWITZERLAND
Zurich
Bern

LIECHTENSTEIN
Vaduz

AUSTRIA
Vienna

CZECH REPUBLIC
Prague
Brno

SLOVAKIA
Bratislava

HUNGARY
Budapest

SLOVENIA
Ljubljana

CROATIA
Zagreb

ITALY
Milan
Venice
Florence
Rome
Naples

MONACO
Monaco

CORSICA (FR.)

SARDINIA (IT.)

SICILY (IT.)

MALTA
Valletta

BOSNIA AND HERZEGOVINA
Sarajevo

YUGOSLAVIA
Belgrade

ALBANIA
Tirana

MACEDONIA
Skopje

GREECE
Athens
Thessaloniki

CRETE (GR.)

Mediterranean Sea

ROMANIA
Bucharest

MOLDOVA
Chisinau

UKRAINE
Odesa

BULGARIA
Sofia

Black Sea

Caspian Sea

ASIA

URAL MOUNTAINS

Volga River

Caspian Sea

Barents Sea

KOLA PENINSULA

White Sea

LAPLAND

Northern Dvina R.

Don River

Dnieper River

CAUCASUS MTS.

Mt. Elbrus
18,510 ft.
(5,642 m)

Sea of Azov

Black Sea

500 miles
500 kilometers
Lambert Azimuthal Equidistant Projection
0   250   500
0   250   500

BALTIC PLAINS

Gulf of Bothnia

SCANDINAVIAN PENINSULA

Lofoten Islands

ARCTIC OCEAN

Gulf of Finland

Baltic Sea

W. Dvina R.

Vistula R.

Oder River

NORTHERN EUROPEAN PLAIN

CARPATHIAN MTS.

Dniester River

Dniester River

Danube River

Danube River

BALKAN PENINSULA

Aegean Sea

Rhodes

30°E

Crete

Mediterranean Sea

20°E

Ionian Sea

ITALIAN PENINSULA

Adriatic Sea

APENNINES

Tyrrhenian Sea

Maltese Islands

Elbe River

ALPS

Po River

Mt. Blanc
15,771 ft.
(4,807 m)

JURA MTS.

Rhine R.

Rhine River

Corsica

Sardinia

Rhône River

Balearic Islands

PYRENEES

Garonne R.

Ebro River

Bay of Biscay

IBERIAN PENINSULA

Tagus River

English Channel

Celtic Sea

British Isles

North Sea

Jutland Peninsula

Faroe Islands

Shetland Islands

Norwegian Sea

Arctic Circle

Iceland

40°W

30°W

20°W

10°W

0°

10°E

20°E

30°E

40°E

50°E

60°N

70°N

40°N

70°N

ATLANTIC OCEAN

AFRICA

Strait of Gibraltar

N
E
S
W

R11

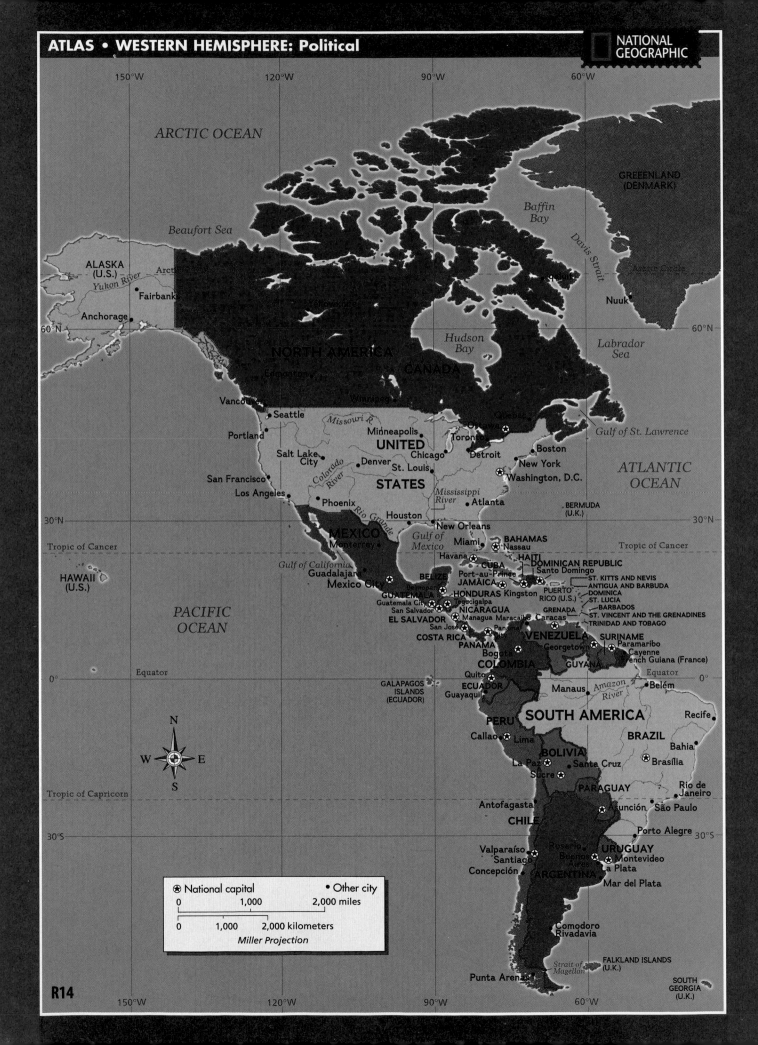

NATIONAL GEOGRAPHIC

ARCTIC OCEAN

GREENLAND (DENMARK)

Baffin Bay

Davis Strait

Arctic Circle

ALASKA (U.S.)

Yukon River

Arctic

Fairbanks

Anchorage

Beaufort Sea

60°N

Nuuk

60°N

Labrador Sea

NORTH AMERICA

Hudson Bay

CANADA

Edmonton

Yellowknife

Vancouver

Winnipeg

Seattle

Quebec

Gulf of St. Lawrence

Portland

Missouri R.

Minneapolis

Ottawa

Toronto

Boston

UNITED

Chicago

Detroit

New York

ATLANTIC OCEAN

Salt Lake City

Denver

St. Louis

Washington, D.C.

Colorado River

San Francisco

STATES

Los Angeles

Phoenix

Mississippi River

Atlanta

BERMUDA (U.K.)

30°N

Houston

30°N

Tropic of Cancer

New Orleans

Tropic of Cancer

Gulf of Mexico

Miami

BAHAMAS

HAWAII (U.S.)

MEXICO

Monterrey

Nassau

Havana

CUBA

HAITI

DOMINICAN REPUBLIC

Gulf of California

Santo Domingo

ST. KITTS AND NEVIS

Guadalajara

BELIZE

Port-au-Prince

PUERTO

ANTIGUA AND BARBUDA

PACIFIC OCEAN

Mexico City

Belmopan

JAMAICA

Kingston

RICO (U.S.)

DOMINICA

GUATEMALA

ST. LUCIA

Guatemala City

HONDURAS

Tegucigalpa

BARBADOS

San Salvador

NICARAGUA

GRENADA

ST. VINCENT AND THE GRENADINES

EL SALVADOR

Managua

Maracaibo

TRINIDAD AND TOBAGO

San José

Caracas

COSTA RICA

Panama

PANAMA

VENEZUELA

SURINAME

Paramaribo

Bogotá

Georgetown

Cayenne

Equator

COLOMBIA

GUYANA

French Guiana (France)

Equator

GALÁPAGOS ISLANDS (ECUADOR)

Quito

ECUADOR

Manaus

Amazon River

Belém

Guayaquil

SOUTH AMERICA

Recife

PERU

BRAZIL

Callao

Lima

Bahia

La Paz

BOLIVIA

Brasília

Santa Cruz

Sucre

Rio de Janeiro

Tropic of Capricorn

PARAGUAY

Antofagasta

Asunción

São Paulo

CHILE

Porto Alegre

30°S

30°S

Valparaíso

Rosario

URUGUAY

Santiago

Buenos Aires

Montevideo

Concepción

La Plata

ARGENTINA

Mar del Plata

⊛ National capital • Other city

0   1,000   2,000 miles

0   1,000   2,000 kilometers

Miller Projection

Comodoro Rivadavia

FALKLAND ISLANDS (U.K.)

Punta Arenas

Strait of Magellan

SOUTH GEORGIA (U.K.)

150°W   120°W   90°W   60°W

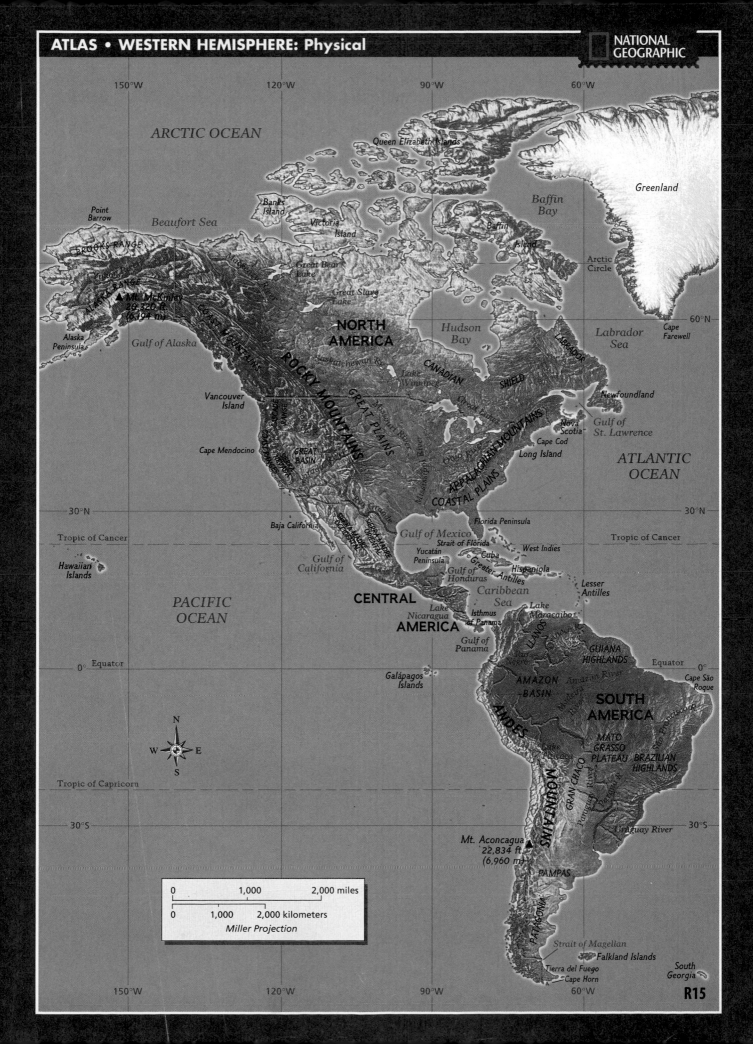

150°W 120°W 90°W 60°N

ARCTIC OCEAN

Queen Elizabeth Islands

Greenland

Banks Island

Point Barrow

Beaufort Sea

Victoria Island

Baffin Bay

Baffin Island

BROOKS RANGE

Great Bear Lake

Arctic Circle

Yukon River

Mackenzie River

ALASKA RANGE

▲ Mt. McKinley 20,320 ft (6,194 m)

Great Slave Lake

60°N

Alaska Peninsula

Gulf of Alaska

NORTH AMERICA

Hudson Bay

Labrador Sea

Cape Farewell

Saskatchewan R.

COAST MOUNTAINS

Lake Winnipeg

CANADIAN

LABRADOR

Vancouver Island

ROCKY MOUNTAINS

GREAT PLAINS

Missouri River

SHIELD

Newfoundland

Nova Scotia

Gulf of St. Lawrence

Cape Mendocino

COAST RANGES

SIERRA NEVADA

GREAT BASIN

Colorado R.

Ohio River

Mississippi River

APPALACHIAN MOUNTAINS

Cape Cod

Long Island

ATLANTIC OCEAN

COASTAL PLAINS

30°N

Rio Grande

Florida Peninsula

30°N

Tropic of Cancer

Baja California

SIERRA MADRE OCCIDENTAL

SIERRA MADRE ORIENTAL

Gulf of Mexico

Strait of Florida

Cuba

West Indies

Tropic of Cancer

Hawaiian Islands

Gulf of California

Yucatán Peninsula

Greater Antilles

Hispaniola

PACIFIC OCEAN

Gulf of Honduras

CENTRAL

Lake Nicaragua

Caribbean Sea

Lesser Antilles

Lake Maracaibo

AMERICA

Isthmus of Panama

Gulf of Panama

LLANOS

Orinoco

GUIANA HIGHLANDS

Equator

Equator

0°

Galápagos Islands

Rio Negro

AMAZON BASIN

Amazon River

Cape São Roque

SOUTH AMERICA

São Francisco R.

Madeira River

ANDES MOUNTAINS

MATO GRASSO PLATEAU

BRAZILIAN HIGHLANDS

Lake Titicaca

Tropic of Capricorn

N
W E
S

GRAN CHACO

Paraguay River

Paraná R.

30°S

Uruguay River

30°S

Mt. Aconcagua 22,834 ft (6,960 m) ▲

PAMPAS

0 1,000 2,000 miles

PATAGONIA

0 1,000 2,000 kilometers

Miller Projection

Strait of Magellan

Tierra del Fuego

Falkland Islands

South Georgia

Cape Horn

150°W 120°W 90°W 60°W

ARCTIC OCEAN

RUSSIA

180°
170°W
160°W
150°W
140°W
130°W

Nome
Fairbanks
ALASKA
CANADA
Anchorage
Juneau

Arctic Circle

PACIFIC OCEAN

Yukon River

0   250   500 miles
0   250   500 kilometers

CANADA

70°N
60°N
50°N
40°N
30°N
20°N

120°W
110°W
130°W

Seattle
Spokane
WASHINGTON
Olympia

Great Falls
Helena
MONTANA
Billings

Columbia River

Portland
Salem
Eugene
OREGON

IDAHO
Boise

Snake River
Pocatello

WYOMING
Casper
Cheyenne

Reno
Carson City
NEVADA

Ogden
Salt Lake City
Provo
UTAH

Great Salt Lake

Denver
Colorado Springs
Pueblo
COLORADO

San Francisco
Oakland
Sacramento
San Jose

Las Vegas

Santa Fe

PACIFIC OCEAN

CALIFORNIA

Los Angeles
Long Beach

San Diego

ARIZONA
Phoenix

Albuquerque
NEW MEXICO

Tucson

El Paso

MEXICO

160°W
155°W
Kauai
Niihau
Oahu
Honolulu
Molokai
Lanai
Maui
Kahoolawe
PACIFIC OCEAN
HAWAII
Hilo
Hawaii
20°N

0   100   200 miles
0   100   200 kilometers

N
W   E
S

CANADA

NORTH DAKOTA
Grand Forks
Fargo
★ Bismarck

SOUTH DAKOTA
★ Pierre
Sioux Falls

MINNESOTA
Duluth
Minneapolis
★ St. Paul

Lake Superior

WISCONSIN
Green Bay
Milwaukee
Madison ★

MICHIGAN
Lake Michigan
Grand Rapids
★ Lansing
Detroit

Lake Huron

CANADA

MAINE
★ Augusta

VERMONT
Montpelier ★

NEW HAMPSHIRE
Concord ★

L. Ontario

NEW YORK
Buffalo
Albany ★
Boston ★
MASSACHUSETTS
Providence
Hartford ★
RHODE ISLAND

Lake Erie
Cleveland

PENNSYLVANIA
Harrisburg ★
Pittsburgh
Philadelphia

New York
Trenton ★ CONNECTICUT
NEW JERSEY
Dover ★ DELAWARE
40°N
70°W

NEBRASKA
Omaha
Lincoln ★

IOWA
Cedar Rapids
Des Moines ★

ILLINOIS
Chicago
Davenport
Gary
Springfield ★

INDIANA
Indianapolis ★
Cincinnati

OHIO
Toledo
Columbus ★

Platte River

KANSAS
Topeka ★
Wichita

Kansas City

MISSOURI
Kansas City
Jefferson City ★
St. Louis

Arkansas River

Louisville
Evansville

KENTUCKY
Frankfort ★

WEST VIRGINIA
Charleston ★

Washington D.C. ★
Annapolis ★ MARYLAND

Richmond ★
VIRGINIA
Norfolk

OKLAHOMA
Tulsa
Oklahoma City ★

ARKANSAS
Fort Smith
Little Rock ★

TENNESSEE
Nashville ★
Knoxville
Memphis

NORTH CAROLINA
Raleigh ★
Charlotte

SOUTH CAROLINA
Columbia ★
Charleston

ATLANTIC OCEAN

TEXAS
Dallas
Fort Worth
Austin ★
San Antonio
Houston
Corpus Christi
Laredo

MISSISSIPPI
Jackson ★

LOUISIANA
Shreveport
Baton Rouge ★
New Orleans
Biloxi

ALABAMA
Montgomery ★
Mobile

GEORGIA
Atlanta ★
Columbus
Savannah

FLORIDA
Jacksonville
Tallahassee ★
Tampa
Miami

30°N

Gulf of Mexico

BAHAMAS

CUBA

⊛ National capital   ★ State capital   • Other city

0   150   300 miles
0   150   300 kilometers
Lambert Azimuthal Equal-Area Projection

100°W   90°W   80°W

ARCTIC OCEAN

RUSSIA

BROOKS RANGE

ALASKA
Mt. McKinley
20,320 ft.
(6,194 m)
ALASKA RANGE

CANADA

Bering
Srait

Bering
Sea

0   250   500 miles
0   250   500 kilometers

170°W   160°W   150°W   140°W

CANADA

60°N

Puget
Sound

Mt. Rainier
14,410 ft.
(4,392 m)

Mt. St. Helens
8,363 ft.
(2,549 m)

ROCKY

Granite Peak
12,799 ft.
(3,901 m)

BLACK
HILLS

40°N

COAST RANGES

CASCADE RANGE

Mt. Hood
11,239 ft.
(3,426 m)

COLUMBIA PLATEAU

MOUNTAINS

GREAT PLAINS

Cape Mendocino

Mt. Shasta
14,162 ft.
(4,317 m)

Great
Salt
Lake

Kings Peak
13,528 ft.
(4,123 m)

San Francisco Bay

COAST

SIERRA NEVADA

CENTRAL VALLEY

GREAT
BASIN

GREAT
SALT LAKE
DESERT

WASATCH RANGE

Pikes Peak
14,110 ft.
(4,301 m)

Mt. Elbert
(14,433 ft.
(4,399 m)

PACIFIC OCEAN

RANGES

Mt. Whitney
14,494 ft.
(4,418 m)

Death Valley
-282 ft.
(-86 m)

MOJAVE
DESERT

Lake
Mead

COLORADO
PLATEAU

30°N

Salton
Sea

SONORAN
DESERT

Humphreys Peak
12,633 ft.
(3,851 m)

Wheeler Peak
13,161 ft.
(4,011 m)

Gila River

Guadalupe Peak
8,749 ft.
(2,667 m)

130°W

PACIFIC
OCEAN

Kauai

Oahu

Maui

HAWAII   Hawaii

Mauna Kea
13,796 ft.
(4,205 m)

0   100   200 miles
0   100   200 kilometers

160°W   155°W

20°N

MEXICO

Gulf of California

R18

120°W   110°W

CANADA

Lake of the Woods

MESABI RANGE

Lake Superior

G R E A T   L A K E S

Lake Michigan

Lake Huron

St. Lawrence River

L. Ontario

Lake Erie

ADIRONDACK MTS.

GREEN MTS.

WHITE MTS.

Mt. Washington
6,288 ft.
(1,917 m)

Cape Cod

Long Island

40°N

ALLEGHENY PLATEAU

ALLEGHENY MTS.

APPALACHIAN MOUNTAINS

PIEDMONT

Delaware Bay

Chesapeake Bay

ATLANTIC COASTAL PLAIN

Cape Hatteras

CENTRAL   PLAINS

Missouri River

Platte River

Wabash River

Ohio River

Mt. Mitchell
6,684 ft
(2,037 m)

INTERIOR PLAINS

OZARK PLATEAU

OUACHITA MOUNTAINS

Mississippi River

ATLANTIC OCEAN

30°N

EDWARDS PLATEAU

GULF COASTAL PLAIN

Mobile Bay

Galveston Bay

Mississippi Delta

Lake Okeechobee

BAHAMAS

Gulf of Mexico

Florida Keys

Straits of Florida

CUBA

0   150   300 miles
0   150   300 kilometers
Lambert Azimuthal Equal-Area Projection

90°W

80°W

The Declaration of Independence

By the summer of 1776, American colonists had been at war with Britain for 14 months. During that time colonists debated whether they were fighting for more rights from Britain or for total independence. As the fighting went on, more and more colonists argued that peace with Britain was no longer possible. In June 1776 members of the Second Continental Congress asked 33-year-old Thomas Jefferson (1743–1826) of Virginia to write a statement explaining why the colonies ought to be independent. Read the Declaration of Independence that Jefferson wrote and the notes of explanation beside it. Notice Jefferson's ideas about government, rebellion, and people's rights. Notice also what injustices he accuses King George III of Great Britain of having committed against the colonists. How do King George's actions take away the rights that Jefferson believes people and governments should have?

The Preamble

At certain times in history, it is necessary for a group of people to break away from the government that has ruled them and to form a new, independent nation. At such a time, their reasons for separation and independence should be clearly stated.

When in the course of human events, it becomes necessary for one people to dissolve the political bands which have connected them with another, and to assume, among the Powers of the earth, the separate and equal station to which the Laws of Nature and of Nature's God entitle them, a decent respect to the opinions of mankind requires that they should declare the causes which impel them to the separation.

A Declaration of Rights

We believe that everyone agrees on certain basic ideas: All people are created equal and they have basic rights that can never be taken away. People have the right to live, the right to be free, and the right to seek happiness.

We hold these truths to be self-evident, that all men are created equal, that they are endowed by their Creator with certain unalienable Rights, that among these are Life, Liberty, and the pursuit of Happiness.

To preserve these rights, people create governments. Every government must have the support of the people it governs.

That, to secure these rights, Governments are instituted among Men, deriving their just Powers from the consent of the governed.

That, whenever any Form of Government becomes destructive of these ends, it is the Right of the People to alter or to abolish it, and to institute new Government, laying its foundation on such Principles, and organizing its powers in such form, as to them shall seem most likely to effect their Safety and Happiness.

Prudence, indeed, will dictate that Governments long established should not be changed for light and transient causes; and, accordingly all experience hath shown, that mankind are more disposed to suffer, while evils are sufferable, than to right themselves by abolishing the forms to which they are accustomed. But, when a long train of abuses and usurpations, pursuing invariably the same Object, evinces a design to reduce them under absolute Despotism, it is their right, it is their duty, to throw off such Government, and to provide new Guards for their future security.

Such has been the patient sufferance of these Colonies; and such is now the necessity which constrains them to alter their former Systems of Government. The history of the present King of Great Britain is a history of repeated injuries and usurpations, all having in direct object the establishment of an absolute Tyranny over these States.

To prove this, let Facts be submitted to a candid world.

He has refused his Assent to Laws the most wholesome and necessary for the public good.

He has forbidden his Governors to pass Laws of immediate and pressing importance, unless suspended in their operation till his Assent should be obtained; and when so suspended, he has utterly neglected to attend to them.

He has refused to pass other Laws for the accommodation of large districts of People, unless those People would relinquish the right of Representation in the Legislature, a right inestimable to them and formidable to tyrants only.

He has called together legislative bodies at places unusual, uncomfortable, and distant from the depository of their Public Records, for the sole purpose of fatiguing them into compliance with his measures.

If a government loses this support or tries to take away basic freedoms, people have the right to change their government or to get rid of it and form a new government that will protect their rights.

However, people should not change governments that have long been in power over minor or temporary problems. We have learned from history that people are usually more willing to put up with a bad government than to get rid of it. But when people see their government misusing its power and mistreating its people time after time, it is the right and duty of the people to get rid of their government and to form a new one.

A List of Abuses

The colonies have suffered patiently long enough, and it is now time to change our government. King George III of Great Britain has ruled badly for many years. His main goal has been to establish total control over the colonies.

These statements are proven by the following facts:

King George III has rejected much-needed laws passed by the colonists.

He has not permitted important laws to be passed by his governors in America.

He has refused to redraw the borders of large voting districts unless the people living there agreed to give up their right to be represented in the legislature.

He has ordered lawmakers in the colonies to meet far from their homes and offices in places that are unusual and difficult to get to. His only reason for doing this has been to tire out the lawmakers so that they will accept his rule.

When lawmakers have criticized the king for attacking their rights, he has broken up the legislature's meetings.

After breaking up their meetings, the king has refused to allow new elections. As a result, colonists have been living in danger, unable to protect themselves or pass new laws.

He has tried to stop colonists from moving west and settling in new lands. He has also tried to prevent people from foreign countries from settling in America by making it hard for newcomers to become citizens.

In some places, he has not let colonists set up a system of courts.

He has forced colonial judges to obey him by deciding how long they can serve and how much they are paid.

He has sent officials from Britain to fill new government offices in the colonies. These officials have mistreated people and demanded unfair taxes.

In times of peace, he has kept soldiers in the colonies even though Americans did not want them.

He has tried to give soldiers power over colonial legislatures.

He and other leaders in Great Britain have passed laws for the colonies that Americans did not want. In these laws the British government has:

forced colonists to house and feed British soldiers;

protected these soldiers by giving them phony trials and not punishing them for murdering colonists;

cut off trade between Americans and people in other parts of the world;

demanded taxes that colonists never agreed to;

prevented colonists accused of crimes from having their trials decided fairly by a jury;

He has dissolved Representative Houses repeatedly, for opposing, with manly firmness, his invasions on the rights of the people.

He has refused for a long time, after such dissolutions, to cause others to be elected; whereby the Legislative Powers, incapable of Annihilation, have returned to the People at large for their exercise; the State remaining in the mean time exposed to all the dangers of invasion from without, and convulsions within.

He has endeavoured to prevent the Population of these States; for that purpose obstructing the Laws of Naturalization of Foreigners; refusing to pass others to encourage their migration hither, and raising the conditions of new Appropriations of Lands.

He has obstructed the Administration of justice by refusing his Assent to Laws for establishing judiciary Powers.

He has made judges dependent on his Will alone, for the tenure of their offices, and the amount and payment of their salaries.

He has erected a multitude of New Offices, and sent hither swarms of Officers to harass our People, and eat out their substance.

He has kept among us, in times of Peace, Standing Armies, without the Consent of our legislature.

He has affected to render the Military independent of and superior to the Civil Power.

He has combined with others to subject us to a jurisdiction foreign to our constitution, and unacknowledged by our laws; giving his Assent to their Acts of pretended Legislation:

For quartering large bodies of armed troops among us:

For protecting them, by a mock Trial, from Punishment for any Murders which they should commit on the Inhabitants of these States:

For cutting off our Trade with all parts of the world:

For imposing Taxes on us without our Consent:

For depriving us, in many cases, of the benefits of Trial by jury:

For transporting us beyond Seas to be tried for pretended offences:

For abolishing the free System of English Laws in a neighbouring Province, establishing therein an Arbitrary government, and enlarging its Boundaries, so as to render it at once an example and fit instrument for introducing the same absolute rule into these Colonies:

For taking away our Charters, abolishing our most valuable Laws, and altering fundamentally the Forms of our Governments:

For suspending our own Legislatures, and declaring themselves invested with Power to legislate for us in all cases whatsoever.

He has abdicated Government here, by declaring us out of his Protection and waging War against us.

He has plundered our seas, ravaged our Coasts, burnt our towns, and destroyed the Lives of our People.

He is at this time transporting large Armies of foreign Mercenaries to compleat the works of death, desolation and tyranny, already begun with circumstances of Cruelty & perfidy scarcely paralleled in the most barbarous ages, and totally unworthy the Head of a civilized nation.

He has constrained our fellow Citizens taken Captive on the high Seas to bear Arms against their Country, to become the executioners of their friends and Brethren, or to fall themselves by their Hands.

He has excited domestic insurrections amongst us, and has endeavoured to bring on the inhabitants of our frontiers, the merciless Indian Savages, whose known rule of warfare, is an undistinguished destruction of all ages, sexes and conditions.

In every stage of these Oppressions We have Petitioned for Redress in the most humble terms: Our repeated Petitions have been answered only by repeated injury. A Prince, whose character is thus marked by every act which may define a Tyrant, is unfit to be the ruler of a free People.

brought colonists falsely accused of crimes to Great Britain to be put on trial;

extended the borders of the neighboring province of Quebec to include lands stretching to the Ohio River, thus forcing colonists in this region to obey harsh French laws rather than English laws. The goal of the British government is to force all colonists to obey these harsh laws;

taken away our charters, or documents that make governments legal, canceled important laws, and completely changed our forms of government;

broken up our legislatures and claimed that Great Britain has the right to pass all laws for the colonies.

King George III has ended government in the colonies by waging war against us and not protecting us.

He has robbed American ships at sea, burned down our towns, and ruined people's lives.

He is right now bringing foreign soldiers to the colonies to commit horrible and brutal deeds. These actions by the king are some of the cruelest ever committed in the history of the world.

He has forced colonists captured at sea to join the British navy and to fight and kill Americans.

He has urged enslaved people in the colonies to rebel, and he has tried to get Native Americans to fight against colonists.

Statement of Independence

For years we have asked King George III to correct these problems and safeguard our rights. Unfortunately, the king has refused to listen to our complaints and he continues to treat us badly. The king is such an unfair ruler that he is not fit to rule the free people of America.

We have also asked the British people for help. We have told them many times of our problems and pointed out the unfair laws passed by their government. We hoped they would listen to us because they believed in reason and justice. We hoped they would listen to us because we are related to each other and have much in common. But we were wrong: The British people have not listened to us at all. They have ignored our pleas for justice. We must, therefore, break away from Great Britain and become a separate nation.

Nor have We been wanting in attention to our British brethren. We have warned them from time to time of attempts by their legislature to extend an unwarrantable jurisdiction over us. We have reminded them of the circumstances of our emigration and settlement here. We have appealed to their native justice and magnanimity, and we have conjured them by the ties of our common kindred to disavow these usurpations, which, would inevitably interrupt our connections and correspondence. They too have been deaf to the voice of justice and of consanguinity. We must, therefore, acquiesce in the necessity, which denounces our Separation, and hold them, as we hold the rest of mankind, Enemies in War, in Peace Friends.

Signers

Button Gwinnett (Ga.)
Lyman Hall (Ga.)
George Walton (Ga.)

William Hooper (N.C.)
Joseph Hewes (N.C.)
John Penn (N.C.)
Edward Rutledge (S.C.)
Thomas Heyward, Jr. (S.C.)
Thomas Lynch, Jr. (S.C.)
Arthur Middleton (S.C.)

John Hancock (Mass.)
Samuel Chase (Md.)
William Paca (Md.)
Thomas Stone (Md.)
Charles Carroll of Carrollton (Md.)
George Wythe (Va.)
Richard Henry Lee (Va.)
Thomas Jefferson (Va.)
Benjamin Harrison (Va.)
Thomas Nelson, Jr. (Va.)
Francis Lightfoot Lee (Va.)
Carter Braxton (Va.)

We, therefore, the Representatives of the United States of America, in General Congress Assembled, appealing to the Supreme judge of the world for the rectitude of our intentions, do, in the Name, and by Authority of the good People of these Colonies, solemnly publish and declare, That these United Colonies are, and of Right ought to be Free and Independent States; that they are Absolved from all Allegiance to the British Crown, and that all political connection between them and the State of Great Britain, is and ought to be totally dissolved; and that as Free and Independent States, they have full Power to levy War, conclude Peace, contract Alliances, establish Commerce, and to do all other Acts and Things which Independent States may of right do. And for the support of this Declaration, with a firm reliance on the protection of divine Providence, we mutually pledge to each other our Lives, our Fortunes and our sacred Honour.

In the name of the American people, we members of the Continental Congress declare that the United States of America is no longer a colony of Great Britain but is, instead, a free and independent nation. The United States now cuts all its relations with Great Britain. As a free nation, the United States has the right and power to make war and peace, make agreements with other nations, conduct trade, and do all the things that independent nations have the right to do. To support this Declaration of Independence, we promise to each other our lives, our fortunes, and our personal honor.

Robert Morris (Pa.)
Benjamin Rush (Pa.)
Benjamin Franklin (Pa.)
John Morton (Pa.)
George Clymer (Pa.)
James Smith (Pa.)
George Taylor (Pa.)
James Wilson (Pa.)
George Ross (Pa.)
Cæsar Rodney (Del.)
George Read (Del.)
Thomas McKean (Del.)

William Floyd (N.Y.)
Philip Livingston (N.Y.)
Francis Lewis (N.Y.)
Lewis Morris (N.Y.)
Richard Stockton (N.J.)
John Witherspoon (N.J.)
Francis Hopkinson (R.I.)
John Hart (N.J.)
Abraham Clark (N.J.)

Josiah Bartlett (N.H.)
William Whipple (N.H.)
Samuel Adams (Mass.)
John Adams (Mass.)
Robert Treat Paine (Mass.)
Elbridge Gerry (Mass.)
Stephen Hopkins (R.I.)
William Ellery (R.I.)
Roger Sherman (Conn.)
Samuel Huntington (Conn.)
William Williams (Conn.)
Oliver Wolcott (Conn.)
Matthew Thornton (N.H.)

The Constitution

of the United States

PREAMBLE

Explanation and Summary

The following text explains the meaning of the Constitution and its Amendments. Crossed out sentences are no longer in effect.

The people of the United States make this Constitution for several reasons: to form a stronger and more united nation; to ensure peace, justice, and liberty; to defend its citizens; and to improve the lives of its people.

We the People of the United States, in Order to form a more perfect Union, establish Justice, insure domestic Tranquility, provide for the common Defense, promote the general Welfare, and secure the Blessings of Liberty to ourselves and our Posterity, do ordain and establish this Constitution for the United States of America.

Article 1. THE LEGISLATIVE BRANCH

Section 1. The Congress

Congress has the power to make laws. Congress is made up of two houses: the Senate and the House of Representatives.

All legislative powers herein granted shall be vested in a Congress of the United States, which shall consist of a Senate and House of Representatives.

Section 2. The House of Representatives

1. Members of the House of Representatives are elected every two years by qualified voters in each state.

1. The House of Representatives shall be composed of members chosen every second year by the people of the several states, and the electors in each state shall have the qualifications requisite for electors of the most numerous branch of the state legislature.

2. To be a member of the House of Representatives, a person must be at least 25 years old, a United States citizen for at least seven years, and live in the state he or she represents.

2. No person shall be a Representative who shall not have attained to the age of twenty-five years, and been seven years a citizen of the United States, and who shall not, when elected, be an inhabitant of that state in which he shall be chosen.

3. The number of Representatives for each state is based on the population, or number of people, who live in that state. Every ten years a census, or count, must be taken to determine the population of each state. At first, this census of the population included indentured servants but not most Native Americans. Each enslaved

3. Representatives a̶n̶d̶ ̶d̶i̶r̶e̶c̶t̶ ̶t̶a̶x̶e̶s̶ shall be apportioned among the several states which may be included within this Union, according to their respective numbers, w̶h̶i̶c̶h̶ ̶s̶h̶a̶l̶l̶ ̶b̶e̶ ̶d̶e̶t̶e̶r̶m̶i̶n̶e̶d̶ ̶b̶y̶ ̶a̶d̶d̶i̶n̶g̶ ̶t̶o̶ ̶t̶h̶e̶ ̶w̶h̶o̶l̶e̶ ̶n̶u̶m̶b̶e̶r̶ ̶o̶f̶ ̶f̶r̶e̶e̶ ̶p̶e̶r̶-̶ ̶s̶o̶n̶s̶,̶ ̶i̶n̶c̶l̶u̶d̶i̶n̶g̶ ̶t̶h̶o̶s̶e̶ ̶b̶o̶u̶n̶d̶ ̶t̶o̶ ̶s̶e̶r̶v̶i̶c̶e̶ ̶f̶o̶r̶ ̶a̶ ̶t̶e̶r̶m̶ ̶o̶f̶ ̶y̶e̶a̶r̶s̶,̶ ̶a̶n̶d̶ ̶e̶x̶c̶l̶u̶d̶i̶n̶g̶ ̶I̶n̶d̶i̶a̶n̶s̶ ̶n̶o̶t̶ ̶t̶a̶x̶e̶d̶,̶ ̶t̶h̶r̶e̶e̶-̶f̶i̶f̶t̶h̶s̶ ̶o̶f̶ ̶a̶l̶l̶ ̶o̶t̶h̶e̶r̶ ̶p̶e̶r̶s̶o̶n̶s̶.̶ The actual enumeration shall be made within three years after the first meeting of the Congress of the United

States, and within every subsequent term of ten years, in such manner as they shall by law direct. The number of Representatives shall not exceed one for every 30,000, but each state shall have at least one Representative; ~~and until such enumeration shall be made, the state of New Hampshire shall be entitled to choose three, Massachusetts, eight, Rhode Island and Providence Plantations, one, Connecticut, five, New York, six, New Jersey, four, Pennsylvania, eight, Delaware, one, Maryland, six, Virginia, ten, North Carolina, five, South Carolina, five, and Georgia, three.~~

4. When vacancies happen in the representation from any state, the executive authority thereof shall issue writs of election to fill such vacancies.

5. The House of Representatives shall choose their Speaker and other officers; and shall have the sole power of impeachment.

Section 3. The Senate

1. The Senate of the United States shall be composed of two Senators from each state, ~~chosen by the legislature thereof,~~ for six years; and each Senator shall have one vote.

2. ~~Immediately after they shall be assembled in consequence of the first election, they shall be divided as equally as may be into three classes. The seats of the Senators of the first class shall be vacated at the expiration of the second year, of the second class at the expiration of the fourth year, and of the third class at the expiration of the sixth year, so that one-third may be chosen every second year; and if vacancies happen by resignation, or otherwise, during the recess of the legislature of any state, the executive thereof may make temporary appointments until the next meeting of the legislature, which shall then fill such vacancies.~~

3. No person shall be a Senator who shall not have attained to the age of thirty years, and been nine years a citizen of the United States, and who shall not, when elected, be an inhabitant of that state for which he shall be chosen.

4. The Vice President of the United States shall be president of the Senate, but shall have no vote, unless they be equally divided.

5. The Senate shall choose their other officers, and also a president pro tempore, in the absence of the Vice President,

person was counted as three-fifths of a free person. Today all people are counted equally. (The crossed-out sections of the Constitution are no longer in effect.)

4. Special elections called by the state's governor must be held to fill any empty seat in the House of Representatives.

5. Members of the House of Representatives choose their own leaders. House members alone have the power to impeach, or accuse, government officials of crimes in office.

1. Each state has two Senators. Each Senator serves a term of six years and has one vote in the Senate. At first, state legislatures elected Senators, but the Seventeenth Amendment changed the way Senators are chosen. Senators are now elected directly by the people.

2. One-third of the Senate seats are up for election every two years. The Seventeenth Amendment changed the way empty seats are filled.

3. To be a Senator, a person must be at least 30 years old, a citizens of the United States for at least nine years, and live in the state he or she represents.

4. The Vice President of the United States is the officer in charge of the Senate but votes only to break a tie.

5. Senators choose their own leaders. When the Vice President is absent, the Senate leader is called the

President *pro tempore* (prō tem′pə rē), or temporary President.

6. The Senate holds all impeachment trials. When the President of the United States is impeached, the Chief Justice of the Supreme Court is the judge for the trial. Conviction, or judgment of guilt, is decided by a two-thirds vote.

7. Impeached officials convicted by the Senate can be removed from office and barred from serving again in government. Regular courts of law can decide other punishments.

1. State lawmakers set rules for Congressional elections. Congress can change some of these rules.

2. Congress meets at least once a year, beginning in December. The Twentieth Amendment changed this date to January 3.

1. The Senate and House of Representatives decide if their members were elected fairly and are qualified to take their seats. At least half the members of each house of Congress must be present for Congress to do most business. Absent members can be required to attend sessions of Congress.

2. Each house of Congress may set its own rules and punish members for breaking them. A two-thirds vote is needed to expel, or force out, a member.

3. Each house of Congress keeps and publishes a record of its activities. Secret matters may be left out of the published record. If one-fifth of the members demand it, a vote on any matter will be published.

or when he shall exercise the office of the President of the United States.

6. The Senate shall have the sole power to try all impeachments. When sitting for that purpose, they shall be on oath or affirmation. When the President of the United States is tried, the Chief Justice shall preside; and no person shall be convicted without the concurrence of two-thirds of the members present.

7. Judgment in cases of impeachment shall not extend further than to removal from office, and disqualification to hold and enjoy any office of honor, trust or profit under the United States; but the party convicted shall nevertheless be liable and subject to indictment, trial, judgment and punishment, according to law.

Section 4. Elections and Meetings of Congress

1. The times, places and manner of holding elections for Senators and Representatives shall be prescribed in each state by the legislature thereof; but the Congress may at any time by law make or alter such regulations, except as to the places of choosing Senators.

2. The Congress shall assemble at least once in every year and such meeting shall be on the first Monday in December, unless they shall by law appoint a different day.

Section 5. Rules of Procedure for Congress

1. Each house shall be the judge of the elections, returns and qualifications of its own members, and a majority of each shall constitute a quorum to do business; but a smaller number may adjourn from day to day, and may be authorized to compel the attendance of absent members, in such manner, and under such penalties as each house may provide.

2. Each house may determine the rules of its proceedings, punish its members for disorderly behavior, and with the concurrence of two-thirds, expel a member.

3. Each house shall keep a journal of its proceedings, and from time to time publish the same, excepting such parts as may in their judgment require secrecy; and the yeas and nays of the members of either house on any question shall, at the desire of one-fifth of those present, be entered on the journal.

4. Neither house, during the session of Congress, shall, without the consent of the other, adjourn for more than three days, nor to any other place than that in which the two houses shall be sitting.

4. During a session of Congress, neither house can stop meeting for more than three days or decide to meet somewhere else unless the other house agrees.

Section 6. Privileges and Restrictions of Members of Congress

1. The Senators and Representatives shall receive a compensation for their services, to be ascertained by law, and paid out of the Treasury of the United States. They shall in all cases, except treason, felony and breach of the peace, be privileged from arrest during their attendance at the session of their respective houses, and in going to and returning from the same; and for any speech or debate in either house, they shall not be questioned in any other place.

1. Each member of Congress receives a salary from the United States government. Except for very serious crimes, no member can be arrested in the place where Congress is meeting while in session. Members cannot be arrested for anything they say in Congress.

2. No Senator or Representative shall, during the time for which he was elected, be appointed to any civil office under the authority of the United States, which shall have been created, or the emoluments whereof shall have been increased during such time; and no person holding any office under the United States, shall be a member of either house during his continuance in office.

2. Senators and Representatives may not hold any other job in the federal government while they serve in Congress.

Section 7. How Laws Are Made

1. All bills for raising revenue shall originate in the House of Representatives; but the Senate may propose or concur with amendments as on other bills.

1. All money and tax bills must begin in the House of Representatives. The Senate can later pass or change these bills.

2. Every bill which shall have passed the House of Representatives and the Senate, shall, before it become a law, be presented to the President of the United States. If he approve he shall sign it, but if not he shall return it, with his objections to that house in which it shall have originated, who shall enter the objections at large on their journal, and proceed to reconsider it. If after such reconsideration two-thirds of that house shall agree to pass the bill, it shall be sent, together with the objections, to the other house, by which it shall likewise be reconsidered, and if approved by two-thirds of that house, it shall become a law. But in all such cases the votes of both houses shall be determined by yeas and nays, and the names of the persons voting for and against the bill shall be entered on the journal of each house respectively. If any bill shall not be returned by the President within ten days (Sundays excepted) after it shall have been presented to him, the same shall be a law, in like manner as if he had signed it, unless the Congress by their adjournment prevent its return, in which case it shall not be a law.

2. After a bill, or suggested law, passes both the House of Representatives and the Senate, it goes to the President. If the President signs the bill, it becomes a law. If the President vetoes, or rejects, the bill, it goes back to Congress. A President's veto can be overridden, or upset, if Congress votes again and two-thirds of the members of each house vote in favor of the bill. The bill then becomes a law. If the President neither signs nor vetoes a bill within ten days (not counting Sundays) of first receiving it, the bill becomes a law. If Congress stops meeting *before* ten days have passed, however, the bill does *not* become a law. This last type of action is called a "pocket veto."

3. Every act passed by Congress must be presented to the President either to be signed or vetoed. The only exception is when Congress votes to adjourn, or stop meeting.

Congress has the power to:

1. raise and collect taxes to both pay debts and to protect and serve the nation, but federal taxes must be the same everywhere in the United States;

2. borrow money;

3. control trade with foreign nations, between states, and with Native Americans;

4. decide how people from foreign countries can become citizens of the United States and to make laws dealing with people and businesses unable to pay their debts;

5. print money, set its value, and set the standards of weights and measures used throughout the nation;

6. punish people who make counterfeit, or fake, money and bonds;

7. set up post offices and roads for mail delivery;

8. protect the rights and creations of scientists, artists, authors, and inventors;

9. create federal, or national, courts lower than the Supreme Court;

10. punish crimes committed at sea;

11. declare war;

12. establish and support an army, but no amount of money set aside for this purpose can be for a term longer than two years;

13. establish and support a navy;

3. Every order, resolution, or vote to which the concurrence of the Senate and House of Representatives may be necessary (except on a question of adjournment) shall be presented to the President of the United States; and before the same shall take effect, shall be approved by him, or being disapproved by him, shall be repassed by two-thirds of the Senate and House of Representatives, according to the rules and limitations prescribed in the case of a bill.

Section 8. Powers Granted to Congress

1. The Congress shall have power to lay and collect taxes, duties, imposts and excises, to pay the debts and provide for the common defense and general welfare of the United States; but all duties, imposts and excises shall be uniform throughout the United States;

2. To borrow money on the credit of the United States;

3. To regulate commerce with foreign nations, and among the several states, and with the Indian tribes;

4. To establish a uniform rule of naturalization, and uniform laws on the subject of bankruptcies throughout the United States;

5. To coin money, regulate the value thereof, and of foreign coin, and fix the standard of weights and measures;

6. To provide for the punishment of counterfeiting the securities and current coin of the United States;

7. To establish post offices and post roads;

8. To promote the progress of science and useful arts, by securing for limited times to authors and inventors the exclusive right to their respective writings and discoveries;

9. To constitute tribunals inferior to the Supreme Court;

10. To define and punish piracies and felonies committed on the high seas and offenses against the law of nations;

11. To declare war, ~~grant letters of marque and reprisal,~~ and make rules concerning captures on land and water;

12. To raise and support armies, but no appropriation of money to that use shall be for a longer term than two years;

13. To provide and maintain a navy;

14. To make rules for the government and regulation of the land and naval forces;

15. To provide for calling forth the militia to execute the laws of the Union, suppress insurrections and repel invasions;

16. To provide for organizing, arming, and disciplining, the militia, and for governing such part of them as may be employed in the service of the United States, reserving to the states respectively, the appointment of the officers, and the authority of training the militia according to the discipline prescribed by Congress;

17. To exercise exclusive legislation in all cases whatsoever, over such district (not exceeding ten miles square) as may, by cession of particular states, and the acceptance of Congress, become the seat of the government of the United States, and to exercise like authority over all places purchased by the consent of the legislature of the state in which the same shall be, for the erection of forts, magazines, arsenals, dockyards, and other needful buildings;—and

18. To make all laws which shall be necessary and proper for carrying into execution the foregoing powers, and all other powers vested by this Constitution in the government of the United States, or in any department or officer thereof.

Section 9. Powers Denied to Congress

1. ~~The migration or importation of such persons as any of the states now existing shall think proper to admit, shall not be prohibited by the Congress prior to the year one thousand eight hundred and eight, but a tax or duty may be imposed on such importation, not exceeding ten dollars for each person.~~

2. The privilege of the writ of habeas corpus shall not be suspended, unless when in cases of rebellion or invasion the public safety may require it.

3. No bill of attainder or ex post facto law shall be passed.

4. No capitation, or other direct, tax shall be laid, unless in proportion to the census or enumeration herein before directed to be taken.

5. No tax or duty shall be laid on articles exported from any state.

14. make rules for the armed forces;

15. call the militia (today called the National Guard) to enforce federal laws, put down rebellions, and fight invasions;

16. organize, train, and discipline the National Guard. States have the power to name officers and train soldiers in the National Guard under rules set by Congress;

17. govern the capital and military sites of the United States; and

18. make all laws necessary to carry out the powers of Congress. This is called the "elastic clause" because it stretches the powers of Congress.

Congress does *not* have the power to:

1. stop enslaved people from being brought into the United States before 1808. In 1808, the first year allowed, Congress passed a law banning the slave trade;

2. arrest and jail people without charging them with a crime. The only exception is during a rebellion or emergency;

3. punish a person without a trial in a court of law; nor punish a person for doing something wrong that was not against the law when the person did it;

4. pass a direct tax (such as an income tax) unless it is in proportion to the population. The Sixteenth Amendment allowed an income tax;

5. tax goods sent out of a state;

6. give ports of one state an advantage over ports of another state; nor can one state tax the ships of another state that enter its borders;

7. spend money without both passing a law and keeping a record of all its accounts;

8. grant any title of nobility (such as king or queen); nor may any worker in the federal government accept any gift or title from a foreign government.

State governments do *not* have the power to:

1. make treaties, print money, or do anything forbidden to the federal government outlined in Section 9 of the Constitution, above;

2. tax goods sent into and out of a state unless Congress agrees;

3. keep armed forces, go to war, or make agreements with others states or foreign countries unless Congress agrees.

1. The President has the power to execute, or carry out, the laws of the United States. The President and Vice President together serve a term of four years.

2. The President is chosen by electors from each state. Today these electors are chosen by the voters and called the *Electoral College*. The number of

6. No preference shall be given any regulation of commerce or revenue to the ports of one state over those of another; nor shall vessels bound to, or from, one state, be obliged to enter, clear, or pay duties in another.

7. No money shall be drawn from the Treasury, but in consequence of appropriations made by law; and a regular statement and account of the receipts and expenditures of all public money shall be published from time to time.

8. No title of nobility shall be granted by the United States; and no person holding any office of profit or trust under them, shall, without the consent of the Congress, accept of any present, emolument, office, or title, of any kind whatever, from any king, prince, or foreign state.

Section 10. Powers Denied to the States

1. No state shall enter into any treaty, alliance, or confederation; grant letters of marque and reprisal; coin money; emit bills of credit; make anything but gold and silver coin a tender in payment of debts; pass any bill of attainder, ex post facto law, or law impairing the obligation of contracts, or grant any title of nobility.

2. No state shall, without the consent of the Congress, lay any imposts or duties on imports or exports, except what may be absolutely necessary for executing its inspection laws; and the net produce of all duties and imposts, laid by any state on imports or exports, shall be for the use of the Treasury of the United States; and all such laws shall be subject to the revision and control of the Congress.

3. No state shall, without the consent of Congress, lay any duty of tonnage, keep troops, or ships of war in time of peace, enter into any agreement or compact with another state, or with a foreign power, or engage in war, unless actually invaded, or in such imminent danger as will not admit of delay.

Article 2. THE EXECUTIVE BRANCH

Section 1. Office of President and Vice President

1. The executive power shall be vested in a President of the United States of America. He shall hold his office during the term of four years, and, together with the Vice President, chosen for the same term, be elected, as follows:

2. Each state shall appoint, in such manner as the legislature thereof may direct, a number of electors, equal to the whole number of Senators and Representatives to which the state may be entitled in the Congress; but no Senator or Representative, or person holding an office or trust or profit under the United States, shall be appointed an elector.

3. ~~The electors shall meet in their respective states, and vote by ballot for two persons, of whom one at least shall not be an inhabitant of the same state with themselves. And they shall make a list of all the persons voted for, and of the number of votes for each; which list they shall sign and certify, and transmit sealed to the seat of the government of the United States, directed to the president of the Senate. The president of the Senate shall, in the presence of the Senate and House of Representatives, open all the certificates, and the votes shall then be counted. The person having the greatest number of votes shall be the President, if such number be a majority of the whole number of electors appointed; and if there be more than one who have such majority, and have an equal number of votes, then the House of Representatives shall immediately choose by ballot one of them for President; and if no person have a majority, then from the five highest on the list the said House shall in like manner choose the President. But in choosing the President, the votes shall be taken by states, the representation from each state having one vote; a quorum for this purpose shall consist of a member or members from two thirds of the states, and a majority of all the states shall be necessary to a choice. In every case, after the choice of the President, the person having the greatest number of votes of the electors shall be the Vice President. But if there should remain two or more who have equal votes, the Senate shall choose from them by ballot the Vice President.~~

4. The Congress may determine the time of choosing the electors, and the day on which they shall give their votes; which day shall be the same throughout the United States.

5. No person except a natural born citizen, ~~or a citizen of the United States, at the time of the adoption of this Constitution,~~ shall be eligible to the office of the President; neither shall any person be eligible to that office who shall not have attained to the age of thirty-five years, and been fourteen years a resident within the United States.

6. In case of the removal of the President from office, or of his death, resignation, or inability to discharge the powers and duties of the said office, the same shall devolve on the Vice President, and the Congress may by law provide for

electoral votes for each state is determined by adding up the number of the state's Senators and Representatives.

3. This part of the Constitution describes an early method of electing the President and Vice President. The Twelfth Amendment changed this method. Originally, the person who received the most electoral votes became President and the person who received the next highest number became Vice President.

4. Congress decides when Presidential electors are chosen and when they vote. The electors vote on the same day throughout the United States. Today people vote for the electors on the Tuesday after the first Monday of November. Presidential elections take place every four years.

5. To be President, a person must be a citizen born in the United States, at least 35 years old, and have lived in the United States for at least 14 years.

6. If the President leaves office for any reason or can no longer serve as President, the Vice President becomes President. If there is no Vice

President, Congress may decide who becomes President. The Twenty-Fifth Amendment changed the method of filling these vacancies, or empty offices.

7. The President receives a set salary that can neither be raised nor lowered during the President's term of office. The President can receive no other gift or salary from the United States or any of the states while in office.

8. Before taking office, the person elected President takes an oath. In this oath, the person promises to carry out the laws of the United States and defend the Constitution.

1. The President is in charge of the armed forces and state militias (today the National Guard) of the United States. The President can demand advice and opinions, in writing, of the people in charge of each executive department. These advisers are called the President's Cabinet. The President also has the power to pardon, or free, people convicted of federal crimes, except in cases of impeachment.

2. The President has the power to make treaties, but they must be approved by two-thirds of the Senate. The President also has the power to name ambassadors, important government officials, and judges of the Supreme Court and other federal courts, with the approval of the Senate.

3. The President has the power to fill empty offices for a short time when the Senate is not meeting.

The President must inform Congress from time to time on the condition of

the case of removal, death, resignation, or inability, both of the President and Vice President, declaring what officer shall then act as President, and such officer shall act accordingly, until the disability be removed, or a President shall be elected.

7. The President shall, at stated times receive for his services, a compensation, which shall neither be increased nor diminished during the period for which he shall have been elected, and he shall not receive within that period any other emolument from the United States, or any of them.

8. Before he enter on the execution of his office, he shall take the following oath or affirmation:—"I do solemnly swear (or affirm) that I will faithfully execute the office of President of the United States, and will to the best of my ability, preserve, protect and defend the Constitution of the United States."

Section 2. Powers Granted to the President

1. The President shall be Commander in Chief of the Army and Navy of the United States, and of the militia of the several states, when called into the actual service of the United States; he may require the opinion, in writing, of the principal officer in each of the executive departments, upon any subject relating to the duties of their respective offices, and he shall have power to grant reprieves and pardons for offenses against the United States, except in cases of impeachment.

2. He shall have power, by and with the advice and consent of the Senate, to make treaties, provided two-thirds of the Senators present concur; and he shall nominate, and by and with the advice and consent of the Senate, shall appoint ambassadors, other public ministers and consuls, judges of the Supreme Court, and all other officers of the United States, whose appointments are not herein otherwise provided for, and which shall be established by law; but the Congress may by law vest the appointment of such inferior officers, as they think proper, in the President alone, in the courts of law, or in the heads of departments.

3. The President shall have power to fill up all vacancies that may happen during the recess of the Senate, by granting commissions which shall expire at the end of their next session.

Section 3. Duties of the President

He shall from time to time give to the Congress information of the state of the Union, and recommend to their consideration such measures as he shall judge necessary and expedient; he may, on extraordinary occasions, convene both houses, or either of them, and in case of disagreement between them, with respect to the time of adjournment, he may adjourn them to such time as he shall think proper; he shall receive ambassadors and other public ministers; he shall take care that the laws be faithfully executed, and shall commission all the officers of the United States.

Section 4. Removal from Office

The President, Vice President and all civil officers of the United States, shall be removed from office on impeachment for, and conviction of, treason, bribery, or other high crimes and misdemeanors.

Article 3. THE JUDICIAL BRANCH

Section 1. Federal Courts

The judicial power of the United States shall be vested in one Supreme Court, and in such inferior courts as the Congress may from time to time ordain and establish. The judges, both of the Supreme and inferior courts, shall hold their offices during good behavior, and shall, at stated times, receive for their services, a compensation, which shall not be diminished during their continuance in office.

Section 2. Powers of Federal Courts

1. The judicial power shall extend to all cases, in law and equity, arising under this Constitution, the laws of the United States, and treaties made, or which shall be made, under their authority; to all cases affecting ambassadors, other public ministers and consuls; to all cases of admiralty and maritime jurisdiction; to controversies to which the United States shall be a party; to controversies between two or more states; between a state and citizens of another state; between citizens of different states, between citizens of the same state claiming lands under grants of different states, and between a state, or the citizens thereof, and foreign states, citizens or subjects.

2. In all cases affecting ambassadors, other public ministers and consuls, and those in which a state shall be party, the

the nation. Today, this speech is called the State of the Union address and is given once a year, usually in late January. In this message, the President recommends laws to improve the nation. The President can also, in time of emergency, call Congress to meet. If, in other situations, Congress cannot decide whether or not to adjourn, the President can make this decision. The President receives foreign officials, makes sure the nation's laws are carried out, and signs orders naming officers in the armed forces.

The President, Vice President, and other non-military officers of the United States may be impeached, or accused of committing crimes, and removed from office if found guilty.

The judicial power, or the power to make decisions in courts of law, is held by the Supreme Court and other lower federal, or national, courts that Congress may set up. Supreme Court and other federal judges hold office for life if they act properly. Judges receive a set salary that cannot be lowered.

1. Federal courts have legal authority over:

a) all laws made under the Constitution;

b) treaties made with foreign governments;

c) cases involving matters occurring at sea;

d) cases involving the federal government;

e) cases involving different states or citizens of different states; and

f) cases involving foreign citizens or governments.

The Eleventh Amendment partly limits which cases federal courts can hear.

2. In cases involving either states or ambassadors and government officials, the Supreme Court is the first and only court that makes a judgment. All other cases begin in lower courts but may later be appealed to, or reviewed by, the Supreme Court.

3. All criminal cases, except those of impeachment, are judged by trial and jury in the state where the supposed crime took place. If a crime occurs outside of any state, Congress decides where the trial takes place.

1. Treason is the crime of making war against the United States or helping its enemies. To be found guilty of treason, a person must confess to the crime or two witnesses must swear to having seen the crime committed.

2. Congress decides the punishment for treason. Relatives of people convicted of treason cannot also be punished for the crime.

Each state must respect the laws, records, and court decisions of every other state in the United States. Congress may pass laws to help carry out these matters.

1. Citizens are guaranteed all their basic rights when visiting other states.

2. A person charged with a crime, who flees to another state, must be returned to the state where the crime took place if the governor of the state so demands.

3. A person enslaved in one state, who escapes to another state, is still considered enslaved and must be returned to the person's owner. The Thirteenth Amendment, which outlawed slavery, nullified, or overturned, this section of the Constitution.

Supreme Court shall have original jurisdiction. In all the other cases before mentioned, the Supreme Court shall have appellate jurisdiction, both as to law and fact, with such exceptions, and under such regulations as the Congress shall make.

3. The trial of all crimes, except in cases of impeachment, shall be by jury; and such trial shall be held in the state where the said crimes shall have been committed; but when not committed within any state, the trial shall be at such place or places as the Congress may by law have directed.

Section 3. The Crime of Treason

1. Treason against the United States shall consist only in levying war against them, or in adhering to their enemies, giving them aid and comfort. No person shall be convicted of treason unless on the testimony of two witnesses to the same overt act, or on confession in open court.

2. The Congress shall have power to declare the punishment of treason, but no attainder of treason shall work corruption of blood, or forfeiture except during the life of the person attainted.

Article 4. RELATIONS AMONG THE STATES

Section 1. Recognition by Each State of Acts of Other States

Full faith and credit shall be given in each state to the public acts, records, and judicial proceedings of every other state. And the Congress may by general laws prescribe the manner in which such acts, records and proceedings shall be proved, and the effect thereof.

Section 2. Rights of Citizens in Other States

1. The citizens of each state shall be entitled to all privileges and immunities of citizens in the several states.

2. A person charged in any state with treason, felony, or other crime, who shall flee from justice, and be found in another state, shall on demand of the executive authority of the state from which he fled, be delivered up, to be removed to the state having jurisdiction of the crime.

3. ~~No person held to service or labor in one state, under the laws thereof, escaping into another, shall, in consequence of any law or regulation therein, be discharged from such service or labor, but shall be delivered up on claim of the party to whom such service or labor may be due.~~

Section 3. Treatment of New States and Territories

1. New states may be admitted by the Congress into this Union; but no new state shall be formed or erected within the jurisdiction of any other state; nor any state be formed by the junction of two or more states, or parts of states, without the consent of the legislatures of the states concerned as well as of the Congress.

2. The Congress shall have power to dispose of and make all needful rules and regulations respecting the territory or other property belonging to the United States; and nothing in this Constitution shall be so construed as to prejudice any claims of the United States, or of any particular state.

Section 4. Guarantees to the States

The United States shall guarantee to every state in this Union a republican form of government, and shall protect each of them against invasion; and on application of the legislature, or of the executive (when the legislature cannot be convened) against domestic violence.

Article 5. AMENDING THE CONSTITUTION

The Congress, whenever two-thirds of both houses shall deem it necessary, shall propose amendments to this Constitution, or, on the application of the legislatures of two-thirds of the several states, shall call a convention for proposing amendments, which, in either case, shall be valid to all intents and purposes, as part of this Constitution, when ratified by the legislatures of three-fourths of the several states, or by conventions in three-fourths thereof, as the one or the other mode of ratification may be proposed by the Congress; provided that ~~no amendment which may be made prior to the year one thousand eight hundred and eight shall in any manner affect the first and fourth clauses in the Ninth Section of the First Article; and that~~ no state, without its consent, shall be deprived of its equal suffrage in the Senate.

Article 6. DEBTS, FEDERAL SUPREMACY, OATHS OF OFFICE

Section 1. Prior Debts of the United States

All debts contracted and engagements entered into, before the adoption of this Constitution, shall be as valid against the United States under this Constitution, as under the Confederation.

---

1. Congress may let new states become part of the United States. No new state can be formed from another state or by joining parts of other states, unless Congress and the legislatures of the states involved approve.

2. Congress has the power to make all laws and rules over territories and government properties of the United States.

The federal government guarantees that the people of each state have the right to elect their leaders. The federal government also promises to protect each state from invasion, rebellion, and violent disorders.

There are two ways to make amendments, or changes, to the Constitution: two-thirds of each branch of Congress can suggest an amendment; or, two-thirds of the state legislatures can call a convention to suggest an amendment. Once the amendment has been suggested, three-fourths of the state legislatures or three-fourths of special state conventions must approve the amendment for it to become part of the Constitution. No state can be denied its equal vote in the Senate without its approval. No amendment could be made before 1808 that affected either the slave trade or certain direct taxes.

The United States government promises to pay back all debts and honor all agreements made by the government under the Articles of Confederation.

The Constitution and all the laws and treaties made under it are the supreme, or highest, law in the United States. If state or local laws disagree with federal law, the federal law must be obeyed. All judges must follow this rule.

Section 2. The Supreme Law of the Land

This Constitution, and the laws of the United States which shall be made in pursuance thereof; and all treaties made, or which shall be made, under the authority of the United States, shall be the supreme law of the land; and the judges in every state shall be bound thereby, anything in the constitution or laws of any state to the contrary notwithstanding.

All officials of the federal and state governments must promise to support the Constitution. A person's religion may never be used to qualify or disqualify a person from holding federal office.

Section 3. Oaths of Office

The Senators and Representatives before mentioned, and the members of the several state legislatures, and all executive and judicial officers, both of the United States and of the several states, shall be bound by oath or affirmation, to support this Constitution; but no religious test shall ever be required as a qualification to any office or public trust under the United States.

The Constitution will become law when special conventions in 9 (of the 13 original) states approve it.

Article 7. RATIFICATION OF THE CONSTITUTION

The ratification of the conventions of nine states, shall be sufficient for the establishment of this Constitution between the states so ratifying the same.

This Constitution is completed by the agreement of everyone at this convention on September 17, 1787, in the twelfth year of the independence of the United States of America.

Done in convention by the unanimous consent of the States present the Seventeenth day of September in the year of our Lord one thousand seven hundred and eighty seven, and of the Independence of the United States of America the Twelfth.

The people present have signed their names below.

In witness whereof we have hereunto subscribed our names.

George Washington, President and deputy from Virginia

DELAWARE
George Read
Gunning Bedford, Jr.
John Dickinson
Richard Bassett
Jacob Broom

MARYLAND
James McHenry
Daniel of St. Thomas
 Jenifer
Daniel Carroll

VIRGINIA
John Blair
James Madison, Jr.

NORTH CAROLINA
William Blount
Richard Dobbs Spaight
Hugh Williamson

SOUTH CAROLINA
John Rutledge
Charles Cotesworth
 Pinckney
Charles Pinckney
Pierce Butler

GEORGIA
William Few
Abraham Baldwin

NEW HAMPSHIRE
John Langdon
Nicholas Gilman

MASSACHUSETTS
Nathaniel Gorham
Rufus King

CONNECTICUT
William Samuel Johnson
Roger Sherman

NEW YORK
Alexander Hamilton

NEW JERSEY
William Livingston
David Brearley
William Paterson
Jonathan Dayton

PENNSYLVANIA
Benjamin Franklin
Thomas Mifflin
Robert Morris
George Clymer
Thomas FitzSimons
Jared Ingersoll
James Wilson
Gouverneur Morris

Attest: William Jackson,
 Secretary

AMENDMENTS TO THE CONSTITUTION

Amendment 1. *Freedom of Religion, Speech, Press, Assembly, and Petition (1791)*

Congress shall make no law respecting an establishment of religion, or prohibiting the free exercise thereof; or abridging the freedom of speech, or of the press; or the right of the people peaceably to assemble, and to petition the government for a redress of grievances.

Amendment 2. *Right to Keep Weapons (1791)*

A well-regulated militia being necessary to the security of a free state, the right of the people to keep and bear arms shall not be infringed.

Amendment 3. *Protection Against Quartering Soldiers (1791)*

No soldier shall, in time of peace, be quartered in any house, without the consent of the owner, nor in time of war, but in a manner to be prescribed by law.

The first ten amendments to the Constitution ensure basic freedoms and are known as the Bill of Rights. Under the First Amendment, Congress cannot make laws:

1) setting up an official religion;

2) preventing people from practicing their religion;

3) stopping people or the press from saying what they want;

4) preventing people from gathering peacefully and asking the government to listen to their complaints and to correct problems.

People have the right to keep weapons and be part of the state militia (today the National Guard).

During peacetime, people cannot be forced to quarter, or house and feed, soldiers in their homes. During time of war, Congress may set other rules.

People are protected against unreasonable arrests and searches of their homes and property. To search a person's home or property, the government must get a search warrant, or special approval, describing exactly what place is to be searched and what items are expected to be found.

A person cannot be charged with a serious crime unless a grand jury, or a group of citizens appointed to study criminal evidence, decides that a good reason exists to put the person on trial. (The only exceptions are cases involving people in the armed forces.) A person judged innocent by a court of law cannot be put on trial again for the same crime. People on trial cannot be forced to testify, or speak in court, against themselves. A person cannot have life, liberty, or property taken away unless fairly decided by a court of law. If the government takes away property for public use, a fair price must be paid the owner.

In all criminal cases, a person accused of a crime has the right to a fast, public trial by a fair jury in the place where the crime took place. All persons accused of a crime have the right to:

1) know the charges against them;

2) hear the evidence and witnesses against them;

3) call witnesses in their defense;

4) have a lawyer.

A person has the right to a trial by jury in civil, or noncriminal, cases involving more than $20.

The government cannot require very high bail, or deposit of money, from a

Amendment 4. *Freedom from Unreasonable Search and Seizure (1791)*

The right of the people to be secure in their persons, houses, papers, and effects, against unreasonable searches and seizures, shall not be violated, and no warrants shall issue, but upon probable cause, supported by oath or affirmation, and particularly describing the place to be searched, and the persons or things to be seized.

Amendment 5. *Rights of Persons Accused of a Crime (1791)*

No person shall be held to answer for a capital, or otherwise infamous, crime, unless on a presentment or indictment of a grand jury, except in cases arising in the land or naval forces, or in the militia, when in actual service in time of war or public danger; nor shall any person be subject for the same offense to be twice put in jeopardy of life or limb; nor shall be compelled in any criminal case to be a witness against himself, nor be deprived of life, liberty, or property, without due process of law; nor shall private property be taken for public use, without just compensation.

Amendment 6. *Right to a Jury Trial in Criminal Cases (1791)*

In all criminal prosecutions, the accused shall enjoy the right to a speedy and public trial, by an impartial jury of the state and district wherein the crime shall have been committed, which district shall have been previously ascertained by law, and to be informed of the nature and cause of the accusation; to be confronted with the witnesses against him; to have compulsory process for obtaining witnesses in his favor, and to have the assistance of counsel for his defense.

Amendment 7. *Right to a Jury Trial in Civil Cases (1791)*

In suits at common law, where the value in controversy shall exceed twenty dollars, the right of trial by jury shall be preserved, and no fact tried by a jury shall be otherwise reexamined in any court of the United States than according to the rules of the common law.

Amendment 8. *Protection from Unfair Fines and Punishment (1791)*

Excessive bail shall not be required, nor excessive fines imposed, nor cruel and unusual punishments inflicted.

Amendment 9. *Other Rights of the People* (1791)

The enumeration in the Constitution, of certain rights, shall not be construed to deny or disparage others retained by the people.

The rights of the people are not limited to those stated in the Constitution.

Amendment 10. *Powers of the States and the People (1791)*

The powers not delegated to the United States by the Constitution, nor prohibited by it to the states, are reserved to the states respectively, or to the people.

Powers not granted to the United States government and not forbidden to the states are left to the states or to the people.

Amendment 11. *Limiting Law Cases Against States (1798)*

The judicial power of the United States shall not be construed to extend to any suit in law or equity, commenced or prosecuted against one of the United States, by citizens of another state, or by citizens or subjects of any foreign state.

A state government cannot be sued in a federal court by people of another state or by people from a foreign country.

Amendment 12. *Election of President and Vice President (1804)*

The electors shall meet in their respective states, and vote by ballot for President and Vice President, one of whom, at least, shall not be an inhabitant of the same state with themselves; they shall name in their ballots the person voted for as President, and in distinct ballots the person voted for as Vice President, and they shall make distinct lists of all persons voted for as President, and of all persons voted for as Vice President, and of the number of votes for each, which lists they shall sign and certify, and transmit, sealed, to the seat of government of the United States, directed to the President of the Senate; the President of the Senate shall, in the presence of the Senate and House of Representatives, open all the certificates and the votes shall then be counted; the person having the greatest number of votes for President shall be the President, if such number be a majority of the whole number of electors appointed; and if no person have such majority, then from the persons having the highest numbers not exceeding three on the list of those voted for as President, the House of Representatives shall choose immediately, by ballot, the President. But in choosing the President, the votes shall be taken by states, the representation from each state having one vote; a quorum for this purpose shall consist of a member or members from two-thirds of the states, and a majority of all the states shall be neces-

This amendment changed the method of choosing a President and Vice President. This method is called the Electoral College. The main change caused by this amendment is that candidates for President and Vice President now run for office together, and each elector casts only one vote. Before, candidates for President and Vice President ran for office separately, and each elector cast two votes. Under the Electoral College, people called electors meet in their home states and vote for President and Vice President. Electors choose one person for President and a different person for Vice President. (One of the people voted for must be from a different state than the elector.) These electoral votes are then sent to the United States Senate where all the electoral votes for President are counted. The person who receives more than half the electoral votes for President is elected President. The person who receives more than half the electoral votes for Vice President is elected Vice President. If no person receives more than half the electoral votes for

person accused of a crime. People convicted of crimes cannot be fined an unfairly high amount. Nor can they be punished in a cruel or unusual way.

President, the House of Representatives chooses the President. A list of the top three vote-getters is sent to the House of Representatives. From this list, the Representatives vote for President with each state entitled to one vote. The person who receives more than half the votes of the states in the House of Representatives is elected President. If no person receives more than half the vote, the Representatives vote again. If the Representatives fail to elect a President by March 4 (later changed to January 20), the Vice President serves as President. If no person receives at least half the electoral votes for Vice President, no one becomes Vice President and a list of the top two vote-getters is sent to the Senate. From this list, the Senators then vote for Vice President, with each Senator entitled to one vote. The person who receives more than half the votes in the Senate becomes Vice President. Qualifications for the office of Vice President are the same as those of President.

Slavery is outlawed in the United States.

Congress can pass any laws necessary to carry out this amendment.

All people born in or made citizens by the United States are citizens of both the United States and the state in which they live. No state can deny any citizen the basic rights outlined in the Fifth Amendment. All states must treat people equally under the law. This amendment made formerly enslaved people citizens of both the United States and the states in which they lived.

The number of a state's Representatives in Congress can be lowered if the state prevents qualified citizens

sary to a choice. ~~And if the House of Representatives shall not choose a President whenever the right of choice shall devolve upon them, before the fourth day of March next following, then the Vice President shall act as President, as in the case of the death or other constitutional disability of the President.~~ The person having the greatest number of votes as Vice President, shall be the Vice President, if such number be a majority of the whole number of electors appointed, and if no person have a majority, then from the two highest numbers on the list, the Senate shall choose the Vice President; a quorum for the purpose shall consist of two-thirds of the whole number of Senators, and a majority of the whole number shall be necessary to a choice. But no person constitutionally ineligible to the office of President shall be eligible to that of Vice President of the United States.

Amendment 13. *Slavery Outlawed (1865)*

Section 1. Abolition of Slavery

Neither slavery nor involuntary servitude, except as a punishment for crime whereof the party shall have been duly convicted, shall exist within the United States, or any place subject to their jurisdiction.

Section 2. Enforcement

Congress shall have power to enforce this article by appropriate legislation.

Amendment 14. *Rights of Citizens (1868)*

Section 1. Citizenship

All persons born or naturalized in the United States and subject to the jurisdiction thereof, are citizens of the United States and of the state wherein they reside. No state shall make or enforce any law which shall abridge the privileges or immunities of citizens of the United States; nor shall any state deprive any person of life, liberty, or property, without due process of law; nor deny to any person within its jurisdiction the equal protection of the laws.

Section 2. Representation in Congress

Representatives shall be apportioned among the several states according to their respective numbers, counting the whole number of persons in each state, ~~excluding Indians not taxed~~. But when the right to vote at any election for the choice of electors for President and Vice President of the United States, Representatives in Congress, the executive and judicial officers of a state, or the members of the legislature thereof, is denied to any of the ~~male~~ inhabitants of such state, being ~~twenty one years of age and~~ citizens of the United States, or in any way abridged, except for participation in rebellion, or other crime, the basis of representation therein shall be reduced in the proportion which the number of such ~~male~~ citizens shall bear to the whole number of ~~male~~ citizens ~~twenty one years of age~~ in such state.

from voting. This section aimed to force states in the South to allow African Americans to vote.

Section 3. Penalties for Confederate Leaders

No person shall be a Senator or Representative in Congress, or elector of President and Vice President, or hold any office, civil or military, under the United States, or under any state, who, having previously taken an oath, as a member of Congress, or as an officer of the United States, or as a member of any state legislature, or as an executive or judicial officer of any state, to support the Constitution of the United States, shall have engaged in insurrection or rebellion against the same, or given aid or comfort to the enemies thereof. But Congress may, by vote of two-thirds of each house, remove such disability.

Any official of the federal or state governments who took part in the Civil War against the United States cannot again hold any federal or state office. But Congress can remove this restriction by a two-thirds vote.

Section 4. Responsibility for Public Debt

The validity of the public debt of the United States, authorized by law, including debts incurred for payment of pensions and bounties for services in suppressing insurrection or rebellion, shall not be questioned. But neither the United States nor any state shall assume or pay any debt or obligation incurred in aid of insurrection or rebellion against the United States ~~or any claim for the loss or emancipation of any slave~~; but all such debts, obligations, and claims shall be held illegal and void.

All money borrowed by the United States government to fight the Civil War is to be paid back. No debts owed to the Confederate states or to the Confederate government to pay for the Civil War are to be paid back by the federal or state governments. No money would be paid to anyone for the loss of people they once held in slavery.

Section 5. Enforcement

The Congress shall have power to enforce, by appropriate legislation, the provisions of this article.

Congress can pass any laws necessary to carry out this amendment.

Amendment 15. *Voting Rights (1870)*

Section 1. Black Suffrage

The right of citizens of the United States to vote shall not be denied or abridged by the United States or any state on account of race, color, or previous condition of servitude.

No federal or state government can prevent people from voting because of their race, color, or because they were once enslaved. This amendment aimed to give black men the right to vote.

Congress can pass any laws necessary to carry out this amendment.

Section 2. Enforcement

The Congress shall have power to enforce this article by appropriate legislation.

Amendment 16. *Income Tax (1913)*

Congress has the power to collect an income tax regardless of the population of any state.

The Congress shall have the power to lay and collect taxes on incomes, from whatever source derived, without apportionment among the several states, and without regard to any census or enumeration.

Amendment 17. *Direct Election of Senators (1913)*

Section 1. Method of Election

Senators are to be elected by the voters of each state. This amendment changed the method by which state legislatures elected Senators as outlined in Article 1, Section 3, Clause 1 of the Constitution.

The Senate of the United States shall be composed of two Senators from each state, elected by the people thereof, for six years; and each Senator shall have one vote. The electors in each state shall have the qualifications requisite for electors of the most numerous branch of the state legislatures.

Section 2. Vacancies

Special elections can be held to fill empty seats in the Senate. State legislatures may permit the governor to name a person to fill an empty seat for a short time until the next election.

When vacancies happen in the representation of any state in the Senate, the executive authority of such state shall issue writs of election to fill such vacancies: *provided* that the legislature of any state may empower the executive thereof to make temporary appointments until the people fill the vacancies by election as the legislature may direct.

Section 3. Those Elected under Previous Rules

This amendment does not affect the election or term of office of any Senator in office before the amendment becomes part of the Constitution.

This amendment shall not be so construed as to affect the election or term of any Senator chosen before it becomes valid as part of the Constitution.

Amendment 18. *Prohibition of Alcoholic Drinks (1919)*

Section 1. Prohibition

Making, selling, or transporting alcoholic, or intoxicating, drinks in the United States is illegal. This amendment was called the Prohibition Amendment because it prohibited, or banned, the use of alcohol.

After one year from the ratification of this article the manufacture, sale, or transportation of intoxicating liquors within, the importation thereof into, or the exportation thereof from, the United States and all territory subject to the jurisdiction thereof for beverage purposes is hereby prohibited.

Section 2. Enforcement

Both Congress and the states can pass any laws necessary to carry out this amendment.

The Congress and the several states shall have concurrent power to enforce this article by appropriate legislation.

Section 3. Time Limit on Ratification

The article shall be inoperative unless it shall have been ratified as an amendment to the Constitution by the legislatures of the several states, as provided in the Constitution, within seven years from the date of the submission hereof to the states by the Congress.

This amendment is to become part of the Constitution only if it is approved within seven years. It was repealed, or canceled, by the Twenty-First Amendment.

Amendment 19. *Women's Right to Vote (1920)*

Section 1. Women Made Voters

The right of citizens of the United States to vote shall not be denied or abridged by the United States or by any state on account of sex.

No federal or state government can prevent people from voting because of their sex. This amendment grants women the right to vote.

Section 2. Enforcement

Congress shall have power to enforce this article by appropriate legislation.

Congress can pass any laws necessary to carry out this amendment.

Amendment 20. *Terms of Office (1933)*

Section 1. Start of Terms of Office

The terms of the President and Vice President shall end at noon on the 20th day of January, and the terms of Senators and Representatives at noon on the 3rd day of January, of the years in which such terms would have ended if this article had not been ratified; and the terms of their successors shall then begin.

The terms of office for the President and Vice President begin on January 20. This date is called Inauguration Day. The terms of office for members of Congress begin on January 3. Originally their terms began on March 4.

Section 2. Meeting Time of Congress

The Congress shall assemble at least once in every year, and such meeting shall begin at noon on the 3rd day of January, unless they shall by law appoint a different day.

Congress must meet at least once a year beginning at noon on January 3. However, Congress may pick a different day to first meet.

Section 3. Providing for a Successor of the President-Elect

If at the time fixed for the beginning of the term of the President, the President-elect shall have died, the Vice President-elect shall become President. If a President shall not have been chosen before the time fixed for the beginning of his term, or if the President-elect shall have failed to qualify, then the Vice President-elect shall act as President until a President shall have qualified; and the Congress may by law provide for the case wherein neither a President-elect nor a Vice President-elect shall have qualified, declaring who shall then act as President, or the manner in which one who is to act shall be selected, and such person shall act accordingly until a President or Vice President shall have qualified.

If the person elected President dies before taking office, the Vice President becomes President. If no person is elected President before the term of office begins, or if the person elected President is not qualified to serve, then the Vice President acts as President until a qualified President is chosen. If both the person elected President and the person elected Vice President are disqualified from holding office, Congress selects the President.

If, during the time Congress is selecting the President and Vice President, one of these two people dies, Congress may pass a law determining how to choose the President and Vice President.

Section 4. Elections Decided by Congress

The Congress may by law provide for the case of the death of any of the persons from whom the House of Representatives may choose a President whenever the right of choice shall have devolved upon them, and for the case of the death of any of the persons from whom the Senate may choose a Vice President whenever the right of choice shall have devolved upon them.

Section 5. Effective Date

Sections 1 and 2 shall take effect on the 15th day of October following the ratification of this article.

Sections 1 and 2 of this amendment take effect on the fifteenth day of October after this amendment becomes part of the Constitution.

This amendment is to become part of the Constitution only if it is approved by three-fourths of the state legislatures within seven years.

Section 6. Time Limit on Ratification

This article shall be inoperative unless it shall have been ratified as an amendment to the Constitution by the legislatures of three-fourths of the several states within seven years from the date of its submission.

Amendment 21. *Repeal of Prohibition (1933)*

Section 1. Prohibition Ends

The Eighteenth article of amendment to the Constitution of the United States is hereby repealed.

The Eighteenth Amendment is repealed, or no longer in effect.

Section 2. Protection of State and Local Prohibition Laws

Any state or territory of the United States may pass prohibition laws.

The transportation or importation into any state, territory, or possession of the United States for delivery or use therein of intoxicating liquors, in violation of the laws thereof, is hereby prohibited.

Section 3. Time Limit on Ratification

This amendment is to become part of the Constitution only if state conventions approve it within seven years.

This article shall be inoperative unless it shall have been ratified as an amendment to the Constitution by conventions in the several states, as provided in the Constitution, within seven years from the date of the submission hereof to the states by the Congress.

Amendment 22. *President Limited to Two Terms (1951)*

Section 1. Limit on Number of Terms

No person can be elected more than two times to the office of President. No person can be elected more than once to the office of President who has served more than two years of another President's term.

No person shall be elected to the office of the President more than twice, and no person who has held the office of President, or acted as President, for more than two years of a term to which some other person was elected President shall be elected to the office of the President more than once. ~~But this Article shall not apply to any person holding the office of President when this Article was proposed by the Congress, and shall not prevent any person who may be holding the office of President, or acting as President, during the term within which this Article becomes operative from holding the office of President or acting as President during the remainder of such term.~~

This amendment does not affect any President who is in office when this amendment becomes part of the Constitution.

Section 2. Time Limit on Ratification

~~This Article shall be inoperative unless it shall have been ratified as an amendment to the Constitution by the legislatures of three-fourths of the several states within seven years from the date of its submission to the states by the Congress.~~

This amendment is to become part of the Constitution only if three-fourths of the state legislatures approve it within seven years.

Amendment 23. *Presidential Elections for the District of Columbia (1961)*

Section 1. Presidential Electors in the District of Columbia

The District constituting the seat of Government of the United States shall appoint in such manner as the Congress may direct: A number of electors of President and Vice President equal to the whole number of Senators and Representatives in Congress to which the District would be entitled if it were a State, but in no event more than the least populous State; they shall be in addition to those appointed by the States, but they shall be considered, for the purposes of the election of President and Vice President, to be electors appointed by a State; and they shall meet in the District and perform such duties as provided by the Twelfth article of amendment.

People living in Washington, D.C. (the District of Columbia), have the right to vote in Presidential elections. The number of electoral votes of Washington, D.C., can never be more than the number of electoral votes of the state with the fewest number of people.

Section 2. Enforcement

The Congress shall have power to enforce this article by appropriate legislation.

Congress can pass any laws necessary to carry out this amendment.

Amendment 24. *Poll Tax Ended (1964)*

Section 1. Poll Taxes Not Allowed in Federal Elections

The right of citizens of the United States to vote in any primary or other election for President or Vice President, for electors for President or Vice President, or for Senator or Representative in Congress, shall not be denied or abridged by the United States or any state by reason of failure to pay any poll tax or other tax.

No person can be prevented from voting in a federal election for failing to pay a poll tax or any other kind of tax.

Congress can pass any laws necessary to carry out this amendment.

Section 2. Enforcement

The Congress shall have the power to enforce this article by appropriate legislation.

Amendment 25. Presidential Succession (1967)

Section 1. Filling the Vacant Office of President

In case of the removal of the President from office or of his death or resignation, the Vice President shall become President.

If the President dies, resigns, or is removed from office, the Vice President becomes President.

Section 2. Filling the Vacant Office of Vice President

Whenever there is a vacancy in the office of the Vice President, the President shall nominate a Vice President who shall take the office upon confirmation by a majority vote of both houses of Congress.

If the office of Vice President becomes empty, the President names a new Vice President, with the approval of both houses of Congress.

Section 3. Disability of the President

Whenever the President transmits to the President pro tempore of the Senate and the Speaker of the House of Representatives his written declaration that he is unable to discharge the powers and duties of his office, and until he transmits to them a written declaration to the contrary, such powers and duties shall be discharged by the Vice President as Acting President.

If the President is unable to carry out the powers and duties of office, the President may inform the leaders of Congress. The Vice President then serves as Acting President. The President may return to office only when he or she informs the leaders of Congress that he or she can again carry out the powers and duties of office.

Section 4. When Congress Designates an Acting President

Whenever the Vice President and a majority of either the principal officers of the executive departments or of such other body as Congress may by law provide, transmit to the President pro tempore of the Senate and the Speaker of the House of Representatives their written declaration that the President is unable to discharge the powers and duties of his office, the Vice President shall immediately assume the powers and duties of the office as Acting President. Thereafter, when the President transmits to the President pro tempore of the Senate and the Speaker of the House of Representatives his written declaration that no inability exists, he shall resume the powers and duties of his office unless the Vice President and a majority of either the principal officers of the executive departments or of such other body as Congress may by law provide, transmit within four days to the President pro tempore of the Senate and the Speaker of the House of Representatives their written declaration that the President is unable to discharge the powers and duties of his office. Thereupon Congress shall decide the issue, assembling within 48 hours for that purpose if not

If the Vice President and at least half the Cabinet, or President's top advisers (or a special committee), inform the leaders of Congress that the President cannot carry out the powers and duties of office, the Vice President immediately becomes Acting President. If the President informs the leaders of Congress that he or she is able to serve as President, he or she again becomes President. But if, within four days, the Vice President and at least half the Cabinet (or a special committee) inform the leaders of Congress that the President still cannot carry out the powers and duties of office, the President does not return to office. Instead, Congress must meet within 48 hours. In the next 21 days, Congress must decide if the President is able to carry out the powers and duties of office. If two-thirds of both houses of Congress vote that the President is unable to in session. If the Congress, within 21 days after receipt of the latter written declaration, or, if Congress is not in session, within 21 days after Congress is required to assemble, determines by two-thirds vote of both houses that the President is unable to discharge the powers and duties of his office, the Vice President shall continue to discharge the same as Acting President; otherwise, the President shall assume the powers and duties of his office.

serve, the President is removed from office and the Vice President becomes Acting President. If two-thirds do not vote this way, the President stays in office.

Amendment 26. *Vote for Eighteen-Year-Olds (1971)*

Section 1. Voting Age

The right of citizens of the United States, who are 18 years of age or older, to vote shall not be denied or abridged by the United States or any state on account of age.

No federal or state government can prevent people 18 years of age or older from voting because of their age. This amendment grants people who are at least 18 years old the right to vote.

Section 2. Enforcement

The Congress shall have the power to enforce this article by appropriate legislation.

Congress can pass any laws necessary to carry out this amendment.

Amendment 27. *Limits on Salary Changes (1992)*

No law, varying the compensation for the services of the Senators and Representatives, shall take effect, until an election of Representatives shall have intervened.

No law changing the salaries of members of Congress can take effect until after the next election of the House of Representatives.

Presidents
of the
United States

George Washington
(1732–1799)

Years in Office 1789-1797
Vice President John Adams
Home State Virginia
Political Party Federalist
First Lady Martha Dandridge Washington
Religion Episcopalian

John Adams
(1735–1826)

Years in Office 1797-1801
Vice President Thomas Jefferson
Home State Massachusetts
Political Party Federalist
First Lady Abigail Smith Adams
Religion Unitarian

Thomas Jefferson
(1743–1826)

Years in Office 1801-1809
Vice Presidents Aaron Burr 1801-1805;
  George Clinton 1805–1809
Home State Virginia
Political Party Democratic-Republican
First Lady (none)
Religion No specific denomination

James Madison
(1751–1836)

Years in Office 1809-1817
Vice Presidents George Clinton 1809-1812,
  died; Elbridge Gerry 1813-1814, died
Home State Virginia
Political Party Democratic-Republican
First Lady Dolley Payne Madison
Religion Episcopalian

James Monroe
(1758–1831)

Years in Office 1817-1825
Vice President Daniel D. Tompkins
Home State Virginia
Political Party Democratic-Republican
First Lady Elizabeth Kortright Monroe
Religion Episcopalian

John Quincy Adams
(1767–1848)

Years in Office 1825-1829
Vice President John C. Calhoun
Home State Massachusetts
Political Party Democratic-Republican
First Lady Louisa Johnson Adams
Religion Unitarian

Andrew Jackson
(1767–1845)

Years in Office 1829-1837
Vice Presidents John C. Calhoun
  1829–1832, resigned;
  Martin Van Buren 1833-1837
Home State Tennessee
Political Party Democrat
First Lady (none)
Religion Presbyterian

Martin Van Buren
(1782–1862)

Years in Office 1837-1841
Vice President Richard M. Johnson
Home State New York
Political Party Democrat
First Lady (none)
Religion Dutch Reformed

William Henry Harrison
(1773–1841)

Years in Office 1841 (one month);
  died in office
Vice President John Tyler
Home State Ohio
Political Party Whig
First Lady Anna Symmes Harrison
Religion Episcopalian

John Tyler
(1790–1862)

Years in Office 1841-1845
Vice President (none)
Home State Virginia
Political Party Whig
First Ladies Letitia Christian Tyler, died 1842; Julia Gardiner Tyler
Religion Episcopalian

James K. Polk
(1795–1849)

Years in Office 1845-1849
Vice President George M. Dallas
Home State Tennessee
Political Party Democrat
First Lady Sarah Childress Polk
Religion Presbyterian

Zachary Taylor
(1784–1850)

Years in Office 1849-1850 (died in office)
Vice President Millard Fillmore
Home State Kentucky
Political Party Whig
First Lady Margaret Smith Taylor
Religion Episcopalian

Millard Fillmore
(1800–1874)

Years in Office 1850-1853
Vice President (none)
Home State New York
Political Party Whig
First Lady Abigail Powers Fillmore
Religion Unitarian

Franklin Pierce
(1804–1869)

Years in Office 1853-1857
Vice President William R. King, died 1853
Home State New Hampshire
Political Party Democrat
First Lady Jane Appleton Pierce
Religion Episcopalian

James Buchanan
(1791–1868)

Years in Office 1857-1861
Vice President John C. Breckinridge
Home State Pennsylvania
Political Party Democrat
First Lady (none)
Religion Presbyterian

Abraham Lincoln
(1809–1865)

Years in Office 1861-1865 (assassinated)
Vice Presidents Hannibal Hamlin 1861–1865; Andrew Johnson 1865
Home State Illinois
Political Party Republican
First Lady Mary Todd Lincoln
Religion No specific denomination

Andrew Johnson
(1808–1875)

Years in Office 1865-1869
Vice President (none)
Home State Tennessee
Political Party Democrat
First Lady Eliza McCardle Johnson
Religion No specific denomination

Ulysses S. Grant
(1822–1885)

Years in Office 1869-1877
Vice Presidents Schuyler Colfax 1869-1873; Henry Wilson 1873-1875, died
Home State Illinois
Political Party Republican
First Lady Julia Dent Grant
Religion Methodist

Rutherford B. Hayes
(1822–1893)

Years in Office 1877-1881
Vice President William A. Wheeler
Home State Ohio
Political Party Republican
First Lady Lucy Webb Hayes
Religion Methodist

James A. Garfield
(1831–1881)

Years in Office 1881 (assassinated)
Vice President Chester A. Arthur
Home State Ohio
Political Party Republican
First Lady Lucretia Rudolph Garfield
Religion Disciples of Christ

Chester A. Arthur
(1829–1886)

Years in Office 1881-1885
Vice President (none)
Home State New York
Political Party Republican
First Lady (none)
Religion Episcopalian

Grover Cleveland
(1837–1908)

Years in Office 1885-1889, 1893-1897
Vice Presidents Thomas A Hendricks, died 1885; Adlai E. Stevenson 1893-1897
Home State New York
Political Party Democrat
First Lady Frances Folsom Cleveland
Religion Presbyterian

Benjamin Harrison
(1833–1901)

Years in Office 1889-1893
Vice President Levi P. Morton
Home State Indiana
Political Party Republican
First Lady Caroline Scott Harrison
Religion Presbyterian

William McKinley
(1843–1901)

Years in Office 1897-1901 (assassinated)
Vice President Garret A. Hobart 1897-1899, died; Theodore Roosevelt 1901
Home State Ohio
Political Party Republican
First Lady Ida Saxton McKinley
Religion Methodist

Theodore Roosevelt
(1858–1919)

Years in Office 1901-1909
Vice President Charles W. Fairbanks 1905-1909
Home State New York
Political Party Republican
First Lady Edith Carow Roosevelt
Religion Dutch Reformed

William Howard Taft
(1857–1930)

Years in Office 1909-1913
Vice President James S. Sherman 1909-1912, died
Home State Ohio
Political Party Republican
First Lady Helen Herron Taft
Religion Unitarian

Woodrow Wilson
(1856–1924)

Years in Office 1913-1921
Vice President Thomas R. Marshall
Home State New Jersey
Political Party Democrat
First Lady Ellen Louise Axson Wilson, died 1914; Edith Bolling Galt Wilson
Religion Presbyterian

Warren G. Harding
(1865–1923)

Years in Office 1921-1923 (died in office)
Vice President Calvin Coolidge
Home State Ohio
Political Party Republican
First Lady Florence Kling DeWolfe Harding
Religion Baptist

Calvin Coolidge
(1872–1933)

Years in Office 1923-1929
Vice President Charles G. Dawes 1925-1929
Home State Massachusetts
Political Party Republican
First Lady Grace Goodhue Coolidge
Religion Congregationalist

Herbert C. Hoover
(1874–1964)

Years in Office 1929-1933
Vice President Charles Curtis
Home State California
Political Party Republican
First Lady Lou Henry Hoover
Religion Quaker

Franklin D. Roosevelt
(1882–1945)

Years in Office 1933-1945 (died in office)
Vice Presidents John Nance Garner 1933-1941; Henry Wallace 1941-1945; Harry S. Truman 1945
Home State New York
Political Party Democrat
First Lady Anna Eleanor Roosevelt
Religion Episcopalian

Harry S. Truman
(1884–1972)

Years in Office 1945-1953
Vice President Alben W. Barkley (1949-1953)
Home State Missouri
Political Party Democrat
First Lady Elizabeth (Bess) Wallace Truman
Religion Baptist

Dwight D. Eisenhower
(1890–1969)

Years in Office 1953-1961
Vice President Richard M. Nixon
Home State Kansas
Political Party Republican
First Lady Marie (Mamie) Doud Eisenhower
Religion Presbyterian

John F. Kennedy
(1917–1963)

Years in Office 1961-1963 (assassinated)
Vice President Lyndon B. Johnson
Home State Massachusetts
Political Party Democrat
First Lady Jacqueline Bouvier Kennedy
Religion Roman Catholic

Lyndon Baines Johnson
(1908–1973)

Years in Office 1963-1969
Vice President Hubert H. Humphrey
Home State Texas
Political Party Democrat
First Lady Claudia (Lady Bird) Taylor Johnson
Religion Disciples of Christ

Richard M. Nixon
(1913–1994)

Years in Office 1969-1974 (resigned)
Vice Presidents Spiro T. Agnew 1969-1973, resigned; Gerald R. Ford 1973-1974
Home State California
Political Party Republican
First Lady Patricia (Pat) Ryan Nixon
Religion Quaker

Gerald R. Ford
(1913–)

Years in Office 1974-1977
Vice President Nelson A. Rockefeller
Home State Michigan
Political Party Republican
First Lady Elizabeth (Betty) Bloomer Ford
Religion Episcopalian

James (Jimmy) Carter
(1924–)

Years in Office 1977-1981
Vice President Walter F. Mondale
Home State Georgia
Political Party Democrat
First Lady Rosalynn Smith Carter
Religion Baptist

Ronald W. Reagan
(1911–)

Years in Office 1981-1989
Vice President George Bush
Home State California
Political Party Republican
First Lady Nancy Davis Reagan
Religion Presbyterian

George Bush
(1924–)

Years in Office 1989-1993
Vice President J. Danforth (Dan) Quayle
Home State Texas
Political Party Republican
First Lady Barbara Pierce Bush
Religion Episcopalian

William Jefferson Clinton
(1946–)

Years in Office 1993-2001
Vice President Albert Gore, Jr.
Home State Arkansas
Political Party Democrat
First Lady Hillary Rodham Clinton
Religion Baptist

George W. Bush
(1946–)

Years in Office 2001–
Vice President Richard Cheney
Home State Texas
Political Party Republican
First Lady Laura Bush
Religion Methodist

White House Technology Firsts

1834	Indoor Plumbing
1845	Central Heating
1848	Gas Lighting
1866	Telegraph
1877	Telephone
1891	Electricity
1921	Radio
1926	Electric Refrigerator
1933	Air Conditioning
1942	Bomb Shelter
1947	Television
1979	Computer
1993	Internet

Sources: *New Columbia Encyclopedia*, 1975; *The Complete Book of U.S. Presidents*, 1993; *World Almanac*, 2000.

Our Fifty States

ALABAMA
★ Montgomery

Date of Statehood 1819

Nickname Heart of Dixie

Population 4,447,100

Area 52,423 sq mi;
    135,776 sq km

Region Southeast

★ Hartford
CONNECTICUT

Date of Statehood 1788

Nickname Constitution State

Population 3,405,565

Area 5,544 sq mi;
    14,359 sq km

Region Northeast

ALASKA
Juneau ★

Date of Statehood 1959

Nickname The Last Frontier

Population 626,932

Area 656,424 sq mi;
    1,700,138 sq km

Region West

★ Dover
DELAWARE

Date of Statehood 1787

Nickname First State

Population 783,600

Area 2,489 sq mi;
    6,447 sq km

Region Northeast

ARIZONA
★ Phoenix

Date of Statehood 1912

Nickname Grand Canyon State

Population 5,130,632

Area 114,006 sq mi;
    295,276 sq km

Region Southwest

Tallahassee ★
FLORIDA

Date of Statehood 1845

Nickname Sunshine State

Population 15,982,378

Area 58,664 sq mi;
    151,939 sq km

Region Southeast

ARKANSAS
★
Little Rock

Date of Statehood 1836

Nickname Land of Opportunity

Population 2,673,400

Area 53,182 sq mi;
    137,741 sq km

Region Southeast

★ Atlanta
GEORGIA

Date of Statehood 1788

Nickname Peach State

Population 8,186,453

Area 59,441 sq mi;
    153,952 sq km

Region Southeast

CALIFORNIA
★
Sacramento

Date of Statehood 1850

Nickname Golden State

Population 33,871,648

Area 163,707 sq mi;
    424,001 sq km

Region West

HAWAII
★
Honolulu

Date of Statehood 1959

Nickname The Aloha State

Population 1,211,537

Area 10,932 sq mi;
    28,314 sq km

Region West

Denver ★
COLORADO

Date of Statehood 1876

Nickname Centennial State

Population 4,301,261

Area 104,100 sq mi;
    269,619 sq km

Region West

IDAHO
★ Boise

Date of Statehood 1890

Nickname Gem State

Population 1,293,953

Area 83,574 sq mi;
    216,457 sq km

Region West

ILLINOIS
★ Springfield

Date of Statehood 1818

Nickname The Prairie State

Population 12,419,293

Area 57,918 sq mi; 150,008 sq km

Region Middle West

MAINE
Augusta ★

Date of Statehood 1820

Nickname Pine Tree State

Population 1,274,923

Area 35,387 sq mi; 91,652 sq km

Region Northeast

INDIANA
★
Indianapolis

Date of Statehood 1816

Nickname Hoosier State

Population 6,080,485

Area 36,420 sq mi; 94,328 sq km

Region Middle West

MARYLAND
Annapolis ★

Date of Statehood 1788

Nickname Free State

Population 5,296,486

Area 12,407 sq mi; 32,134 sq km

Region Northeast

IOWA
★
Des Moines

Date of Statehood 1846

Nickname Hawkeye State

Population 2,926,324

Area 56,276 sq mi; 145,755 sq km

Region Middle West

Boston ★

MASSACHUSETTS

Date of Statehood 1788

Nickname Bay State

Population 6,349,097

Area 10,555 sq mi; 27,337 sq km

Region Northeast

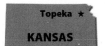

Topeka ★

KANSAS

Date of Statehood 1861

Nickname Sunflower State

Population 2,688,418

Area 82,282 sq mi; 213,110 sq km

Region Middle West

MICHIGAN
★
Lansing

Date of Statehood 1837

Nickname Wolverine State

Population 9,938,444

Area 96,810 sq mi; 250,738 sq km

Region Middle West

KENTUCKY
★
Frankfort

Date of Statehood 1792

Nickname Bluegrass State

Population 4,041,769

Area 40,411 sq mi; 104,664 sq km

Region Southeast

MINNESOTA

St. Paul ★

Date of Statehood 1858

Nickname North Star State

Population 4,919,479

Area 86,943 sq mi; 225,182 sq km

Region Middle West

LOUISIANA

Baton Rouge ★

Date of Statehood 1812

Nickname Pelican State

Population 4,468,976

Area 51,843 sq mi; 134,273 sq km

Region Southeast

MISSISSIPPI
★
Jackson

Date of Statehood 1817

Nickname Magnolia State

Population 2,844,658

Area 48,434 sq mi; 125,444 sq km

Region Southeast

Our Fifty States
Missouri • Oregon

MISSOURI
★ Jefferson City

Date of Statehood 1821

Nickname Show Me State

Population 5,595,211

Area 69,709 sq mi;
180,546 sq km

Region Middle West

MONTANA
★ Helena

Date of Statehood 1889

Nickname Treasure State

Population 902,195

Area 147,046 sq mi;
380,849 sq km

Region West

NEBRASKA
Lincoln ★

Date of Statehood 1867

Nickname Cornhusker State

Population 1,711,263

Area 77,358 sq mi;
200,357 sq km

Region Middle West

NEVADA
★ Carson City

Date of Statehood 1864

Nickname Silver State

Population 1,998,257

Area 110,567 sq mi;
286,369 sq km

Region West

NEW HAMPSHIRE
Concord ★

Date of Statehood 1788

Nickname Granite State

Population 1,235,786

Area 9,351 sq mi;
24,219 sq km

Region Northeast

NEW JERSEY
★ Trenton

Date of Statehood 1787

Nickname Garden State

Population 8,414,350

Area 8,722 sq mi;
22,590 sq km

Region Northeast

NEW MEXICO
★ Santa Fe

Date of Statehood 1912

Nickname Land of Enchantment

Population 1,819,046

Area 121,598 sq mi;
314,939 sq km

Region Southwest

NEW YORK
Albany ★

Date of Statehood 1788

Nickname Empire State

Population 18,976,457

Area 54,475 sq mi;
141,090 sq km

Region Northeast

NORTH CAROLINA
Raleigh ★

Date of Statehood 1789

Nickname Tar Heel State

Population 8,049,313

Area 53,821 sq mi;
139,396 sq km

Region Southeast

NORTH DAKOTA
Bismarck ★

Date of Statehood 1889

Nickname Peace Garden State

Population 642,200

Area 70,704 sq mi;
183,123 sq km

Region Middle West

OHIO
★ Columbus

Date of Statehood 1803

Nickname Buckeye State

Population 11,353,140

Area 44,828 sq mi;
116,105 sq km

Region Middle West

OKLAHOMA
★ Oklahoma City

Date of Statehood 1907

Nickname Sooner State

Population 3,450,654

Area 69,903 sq mi;
181,049 sq km

Region Southwest

OKLAHOMA

OREGON
★ Salem

Date of Statehood 1859

Nickname Beaver State

Population 3,421,399

Area 98,386 sq mi;
254,820 sq km

Region West

PENNSYLVANIA

Harrisburg ★

Date of Statehood 1787

Nickname Keystone State

Population 12,281,054

Area 46,058 sq mi;
119,290 sq km

Region Northeast

VERMONT

★
Montpelier

Date of Statehood 1791

Nickname Green Mountain State

Population 608,827

Area 9,615 sq mi;
24,903 sq km

Region Northeast

RHODE ISLAND

Providence ★

Date of Statehood 1790

Nickname Ocean State

Population 1,048,319

Area 1,545 sq mi;
4,002 sq km

Region Northeast

VIRGINIA

Richmond ★

Date of Statehood 1788

Nickname Old Dominion

Population 7,078,515

Area 42,769 sq mi;
110,772 sq km

Region Southeast

SOUTH CAROLINA
★
Columbia

Date of Statehood 1788

Nickname Palmetto State

Population 4,012,012

Area 32,007 sq mi;
82,898 sq km

Region Southeast

★ Olympia
WASHINGTON

Date of Statehood 1889

Nickname Evergreen State

Population 5,894,121

Area 71,303 sq mi;
184,675 sq km

Region West

Pierre ★
SOUTH DAKOTA

Date of Statehood 1889

Nickname Mount Rushmore State

Population 754,844

Area 77,121 sq mi;
199,743 sq km

Region Middle West

WEST VIRGINIA

★ Charleston

Date of Statehood 1863

Nickname Mountain State

Population 1,808,344

Area 24,231 sq mi;
62,758 sq km

Region Southeast

TENNESSEE

★ Nashville

Date of Statehood 1796

Nickname Volunteer State

Population 5,689,283

Area 42,146 sq mi;
109,158 sq km

Region Southeast

WISCONSIN

Madison
★

Date of Statehood 1848

Nickname Badger State

Population 5,363,675

Area 65,503 sq mi;
169,653 sq km

Region Middle West

TEXAS

Austin ★

Date of Statehood 1845

Nickname Lone Star State

Population 20,851,820

Area 268,601 sq mi;
695,677 sq km

Region Southwest

★
Salt Lake City

UTAH

Date of Statehood 1896

Nickname Beehive State

Population 2,233,169

Area 84,904 sq mi;
219,901 sq km

Region West

WYOMING

Cheyenne
★

Date of Statehood 1890

Nickname Equality State

Population 493,782

Area 97,818 sq mi;
253,349 sq km

Region West

Sources: Population — U.S. Bureau of Census, 2000; Area — U.S. Bureau of Census, 2000.

Dictionary of Geographic Terms

STRAIT (strāt) A narrow waterway that connects two larger bodies of water.

GULF (gulf) Part of an ocean that extends into the land; larger than a bay.

RESERVOIR (rez'ər vwär) A natural or artificial lake used to store water.

PLATEAU (pla tō') A high, flat area that rises steeply above the surrounding land.

DAM (dam) A wall built across a river, creating a lake that stores water.

CANYON (kan'yən) A deep, narrow valley with steep sides.

MESA (mā'sə) A hill with a flat top; smaller than a plateau.

DUNE (dün) A mound, hill, or ridge of sand heaped up by the wind.

BUTTE (būt) A small, flat-topped hill; smaller than a mesa or plateau.

OASIS (ō ā'sis) A fertile area in a desert that is watered by a spring.

HILL (hil) A rounded, raised landform; not as high as a mountain.

VALLEY (val'ē) An area of low land between hills or mountains.

DESERT (dez'ərt) A dry environment with few plants and animals.

COAST (kōst) The land along an ocean.

BAY (bā) Part of an ocean or lake that extends deeply into the land.

ISTHMUS (is'məs) A narrow strip of land that connects two larger bodies of land.

ISLAND (ī'lənd) A body of land completely surrounded by water.

PENINSULA (pə nin'sə lə) A body of land surrounded on three sides by water.

R58

VOLCANO (vol kā′nō) An opening in Earth's surface through which hot rock and ash are forced out.

MOUNTAIN (moun′tən) A high landform with steep sides; higher than a hill.

HARBOR (här′bər) A sheltered place along a coast where boats dock safely.

PEAK (pēk) The top of a mountain.

GLACIER (glā′shər) A huge sheet of ice that moves slowly across the land.

CANAL (kə nal′) A channel built to carry water for irrigation or transportation.

LAKE (lāk) A body of water completely surrounded by land.

TRIBUTARY (trib′yə ter ē) A smaller river that flows into a larger river.

SOURCE (sôrs) The starting point of a river.

PORT (pôrt) A place where ships load and unload their goods.

TIMBERLINE (tim′bər līn) A line above which trees do not grow.

WATERFALL (wô′tər fôl) A flow of water falling vertically.

PLAIN (plān) A large area of nearly flat land.

RIVER BASIN (riv′ər bā′sin) All the land that is drained by a river and its tributaries.

MOUNTAIN RANGE (moun′tən rānj) A row or chain of mountains.

RIVER (riv′ər) A stream of water that flows across the land and empties into another body of water.

BASIN (bā′sin) A bowl-shaped landform surrounded by higher land.

DELTA (del′tə) Land made of soil left behind as a river drains into a larger body of water.

MOUNTAIN PASS (moun′tən pas) A narrow gap through a mountain range.

MOUTH (mouth) The place where a river empties into a larger body of water.

OCEAN (ō′shən) A large body of salt water; oceans cover much of Earth's surface.

Gazetteer

This Gazetteer is a geographical dictionary that will help you to pronounce and locate the places discussed in this book. Latitude and longitude are given for cities and some other places. The page numbers tell you where each place appears on a map or in the text.

A

Abilene (ab'ə lēn) A city in central Kansas; in the 1860s, Abilene was the northern end of the Chisholm Trail; 39°N, 97°W. (m. 485, t. 484)

Acadia (ə kā' dē ə) A French-speaking region in Canada where Cajuns originally came from; 48°N, 65°W. (t. 31)

Acapulco (a kə' pul kō) A resort city on Mexico's Pacific coast; 17°N, 100°W. (m.617, t. 620)

Africa (af'ri kə) One of Earth's seven continents. (m. R6, t. 106)

Alamo, the (al'ə mō) A mission in San Antonio, Texas, where Mexican troops defeated Texan defenders in 1836; 30°N, 98°W. (t. 395)

Alaska Range (ə las'kə rānj) A mountain range in southern Alaska. (m. R18)

Alberta (al bûr'tə) A province of Canada in the southwestern part of the country. (m. 611)

Allegheny Mountains (al ə gā'nē moun'tənz) A mountain range in Pennsylvania, Virginia, and West Virginia, part of the Appalachians. (m. R18)

Amazon River (am'ə zon riv'ər) The longest river in South America, flowing from the Andes Mountains to the Atlantic Ocean. (m. 629, t. 629)

Anchorage (ang'kər ij) A city in southern Alaska, the largest city in the state and an important port; 61°N, 150°W. (m. R16, t. 77)

Andes Mountains (an'dēz moun'tənz) A mountain range along the west coast of South America, the world's longest chain of mountains. (m. 629, t. 48)

Angel Island (ān'jəl ī'lənd) An island in San Francisco Bay, California, which served as the west coast entry point for immigrants from the 1880s to the early 1920s; 38°N, 122°W. (t. 512)

Annapolis (ə nap'ə ləs) Capital of Maryland and site of the U.S. Naval Academy; 39°N, 76°W. (m. R16, t. 316)

Antarctic Circle (ant ärk'tik sûr'kəl) A line of latitude at 66°33'S. (m. R4)

Antarctica (ant ärk'ti kə) One of Earth's seven continents. (m. R4)

Antietam (an tē'təm) A creek near the town of Sharpsburg, Maryland, site of a major Civil War battle in 1862; 39°N, 78°W. (m.451, t.443)

Appalachian Mountains (ap ə lā'chē ən moun'tənz) Chain of mountains stretching from Canada to Alabama. (m. R16, t. 5)

Appomattox Court House (ap ə mat'əks kôrt hous) A town in central Virginia, where Confederate General Lee surrendered to Union General Grant in 1865, ending the Civil War; 37°N, 79°W. (m. 451, t. 452)

Arctic Circle (ärk'tik sûr'kəl) A line of latitude at 66°/30'N. (m. R4)

Arctic Ocean (ärk'tik ō'shən) The smallest of Earth's four oceans. (m. R4)

Argentina (är jən tē'nə) A country in South America. (m.629, t.630)

Asia (ā'zhə) The largest of Earth's seven continents. (m. R8, t.98)

Atlanta (at lan'tə) The capital and largest city of Georgia; 34°N, 84°W. (m. R9, t. 449)

Atlantic Ocean (at lan'tik ō'shən) One of Earth's four oceans. (m. R4)

Australia (ôs trāl'yə) The smallest of Earth's seven continents. (m. R5)

pronunciation key

a	at	ī	ice	u	up	th	thin
ā	ape	îr	pierce	ū	use	th	this
ä	far	o	hot	ü	rule	zh	measure
âr	care	ō	old	ù	pull	ə	about, taken,
e	end	ô	fork	ûr	turn		pencil, lemon,
ē	me	oi	oil	hw	white		circus
i	it	ou	out	ng	song		

B

Bahamas (bə hä′məz) A chain of islands in the West Indies, southeast of Florida. (m. 121, t. 121)

Baja California (bä′hä kal i fôr′nyə) A long, narrow peninsula at the northwest corner of Mexico. (m. 617)

Baltimore (bôl′ tə môr) The largest city in Maryland and a port on Chesapeake Bay; 39°N, 77°W. (m. R16, t. 193)

Bay of Pigs (bā əv pigz′) Site of a failed attempt by a small Cuban force to overtake the communist government; 25°N, 82°W. (t. 570)

Belize (bā lēz′) A country on the northeastern coast of Central America, on the Caribbean Sea. (m. R4, t. 626)

Bering Strait (ber′ing strāt) A narrow waterway connecting the Bering Sea and the Arctic Ocean. (m. R4, t. 80)

Beringia (bə rin′jē ə) A sunken land bridge that once connected North America and Asia at what is now the Bering Strait; 62°N, 167°W. (t. 41)

Berlin (bûr lin′) The capital of Germany, divided from 1945 to 1989; 53°N, 13°E. (m. 563, t. 570)

Berlin Wall (bûr lin′ wôl) A wall that separated communist East Berlin and democratic West Berlin. It was torn down in 1989. (t. 570)

Birmingham (bûr′ming ham) A city in north-central Alabama, the largest city in the state; 34°N, 87°W. (m. R16, t. 580)

Black Hills (blak hilz) A mountain range in southwestern South Dakota and northeastern Wyoming. (m. R18, t. 72)

Bolivia (bə liv′ē ə) A country in west-central South America. (m. 629)

Boonesborough (bünz′bər ə) A town in east-central Kentucky, now Boonesboro; site of fort founded in 1775 by Daniel Boone; 38°N, 84°W. (m. 349, t. 348)

Bosnia (boz′ nē ə) One of the many countries that came out of the former Yugoslavia. (m. R10, t. 595)

Boston (bôs′tən) Capital and largest city of Massachusetts; 42°N, 71°W. (m. 181, t. 181)

Brazil (brə zil′) The largest country in South America, in the eastern part of the continent. (m. 629, t. 629)

Brooks Range (brüks rānj) A mountain range extending across the northern part of Alaska. (m. R18)

Buenos Aires (bwā′nəs ī′rəs) The capital of Argentina; 35°S, 58°W. (m. 629, t. 632)

Bull Run (bùl run) A stream in northeastern Virginia near Washington, D.C.; site of two major Civil War battles in which the Union forces were defeated (1861 and 1862); 39°N, 77°W. (m. 451, t. 437)

Bunker Hill (bung′ kər hil) Site of a Revolutionary War battle where the Patriots proved their will to fight. (m. 299, t. 273)

C

California Trail (kal i fôr′nyə trāl) A trail through the Rocky Mountains and the Sierra Nevadas to the California gold fields used by "forty-niners" in 1849. (m. 385, t. 386)

Cambodia (kam bō′dē ə) A country in southeastern Asia. (m. 587, t. 586)

Canada (kan′ə də) A country in northern North America, bordering the United States. The second-largest country in the world, it is made up of ten provinces and two territories. (m. 611, t. 153)

Canadian Shield (kə nā′dē ən shēld) A plateau of ancient rocks covering more than half of Canada. (m. 611, t. 611)

Canyon de Chelly (kan′ yən də shā) A fertile canyon in Arizona that became home to the Navajo during the 1700s. (m. 59, t. 60)

Cape Cod (kāp kod) A peninsula in southeastern Massachusetts, enclosing Cape Cod Bay. (m. 181, t. 165)

Cape Horn (kāp hôrn) The southernmost tip of South America. (m. 629, t. 629)

Cape of Good Hope (kāp əv gùd hōp) The southernmost tip of Africa; 34°S, 18°E. (m. 110, t. 110)

Cape Verde (kāp vûrd) The westernmost point of Africa; 25°N, 25°W. (m. 110, t. 110)

Caribbean Sea (kar ə bē′ən sē) A part of the Atlantic Ocean, due east of Central America. (m. 623, t. 117)

Cascade Range (kas kād′ rānj) A mountain range extending from northern California through Oregon and Washington. (m. R18)

Catskill Mountains (kats′kil moun′tənz) A mountain range in New York, part of the Appalachians. (m. 196)

Central America (sen′trəl ə mer′i kə) A region between the Pacific Ocean and the Caribbean Sea, occupying the southern part of the North American continent south of Mexico. (m. 623, t. 622)

Chapultepec (chə pul′tə pek) A rocky hill in Mexico City, Mexico, site of a fortress captured by United States forces in 1847 in the Mexican War; 19°N, 99°W. (t. 398)

Charleston (chärlz′tən) Capital and largest city in West Virginia; 38°N, 82°W (m. 33); and a coastal city in southeastern South Carolina, originally Charles Town; 33°N, 80°W. (m. 208, t. 206)

Charlestown (chärlz′taun) A town in Massachusetts across the Charles River from Boston; the Battle of Bunker Hill was fought near there in 1775; 42°N, 71°W. (m. 271, t. 273)

Chesapeake Bay (ches′ə pēk bā) A long arm of the Atlantic Ocean surrounded by Maryland and Virginia. (m. 160, t. 160)

Chicago (shi kä′gō) A city in northeastern Illinois, the largest city in the state, a transportation and manufacturing center; 42°N, 88°W. (m. R16, t. 241)

Chile (chil′ē) A country in southwestern South America. (m. 629, t. 629)

Chimney Rock (chim′ nē rok′) A point on the Oregon Trail where travelers often got rid of extra weight such as furniture and other possessions. (t. 387)

China (chī′nə) A country in eastern Asia, the most populous in the world. (m. R8, t. 97)

Chisholm Trail (chiz′əm trāl) A cattle trail from San Antonio, Texas, to Abilene, Kansas, in use from 1867 to 1886. (m. 485, t. 484)

Coast Ranges (kōst rānj′əz) The mountain ranges along the Pacific Coast of North America. (m. R18)

Coastal Plain (kōst′əl plān) Flat lowland along the Atlantic Coast and the Gulf Coast. (t. 6)

Colorado River (kol ə rad′ō riv′ər) A river in the southwestern United States, flowing from Colorado to the Gulf of California. (m. R18)

Columbia River (kə lum′bē ə riv′ər) A river in northwestern North America. (m. 352, t. 354)

Concord (kong′kərd) A town in eastern Massachusetts, site of one of the first battles of the American Revolution; 42°N, 71°W. (m. 271, t. 270)

Costa Rica (kōs′tə rē′kə) A country in southern Central America. (m. 623)

Cuba (kū′bə) An island country in the Caribbean Sea, the largest of the West Indies. (m. 520, t. 518)

Cumberland Gap (kum′bər lənd gap) A natural pass through the Appalachian Mountains in Kentucky; 37°N, 84°W. (m. 349, t. 348)

Cuzco (cùz′ ko) The Incan capital city, located in modern-day Peru; 14°S, 72°W. (m. 51, t. 50)

D

Detroit (di troit′) A city in southeastern Michigan, the largest city in the state, and an important manufacturing center; 42°N, 83°W. (m. R16, t. 241)

District of Columbia (dis′trikt uv kə lum′bē ə) The capital district of the United States; 39°N, 77°W. (m. R16, t. 350)

Dodge City (doj sit′ē) A city in southwestern Kansas. In the 1870s and 1880s, Dodge City was a railhead at the end of a major cattle trail; 38°N, 100°W. (m. 485, t. 484)

Dominican Republic (də min′i kən ri pub′lik) A country in the West Indies occupying the eastern part of the island of Hispaniola. (m. 623)

Dust Bowl (dust bōl) A 150,000-square-mile area of the Great Plains that suffered years of drought and dust storms in the 1930s. (m. 553, t. 553)

E

Ecuador (ek′wə dôr) A country on the northwestern coast of South America. (m. R14, t. 50)

Egypt (ē′ jipt) A country in the Middle East. (m. R6, t. 594)

El Camino Real (el cä mē′nō rä äl) A number of routes that connected Spain's colonies in the American Southwest to Mexico from the late 1500s to the middle 1800s. (m. 238, t. 239)

El Salvador (el sal′və dôr) A country in western Central America. (m. 623, t. 625)

Ellis Island (el′is ī′lənd) A small island in upper New York Bay that served as the chief United States point of arrival for immigrants from 1892 to 1943; 41°N, 74°W. (t. 28)

England (ing′lənd) A part of the United Kingdom of Great Britain and Northern Ireland. England occupies the southern part of the island of Great Britain. (m. R10, t. 151)

equator (i kwā′tər) An imaginary line encircling Earth halfway between the North Pole and the South Pole, designated as 0° latitude. (m. H12, t. H12)

Erie Canal (îr′ē kə nal′) A human-made waterway across New York State, connecting the Hudson River with Lake Erie. (m. 374, t. 373)

Europe (yür′əp) One of Earth's seven continents, between Asia and the Atlantic Ocean. (m. R10, t. 96)

F

Fort Duquesne (fôrt dü kān′) A fort built by the French in 1754 where Pittsburgh stands today. (t. 247)

Fort McHenry (fôrt mək hen′rə) A fort protecting the harbor of Baltimore, Maryland. (t. 360)

Fort Necessity (fôrt nə ses′i tē) A temporary fort built 60 miles south of Fort Duquesne in 1754 by troops under George Washington's command; 40°N, 80°W. (t. 247)

Fort Sumter (fôrt sum′tər) A fort guarding the entrance to Charleston Harbor, South Carolina; site of the first battle of the Civil War; 33°N, 80°W. (m. 451, t. 434)

Fort Ticonderoga (fôrt tī kon də rō′gə) A fort on Lake Champlain, New York; site of important battles in the American Revolution; 44°N, 74°W. (m. 299, t. 273)

Fort Vincennes (fôrt vin senz′) A fort on the Wabash River; 39°N, 88°W. (t. 298)

Fort Wagner (fôrt wag′nər) A fort on Morris Island in Charleston harbor, South Carolina; 33°N, 80°W. (t. 444)

Four Corners (fôr kôr′nərz) The place at which the states of Arizona, New Mexico, Utah, and Colorado meet; 37°N, 109°W. (m. 59, t. 59)

France (frans) A country in western Europe. (m. R10, t. 97)

French Guiana (french gē an′ə) A common wealth of France on the Atlantic coast of South America. (m. 629, t. 630)

G

Gettysburg (get′iz bûrg) A town in south-central Pennsylvania, site of a major Union victory during the Civil War; 40°N, 77°W. (m. 451, t. 446)

Ghana (gä′ nə) A country in West Africa from which many enslaved African Americans were abducted. Also see **Nigeria**. (m. R6, t. 212)

Goliad (gō′lē ad) A city in Texas where Texan defenders were defeated by Mexican troops in 1836; 29°N, 97°W. (t. 395)

Grand Banks (grand bangks) A fishing area off the coast of Canada, discovered by John Cabot in 1497; 45°N, 62°W. (t. 151)

Grand Canyon (grand kan′yən) A vast and richly colored canyon on the Colorado River in northwestern Arizona. (t. 7)

Great Lakes (grāt lāks) A group of five large fresh-water lakes in North America along the border between Canada and the United States. The Great Lakes are Lake Superior, Lake Michigan, Lake Huron, Lake Erie, and Lake Ontario. (m. R19, t. 6)

Great Lakes–St. Lawrence Lowlands (grāt lāks sānt lôr′ əns lō′ landz) The most populated region in Canada, located near the Great Lakes. (m. 611, t. 611)

Great Plains (grāt plānz) A flat, dry land area with rich soil in the Midwest. (m. R18, t. 6)

Great Salt Lake (grāt sôlt lāk) A lake in northwestern Utah, the largest salt lake in North America; 41°N, 113°W. (m. R18, t. 386)

Greensboro (grēnz′bûr ō) A city in north-central North Carolina; 36°N, 80°W. (t. 580)

Guadalajara (gwä də lə här′ə) The second largest city in Mexico, located northwest of Mexico City; 21°N, 103°W. (m. 617, t. 620)

Guam (gwäm) An island in the western Pacific Ocean; 14°N, 143°E. (m. 520, t. 521)

Guatemala (gwä tə mä′lə) A country in the northern part of Central America. (m. 623, t. 623)

Guilford Court House (gil′ fərd kôrt hous) Site of a 1781 revolutionary battle where Cornwallis lost one-fourth of his soldiers. (m. 338, t. 301)

Gulf Coastal Plains (gulf kō′ stəl plānz) A flat lowland along the Atlantic Coast and Gulf Coast that has sandy beaches, wetlands, and rich farmland. (m. R19, t. 6)

Gulf of Mexico (gulf əv mek′si kō) An arm of the Atlantic Ocean between the United States and Mexico. (m. R15)

Guyana (gī an′ə) A country on the northeastern coast of South America. (m. 629, t. 630)

H

Haiti (hā′tē) A country in the West Indies, occupying the western part of the island of Hispaniola. (m. 623, t. 624)

Harlem (här′ləm) A district of New York City. (t. 547)

Harpers Ferry (här′pərz fer′ē) A town in northeastern West Virginia; 39°N, 78°W. (t. 427)

Havana (hə van′ ə) The capital of Cuba; in 1898, the USS *Maine* exploded here, starting the Spanish-American War. 25°N, 82°W. (m. 623, t. 518)

Hiroshima (hîr ə shē′mə) A port city in southwestern Japan on the island of Honshu; the first city where an atomic bomb was dropped; 34°N, 132°E. (m. 562, t. 564)

Hispaniola (his pən yō′lə) An island in the Greater Antilles in the Caribbean. (m. 117)

Hodenosaunee Trail (hō den ō sä′nē trāl) A 250-mile path connecting the homelands of five Iroquois peoples in the 1500s. (m. 65, t. 64)

Honduras (hon dùr′əs) A country in northern Central America. (m. 623)

Houston (hüs′tən) The largest city in Texas and a major port; 30°N, 95°W. (m. R16, t. 396)

Hudson Bay (hud′sən bā) A large inland sea in north-eastern Canada. (m. 611)

Hudson River (hud′sən riv′ər) A tidal river in eastern New York that empties into the Atlantic Ocean. (m. 254, t. 152)

I

India (in′dē ə) A large peninsular country in southern Asia. (m. R8, t. 105)

Indian Ocean (in′dē ən ō′shən) One of Earth's four largest bodies of water, south of Asia, between Africa and Australia. (R5)

Indian Territory (in′dē ən ter′i tôr ē) Land set aside by the Indian Removal Act of 1830 as a place for Native Americans forced from their homelands. (m. 379, t. 379)

Interior Plains (in tîr′ ē ər plānz) A vast area of flat land that stretches between the Appalachian and Rocky mountains. (m. 218, t. 6)

Iraq (i rak′) A country in southwestern Asia. (m. 596, t. 596)

Israel (iz′ rē əl) A country in the Middle East. (m. 596, t. 594)

Isthmus of Panama (pan′ə mä) A narrow strip of land connecting North America and South America. (m. 525, t. 525)

Italy (it′ə lē) A country in southern Europe. (m. R10, t. 97)

---J---

Jamaica (jə māʹkə) An island country in the West Indies, south of Cuba. (m. 623)

Jamestown (jāmzʹtoun) A town in southeastern Virginia; the first permanent English settlement in North America, founded in 1607; 37°N, 77°W. (m. 160, t. 158)

Japan (jə panʹ) A country in eastern Asia. (m. R8, t. 558)

---K---

Kansas City (kanʹzəs sitʹē) A city in western Missouri, the largest city in the state; 39°N, 95°W. (m. R16)

Kitty Hawk (kitʹē hôk) A village on the Outer Banks off the coast of North Carolina. Wilbur and Orville Wright made the first successful airplane flight there in 1903; 36°N, 76°W. (t. 526)

Kuwait (kü wātʹ) A country in the Middle East. (m. 596, t. 596)

---L---

La Venta (lä venʹ tə) A popular Olmec trading city, circa 1300 to 400 B.C. along the Gulf Coast of what is now southern Mexico; 15°N, 95°W. (m. 43, t. 42)

Lake Erie (lāk irʹē) The southernmost of the Great Lakes, bordering Canada and the United States. (m. R19, t. 373)

Lake Huron (lāk hyürʹən) Second largest of the Great Lakes, bordering Canada and the United States. (m. R19)

Lake Michigan (lāk mishʹi gən) Third largest of the Great Lakes, between Michigan and Wisconsin. (m. R19)

Lake Ontario (lāk on târʹē ō) The smallest and eastern-most of the Great Lakes, bordering Canada and the United States. (m. R19)

Lake Superior (lāk sə pîrʹē ər) The largest and northern-most of the Great Lakes, bordering Canada and the United States. (m. R19)

Latin America (latʹin ə merʹi kə) The part of the Western Hemisphere south of the United States—including Mexico, Central America, South America, and the West Indies. (m. R14, t. 620)

Lexington (lekʹsing tən) A town in eastern Massachusetts, site of one of the first battles of the American Revolution; 42°N, 71°W. (m. 271, t. 270)

Lima (lēʹmə) The capital of Peru, built by Pizarro in 1534; 13°S, 78°W. (m. R5, t. 144)

Little Bighorn River (litʹəl bigʹhôrn rivʹər) A river in northern Wyoming and southern Montana. (t. 496)

Lowell (lōʹəl) A city in northeastern Massachusetts; 42°N, 71°W. (t. 370)

---M---

Massachusetts Bay Colony (mas ə chüʹ sits bā kolʹ ə nē) The first colony settled by Puritans in 1629 in what is today Massachusetts. (m. 181, t. 180)

Menlo Park (menʹlō pärk) A town in central New Jersey, site of Thomas Edison's laboratory; 41°N, 74°W. (t. 505)

Mesa Verde (māʹsə verdʹē) An Anasazi village built around A.D. 900, located in present-day Colorado; 57°N, 108°W. (m. 45)

Mexico (mekʹsi kō) A North American country on the southern border of the United States. (m. 617, t. 41)

Mexico City (mekʹsi kō sitʹē) Capital and largest city in Mexico, the second largest city in the world; 19°N, 99°W. (m. 617, t. 144)

Middle Colonies (midʹəl kolʹə nēz) The colonies of Delaware, New Jersey, New York, and Pennsylvania before the American Revolution. (m. 191, t. 189)

Middle East (midʹəl ēst) An area that includes the countries located in southwest Asia and northern Africa. (m. 596, t. 594)

Mississippi River (mis ə sipʹē rivʹər) The longest river in the United States, flowing from Minnesota to the Gulf of Mexico. (m. R18, t. 6)

Missouri River (mi zürʹē rivʹər) A large tributary of the Mississippi, flowing from Montana to the Mississippi River north of St. Louis. (m. 381, t. 355)

Montgomery (mont gumʹə rē) Capital of Alabama; 32°N, 86°W. (m. 583, t. 581)

Montreal (mon trē älʹ) A port city in southern Quebec; Canada's largest city; 46°N, 74°W. (m. 611, t. 614)

Mormon Trail (môrʹmən trāl) A route west named for the 20,000 Mormons who migrated from Nauvoo, Illinois, between 1837 and 1847. (m. 385, t. 386)

Mount McKinley (mount mə kinʹlē) The highest mountain in North America, elevation 20,320 feet (6,194 m), located in the Alaska Range in south-central Alaska; also known as Denali, or "Great One"; 64°N, 153°W. (m. R18, t. 5)

Mount Vernon (mount vûrʹnən) The home of George Washington, on the Potomac River; 39°N, 77°W. (t. 291)

Mount Whitney (mount hwitʹnē) The highest mountain in the continental United States, elevation 14,494 (4,418 m), located in southeast California; 37°N, 118°W. (m. R19)

---N---

Nagasaki (nä gə säʹkē) A city in Japan on the western coast of the island of Kyushu. It was the second city struck by an atomic bomb; 33°N, 130°E. (m. 562, t. 564)

Nanjing (nanʹ jēngʹ) A Chinese city where more than 200,000 civilians were killed by the Japanese in 1937; 32°N, 118°E. (m. 106, t 564)

National Road (nash'ə nəl rōd) A road built for pioneers in the first half of the 1800s. It ran from Maryland to the Mississippi River. (m. 374, t. 372)

New Brunswick (nü brunz'wik) A province of Canada in the southeastern part of the country. (m. 611, t. 613)

New England (nü ing'lənd) Region of the United States containing the states of Maine, Vermont, New Hampshire, Massachusetts, Connecticut, and Rhode Island. (m. 186, t. 165)

New France (nü frans) French possessions in North America during colonial times. It included large parts of what are now Canada and the United States. (m. 241, t. 153)

New Netherland (nü neth'ər lənd) A Dutch colony from 1609 to 1664 that included parts of present-day New York, New Jersey, and Connecticut. (t. 188)

New Orleans (nü ôr'lē ənz) Largest city in southern Louisiana, and a major port; 30°N, 90°W. (m. R17, t. 243)

New Spain (nü spān) Colonial lands held by Spain, mainly in North America. New Spain included parts of what are now the United States, Mexico, Central America, and islands in the West Indies. (m. 143, t. 132)

New York City (nü yôrk sit'ē) The largest city in the United States, located in southeastern New York State; 41°N, 74°W. (m. R17, t. 206)

Nicaragua (nik ə rä'gwə) The largest country in Central America, located in the middle part of the region. (m. 623, t. 625)

Nicodemus (nik ə dē'məs) A town in Kansas formed by freed African Americans from Kentucky following the Civil War; 39°N, 100°W. (t. 490)

Nigeria (nī jir' ē ə) A country in west Africa (m. R6, t. 212)

Normandy (nôr' mən dē) A town in France; also the beach where the Allies invaded Europe during World War II; 48°N, 5°W. (m. 563, t. 562)

North America (nôrth ə mer'i kə) The third largest of Earth's seven continents. It includes Canada, Mexico, the West Indies, and the United States. (m. R4, t. 41)

North Korea (nôrth kə rē'ə) A country occupying the northern part of the Korean peninsula. (m. R8, t. 568)

North Vietnam (nôrth vī et näm') From 1954 to 1975, a country in southeast Asia; now part of Vietnam. (m. 587, t. 586)

Northwest Territories (nôrth west' ter'i tôr ēz) An administrative division of Canada in the northern part of the country. (m. 611)

Northwest Territory (nôrth west' ter'i tôr ē) The land claimed by the United States after the Revolutionary War and organized as a territory in 1787, including what became the states of Indiana, Wisconsin, Ohio, Michigan, and Illinois. (m. 314, t. 314)

Nova Scotia (nō'və skō'shə) A province of Canada in the southeastern part of the country. (m. 611, t. 613)

Nunavut (nun'ə vut) A vast section of Canada's Northwest Territories and homeland of the Inuit. (m. 611, t. 613)

O

Ohio River (ō hī'ō riv'ər) A river in the east-central United States, flowing from Pittsburgh, Pennsylvania, southwest into the Mississippi River. (m. R19)

Ohio River valley (ō hī'ō riv'ər val'ē) The region along the banks of the Ohio River, known for its industry and farming. (m. R19, t. 247)

Old Oraibi (ōld ō rä ē'bē) A pueblo in Arizona inhabited by the Hopi for about 800 years, one of the oldest continuously populated settlements in the United States; 36°N, 111°W. (m. 59, t. 57)

Ontario (on târ'ē ō) A province of Canada in the southeastern part of the country. (m. 611, t. 613)

Oregon Territory (ôr'i gən ter'i tôr ē) The area of the Western region of the United States during the middle 1800s. (m. 385, t. 385)

Oregon Trail (ôr'i gən trāl) A route west used by pioneers in the 1840s. (m. 385, t. 385)

Ottawa (ot'ə wə) The capital of Canada in the province of Ontario; 45°N, 76°W. (m. 611, t. 613)

P

Pacific Ocean (pə sif'ik ō'shən) The largest of Earth's four oceans. (m. R4)

Palestine (pal'ə stīn) An area in the Middle East whose territory is the West Bank and Gaza Strip, partly controlled by Israel. (t. 601)

Pampas (pam' pəs) Southern region of South America, which is much like the Great Plains in the United States. (m. R15, t. 629)

Panama (pan'ə mä) The southernmost country in Central America. (m. 623, t. 625)

Panama Canal (pan'ə mä kə nal') A human-made waterway across the Isthmus of Panama that connects the Atlantic and Pacific oceans. (m. 525, t. 525)

Paraguay (par'ə gwā) A country in south-central South America. (m. 629, t. 630)

Pearl Harbor (pûrl här'bər) A major United States naval base near Honolulu, Hawaii, on the island of Oahu. Japan bombed Pearl Harbor on December 7, 1941, bringing the United States into World War II; 21°N, 158°W. (m. 562, t. 558)

Peru (pə rü') A country in northwestern South America. (m. 629, t. 50)

Petersburg (pēt'erz bûrg) A city in southeastern Virginia; 37°N, 77°W. (t. 452)

Philadelphia (fil ə del'fē ə) The largest city in Pennsylvania. From 1790 to 1800 it was the capital of the United States; 40°N, 75°W. (m. 191, t. 190)

Philippines (fil'ə pēnz) A group of islands off the coast of southeast Asia. (m. 520, t. 520)

Pittsburgh (pits'bûrg) A city in Pennsylvania, a leading producer of iron and steel; 40°N, 80°W. (m. R17, t. 248)

Plymouth (plim'əth) A town in southeastern Massachusetts founded by the Pilgrims in 1620; 42°N, 71°W. (m. 166, t. 167)

Portsmouth (pôrts'məth) A town in southeastern Rhode Island founded in 1637 by Anne Hutchinson; 43°N, 71°W. (m. 186, t. 182)

Portugal (pôr'chə gəl) A country in southwestern Europe. (m. R10, t. 109)

prime meridian (prīm mə rid'ē ən) The line of longitude from which longitudes east and west are measured; 0° longitude. (m. H12, t. H12)

Promontory Point (prom'ən tōr ē point) The place in Utah where the first transcontinental railroad in the United States was completed in1869; 41°N, 113°W. (m. 478, t. 478)

Providence (prov'i dəns) The capital and largest city of Rhode Island; founded by Roger Williams in 1636; 42°N, 72°W. (m. 186, t. 182)

Puerto Rico (pwer'tō rē'kō) An island in the West Indies, a commonwealth of the United States. (m. 520, t. 520)

Quebec (kwi bek') The largest province of Canada in the eastern part of the country; also the capital city of this province; 47°N, 71°W. (m. 611, t. 153)

R

Richmond (rich'mənd) Capital of Virginia; Confederate capital from 1861 to 1865; 38°N, 78°W. (m. 451, t. 436)

Rio Grande (rē'ō grand') A river in southwestern United States. It forms part of the border between the United States and Mexico. (m. 238, t. 235)

Roanoke Island (rō'ə nōk ī'lənd) An island off the coast of North Carolina, the site of the "Lost Colony" founded by Sir Walter Raleigh in 1587; 36°N, 76°W. (m. 159, t. 158)

Rocky Mountains (rok'ē moun'tənz) A high, rugged mountain chain in western North America, stretching from Alaska into Mexico. (m. R18, t. 5)

S

Sahara (sə har'ə) The largest desert in the world, stretching across most of North Africa. (m. 106, t. 106)

Salt Lake City (sält lāk sit'ē) Capital and largest city of Utah; 41°N, 112°W. (m. 385, t. 386)

San Antonio (san an tō'nē ō) A city in south-central Texas; 29°N, 99°W. (m. 238, t. 238)

San Diego (san dē ā'gō) A port city in southern California; 33°N, 117°W. (m. 238, t. 238)

San Francisco (san frən sis'kō) A city in west-central California; 38°N, 122°W. (m. 238, t. 239)

San Jacinto River (san jə sin' tō riv'ər) A river in southeastern Texas. (t. 395)

San Salvador (san sal'və dôr) Capital and largest city of El Salvador; 14°N, 89°W. (m. 623); also one of the Bahamas, known as Watling Island. It is believed to be the site of Columbus's first landing in North America in 1492; 24°N, 75°W. (m. 121, t. 121)

Santa Fe (san'tə fā) The capital of New Mexico; the Spanish established a settlement here in 1609 on the site of ancient Native American ruins; 35°N, 106°W. (m. 238, t. 235)

São Paulo (sou pou'lō) The largest city in Brazil; 24°N, 47°W. (m. 629, t. 632)

Saratoga (sar ə tō'gə) Site in New York of a Patriot victory in the Revolutionary War; 43°N, 75°W. (m. 299, t. 296)

Savannah (sə van'ə) A port city in southeastern Georgia, site of important battles in the American Revolution and the Civil War; 32°N, 81°W. (m. 193, t. 194)

Selma (sel' mə) A city in Alabama where police beat civil rights marchers on March 7, 1965, known as "Bloody Sunday"; 32°N, 88°W. (m. 583, t. 581)

Seneca Falls (sen'i kə fälz) In New York, site of the first women's rights convention in the United States, in 1848; 43°N, 77°W. (t. 420)

Seneca Village (sen'i kə vil'ij) African American community in New York City in the early 1800s; 41°N, 74°W. (t. 414)

Shiloh (shī'lō) The site of a bloody Union victory in southwestern Tennessee in 1862; 35°N, 88°W. (m. 451, t. 445)

Sierra Madres (sē er'ə mä'drä) A mountain system in Mexico. (m. 617, t. 617)

Sierra Nevada (sē er'ə nə vad'ə) A mountain range in eastern California. (m. R18, t. 475)

Silk Road (silk rōd) An ancient network of overland trade routes that stretched from China to what is now Iran. (m. 106, t. 100)

Sitka (sit'kə) A city on Baranof Island, Alaska, in the Alexander chain of islands; 57°N, 135°W. (t. 78)

Snake River (snāk riv'ər) A river that flows into the Columbia River. (m. R18, t. 354)

Songhai (song'hī) A powerful and wealthy kingdom that ruled West Africa in the 1400s. (m. 106, t. 106)

South America (south ə mer'i kə) One of Earth's seven continents; located in the Western Hemisphere. (m. 629, t. 48)

South Korea (south kə rē'ə) A country occupying the southern part of the Korean peninsula. (m. R8, t. 568)

South Vietnam (south vī et näm') From 1954 to 1975, a country in southeast Asia; now part of Vietnam. (m. 587, t. 586)

Southern Colonies (suth′ərn kol′ə nēz) The colonies of Georgia, Maryland, North Carolina, South Carolina, and Virginia before the American Revolution. (m. 193, t. 192)

Spain (spān) A country in southwestern Europe. (m. R10, t. 120)

St. Augustine (sānt ô′gə stēn) A port city in Florida; the oldest city in the United States; 30°N, 81°W. (t. 234)

St. Lawrence River (sānt lôr′əns riv′ər) A river in eastern North America between the United States and Canada. (m. R15, t. 153)

Strait of Magellan (strāt əv mə jel′ən) The narrow waterway between the southern tip of South America and Tierra del Fuego that links the Atlantic Ocean to the Pacific Ocean. (m. 136)

Suriname (sur′ə näm) A country on the northeastern coast of South America. (m. 629, t. 630)

Sutter's Mill (su′tərz mil) The sawmill on the American River where gold was discovered in California in 1848, starting the California gold rush; 39°N, 121°W. (t. 388)

Tenochtitlán (te nōch tē tlän′) The capital of the ancient Aztec Empire on the site of present-day Mexico City; 19°N, 99°W. (m. 49, t. 49)

Tikal (ti käl′) An ancient Mayan city in northern Guatemala; 17°N, 90°W. (m. 43, t. 43)

Timbuktu (tim buk tü′) A West African city in the present-day country of Mali; 17°N, 3°W. (m. 106, t. 106)

Toronto (tə ron′tō) Capital and largest city of the Canadian province of Ontario; 44°N, 79°W. (m. 611, t. 614)

Trenton (tren′tən) Capital of New Jersey, site of an important battle in the American Revolution; 40°N, 75°W. (m. 306, t. 295)

Tsenacomacoh (sen ə käm′ə kō) The name the Powhatan peoples of eastern Virginia had given to their homeland. (t. 160)

Umbler (um′blər) A community of free African Americans in central Virginia that began during the 1700s. (t. 414)

Uruguay (yur′ə gwā) A country on the southeastern coast of South America. (m. 629, t. 630)

Valley Forge (val′ē fôrj) A village in Pennsylvania where George Washington's army camped during the winter of 1777–1778; 40°N, 75°W. (m. 306, t. 297)

Valley of Mexico (val′ē əv mek′si kō) An area of lower-lying land in central Mexico. (t. 48)

Vancouver (van kü′vər) A port city in southwestern British Columbia, Canada; 49°N, 123°W. Also an island of British Columbia, Canada. (m. 611)

Venezuela (ven ə zwā′lə) A country in northwestern South America, on the Caribbean Sea. (m. 629, t. 630)

Versailles (vâr sī′) A city southwest of Paris, France, and site of international peace conferences such as the one that ended World War I; 49°N, 2°E. (t. 542)

Vicksburg (viks′bûrg) A city in west-central Mississippi on the Mississippi River, site of a major battle during the Civil War; 32°N, 91°W. (m. 451, t. 445)

Wallowa River (wä lau′ə riv′ər) A river in northeastern Oregon. (t. 497)

Washington, D.C. (wä′shing tən) Capital of the United States; 39°N, 77°W. (m. R16, t. 350)

Weeksville (wēks′vil) A community of free African Americans in Brooklyn, New York. (t. 414)

West Indies (west in′dēz) The islands stretching from Florida in North America to Venezuela in South America. (m. 220, t. 217)

Wilderness Road (wil′dər nis rōd) An early road across the Appalachians to Kentucky. (m. 349, t. 348)

Williamsburg (wil′yəmz bûrg) Colonial capital of Virginia from 1699 to 1779 where the House of Burgesses met; 37°N, 77°W. (m. 208, t. 225)

Yorktown (yôrk′toun) A town in southeastern Virginia, site of the last major battle of the American Revolution; 37°N, 77°W. (m. 306, t. 302)

Yosemite National Park (yō sem′i tē) A national park in east-central California noted for its valleys, waterfalls, and sequoia trees; 38°N, 120°W. (t. 3)

Yucatán peninsula (ū kə tan′ pə nin′sə lə) A peninsula in southeastern Mexico. (m. 617, t. 133)

Biographical Dictionary

The Biographical Dictionary tells you about the people you have learned about in this book. The Pronunciation Key tells you how to say their names. The page numbers tell you where each person first appears in the text.

A

Adams, Abigail (ad'əmz), 1744–1818 First Lady to President John Adams. (p. 265)

Adams, Henry (ad'əmz), 1843–1884? Former slave who led thousands of African American exodusters to Kansas in 1879. (p. 490)

Adams, John (ad'əmz), 1735–1826 Second President of the United States from 1797 to 1801. (p. 265)

Adams, John Quincy (ad'əmz), 1767–1848 Sixth President of the United States from 1825 to 1829. (p. 376)

Adams, Samuel (ad'əmz), 1722–1803 Patriot and leader in the American Revolution. (p. 263)

Addams, Jane (ad'əmz), 1860–1935 Reformer who founded Hull House in Chicago in 1889, the first settlement house in the United States. (p. 514)

Allen, Ethan (al'ən), 1738–1789 Leader of the "Green Mountain Boys," the Vermont militiamen who captured Fort Ticonderoga in the American Revolution. (p. 273)

Allen, Richard (al'ən), 1760–1831 Abolitionist and founder of the Free African Society in 1787. He helped found the first African Methodist Episcopal Church in 1816 with Absalom Jones. (p. 314)

Anthony, Susan B. (an'thə nē), 1820–1906 A leader in the movement for women's suffrage. (p. 549)

Armistead, James (är'mə sted), 1760–1832 Patriot spy who helped defeat the British general Charles Cornwallis at Yorktown in 1781. (p. 302)

Armstrong, Neil (ärm' strong), 1930– First man to walk on the moon in 1969. (p. 602)

Arnold, Benedict (är'nəld), 1741–1801 Colonial general in the Continental army who later became a traitor to the American Revolution. (p. 273)

Atahualpa (ä tə wäl'pə), 1500?–1533 Last ruler of the vast Inca Empire who was captured and killed by the Spaniards. (p. 134)

Attucks, Crispus (at'əks), 1723?–1770 Patriot and former slave who was one of the first people killed in the Boston Massacre in 1770. (p. 264)

Austin, Stephen F. (ôs'tən), 1793–1836 Pioneer who led about 300 American families to Texas in 1822. (p. 393)

B

Balboa, Vasco Núñez de (bäl bō'ə, väs'kō nü'nyes de), 1475–1519 Explorer who led the first European expedition across the Isthmus of Panama to the Pacific Ocean in 1513. (p. 143)

Banneker, Benjamin (ban'i kər), 1731–1806 Scientist, writer, and planner of the District of Columbia. (p. 350)

Barton, Clara (bär'tən), 1821–1912 Nurse for the Union forces during the Civil War known as the "Angel of the Battlefield." She later founded the American Red Cross. (p. 445)

Beckwourth, James (bek' wûrth), 1798–1867 A "Mountain Man," or fur trader. (p. 387)

Bell, Alexander Graham (bel), 1847–1922 Inventor who built the first working telephone in 1876. (p. 505)

Bickerdayke, Mary Ann (bik ûr dīk), 1817–1901 A nurse who served the Union during the Civil War. (p. 445)

Bolívar, Simón (bō lē'vär, sē mōn'), 1783–1830 Venezuelan military and revolutionary leader who helped free much of northern South America in the early 1800s; known as "The Liberator." (p. 628)

Bonaparte, Napoleon (bō'nə pärt, nə pō'lē ən), 1769–1821 Emperor of France who sold the Louisiana Territory to the United States in 1803. (p. 351)

pronunciation key

a	at	ī	ice	u	up	th	thin
ā	ape	îr	pierce	ū	use	th	this
ä	far	o	hot	ü	rule	zh	measure
âr	care	ō	old	u̇	pull	ə	about, taken,
e	end	ô	fork	ûr	turn		pencil, lemon,
ē	me	oi	oil	hw	white		circus
i	it	ou	out	ng	song		

Boone, Daniel (bün), 1734–1820 Virginia pioneer and trailblazer who guided settlers through the Cumberland Gap into Kentucky. (p. 348)

Bowie, Jim (bō'ē), 1796–1836 Soldier who died defending the Alamo in 1836. (p. 394)

Bradford, William (brad'fərd), 1590–1657 Governor of the Plymouth Colony beginning in 1621. (p. 167)

Brant, Joseph (brant), 1742–1807 Mohawk leader who sided with the British in the American Revolution. (p. 304)

Bridger, James (brij' ər), 1804–1881 A "Mountain Man," or fur trader, who established a fort near the Mormon Trail and the California Trail. (p. 386)

Brown, John (broun), 1800–1859 Abolitionist who led a raid on Harpers Ferry, Virginia, in 1859. (p. 427)

Burgoyne, John (bər goin'), 1722–1792 British general who was defeated at the Battle of Saratoga in 1777. (p. 296)

Bush, George (bush), 1924– The forty-first President of the United States from 1989 to 1993. (p. 596)

Bush, George W. (bush), 1946– Forty-third President of the United States, elected in 2000. (p. 597)

C

Cabeza de Vaca, Álvar Núñez (kä be'sä de vä'kä, äl'vär nün' yes), 1490?–1560? Spanish explorer who was the first to reach Texas. (p. 142)

Cabot, John (kab'ət), 1450?–1498? Italian sea captain in the service of England who was the first European to explore North America in search of a Northwest Passage. (p. 151)

Carnegie, Andrew (kär'ni gē), 1835–1919 Business leader who developed the steel industry and philanthropist who established many charities. (p. 504)

Carter, James E. (kär'tər), 1924– The thirty-ninth President of the United States from 1977 to 1981. (p. 594)

Carter, III, Robert (kär'tər), 1728–1804 Virginia planter and slave-owner who freed the 500 people enslaved on his plantation, beginning in 1791. (p. 214)

Cartier, Jacques (kär tyä' zhäk), 1491–1557 French explorer who became the first European to navigate the St. Lawrence River in 1535. (p. 153)

Castro, Fidel (käs'trō), 1926– Communist leader of Cuba since 1959. (p. 570)

Catt, Carrie Chapman (kat), 1859–1947 Women's rights leader who helped bring about the passage of the Nineteenth Amendment in 1920. (p. 549)

Champlain, Samuel de (sham plān'), 1567–1635 Explorer and founder of Quebec, the first permanent French settlement in North America, in 1608. (p. 153)

Charles I (chärlz), 1600–1649 King of England who gave the Puritans a charter to form the Massachusetts Bay Colony in 1629. (p. 181)

Charles II (chärlz), 1630–1685 King of England when England made the Dutch colony of New Netherland a part of the Middle Colonies. (p. 188)

Chávez, César (chä'ves, se'sär), 1927–1993 A founder of the United Farm Workers labor union. (p. 585)

Chisholm, Shirley (chiz'əm), 1924– United States Representative from New York from 1969 to 1983. She was the first African American woman to be elected to Congress. (p. 593)

Clark, George Rogers (klärk), 1752–1818 Revolutionary War general and frontier leader who defeated the British at Fort Vincennes in 1779. (p. 298)

Clark, William (klärk), 1770–1838 Explorer of the Louisiana Territory with Meriwether Lewis. He was the brother of George Rogers Clark. (p. 352)

Clay, Henry (klā), 1777–1852 United States Senator who helped work out the Missouri Compromise in 1820 and the Compromise of 1850. (p. 358)

Clinton, DeWitt (klin'tən), 1769–1828 New York governor who supported the building of the Erie Canal. (p. 372)

Clinton, William J. (klin'tən), 1946– The forty-second President of the United States from 1993 to 2001. (p. 596)

Coffin, Levi (ko'fin), 1798–1877 Quaker conductor on the Underground Railroad in Indiana. (p. 419)

Columbus, Christopher (kə lum'bəs), 1451?–1506 Italian sea captain and explorer. Sailing under the flag of Spain, he reached the Americas in 1492. (p. 120)

Cook, James (kuk), 1728–1779 British sea captain and explorer who reached Hawaiian Islands in 1778. (p. 519)

Cooper, Peter (kü'pər), 1791–1883 New York merchant and inventor of a steam-driven train, the *Tom Thumb*. (p. 374)

Corbin, Margaret (kôr' bin), late 1700s A Revolutionary War hero who took over her husband's cannon after he was killed in battle. (p. 291)

Cornwallis, Charles (kôrn wol'is), 1738–1805 British general who surrendered at Yorktown, the last major battle of the American Revolution in 1781. (p. 301)

Coronado, Francisco de (kô rō nä'dō, fran sēs' kō de), 1510–1554 Spanish explorer of the American Southwest from 1540 to 1542. (p. 139)

Cortés, Hernando (kôr tes', er nän'dō), 1485–1547 Conquistador who defeated the Aztec in 1521. (p. 131)

Crazy Horse (krā′zē hôrs), 1849?–1877 Lakota chief who, with Sitting Bull, defeated Colonel Custer at the Battle of the Little Bighorn in 1876. (p. 495)

Crocker, Charles (krok′ər), 1822–1888 Business leader who directed the building of the Central Pacific Railroad. (p. 475)

Crockett, David (krok′it), 1786–1836 United States Representative and frontier scout who died defending the Alamo. (p. 394)

Cuauhtémoc (kwä tā′mok), 1495?–1525 Aztec ruler following the death of Moctezuma II who led the Aztec in the final battle for Tenochtitlán. (p. 132)

Custer, George (kus′tər), 1839–1876 United States Army colonel defeated at the Battle of the Little Bighorn in 1876. (p. 496)

 D

Da Gama, Vasco (də gäm′ə, väs′kō), 1460–1524 Portuguese navigator who was the first European to sail from Europe to Asia in 1498. (p. 111)

Davis, Jefferson (dā′vis), 1808–1889 United States Senator who was President of the Confederate States of America from 1861 to 1865. (p. 428)

Dawes, William (dôz′), 1745–1799 Patriot who rode with Paul Revere on April 18, 1775, to warn colonists that British troops were coming. (p. 271)

De Soto, Hernando (de sō′tō, er nän′dō), 1500?–1542 Spanish explorer of the Southeast from 1539 to 1542. He was the first European to see the Mississippi River. (p. 143)

Deere, John (dîr), 1804–1886 Illinois blacksmith who invented the steel plow in 1837. (p. 370)

Deganawida (dä gän ə wē′ də), 1400s A founder of the Iroquois Confederacy in 1570. (p. 65)

Dewey, George (dü′ē), 1837–1917 United States admiral who defeated the Spanish in the Philippines during the Spanish-American War in 1898. (p. 520)

Dias, Bartolomeu (dē′əsh, bâr tù lù mā′ù), 1450?–1500 Portuguese ship captain who reached the Cape of Good Hope in 1487. (p. 110)

Dickenson, Suzanna (dik′ən sən), 1820–1883 Alamo survivor who carried word of the Texans' defeat to Sam Houston, leader of the Texas forces. (p. 395)

Dodge, Grenville (doj), 1831–1916 Former Union general in charge of building the Union Pacific Railroad. (p. 475)

Douglass, Frederick (dug′ləs), 1817–1895 Abolitionist who led the attack on slavery in the middle 1800s. (p. 412)

Du Bois, W.E.B. (dü boiz′), 1868–1963 A founder of the National Association for the Advancement of Colored People (NAACP) in 1909. (p. 544)

Du Sable, Jean Baptiste Point (dü sä′blə, zhän′ bap tēst′ pwän′), 1745–1818 Haitian fur trader who established a trading post that later became the city of Chicago. (p. 241)

 E

Earhart, Amelia (âr′härt), 1898–1937 Airplane pilot who was the first woman to fly across the Atlantic in 1928. (p. 548)

Edison, Thomas Alva (ed′ə sən), 1847–1931 Inventor of the light bulb in 1879, the phonograph, and more than 1,000 other inventions. (p. 505)

Eisenhower, Dwight D. (ī′zən hou ər), 1890–1969 The thirty-fourth President of the United States from 1953 to 1961. Supreme Allied Commander in World War II, he directed the Allied invasion of Europe from 1944 to 1945. (p. 562)

Elizabeth I (i liz′ə bəth), 1533–1603 Queen of England during the founding of the Roanoke colony and the defeat of the Spanish Armada. (p. 159)

Ellington, Duke (el′ing tən), 1889–1974 African American composer and musician who brought jazz to a wide audience in the 1920s. (p. 547)

Equiano, Olaudah (i kwē ä′nō, ōl′ə dä), 1750–1797 African who wrote of being kidnapped, enslaved, and transported to North America. (p. 202)

Estevanico (es te vä nē′kō), 1500s African whose story of the "Seven Cities of Gold" led Francisco de Coronado to explore the Southwest in 1540. (p. 139)

 F

Ferdinand (fûr′də nand), 1452–1516 King of Spain who, with his wife, Queen Isabella, paid for Columbus's voyages to the Americas. (p. 120)

Findley, John (find′lē), 1722–1772? Frontier trader who blazed trails with Daniel Boone over the Cumberland Gap to Kentucky. (p. 348)

Fitzgerald, F. Scott (fits jer′əld), 1896–1940 Writer of the Roaring Twenties. (p. 547)

Ford, Gerald (fôrd), 1913– The thirty-eighth President of the United States from 1974 to 1977. (p. 591)

Ford, Henry (fôrd), 1863–1947 Automaker who introduced assembly line mass production to the auto industry. (p. 526)

Franklin, Benjamin (frang′klin), 1706–1790 Writer, scientist, delegate to the Continental Congress, and signer of the Declaration of Independence. (p. 206)

Fray Marcos de Niza (frī mär′kōs de nē′sä), 1500s Roman Catholic priest who accompanied Coronado on his search for the "Seven Cities of Gold." (p. 139)

Fulton, Robert (fûl′tən), 1765–1815 Builder of the first successful steamboat, the *Clermont,* in 1807. (p. 372)

 G

Gage, Thomas (gāj), 1721–1787 Commander of the British forces in North America during the American Revolution. (p. 271)

Garrison, William Lloyd (gar′ə sən), 1805–1879 Abolitionist and founder of the newspaper *The Liberator* in 1831. (p. 416)

George II (jôrj), 1683–1760 King of England during the French and Indian War. (p. 193)

George III (jôrj), 1738–1820 King of England during the American Revolution. (p. 265)

Glidden, Joseph F. (glid′ən), 1813–1906 Inventor of barbed wire in 1873. (p. 489)

Gompers, Samuel (gom′pərz), 1850–1924 Labor union leader who founded the American Federation of Labor in 1886. (p. 508)

Gorbachev, Mikhail (gôr′bə chəf, mi kīl′), 1931– Last leader of the Soviet Union from 1984 to 1991. (p. 595)

Gore, Jr., Albert (gôr), 1948– Vice President of the United States under William J. Clinton. (p. 597)

Gorgas, William (gôr′gəs), 1854–1920 United States Army doctor who helped control the spread of malaria during the building of the Panama Canal from 1904 to 1914. (p. 525)

Gorges, Ferdinando (gôr jəs′), 1566–1647 Proprietor of Maine, until it became part of the Massachusetts Bay Colony. (p. 182)

Grant, Ulysses S. (grant), 1822–1885 The eighteenth President of the United States from 1869 to 1877. He was commander of the Union army from 1864 to 1865. (p. 445)

Greene, Nathanael (grēn), 1742–1786 Patriot general during the American Revolution who forced the British out of Georgia and the Carolinas. (p. 301)

Grimké, Angelina Emily (grim′kē), 1805–1879 Southern abolitionist who, with her sister Sarah, spoke out against slavery. (p. 417)

Grimké, Sarah Moore (grim′kē), 1792–1873 Southern abolitionist who, with her sister Angelina, spoke out against slavery. (p. 417)

 H

Hale, Nathan (hāl), 1755–1776 Patriot hanged by the British as a spy in the American Revolution. (p. 294)

Hamilton, Alexander (ham′əl tən), 1757–1804 Colonial assembly member, delegate to the Constitutional Convention, and first Secretary of the Treasury from 1789 to 1795. (p. 316)

Hancock, John (han′kok), 1737–1793 Patriot and president of the Continental Congress from 1775 to 1777. (p. 270)

Hays, Mary Ludwig (hāz), 1752–1832 American patriot; known as "Molly Pitcher." (p. 291)

Henry, Patrick (hen′rē), 1736–1799 Virginia Burgess who encouraged the colonists to fight for their independence from Great Britain. (p. 263)

Henry, Prince (hen′rē), 1394–1460 Prince of Portugal who established a school for sailors; known as "the Navigator." (p. 109)

Hiawatha (hī ə wä′thə), 1400s A founder of the Iroquois Confederacy. (p. 65)

Hidalgo, Miguel (ē däl′gō, mē gel′), 1753–1811 Roman Catholic priest and leader who started Mexico's war for independence from Spain in 1810. (p. 616)

Hitler, Adolf (hit′lər), 1889–1945 Nazi dictator of Germany whose actions led to World War II and the Holocaust. (p. 559)

Hooker, Thomas (hük′ər), 1586–1647 Puritan minister who founded the colony of Connecticut in 1639. (p. 182)

Hoover, Herbert (hü′vər), 1874–1964 The thirty-first President of the United States from 1929 to 1933 who served during the beginning of the Great Depression. (p. 554)

Houston, Sam (hūs′tən), 1793–1863 Leader of the Texas army during the Texas Revolution and first president of the Republic of Texas in 1836. (p. 395)

Howe, William (hou), 1729–1867 Commander of British forces in the American colonies from 1775 to 1778. (p. 277)

Hudson, Henry (hud′sən), ?–1611 English explorer who searched for a Northwest Passage through North America beginning in 1609. (p. 152)

Huerta, Dolores (wer′tä), 1929– A founder of the United Farm Workers labor union. (p. 585)

Hughes, Langston (hūz), 1902–1967 Major African American writer of the Harlem Renaissance. (p. 547)

Hutchinson, Anne (huch′ən sən), 1591–1643 Puritan founder of the Portsmouth, Rhode Island, in 1636. (p. 182)

 I

Idar, Jovita (ī där), 1885–1946 Texas woman who worked to improve living conditions and education among Mexican Americans. (p. 524)

Biographical Dictionary

Isabella (iz ə bel'ə), 1451–1504 Queen of Spain who, with her husband, King Ferdinand, paid for Columbus's voyages to the Americas. (p. 120)

J

Jackson, Andrew (jak'sən), 1767–1845 Seventh President of the United States from 1829 to 1837. He defeated the British at the Battle of New Orleans during the War of 1812. (p. 360)

Jackson, Helen Hunt (jak'sən), 1830–1885 Massachusetts writer who criticized treatment of Native Americans in the late 1800s. (p. 498)

Jackson, Thomas "Stonewall" (jak'sən), 1824–1863 General who played an important role in the Confederate victories at both battles of Bull Run. (p. 437)

James I (jāmz), 1566–1625 King of England for whom Jamestown was named. (p. 161)

Jefferson, Thomas (jef'ər sən), 1743–1826 Third President of the United States from 1801 to 1809. He was author of the Declaration of Independence and responsible for the Louisiana Purchase. (p. 277)

Jennings, Elizabeth (jen' ings), circa 1850 An African American who sued a bus company after she was forced to exit the bus because she was not white. (p. 414)

Johnson, Andrew (jon'sən), 1808–1875 The seventeenth President of the United States from 1865 to 1869. He took office after President Lincoln's assassination. (p. 457)

Johnson, Lyndon Baines (jon'sən), 1908–1973 The thirty-sixth President of the United States from 1963 to 1969. He took office after President Kennedy's assassination. (p. 581)

Jolliet, Louis (jō'lē et), 1645–1700 French explorer who sailed with Jacques Marquette through the Great Lakes and down the Mississippi to the mouth of the Arkansas River in 1673. (p. 154)

Jones, Absalom (jōnz), 1746–1818 Abolitionist who, with Richard Allen, helped found the first African Methodist Episcopal Church in 1816. (p. 362)

Jones, John Paul (jōnz), 1747–1792 American sea captain who commanded the *Bonhomme Richard* and defeated the British ship *Serapis* in 1779. (p. 298)

Jones, Mary Harris (jōnz), 1830–1930 American labor union leader. She fought against child labor and was known as "Mother Jones." (p. 509)

Joseph, Chief (jō'zəf), 1840–1904 Leader of the Nez Percé, whose people were captured and forced onto a reservation. (p. 497)

Juárez, Benito (hwä'res, be nē'tō), 1806–1872 Zapotec Indian who, as Mexico's president in the middle 1800s, tried to make conditions fairer for all. (p. 619)

K

Kennedy, John F. (ken'i dē), 1917–1963 The thirty-fifth President of the United States from 1961 to 1963 and the youngest person to be elected President. (p. 570)

Key, Francis Scott (kē), 1779–1843 Writer of "The Star-Spangled Banner" during the War of 1812. This poem later became the national anthem. (p. 360)

Khrushchev, Nikita (krüsh' chev), 1894–1971 The leader of the Soviet Union during the Cuban Missile Crisis. (p. 570)

King, Jr., Martin Luther (king), 1929–1968 Baptist minister and major civil rights leader during the 1950s and 1960s. (p. 579)

Knox, Henry (noks), 1750–1806 Revolutionary War officer who helped drive the British from Boston in 1776. (p. 277)

Kosciuszko, Thaddeus (kos ē üs'kō), 1746–1817 Patriot from Poland who served in the Continental army from 1776 to 1784. (p. 296)

Kublai Khan (kü' blə kähn), 1214–1294 Mongol ruler of China who befriended Marco Polo. (p. 98)

L

La Salle, René Robert Chevalier Sieur de (lə sal'), 1643–1687 French explorer who reached the mouth of the Mississippi River in 1682. (p. 242)

Lafayette, Marquis de (laf ē et', mär kē' də), 1757–1834 French general who joined the Continental army during the American Revolution. (p. 297)

Las Casas, Bartolomé de (läs kä'säs, bär tō lō mā' de), 1474–1566 Roman Catholic missionary who opposed the mistreatment of Indians in New Spain. (p. 140)

Latimer, Lewis (lat'ə mər), 1848–1928 African American inventor who assisted in the invention of Bell's telephone and Edison's light bulb. (p. 505)

Le Moyne de Bienville, Jean-Baptiste (lü moin' də bē ən' vēl), 1680–1768 With his brother, Pierre Le Moyne d'Iberville, established the first settlement in Louisiana in 1699. (p. 243)

Le Moyne d'Iberville, Pierre (lü moin' də bûr vēl), 1661–1706 With his brother, Jean-Baptiste Le Moyne de Bienville, established the first settlement in Louisiana in 1699. (p. 242)

Lee, Richard Henry (lē), 1732–1794 Virginia planter, patriot, and signer of the Declaration of Independence. (p. 227)

Lee, Robert E. (lē), 1807–1870 Army officer who commanded the Confederate army during the Civil War. (p. 435)

L'Enfant, Pierre (län fän', pē yâr'), 1754–1825 French engineer and architect who designed the plan of the District of Columbia. (p. 350)

Lewis, Meriwether (lü'is), 1774–1809 United States army officer and scout who explored the Louisiana Territory with William Clark from 1803 to 1806. (p. 352)

Liliuokalani (lē lē ü wō kä lä'nē), 1838–1917 Last queen of Hawaii from 1891 to 1893 who was overthrown by American planters. (p. 519)

Lincoln, Abraham (ling'kən), 1809–1865 The sixteenth President of the United States from 1861 to 1865 who led the country during the Civil War. He wrote the Gettysburg Address. (p. 426)

Lindbergh, Charles (lind'bûrg), 1902–1974 Became the first person to fly solo nonstop across the Atlantic Ocean in 1927. (p. 548)

Locke, John (lok), 1632–1704 English philosopher whose thinking influenced Thomas Jefferson in the writing of the Declaration of Independence. (p. 228)

L'Ouverture, Toussaint (lü vûr tyûr, tü san'), 1743?–1803 Haitian military leader and former slave who fought for the independence of Haiti and end of slavery. (p. 624)

Love, Nat (luv), 1854–1921 American cowboy and writer who had been enslaved. (p. 483)

Lowell, Francis Cabot (lō'əl), 1775 –1817 Cloth factory owner who built the first power loom in the United States in 1813. (p. 370)

M

Madison, Dolley (mad'ə sən), 1768–1849 First Lady to President James Madison who saved George Washington's portrait from British forces invading Washington, D.C., during the War of 1812. (p. 360)

Madison, James (mad'ə sən), 1751–1836 Fourth President of the United States from 1809 to 1817 and author of *The Federalist Papers*. (p. 318)

Magellan, Ferdinand (mə jel'ən, fûr'də nand), 1480?–1521 Portuguese explorer sailing for Spain who led the first known voyage around the world. (p. 136)

Malcolm X (mal'kəm eks), 1925–1965 African American civil rights leader in the early 1960s. (p. 585)

Marina, Doña (mä rē'nä, dōn'yä), 1501?–1550 Indian also called Malinche (mä lēn' chä) who aided Hernando Cortés in his conquest of Tenochtitlán in 1521. (p. 131)

Marion, Francis (mâr'ē ən), 1732–1795 Revolutionary War commander who fought the British army throughout the Carolinas; known as the "Swamp Fox." (p. 301)

Marquette, Jacques (mär ket', zhäk), 1637–1675 Roman Catholic priest from France who sailed with Louis Jolliet through the Great Lakes and down the Mississippi to the mouth of the Arkansas River in 1673. (p. 154)

Marshall, Thurgood (mär'shəl), 1907–1993 Lawyer who helped end segregation in public schools in 1954. He was also the first African American Supreme Court justice from 1967 to 1991. (p. 579)

Mason, George (mā'sən), 1725–1792 Delegate to the Constitutional Convention who called for a Bill of Rights. (p. 330)

Mason, John (mā sən), 1586–1630 Proprietor of New Hampshire. (p. 182)

Massasoit (mas'ə soit), 1580?–1661 Main Wampanoag sachem who made a peace agreement with the Pilgrims at Plymouth. (p. 166)

McCarthy, Joseph (mə kär'thē), 1908–1957 United States Senator who led an anticommunist campaign from 1950 to 1954 that unjustly accused many government and military officials. (p. 568)

McCormick, Cyrus (mə kôr'mək), 1809–1884 Inventor of the reaper in 1831. (p. 370)

McCoy, Elijah (mə koi'), 1843–1929 Inventor of the oil cup called the "real McCoy" in 1872. (p. 506)

McCoy, Joseph (mə koi'), 1837–1915 Business leader who made Abilene, Kansas, a center of the cattle industry in 1866. (p. 484)

McKinley, William (mə kin'lē), 1843–1901 The twenty-fifth President of the United States from 1897 to 1901. (p. 520)

Meade, George (mēd), 1815–1872 General who commanded the Union forces at the Battle of Gettysburg in 1863. (p. 447)

Menchú, Rigoberta (men chü'), 1959– Guatemalan whose campaign for equal treatment for Guatemalan Indians won her the Nobel Peace Prize in 1992. (p. 627)

Metacomet (met ə käm'ət), 1639?–1676 Wampanoag sachem known to the English colonists as King Philip. He led one of the last Native American battles against the colonists in New England in 1676. (p. 184)

Moctezuma II (mäk tə zü'mə), 1480?–1520 Aztec emperor defeated by Hernando Cortés in 1520. (p. 129)

Monroe, James (mən rō'), 1758–1831 Fifth President of the United States from 1817 to 1825. He proclaimed the Monroe Doctrine, which opposed European interference in the Western Hemisphere. (p. 362)

Morris, Gouverneur (môr' is), 1752–1816 The delegate of the Constitutional Convention who wrote down the Constitution. (p. 317)

Mott, Lucretia (mot), 1793–1880 Abolitionist and women's rights leader who helped organize the Seneca Falls Convention in 1848. (p. 420)

Muir, John (myùr), 1838–1914 Conservationist who worked to establish Yosemite National Park in 1890. (p. 527)

Mussolini, Benito (mü sə lē'nē), 1883–1945 Italian dictator who joined the Axis in World War II. (p. 559)

N

Nixon, Richard (nik'sən), 1913–1994 The thirty-seventh President of the United States from 1969 to 1974 who resigned from office. (p. 586)

O

O'Connor, Sandra Day (ō kon'ər), 1930– Arizona judge who became the first woman to serve on the United States Supreme Court in 1981. (p. 593)

Oglethorpe, James (ō'gəl thôrp), 1696–1785 British military officer who founded the colony of Georgia in 1732. (p. 194)

Oliver, James (äl'iv ər), 1823–1908 Inventor of a new type of "sodbusting" steel plow in 1877. (p. 488)

Oñate, Don Juan de (ō nyä'tə, dōn hwän' de), 1549?–1628? Conquistador from Mexico who founded Santa Fe, New Mexico, about 1609. (p. 235)

Osceola (ä sē ō'lə), 1800–1838 Seminole chief who resisted his people's removal from Florida. (p. 381)

Otermín, Antonio de (ō ter mēn'), late 1600s Spanish governor of New Mexico in 1680. (p. 237)

P

Pachakuti Inca (päh chäh kü tē), 1400s Emperor who enlarged the Inca Empire. (p. 50)

Paine, Thomas (pān), 1737–1809 American Patriot who wrote *Common Sense* in 1776. (p. 278)

Parker, Dorothy (pär' kər), 1893–1967 A popular writer from the 1920s, known for her rebellious spirit. (p. 547)

Parker, John (pär'kər), 1729–1775 Patriot captain at the Battle of Lexington on April 19, 1775, where the first shots in the American Revolution were fired. (p. 271)

Parks, Rosa (pärks), 1913– African American who fought segregation on city buses in Montgomery, Alabama, in 1955. (p. 579)

Penn, William (pen), 1644–1718 Quaker leader who founded the colony of Pennsylvania in 1681. (p. 189)

Perry, Oliver Hazard (per'ē), 1785–1819 United States Navy captain who defeated the British in the Battle of Lake Erie during the War of 1812. (p. 359)

Pickett, George (pik'ət), 1825–1875 Confederate general who led "Pickett's Charge" at the Battle of Gettysburg in 1863. (p. 447)

Pinckney, Elizabeth Lucas (pink'nē), 1722?–1793 South Carolina planter who made indigo a major cash crop for the Southern Colonies. (p. 217)

Pitt, William (pit), 1759–1806 A major supporter of the British during the French and Indian War. (p. 248)

Pizarro, Francisco (pē sär'rō), 1471?–1541 Spanish conquistador who defeated the Inca in 1533. (p. 134)

Pocahontas (pō kə hon'təs), 1595?–1617 Daughter of Chief Powhatan whose marriage to John Rolfe led to the "Peace of Pocahontas" from 1614 to 1617. (p. 162)

Polk, James K. (pōk), 1795–1849 Eleventh President of the United States from 1845 to 1849, during the Mexican War. (p. 396)

Polo, Marco (pō'lō), 1254?–1324? Italian merchant whose book about his travels through China from 1274 to 1292 stirred European interest in Asia. (p. 98)

Ponce de León, Juan (pōn' se de le ōn'), 1460?–1521 Spanish explorer who reached Florida in 1513. (p. 143)

Pontiac (pon'tē ak), 1720–1769 Ottawa chief who led attacks against the British after losing the French and Indian War in 1763. (p. 249)

Popé (pō pā'), ?–1688 Pueblo leader who drove the Spanish out of New Mexico for 12 years, beginning in 1680. (p. 237)

Powell, Colin (pou' əl), 1937– Chairman of the Joint Chiefs of Staff during the Gulf War and Secretary of State under George W. Bush. (p. 596)

Powhatan, Chief (pou ə tan'), 1550?–1618 Chief of the Powhatan tribe who helped the English settlement at Jamestown. (p. 160)

Punch, John (punch), c. 1640 An enslaved African in the English colonies in 1640. (p. 211)

R

Raleigh, Sir Walter (rô'lē), 1552?–1618 English explorer, historian, and soldier who started two unsuccessful colonies at Roanoke Island, in 1584 and 1587. (p. 159)

Reagan, Ronald (rā'gən), 1911– The fortieth President of the United States from 1981 to 1989. (p. 594)

Reed, Ester De Berdt (rēd), 1746–1780 Founder of the Ladies Association, the first women's organization in the United States. (p. 291)

Revels, Hiram R. (rev'əlz), 1822–1901 First African American Senator, who finished the term of Jefferson Davis from 1870 to 1871. (p. 459)

Revere, Paul (rə vîr'), 1735–1818 Boston Patriot and silversmith who, on the night of April 18, 1775, rode to warn the people of Lexington that British troops were coming. (p. 271)

Rockefeller, John D. (rok'ə fel ər), 1839–1937 Business leader who started the Standard Oil Company. (p. 507)

Rolfe, John (rälf), 1585–1622 Jamestown leader whose method of curing tobacco made it a successful cash crop; married Pocahontas. (p. 161)

Roosevelt, Eleanor (rō'zə velt), 1884–1962 Writer and First Lady to thirty-second President Franklin D. Roosevelt. (p. 554)

Roosevelt, Franklin D. (rō'zə velt), 1882–1945 The thirty-second President of the United States from 1933 to 1945. He created the New Deal to fight the Great Depression and led the country during World War II. (p. 554)

Roosevelt, Theodore (rō'zə velt), 1858–1919 The twenty-sixth President of the United States from 1901 to 1909. He led the Rough Riders during the Spanish-American War in 1898. (p. 522)

Ross, John (rôs), 1790–1866 Cherokee chief from 1828 to 1866 whose people were forced to march to the Indian Territory in 1838. (p. 380)

Sacagawea (sak ə jə wē'ə), 1787?–1812 Shoshone translator for the Lewis and Clark Expedition from 1805 to 1806. (p. 352)

Samoset (sam'ə set), 1590?–1655 Wampanoag sachem who was among those who first met the Pilgrims at Plymouth in 1620. (p. 166)

San Martín, José de (sän mär tēn'), 1778–1850 Argentinian military leader who freed Argentina and Chile from Spanish rule in the early 1800s. (p 631)

Santa Anna, Antonio López de (sän'tä än'ä), 1795–1876 Mexican general who defeated the Texans defending the Alamo in 1836. (p. 394)

Scott, Winfield (skot), 1786–1866 United States general during the Civil War who proposed the Anaconda Plan. (p. 436)

Sequoyah (si kwoi'ə), 1766?–1843 Cherokee leader who invented an alphabet for his people's language. (p. 379)

Serra, Junípero (she' ra), 1713–1784 Founder of the first Spanish mission in California, Mission San Diego de Alcalá. (p. 238)

Shays, Daniel (shāz), 1747?–1825 American Revolutionary officer who led a rebellion of Massachusetts farmers against state courts in 1786. (p. 313)

Sherman, Roger (shûr'mən), 1721–1793 Patriot who proposed the Great Compromise at the Constitutional Convention in 1787. (p. 449)

Sherman, William Tecumseh (shûr'mən, wil'yəm tə kum'sə), 1820–1891 Union general whose destructive march through Georgia in 1864 helped defeat the Confederacy. (p. 489)

Sinclair, Upton (sin klâr'), 1878–1968 Writer whose novel *The Jungle* in 1906 exposed unsafe practices in the meat-packing industry. (p. 523)

Sitting Bull (sit'ing bùl'), 1834–1890 Lakota chief who, with Crazy Horse, defeated Colonel Custer at the Battle of the Little Bighorn in 1876. (p. 496)

Slater, Samuel (slā'tər), 1768–1835 English engineer who built the first water-powered spinning mill in the United States in 1789. (p. 369)

Smith, John (smith), 1579?–1631 English army captain whose strict discipline helped the Jamestown settlement to survive. (p. 161)

Squanto (skwon'tō) 1585?–1622 Native American who helped the Pilgrims at Plymouth to survive. (p. 166)

Stalin, Josef (stä'lin), 1879–1953 Dictator of the Soviet Union from 1923 to 1953. (p. 560)

Standish, Miles (stan'dish), 1584?–1656 English army captain at Plymouth who helped defend the Pilgrim colony. (p. 169)

Stanton, Elizabeth Cady (stant'ən), 1815–1902 Abolitionist and women's rights leader who helped write the "Declaration of Rights and Sentiments" at the Seneca Falls Convention in 1848. (p. 420)

Steuben, Friederich von (stü'bən), 1730–1794 Patriot officer from Germany who helped train the Continental army at Valley Forge. (p. 297)

Stowe, Harriet Beecher (stō), 1811–1896 Abolitionist and writer of *Uncle Tom's Cabin* in 1851. (p. 417)

Stuyvesant, Peter (stī'vis ənt), ?–1672 Colonial governor of New Netherland. (p. 188)

Sunni Ali (sù'nē ä'lē), ?–1492 King of Songhai in West Africa in the late 1400s. (p. 106)

Tarbell, Ida (tär'bəl), 1857–1944 Muckraker and writer whose articles described the unfair business practices of the Standard Oil Company in 1903. (p. 523)

Taylor, Zachary (tā'lər), 1784–1850 The twelfth President of the United States from 1849 to 1850. He led United States forces during the war with Mexico. (p. 396)

Tecumseh (tə kum'sə), 1768–1813 Shawnee chief who attempted to unite Native American peoples against new settlers in the Northwest Territory. (p. 358)

Tomochichi (tō mä chē'chē), 1650?–1739 Chief of the Yamacraw who gave James Oglethorpe land for the Savannah settlement. (p. 194)

Tompkins, Sally (täm'kənz), 1833–1916 Confederate nurse who ran a hospital in Richmond, Virginia, during the Civil War. (p. 445)

Travis, William (trav'əs), 1809–1836 Commander of the Texas army at the Alamo in 1836. (p. 394)

Truman, Harry S. (trü'mən), 1884–1972 The thirty-third President of the United States from 1945 to 1953. He led the country at the end of World War II. (p. 564)

Truth, Sojourner (trüth), 1797?–1883 Abolitionist who escaped from slavery in 1827 and spoke out for women's rights. (p. 420)

Tubman, Harriet (tub'mən), 1820?–1913 Abolitionist and Underground Railroad conductor who helped hundreds of enslaved African Americans escape to freedom. (p. 419)

Turner, Nat (tûr'nər), 1800–1831 Leader of a slave revolt in Virginia in 1831. (p. 412)

Vargas, Diego de (vär'gäs, dē e'gō de), 1643–1704 Commander of the Spanish army that recaptured New Mexico from the Pueblo people in 1692. (p. 237)

Verrazano, Giovanni da (vâr ə zä'nō, jō vän' nē də), 1485?–1528? Italian sea captain in the service of France who searched for a Northwest Passage in 1524. (p. 151)

Washington, Booker T. (wô'shing tən), 1856–1915 Educator and founder of the Tuskegee Institute, an African American college, in 1881. (p. 544)

Washington, George (wô'shing tən), 1732–1799 First President of the United States from 1789 to 1797. He fought in the French and Indian War and led the Continental army during the American Revolution. (p. 247)

Washington, Martha (wô'shing tən), 1731–1802 First Lady to President George Washington. She assisted the Continental army during the American Revolution. (p. 291)

Wells–Barnett, Ida (welz' bär'nət), 1862–1931 A founder of the National Association for the Advancement of Colored People (NAACP) in 1909. (p. 544)

Wheatley, Phillis (hwēt'lē), 1753?–1784 Enslaved African American poet whose poems called for fair treatment for all people. (p. 228)

White, John (hwīt), 1500s Leader of the English colony of Roanoke in 1587. (p. 159)

Whitman, Marcus (hwit'mən), 1802–1847 Missionary who traveled to the Oregon Territory in 1836 with his wife, Narcissa Whitman. (p. 386)

Whitman, Narcissa (hwit'mən), 1808–1847 American missionary who traveled to the Oregon Territory in 1836 with her husband, Marcus Whitman. (p. 386)

Whitney, Eli (hwit'nē), 1765–1825 Inventor of the cotton gin in 1793. (p. 369)

Williams, Roger (wil'yəmz), 1603–1684 Puritan minister who founded the colony of Rhode Island in 1636. (p. 182)

Wilson, Woodrow (wil'sən), 1856–1924 The twenty-eighth President of the United States from 1913 to 1921. He led the United States during World War I and helped found the League of Nations. (p. 541)

Winthrop, John (win'thrəp), 1588–1649 First governor of the Massachusetts Bay Colony in 1630. (p. 181)

Woolman, John (wŭl'mən), 1720–1772 Quaker who spoke out against slavery in the colonies. (p. 214)

Wright, Orville (rīt), 1871–1948 Inventor who, with his brother Wilbur, made the world's first successful airplane flight in 1903. (p. 526)

Wright, Wilbur (rīt), 1867–1912 Inventor who, with his brother Orville, made the world's first successful airplane flight in 1903. (p. 526)

Yanga (yang'gə), 1500s–1600s Leader of a slave revolt in New Spain in 1609. (p. 141)

York (yôrk), 1770–1832? William Clark's slave and a member of the Lewis and Clark Expedition from 1804 to 1806. (p. 354)

Young, Brigham (yung), 1801–1877 Leader of the Mormons who brought the Mormons from Illinois to Utah, where they founded Salt Lake City. (p. 386)

Zavala, Lorenzo de (zä vä'lä), 1788–1836 The first vice president of the Texas Republic in 1836. (p. 396)

Zenger, John Peter (zeng'ər), 1697–1746 Newspaper printer whose trial in 1734 helped to establish the idea of freedom of the press. (p. 228)

Zheng He (jäng hə), 1371?–1433? Chinese sea captain whose voyages opened Chinese exploration and trade in the early 1400s. (p. 107)

Zhu Di (zhü dē), 1360–1424 Emperor of China who encouraged exploration in the early 1400s. (p. 106)

Glossary

This Glossary will help you to pronounce and understand the meanings of the vocabulary in this book. The page number at the end of the definition tells where the word first appears.

A

A.D. (ā dē) "Anno Domini," Latin for "in the year of the Lord." Used before a numeral to indicate a year occurring since the birth of Jesus Christ. (p. 47)

abolitionist (ab ə lish′ə nist) A person who wanted to end slavery in the United States. (p. 417)

activist (ak′ tə vist) A person who supports or takes actions in something he or she belives in. (p. 580)

adobe (ə dō′bē) A type of clay used for building by Native Americans and Spanish colonists in the Southwest. (p. 58)

agriculture (ag′ri kul chər) The business of farming. (p. 217)

alliance (ə lī′ əns) A friendship with people, powers, or countries for purposes of protection. (p. 541)

Allied Powers (al′līd pou′ərz) The name given to the forces led by Great Britain, France, and Russia during World War I. See Central Powers. (p. 541)

Allies (al′līz) The name given to the countries allied against the Axis powers in World War II, including the United States, Britain, France, the Soviet Union, and China. See Axis. (p. 559)

alternative (ôl tûr′nə tiv) Another way of doing something. (p. 156)

amendment (ə mend′mənt) An addition to the Constitution. See Constitution (p. 324)

American Revolution (ə mer′i kən rev ə lü′shən) The war between Great Britain and its thirteen American colonies from 1775 to 1783. (p. 286)

Americans with Disabilities Act (ə mer′i kənz with dis′ ə bil′itēz akt) A law that made it illegal for employers to discriminate against people with disabilities. (p. 590)

Anaconda Plan (an ə kon′də plan) The Union's plan for defeating the Confederacy in the Civil War. (p. 436)

Antifederalist (an′tē fed′ər ə list) An opponent of a strong central government in the late 1700s. See Federalist. (p. 329)

apprentice (ə pren′ tis) A person who works for a skilled person to learn a trade or art. (p. 205)

armada (är mä′dä) A large fleet of ships, especially warships. (p. 159)

arms race (ärmz rās) A race to build the most powerful weapons. (p. 568)

Articles of Confederation (är′ti kəlz əv kən fed ə rā′shən) The first plan of government of the United States, in effect from 1781 to 1789. (p. 313)

assembly (ə sem′blē) A lawmaking body. (p. 225)

assembly line (ə sem′blē līn) A method of mass production in which the product is carried on a moving belt past workers who remain in place. (p. 526)

atlas (at′ləs) A book of maps. See reference source. (p. 598)

atomic bomb (ə tom′ik bom) A bomb that produces massive amounts of energy by splitting atoms. (p. 564)

autobiography (ô tə bī og′rə fē) The story of a person's own life written by himself or herself. (p. 202)

Axis (ak′sis) Countries that fought the Allies in World War II, including Germany, Italy, and Japan. See Allies. (p. 559)

B

B.C. (bē sē) "Before Christ." Used to indicate a year occurring before the birth of Jesus Christ. (p. 47)

backcountry (bak′kən trē) In colonial times, the name of the eastern foothills of the Appalachians. (p. 208)

Bank of the United States (bangk əv thə ū nī′ tid stāts) Second national bank of the United States, which ended when President Jackon withdrew all federal funds in 1833. (p. 378)

Battle of Bunker Hill (ba′təl əv bung′kər hil) Costly British "victory" in 1775 over Patriot forces at a site near Charlestown, Massachusetts. (p. 273)

pronunciation key

a	at	ī	ice	u	up	th	thin
ā	ape	îr	pierce	ū	use	th	this
ä	far	o	hot	ü	rule	zh	measure
âr	care	ō	old	ù	pull	ə	about, taken,
e	end	ô	fork	ûr	turn		pencil, lemon,
ē	me	oi	oil	hw	white		circus
i	it	ou	out	ng	song		

Battle of Gettysburg (ba'təl əv get'iz bûrg) The Civil War battle in southeastern Pennsylvania in July 1863 in which Confederate forces under General Robert E. Lee were defeated. (p. 446)

Battle of New Orleans (bat'əl əv nü ôr'lē ənz) A United States victory over British forces in the last battle of the War of 1812. See War of 1812. (p. 362)

bilingual (bī ling'gwəl) Having the ability to speak two languages equally well. (p. 610)

Bill of Rights (bil əv rīts) The first ten amendments to the Constitution, ratified in 1791. See amendment and Constitution. (p. 330)

black codes (blak kōdz) Laws passed by the Southern states after the Civil War that severely limited the rights of the newly freed African Americans. (p. 457)

blockade (blo kād') The closing of an area, especially during wartime, to keep people or supplies from moving in or out. (p. 436)

Boston Massacre (bôs'tən mas'ə kər) The killing of five colonists during a conflict with British soldiers in Boston in 1770. (p. 264)

Boston Tea Party (bos'tən tē pär'tē) A 1773 protest against British taxes; colonists disguised as Mohawks dumped tea into Boston Harbor. (p. 265)

boycott (boi'kot) To refuse to do business or have contact with a person, group, country, or product. (p. 264)

Buffalo Soldiers (buf' ə lō sōl' jer) The name given to the African American cavalry unit that fought in the Plains Wars and the Spanish-American War. (p. 521)

C

Cabinet (kab'ə nit) The officials appointed by the President to be advisers and to head each department in the executive branch. (p. 331)

call number (kôl num'bər) The numbers that tell exactly where to find a book in the library. (p. 598)

canal (kə nal') A human-built waterway. (p. 372)

caravan (kâr'ə van) A group of people traveling together for safety, especially through desert areas. (p. 106)

caravel (kâr'ə vel) A fast sailing ship that could be steered easily and hold large amounts of cargo. (p. 109)

cardinal direction (kär'də nəl di rek'shən) One of the four main points of the compass; north, south, east, and west. See compass rose. (p. H13)

cash crop (kash krop) A crop that is grown to be sold for profit. See profit. (p. 161)

cattle drive (kat'əl drīv) A long journey in which cowboys brought cattle from the ranch to the railroad, from about the 1860s to the 1880s. See railhead. (p. 483)

cause (kôz) Something that makes something else happen. See effect. (p. 68)

CD-ROM (sē dē räm') A type of reference source similar to a compact disc that is "read" by a computer. It combines text, sound, and even short films. See reference source. (p. 598)

census (sen'səs) An official count of all the people living in a country or region. (p. 20)

Central Powers (sen'trəl pou'ərz) The forces led by Germany, Austria-Hungary, and Turkey in World War I. See Allied Powers. (p. 541)

century (sen'chə rē) A period of 100 years. (p. 47)

charter (chär'tər) An official document giving permission to do something, such as settle in an area. (p. 159)

checks and balances (cheks and bal'ən səz) The system in which each branch of government is balanced by the others. (p. 326)

circle graph (sûr'kəl graf) A kind of graph that shows how something can be divided into parts. (p. 102)

citizen (sit'ə zən) A person born in a country or who becomes a member of that country by law. (p. 23)

civil rights (siv'əl rīts) The individual rights of all citizens to be treated equally under the law. (p. 461)

Civil Rights Act (siv'əl rīts akt) A law that bans discrimination because of a person's color, race, national origin, religion, or sex. (p. 581)

Civil War (siv' əl wôr) The war between the Union and the Confederacy from 1861 to 1865. (p. 435)

civilian (si vil' yən) A person who is not in the armed forces. (p. 438)

civilization (siv ə lə zā'shən) A culture that has complex systems of government, education, religion, and often many people living in cities. (p. 42)

clan (klan) Families who share the same ancestor. (p. 64)

climate (klī'mit) The general weather of an area. (p. 8)

Cold War (kōld wôr) The conflict from 1945 to 1991 between the United States and the Soviet Union, involving ideas, words, money, and weapons. (p. 567)

colony (kol'ə nē) A settlement far away from the country that rules it. (p. 122)

Columbian Exchange (kə lum'bē ən eks chänj') The movement of people, plants, animals, and germs across the Atlantic Ocean following the voyages of Columbus. (p. 122)

Committees of Correspondence (kə mit'ēz əv kôr ə spon'dəns) Groups organized in the 1770s to keep colonists informed of important events. (p. 265)

commonwealth (kom' ən welth) A country or state governed by its people. (p. 627)

communism (kom'yə nizm) A system in which the government owns all property and makes nearly all decisions for its citizens. (p. 560)

compass rose (kum'pəs rōz) A drawing that indicates directions on a map, especially cardinal and intermediate directions. See cardinal direction and intermediate direction. (p. H13)

compromise (kom'prə mīz) The settling of a dispute by each side agreeing to give up part of its demands. (p. 67)

Compromise of 1850 (kom'prə mīz uv āt'tēn' fif'tē) A law admitting California to the Union, allowing territories to decide on slavery, and requiring the North to obey the Fugitive Slave Law. See Fugitive Slave Law of 1850. (p. 425)

concentration camp (kon sen trā'shən kamp) A type of prison in which the Nazis enslaved and murdered millions of people during World War II. See Holocaust. (p. 564)

conclusion (kən klü'zhən) A statement reached by considering all information. (p. 572)

confederacy (kən fed'ər ə sē) A group of countries, states, or people who join for a common purpose. (p. 194)

Confederacy (kən fed'ər ə sē) The Confederate States of America that seceded from the Union during the Civil War. (p. 428)

conquistador (kōn kēs tä dôr') A Spanish conqueror who first came to the Americas in the 1500s. (p. 132)

consequence (kōn si kwens) A result of an action. (p. 16)

conservation (kon sər vā'shən) The protection and careful use of natural resources. (p. 15)

conservationist (kon' sər vā'shə nist) Person who works to preserve the environment. (p. 527)

constable (kon stə-bəl) A town officer. (p. 227)

Constitution (kon stī tü'shən) A plan of government. In the United States it is the supreme law and plan of the national government, adopted in 1789. (p. 22)

Constitutional Convention (kon stī tü'shə nəl kən ven'shən) The meeting of twelve states' delegates in Philadelphia, Pennsylvania, that replaced the Articles of Confederation with a new Constitution. See Articles of Confederation and Constitution. (p. 316)

consumer (kən sōō'-mər) A person who buys and uses goods and services. (p. 27)

Continental army (kon'tə nen'təl är'mē) The army created by the Second Continental Congress in 1775 with George Washington as commander in chief. See Second Continental Congress. (p. 277)

convert (kən vûrt') To cause a person to change a belief. (p. 235)

cooperation (kō op ər ā shən) When more than one group works together. (p. 189)

corporation (kôr pə rā'shən) A business that is owned by individuals who invest in that company. (p. 507)

cotton gin (kot'ən jin) A machine that separates cotton from its seeds, invented by Eli Whitney in 1793. (p. 369)

coup stick (kü stik) A special weapon used by a Lakota Sioux soldier to show bravery by touching, not killing, his enemy. (p. 72)

coureur de bois (kü rər' də bwä') In New France, a person who trapped furs without permission from the French government. (p. 241)

covenant (kuv'ə nənt) A special agreement. (p. 181)

cowtowns (kou tounz) Entire towns developed for cowboys passing through (p. 484)

Cuban Missile Crisis (kyū'bən mis'əl krīs'is) A confrontation in 1962 between the United States and the Soviet Union over nuclear missiles in Cuba. (p. 571)

cultural region (kul' chər-əl rə'jən) Area where people share the same beliefs and customs (p. 13)

currency (kûr' ən sē) The coins, paper, or gold used as money in a country (p. 105)

Custer's Last Stand (kus'tarz last stand) The last major Native American victory on the Plains. (p. 497)

D

DNA (dē en ā) A substance which carries genetic information. (p. 602)

database (dā' tə-bās') A reference source that contains information, such as articles, pictures, maps, and music that has been stored electronically. (p. 598)

debtor (det'ər) A person who owes money. (p. 194)

decade (dek'ād) A period of ten years. (p. 47)

decision (dis izh'ən) A choice made from a number of alternatives. See alternative. (p. 156)

decision making (dis izh'ən māking) Choosing from a number of alternatives to achieve a goal. (p. 156)

Declaration of Independence (dek lə rā'shən əv in di pen'dəns) The document issued by the Second Continental Congress on July 4, 1776, explaining why the colonies were breaking away from Great Britain. (p. 278)

delegate (del'i git) A member of an elected assembly. See assembly. (p. 226)

democracy (di mok'rə sē) A form of government in which the people make the laws and run the government. (p. 324)

democratic republic (dem' ə kratic repub'lik) A form of government where people choose representatives to run the government. (p. 22)

dictator (dik'tā tər) A leader with complete authority over the government. (p. 559)

discrimination (di skrim'ə nā shən) An unfair difference in the treatment of people. (p. 544)

distribution map (dis trə-byü' shən map) A map that shows how features such as language, climate, and products are spread out over an area. (p. 440)

Glossary

diversity (di vûr'si tē) Variety; differences. (p. 18)

draft (draft) The process of selection of men for compulsory military service. (p. 448)

Dred Scott Decision (dred skät di sizh'ən) An 1857 Supreme Court decision that said slaves were private property. (p. 427)

Dust Bowl (dust bōl) Years of drought in the 1930s that turned 150,000 square miles of the Great Plains into dust. (p. 533)

E

ecosystem (ē' kō-sis təm) All the living and nonliving things in a certain area. (p.13)

editorial (ed i tôr'ē əl) A newspaper article in which the editors give their opinions on issues. (p. 422)

effect (i fekt') Something that happens as a result of a cause. See cause. (p. 68)

elevation (el ə vā'shən) The height of an area above sea level. See elevation map. (p. 186)

elevation map (el ə vā'shən map) A physical map that uses colors to show the elevation, or height, of land above sea level. See physical map. (p. H17)

Emancipation Proclamation (ē man si pā'shən prok lə mā'shən) An official announcement issued by President Abraham Lincoln in 1862 that led to the end of slavery in the United States. (p. 443)

empire (em'pīr) A large area where different people are controlled by one ruler or government. (p. 49)

encomienda (en kō mē en'dä) A very large piece of land in New Spain given by the Spanish government to certain Spanish colonists during the 1500s. (p. 140)

encyclopedia (en sī klə pē'dē ə) A book or set of books that gives information about people, places, things, and past events. (p. 598)

entrepreneur (än' trə prə nûr') A person who forms, runs, and takes the risk for a business. (p. 26)

environment (en vī'rən mənt) All the surroundings in which people, plants, and animals live. (p. 12)

Era of Good Feelings (ir'ə uv güd fē'lingz) The name given to the period of peace and prosperity that followed the War of 1812. (p. 362)

ethnic group (eth'nik grüp) People with the same customs and language, often having a common history. (p. 19)

executive branch (eg zek'yə tiv branch) The part of government, headed by the President, that carries out the laws. (p. 318)

exoduster (ek'sō dus tər) The term used for the African Americans from the South who went to Kansas in the 1860s. (p. 490)

expedition (ek spi dish'ən) A journey made for a special purpose. (p. 99)

export (ek'spôrt) To send goods to other countries for sale or use. (p. 216)

F

fact (fakt) A statement that can be proven true. (p. 390)

favela (fä vä'lä) The name for any slum near São Paulo, Brazil. See slum. (p. 632)

feature article (fē'chər är'ti kəl) A newspaper article focusing on a person, issue, or event. (p. 422)

federal (fed'ər əl) The word describing a central, or national, government. (p. 22)

federal system (fed'ər əl sis'təm) A system of government in which power is shared between the central government and state governments. (p. 325)

Federalist (fed'ər ə list) A supporter of a strong federal system of government in the late 1700s. See Antifederalist. (p. 329)

Fifteenth Amendment (fif'tēnth' ə mend'mənt) An amendment to the Constitution, ratified in 1870, that made it illegal to withhold voting rights "on account of race or color." (p. 460)

First Continental Congress (fûrst kon'tə nen'təl kong'gris) The assembly of colonial delegates that met in 1774 in Philadelphia to oppose the Intolerable Acts. (p. 266)

forty-niners (fôr'tē nī'nərz) People who came to California in 1849 in search of gold. (p. 388)

fossil fuel (fos'əl fū'əl) A fuel, such as oil, natural gas, and coal, that is formed from the remains of plants and animals that lived millions of years ago. (p. 12)

Fourteenth Amendment (fôr'tēnth' ə mend'mənt) An amendment to the Constitution, ratified in 1868, that officially established blacks as citizens with the same legal rights as whites. (p. 457)

frame of reference (frām əv ref'rəns) The basis a person uses when forming a point of view. (p. 492)

free enterprise (frē en'tər prīz) An economic system in which people can own property and businesses and are free to decide what to make, how much to produce, and what price to charge. (p. 26)

Freedmen's Bureau (frēd'mənz byúr'ō) A government agency created in 1865 that provided food, schools, and medical care for freed slaves in the South. (p. 458)

French and Indian War (french ənd in'dē ən wôr) A conflict between Great Britain and France in North America from 1756 to 1763. (p. 246)

frontier (frun tîr') A word used by settlers to describe land beyond their settlements. (p. 204)

Fugitive Slave Law (fū'ji tiv slāv lô) A law of 1850 that required police in free states to help capture escaping slaves. (p. 425)

G

gene (jēn) A cell that contains all the information that gives living things their characteristics. (p. 602)

generalization (jen ər ə lə zā'shən) A broad statement that ties together separate facts or ideas. (p. 244)

Gettysburg Address (get'iz bûrg ə dres') The speech made by President Lincoln at the site of the Battle of Gettysburg in 1863. (p. 446)

glacier (glā shər) A huge sheet of ice. (p. 41)

gold rush (gōld rush) The rush of people to an area where gold has been discovered, as in California in 1849. (p. 388)

graph (graf) A diagram that presents information in a way that makes it easy to detect patterns, trends, or changes over time. (p. 102)

Great Chicago Fire (grāt shi kä'gō fīr) A fire in 1871 that destroyed a third of the city in 24 hours. (p. 512)

Great Compromise (grāt kom' prə mīz) The plan drawn up at the Constitutional Convention in 1787 to form two houses of Congress. (p. 319)

Great Depression (grāt di presh'ən) The period of widespread economic hardship in the 1930s. (p. 553)

Great Migration (grāt mī grā'shən) The journey of African Americans from the South to northern manufacturing cities that peaked in the early 1900s. (p. 544)

grid (grid) A set of criss-crossing lines that can help you to determine locations, such as on a map or globe. (p. 11)

H

historian (hi stôr'ē ən) A person who studies the past. (p. 28)

historical map (hi stôr'i kəl map) A map that shows information about the past or past events. (p. H17)

hogan (hō' gən) Dome-shaped Navajo dwellings made with log or stick frames and covered with mud or sod. (p. 59)

Holocaust (hol'ə kost) The murder of six million Jews by Nazi Germany during World War II. (p. 564)

Homestead Act (hōm'sted akt) A law that gave free farmland to any adult male or widow who agreed to work it for five years. (p. 487)

homesteader (hōm'sted ər) One who claimed land on the Great Plains under the Homestead Act of 1862. (p. 487)

House of Burgesses (hous əv bûr'jis əz) The lawmaking body of colonial Virginia, established in Jamestown in 1619. (p. 162)

House of Representatives (hous əv rep ri zen'tə tivz) The house of Congress in which each state's number of representatives is determined according to its population. See legislative branch. (p. 319)

humid (hū'mid) Wet; moist. (p. 8)

hurricane (hûr'i kān) A storm with violent winds revolving around a calm center. It is accompanied by heavy rains, high tides, and flooding. (p. 623)

hydroelectricity (hī drō i lek tris'i tē) Electricity generated by the force of running water. (p. 556)

I

Ice Age (īs āj) A period of extreme cold during which much of Earth's water was frozen into glaciers. (p. 41)

immigrant (im'i grənt) A person who comes to a country from another to live. (p. 18)

impeach (im pēch') To charge a government official with wrongdoing. (p. 459)

indentured servant (in den'chərd sûr'vənt) A person who bounds himself or herself to serve someone for a certain period of time in exchange for something. (p. 162)

Indian Removal Act (in'dē ən ri mü'vəl akt) An 1830 law forcing Native Americans of the Southeast to move to what is now Oklahoma. (p. 379)

indigo (in'di gō) A plant used to produce a blue dye. (p. 195)

Industrial Revolution (in dus'trē əl rev ə lü'shən) The dramatic change from making goods by hand at home to making them by machine in factories. (p. 368)

industry (in'də strē) All the businesses that make one kind of product or provide one kind of service. (p. 218)

inference (in' fər əns) Something you figure out based on clues and information that you already know. (p. 454)

inflation (in flā' shən) A rise in the usual prices of goods and services. (p. 633)

integrate (in' ti grāt) To bring groups of different people together, such as blacks and whites after segregation. (p. 580)

interchangeable parts (in tər chān'jə bəl pärts) Parts of a product built to a standard size so that they can be easily replaced. (p. 370)

intermediate direction (in tər mē'dē it di rek'shən) A direction halfway between two cardinal directions; northeast, northwest, southwest, southeast. (p. H13)

Iron Curtain (ī'ərn kûr'tin) The imaginary borders dividing Europe into communist and noncommunist countries from 1948 to 1991. (p. 566)

Iroquois Confederacy (ir'i kwä kən fed'ər ə sē) The union of the five major Iroquois nations. (p. 65)

irrigation (ir i gā'shən) A method of supplying dry land with water through a series of ditches or pipes. (p. 44)

J

jazz (jaz) The form of popular music that grew out of African American culture in the 1920s. (p. 547)

jerky (jûr'kē) Thin strips of sun-dried meat. (p. 74)

Glossary

Jim Crow laws (jim krō lōz) Laws passed by Southern states after Reconstruction that established segregation, or separation of the races. (p. 461)

judicial branch (jū dish'əl branch) The part of government that decides the meaning of the laws. See Supreme Court. (p. 318)

K

kachina (kə chē'nə) In the Pueblo religion, the living spirit of an ancestor. (p. 58)

Kansas-Nebraska Act (kan'zəs nə bras'kə akt) An 1854 law that allowed the Kansas and Nebraska territories to decide whether to become free or slave states. (p. 426)

kiva (kē və) Underground rooms used by the Anasazi for religious ceremonies. (p. 58)

Korean War (kə rē'ən wôr) A war between communist North Korea, supported by China, and South Korea, supported by the United States and other United Nations members. It lasted from 1950 to 1953. (p. 568)

L

La Causa (lä kōza) The name given to the labor union for migrant workers. In English, "the cause." (p. 585)

labor union (lā'bər ūn'yən) A group of workers united to gain better wages and working conditions. (p. 508)

landform (land'fôrm) A shape on Earth's surface, such as a mountain or hill. (p. 4)

large-scale map (lärj skāl map) A map that shows a smaller area in greater detail. See small-scale map. (p. 306)

latitude (lat'i tüd) An imaginary line, or parallel, measuring distance north or south of the equator. See parallel. (p. H12)

League of Nations (lēg əv nā'shənz) An international organization set up after World War I to prevent future wars. (p. 542)

League of Women Voters (lēg əv wim'ən vōt'ərz) A volunteer organization founded in 1920 to inform people about politics. (p. 550)

legislation (lej i slā'shən) The making or passing of laws. (p. 225)

legislative branch (lej'is lā tiv branch) The lawmaking part of government. See House of Representatives and Senate. (p. 318)

line graph (līn graf) A kind of graph that shows changes over time. See graph. (p. 102)

locator (lō kā'tər) A small map inset in the corner of a larger map that helps you understand where the subject area of the larger map is located on Earth. (p. H15)

lodge (loj) A type of home made of logs, grasses, sticks, and soil which the Native Americans of the Plains used. (p. 71)

log (log) A record, usually of a voyage or experiment. (p. 120)

longhouse (lông'hous) A home shared by several related Iroquois families. (p. 64)

longitude (lon'ji tüd) An imaginary line, or meridian, measuring distance east or west of the prime meridian. See meridian. (p. H12)

Louisiana Purchase (lü ē zē an'ə pûr'chəs) The territory purchased by the United States from France in 1803, reaching from the Mississippi River to the Rocky Mountains and from the Gulf of Mexico to Canada. (p. 352)

Loyalist (loi'ə list) A colonist who supported Great Britain in the American Revolution. (p. 274)

M

manifest destiny (man' ə fest des' tənē) A belief in the right of the United States to claim new lands. (p. 399)

map key (map kē) A guide that shows what each symbol on a map stands for. See symbol. (p. H15)

map scale (map skāl) A line like a measuring stick drawn on a map which uses a unit of measurement, such as an inch, to represent a real distance on Earth. (p. 306)

Marshall Plan (Mär' shəl plan) Plan that provided $13 billion in goods to help Western Europe recover from World War II. (p. 567)

Mayflower Compact (mā'flou ər kom'pakt) An agreement the Pilgrims made before landing in New England to make and obey "just and equal laws." (p. 166)

media (mē'dē ə) Any method of communication that reaches a large number of people, including radio, newspapers, television, magazines, and computer networks. (p. 549)

mercenary (mûr'sə ner ē) A soldier paid to fight for another country. (p. 289)

merchant (mûr'chənt) A shop owner. (p. 97)

meridian (mə rid'ē ən) Any line of longitude east or west of Earth's prime meridian. See longitude. (p. H12)

mesa (mā' sə) A mountain or hill with a flat top and steep sides. (p. 57)

mestizo (me stē'zō) A person who has both Indian and Spanish ancestors. (p. 618)

Mexican War (mek'si kən wôr) A war between the United States and Mexico from 1846 to 1848. (p. 396)

Middle Ages (mid'l ā' jes) The period of European history from around 500 to 1500. (p. 97)

Middle Passage (mid'əl pas'ij) The middle leg of the triangular trade route in colonial times in which captive Africans were shipped to the West Indies to be sold into slavery. See triangular trade. (p. 220)

migrant (mī' grənt) A worker who moves from farm to farm picking different crops. (p. 585)

militia (mi lish'ə) A group of volunteers who fought in times of emergency during the colonial period and the American Revolution. See minutemen. (p. 226)

minutemen (min'it men) Volunteer soldiers who defended the colonies against the British at a minute's notice. (p. 266)

mission (mish'ən) A settlement where missionaries lived and worked. (p. 235)

missionary (mish'ə ner ē) A person who teaches his or her religion to people of different beliefs. (p. 140)

Missouri Compromise (mi zur'ē kom'prə mīz) A law passed by Congress in 1820 that divided the Louisiana Territory into areas allowing slavery and areas outlawing slavery. (p. 424)

monopoly (mə nop'ə lē) A company that controls an entire industry. (p. 507)

Monroe Doctrine (mən rō dok'trin) A declaration by President Monroe in 1823 that opposed European interference in the Western Hemisphere. (p. 363)

Mountain Men (moun't ən men) Fur trappers of the western mountains during the 1800s. (p. 386)

national anthem (nash'ə nəl an'thəm) A country's official song, such as "The Star-Spangled Banner." (p. 360)

National Association for the Advancement of Colored People (NAACP) (nash'ə nəl ə sō sē ā'shən fôr thē ad vans'mənt əv kul'ərd pē'pōl) An organization, founded in 1909 by blacks and whites, to fight prejudice and discrimination. (p. 544)

national debt (nash'ə nəl det) The amount of money the government owes. (p. 594)

national park (nash'ə nəl pärk) An area set aside by the national government for the public to enjoy. (p. 527)

natural resource (nach'ər əl rē'sôrs) A material found in nature that people use. (p. 12)

navigation (nav i gā'shən) The science of determining a ship's location and direction. (p. 109)

neutral (nū'trəl) Not taking sides. (p. 359)

New Deal (nū dēl) Government programs started by President Franklin D. Roosevelt in the 1930s to help recover from the Great Depression. (p. 555)

New Jersey Plan (nū jur'zē plan) The plan offered by the small states at the Constitutional Convention of 1787 that would have given all states an equal number of representatives in Congress. (p. 319)

news article (nūz är'ti kəl) A newspaper story that factually describes an important recent event. (p. 422)

Nineteenth Amendment (nīn'tēnth ə mend'mənt) An amendment to the Constitution, ratified in 1920, that gave women the right to vote. (p. 547)

nonrenewable resource (non ri nū'ə bəl rē'sôrs) A material found in nature that cannot be replaced, such as coal, oil, and natural gas. (p. 12)

North American Free Trade Agreement (nôrth ə mer'i kən frē trād ə grē'mənt) A treaty signed by Canada, Mexico, and the United States in 1992 that makes all of North America one trading area. (p. 615)

Northwest Ordinance (north'west' ôr'də nəns) A law of 1787 organizing the Northwest Territory for settlement and eventual statehood. (p. 314)

Northwest Passage (north'west' pas'ij) A water route believed to flow through North America that explorers searched for from the 1500s to the 1700s. (p. 151)

opinion (ə pin' yən) A personal view or belief. (p. 390)

outline (out'līn) A plan for organizing written information about a subject. (p. 24)

overseer (ō'vər sē ər) The boss of a plantation. (p. 213)

P

Pacific Railroad Act (pə sif'ik rāl'rōd akt) An 1862 law offering government loans and free land to the two companies building the transcontinental railroad. See transcontinental railroad. (p. 475)

parallel (par'ə lel) A line of latitude. See latitude. (p. H12)

Patriot (pā'trē ət) An American colonist who supported the fight for independence. (p. 274)

patriotism (pā'trē ə tiz əm) A love for and loyal support of one's country. (p. 18)

Persian Gulf War (pur'zhən gulf wôr) A war in 1991 in which international armed forces led by the United States drove Iraqi forces from Kuwait. (p. 596)

physical map (fiz'i kəl map) A map that highlights Earth's natural features. (p. H17)

pioneer (pī ə nir') A person who creates a path, usually to make a new home and lead a settlement. (p. 347)

plantation (plan tā'shən) A large farm that often grows one crop. (p. 210)

point of view (point əv vū) The position from which a person looks at an issue or situation. (p. 322)

political cartoon (pə lit'i kəl kär tün') A drawing that shows a cartoonist's opinion about a political person, event, or issue. (p. 268)

political map (pə lit'i kəl map) A map that shows the boundaries of states and countries. (p. H17)

political party (pə lit'i kəl pär'tē) A group of people who share similar ideas about government. (p. 332)

pollution (pə lü'shən) Unclean matter. (p. 13)

portage (pôr'tij) A land route between bodies of water. (p. 155)

potlatch (pot'lach) A special feast given by Native Americans of the Northwest Coast. (p. 78)

prairie (prâr'ē) Flat or gently rolling land covered mostly with grasses and wildflowers. (p. 71)

Glossary

Preamble (prē′am bəl) The introduction to the Constitution. (p. 325)

precipitation (pri sip i tā′shən) The moisture that falls to Earth as rain or snow. (p. 8)

prejudice (prej′ə dis) A negative opinion formed without proof. (p. 414)

presidio (pri sē′ dē ō) A military fort where soldiers live. (p. 238)

primary source (prī mer′ē sôrs) A firsthand account of an event or an artifact. (p. 29)

Proclamation of 1763 (prok lə mā′shən) An announcement by King George III of Britain outlawing colonial settlement west of the Appalachians. (p. 249)

profit (prof′it) The money remaining after the costs of a business have been paid. (p. 151)

property rights (prop′ər tē rīts) The rights to own or use something. (p. 495)

proprietor (prə prī′i tər) A person who owns a property or a business. (p. 193)

province (prov′ins) A political division of a country, as in Canada. (p. 611)

pueblo (pweb′lō) A Spanish word meaning "village" used to refer to the apartment-style homes of the Native Americans of the Southwest. (p. 57)

R

railhead (rāl′hed) Any town on a railroad line where a cattle drive usually ends. (p. 484)

rain forest (rān fôr′ist) A dense, usually tropical forest that has lots of rain year round. (p. 617)

ratify (rat′ə fī) To give official approval, for example, to the Constitution or amendments to it. (p. 328)

reaper (rē′pər) A machine that uses sharp blades to harvest grain. (p. 370)

Reconstruction (rē kən struk′shən) The period after the Civil War in which Congress passed laws designed to bring Southern states back into the Union. (p. 456)

recycle (rē sī′kəl) To save discarded items, like cans or bottles, so that they can be used again. (p. 15)

reference source (ref′ər ens sôrs) A book or other source that has facts about many different subjects. (p. 598)

reform (ri fôrm′) A change to make government or business work better. (p. 523)

relief (ri lēf′) The difference in height between land areas. (p. 186)

relief map (ri lēf′ map) A physical map that uses shading to show the difference in height between areas of land. See relief and physical map. (p. H17)

relocation camp (rē lō kā′shən kamp) Prison camps in which Japanese Americans were held in the western United States during World War II. (p. 561)

renewable resource (ri nü′ə bəl rē′sôrs) A material found in nature that can be replaced, such as forests. (p. 12)

repeal (ri pēl′) To withdraw or cancel. (p. 263)

republic (ri pub′lik) A form of government in which the people elect representatives to run the country. (p. 325)

reservation (rez ər vā′shən) An area set aside for Native Americans. (p. 495)

road map (rōd map) A map that indicates cities, highways, and points of interest. (p. H18)

Roaring Twenties (rôr′ing twen′tēz) The decade of the 1920s, which got this nickname because of the time's prosperity and excitement. (p. 546)

Rough Rider (ruf rī′dər) One of Theodore Roosevelt friends who voluteered to fight in Cuba during the Spanish-American War. (p. 520)

rural (rür′ əl) Of the countryside. (p. 15)

S

sachem (sā′chəm) A Native American chief in the Eastern Woodlands and Great Lakes regions. (p. 166)

satellite (sat′ə līt) An object that circles a larger object, such as the moon around Earth. (p. 569)

scale (skāl) A guide that explains the relationship between real distances on Earth and distances on a map. (p. H14)

secede (sə sēd′) To break away from a group, such as the Southern states seceding from the Union in 1861. (p. 428)

Second Continental Congress (sek′ənd kon′tə nen′təl kong′gris) A meeting in Philadelphia in 1775 of delegates from all 13 colonies that established a colonial army and declared American independence. See Declaration of Independence. (p. 276)

Second Treaty of Fort Stanwix (sek′ ənd trē′tē əv fôrt stan′ wiks) The treaty by which the Iroquois lost their land in the Ohio River valley after the American Revolution. (p. 304)

secondary source (sek′ən der ē sôrs) An account of the past based on information from primary sources and written by someone who was not an eyewitness to those events. See primary source. (p. 29)

secretary (sek′rə ter ē) The head of each department in the executive branch of government. As a group the secretaries are called the President's Cabinet. See Cabinet. (p. 331)

segregation (seg ri gā′shən) The separation of people, usually based on race or religion. (p. 461)

Senate (sen′it) The house of Congress in which each state has an equal number of representatives, or Senators, regardless of population. See legislative branch and House of Representatives. (p. 319)

Seneca Falls Convention (sen′i kə fôlz kən ven′shən) The country's first women's rights meeting, held in Seneca Falls, New York, in 1848. (p. 420)

settlement house (set'əl mənt hous) In the late 1800s and early 1900s, a community center for the poor, immigrants, and others in need of child care, education, and so on. (p. 514)

sharecropping (shâr'krop ing) In the late 1800s and early 1900s, a system in which farmers rented land from a landowner and paid the owner with a share of their crop. (p. 458)

Shays's Rebellion (shāz ri bel'yən) A revolt in 1786 of Massachusetts farmers, led by Daniel Shays, who opposed tax decisions of the state courts. (p. 313)

slave codes (slāv cōdz) Rules made by colonial planters that controlled the lives of enslaved Africans. (p. 211)

slave trade (slāv trād) The business of buying and selling people for profit. See triangular trade. (p. 202)

slavery (slā'və rē) The practice of people owning other people and forcing them to work. (p. 49)

slum (slum) A poor, crowded section of a city with rundown and often unsafe housing. See favela. (p. 512)

small-scale map (smôl skāl map) A map that shows a large area but not much detail. See large-scale map. (p. 306)

sodbuster (sod'bus tər) A settler on the Great Plains who had to "bust" through thick sod to plant crops. (p. 488)

soddies (sod'ēs) Houses made of sod by the Great Plains settlers. (p. 488)

Sons of Liberty (sunz əv lib'ər tē) Colonists who organized to protest against the British government. (p. 263)

Spanish-American War (span'ish ə mer'i kən wôr) The war in which the United States gained control of Puerto Rico, Guam, and the Philippines from Spain in 1898. (p. 521)

specialize (spesh'ə līz) To spend most of one's time doing one kind of job. (p. 42)

Stamp Act (stamp akt) A law passed by Britian in 1765 requiring colonists to pay a tax on newspapers, pamphlets, legal documents, and even playing cards. (p. 263)

statehood (stāt'hūd) Becoming a state in the United States. (p. 314)

states' rights (stāts rīts) The belief that each state should be allowed to make its own decisions. (p. 427)

steam engine (stēm en'jin) An engine powered by the energy produced from steam. (p. 372)

stock (stok) Shares of ownership in a company. (p. 160)

stock exchange (stok eks chānj') A special market where shares of stocks are bought and sold. (p. 553)

stockyard (stok' yärd) A cattle pen. (p. 484)

strike (strīk) A refusal of all the workers in a business to work until the owners meet their demands. (p. 508)

suffrage (suf'rij) The right to vote. (p. 549)

summary (sum' ə rē) A brief way of telling the main points of an event or an idea. (p. 222)

Supreme Court (sə prēm' kôrt) The head of the judicial branch of the federal government. It is the highest court in the country. See judicial branch. (p. 318)

surveyor (sər vā ər) A person who measures land. (p. 290)

sweatshop (swet'shop) A small, crowded factory where people work in unsafe conditions. (p. 508)

symbol (sim'bəl) Something that stands for something else. See political cartoon. (p. H15)

Tea Act (tē akt) Legislation in which Great Britain made the colonists pay a tax on tea imported from Britain. (p. 265)

technology (tek nol'ə jē) The design and use of tools, ideas, and methods to solve problems. (p. 78)

teepee (tē'pē) A cone-shaped tent made of animal skins used by Native Americans of the Plains. (p. 72)

tenement (ten'ə mənt) An apartment building divided into many small, cramped apartments. (p. 512)

territory (ter'i tôr ē) An area of land that belongs to a government. (p. 314)

terrorism (târ' ər iz' əm) The use of fear and violence to gain political goals. (p. 601)

Thirteenth Amendment (thûr'tēnth' ə mend'mənt) An amendment to the Constitution, ratified in 1865, that abolished slavery. (p. 450)

time line (tīm' līn) A diagram showing the order in which events took place. (p. 46)

time zone (tīm zōn) One of the 24 areas into which Earth is divided for measuring time. (p. 480)

tolerate (tol'ə rāt) To allow people to have different beliefs from your own. (p. 182)

total war (tō'təl wôr) A war in which both sides not only strike against one another's soldiers, but against civilians and the economic system of the enemy. (p. 438)

totem pole (tō'təm pōl) A tall carved log used by Native Americans of the Northwest Coast to honor an important person or to mark a special event. (p. 79)

Trail of Tears (trāl əv tîrz) Name given to the forced march of 15,000 Cherokee in 1838 from Georgia to the Indian Territory. (p. 381)

traitor (trā'tər) Someone who turns against his or her country. See treason. (p. 277)

transcontinental railroad (trans kon ti nen'təl rāl'rōd) A railroad that crosses an entire continent. See Pacific Railroad Act. (p. 474)

travois (trə voi') A sled-like device constructed by Native Americans of the Plains. (p. 71)

treason (trē'zən) The betrayal of one's country by giving help to an enemy. See traitor. (p. 227)

Treaty of Alliance (trē'tē əv ə-lī' əns) The treaty the French signed with the United States during the American Revolution. (p. 297)

Treaty of Guadalupe Hidalgo (trē'tē əv gwä dä lü' pē ē däl'gō) The treaty signed in 1848 that ended the Mexican War. See Mexican War. (p. 398)

Treaty of Paris of 1763 (trē'tē əv par'is) An agreement signed by Great Britain and France that brought an end to the French and Indian War. (p. 248)

Treaty of Paris of 1783 (trē'tē əv par'is) The peace treaty in which Great Britain recognized the United States as an independent country. (p. 304)

Treaty of Versailles (trē'tē əv vâr sī') The peace treaty of 1919, officially ending World War I. (p. 542)

triangular trade (trī ang'gyə lər trād) The three-sided trade route between Africa, the West Indies, and colonial New England. (p. 220)

tribute (trib'ūt) Forced payment, usually made in the form of valuable goods. (p.129)

trust (trust) A secret agreement by leaders of an industry to fix prices and end competition. (p.523)

U

Underground Railroad (un'dər ground rāl'rōd) A system of secret routes used by escaping slaves to reach freedom in the North or in Canada. (p. 418)

unemployment (un em ploi'mənt) The number of workers without jobs. (p. 556)

United Nations (ū nīt'əd nā'shenz) An international organization, founded in 1945 following World War II, which works to preserve world peace. (p. 567)

urban (ur' bən) Of the city. (p. 15)

urbanization (ur' bə ni zā shən) The development and growth of cities. (p. 15)

V

values (val'ūz) Beliefs or ideals that guide the way people live. (p. 18)

veto (vē'tō) To refuse to approve. (p. 327)

Vietnam War (vī et näm' wôr) A war between South Vietnam and North Vietnam from 1954 to 1975, when North Vietnam defeated South Vietnam. (p. 586)

Virginia Plan (vər jin'yə plan) The plan, adopted by the Constitutional Convention in 1787, that established three branches of the federal government. (p. 318)

Voting Rights Act (vōt'ing rīts akt) A law that banned the use of a poll tax and required Southern voting laws to be approved by the Department of Justice. (p. 581)

voyageur (vwä yä zhûr') A trader who transported furs by canoe in New France. (p. 241)

W

wagon train (wag ən trān) A large group of wagons that travels west together for safety. (p. 385)

wampum (wom'pəm) Polished beads used in gift-giving and trading by Native Americans. (p. 64)

War Hawks (wôr hôks) Members of Congress who wanted the United States to go to war against Great Britain. See War of 1812. (p. 359)

War of 1812 (wôr uv ā'tēn'twelv) War between Great Britain and the United States from 1812 to 1815. (p. 359)

wigwam (wig' wom) Native American home built with bent sapling frames, then covered with cattail mats or elm bark. (p. 63)

World War I (wûrld wôr wun) A war that began in Europe in 1914 between the Central Powers and the Allied Powers. See Allied Powers and Central Powers. (p. 540)

World War II (wûrld wôr tü) War between the Axis and the Allies that involved most of the countries of the world. It was fought from 1939 to 1945. (p. 559)

Index

This index lists many topics that appear in the book, along with the pages on which they are found. Page numbers after a *c* refer you to a chart, after a *g* refer you to a graph, after an *m* refer you to a map, after a *p* refer you to photographs or artwork, after a *q* refer you to a quote.

Index

Credits

Cover Design: The Mazer Corporation

Maps: National Geographic

Charts: Doug Horne

Chapter Opener map: Joe Lemonnier

Illustrations: Thomas Buchs: 340-341; Anthony Carabucci: 534-535; Raul Colón: 468-469; Richard Cowdry: 436, 506, 612; Daniel DelValle: 33, 157, 307, 339, 357, 383, 589; David Diaz: 34-35; John Edens: 44, 132, 133, 142-143, 190, 362, 449, 548; John Edwards: 373; Luigi Galante: 60, 64, 84, 165, 182, 212, 236, 290; Keith Garletts: 256-257; Patrick Gnan: 438-439, 511, 602; Steve Harrington: 371; Albert Lorenzo: 120; Michael Maydak: 13; Greg Newbold: 361, 477; Ortelious Design, Inc.: pp. A1-16 maps; Larry Reinhart: 174-175; Mark Schroder: 404-05; Rob Schuster: 391, 400; Bleu Tirrell: 88-89, 90-91; George Ulrich: 33, 83, 87, 173, 225, 245, 251, 338, 403, 467, 533, 573, 599, 607, 635; Andrew Wheatcroft: 283, 296, 303, 370; Phil Wilson: 248, 278, 279.

Photography Credits: All photographs are by Macmillan/McGraw-Hill except as noted below.

Cover, i: Richard Beneholtz/Corbis Stock Market; Terry Donnelly/Stone. A2: t.r. ©Richard T. Nowitz/Photo Researchers; b.r. ©Joseph Sohm/Corbis. A3: t.r. ©Joseph Sohm/Visions of America/Corbis; b.l. ©National Archives A6: b. ©The Granger Collection. A6–A7: ©Jim Cummins/FPG. A8: t.r. ©Bettmann/Corbis; b.l. ©The Granger Collection. A9: b.l. ©Associated Press, AP; bkgd. ©The Granger Collection. A10: t.l. ©Emil Muench/Photo Researchers; A10: t.r. ©1998 Ken Martin/Visuals Unlimited; b.l. John D. Cunningham/Visuals Unlimited. A11: b.r. ©Robert Ratue/Stock Boston; b.l. ©Bill Goulet/Bruce Coleman; t.r. ©Jim Steinberg/Photo Researchers. A12: m.b. ©M.E. Warren/Photo Researchers; m.t. ©Charles Gupton/The Stock Market; bg. ©Inga Spence/Visuals Unlimited; b. ©John B. Boykin/The Stock Market; t. ©John B. Boykin/The Stock Market. A13: t.c. ©National Archives; c. ©Reuters NewMedia Inc./Corbis; t.r. ©Corbis; bg. ©Art Stein/Photo Researchers. A14: b.c. ©Bettmann/Corbis; b.l. ©Bettmann/Corbis; b.r. ©Flip Schulke/Corbis; t.r. ©Terry Farmer/Pictor. A15: ©Jose Carrillo/Stock Boston. A16: bkgd. ©ESA/PLI/Corbis Stock Market; t.l. ©David Ducros/Science Photo Library/Photo Researchers; m.l. ©R.W. Jones/Corbis; c.r. Chris Collins/The Stock Market; b.r. Don Mason/The Stock Market; b.l. Ariel Skelley/The Stock Market; c.l. Ed Bock/The Stock Market. H4: b.l. Hulton Archive. H5: b. Bridgeman Art Library. H6: t. Corbis/Bettmann. H9: b.l. Everett C. Johnson/Folio, Inc. t. AP/Wide World Photos. b.r. Jim Pickerell/Stock Connection/Picture Quest. H10: t.r.©Steve Cole/PictureQuest; b.r. ©John Hartman/StockConnection/PictureQuest; b.l. Mark Thiessen; t.l. Satellite image by: spaceimaging.com. 2-3: bg. ©Bill Ross/Corbis. 4: t.r. ©Telegraph Colour Library/FPG International; bl. ©MCMXCVII/Imagebank. 4-5: b. ©Jeremy Woodhouse/DRK Photo; bg. ©Superstock. 5: lc. ©Carr Clifton. 6: tr. ©Bryan Timlinson. 6-7: bg. ©Grant Heilman/Grant Heilman Photography, Inc. 7: bl. ©Fred Bruemmer; t. ©Ron Watts/Corbis. 8-9: bg. ©Warren Faidley/Weatherstock. 9: c. ©Tom Bean/Corbis. 12: tr. ©Larry Lefever/Grant Heilman Photography. 12-13: bg. ©Superstock. 14: tr. ©Mark E. Gibson/Visuals Unlimited; b. ©Calvin Larsen/Photo Researchers, Inc.; c. ©D. Mason/Woodfin Camp & Associates. 14-15: bg. ©Larry Lefever/Grant Heilman Photography. 15: tl. ©Joseph Sohm; ChromoSohm Inc./Corbis; b. ©1993 Alan L. Detrick/Photo Researchers, Inc. 16. ©Jack K. Clark/Comstock. 17: bl. ©Arthur Tilley/FPG International; br. ©Judy Canty/Stock Boston Inc./Picture Quest. 18: tr. ©2000 Don Mason/Corbis Stock Market; b. ©Jimmy Rudnick/The Stock Market. 18-19: bg. ©Reuters NewMedia Inc./Corbis. 19: c. ©2000 John Henley/Corbis Stock Market; bl. ©Ken Chernus/FPG International; t. ©2000 Ronnie Kaufman/Corbis Stock Market. 20-21: bg. ©VCG 1998/Getty Images; c. ©Getty Images. 22: b. ©Dallas and John Heaton/Corbis. 22-23: bg. ©The Imagebank. 23: br. ©1976 Bob Fitch/Take Stock; cl. ©Corbis; bl. ©Bettmann/Corbis; tl. 24:Pictor International/Picturequest 25: ©AP Wide World Photo. 26: tr. ©The Image Works; b. ©Richard Hutchings/Photo Researchers, Inc.; c. ©MCMXCIX/Imagebank. 26-27: bg. ©Royalty Free/Corbis. 27: tl. ©James Marshall/Corbis; bl. ©Felicia Martinez/Photoedit. 28: tr. ©Bettman/Corbis. 28-29. b. ©Joseph Sohm; ChromoSohm Inc./Corbis; bg. ©Joseph Sohm; ChromoSohm Inc./Corbis. 29: br. ©92 Geri Engberg/Corbis Stock Market; Dennis Brack/Blackstar Publishing/Picturequest 30: tr. ©Pete Laloutas/The Stock Market. 30-31: bg. ©DRA/Still Pictures/Peter Arnold, Inc.; bg. ©Bill Varie/Corbis. 31: tl. ©Eric Horan 2000; lc. ©W. Geiersperger/The Stock Market; b. ©1995 YVA Momatiuk & John Eastcott. 36-37: ©Superstock. 38-39: b. ©LLoyd Townsend/The Native Americans/Turner Publishing. 39: tl. ©Werner Forman Archive/Art Resource, NY; tr. ©Robert Frerck/Natural Museum of Anthropology, New Mexico. 40: ©Kenneth Garrett/National Geographic Image Collection. 41: br. ©Jonathon Blair/Corbis. 42: br. ©Robert Frerck/Woodfin Camp and Associates. 43: br. ©John Neubauer/Photoedit. 44: b. ©Richard J. Green/Photo Researchers, Inc. 46: tl. ©George H.H. Huey. 48: r. ©Lawrence Migdale/Photo Researchers, Inc. 50: b. ©Robert Frerck/Woodfin Camp and Associates. 51: Museum Fur Vokerkunde, Berlin/Werner Forman Archive/Art Resource. 54: bl. ©Superstock; br. ©National Gallery of Art, Washingon. 55: t. ©Smithsonian American Art Museum, Washington, DC/Art Resource, NY; bl. ©Merril Sitka/Museum of History and Industry. 56: b. ©Superstock. 57: br. ©Dan Budnik/Woodfin Camp & Associates, Inc. 58: c. ©Jerry Jacka/Jerry Jacka Photography. 59: ©Jerry Jacka Photography. 61: tr. ©Daemmrich/The Image Works; cr. ©Daemmrich/The Image Works. 62: ©Saint Louis Historical Society. 63: tr. ©James P. Rowan; cr. ©Canadian Museum of Civilization. 65: b. ©M. Greenlar/The Image Works. 66: ©The Granger Collection. 67: ©The Granger Collection. 68-69: c. ©Library of Congress. 70-71: b. ©The Newberry Library/Stock Montage, Inc. 72: b. ©Museum of the South Dakota State Historical Society, Pierre. 74: b. ©Francis G. Mayer/Corbis. 75: c. ©W. S. Nawrocki ASMP; tl. ©83 Wm. S. Nawrocki. 76: ©2001 Getty Images. 78: b. ©Lawrence Migdale. 79: tr. ©Lawrence Migdale; cr. ©Lawrence Migdale; br. ©Lawrence Migdale; c. ©Lawrence Migdale. 80: b. ©University of Washington Libraries, E. J. Partridge Collection. 81: cr. Courtesy of the Division of Anthropology, American Museum of Natural History. 82: tr. ©Native Images Photography; bl. ©Native Images Photography. 92-93: Corbis. 94: b. Bridgeman Art Library International, Ltd. 95: t. The Bridgeman Art Library International, Ltd.; b. ©The Granger Collection. 96: b. ©Northwind Picture Archives. 97: ©Gianni Dagli Orti/Corbis. 98: bl. ©Stock Montage; tr. Ancient Art and Architecture Collection Ltd. 99: br. Ancient Art and Architecture Collection Ltd.; bl. Ancient Art and Architecture Collection Ltd. 100: tl. photo: ©Corbis, colorization: @Walter Stuart; br. Ancient Art & Architecture Collection Ltd. 101: t. The Bridgeman Art Library International, Ltd. 104: Granger Collection. 105: tr. The Granger Collection. 106-107: t. Asian Art Museum of San Francisco/The Avery Brundage Collection. 108: b. ©Kinuko Y. Craft/National Geographic Society. 109: br. The Granger Collection; b. ©Kinuko Y. Craft/National Geographic Society. 110: t. ©Jeff J. Daly/Visuals Unlimited. 111: Tony Arruza/Corbis. 114: Museo Navale, Genoa-Pegli/Superstock. 115: b. ©Virginia Ferrero/DDB Stock Photography; t. ©The Granger Collection. 116-117: b. ©Steve Simonsen. 118: b. ©Michael Pole/Corbis. 119: tl. ©Museo del Hombre Dominicano, Santo Domingo; bl. ©National Museum of the American Indian, Smithsonian Institution, New York; r. ©Museo Nazionale Preistorico ed. 120: b. ©Christie's Images/Superstock. 122: b. ©Dave G. Houser/Corbis. 123: tl. ©Alan & Linda Detrick/Photo Researchers, Inc.; lc. ©Barry L. Runk/Grant Heilman; bl. ©Townsend P. Dickinson; tr. ©Coco McCoy/Rainbow/Picture Quest; rc. ©Grant Heilman/Grant Heilman Photography,Inc.; br. ©1998/Foodpix. 124: tr. photo: ©University of California Berkeley; colorization: Walter Stuart; br. photo: ©University of California Berkeley, colorization: Walter Stuart. 125: tr. Michael Holford. 126: tl. Courtesy of Henrietta Mann; br. Courtesy of Emanuele Alfano. 127: Courtesy of Irene S. Vernon. 128: b. Lotos Film. 130: ©Archivo Iconografico, S.A./Corbis. 131: t. ©Stock Montage; br. ©The Granger Collection. 134: b. ©Charles & Josette Lenars/Corbis. 135: ©Nierling/Treasure Savors Inc./Mel Fisher Maritime Museum. 138: ©D. Donne Bryant. 139: ©Archivo Iconografico, S.A./Corbis. 140: ©The Granger Collection. 141: ©Schalkwijk/Art Resource. 144: ©Robert Frerck/Woodfin Camp and Associates. 145: ©The Granger Collection. 148: b. ©David Harp/Folio, Inc. 149: t. ©1994 North Wind Pictures; b. ©The Bridgeman Art Library International, Ltd. 150-151: b. ©The Mariners Museum; 151: t. ©The Bridgeman Art Library International. 152: ©Lee Snider/The Image Works. 153: ©The Granger Collection. 154: ©1998 North Wind Pictures. 155: Stock Montage. 158: ©Richard T. Nowitz/Corbis. 159: National Portrait Gallery, London/Superstock. 160: The Ashmolean Museum, Oxford. 161: t. The Granger Collection; b. ©Grant Heilman Photography. 162: National Portrait Gallery, Smithsonian Institution/Art Resource. 163: The Chrysler Museum. 164: c. Bridgeman Art Library, International Ltd. 164-165: b. ©Index Stock Imagery. 166: ©The Granger Collection. 167: ©Getty Images. 168: ©Stock Montage. 169: ©2000 Paul Rezendes. 176-177: Connecticut Historical Society. 178: b. ©Stock Montage. 179: t. Superstock; bl. photo: ©Art Resource, colorization: Walter Stuart. 180: ©Pilgrim Hall Museum. 183: ©Stock Montage. 184: t. photo: Bettmann Archive/Corbis, colorization: Walter Stuart; b. Shelburne Museum, Vermont. 185: The Granger Collection. 186: b. ©Corbis. 188: ©The Bridgeman Art Library. 189: ©Andre Jenny/Focus Group/PictureQuest. 190: bl. ©Graydon Wood/Corbis. 191: ©Superstock. 192: photo: ©Corbis, colorization: Walter Stuart. 193: photo: ©The Granger Collection, colorization: Walter Stuart. 194: ©The Granger Collection. 195: The LuEsther T. Mertz Library, The New York Botanical Garden. 198: t. ©The Granger Collection; b. ©The Claude Moore Colonial Farm. 199: tl. Private Collection/Bridgeman Art Library, London/Superstock; tr. Colonial Williamsburg; b. ©Bryan Hemphill/Index Stock Imagery. 200: ©Jeff Greenberg/Index Stock Imagery. 201: Bettmann Archives/Corbis. 202: tl. ©The Granger Collection; b. ©Getty Images. 203: ©The Bridgeman Art Library International Ltd. 204: ©Breton Littlehales/National Geographic Society. 205: ©Cary Wolinsky/Aurora Photos. 207: ©National Portrait Gallery,London/Superstock. 209: ©Richard T. Nowitz/Corbis. 210: Private Collection/Bridgeman Art Library, London/Superstock. 211: The Granger Collection. 213: ©Nik Wheeler/Corbis. 214: b. Haverford College. 214-215: t. ©Folio, Inc. 215: br. ©Tim Wright/Corbis. 216: ©Catherine Karnow/Folio, Inc. 217: ©Getty Images. 218: b. ©The Granger Collection; c. ©The Mariners' Museum. 219: b. ©Grant Heilman Photography; tl. ©Photodisc. 221: cl. ©The Corning Museum of Glass; cr. ©The Corning Museum of Glass. 222: ©1998 North Wind Pictures. 223: ©Michael Schwarz/The Image Works. 224: ©Andre Jenny/Focus Group/Picture Quest. 225: ©The Granger Collection. 226: ©The Granger Collection. 227: photo: ©Bettmann/Corbis, colorization: Walter Stuart. 228: ©The Granger Collection. 229: Bettmann Archive/Corbis. 232: ©Daemmrich/The Image Works. 233: t. ©The Bridgeman Art Library; b. ©Superstock. 234: ©Index Stock Imagery. 235: ©Reynaldo Rivera/Onate Monument & Visitor's Center. 237: ©Museum of New Mexico. 239: The Granger Collection. 240: ©Pictor International/Pictor International, Ltd./PictureQuest; Buffalo Bill Historical Center. 242: bl. Chuck Fishman/Woodfin Camp & Associates Inc.; tr. ©The Granger Collection. 242-243: spread ©Greg Ryan/Sally Beyer; 243: cr. ©2001 The Smithsonian Institution; cl. ©Smithsonian Institution. 244: c. The Granger Collection; l. Collection, Haggerty Museum of Art Marquette University, Milwaukee, WI; c. 1991 Marquette University; r. The Granger Collection. 245: bl. ©The Bridgeman Art Gallery. 246: ©Hulton Archive. 247: ©Bettmann/Corbis. 249: Superstock. 250: bl. Courtesy of Alexandra Cerda; tr. Courtesy of Alan Givez. 258-259: spread ©Superstock. 260: The Granger Collection. 261: t. ©The Granger Collection; b. Superstock. 262: The Granger Collection. 263: Northwind Picture Archives. 264: tl. Bettmann Archives/Corbis; c. The Granger Collection. 265: Colonial Williamsburg Foundation. 266: bl. ©Joseph Nettis/Photo Researchers, Inc.; br. John Coletti/Stock Boston. 267: Bettmann Archives/Corbis. 268: ©The Granger Collection. 269: ©Jim Borgman. 270: ©Folio, Inc. 272: b. The Granger Collection; t. ©Concord Museum. 273: ©Lee Snider; Lee Snider/Corbis. 274: Yale University Art Gallery. 275: The Granger Collection. 276: b. ©The Granger Collection. 277: ©Superstock. 280: The Granger Collection. 281: ©Bettmann/Corbis. 282: b. ©Archive Photos/PictureQuest. 283: ©Barry Goldring. 284: ©The Bridgeman Art Library. 286: The Granger Collection. 287: t. ©The Granger Collection; b. ©The Granger Collection. 288: b. ©Historical Society of Delaware. 289: ©Ted Spiegel/Corbis. 291: t. The Granger Collection; b. The Granger Collection; c. The Granger Collection. 292: ©David Wagner. 293: Paul Vincze/Jewish-American Hall of Fame; Paul Vincze/Jewish-American Hall of Fame. 294-295: b. The Granger Collection. 295: tr. ©Superstock. 297: t. ©The Granger Collection. 298: Larry Fisher/Masterfile. 299: ©Nawrocki Stock Photo, Inc. 300: ©Library of Congress, Washington DC/Superstock. 301: ©The Granger Collection. 302: t. ©The Granger Collection; b. ©David Stover/Stock South/PictureQuest. 304: ©The Granger Collection. 305: tl. Thaw Collection Fenimore House Museum, Cooperstown, NY. Photo by John Bigelow Taylor, NYC.; rc. ©l. MurrayAlcosser/The Image Bank; r. Ted Spiegel. 310: br. ©Superstock; bl. ©Hulton Archive. 311: t. ©Dennis Brack/Black Star Publishing/PictureQuest; b. ©The Granger Collection. 312: ©Stock Montage. 313: ©The Granger Collection. 314: ©The Granger Collection. 315: tl. ©The Granger Collection. 316: ©Dennis Degnan/Corbis. 317: ©The Granger Collection. 318: Library of Congress. 320: b. The Granger Collection; lc. ©Library of Congress. 321: Pennsylvania Academy of the Fine Arts. 323: ©Corbis. 324: ©Jim Pickerell/The Image Works. 325: ©Joseph Sohm/Stock Boston, Inc./PictureQuest. 327: ©J. Sohm/The Image Works. 328: ©Michal Bryant/Woodfin Camp and Associates. 329: b. ©Lee Snider/Corbis; tr. ©National Portrait Gallery, Smithsonian Institution/Art Resource, NY. 330: ©The Granger Collection. 331: tr. ©The Granger Collection; rc. Smithsonian Institute. 332: ©Bettmann/Corbis. 333: tr. Independence National Historic Park. 334: tl. Courtesy of Trevor Austin; br. Courtesy of Ebony Kennedy. 335: Courtesy of Matthew Lee. 336: ©National Portrait Gallery, Smithsonian Institution/Art Resource, NY. 342–343: Greg Ryan/Sally Beyer. 344: photo: ©Bettmann/Corbis, colorization: Walter Stuart. 345: bl. ©The Granger Collection; t. ©Bettmann/Corbis. 346: ©1992 North Wind Pictures. 348: tr. ©The Granger Collection; b. photo: ©Corbis, colorization: Walter Stuart. 349: ©Michael Freeman/Corbis. 350: Smithsonian Institute; rc. The Granger Collection. 351: t. ©Nawrocki Stock Photo; br. ©Erich Lessing/Art Resource. 352: ©The Bridgeman Art Library. 353: r. ©Pat Hertz/North Dakota Tourism Department; br. ©2001 Smithsonian Institute; bl. ©2001 Smithsonian Institution. 354: t. ©Jack Zehrt; br. ©Ray Richardson/Animals Animals. 355: c. ©1970, Missouri Historical Society. 357: ©American Museum of Natural History/DK. 358: ©The Granger Collection. 359: br. ©Christie's Images/Superstock; bl. photo: ©Corbis, colorization: Walter Stuart. 360: tl. Archive Photos; tr. New York Historical Society. 362: br. Courtesy of Mother Bethel AME Church, Photo by Gary Reed; tr. National Portrait Gallery/Smithsonian Institute. 363: National Portrait Gallery/Smithsonian Institute. 366: bl. ©Superstock; br. photo: ©Bettmann/Corbis, colorization:©Walter Stuart. 367: t. ©Getty Images; bl. photo: ©Getty Images, colorization: Walter Stuart. 368: ©1996 North Wind Pictures. 369: ©Bettman Archives/Corbis; ©Science Museum/Science and Society Picture Library, London. 372: bl. ©Superstock; t. ©Nawrocki Stock Photo. 374-375: ©Superstock. 376: ©Photri-Microstock. 377: tr. photo: ©Corbis, colorization: ©Walter Stuart; rc. New York Historical Society. 378: bl. Bettmann Archive/Corbis; tr. ©American Museum of Natural History/DK. 380: ©The

Granger Collection. 382: Courtesy of Sandra Starner. 384-385: ©Superstock. 386: ©The Oakland Museum. 387: br. ©Davis Muench/Corbis; t. Nawrocki Stock Photography, Inc. 388: California State Library. 389: tr. Bettmann/Corbis; rc. ©Nowracki Stock Photography, Inc. 390: California State Library/Tom Meyers. 391: Underwood Photo Archives. 392: ©Bob Daemmrich/Stock Boston, Inc./PictureQuest. 393: Institute Of Texan Cultures, San Antonio, Texas. 394: bl. ©2000 North Wind Pictures; br. ©National Portrait Gallery, Smithsonian Institution/Art Resource, NY; c. Texas State Library, Archives Division. 395: ©Superstock. 396: t. Star of Republic Museum; br. San Jacinto Museum of History. 397: ©The Granger Collection. 398: t. Archives Division, Texas State Library; b. Archives Division, Texas State Library. 399: ©National Portrait Gallery/Smithsonian Institution/Art Resource. 406-407: ©Courtesy of Army Art Collection, U.S. Army Center of Military History. 408: ©The Bridgeman Art Library. 409: t. ©The Granger Collection; bl. ©Getty Images. 410: ©1997 North Wind Pictures. 411: ©Grant Heilman Photography. 413: ©Bettmann/Corbis. 414: ©Brooklyn Public Library-Brooklyn Collection. 416: bc. Harriet Beecher Stowe Center; r. Courtesy: National Park Service, Frederick Douglass NHS. 417: ©Brown Brothers. 419: ©Corbis. 420: Archive Photos. 421: ©Andre Jenny/Focus Group/PictureQuest. 422: ©Michelle D. Bridwell/PhotoEdit. 423: McGraw-Hill. 424: ©The Granger Collection. 427: tr. ©The Granger Collection; tl. photo: ©Culver Pictures, colorization: Walter Stuart. 428: b. ©The Bridgeman Art Library; t. ©The Granger Collection. 429: ©The Granger Collection. 432: ©1994 North Wind Pictures. 433: tl. ©The Granger Collection; tr. Appomattox Court House National Historic Park; bl. ©The Granger Collection. 434: photo: ©Bettmann/Corbis, colorization: Walter Stuart. 435: ©Superstock. 437: br. ©Getty Images. 438: ©Charles Harrington, Cornell University Photo. 442: ©Larry Sherer/High Impact Photography. 443: ©The Granger Collection. 444: b. photo: ©Brown Brothers, colorization: Walter Stuart; t. ©Bettmann/Corbis. 445: ©US Army Military History Institute. 446: ©The Bridgeman Art Library. 447: The Granger Collection. 448: ©The Granger Collection. 450: br. ©The Bridgeman Art Library; bl. ©David J. & Janice L. Frent Collection/Corbis; t. ©Bettmann/Corbis. 452: bl. ©Corbis; rc. ©Smithsonian Institute, br. ©Bettmann/Corbis. 453: photo: ©Smithsonian, colorization: Walter Stuart. 454: McGraw-Hill. 455: ©1994 North Wind Pictures. 456: ©The Museum of the Confederacy. 457: Stock Montage. 458: ©Cook Collection Valentine Museum. 459: t. ©The Bridgeman Art Library; b. ©Nawrocki Stock Photos, Inc. 460: ©Corbis. 461: photo: ©Thomas Nast/Library of Congress, colorization: Walter Stuart. 462: t. Courtesy of Robert F. Engs; b. Courtesy of Rebecca Plant. 463: Courtesy of Cathy Nelson. 466: ©Bettmann/Corbis. 470-471: ©Museum of the City of New York/Corbis. 472: ©The Granger Collection. 473: tl. ©W.R. Leigh/Wood River Gallery/PictureQuest; tr. ©Nebraska State Historical Society; bl. ©Bettmann/Corbis. 474: ©Wolfgang Kaehler/Corbis. 475: ©Hulton-Deutsch Collection/Corbis. 476: ©MMSD (Southern Pacific Photos). 479: tr. ©The Granger Collection; tl. ©Underwood Photo Archives. 481: l. ©George Hall/Corbis; r. Union Pacific Railroad Museum. 482-483: b. ©Superstock; 483: tr. ©Thomas Wiewandt/Index Stock Imagery/PictureQuest. 484: ©Bettmann/Corbis. 485: ©John Eastcott & Yva Momatiuk/The Image Works. 486-487: b. ©Bettmann/Corbis. 487: rc. ©Joseph H. Bailey/National Geographic Society. 489: t. ©The Granger Collection; rc. John Lund/Tony Stone Images. 490: b. ©Kansas State Historical Society; br. ©Kansas Historical Society. 491: b. ©John and Diane Harper/New England Stock Photo; tl. ©Kansas Historical Society. 492: ©Smithsonian American Art Museum, Washington, DC/Art Resource, NY. 493: bl. ©D. Boone/Corbis; tr. ©Tony Freeman/Photoedit. 494-495: b. Denver Public Library, Western History Collection. 495: bl. ©Darrell Gulin/Corbis. 496: lc. ©Corbis; t. ©Corbis. 497: ©Bettmann/Corbis. 498: ©Alvis Upitis/The Imagebank. 499: c. John Elk III; tl. Jim Argo. 502: ©John Ferguson Weir/Putnam County Historical Society. 503: tl. Brown Brothers; tr. The Granger Collection; bl. The Granger Collection; tr. ©Brown Brothers. 504: ©Bettmann/Corbis. 505: ©The Granger Collection. 507: tr. ©The Granger Collection; bl. ©Brown Brothers. 508: ©The Granger Collection. 509: r. ©Corbis; l. ©Library of Congress. 510: tr. ©Museum Fur Vokerkunde, Berlin/Werner Forman Archive/Art Resource; ©1996 North Wind Pictures. 512: ©The Granger Collection. 514: c. ©National Portrait Gallery, Washington DC/Art Resource; bl. ©Bettmann/Corbis. 515: ©The Collection of Walter and Naomi Rosenbloom. 516: ©Bettmann/Corbis. 517: br. ©The Library of Congress; c. ©The Library of Congress. 518: The Granger Collection. 519: ©Chris Arend/Alaska Stock. 521: c. ©The Granger Collection; r. ©Ecoscene/Corbis. 522: ©David L. Brown/Panoramic Images. 523: ©The Granger Collection. 524: ©Courtesy of Jovita F. Lopez/The UT Institute of Texan Cultures at San Antonio. 525: tr. ©Underwood & Underwood/Corbis. 526: b. ©The Granger Collection; tr. ©Cindy Lewis Photography. 527: ©Folio, Inc. 528: b. Courtesy of Scott E. Perwin; t. Courtesy of Kathleen DuRousseau. 529: t. Courtesy of Seth Cotlar. 536-537: ©Roger Ressmeyer/Corbis. 538: l. ©KJ Historical/Corbisstockmarket.com; r. The Granger Collection. 539: tl. Brown Brothers; tr. The Granger Collection; bl. Globe Photos. 540: Culver Pictures. 541: tr. The Granger Collection; c. photo: ©Bettmann/Corbis, colorization: Walter Stuart. 542: bl. Brown Brothers; t. ©Corbis. 544: t. ©Bettmann/Corbis. 545: ©2000 Owen/Black Star. 546: Underwood Photo Archives, Inc. 547: tr. Underwood Photo Archives, Inc.; cr. ©Getty Images. 549: ©Bettmann/Corbis. 550: State Historical Society of Wisconsin Visual Archives. 551: Photo Courtesy of the Kent State University Museum. 552: ©Bettmann/Corbis. 554: Associated Press; FDR Library. 555: ©Underwood & Underwood/Corbis. 556: ©Bettmann/Corbis. 557: The Granger Collection. 558: The Granger Collection. 559: Hulton-Deutsch Collection/Corbis. 560: bl. Underwood Photo Archives, Inc.; br. Library of Congress. 561: Archive Photos. 562: ©Archive Photos. 563: Associated Press, TASS. 564-565: ©UPI/Bettmann. 566: ©Bettmann/Corbis. 567: The Granger Collection. 568: ©UPI/Bettmann. 569: tr. ©Bettmann/Corbis; t. ©Archive Photos/Blank Archives. 570: Underwood Photo Archives, Inc. 571: ©Chuck Carlton/Index Stock Imagery/PictureQuest. 572: ©Bettmann/Corbis. 573: ©Bettmann/Corbis. 574: ©Bettmann/Corbis. 576: l. ©Charles Moore/Black Star; r. ©Bettmann/Corbis. 577: t. ©Seattle Post-Intelligencer Collection; Museum of History & Industry/Corbis; b. ©NASA/Roger Ressmeyer/Corbis. 578: ©Steve Shapiro/Black Star Publishing/PictureQuest. 579: Bettmann Archives/Corbis. 580: ©Smithsonian. 581: lc. ©Bruce Roberts/Photo Researchers, Inc.; b. ©2001 Getty Images. 582: ©Flip Schulke/Corbis. 583: ©Wally McNamee/Corbis, colorization: ©Walter Stuart. 584: ©Bettmann/Corbis. 585: ©Corbis. 586: Associated Press, AP. 587: t. ©David J. & Janice L. Frent Collection/Corbis; b. ©David J. & Janice L. Frent Collection/Corbis. 588: b. Courtesy of Sandra Stein. 590: ©Corbis. 591: ©2000 Dennis Brack/Black Star. 592: b. ©UPI/Corbis-Bettmann. 592-593: t. ©Frank Johnston/Black Star Publishing/PictureQuest; 593: br. Globe Photos, Inc. 594: b. ©Brad Markel/Gamma Liaison; t. ©McEhinley-Sygma. 595: ©S. Sherbell/Corbis SABA. 596: ©Corbis. 598: ©White House Press/Corbis SABA. 599: ©Reuters New Media Inc./Corbis. 600: NASA. 601: ©Thomas E. Franklin/The Record (Bergen County, NJ)/Corbis SABA. 603: ©Richard Nowitz/Phototake/PictureQuest. 604: ©Bettmann/Corbis. 606: ©Nik Wheeler/Black Star Publishing/PictureQuest. 608-609: 610: ©Ron Stroud/Masterfile. 613: b. ©Serman Hines/Masterfile; t. ©Bill Brooks/Masterfile. 614: ©Gunter Marx Photography/Corbis. 615: ©P. Renault/Explorer/Photo Researchers, Inc. 616: ©Schalkwijk/Art Resource, NY. 618: b. ©Andrew Rakoczy/Photo Researchers, Inc.; inset ©Andrew Rakoczy/Photo Researchers, Inc. 619: b. ©Schalkwijk/Art Resource, NY; t. ©Robert Frerck/Odyssey/Chicago. 620: ©Danny Lehman/Corbis. 621: l. David Hiser/The Imagebank; tr. ©Joel Salcido/Daemmrich Assoc. 622-632: ©Stephen and Donna O'Meara/Photo Researchers, Inc. 624: b. ©Charles O'Rear/Corbis; t. The Granger Collection. 625: t. ©Russell Gordon/Odyssey/Chicago; inset ©Inga Spence/DDB Stock Photo. 626: l. ©Ernesto Bazan/SABA; t. ©Steve Winter/NGS Image Collection. 628: Owen Frankin/Stock Boston. 630: t. ©George D. Lepp/Corbis; b. ©Hubert Stadler/Corbis. 631: tr. ©Corbis. 632: tr. ©Frank Staub/Index Stock Imagery/PictureQuest; bl. ©Georg Gerster/Photo Researchers, Inc. 633: tl. ©TempSport/Corbis. R42: br., ml. Art Resource. R43: bc. The Granger Collection, NY. R44: tc. The Granger Collection, NY; bl. Art Resource. R45: tl. The Granger Collection, NY. R50: tl. Peter Gridley/FPG International. R53: tr. Eric Draper/The White House; tl. Peter Gridley/FPG International.

Acknowledgments *(continued from page ii)*

From **Big Men, Big Country: A Collection of American Tall Tales** by Paul Robert Walker and James Bernardin, illustrator. Copyright © 1993 by Paul Robert Walker. Harcourt, Brace, Jovanovich. Used by permission. From **A Century of Dishonor: A Sketch of the United States Government's Dealings with Some of the Indian Tribes** by Helen Hunt Jackson. Copyright © 1995. University of Oklahoma Press. Used by permission. From **The Civil War Diary of General Josiah Gorgas** by Frank E. Vandiver. Copyright © 1947. University of Alabama Press. Used by permission. From **Blacks and Jews: Are They Really Sworn Enemies?** by Educational Video Center. Copyright © 1992. Educational Video Center. Used by permission. Einstein, Albert. "The unleashed power. . ." **The Columbia World of Quotations**. New York: Columbia University Press, 1996. 13 August, 2001. www.bartleby.com/66/ Used by permission. From **The Log of Christopher Columbus** by Christopher Columbus; selections by Steve Lowe. Copyright © 1992 by Steve Lowe. Philomel Books, a Division of Putnam and Grosset Book Group. Used by permission. From **The Presidency of Gerald R. Ford (American Presidency)** by John Robert Greene. Copyright © 1995. University Press of Kansas. Used by permission. From **History Speaks: John F. Kennedy's Inaugural Address** by Julia Hargrove and Judy Mitchell, ed. Copyright © 2000. Teaching & Learning Company. Used by permission. From **Sinews of Peace Post War Speeches** by Winston S. Churchill and Randolph S. Churchill, ed. Copyright © 1949. AMS Press, Inc. Used by permission. From **A Testament of Hope: The Essential Speeches and Writings of Martin Luther King, Jr.**, by Martin Luther King, Jr., and James M. Washington, ed. Copyright © 1986. HarperSanFrancisco. Used by permission. From **The Greatest Speeches of President John F. Kennedy** by John F. Kennedy. Copyright © 2000. Titan Publishing. Used by permission. From **The Essential Franklin Delano Roosevelt: FDR's Greatest Speeches, Fireside Chats Messages and Proclamations** by Franklin Roosevelt and John Gabriel Hunt, ed. Copyright © 1998. Grammercy Publishing. Used by permission. From **Farewell to Manzanar** by Jeanne Wakatsuki Houston and James D. Houston. Copyright © 1973 by James D. Houston. Random House Inc. Used by permission. From **Writings** by W. E. B. Du Bois. Copyright © 1986. Library of America. Used by permission. From **The Norton Anthology of African-American Literature** by Henry Louis Gates, Jr., and Nellie Y. McKay, ed. Copyright © 1997. W. W. Norton and Company. Used by permission. Excerpt from "Harlem Night Song" from **Collected Poems of Langston Hughes** by Langston Hughes. Copyright © 1994 by Estate of Langston Hughes. Reprinted by permission of Alfred A. Knopf, Inc. Reprinted by permission of Harold Olber Associates, Inc. Copyright © 1951 by Langston Hughes. Copyright © renewed 1982 by George Houston Bass. Used by permission. From **Crack-Up** by F. Scott Fitzgerald. Copyright © 1945. New Directions. Used by permission. From **More than a Muckraker: Ida Tarbell's Lifetime in Journalism** by Ida M. Tarbell. Copyright © 1996. University of Tennessee Press. Used by permission. From **Jane Addams of Hull House, 1860–1935**; **A Centenary Study** by Margaret Times. Copyright © 1961. Macmillan. Used by permission. From **Twenty Years at Hull House: With Autobiographical Notes** by Jane Addams. Copyright © 1981. Penguin Books, Signet Classic. Used by permission. From **They Saw the Elephant: Women in the California Gold Rush** by JoAnn Levy. Copyright © 1992. University of Oklahoma Press. Used by permission. From **The Jungle** by Upton Sinclair. Copyright © 1981. Random House, Inc. Bantam Classics. Used by permission. From **Me and Mine: The Life Story of Helen Sekaquaptewa** by Helen Sekaquaptewa and Louis Udall. Copyright © 1969. University of Arizona Press. Used by permission. From **Timarion** by (Anonymous) and Barry Baldwin, ed. Copyright © 1984. Wayne State University Press. Used by permission. From **Life of Olaudah Equiano, or Gustavus Vassa, the African** by Olaudah Equiano. Copyright © 1999. Dover Publications. Used by permission. From **The Concord Hymn and Other Poems** by Ralph Waldo Emerson. Copyright © 1996. Dover Publications. Used by permission. From **Native American Legends of the Great Lakes and the Mississippi Valley** by Katharine B. Judson, ed. Copyright © 2000 by Northern Illinois University Press. Used by permission. From **The Journal of Jasper Jonathan Pierce: A Pilgrim Boy** by Ann Rinaldi. Copyright © 2000 by Ann Rinaldi. Scholastic. Used by permission. **Patrick Breen Dlary, November 20, 1846–March 1, 1847** by Patrick Breen. 1868. The Bancroft Library, University of California, Berkeley. Copyright © 1997 by the Regents of University of California. 24 October, 2001. http://www.oac.cdlib.org/dynaweb/ead/calher/breen/@GenericBookTextView/;uf=0#X Used by permission. From **The Travels of Marco Polo** by Marco Polo, Ronald Letham, ed. Copyright © 1958. Viking Press, a division of Penguin Putnam. Used by permission. Excerpt from "The First Americans" by Sharon Begley and Andrew Murr; *Newsweek*, April 26, 1999. Used by permission. Excerpt from "Pioneer Life in America" by Jerome O. Steffen. Discovery Channel School. Original content provided by World Book Online. 24 October, 2001. http://www.discoveryschool.com/homeworkhelp/worldbook/atozhistory/p/431660.html Used by permission. Sawhook, Georgia. Link from home page. 1970. 24 October, 2001. http://www.geocities.com/Heartland/Pointe/5892/Grandpa.html Used by permission. From **Jane Addams**. Ed. Julie Johnson and Henry Steele Commager. National-Louis University. 13 August, 2001. http://nlu04.nl.edu/ace/Resources/Addams.html Used by permission. Aiello, Jo Ann and George. Link from Homepage. Copyright © 1997–2001 by Jo Ann and George Aiello. 17 July, 2001. http://www.glittering.com/letters/rolfe1.html Used by permission. From **New York to Niagara, 1836, the Journal of Thomas S. Woodcock** by Deoch Fulton. New York, 1938. *Houghton Mifflin Education Place.* Copyright © 1999. Houghton Mifflin Company. 18 July, 2001. http://www.eduplace.com/ss/hmss/8/unit/act4.1.1.html Used by permission.